CW01655317

[illegible] de to

DOING YOUR RESEARCH PROJECT

The Essential Guide to

DOING YOUR RESEARCH PROJECT

5th Edition

Zina O'Leary
Emma Tennent

Sage

Sage

1 Oliver's Yard
55 City Road
London EC1Y 1SP

2455 Teller Road
Thousand Oaks
California 91320

Unit No 323-333, Third Floor, F-Block
International Trade Tower
Nehru Place, New Delhi 110 019

8 Marina View Suite 43-053
Asia Square Tower 1
Singapore 018960

Editor: Charlotte Bush
Editorial assistant: Pippa Wills
Production editor: Rabia Barkatulla
Copyeditor: Neil Dowden
Proofreader: Tom Bedford
Indexer: Elizabeth Ball
Marketing manager: Fauzia Eastwood
Cover design: Shaun Mercier
Typeset by: C&M Digitals (P) Ltd, Chennai, India
Printed in the UK by Bell and Bain Ltd, Glasgow
BB0350111

© Zina O'Leary and Emma Tennent 2025

Apart from any fair dealing for the purposes of research, private study, or criticism or review, as permitted under the Copyright, Designs and Patents Act, 1988, this publication may not be reproduced, stored or transmitted in any form, or by any means, without the prior permission in writing of the publisher, or in the case of reprographic reproduction, in accordance with the terms of licences issued by the Copyright Licensing Agency. Enquiries concerning reproduction outside those terms should be sent to the publisher.

Library of Congress Control Number: 2024936839

British Library Cataloguing in Publication data

A catalogue record for this book is available from the British Library

ISBN 9781529672237
ISBN 9781529672220 (pbk)

TABLE OF CONTENTS

About the Authors vii
Acknowledgements ix
Online Resources xi

1 Taking the Leap into the Research World 1
2 Setting Up and Getting Started 23
3 Developing Your Research Question 39
4 Undertaking Credible and Ethical Research 59
5 Crafting a Research Proposal 89
6 Reviewing Literature 103
7 Designing a Research Plan 125
8 Understanding Methodologies: Quantitative and Qualitative Approaches 141
9 Understanding Methodologies: Mixed Approaches 173
10 Understanding Methodologies: Evaluative, Action-Oriented and Emancipatory Strategies 187
11 Identifying and Selecting Samples, Informants and Cases 215
12 Primary Data: Surveys, Interviews and Observation 237
13 Secondary Data 277
14 Online-Generated Data 297
15 Analysing Quantitative Data 317
16 Analysing Qualitative Data 341
17 The Challenge of Writing Up 367
18 Final Hurdles 387

Glossary 403
References 419
Index 431

ABOUT THE AUTHORS

Zina O'Leary is an internationally recognized leader in research methodologies and has a keen interest in the application of research to evidence-based decision-making. She is an Adjunct Professor at the Jospeh R. Biden School of Public Policy and Administration at the University of Delaware and a Senior Fellow at the Australia and New Zealand School of Government where she coordinates research and project units for their Executive Masters and Executive Education Programmes. She also has an extensive history as a consultant to both government and the private sector and was the research coordinator for the Centre for Environmental Health Development at the World Health Organization Collaborating Centre. She is the author of *Researching Real World Problems*, *The Social Science Jargon Buster*, *Workplace Research* and three books in Sage's Little Quick Fix Series: *Research Questions*, *Research Proposals* and *Presenting Your Research*.

Emma Tennent is a senior lecturer at Te Herenga Waka – Victoria University of Wellington. She has experience teaching research methods and research paradigms to undergraduate and postgraduate students across a range of disciplines. She is the recipient of an Early Career Teaching Excellence Award and an accredited Fellow of the Higher Education Academy. She works with Zina at the Australia and New Zealand School of Government as a research project advisor for the Executive Master of Public Administration. She has co-published with students and academic colleagues in the open-access book *The Power of Partnership: Students, Staff, and Faculty Revolutionizing Higher Education*.

ACKNOWLEDGEMENTS

Zina

I have a new co-author! Emma... I wasn't sure about sharing my book with anyone, but it was time, and I could not be happier sharing this journey of learning and teaching with you. You have been a real joy to work with and your voice is a wonderful addition to this work. It is a better book because of you. As for everyone else, well we are on the fifth edition, so you've all been acknowledged several times before! So blah blah blah to family and friends, thank you for making academia just one part of my life. And thank you to the tremendous staff at Sage for working so seamlessly with us to produce a super-slick work. Finally, a gigantic shout-out to Jack, who makes anywhere and everywhere we are, home. Over to you, Emma...

Emma

Zina, thank you for welcoming me onto this new edition with open arms. You trusted me with a book you've put so much time and effort into and I've appreciated your generosity throughout the process. Thanks to Kathryn and Amanda for putting Zina and me in touch and making this collaboration possible. To my beautiful friends – Gloria, Jess S. and Jess L., Fiona, Kate, Kealagh, Lucy and Sophie – thanks for challenging and inspiring me. The team at Sage has made the publishing experience a breeze. Final thanks to my love, for helping me see things differently, and to my family for being proud of all that I do.

ONLINE RESOURCES

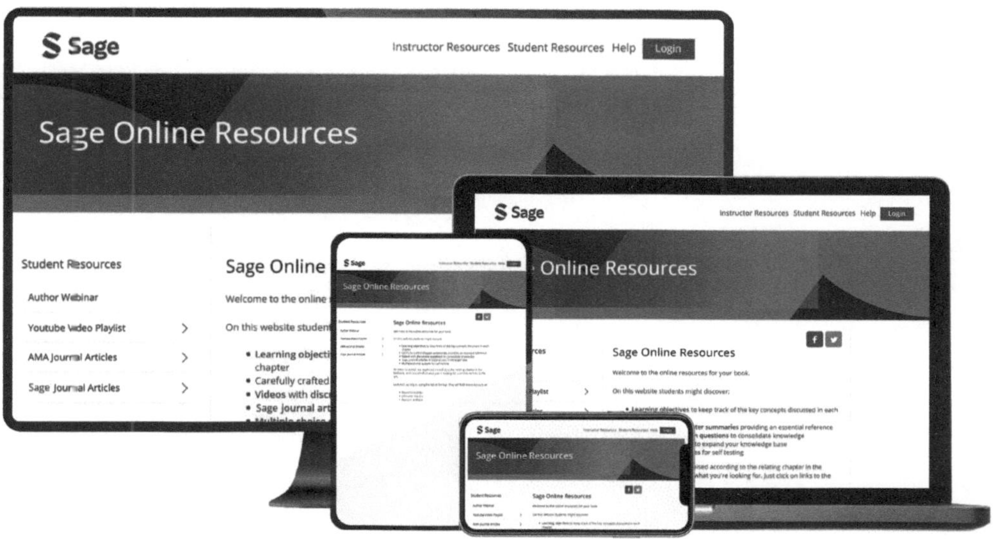

Designed to support students through every step of the research process, the fifth edition of The Essential Guide to Doing Your Research Project offers a range of online resources for lecturers. Find them at: **https://study.sagepub.com/olearyandtennent5e**.

FOR LECTURERS

A detailed **Lecturer's guide** supports you to teach using the book, featuring case studies, real datasets, teaching suggestions, checklists, as well as additional further reading resources for each chapter.

Download **PowerPoint slides** for each chapter featuring content summaries, key figures, examples and discussion point which can be customized for use in your own lectures and presentations.

1

TAKING THE LEAP INTO THE RESEARCH WORLD

Learning Objectives

- The challenge of tackling a research project
    - To understand research as both a challenge and an opportunity
    - To understand the responsibility inherent in producing 'truth'
- So what is this thing called research and why do it?
    - To understand the need for research
    - To understand the power of research as a tool for situation improvement
- Delving into the 'construct' of research
    - To understand the thorny worlds of epistemology and ontology
    - To understand the paradigms that drive research
    - To become comfortable with the concept of reflective practice and mixed methodologies
    - To understand the difference between methodology and method
- Getting help along the way
    - To understand how to get the most from this book

Research is formalized curiosity. It is poking and prying with a purpose.

Zora Neale Hurston (1942)

THE CHALLENGE OF TACKLING A RESEARCH PROJECT

It's actually quite exciting. Before you lies the opportunity to tackle your own **research** project! You get to drive the process and make all the calls. But we get it – it can also be a bit daunting.

After all, you're not an expert on research and suddenly you are confronted with a need to manage the entire process: pick a topic, develop a researchable question, navigate your way through **ethics**, work with literature, develop a methodological approach, design **methods**, construct a coherent proposal, find **respondents**, collect data, analyse that data and write it up – all within a timeframe that can seem completely unrealistic!

Well, you're not alone if you find yourself asking: How in the world am I going to manage all that? Believe it or not, the answer is pretty straightforward. Whether you are tackling a one-semester project at the end of your undergraduate degree or undertaking a PhD, the answer is the same. You do it one step at a time. There is a logic and rhythm to doing research, a logic and rhythm that you need not only to become familiar with, but also to be able to apply with some level of confidence and competence.

But, yes, it can be intimidating. Even if you do not consciously recognize it, 'doing' research represents a huge shift in your learning journey. Up until this point, you've probably been limited to being a knowledge consumer. The information is already out there – you just need to find it, memorize it, engage with it, synthesize it and, as your skills build, form opinions about it and maybe even critique it. But undertaking research is a whole new world. You move from being a knowledge consumer to a knowledge producer, someone who must use their critical thinking skills to create and transmit knowledge. And this means taking on a whole new realm of responsibility and gaining competence with a host of new skills. This is the challenge of 'doing', and not just knowing about, research.

So What Is This Thing Called Research and Why Do It?

It is easy to think you've got a broad grasp of this concept we call 'research'. After all, it's something you probably do in your daily life on a regular basis. You do 'research' when you are deciding what car to buy. You do 'research' to help you determine what university you should attend. And, of course, you do 'research' when you have to find things out for an assignment.

But there is a distinct difference between this kind of everyday research and the construct of research that you're about to tackle. The author Zora Neale Hurston said: 'Research is formalized curiosity. It is poking and prying with a purpose' (Hurston, 1942: 143). And this is certainly one part of it. Research demands formalization, systemization and rigorous processes. But 'formalized curiosity' is also required in order to make a new contribution to knowledge. As the *Oxford English Dictionary* (2012) puts it, research is 'the systematic study of materials and sources in order to establish facts and reach new conclusions'. So more than engaging in what might be haphazard processes to find out something *you* did not know, academic research is about systematically finding out something not known in the wider world. It is your opportunity to contribute to a body of knowledge.

If you think about it, that's actually quite exciting. Through research, you have the capability to create knowledge, knowledge that just might impact on real change. After all, knowledge for knowledge's sake is a luxury many argue we cannot afford. Rarely is research undertaken simply to satisfy curiosity. Much more often we are after knowledge that can help us tackle pressing problems and issues, and help improve situations.

The Need for Research Knowledge

We know that for some of you, the main driver for undertaking a research project is simply the requirement that exists within your degree. But beyond requirements, the potential to have your research make a contribution to the betterment of some situation should be a real motivator. As the physicist Richard Feynman said, 'We are at the very beginning of time for the human race. It is not unreasonable that we grapple with problems. ... Our responsibility is to do what we can, learn what we can, improve the solutions, and pass them on' (Feynman, 1997: 102).

Research is about facilitating situation improvement. It is about offering ways forward. And we need that. There are so many areas where we can, and need to, make a difference. Governments, for example, are riddled with problems – in fact, governments themselves can be a problem. The environment is under stress. Our planet is turning into a giant greenhouse, there is salinity in the soil, and we do not have enough clean and safe drinking water to go around. In fact, we can't find a way to distribute money, food or medicine so that everyone with a need gets a share. Health care and education are far from adequate and/or equitable, and from the global arena to the local playground we cannot seem to overcome racism, sexism, prejudice or discrimination. Domestic violence and child abuse occur daily in every corner of the world, and child pornography is a multi-billion-dollar industry.

We also have to deal with the threat of terrorism as well as our fear of that threat. We poison ourselves daily with toxic chemicals – from alcohol, cigarettes, factories and automobiles. Children are starving – some due to war and political upheaval, some from mass-media-induced anorexia. Meanwhile, schools struggle with violence, drugs, and sexual and racial tension.

And then there is the workplace, where more than 6,300 people die every day owing to work-related accidents and disease (International Labour Organization, 2016). Meanwhile, 'survivors' deal with significant stress from the boss, massive bureaucratic inefficiencies, gross inequities and the need to balance work with a thousand other responsibilities.

So, the stakes are high, and researchers are but one group, among many, dedicated to situation improvement.

The Potential of Research Knowledge

So what is the role of research in making the world a better place? Well, research is the process of gathering data in order to answer a particular question and this question will generally relate to a need for knowledge that can facilitate problem-solving. More broadly, research can highlight how we think about problems and solutions, and help us understand which problems need solving.

Does this then make research the answer to our problems? Well, unfortunately no – but research can be an instrumental part of problem resolution. Research can be a key tool in informed decision-making. It can be central to determining what we should do, what we can do, how we will do it and how well we have done it. Research may not be the answer to our problems, but it can supply some of the data necessary for us to begin to tackle challenges we all face.

Research can help us:

- understand more about particular issues and problems – including all the complexities, intricacies and implications thereof;
- find workable solutions – vision futures, explore possibilities;
- work towards that solution – implement real change;
- evaluate success – find out if problem-solving/change strategies have been successful;
- offer robust recommendations – as an extension of findings, recommendations can be used to influence practice, programmes and policy.

If you think about it, from local to global levels, all of these activities can be, and should be, informed by research. Research can be the key to finding out more; that is, uncovering and understanding the complexity of the issues that surround us. It can also help us in our quest for solutions. It can be key to assessing needs, envisioning futures, and finding and assessing potential answers. It can also allow us to enact and learn from change through the use of '**action research**' strategies. And finally, **evaluative research** can be central to monitoring and refining our attempts at problem-solving. In short, research may not be the answer – but it is certainly a tool that can help us move forward.

I Have a Question!

Does My Research Really Have the Potential to Solve the World's Problems?

It's about scale. Sure you might like to save the world's children from hunger, do away with the evils of terrorism or put a stop to religious persecution, but few of you will be in a position to fully address these types of problems through research processes. Generally speaking, conducting a research project will find you engaged in issues, or aspects of issues, that, while still important and significant, are local, grounded and practical. Even more so than projects that are overly grandiose and theoretical, there can be genuine value in projects that respond to real and tangible needs. Your goal should be to do what you can to add to a body of knowledge and see if you can offer some evidence that can aid evidence-based decision-making for situation improvement.

Delving into the 'Construct' of Research

Now that you have some sense of what research is and why you might be motivated to take it on, it is time to delve a bit deeper into the philosophical underpinning of the research game. You might think that there's only one way to do research, but in fact there are huge differences (and debates!) about what research even is and how it should happen. Now, for many of you the first image of 'research' that might come to mind is the **scientific method**, a technical rule-following enterprise to observe both natural/physical and social worlds. But the scientific approach to research is just one paradigm and many of its key assumptions are critiqued by other paradigms. The tricky thing about assumptions is they often go unstated (both in our personal lives and research endeavours). But it's important to understand how assumptions about reality and knowledge shape different approaches to research.

Ontology and Epistemology

These long and somewhat frightening terms refer to sets of assumptions about reality and assumptions about knowledge. It is important to become familiar with these terms since they help us understand debates and diversity related to the production of knowledge and, consequently, the research processes you are about to engage in.

All right, so let's break this down. The main question addressed by **ontology** is 'What types of things actually exist?', while the main question addressed by **epistemology** is 'What are the rules for knowing what exists?' Now these two questions actually work in concert and have a tendency to lead to great debate. Because there are different rules for knowing (epistemologies), there can be quite varied conceptions of what exists or what is 'real' (ontology).

Consider the following. 'Empiricists' believe that all knowledge is limited to what can be observed by the senses (their epistemology). They therefore have a difficult time acknowledging as real anything that cannot be measured and tend to believe in an objective reality (their ontology). But there are other ways of knowing (competing epistemologies) which lead to differing conceptions of what's 'real' (alternative ontologies). For example, those with religious epistemologies based on faith (rather than measurement) would say God is real even if you cannot physically touch Him or Her. Postmodernists, however, may question whether there is any way we can find 'truth', and might suggest that 'truth' is a slippery concept that is always political.

In the world of social science research, the tension and debate between competing epistemologies and ontologies requires researchers to consider their own orientation to knowledge and truth. Even new researchers need to consider their positioning. For example, do you have a sense that the truth is 'out there' and believe you can only know what you can physically observe? As a researcher, what limits will this put on your research? Or do you have a sense that truth is actually ambiguous, fluid and relative, and people play a large part in the construction of knowledge? Certainly, holding those beliefs will impact on how you approach your research.

Okay, so let's say the Department of Education is reviewing its indicators for educational success of third-graders. Are you in the empiricist camp ready to review and measure traditional indicators of mathematical and English literacy? Or are you from a more postmodern camp ready to delve into the world of the students to get a genuine feel for experiences of worth, contentment, creativity and ingenuity?

Within social science research, the debate that rages between such differing ways of knowing is enormous, leading to an overly defensive, emotive and often unproductive divide between empiricists and more postmodern researchers. Both camps believe they hold the key to legitimate knowing, which unfortunately lessens the potential for them to work together down a path of holistic knowing (see Figure 1.1).

There's one other 'ology' worth knowing about. **Axiology** gets less attention than ontology and epistemology but is an important principle that acknowledges the role of ethics and values in research. The research questions we ask, our personal values, the values embedded in our culture or community, and even how we conceptualize research all reflect ethics and values. We cover this in detail in Chapter 4.

Competing Positions

Let's pause here and have a quick look at some of the ways in which we can come to have an understanding of our world, and how a particular way of knowing might influence research processes. Now it would be helpful if these terms were mutually exclusive – but given their varied disciplinary roots, many overlap, which, we know, can be confusing. We'll give a brief overview here, but if you really want to get into the nitty-gritty of each of these 'isms', have a look at the readings recommended at the end of this chapter.

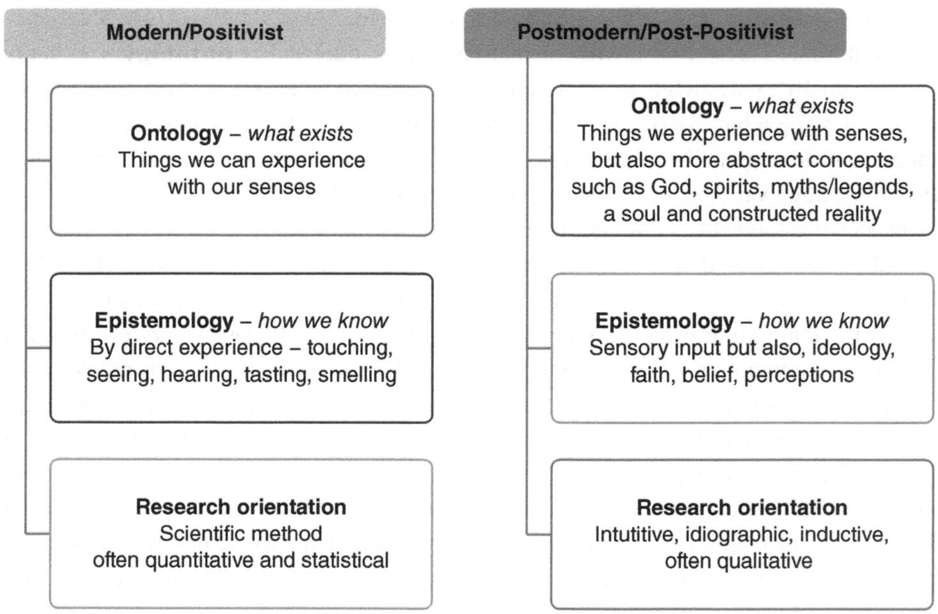

Figure 1.1 Modern/positivist vs postmodern/post-positivist

In combination, the three terms – **realism**, **empiricism**, **positivism** – present a relatively straightforward approach to attaining a single truth about an objective world. In the conduct of research, they suggest that what we can know comes from sensory experience best served through scientific method. These terms represent an approach to research that has been dominant since the Enlightenment.

In the social science research world, this approach to knowing is often the underlying assumption of how the world works, and what needs to be studied. We, as social scientists, are in the business of looking for evidence: evidence of better sales; evidence of increased consumption; evidence of weight loss; evidence of increased life expectancy; evidence of smoking cessation; evidence of better test scores. We measure what people did, what people do and how often they do it.

However, this black and white way of seeing is increasingly being called into question. Physicists now recognize the role of chaos and complexity in a universe that we may never 'capture'. And what about the nature of truth in the social world? Whose truth is it anyway? There are many '**post-positivist**' philosophers and researchers alike who question the assumptions of these ways of knowing and openly critique, oppose and/or reject positivism's central tenets.

This has led to acceptance of alternative paradigms that can be broadly classed under the umbrella of a 'postmodern' or 'post-positivist' worldview. For these approaches, the certainty implied above is replaced by an acceptance of chaos, complexity, the unknown, incompleteness, diversity, plurality, fragmentation and multiple realities.

In social sciences this means complexity in research methods themselves. For example, how do we judge the quality of parenting when sibling memories and perceptions are completely at odds with each other? What is the best approach for understanding why people speed even when we have objective measures of risk? People are complex, their social systems are complex, their morals and values and where they come from are complex. Postmodern researchers try to be true to this complexity, while still doing 'research'.

I Have a Question!

Do I Really Need to Engage with All These 'isms' and 'ologies'?

The short answer is yes. These concepts might seem vague and abstract (after all, they are philosophical terms) but they're actually fundamental to how we see ourselves, the world and our research. We might go through our lives without explicitly declaring our 'ontology' but when you are doing research, you are producing knowledge. And as someone who is going to conclude something, you need to put your cards on the table; you need to declare your positioning in relation to knowledge, and that means knowing what your positioning is and being able to articulate it to others. So it's time to embrace your 'isms' and 'ologies'.

Quantitative, Qualitative and Mixed Approaches

In common research parlance, we often refer to the realist, empirical, 'truth is out there' approach as **quantitative** – an unfortunate label that confuses the assumptions of various paradigms with the practice of quantifying data through the use of numbers. Similarly, the assumption of multiple, constructed, **subjective** truths and complexity is aligned with what is referred to as **qualitative** – again an unfortunate term that also confuses the assumptions of various paradigms, but this time with the practice of preserving the spoken word. Quantitative and qualitative are, therefore, often loaded terms that point to belief systems and value judgements. In other words, a continuation of paradigm wars. We, however, are strong advocates of adopting research approaches based not on tradition, but on the goal of best answering a well-considered research question. This may indeed take researchers down the path of **mixed methodology** – approaches that draw on the methods of both quantitative and qualitative traditions and demand a highly reflexive researcher (a much richer discussion of the quantitative and qualitative and mixed approaches is taken up in Chapters 8 and 9).

One way to think about the dichotomies between positivism and post-positivism, and between the quantitative and qualitative, is the distinction between the right and left brain. The logical left brain likes the certainty, **objectivity** and rules and processes associated with positivism and the 'quantitative', while the rebellious right gives much less credence to structure and is more comfortable with the uncertainty, complexity and **relativism** of the post-positivist, 'qualitative' paradigm.

So just maybe these various ways of knowing represent more than simply paradigmatic shifts over time. Perhaps they represent a more fundamental division within the perception of each individual. We certainly have the capacity to see in more than one way. We can exercise both sides of the brain. We can even work towards a whole-brain, more integrated approach.

And this is certainly true of research. If we accept that these two ways of knowing are both valuable, and that they can and do coexist, then, within the research world, both approaches should be validated and, as discussed below, traversed.

The Position of the Reflexive Researcher

Being reflexive as a researcher is more than just reflecting on the research process. **Reflexivity** is about critically reflecting on your role as the researcher. How does your position (what you know and believe) shape how you act? What are the taken-for-granted assumptions that underlie your approach to research?

Undeniably, there is a divide in the research world between those who accept chaos, complexity, the unknown and multiple realities, and those who do not. But we would argue that this divide can and should be traversed. Many researchers feel a need to identify themselves with a particular way of knowing and only engage in methodological approaches that sit under their own epistemology.

There are even researchers who rely on, and even come to 'believe' in, particular methodological approaches. Janesick actually coined the term 'methodolatry' – a combination of method and idolatry that she defines as a 'preoccupation with selecting and defending methods to the exclusion of the actual substance of the story being told'; she describes methodolatry as a 'slavish attachment and devotion to methods' (2007: 48). It is, therefore, well worth considering whether divergent, disparate and distinct ways of knowing can each offer credible knowledge production.

Critical Thinking Challenge 1

Researcher Identity

Good research is a thinking person's game. It is a creative and strategic process that involves constantly assessing, reassessing and making decisions about the best possible means for obtaining trustworthy information, carrying out appropriate analyses and drawing credible conclusions. And this starts with you.

Think about your own ontology and epistemology. How do you see the world? How do you understand the world? And how will this influence how you research the world?

I Have a Question!

What Is Better, Quant. or Qual.?

Put simply, there is no 'best type' of research. Particular research strategies are good or bad to the exact degree that they fit with the questions at hand. Good questions need to be matched with appropriate procedures of inquiry, and this is always driven by the researcher, not the methodology. The perspectives you will adopt and the methods you will use need to be as fluid, flexible and eclectic as is necessary to answer the questions posed.

Box 1.1 highlights the advantages of not being pigeonholed. Each research situation and research question is unique, and assumptions can be as varied as the situations. The trick is to understand what assumptions you are working under and how they might affect your study.

Box 1.1

Banana Consumption Assumptions!

Zina once had a student who wanted to explore whether recycled 'grey' water could be used to irrigate bananas. She did this in two phases. The first phase involved the formulation of a **hypothesis** that stated there would be no biophysical differences between bananas irrigated with town water and those irrigated with recycled grey water. For this phase of the study she (quite appropriately) accepted the positivist assumptions and conducted her research according to the 'rules' of scientific method - she was the consummate lab-based objective scientist.

Her second phase explored whether consumers would buy bananas irrigated with recycled water regardless of 'no difference' in quality. For this phase of the study, the student thoughtfully explored her assumptions and realized that, in relation to this particular question, she found herself moving into 'post-positivist' territory. She struggled with her own subjectivity and realized that 'truth' and 'reality' can be two different things (many consumers who believed findings of 'no difference' claimed they still would not purchase the bananas irrigated with recycled water). There was no defined set of rules to best answer this question, but her willingness to 'think' her way through the process and be flexible in her approach allowed her to draw conclusions that were seen as both credible and valuable.

Methodology, Methods and Tools

Once you have worked your way through the paradigm question, there is still a need to be clear about constructs that sit within any research approach. We're talking here about methodologies and methods. While we will delve into the details of various approaches throughout the book, it's important to underscore the difference between methodologies and methods now and how they are related to the design of a study.

As you begin to develop a plan for your research, you will need to come to grips with elements that are as broad as questions related to paradigm, and as specific as questions dealing with the nuts and bolts of who, where, when, how and what.

Now it is not uncommon for students to want to jump straight into the details of their research methods without engaging at the level of research **methodology**. They want to fast-forward to designing strategies for data collection and cannot understand why it's important to grasp, adopt and apply frameworks that sit at a higher macro level.

But methodologies are crucial to the research process and, in fact, provide us with much more than just research strategies. They actually provide us, as researchers, with legitimization for knowledge production. They are our means of showing the outside world that we are not just random people with an opinion, but that we are researchers who are engaging with well-considered, rigorous processes. The adopting of various methodological positions (as discussed in Chapters 8 and 9) shows that we have grappled with the responsibilities and controversies associated with the production of knowledge.

Credible research design therefore requires more than just the adoption of data collection and data analysis methods. It requires that such methods are nested within more macro-level frameworks, or methodologies, that work in concert with methods to provide researchers with a voracious design that can stand up to the highest level of scrutiny. Figure 1.2 from Brown and Dueñas (2020) details this.

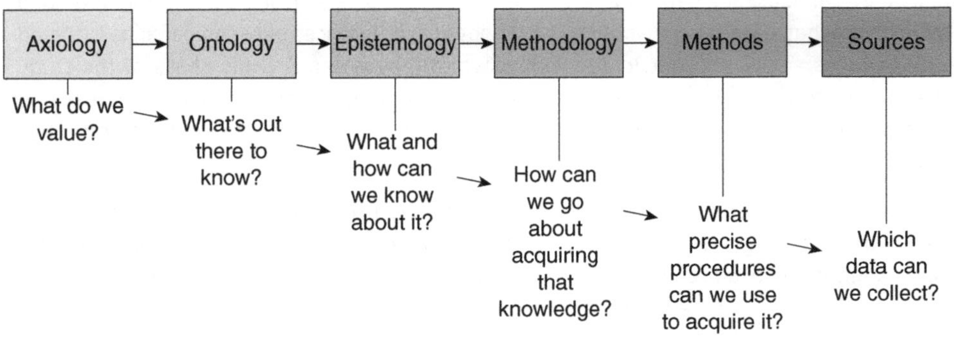

Figure 1.2 Methods and methodologies: the building blocks

GETTING HELP ALONG THE WAY

By now you are probably getting some sense of why research is often referred to as a journey. You haven't even finished the first chapter of this book, and already there's a whole lot you've been asked to consider. And that's before you even start thinking about your own research project. But don't worry, you are not alone. The goal of this book is to be your guide. It is designed to accompany you on your journey; to lay out the processes and procedures you will need to engage with; to help you through the logic of research; to offer guidance on all the decisions that are part and parcel of conducting a research project; and to send you down the right road when you need to delve deeper into relevant methodologies and methods.

At the same time, it is important to know that this is not a 'recipe book'. It does not lay out sets of 'steps' that you blindly follow. Yes, it will logically work you through the processes and procedures, but this is a book that recognizes that good research is always reliant on reflexive researchers, researchers who must weigh up all decisions in light of a quest for credible data and findings, limited by unavoidable practicalities.

So whether you are about to tackle a small-scale project, or undertake a major thesis, this book will engage your critical thinking skills to take you on a journey of rich discovery, a journey that will have you unearth not only 'findings' related to your research question, but also the process of research, as well as the thorny challenges associated with project management.

I Have a Question!

What Does AI Mean for Research?

(Zina O'Leary, Emma Tennent and Gemini AI)

The last few decades have left us with unprecedented access to a vast array of research studies, as well as the ability to access an extraordinary amount of data. This makes AI the tool researchers have been waiting for.

AI can locate, identify, extract, summarize, synthesize, analyse and write. And the programs and apps using AI are proliferating and advancing at lightning speed. So we need to know how to manage this technological juggernaut.

We thought it might be fun to ask Gemini AI a few questions about AI and the research process. Here are its answers, some good advice we think. (Please note, this is the only section of this book written by our friend Gemini AI!)

Can AI write a literature review?

AI can be a valuable tool in writing a **literature review**, but it's important to *remember its limitations and utilize it responsibly*. Here's how AI can assist you in the process:

1. Identifying Relevant Literature:
   - Some AI tools can *search vast databases* based on your keywords and research topic. They can help you discover a wider range of relevant literature, including obscure sources you might miss through conventional methods.
2. Summarizing and Extracting Information:
   - AI tools can **summarize papers automatically** and extract key points, saving you time and effort in reading through large volumes of text. This can be particularly helpful when dealing with a large pool of research.
3. Identifying Themes and Trends:
   - AI can **analyse the content of multiple papers** and identify overarching themes, trends and debates within the field. This can help you organize your review and understand the current state of knowledge on your topic.
4. Identifying Gaps in the Literature:
   - Some AI tools can **analyse the themes and methodologies present in existing research** and suggest potential gaps or areas where further research is needed. This can help you identify your niche and refine your research question.

(Continued)

However, it's crucial to remember:

- **AI cannot replace critical thinking and analysis.** You need to evaluate the information AI provides, assess its accuracy and relevance, and avoid relying solely on AI-generated summaries or interpretations.
- **AI systems can be biased based on the data they are trained on.** Be aware of potential biases and critically evaluate the information retrieved through AI tools.
- **AI cannot write a literature review for you.** It can provide tools and insights, but you still need to synthesize the information, formulate arguments and structure the review following proper academic conventions.

Here are some **ethical considerations** when using AI for literature reviews:

- **Be transparent about the use of AI.** Acknowledge that you used AI tools as part of your research process, but clearly state that the final review and interpretations are your own.
- **Cite all sources correctly.** Even if you use AI to identify relevant literature, you still need to properly cite all the sources you use in your final review.

Overall, AI can be a valuable **supplementary tool** in writing your literature review, but it cannot replace your own critical thinking, analysis and writing skills. Use AI responsibly, be aware of its **limitations** and focus on utilizing it to enhance your own research efforts.

Can AI write up a research report?

AI currently cannot **independently** write up research in its entirety. While AI offers valuable tools that can assist in various stages of research, it lacks the critical thinking, creativity and understanding of the research context that are essential for generating original, accurate and well-structured research outputs. Here's a breakdown of AI's current capabilities and limitations in research:

What AI can do:

- **Data Processing and Analysis:** AI excels at handling and analysing large datasets, summarizing and extracting key information, and identifying patterns and trends. This can be helpful in tasks like data cleaning, preparing research materials and conducting preliminary exploratory analysis.
- **Literature Review Support:** AI tools can assist in searching for relevant literature, summarizing research papers, and identifying themes and gaps in existing research. This can save researchers time and effort and help them refine their research questions.
- **Generating Textual Content:** Some AI tools can generate text based on specific prompts and parameters. However, this generated content often lacks originality, depth and critical analysis, and may require significant revision or human intervention to be accurate and relevant to the research question.

What AI cannot do (yet):

- **Formulate Research Questions and Hypotheses:** AI cannot independently define research questions or develop testable hypotheses. These require a deep understanding of the research field, existing knowledge and creative problem-solving skills that AI currently lacks.

- **Design Research Methods:** Designing a research method that is robust, ethical and appropriate for the topic requires a nuanced understanding of the research problem, potential biases and ethical considerations involved. This level of critical thinking and ethical awareness are beyond the current capabilities of AI.
- **Analyse and Interpret Data:** While AI can perform statistical analysis and identify patterns, it lacks the ability to critically interpret the results, draw meaningful conclusions or connect them to broader theoretical or real-world implications. This requires human judgement, expertise in the research field, and the ability to consider alternative explanations and potential biases.
- **Write Cohesive and Informative Research Reports:** AI cannot currently write a complete and well-structured research report that seamlessly integrates different elements like literature review, methodology, findings, discussion and conclusion. This requires the ability to organize information logically, write with clarity and coherence, and present findings in a way that is relevant and meaningful to the target audience.

Overall, while AI is a powerful tool that can significantly enhance the research process, it cannot replace the critical thinking, creativity and overall intellectual contribution of human researchers. AI should be viewed as a valuable assistant that can automate certain tasks and provide insights, but not as a replacement for the human mind's capabilities in conducting rigorous and meaningful research.

How can AI Best Help in the Conduct of Social Science Research?

AI plays a **supportive and transformative role** in social science research, offering valuable assistance at various stages of the process. Here's how AI can best contribute:

1 Enhanced Data Analysis:

- AI excels at analysing **large, complex datasets** from diverse sources like social media, surveys and online platforms. This allows researchers to extract **unprecedented insights** into human behaviour, social trends and public opinion.
- AI algorithms can identify **hidden patterns and correlations** within data that might be missed by human analysis, leading to breakthroughs in understanding complex social phenomena.

2 Streamlined Research Tasks:

- AI tools can **automate repetitive tasks** like data cleaning, preparing research materials and conducting preliminary analysis. This frees up valuable time for researchers to focus on more **complex tasks** like designing research methods, interpreting results and drawing meaningful conclusions.

3 Advanced Text Analysis:

- **Sentiment analysis** utilizes AI to analyse the tone and emotions expressed in text data, offering deeper insights into public opinion, cultural trends and individual attitudes.
- AI can also **extract key information and summarize textual content** from documents, interviews and online forums, allowing researchers to efficiently capture important details from large volumes of data.

(Continued)

4 Predictive Modelling and Simulation:

- Machine Learning, a branch of AI, allows researchers to create **predictive models** that forecast future outcomes based on historical data and current trends. This can be helpful in understanding the potential impact of policies, predicting social unrest and anticipating changing demographics.
- **Agent-based models** powered by AI can simulate interactions within social systems, helping researchers test hypotheses and understand the dynamics of group behaviour under various cnditions.

5 Facilitating Research Collaboration:

- AI tools can **bridge the gap between geographically dispersed researchers**, enabling efficient collaboration by facilitating data sharing, analysis and report generation.

However, it's crucial to remember:

- **AI is a tool, not a replacement for human expertise.** Researchers must critically analyse AI-generated insights, ensuring data quality, identifying potential biases and maintaining ethical considerations throughout the research process.
- **Transparency and responsible use** are critical. Researchers should be transparent about the use of AI in their work and ensure the algorithms and data used are unbiased and ethically sourced.

In conclusion, AI empowers social science research by:

- Unlocking deeper insights from data
- Facilitating broader analysis
- Streamlining research workflows
- Enhancing collaboration

As AI continues to evolve, its impact on social science research will likely **expand significantly**. However, ethical considerations and responsible use remain paramount to ensure AI truly facilitates meaningful and trustworthy research.

THE STRUCTURE OF THE BOOK

This book consists of 18 chapters that will take you logically through all aspects of conducting a research project from conception to dissemination. In other words, the chapters mirror the processes necessary for the conduct of most research projects.

PRELIMINARIES – As well as introducing the book's objectives and offering guidelines for how to get the most out of the work, this section will take you through foundational work needed before embarking on research.

- Chapter 1 introduces you to some of the more fundamental and theoretical aspects of research, including an understanding of how knowledge is understood and produced. This level of understanding can go a long way in helping to ground your own research approach.

- Chapter 2 is about practicalities. This chapter acknowledges that undertaking research can be a difficult and alienating activity, and attempts to offer strategies for staying on top of the process. It covers: what you need to know to start your research journey; how to best navigate the research process; and how to stay on track.
- Chapter 3 takes you through the art and science of knowing what you want to know. It guides you through the process of defining a feasible, clearly articulated research question that acts to direct 'methods'. It is amazing how much simpler it is to adopt, adapt or create appropriate methodological approaches when you are absolutely clear about what it is you want to know.
- Chapter 4 covers the concept of integrity. The chapter starts with an exploration of power and politics in research processes before moving on to traditional indicators of credibility as well as alternatives more appropriate to qualitative data. The chapter then discusses ethical responsibilities and ethics approval processes.

PLANNING – The next three chapters are about effective planning.

- Chapter 5 covers research proposals and the opportunity they present to clarify thinking, bed down ideas, articulate thoughts in a way that provides a blueprint for future action and, most importantly, 'sell your project'.
- Chapter 6 explores the varied ways in which literature informs research. Zina often tells students that before 'doing' research, they need to convince her of three things: that the questions they wish to answer are worthy of research; that they are the right person to add to a body of knowledge (they know their stuff); and that their methodological approach is the best 'doable' way of getting the answers to their question. And to do this, they need to read. This chapter covers issues related to sourcing, managing and utilizing the literature to its full potential.
- Chapter 7 looks at designing your study such that it grows from questions rather than falls from paradigms, and offers a framework for delving into the basic questions that drive method.

METHODOLOGY – The design of social science studies has become incredibly diverse over the past 30 or so years, and can be a daunting realm of exploration for those new to research. Chapters 8, 9 and 10 delve more specifically into methodologies that inform research.

- Chapter 8 takes you through what are often described as qualitative and quantitative methods.
- Chapter 9 explores the opportunities, challenges and methods associated with mixed methodologies.
- Chapter 10 explores more purposive approaches such as evaluative, action-oriented and emancipatory strategies.

DATA COLLECTION – The focus of the next four chapters is effective data collection.

- Chapter 11 looks at who holds the data you seek, your 'respondents', and covers the logistics, challenges and methods of defining and selecting samples, key informants and cases.

- Chapter 12 concentrates on the opportunities and challenges associated with primary data collection, such as surveys and interviews.
- Chapter 13 takes you through options for collecting and working with secondary data sources.
- Chapter 14 explores the ever-expanding world of online-generated data.

DATA ANALYSIS – Next comes making sense of, and presenting, your data.

- Chapter 15 takes you through the basics of quantitative data management and analysis, and covers variable types, measurement scales, descriptive and inferential statistics, the selection of statistical tests and data presentation.
- Chapter 16 focuses on qualitative data and takes you through the logic and methods of general qualitative analysis, as well as specific branches of analysis such as content, discourse, conversation and narrative analysis, plus semiotics and hermeneutics. The chapter concludes with examples of how to present qualitative data.

FINISHING UP – Finally, writing it all up and sharing your work.

- Chapter 17 will help you tackle the challenge of writing your report in impactful ways. It explores writing as a communication exercise that demands a convincing narrative. It then takes you through all required sections of a credible research report.
- Chapter 18 covers those incredibly important post-write-up aspects of the research process, namely disseminating your research, presenting your research and making the transition from student to professional.

HOW TO GET THE MOST OUT OF THE BOOK

There are actually a few ways you can use this book and you may find yourself dipping in and out of these four strategies:

1. Read it through. You will become familiar with the processes and procedures associated with research.
2. Use it as a reference. As you progress through your research project, you will inevitably need to look things up. You are likely to find the answers within this book's 18 chapters. And if you can't, the recommended readings should give you some good leads.
3. Use this book as a companion to your research processes. This is where the book really comes into its own. While each chapter will introduce you to a new area of content, the main goal is to take you through the development processes you need to undertake when doing your own project. The emphasis is to arm you with the knowledge and skills you will need to get you from 'clueless' to 'completed'. When using the book in this way, a good approach is to read as you go. We would recommend starting here and working your way through to the last page of Chapter 18, when you will be ready to submit your work.

Chapter Summary

- Research is the process of developing new knowledge by gathering data that answer a particular question. It is your opportunity to contribute to a body of knowledge and perhaps even influence change. It can also be a key tool in informed decision-making. It can be central to determining what we should do, what we can do, how we will do it and how well we have done it.
- Scientific research was born of 'positivism' and adopted the assumptions of that paradigm. These assumptions include: a knowable and predictable world; empirical and reductionist research; objective and expert researchers; hypothesis-driven methods; and statistically significant, quantitative findings.
- Largely based on critiques of positivism, a range of post-positivist approaches acknowledge: an ambiguous and variable world that is ambiguous and variable; intuitive and holistic research; subjective and collaborative researchers; inductive and exploratory methods; and qualitative findings.
- Rather than positioning the researcher according to paradigmatic assumptions, the reflexive researcher can consider whether it is possible to explore the assumptions of various paradigms as they relate to particular research questions.
- While undertaking a research project can be somewhat intimidating, using this book as a guide to your journey will help you best navigate all the ins and outs of the research process.

FIND YOUR NEXT STEP

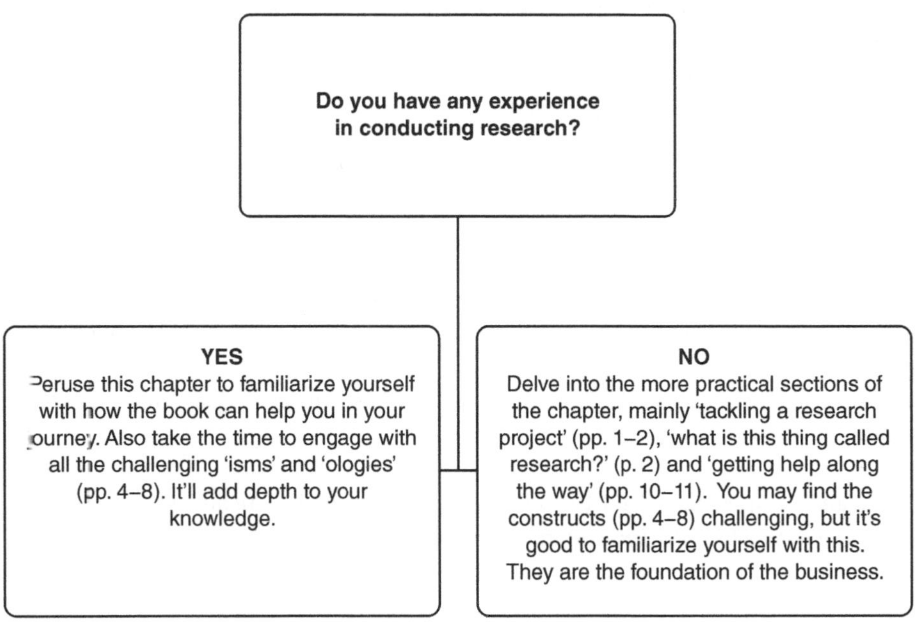

FURTHER READING

There are some heavy theoretical concepts in this chapter that you may want to explore in a bit more depth. There are some accessible reads below, but we thought we'd start with two more general reads.

Killman, L. (2013) *Research Terminology Simplified: Paradigms, Axiology, Ontology, Epistemology and Methodology*. Sudbury, ON: Author.
We like this book because it has all the relevant terms in one place. It is self-published but could be extremely helpful.

O'Leary, Z. (2007) *The Social Science Jargon Buster*. London: Sage.
Honestly, Zina would say this is the book she's most proud of. It covers key terms across the social sciences and includes all relevant research terminologies.

Paradigms

Smith, L. T. (2022) *Decolonizing Methodologies: Research and Indigenous Peoples.*
Third edition. London: Zed Books
This influential book points out how scholarly research is implicated in legacies of colonialism and offers a visionary new 'decolonizing' approach to research methodology. Challenging and inspiring.

Blaikie, N. and Priest, J. (2017) *Social Research: Paradigms in Action*. Cambridge: Polity Press.
The conduct of social research rests on paradigmatic assumptions. We like the way this book acknowledges this and guides researchers with illustrative examples.

Bingham A. J., Mitchell, R. and Carter, D. S. (2024). *A Practical Guide to Theoretical Frameworks for Social Science Research*. Abingdon: Routledge.
A good overview that includes examples of studies within the different theoretical frameworks from a broad range of academic disciplines

The 'ologies'

Moon, K. and Blackman, D. (2017) 'A guide to ontology, epistemology, and philosophical perspectives for interdisciplinary researchers'. https://i2insights.org/2017/05/02/philosophy-for-interdisciplinarity/
A blog post summarizing the authors' research article with some great diagrams and links to the whole thing if you want to read it.

McCain, K. and Kampourakis, K. (2019) *What Is Scientific Knowledge? An Introduction to Contemporary Epistemology of Science*. Abingdon: Routledge.
Accessible introductory chapters around the key debates about scientific knowledge. We like the range of different perspectives here.

Goldman, A. and McGrath, M. (2014) *Epistemology: A Contemporary Introduction*. Oxford: Oxford University Press.
Written by two important contributors to the field, this is a solid and accessible introduction. We particularly liked the section on evidence.

Martin, R. (2010) *Epistemology: A Beginner's Guide*. London: Oneworld Publications.
We like this beginner's guide. It is designed to make you think about what knowledge is, how to obtain it and whether we can trust it. Very accessible.

Conee, E. and Sider, T. (2015) *Riddles of Existence: A Guided Tour of Metaphysics*, 2nd edition. Oxford: Oxford University Press.
While highly philosophical, this book actually makes ontology somewhat accessible. The challenge of thinking through what exists is a worthwhile exercise for any researcher.

Effingham, N. (2013) *An Introduction to Ontology*. Cambridge: Polity Press.
An accessible introduction to the aims and methods of ontology. We like that it's clear and conversational.

Positivism and Empiricism

Carey, S. S. (2011) *A Beginner's Guide to Scientific Method*. Belmont, CA: Wadsworth.
While strongly rooted in the belief that scientific method is 'the way', this is nonetheless a good introduction to both 'what is' and 'how to do' scientific method.

Robinson, D. (2013) *Introducing Empiricism: A Graphic Guide*. New York: Totem Books.
Good critical introduction to what we experience and if/how we can trust it. Engaging graphics in this book make it more accessible.

Steinmetz, G. (ed.) (2005) *The Politics of Method in the Human Sciences: Positivism and its Epistemological Others (Politics, History, and Culture)*. Durham, NC: Duke University Press.
Good comparative read. Varieties of positivism and alternative ways of seeing are explored by their assumptions and applications.

Realism and Relativism

Oreskes, N. (2021) *Why Trust Science?* Princeton, NJ: Princeton University Press.
With the trustworthiness of science coming under increasing scrutiny, it's important to understand how and why science continues to give us some of the best evidence we have around. Clearly written and engaging.

Wei, W. (2017) *Philosophy of Science: An Introduction to the Central Issues*. Abingdon: Routledge.
An English translation of a widely used Chinese textbook, this provides a concise introduction to the Western philosophy of science alongside Chinese perspectives.

Chakravartty, A. (2010) *A Metaphysics for Scientific Realism: Knowing the Unobservable.* Cambridge: Cambridge University Press.
A useful look at how realism has evolved in the social sciences, culminating in an argument for scientific realism underpinning scientific knowledge.

Finkelde, D. and Livingston, P. (eds) (2020) *Idealism, Relativism and Realism: New Essays on Objectivity Beyond the Analytic-Continental Divide.* Berlin: De Gruyter.
An interesting set of essays that explores the challenges of objectivity under various paradigms.

Boghossian, P. A. and Coliva, A. (2019) *Fear of Knowledge: Against Relativism and Constructivism.* Abingdon: Routledge.
Relativism can be seen as a threatening enemy – and the goal of this book is to take the enemy down. This is a great read if you want to understand the arguments against relativism (and constructivism) as well as the passion paradigm wars can evoke.

Baghramian, M. & Coliva, A. (2019) *Relativism*. Abingdon: Routledge.
A deep dive into the principles of relativism as well as arguments for and against. A good companion piece to Boghossian and Coliva (above).

Social Constructionism

Berger, P. L. and Luckman, T. (1967*) The Social Construction of Reality: A Treatise in the Sociology of Knowledge*. New York: Anchor.
This is a classic work that challenges the proposition that there is a single truth 'out there'. It argues that we can only understand the world by understating those who seek to know it. Beyond this, these seekers of knowledge are also the creators of it.

Burr, V. (2015) *Social Constructionism*, 3rd edition. New York: Psychology Press.
A good introduction – sympathetic yet critical. We like the use of examples to explain and articulate key concepts.

Hjelm, T. (2014) *Social Constructionisms: Approaches to the Study of the Human World.* London: Red Globe Press.
We like the way this book breaks down the construct, links it to our understanding of the social world and discusses relevant critiques.

Walker, C. A. (2015) 'Social constructionism and qualitative research', *Journal of Theory Construction & Testing*, 19(2): 37–8.
It is good to see a direct connection between theory and method.

Objectivity and Subjectivity

Gaukroger, S. (2012) *Objectivity: A Very Short Introduction.* Oxford: Oxford University Press.
Like it says, this is a very short introduction that gives you quick answers and starting points for further exploring objectivity.

John, S. (2021) *Objectivity in Science*. Cambridge: Cambridge University Press.
Is it possible to do value-free research? This book tackles that claim (amongst others) in a thorough discussion of objectivity. A more expansive read within the philosophy of science.

Letherby, G., Scott, J. and Williams, M. (2012) *Objectivity and Subjectivity in Social Research*. London: Sage.
We like the practical approach taken in this book and the resistance to dichotomizing objectivity and subjectivity. An informative look at how they work in concert.

2

SETTING UP AND GETTING STARTED

Learning Objectives

- Getting started
  - To appreciate the personal and professional development associated with research
- Navigating the process
  - To understand the value of becoming familiar with the requirements of your university/discipline/programme
  - To understand the importance of acquiring the right resources, equipment, supervision and literature
  - To develop skills in workload management
- Staying on course
  - To develop strategies for finding balance and overcoming challenges

> The scariest moment is always just before you start.
>
> Stephen King (2010)

GETTING STARTED

You know what would make Stephen King's advice even more valuable? If we knew the best way to make a start. Most students getting ready to tackle a research project have little idea of how to make a start or what they need to get them on their way.

Well, one thing is for sure, research does not just happen. Researching is a process that demands planning, forethought, commitment and persistence. In fact, research is more of a journey than a task; and, like any journey, it needs to be managed, navigated and negotiated from early conception to final destination. Now it is not unusual for students to question their ability to successfully navigate this journey. After all, researching is a skill that is only just beginning to develop, so the thought of embarking on it can be quite daunting. Some jump in without a strategic plan, while others wallow too long in the planning stages. Some will make a good start but get lost or lose motivation along the way. As you begin to contemplate the task ahead, it's worth keeping in mind that completing a research project in good time is much more than a test of your intellectual ability; it is also a test of your persistence and tenacity.

As you travel on your journey, you are likely to find that your quest to produce new knowledge will be a learning experience far richer than you might have ever expected. Conducting a research project allows you to:

- Capitalize on existing skills – You bring with you a host of skills. A research project will allow you to inventory your own skills and apply them to the challenge of conducting a research project.
- Exercise critical thinking skills – Conducting research is a process of constant considered decision-making. Rather than being prescribed, research demands critical reflection and critical decision-making at every turn.
- Engage in 'problem-based learning' – The thinking behind problem-based learning is that the best starting point for learning is working through a problem that needs to be solved in a hands-on fashion. The learning here is 'double loop'. Not only do you learn about a problem you are exploring, but you also learn how to tackle that problem, hopefully in a manner that will allow you to transfer problem-solving skills to a variety of new challenges. The nature of conducting research (and stumbling a bit along the way) embeds problem-based learning into the research process.
- Engage in 'action learning' – Kolb (1984) stressed the importance of the creation of knowledge through 'transformation of experience'. He suggested that experiential or action learning is dependent on cycles that include (1) engagement in real experiences (concrete experimentation) that need to be followed by (2) thoughtful review and consideration (reflexive **observation**) as well as (3) broader theorizing (abstract conceptualization) and (4) attempts to improve action (active experimentation). Such processes are embedded in various aspects of conducting research. To 'do' research is to engage in cycles of action learning.
- Enhance communication skills – Gathering credible data is not a task for the shy or faint-hearted. It is a process that is highly dependent on your ability to communicate with others. Whether it is the challenge of gaining access, conducting interviews or engaging in **participant observation**, boosting your communication skills is often a side benefit of doing research.
- Develop research skills – Even though we write research methods texts, we'll still tell you there is only so much you can learn from 'reading' about the conduct of research – the real learning comes from the 'doing'. Without a doubt, it is reflectively conducting research that will teach you how to do it.

- Produce new knowledge – You will find out something. You will hopefully get an answer to your research question. You will have produced new knowledge that will add to a body of knowledge.
- Engage in, or facilitate, evidence-based decision-making – It is a really good feeling to know that common-sense, practical decisions are being influenced by data you generate. If well managed from conception through to dissemination, your research project might just have the ability to influence change.
- Offer a pathway for gaining academic qualifications or getting a raise – Perhaps these goals are not as noble as the learning objectives above, but let's face it, this kind of stuff is often important to us.

NAVIGATING THE PROCESS

Research is a process that simultaneously demands imagination, creativity, discipline and structure, and needs to be navigated strategically from start to finish. So, right from the start, it is worth considering a number of practicalities related to the process. In order to hit the ground running it is a good idea to: familiarize yourself with your institution/programme's resources and requirements; get appropriately set up; negotiate the advisory process; and manage your workload in ways that will see you complete on time and still manage to maintain a life!

Understanding Your Programme

In order to move strategically through the research process, you need to become familiar with the requirements and resources of your university. If you do not, you might just end up wasting a lot of time undertaking and producing research that falls outside set guidelines and/or not taking full advantage of the resources available to you.

Requirements

One of the greatest frustrations for students and lecturers alike is when good work does not meet set requirements. The best way to ensure that university protocols are met is to find out what they are early on, and to keep them in mind throughout the research project. Common research requirements include:

- Meeting deadlines – Perhaps one of the biggest hurdles you will face, but extremely important to manage. Late submissions might not be accepted or may be subject to penalties. It is well worth knowing your deadlines and familiarizing yourself with policies for late submission and extensions before you even start the journey.
- Staying within word limits – Word limits vary with level of study, discipline and university. But whatever the limit is, it is generally expected that it will take close to this to produce a quality research paper/thesis. As a lecturer, seeing a very 'thin' paper is almost (but not quite) as disappointing as seeing one you will have to get home with

a trolley. Try not to go too far under or over the prescribed word count. Some lecturers/institutions can be quite strict with works that fall outside set limits.

- Gaining ethics approval – This is essential for most research that involves human (or animal) participants and is discussed fully in Chapter 4. Each university will have its own requirements, committees and deadlines for gaining such approval.
- Progress reports/seminars – For longer projects, universities often require reports to be submitted by students, supervisors or both, on an annual or biannual basis. Students might also be expected to present in regularly scheduled seminars.
- An examination process – This too varies by level of study and university. Some research write-ups will be given a grade or level, while others are simply deemed satisfactory/unsatisfactory. For higher degrees, the examination process often involves external examiners that the student may or may not have a say in determining. It may also involve an oral defence (or viva voce) of the work. It is highly advisable to discuss the issue of examination/examiners with your supervisor quite early in the process. There can be great benefit in knowing what to expect.
- Originality and avoidance of **plagiarism** – Virtually all universities have clear policies on originality and plagiarism. Familiarizing yourself with what constitutes plagiarism can help you avoid some deadly grey areas.

Resources

When it comes to resources, many students do not bother to ask, therefore they do not receive. Finding out what your university/programme offers research students should be high on the list of initial priorities. As highlighted in Box 2.1, nothing is more frustrating than finding out about an excellent service or facility just a bit too late.

Box 2.1

Damn! I Wish I Knew That Six Months Ago

Scenario 1

'$1,300! You got $1,300 for your field trip? How in the world did you get that?'

'All research students are entitled to $2,500 a year to help cover costs; you just have to put in a form.'

'You're kidding me. How come I wasn't told?'

Scenario 2

'This great article I need to read is behind a paywall. I guess I'll have to pay if I want to read it ...'

'Don't you know you can do an inter-campus loan through the library website? They can send a PDF right to you.'

'You are joking ... since when?'

Some of the resources you may want to check on are:

- Accommodation – Is dedicated or shared office space available?
- Equipment – Will you have access to desk, computer, printer?
- Software – What software is supported by the university? Is it willing to acquire any software you might need?
- Funds – Is there any money available to help with costs such as university fees, books, photocopying, consumables (paper, ink cartridges, recording media), travel costs (site visits, conference attendance) and equipment (recorder, transcription machine, PC, laptop, software, etc.)?
- Library facilities – What databases are available? Is there a system of inter-library loans?
- Workshops – Does the university offer any methods workshops or writing circles?
- Methods assistance – Is there any assistance available for questionnaire design, transcription, data entry? Is statistics advice available?
- Writing assistance – Is there anyone who can help you put together a proposal, or structure a final draft? Is there anyone to help with editing?

Getting Set Up

Researching is an activity that requires more independence and autonomy than most types of learning you are likely to have attempted and requires that you spend a fair amount of time reading or working at a computer. Getting set up therefore requires access to a quiet place to work, a good reliable computer and proficiency in the software you need to use:

- The study/office – Having a comfortable place to lock yourself away is essential. Researching can be an alienating activity and creating or finding a space where you can work comfortably is well worth the effort.
- The computer – You may need to run statistical and/or **qualitative data** management programs that can be demanding on the system so it may be worth using university-provided desktops in addition/instead of a personal laptop.
- Proficiency – Whether you're using specialist software, or even just managing large documents, working with graphics, and conducting advanced searches, it's important to feel confident in your technical skills. There are lots of helpful online tutorials and your university may offer workshops so take this opportunity to upskill.

Getting the Right Advice

Doing a research project usually involves working with the guidance and support of a mentor or supervisor. For many this is a new and somewhat daunting experience. Now we would like to be able to say that this experience will be highly rewarding – and more often than not it is. But at times it can be tumultuous, frustrating, aggravating and just plain unsatisfactory. Supervisors can be busy, dismissive, muddled and sometimes even arrogant. So it is extremely important to negotiate expectations right from the outset and work towards open, clear and comfortable communication.

If you are new to supervisory relationships, you may not be aware of just how varied they can be. Some relationships are based on student autonomy and independence, while others are much more collaborative and dependent. The only way to know where you stand is to negotiate both student and supervisor expectations. Keep in mind that if you do not do this early, you may be setting yourself up for a tremendous amount of frustration and angst. Emma uses a supervisor expectations checklist where students and supervisor independently rank which tasks are each other's responsibility and use that as a prompt for discussion. Box 2.2 highlights some of the expectations you may want to openly negotiate with your supervisor.

Box 2.2

Negotiating Expectations

Expectations that need to be clarified in student-supervisor relationships include:

Autonomy:

- Who is responsible for orienting the student to university resources/requirements?
- Who sets the timelines?
- How much advice/direction can/will the supervisor provide on the selection of topic, question, methodological and theoretical frameworks?
- Will the student be expected to submit all drafts for review/comment?
- Do all new directions need to be cleared with the supervisor?
- Will writing/editing assistance be provided by the supervisor?
- Who makes the final decision on acceptability?

The programme:

- How regularly will you meet? Whose responsibility is it to schedule meetings?
- What is the expected turnaround time for getting and responding to feedback?
- Are seminar presentations required?

The nature of the relationship:

- Will the relationship be purely professional or professional/personal?
- Will emotional support be provided?
- Is open and frank discussion on progress expected/welcomed?

Your supervisor–student relationship is likely to be closer than any other relationship previously experienced with an academic. One reason this can be a bit nerve racking is that it is a relationship of very unequal power. On one side you have the professor and expert, while on the other you have the student and novice. Yes, the goal should be mentoring, growth and mutual respect, and this is usually the case. But, as highlighted in Box 2.3, it is a relationship that can easily leave students feeling patronized or even a bit intimidated.

Box 2.3

The Power of the Red Pen – Kate's Story

When I switched universities, I was assigned to a supervisor who had just received her PhD and had research interests similar to my own. We met a few times, and I can't say it went very well. While her PhD was in an area similar to mine, our approaches seemed worlds apart, and I got the distinct feeling that she thought my approach was not just different, but wrong. No one wants to be 'judged', so it was with much trepidation that I handed her an early chapter of my thesis. I hated the thought of her passing judgement as she read and dreaded receiving her feedback.

I got the chapter back a few weeks later and it was even worse than I thought. The paper was literally covered in red ink. Angry, vile, 'I have power over you', 'You are wrong' red ink. Well, I went from feeling apprehensive to angry. There was no need to exercise that type of power trip on me. I did not need hypercritical judgement, what I needed was support, guidance, advice and perspective. In the end, what I actually needed was a new supervisor.

This does not mean that you and your supervisor need to be on the same 'wavelength'. A lot can be learned from a supervisor whose style pushes your boundaries and helps you grow in ways you might not have even considered. The thesis acknowledgement below sums this up quite well:

> My thanks to Dr Sherman who was a great supervisor for the way my mind works. And my thanks to Dr Hakim who was an equally great supervisor for the way it doesn't.

In sum, we would recommend three strategies for facilitating a positive supervisor–student relationship. First, know what your supervisor expects of you and what you can expect from your supervisor right from the start of your relationship. Second, be open – do not bottle up concerns and frustration. Share them with your supervisor in as non-threatening a way as possible as soon as issues arise. Third, if you cannot see a way to make the relationship work, talk to someone about it: a course coordinator, the research office, an academic you trust. Not every relationship may be destined for success but working towards this is the goal. It's important to remember that if you can develop a healthy rapport with your supervisor, you will make your journey that much easier.

Using Literature

One of the biggest challenges in starting a research project is feeling overwhelmed by the task of narrowing into your research topic and eventual question. Our advice here is to turn to the literature and turn to it quite early. Yes, talk to your supervisor, but also become independently knowledgeable, and maybe even an expert, in your topic.

Do the background reading, do the contextual reading, do the academic reading. Understand the pressing issues, understand the political agendas, understand the gaps in knowledge. If you have your head around all this, imagine how much less daunting it will be to engage in a fruitful conversation about the direction of your research!

So, for example, say you were interested in health promotion; in particular, you are interested in obesity in youth, but you are having a difficult time focusing in more than this. Read! Read the background statistics on obesity and youth – in your area, your state, your country, internationally. Read the media coverage – local and beyond. Read about what the local/state health promotion units are doing. Read through journal articles that cover past research on youth obesity. Gather it all in. It is needed to help you focus. It is needed to help you articulate that research question.

Now there's no shortage of literature available to the budding researcher. An array of library databases allows you to explore almost any topic. And with tools like Google Scholar, you can search for abstracts, peer-reviewed articles, books, theses and technical reports across a variety of disciplines. Even if you haven't done this type of literature search before, your day-to-day Internet searching already has you fairly skilled in this area. And as you become familiar with your university's databases and begin to think more and more strategically about how you can expand and limit your searches, appropriate literature will only be a few clicks away. We'll leave it here for now, but you can turn to Chapter 6 for a more step-by-step guide to searching and finding relevant literature.

Working with Others

The conduct of research can be challenging enough when you are working on your own but add a group element and the challenges can be exponential. That's not to say there aren't benefits. Conducting research with others will not only give you the ability to increase the scale and scope of your work, it will also allow you to develop other professional skills such as delegation, teamwork and communication (face-to-face and virtual).

There are strategies that can make the conduct of group research travel along with as little stress as possible:

- Align incentives
  - Discuss team and individual performance objectives
  - Ensure that team members know how excellent work for the team will affect their own performance evaluation
  - Aim to have each member derive a sense of purpose and belonging from being on the project team
  - Discuss how members need to understand that a negative team outcome will reflect negatively on them
- Establish ground rules
  - Develop rules to govern expectations and appropriate behaviours. Once set, these rules can be invoked if problems arise

- Assign tasks
  - Tasks should be broken into their component parts
  - An inventory should be made of what each member could contribute
  - Clarify the process
  - Develop a timeline, including meeting dates
  - Identify the end product and work back to the present
  - Establish completion dates for subtasks
- Keep communication open
  - Ensure that everyone knows what is expected of them, and when it is expected
  - Regular meetings are essential to maintaining good team relationships
- Accentuate the positive
  - Dialogue is critical for understanding each other's points of view
  - Ways must be found to break down language and status barriers
  - Strive to be a 'glue person' that holds the team together
- Manage team crises
  - Consider ways to get the team back on track
  - Discuss problems in a special meeting
  - Take stock of what has been achieved
  - Strive to achieve some quick 'small gains' that will help the broader team process
  - Remind everyone of 'the shadow of the future'
- End well
  - When the project has been completed, find ways to celebrate
  - Efforts to formally end the project can ensure that ties created during the life of the team are respected
  - Seeking good endings is especially vital when the team process has been difficult

Managing the Workload

One word that we stress in all student research projects, regardless of level or discipline, is 'doability'. Is it doable? Well, assessing doability involves more than just looking at the quality of the research design. It also involves looking at the full gamut of pressures and responsibilities that you as an individual need to manage. Realistically assessing and managing your workload is essential. If you don't, time will simply slip away.

There are no set rules for time management. You might be a night owl, an early bird, someone who can multi-task, someone who can only tackle one task at a time, someone who feels anxious without a defined schedule or someone who is more spontaneous. Recognizing your own approach, working with its strengths and addressing its shortcomings will be important to timely completion. If you can work your own style into a plan, it can help you manage what is likely to end up a very complex and, at times, seemingly unending task.

One useful tool is a Gantt chart. As shown in Table 2.1, a Gantt chart can be used to map out a project from start to finish. Now keep in mind that researching is often a fluid and flexible exercise likely to incorporate the unexpected, and your chart will invariably need to shift in order to reflect the dynamic nature of your project. However, having a document that can be negotiated and modified is more likely to keep you true to deadlines than not having one at all.

Table 2.1 Gantt chart

	Jan.	Feb.	Mar.	Apr.	May	June	July	Aug.	Sept.	Oct.	Nov.	Dec.
Groundwork	xx	xx										
Literature review		xx	xx	xx	xx	xx						
Defining methods			xx	xx								
Data collection					xx	xx	xx					
Progress seminar						12th						
Data analysis							xx	xx	xx			
Write first draft		xx	xx	xx	xx	xx	xx	xx				
Write second draft								xx	xx	xx		
Final seminar											27th	
Write final draft										xx	xx	xx
Thesis due												15th

For some, the discipline it takes to stick to a Gantt chart comes naturally. These amazing individuals are able to get up at a specified time, work diligently to a plan, and take only minimal food and toilet breaks. And they manage to do this five days a week. For us ordinary humans, however, the procrastination skills we have developed over many years of formal schooling are much too sophisticated to see us succumb to that level of discipline. Instead, we wait for inspiration. Which is fine if inspiration strikes with enough frequency and regularity – but what if it doesn't? Well, then, you may have to 'trick' yourself into some sort of pseudo-inspirational state. Some things you might want to try are:

- Working on/reading over your research journal – An invaluable tool for any researcher is a good journal that can capture creative inspiration and help you manage the process. Your journal might include observations, notes on method and theory, lists of relevant contacts, notes/reminders to yourself and any other ideas, doodles, concept maps, etc. that come to mind. Adding to your journal, or simply reading it over, may get the creative juices flowing. Recording your thoughts and documenting your progress is also an essential part of being a reflexive researcher.

- Forcing yourself to get on the computer – Engaging in some menial task can be a catalyst for doing richer work. Try starting with relatively mindless editorial work, data cleaning or referencing, and then try to move to whatever you are procrastinating over. If you don't approach the computer at all, then nothing gets done. But if you sit down to a task, not only is the task accomplished, but the real work might get going as well.
- Forcing yourself to get off your phone. Putting your phone away in a drawer, putting it on aeroplane mode, or using one of the Internet-blocking apps can help if you find yourself reaching for distraction.
- Writing a letter to a real or fictional friend – If you are feeling stuck, try writing an informal letter that tells 'whoever' what you are trying to do. Freeing yourself from academic writing can often help liberate ideas.
- Going for a walk – Sometimes a good head-clearing walk can be a trigger for a flood of fresh ideas. You might like to take notes or voice recordings on your travels if you are struck by inspiration.

Staying on Course

Nearly every student agonizes over the research journey. For most, their research project is likely to be the biggest academic project ever undertaken. Knowing a field, being responsible for the production of 'new knowledge', designing methods, collecting and analysing data, and writing it all up can be an intimidating challenge – particularly for those whose roles and responsibilities in the real world extend beyond those of being a student. But rest assured, feelings of frustration, confusion and even incompetence are both commonplace and surmountable. Being able to find a balance and deal with a crisis are part and parcel of researching.

Finding a Balance

Student, employee, parent, child, partner – no student is a student alone. We all have a variety of roles to play. Yet sometimes those around us, ourselves included, forget that we need to manage and balance all of these simultaneously, even if they are sometimes incompatible. Balance is essential. No one can reach or work to their potential if they are neglecting important areas of their life.

So how do you find balance when you know you need to focus on your studies, yet you are feeling pressure at work, and you realize that you must reprioritize family? Well, as highlighted in Box 2.4, whether at work, home or university, being honest and open about your needs is a good start. That, combined with the ability to say 'no', can go a long way to staying on top of it:

- At work – Try taking the time to discuss the demands of study with your managers. Hopefully, they will be supportive. If not, at least you know where you stand. If your research is work-related, it may be possible to negotiate time and resources for your project, particularly if you explain the significance and potential benefits of your research to the workplace.

- At home – Having the support of family is essential, not only for the practical support that can come from assistance with domestic duties, childcare, etc., but also for the emotional support that can be quite crucial during the process. Unfortunately, some partners can be threatened by, or envious of, your achievements. Working through this dilemma, or again at least knowing where you stand, can put you in a stronger position.
- At university – We think the best advice is to be professional but put your concerns on the table for legitimization. Being open and honest with your supervisor is crucial to your ability to set realistic and, most importantly, achievable goals.

Critical Thinking Challenge 2

Overcoming Obstacles

What do you imagine will be the biggest threat to successful on-time completion of your research project? What are one or two strategies you can use to avoid and/or manage this situation?

Dealing with Challenges

> If there is no struggle, there is no progress.
>
> Frederick Douglass (attributed)

You know what? It would actually be unrealistic to undertake a major research project without expecting it to intersect with some sort of challenge – our lives are full of them. It is easy to find it becoming too much, to start doubting yourself, or doubting what you're doing. For example, you may experience periods of waning motivation. It can be difficult to stay motivated for an extended period of time. What starts as an exciting and interesting project can sometimes end up being one you just want to finish. Developing a supportive research culture can go a long way in keeping up motivation. Whether it be an attentive/sympathetic ear at home, interested work colleagues, a peer support network or a relevant online group, engaging with others can help keep your interest up. It might also be worth reminding yourself to 'enjoy the process' and that 'the finish line will appear'.

Another common challenge is a lack of confidence. There are a lot of people who start their 'research' careers at the end of very successful 'learning' careers. These are people who are used to competence and success. Well, research students generally set their own agenda, work independently and attempt to work to their potential; and herein lies the problem. Working to your potential pushes at your own personal limits, often in ways prior learning has not. Feeling like an impostor, thinking that it is beyond your capabilities and believing that your work is not good enough are, believe it or not, fears widely shared. Getting a more objective sense of how you are doing can help put things in perspective. If you talk to your supervisor and your peers, you will often find that others have more faith in you than you have in yourself. We often tell students who are facing a crisis of confidence that they are in the midst of a learning process; skills and confidence will grow with time.

At times you might also feel lost. And this can happen even within the parameters of a shorter project. Research often starts with broad-ranging exploration that can take you down many tangents. The upside is that this exploration will undeniably increase your learning and often lead to new insights. The downside, however, is that you risk feeling lost. It is pretty easy to be blown off course and feel like you have no idea where you are going. Finding direction can come from reflecting on what it is that you really want to know, having open and candid discussions with your supervisor, and in the end remembering that the answers may not simply appear. You may need to make some hard decisions about the direction you will take.

Becoming disorganized can also get the better of you; and it's too easy to say, 'You need to be organized'. You probably knew that before you got that out-of-control feeling. The need for self-discipline may be obvious, but the ability to exercise it is much harder. If physical disorganization is your downfall, take a week or two off from 'doing' research and just clean up your workspace and organize yourself. If, however, disorganization is more in your mind and you feel as though you cannot think straight, you can (1) try the above – an organized desk and office can pave the way for an organized mind – or (2) get away from it all. Sometimes a good weekend away is all you need to recharge the mental batteries.

Finally, your research project may intersect with some level of personal crisis. It was John Lennon who said 'Life is what happens to you while you're busy making other plans'. It would be nice if the world stopped while you got on with your research, but that simply doesn't happen. Whether it's finances, partners, parents, children, work, in fact any variety of drama, the research process necessarily coincides with life's inevitable ups and downs. Reach out to your support network and speak openly with your supervisor. Our experience is that people are generally supportive. Perhaps most important of all, don't put too much pressure on yourself. Get support and then make a guilt-free decision to press on, take it slower or have a hiatus until the crisis subsides.

What is important is to know that you're not alone. As shown in Box 2.4, knowing what to expect, knowing how others cope, and developing and using a support system can help you through inevitable rough patches.

Box 2.4

Zina's Research Story

I think there are several reasons why I (Zina) was able to manage my research project from start to finish without too much undue stress. For one, I was pretty organized. I set myself timelines that were realistic - including life-balance and making sure that my plan did not involve taking me away for my other commitments. And I made sure that my supervisor thought my plan was achievable. So not only did I try to honestly assess my own work-life challenges, I also had an expert assess the research end of things.

Another factor was trying to remember that, in most cases, stress does pass. When I did feel a bit overwhelmed, I did my best to breathe through it and believe it would pass. I also quickly sought reassurance and support at these times and did not let myself wallow for too long.

(Continued)

I think we need to do that more - a lot of my peers seemed to sit in their stress rather than take steps to get past it.

So that's my advice. Know where you want to go, make sure your supervisor thinks your approach is achievable, be organized and get support when you need it. Believe it is doable and try not to let doubts double down in your mind.

I Have a Question!

My Project Is Pretty Small-Scale, It's Not a PhD or Anything. Do All These Challenges and Strategies Apply to Me?

Absolutely. Here is the thing about research. Regardless of whether it is a PhD, master's, honours or a research component within a capstone unit, most students are navigating uncharted waters and feeling a lot of time pressure. Your project scope tends to be just a little too big for your timeframe, and it is easy to feel out of your depth. Knowing what to expect and having strategies to call on can certainly facilitate the journey, regardless of scope.

Chapter Summary

- Research is a process that needs to be actively managed. Being strategic in your preliminary planning, being organized and prepared, and creating the mental space necessary for research are important parts of the process.
- In order to produce research that falls within university guidelines, you will need to familiarize yourself with your institution's requirements. This will allow you to access all resources and navigate a path through the research process.
- Getting the right advice can be a challenge. Working towards good communication and clear expectations with your supervisor is essential. Also be ready to engage with literature early on so you can be on top of your topic.
- If you are working with others, you will need to actively manage that process. While group work can definitely add elements of stress do not underestimate the professional skill development it can offer.
- Conducting research can throw up some real challenges. Using Gantt charts and working with both discipline and inspiration can help you manage workload and timelines, but it is also important to remember how important balance is to well-being.
- The research process is rarely an easy and straightforward journey. It often involves challenges associated with confidence and motivation and coincides with life's ups and downs. Knowing that you are not alone and that there is support can help get you through.

FIND YOUR NEXT STEP

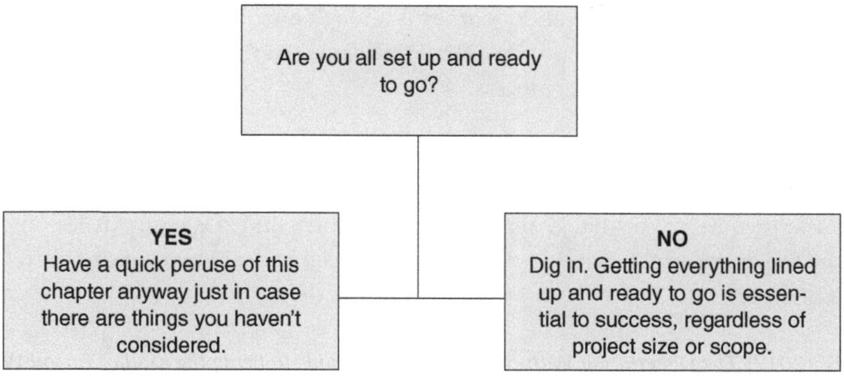

FURTHER READING

There's an incredible blog called The Thesis Whisperer run by Professor Inger Mewburn which you can check out at thesiswhisperer.com; subscribe to as an email list; or listen to the podcast On the Reg. Compilations of the last ten years of blog posts are available in physical form with the book:

Mewburn, I. (2020). *How to Tame your PhD*, 2nd edition. Thesis Whisperer Books.
There are quite a few research project survival guides out there. The following might be worth a look.

Jegede, F. (2021). *Doing a PhD in the Social Sciences: A Student's Guide to Post-Graduate Research and Writing*. Abingdon: Routledge.
From getting set up, working with your supervisor, to the dreaded viva/oral defence, this guide covers each stage of the process with helpful tips and examples.

Cooksey, R. W. and McDonald G. (2019) *Surviving and Thriving in Postgraduate Research.* Singapore: Springer.
It may not feel possible to do more than just survive, but this book shows that enjoying and thriving is possible with the right strategies and mindset.

Hall, G. and Longman, J. (2016) *The Postgraduate's Companion*. London: Sage.
Some good information here on topics such as what a research degree involves; selecting the right university; getting in; and getting funding. It also takes you through the thesis process and what you can expect when you complete. Quite a comprehensive guide.

Roberts, C. and Hyatt, L. (2018) *The Dissertation Journey: A Practical and Comprehensive Guide to Planning, Writing, and Defending Your Dissertation*, 3rd (revised) edition. Thousand Oaks, CA: Corwin Press.
There is no doubt that the dissertation journey is a tough one. We like how this guide is there to accompany you. It is stronger on the overall challenge than research methods, but worth a look if you are struggling with the process.

Townsend, K. (2018) *How to Keep Your Research Project on Track: Insights from When Things Go Wrong*. Cheltenham: Edward Elgar.
We love the premise of this book. Yes, things do go awry and the resultant lessons become part of the learning journey. But do you know what's even better? Being able to learn from the mistakes of others.

White, G. (2017) *The Dissertation Warrior: The Ultimate Guide to Being the Kind of Person Who Finishes a Doctoral Dissertation or Thesis*. Happy Valley, OR: Triumphant Heart International.
Less about the thesis, and more about the thesis writer. This is terrific, because the journey of producing a thesis, at any level, is a journey of growth.

3

DEVELOPING YOUR RESEARCH QUESTION

Learning Objectives

- The importance of good questions
    - To understand why the articulation of a research question is so crucial
    - To be able to use a research question to define an investigation and provide direction
- The preliminaries: defining your topic
    - To understand the value of creativity and inspiration in defining a topic
    - To understand how literature can be used to narrow into topic
    - To be mindful of the practicalities that can set parameters for research
- From interesting topics to researchable questions
    - To be able to engage in a process that moves topics to researchable questions
    - To understand the iterative nature of question development
    - To understand how and when hypotheses are appropriate for research
- Characteristics of good questions
    - To be able to assess the efficacy and researchability of potential research questions

THE IMPORTANCE OF GOOD QUESTIONS

The scientific mind does not so much provide the right answers as ask the right questions.

Claude Lévi-Strauss (1964)

You're ready. You have got yourself set up and have a pretty good idea of what you are in for. You even have a few research ideas. Next step? To develop and articulate a clear research question.

Now you may be thinking, 'I have a pretty good idea about what I want to research. Is working on my actual question so important?' Well, the answer is an unequivocal 'yes'. There are a lot of students who want to jump right into their research project without taking the time to really think through and develop their research question. Some have ideas about their topic, but they are not clear on the aspects they want to explore. Others will have their ideas pretty much narrowed down but have not clearly articulated this in a researchable question.

We have to say that we are real sticklers for good research questions. We believe they are absolutely fundamental to good research; and your ability to articulate one is essential. After all, how will you know when you have found the answer to your question, if you can't say what your question is?

Remember: research is a decision-making journey. The process, in fact, demands that you constantly engage in decision-making that is logical, consistent and coherent. And what do you think is the benchmark for logical, consistent and coherent decision-making? It's that the choices you make take you one step closer to being able to answer your research question credibly. So without clear articulation of your question, you are really travelling blind.

Research questions are essential because they:

- Define an investigation – A well-articulated research question can provide both you and your eventual readers with information about your project. It can:
    - define the topic – youth suicide, environmental degradation, secularization, etc.;
    - define the nature of the research endeavour – to discover, explore, explain, describe or compare;
    - define the questions you are interested in – what, where, how, when, why;
    - define your constructs and **variables** – income, age, education, gender, self-esteem, pollution, etc.;
    - and indicate whether you foresee a relationship between variables – impacts, increases, decreases, relationships, correlations, causes, etc.
- Set boundaries – Along your research journey you are likely to find yourself facing plenty of tangents, detours and diversions, and a well-defined question can help you set boundaries. When faced with an interesting tangent, ask yourself: 'What does this have to do with my question?' We would suggest that there are three potential answers:
    - (1) actually very little – I will have to leave it and maybe pick it up in my next project;
    - (2) actually it is quite relevant – if you think about it, it really does relate to … (this can be exciting and add new dimensions to your work); and
    - (3) well, nothing really, but I actually think this is at the heart of what I want to know – perhaps I need to rethink my question.
- Provide direction – A well-defined, well-articulated research question will act as a blueprint for your project. It will point you towards the theory you need to explore; the literature you need to review; the data you need to gather; and the methods you need to call on. In fact, we would suggest that it is nearly impossible to define a clear

methodology for an ill-defined research question. If you do not know what you want to know, you will not be in a position to know how to find it out.

- Act as a frame of reference for assessing your work – Not only does your question provide continuity and set the agenda for your entire study, but it also acts as a benchmark for assessing decision-making. The criteria for all decisions related to your project will be whether or not choices lead you closer to credible answers to your research question.

Now we don't want to make it sound like research questions are reductionist devices that take all exploration, creativity and fluidity out of the research process. Not at all. Research questions themselves can be designed so that they are open and exploratory. As well, research questions can, and often do, change, shift and evolve during the early stages of a project. This is as it should be, since your engagement in the literature evolves both your knowledge and thinking. Yes, research questions define an investigation and provide direction, but it is up to the researcher to define and redefine questions so that they can most appropriately accomplish these tasks.

THE PRELIMINARIES: DEFINING YOUR TOPIC

All this talk about the importance of research questions is fine, but what if you're not even sure what interests to pursue? Well, you are not alone. Yes, there are plenty of students who are quite clear about what they want to research, but there are also a lot who really struggle with the idea of generating a research topic. In fact, many feel that coming up with something worthy of research is beyond them.

So how do you focus in on a topic? Well, as highlighted below and in Box 3.1, you work on generating ideas by homing in on your curiosity and creativity; looking for inspiration; and exploring your options with an eye towards practicalities. It is the first step in moving from real challenges and opportunities to research questions.

Curiosity and Creativity

> The most precious thing I had then is the most precious thing I have now – my own curiosity.
>
> Ta-Nehisi Coates (2018)

Ideas for research are generated any time curiosity or passion is aroused. Every day we are surrounded by events, situations and interactions that make us wonder, stop and think, or bring joy, frustration, relief or anger bubbling to the surface. This is the rich and fertile ground from which research ideas are born. Think about what stirs you, what you argue about with your friends, family and peers, and what issues are topical in the world, at home or in your workplace. You will soon find that research topics abound. If you can learn to catch yourself thinking, 'Gee, I wonder ...', you will have an unending supply of ideas.

An option worth trying here is a concept map. Mapping allows you the freedom to think laterally as well as linearly. It uses free association to encourage the mind to jump from one idea to another, thereby enhancing creative processes. Concept mapping can facilitate brainstorming, drawing out connections and building themes; and can also be a great tool for overcoming writer's block. Figure 3.1 shows a simple concept map used to draw out potential research topics.

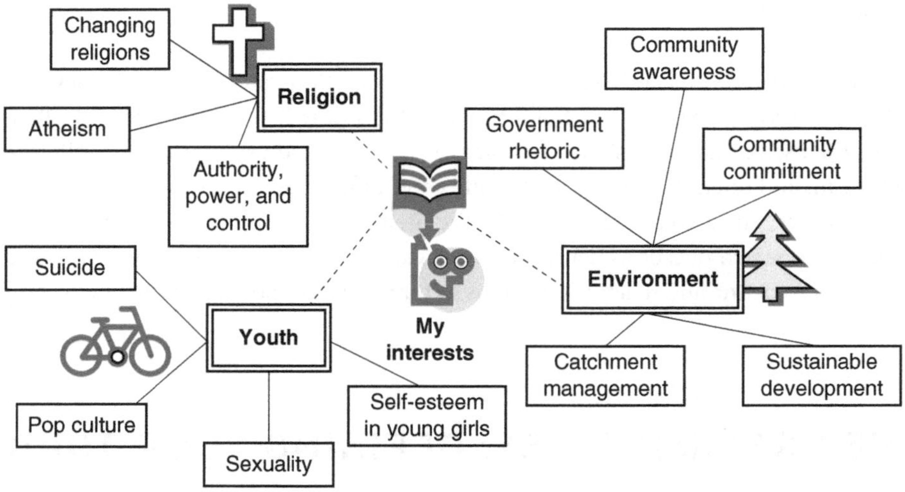

Figure 3.1 Concept map of potential research topics

Turning to Literature

The importance of reading for research cannot be overemphasized. Never do we know everything about our topic, and rarely do we know enough. Getting abreast of the background, context, controversies, academic debates and political agendas surrounding your area of interest is time well spent. It will certainly help you identify research interests and research needs. You may find yourself drawn to the exploration of an important aspect of a problem that has been ignored in the literature. You may want to question some of the assumptions that underpin common understandings. You may decide to add to a raging debate with an innovative approach. You may want to take up an opportunity to gather definitive data evidence for much needed evidence-based decision-making. You may want to take up the challenge of answering further questions posed at the end of a research paper.

In addition to topical literature, you might also develop questions through your engagement with theory. This happens when you are reading 'theory' and it suddenly resonates. You think 'aha', maybe that is why a particular situation is the way it is, or perhaps that is why they do what they do. A student of Zina's had such a moment when he read a work by Althusser highlighting the role that institutions such as the family, schools and the Church have in embedding government ideology into individual consciousness. The student began to view the role of the Church in a new light and decided to investigate if and how the Irish Catholic Church operates as an arm of the government in the socialization of its citizens.

An early literature task is the preliminary literature review (see Chapter 6). This is an attempt to become aware of the scope of research that has been conducted in your area. By understanding what has been researched, what has not been researched, the methods employed and the efficacy of those methods/projects, you can begin to understand the need for and scope of potential projects in your space. This is also an important time to notice and reflect on whose voices are represented in the literature and which perspectives might be overlooked. An early literature review is an excellent way to begin to narrow into your research.

Looking for Inspiration

Another approach for narrowing in on your topic (see Box 3.1) is to be highly attuned to the world around you. Inspiration might be drawn from:

- Personal insights and experiences – Everyone has experience and insight they can draw on. Take the workplace, for example. Just about anyone who has ever had a job will tell you that workplaces are rife with problems: red tape, inefficiencies, ineptitude, incompetence, decision-makers not in touch with the coal-face, corruption, profit before service, morale and motivation. Your own frustrations are often tied to the frustrations of many – and if they can also be tied to the goals, aims, objectives and vision of the organization, community or institution in which they sit, then there is a good chance those very frustrations will have 'research' potential.
- An observation – It can be quite hard to see what surrounds us, so viewing the world through fresh eyes can provide powerful research insights. This happened to a student of Zina's who was on a train when he suddenly became fascinated by the unwritten rules of personal space. He found himself intrigued by the rules that governed who sat where, how close they sat, who moved away from whom and under what circumstances. He watched with fascination as people jockeyed for seats as the number of carriage occupants changed with each stop, and decided that he wanted to study the rules that govern such behaviour.
- Contemporary/timely issues – Sometimes an old topic can take on fresh life. A topic might suddenly become an agenda at the workplace or may even become the focus of global attention. The Western world's interest in, fascination with and judgement of Islamic faith is a case in point. 'Angles' become easy to find and questions such as 'How are the media covering the topic?', 'What are the policy, practice and rhetoric of government?' and 'What impact is this having on schoolyard racism?' become quite easy to generate.
- Identifying **stakeholder** needs – Stakeholder needs can be extremely broad and can range from the need for an equitable health-care system, to a need for remediation of blue-green algae blooms in the local area, to a need to motivate students to stay in school. Identifying needs can come from following media coverage, reading letters to the editor or listening to stakeholders at various forums including town council meetings, workplace meetings or any other place where stakeholders may gather to express their concerns.
- Community engagement – You may be a member of a community and want to use your research to solve a pressing need. Or you might want to develop research to be useful to

communities you are not a part of. In either case, talking to people is essential. What do community members see as problems and issues? What do they want and need? If you want to do research with and for communities (rather than 'on' or 'to'), it's essential to get out there and *listen*.

Box 3.1

Selecting Issues Suitable for Research

Below is a list of research topics some of our students are working on and how/why these issues were selected.

- The impact of the accessibility of pornography on the sexual expectation of teens - Selected by a high-school counsellor concerned over what he sees as a worrying trend.
- The inclusion of climate change risk as a factor in fire-management planning - Selected by a manager in the New South Wales Rural Fire Service who recognized the need for currency in planning processes.
- A large percentage of non-recyclable materials in household recycle bins - Selected by a frustrated council officer in charge of waste management who was undertaking a higher degree.
- Decision-making in a health-promotion centre without any evidence base - Selected by the new centre director who was unsure how to prioritize issues.
- Violence towards nursing staff in emergency wards - Selected by a former nurse undertaking an occupational health and safety postgraduate degree after being forced into a career change by a patient attack.
- Bastardization and ritual hazing at university - Selected by a student who went through such practices in her first year at university.
- Subcontractors in the construction industry with poor safety records - Selected by an occupational health and safety student because of current media coverage related to the topic.
- Underutilization of experiential learning in the classroom - Selected by an education student through the literature she came across in the course of her degree.
- The motivations of individuals adopting strategies to mitigate climate change - Selected by a student fascinated by apathy in spite of individuals' knowledge of a threat.
- Disregard of fire alarms in Hong Kong high-rises - Selected by a fire-safety officer undertaking a higher degree, who was in charge of an investigation where seven people died because they ignored an alarm.

I Have a Question!

Do I Have Unlimited Scope in Choosing My Research Topic?

In a word, no. As limiting as it may seem, all budding topics need to be checked against practicalities. No matter how interesting a topic appears, in the end your project must be 'doable'. At the stage of topic definition 'doability' includes:

1 Appropriateness - some ideas are simply not relevant to the degree you are undertaking. Even if a topic has potential, it may be at odds with your academic programme. If this is the case, it is a signal to sit down and really think about your research, academic and career goals ... and seek alignment.
2 Supervision - not many students manage to negotiate a major research project without a great deal of supervisory support. Finding out whether appropriate supervision for your topic is available before you lock yourself into a project is well advised.
3 Funding body/employer requirements - if a funding body or employer has sponsored you to conduct research in a particular area, you may not be able to shift topics. Keep in mind, however, that even within a defined project, there can be scope to concentrate on particular aspects or bring a fresh perspective to an issue. Open negotiation and even a 'sales pitch' covering the relevance and possible benefits of your proposed research can give you more creative potential.

FROM INTERESTING TOPICS TO RESEARCHABLE QUESTIONS

Hopefully you now recognize the importance of developing a clear research question and have an interesting topic in mind. It's time to begin narrowing in on your question.

Narrowing In

While expansive questions can be the focus of good research, ambiguity can arise when questions are broad and unwieldy. Being bounded and precise makes the research task easier to accomplish. If you are worried about being too limited, keep in mind that each question can be likened to a window that can be used to explore rich theory and depth in understanding. 'Focused' is not a synonym for 'superficial'. There are two strategies we recommend for narrowing in. The first is to revisit your concept map, while the second is to work through the four-step question generation process outlined below.

The Concept Map Revisited

Just as a concept map can be used to brainstorm research topics, it can also be used for question clarification. The map in Figure 3.2 explores 'Why young girls have poor self-image'. The student has mapped out some major influences – peers, parents and the media – and has begun to think about causes of the 'problem'. This leads to some interesting ideas that might all be researchable. The student then takes this further by asking two things:

1 what aspects am I most interested in; and
2 do I have any insights that I might be able to add? From this, the student has two 'aha' moments, and research questions begin to come into focus. The first looks at the role of the media as a whole and asks: 'What do young girls consider normal in terms of

body image?' The second comes from an interesting reflection on the compliments parents give to daughters, and how often they relate to how 'pretty they are'. The student begins to wonder whether parents are subconsciously teaching their daughters that worth is determined by external beauty.

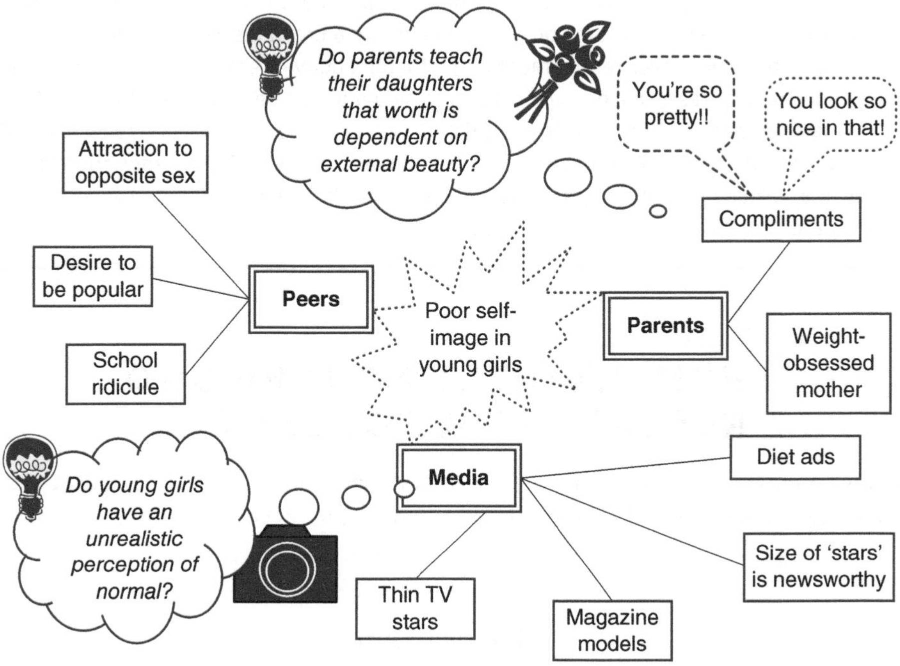

Figure 3.2 Mapping your questions

Four-Step Question Generation Process

A more linear process than concept mapping is to work through the following four steps:

1 Using only one- or two-word responses, write down the answers to the following questions:
   a What is your topic? For example, back pain, recycling, independent learning, social media bullying …
   b What is the context for your research? For example, a school, local authority, hospital, community …
   c What do you want to achieve? For example, to discover, to describe, to change, to explore, to explain, to develop, to understand …
   d What is the nature of your question? Is it a what, who, where, how, when or why question?
   e Are there any potential relationships you want to explore? For example, impacts, increases, decreases, relationships, correlations, causes …
2 Starting with the nature of the question – who, what, where, how, when – begin to piece together the answers generated in step 1 until you feel comfortable with the eventual

question or questions. Suppose your problem was the large percentage of non-recyclable materials in household recycle bins (as discussed in Box 3.1). The answers from step 1 might lead to a number of questions:

a Topic: recycling. Context: domestic/community. Goal: to explore why there is a lack of efficiency. Nature of your question: who and why. Relationship: correlation between demographic characteristics and inefficient recycling.

Question: Is there a relationship between household recycling behaviours and demographic characteristics?

b Topic: recycling. Context: domestic/households. Goal: to understand how individuals go about the task of recycling. Nature of your question: how. Relationship: N/A.

Question: How do individuals engage in decision-making processes related to household domestic waste management?

c Topic: recycling. Context: domestic/community. Goal: to describe the nature of recycling inefficiencies so that an effective community awareness campaign can be developed. Nature of your question: what. Relationship: N/A.

Question: What are the most common non-recyclable items found in household recycle bins?

3 If you have developed more than one question (remember: any one problem can lead to a multitude of research questions), decide on your main question based on interest and practicalities as well as the advice of your supervisor.
4 Narrow and clarify until your question is as concise and well articulated as possible. Remember: the first articulation of any research question is unlikely to be as clear, helpful and unambiguous as the third, fourth or even fifth attempt.

These two processes should go a long way in helping you define a solid research question – something essential for setting you on the right methodological path. But getting there can be a process. Box 3.2 gives you a few examples of research question evolution.

Box 3.2

The Evolution of a 'Good' Research Question

Initial Question: How should schools deal with child abuse?

Problems: High ambiguity - need to define schools; need to define child abuse; need to define 'abusers'; need to define 'deal with'.

After several iterations that included consultation with literature, key stakeholders and supervisor ...

Final Question: What is best practice for UK primary schools in managing allegations of physical, emotional or sexual mistreatment of school children by school staff?

(Continued)

Initial Question: Does mandatory reporting decrease domestic violence?

Problems: Ambiguity - need to define mandatory reporting; need to define domestic violence; need to define stakeholders. Possibly wrong question - questions that start with 'Does' are yes/no questions; not generally what you want.

After several iterations that included consultation with literature, key stakeholders and supervisor ...

Final Question: Have the Northern Territory Domestic and Family Violence Act amendments introducing mandatory reporting of domestic violence decreased incidents of violence, in spite of statistics that show an increase in reported events?

Initial Question: Should Facebook be open to exploration by researchers?

Problems: Ambiguity - need to define what aspects of Facebook; need to define researchers; need to define exploration. Possibly wrong question - another yes/no question; worth reconsidering what you really want to know that sits under this articulation.

After several iterations that included consultation with literature, key stakeholders and supervisor ...

Final Question: Under what circumstances might an analysis of Facebook posts be warranted by professional researchers and how can this be managed in an ethical fashion?

The Need to Redefine

You now have the perfect research question. You are on track and ready to set that question in stone. Well, perhaps not – research questions can, and often do, change, shift and evolve during the early stages of a project; and not only is this fine, it is actually appropriate as your engagement in the research process evolves both your knowledge and thinking. Developing a clear question is essential for direction setting, but it is important to remember that the research journey is rarely linear. It is a process that generates as many questions as it answers and is bound to take you in unexpected directions.

Consider the following. In order to do research, you need to:

1. Define your research question so that you can identify the body of literature you need to become conversant with and eventually review.
2. Read and review a body of literature so that you are in a position to form appropriate, researchable questions.

So what comes first, the chicken or the egg? In the case of reading and question setting, one does not necessarily precede the other. They should, in fact, be intertwined. Research generally starts with an idea, which might come from any number of sources. The idea should then lead to reading; this reading should lead to the development of a potentially researchable question; the potential question should lead to more specific reading; and the specific reading should modify the question. As shown in Figure 3.3, forming a question is an iterative process, one that needs to be informed by reading at all stages.

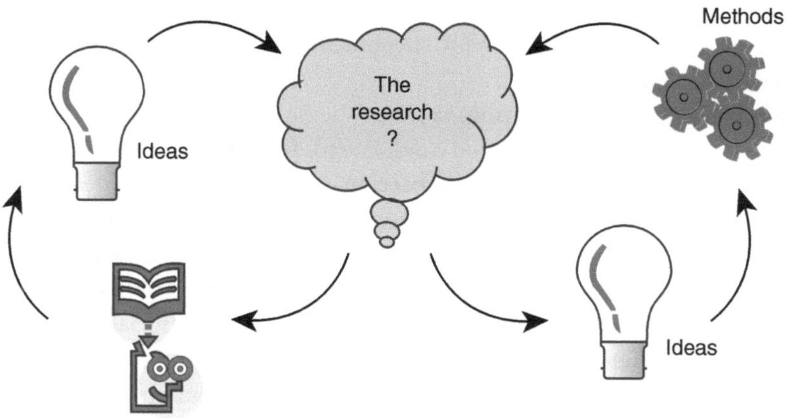

Figure 3.3 Cycles of research question development

A similar situation can occur when you begin to explore your methodology. Delving into 'how' your research might unfold can pique your interest in aspects of your topic not reflected in your currently defined question. Yet without that defined question, you might not have gone as far in exploring potential methods.

In fact, as you get going with your research, you may come across any number of factors that can lead you to: query your aims and objectives; modify your question; add questions; or even find new questions. The challenge is assessing whether these factors are sending you off the track, or whether they represent developments and refinements that are positive for your work. Discussing the issues with your supervisor can provide invaluable support in making such determinations.

The Hypothesis Dilemma

'Do I need a "hypothesis"?' This must be one of the most common questions asked by students, and there seem to be two clearly defined paradigmatic schools of thought driving the answers. Positivists (see Chapter 1) believe that the hypothesis is the cornerstone of scientific method and that it is an absolutely necessary component of the research process. Post-positivists, however, often view the hypothesis as a reductionist device designed to constrain social research.

Unfortunately, this tendency for dichotomization offers little assistance to students struggling to figure out if a hypothesis should drive their research. To answer this question, students need to know two things: what a hypothesis actually does; and whether a hypothesis is appropriate given their research question.

A hypothesis takes your research question a step further by offering a clear and concise statement of what you think you will find in relation to your variables, and what you are going to test. It is a tentative proposition that is subject to verification through subsequent investigation. And it can be very useful in the right context.

Suppose you are interested in research on divorce. Your research question is: 'What factors contribute to a couple's decision to divorce?' Your hunch is that it has a lot to do with money – financial problems lead to divorce. Here you have all the factors needed for a hypothesis: logical conjecture (your hunch); variables (divorce and financial problems); and a relationship that can be tested (leads to). It is therefore a perfect question for a hypothesis – maybe something like 'Financial problems increase the likelihood of divorce'.

A question like 'Is there a relationship between the hours teenagers spend on social media and their self-esteem?' is also a fairly good candidate for hypothesis development. Your hunch is that social media engagement has an impact on self-esteem. You can leave this broad (a non-directional hypothesis) with something like: hours on social media impact on self-esteem. Or you can focus it more with directionality in the relationship. Do you suspect that self-esteem is positively or negatively correlated with social media engagement? This would mean your hypothesis consists of a logical conjecture (your hunch); variables (social media engagement and self-esteem); and a relationship that can be tested (self-esteem increases or decreases in relation to media engagement). A directional hypothesis might end up as 'Teens who spend a large amount of free time on social media have high levels of self-esteem'.

Basically, if you have (1) a clearly defined research question, (2) variables to explore and (3) a hunch about the relationship between those variables that (4) can be tested, a hypothesis is quite easy to formulate.

Now not all research questions will lend themselves to hypothesis development. Take the question 'How do high-school students engage in decision-making processes related to career/further study options?' Remember: a hypothesis is designed to express 'relationships between variables'. This question, however, does not aim to look at variables and their relationships. The goal of this question is to uncover and describe a process, so a hypothesis would not be appropriate.

Generally, a hypothesis will not be appropriate if:

- You do not have a hunch or educated guess about a particular situation – For example, you may want to study alcoholism in Scandinavia, but you do not feel you are in a position to hypothesize because you are without an appropriate cultural context for educated guessing.
- You do not have a set of defined variables – Your research may be explorative in a bid to name the contributing factors to a particular situation. In the case of alcoholism in Scandinavia, your research aim may be to identify the factors or variables involved.
- Your question centres on phenomenological description (see Chapter 8) – For example, you may be interested in the question, 'What is the experience of drinking like for Scandinavians?' A relationship between variables does not come into play.
- Your question centres on an ethnographic study of a cultural group (see Chapter 8) – For example, you might want to ask, 'What is the cultural response to a defined problem of alcoholism in a Scandinavian country?' In this situation, force-fitting a hypothesis can limit the potential for rich description.
- Your aim is to engage in, and research, the process of collaborative change (see Chapter 10) – In 'action research', methodology is both collaborative and emergent, making predetermined hypotheses impractical to use.

In short, whether a hypothesis is appropriate for your question depends on the nature of your inquiry. If your question boils down to a 'relationship between variables', then a hypothesis can clarify your study to an extent even beyond a well-defined research question. If your question, however, does not explore such a relationship, then force-fitting a hypothesis simply won't work.

Critical Thinking Challenge 3

Interrogating the Topic

Write down the topic you want to explore in your research. Now think of all the things you could ask of that topic and why knowing it might be important.

- What is the problem?
- What is the answer?
- Why is this happening?
- Who is responsible?
- Who is this happening to?
- Where is this occurring?
- When is this occurring?
- How does this manifest?
- How can it be controlled?
- How can it be fixed?
- Are there options?
- Which options should be taken?
- How many......, how long......, how much......, how far-reaching......, how expensive......?

Now try to figure out what's already known and what needs to be found out. This may also lead you to much broader questions, like:

- What is the history of my academic discipline's approach to this question/topic?
- What other questions could be asked?
- Who do I want to benefit from my research?

Talk to your supervisor for more guidance on these matters, and don't freak out! Coming up with a good research question takes a bit of interrogation and investigation.

CHARACTERISTICS OF GOOD QUESTIONS

Once you come up with a research question, you need to assess if it is going to be researchable at a practical level. Try running through the following checklist (summarized in Box 3.3). If you find yourself feeling uncomfortable with the answers, it may indicate a need to rethink your question.

Is the Question Right for Me?

Common wisdom suggests that setting a realistic research plan involves assessing (1) your level of commitment and (2) the hours you think you will need to dedicate to the task – then double both. You need to consider whether your question has the potential to hold your interest for the duration. As discussed in Chapter 2, it is very easy to lose motivation, and you are likely to need a genuine interest to stay on track.

There is, however, a flipside. Questions that can truly sustain your interest are usually the ones that best bring out your biases and subjectivities. As discussed in Chapter 4, these subjectivities need to be carefully explored and managed in ways that will ensure the integrity of the research process. You may want to give careful consideration to:

- Researching questions where you know you have an axe to grind. Deep-seated prejudices do not generally lend themselves to credible research.
- Researching issues that are close to home, such as domestic violence or sexual abuse. Having lived experience can be a powerful motivation, but it's important to have the right supports in place if your research will bring up challenging or traumatic things for you. Emma encourages students researching violence to have personal and professional support networks (e.g. counsellors, colleagues, supervisors), but mixing work and lived experience can be intense and is not for everyone.

Is the Question Right for the Field?

The role of research is to do one or more of the following: advance knowledge in a particular area/field; improve professional practice; impact on policy; or aid individuals. Research questions need to be significant – not only to you, but to a wider academic or professional audience as well.

Zina often asks her students to imagine they are applying for competitive funds that will cover the cost of their research. Before they can even begin to make arguments that will convince a funding body they are competent to do the research and that their approach is likely to give meaningful and credible results, they will need to convince the body that the topic itself is worth funding. They need to be able to articulate:

- Why the knowledge is important.
- What the societal significance is.
- How the findings will lead to societal advances.
- What improvements to professional practice and/or policy may come from their research.

An early task in the research process is to be able to clearly articulate a rationale for your study that outlines the significance of the project. Your question needs to be informed by the literature and be seen as significant.

Is the Question Well Articulated?

A research question not only indicates the theory and literature you need to explore and review, but also points to the data you will need to gather, and the methods you will need to adopt. This makes clear articulation of research questions particularly important. Terms need to be unambiguous and clearly defined.

Take the question 'Is health care a problem in the USA?' As a question for general debate, it is probably fine. As a research question, however, it needs a fair bit of clarification. How are you defining 'health care'? What boundaries are you putting on the term? How are you defining 'problem'? Social, moral, economic, legal or all of these? And who are you speaking for? A problem for whom? The more clarity in the question, the more work the question can do, making the direction of the study that much more defined.

Another point to consider is whether your question rests on unfounded assumptions. Take the question 'How can women in Fijian villages overthrow the patriarchal structures that oppress them?' There are a few assumptions here that need to be checked:

1. That there are patriarchal structures. This information might exist and be found in literature. Assuming this is true ...
2. That these patriarchal structures are indeed oppressive to the women concerned.
3. That there is a desire on the part of Fijian women to change these patriarchal structures.
4. That 'overthrowing' is the only option mentioned for change. It is a loaded term that alludes to strong personal subjectivities.

Your position/subjectivity is also important to consider for a question like this. Are you a Fijian woman working towards this aim in the community? Or are you a 'cultural outsider' whose views and assumptions are shaped by a different sociocultural context? There is a long and damaging history of Western researchers seeking to problematize and/or 'fix' indigenous and marginalized peoples. Although you might have good intentions, it's important to carefully scrutinize assumptions underlying your research questions and reflect on their consequences. From what position are you approaching your research?

Is the Question Doable?

Perhaps the main criterion of any good research question is that you will be able to undertake the research necessary to answer the question. Now that may sound incredibly obvious, but there are many questions that cannot be answered through the research process. Take, for example, the question 'Does a difficult labour impact on a newborn's ability to love its mother?' Not researchable. How do you define 'love'? And even if you could define it, you would need to find a way to measure a newborn's ability to love. And even if you could do that, you are left with the dilemma of correlating that ability to love to a difficult labour. Interesting question, but not researchable.

Other questions might be researchable in theory, but not in practice. Student research projects are often constrained by:

- a lack of time;
- a lack of funds;
- a lack of expertise;
- a lack of access;
- a lack of ethical clearance.

Making sure your question is feasible and that it can lead to a completed project is worth doing early. Nothing is worse than realizing your project is not doable after investing a large amount of time and energy.

Does the Question Get the Tick of Approval from Those in the Know?

When it comes to articulating the final question, it makes sense to ask the advice of those who know and do research. Most supervisors have a wealth of research and supervisory experience, and generally know what questions are 'researchable' and what questions will leave you with a massive headache. Run your question past lecturers in the field, your supervisor and any 'experts' you may know.

Box 3.3

The Good Question Checklist

Is the question right for me?

- Will the question hold my interest?
- Can I manage any potential biases/subjectivities I may have?
- Do I have the right support in place if the research will be personally challenging?

Is the question right for the field?

- Will the findings be considered significant?
- Will it make a contribution to knowledge?
- Does it have the ability to effect change?
- Who will benefit from the research?

Is the question well articulated?

- Are the terms well defined?
- Are there any unchecked assumptions? What other questions could be asked? Have I considered alternative ways of knowing and doing?

Is the question doable?

- Can information be collected in an attempt to answer the question?
- Do I have the skills and expertise necessary to access this information? If not, can the skills be developed?
- Will I be able to get it all done within my time constraints?
- Are costs likely to exceed my budget?
- Are there any potential ethical problems?

Does the question get the tick of approval from those in the know?

- Does my supervisor think I am on the right track?
- Do 'experts' in the field think my question is relevant/important/doable?

I Have a Question!

I Am Having a Hard Time Getting Down to One Single Research Question. In Fact, I Have About Five Questions. Do I Really Need to Narrow Down to One?

We would certainly advise it. Sub-questions are fine - but our suspicion is that one of your questions is the main game. Or that a main-game question is still unspoken. Identifying/articulating this question is quite important. It is your way of centring into your research. Your thinking will become much clearer and more manageable once you can confidently articulate, in one sentence, what your research attempts to discover.

Chapter Summary

- Developing a well-articulated research question is essential because it defines the project, sets boundaries, gives direction and acts as a frame of reference for assessing your work.
- The ability to generate topics for research can be a real challenge. Research inspiration can come from any number of areas, including literature; personal insights and experiences; observations; contemporary/timely issues; and stakeholder needs.
- Research directions are not always at the full discretion of the researcher. Practicalities you need to be mindful of include: appropriateness of the topic; your ability to get supervisory support; and funding opportunities and commitments.
- Moving from topics to researchable question can be daunting. Using a concept map or development process, as well as continued refining, will help you develop a researchable question as well as a strong hypothesis, as appropriate.
- Good research questions need to be: right for you; right for the field; well articulated; doable; and get the tick of approval from those in the know.

FIND YOUR NEXT STEP

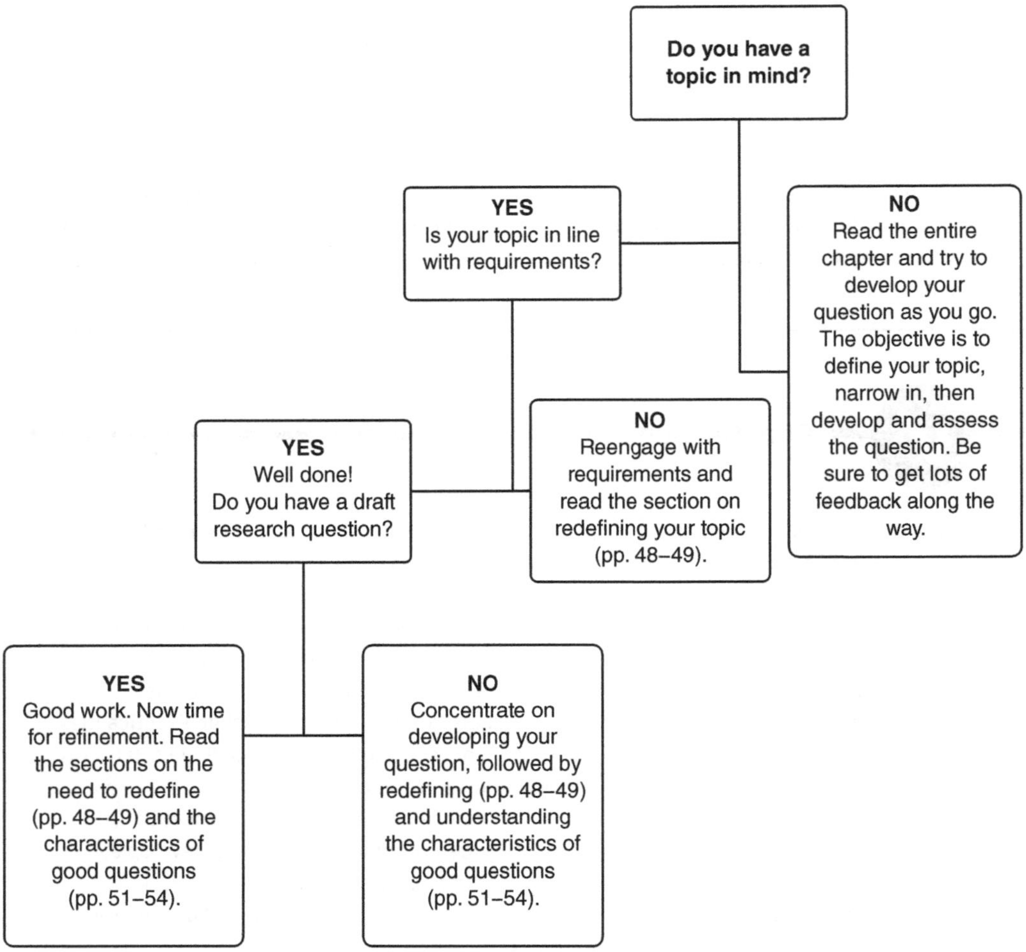

FURTHER READING

Most research methods texts give some coverage to developing research questions. Books with particularly good chapters on question development worth a look are:

Booth, W. C., Colomb, G. C. and Williams, J. M. (2016) *The Craft of Research*. Chicago: University of Chicago Press.

Clark, T., Foster, L., Sloan, L. and Bryman, A. (2021) *Bryman's Social Research Methods*, 6th edition. Oxford: Oxford University Press.

Robson, C. (2016) *Real World Research*. Oxford: Blackwell.

There are, however, three books that are solely dedicated to the challenge of research question development:

Alvesson, M. and Sandberg, J. (2024) *Constructing Research Questions: Doing Interesting Research*, 2nd edition. London: Sage.
This book delves into the power of a well-conceived research question, not just to accept and expand on current theory, but to challenge existing theories and develop new ways of seeing.

O'Leary, Z. (2018b) *LQF: Research Questions*. London: Sage.
This is a super short book from a Sage series on research methods. It doesn't go into theory, but it will definitely spark your thinking when it comes to research questions. And in addition, it's written by one of your favourite authors.

White, P. (2017) *Developing Research Questions: A Guide for Social Scientists*. Basingstoke: Palgrave Macmillan.
This book takes students through common questions such as: what makes topics suitable for research; how you go from topics to questions; and how you refine to the point of 'researchability'. Lots of grounded tips here.

4

UNDERTAKING CREDIBLE AND ETHICAL RESEARCH

Learning Objectives

- Credibility: integrity in the production of knowledge
    - To appreciate the need for credible research regardless of paradigm
    - To become familiar with both positivist and post-positivist indicators of research credibility
- Ethics: integrity and the 'researched'
    - To understand the legal, moral and ethical obligations inherent in the conduct of research
    - To become familiar with basic elements of the ethics approval process

RESEARCH INTEGRITY

All our science, measured against reality, is primitive and childlike – and yet it is the most precious thing we have.

Albert Einstein (date unknown, quoted by Hoffmann and Dukas, 1972)

From the vantage point of the colonized, a position from which I write, and choose to privilege, the term 'research' is inextricably linked to European imperialism and colonialism. The word itself, 'research', is probably one of the dirtiest words in the indigenous world's vocabulary.

Linda Tuhiwai Smith (2021, p. 1)

Science is 'primitive and childlike', yet it is 'precious'. What did Einstein mean by this, and what implications does it have for researchers? Well, science is primitive and childlike simply because the quest to capture reality is a challenge we have not fully met, and probably never will. But it is precious because it is so central to our ability to learn, to grow, to shift, to change – to make a difference. But research is not an innocent enterprise. The word itself is one of the 'dirtiest words' for indigenous people like Linda Tuhiwai Smith, an international expert on decolonial research. To do research with integrity, we need to acknowledge this damning legacy and work towards better ways to produce knowledge.

Integrity in research plays out in two broad arenas in which power and politics both play a role. The first is in your quest to produce knowledge – your responsibility here is to make sure you have captured 'truth'; reached conclusions not tainted by error and unrecognized bias; and have conducted your research with professional integrity. The second is in working with others – your responsibility here is an ethical one that ensures that the rights and well-being of those involved with your study are protected at all times.

CREDIBILITY: INTEGRITY IN THE PRODUCTION OF KNOWLEDGE

If the goal of conducting research is to produce new knowledge, knowledge that others will come to trust and rely on, then the production of this knowledge needs to be credible. It must have the 'power to elicit belief'.

But this is easier said than done. Social science research generally involves working with people – and research that involves people provides a host of challenges to research integrity. In fact, people are extremely difficult. Bacteria, cells, DNA, etc. generally behave in the laboratory – you know what to expect, and the little bacteria are not attempting to consciously or subconsciously throw you.

But people are tough. They have hidden agendas, fallible memories and a need to present themselves in certain ways. They can be helpful, defensive and/or deferential – and there will be plenty of times when you won't know when they are being what. And then there is the researcher. Also a fallible, biased or subjective human entity, faced with the challenge of producing 'unbiased', trustworthy results. Now when you combine a subjective researcher with an unpredictable 'researched' it makes the production of credible knowledge no easy feat.

Outside the research world **credibility** can come from that which is believable, plausible, likely, probable or realistic. But within the research world, credibility takes on a more specialized meaning and is demonstrated by a range of indicators such as **reliability**, **validity**, **authenticity**, **neutrality** and **auditability**. Such indicators point to research that has been approached as disciplined rigorous inquiry and is therefore likely to be accepted as a valued contribution to knowledge.

Working with Appropriate Indicators

Knowing what indicators are relevant and appropriate for a particular research project is not without ambiguity. As the assumptions that underpin research expand beyond the realms of positivist knowing (see Chapter 1), debate over how research should be critically evaluated intensifies. For some researchers, indicators of good research are premised around a world that can be quantifiably measured through defined rules of inquiry, can be approached with objectivity and is, in fact, knowable. These assumptions, however, have been called into question by those critiquing the positivist paradigm. It is now recognized that an alternative set of indicators is more appropriate for research premised around a post-positivist/postmodern world – a world that is recognized as infinitely complex and without a defined 'truth'; recognizes and values subjectivities; and is unlikely to be captured by statistics alone.

The difficulty for many researchers is that the assumptions that underpin their research may not fit neatly into one paradigmatic way of knowing. To pigeonhole themselves and their research into either positivist or post-positivist frameworks limits their ability to think and act reflexively. Designing studies that can cross the constructed boundaries dividing these two camps is difficult when researchers adopt frameworks derived from within the paradigms.

So in the face of such complexity, how do you begin to work towards indicators of credibility? Well, rather than use a paradigmatic base, we suggest you look at the underlying challenges that need to be met in order to ensure good research, namely:

- Have subjectivities been acknowledged and managed?
- Has 'true essence' been captured?
- Are methods approached with consistency?
- Are arguments relevant and appropriate?
- Can the research be verified?

These questions can act as a framework for evaluating the credibility of your own work as well as the work of others. It is then up to you as a researcher to determine the appropriate indicators for each of these questions through an examination of your own worldview and assumptions; the aims and objectives of the research; and the methodological approaches adopted (see Table 4.1 on p. 74).

Managing Subjectivities

The question here is not whether researchers are subjective entities (everyone is), but whether we recognize ourselves as subjective, and whether we can manage our personal biases.

There is no doubt that we make sense of the world through the rules we are given to interpret it. But because we are immersed in these rules and surrounded by them, they can be very hard to see. For example, those born into a religious faith do not often remember when they first heard about God; He or She simply is. Our sense of patriotism, our understandings of family, our belief in justice and equity – our morals and most core beliefs – are established within us before we have the ability to recognize or reflect on them as constructs. These beliefs are embedded within us. They are a part of how we understand and make sense of the world – and how we might research it. Working towards credible research therefore demands reflexive awareness of our worldviews and a conscious effort for us to take them into account as we enter into the research journey.

Reflexivity

Now for scientists, such as those working in a laboratory, this means putting aside any preconceived notions and aiming for pure objectivity. Strict methodological protocols and a 'researched' that is outside the self generally make striving for this indicator a manageable task. For social science researchers, however, the challenge is somewhat more difficult. It is society itself that is being researched, and as products of society, social science researchers need to recognize that their own worldview makes them value bound. If who we are colours what we see and how we interpret it, then the need to hear, see and appreciate multiple perspectives or realities is essential to rigorous research. Feminists, for example, have long critiqued the social sciences for their tendency to analyse and interpret the world from a privileged, white, male perspective, while indigenous peoples have pointed out how assumptions about an objective world are connected to colonialism, imperialism and racism.

Objectivity is never a given. If you as a researcher don't take subjectivities into account and actively work towards the criteria of neutrality, you can readily fall into the trap of judging the reality of others in relation to your own. In fact, researchers who do not act to consciously manage their own positioning run the risk of conducting 'self-centric' analysis; that is, being insensitive to issues of race, class or gender; hearing only the dominant voice; and disregarding the power of language.

Being Insensitive to Issues of Power

Zina admits that when she began doing research, she didn't feel powerful. She was just a student and didn't see how power might impact on her ability to conduct credible research. However, looking back she realizes she did have power. It was power derived from being well educated and middle class, power derived from being in a position to conduct research, power that comes from being in a position of control and authority. Emma is Pākehā, a descendant of white settlers in Aotearoa New Zealand. She wasn't taught much about local colonial history at school and so has had to 'unlearn' many of the myths about hard work and individualism to acknowledge the privilege that comes with her identity.

Features like gender, age, ethnicity, religion and social class structure our societies and shape how we see the world (and thus how we approach research). If you are at the start of your research journey, you may not feel particularly powerful compared to professionals and academics in your field. But it's important to consider dimensions of privilege and marginalization for both you and your research. Certain aspects of this may appear invisible to us, like fish who can't see the water they swim in. Other aspects may be undeniable, particularly if you experience marginalization or discrimination.

The impact of unrecognized power can be profound. For years, anthropologists conducted research without this reflexive awareness of self, and for years their findings were imprinted with the biases and assumptions of white, patriarchal, Western society. Both the integrity of the knowledge produced and the well-being of the researched are dependent on the ethical negotiation of power and power relationships.

Many of us live in lands that have been colonized. If you haven't had to consider your ways of knowing before, it's likely you have some element of privilege. For example, many indigenous people know all too well the devastating impacts of different ideas about reality, the world, human nature and truth. These are far from metaphysical abstractions but have very material consequences.

Insensitivity to issues of race, class, gender, etc. refers to the practice of ignoring these constructs as important factors or variables in a study and can be a by-product of 'self-centric' analysis. Researchers need to recognize and appreciate the reality of the researched, otherwise they run the risk of ignoring unique and significant attributes. For example, a study of student motivation in a multicultural setting would not be very meaningful without ethnicity as one significant variable. Yes, career ambitions, study enjoyment, perceived relevance, etc. can be important predictors of motivation, but all of these factors can be motivated by family and culture. For example, in many Anglo-Asian households, student success and failure are seen as parental success and failure, and this can be a huge student weight and/or motivator.

Insensitivity to issues of race, class and gender can also lead to dichotomization, or the tendency to put groups at two separate ends of the spectrum without recognition of overlapping characteristics. We do this when we talk in absolute terms about 'men' and 'women' or 'Black people' and 'white people'. Research that dichotomizes is often research that has fallen prey to stereotypes.

Finally, insensitivity to race, class and gender can lead to double standards where the same behaviours, situations or characteristics are analysed using different criteria depending on whether respondents are Black or white, male or female, rich or poor, etc. Suppose you wanted to explore reasons for marital infidelity. If you were to use different sets of responses for males and females in which your preconceived notions about men being 'easily bored' and women being 'quite needy' came through, you would have a double standard. Remember that in the conduct of research, there is an essential need to guard against the assumptions and biases inherent within our society.

Critical Thinking Challenge 4

You the Researcher

There are many intersecting aspects that make up our identities. Figure 4.1 below is not exhaustive but captures some key domains on which power and privilege are structured. For different spokes of the wheel, you may be closer or further away from power. Take some time to reflect on where you are situated. How does this shape how you understand yourself, the world and the research you want to do? Are the people you want to work with similarly or differently situated? What impacts will this have on your approach to research?

(Continued)

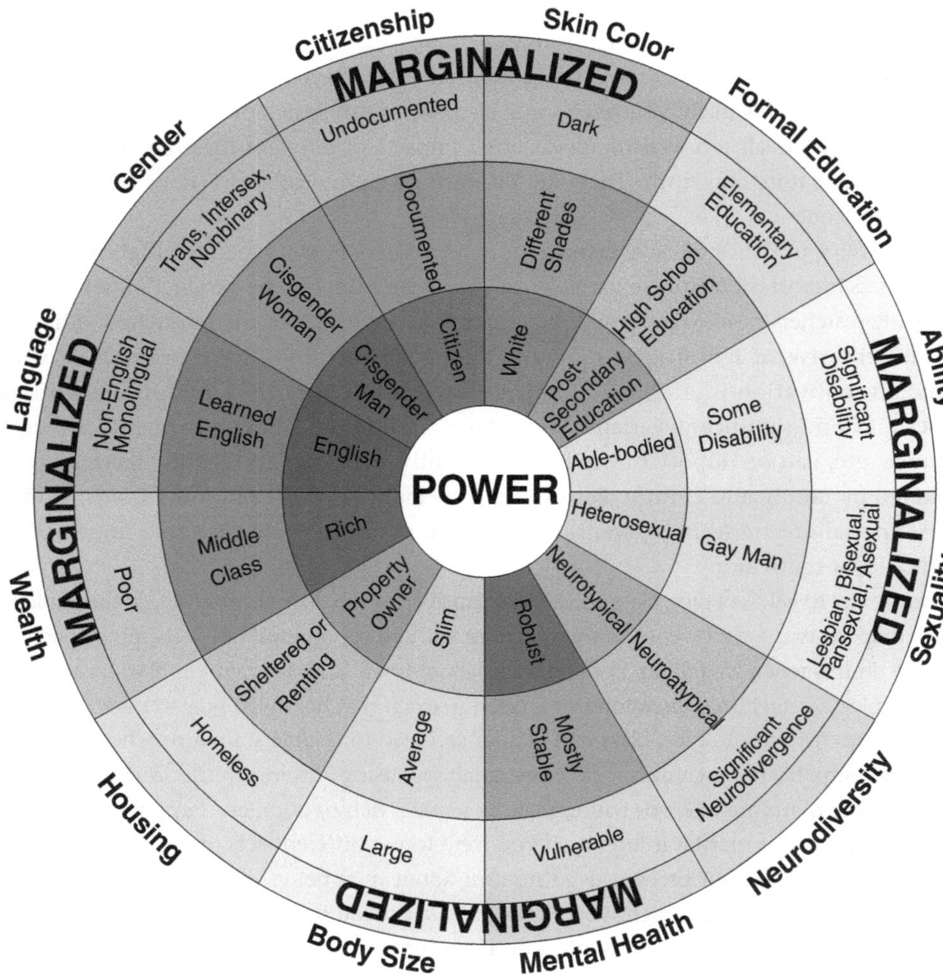

Figure 4.1 Some of the many axes that make up a position of privilege. You may be closer to the centre on some domains and further away on others

Source: 'Adapted from James R Vanderwoerd ("Web of Oppression"), and Sylvia Duckworth ("Wheel of Power/Privilege")'

Hearing Only the Dominant Voice

> There's really no such thing as the 'voiceless'. There are only the deliberately silenced, or the preferably unheard.
>
> Arundhati Roy (2004)

It is very easy to listen to those who are speaking the loudest or to those who are speaking your 'language'. But when you do this, you're likely to end up missing an important undercurrent, a whole other voice. Zina has struggled with this in her own teaching. When she gives a workshop, she tries very hard to relate to her students – to communicate with them rather than lecture at them. She tries to engage in 'dialogue' and get a two-way conversation going. And she does this fairly well. In every class a core group of students makes this easy for her.

But who is in this core group? Well, it can be a mixed bag, but it's clear who isn't. It is not generally the international students; they tend to stay in the background. Now there are a number of reasons for this. For one, many come from an educational system where they are not invited to participate. Others struggle with English as a second language. But another factor could be Zina and her reality. The examples she uses, the personal anecdotes she shares, her 'in your face' American style can all conspire so that those with demographic characteristics similar to hers are the ones who speak up the most. So it is the East Asian and Indian students in her class who can go unheard (as they are likely to do throughout their Western university careers).

When she is teaching, her challenge is to find a way to engage all of her class and to make sure she is reaching every student – and that they are reaching her. The challenge when researching is similar (see Box 4.1). If you do not consciously work on strategies for appreciating diversity and hearing the marginalized, you run the risk of gathering data and reaching conclusions that ignore those in society who often go unheard. Attempting to empower traditionally marginalized voices is essential in responsible research. Indigenous peoples, minorities, children, women and LGBTQ+ people are often not heard, yet their voices are essential to any full understanding.

Box 4.1

The People in My Shire – Keith's story

I was conducting research with a local council and had already interviewed the mayor and a few of the local councillors about the community when I attended my first council meeting. The meeting was a real eye-opener. The ethnic background for the region I was studying was about 45% Anglo-Australian, 25% Asian, 20% Indian and 10% Greek, with at least seven different religions. Yet, when I walked into the meeting, I was asked to give my 'Christian' name, and the meeting started with a prayer from the Protestant minister. At that stage, I took a good look around and realized that all of the councillors looked to be of Anglo-Australian descent. In fact, almost everyone present at the meeting was Anglo-Australian.

I then thought of all the times the mayor and councillors had spoken of their 'community'. I was left wondering what their 'community' was. Was their frame of reference the range of constituents in their jurisdiction, or was their frame of reference individuals with the same demographic background as themselves – in other words, 'community' as the white Christians who came to the council meetings? From that point on I was committed to ensuring that my research reflected the 'real' community, not just those with the ability/propensity to be heard.

Disregard for the Power of Language

Research is coloured by our use of language in a number of ways. First, there is the subtle yet formidable power of words themselves. The words we use to speak to respondents, and they use to speak to us, can be easily misunderstood and misrepresented. For example, language that might be 'shocking' for one group might be quite 'everyday' for another. It is worth remembering that analysis of words needs to come from the perspective and reality of the researched, not the researcher.

Working with respondents with whom you do not share a common language presents an added level of difficulty. There isn't a single computer program that can accurately translate one language to another; and that is because languages are highly metaphorical, mythical, poetic and full of hidden meanings, riddles and assumptions. Accurate interpretations, let alone the nuances of language and speech, are often lost through interpreters or in the process of translation. The researcher who assumes that English can capture thoughts processed in a different language with any sophistication risks reducing the richness and complexity of a respondent's ideas and views (and imposes an Anglocentric bias on the research). Researchers working outside their first language need to find ways to confirm that the accuracy and richness of their data are not lost in the process of interpretation and translation.

Strategies for Managing Subjectivities

Managing subjectivities is more than something you should do. It is, in fact, a task which is crucial to the production of credible data and trustworthy results. Strategies you can adopt include:

- Appreciating your own worldview – Your ability to manage subjectivities is dependent on being able to recognize and articulate them. In fact, the first chapter of many theses now includes a section on researcher positioning.
- Appreciating alternative realities – Actively explore the personal and societal assumptions that underpin the understandings of the researcher and the researched and accept that these might be quite distinct.
- Suspending initial judgements – We live in a society where it is common to judge what we do not understand. Yet as researchers, not understanding is precisely why it is important not to judge.
- Checking your interpretation of events, situations and phenomena with 'insiders' – This is particularly relevant in cross-cultural research. Finding out how someone from within a cultural reality understands a situation can help illuminate your own biases.
- Getting the full story – Those we seek out and those willing to participate are often those with the strongest voices. Your research design should seek representation from all those you wish your research to speak for or about, including those often silenced.
- Seeking out and incorporating alternative and pluralistic points of view – Even when crystallizing interpretations, hold on to the richness and complexity that can come from outside viewpoints.

Capturing 'Truth'

It could be said that research is all about the elusive concept of 'truth' and our desire to capture it. Traditionally, we are talking here about a knowable world in which a singular truth can be assessed by the indicator of validity. In other words, we assess whether our findings are 'correct'. Suppose you were exploring whether 'gender identification causes girls to relate better to their mothers than do boys'. Validity would rest on:

1 showing that how you measured 'relate' truly reflected 'relating';
2 showing that you had a sample size large enough and representative enough to make the claim about girls and boys in general;
3 showing that it truly is gender identification that is affecting the ability to relate, and not any other factors (see Box 4.4 on p. 70).

In a world where we accept the possibility of multiple realities, however, authenticity is more likely to be an appropriate indicator. Authenticity indicates that rigour and reflexive practice have assured that conclusions are justified, credible and trustworthy even when truth is dependent on perspective (see Box 4.2).

Box 4.2

Whose Reality Is It Anyway?

Zina once took a group of humanities students to a local school to look at the layout of the fifth-grade classroom. There were 42 children aged 10 sitting down in seven rows of six, all facing forward. The teacher was standing in the middle of the front of the classroom, facing the children. Zina broke her students up into two groups and asked them to find out why the classroom was set up in this manner.

The eventual responses were quite distinct. The first group attempted to answer the question from the perspective of the teacher. They interviewed her and found that this was the best set-up, and that there is no other logical way the room could be arranged. The children need to face both the teacher and the blackboard. The students also found that this set-up minimized the propensity for the children to distract or be distracted by each other and allowed them to direct their focus on the teacher.

Photo 4.1 Classroom rows

Source: National Archives and Records Administration (public domain)

The analysis of the second group was completely different. They answered the question from the perspective of critical literature and claimed that the structure was typical of how most

(Continued)

classrooms are set up, which is a clear mechanism of control. The seating arrangement exists because it facilitates a relationship of power between teacher and student that is all one-way. There is no respect for what peers can give to each other. This structure alienates the children from each other, making them unable to act as a collective and therefore rendering them powerless. It also limits learning because it tends to facilitate rote memorization, rather than hands-on engagement.

Which group was right? Well this is the point - it is not a matter of right or wrong. It is simply a matter of reality and perspective. You need to be cognizant of the realities you are presenting as well as those you are not.

Building Trust

Your ability to capture truth, whether you understand it as a single valid truth or an authentic truth that may sit alongside other interpretations, will be highly dependent on your ability to get your respondents to talk to you with openness and honesty. And while there are no techniques that can guarantee candour, building trust is essential. It is therefore absolutely crucial to minimize any real or perceived power differential between you and the 'researched'. If you can't do this, the 'researched' are likely to feel alienated, intimidated and/or uninterested by the research process.

There are any number of factors that can influence your ability to build rapport and trust, including:

- Gender – The rapport and trust you build, the slant on stories you hear and the memories you draw out can be very dependent on gender. For example, some women might only feel comfortable talking about the loss of a child with another woman. Or imagine conducting an interview on promiscuity; the answers you might elicit could be highly dependent on your own gender. Now there are no hard-and-fast rules here. What is important is to consciously think through the issue of gender and whether it is likely to be a factor in building trust.
- Age – Trust is often dependent on your ability to relate to your respondents and their ability to relate to you, and age can certainly be a factor. For example, there are very few parents who can ask their teenagers 'What did you do this weekend?' and get the full story – especially if the weekend was any good! Like it or not, age can be a critical factor in credible data collection. And again there are no hard-and-fast rules, just a mandate that you consider how age might influence researcher–researched relationships.
- Ethnicity – The ethnic and cultural background of the researcher can certainly influence the research process. Sad to say, we still have much inequity, suspicion and mistrust running across ethnic and racial lines. But that is a reality – and it is a reality that can affect your ability to gain trust. Suppose you wanted to research attitudes towards education in a Latinx community. While a white outsider might struggle to gain trust, a Latinx insider might have an easier time opening up honest and open lines of communication.

- Socioeconomic status/education – Societal position can also have great bearing on the research process. Researchers often come from a position of privilege, so you need to think about breaking down barriers, and convince the 'researched' that you are not sitting in judgement. Being aware of your own socioeconomic status and educational background, as well as that of the researched, puts you in a position to manage any potential power-related issue that might influence your study.
- Position of power and privilege within a culture or subculture – An imbalance of power can be a common difficulty for researchers working within a culture where they are cast as a 'scientist' or 'expert'. Gary Larson once drew a cartoon showing 'natives' in a hut frantically hiding their VCRs and TVs while yelling out 'Anthropologists!' He very insightfully illustrates how deference to the expert changes the researched. A major dilemma when understanding cross-cultural studies is knowing how you can conduct 'authentic' research when you are immersed in a culture where your position of power and privilege finds those you are researching acting in ways that may not be 'natural'.

Box 4.3

Insiders and Outsiders in Research

In her landmark book *Decolonizing Methodologies*, Linda Tuhiwai Smith talks about the struggles of being both insider and outsider as an indigenous researcher. All of us have multiple identities and we can be at once insider and outsider to the communities we research. This can be difficult when you are judged by 'insider' criteria (e.g. family background, status, politics, age, gender, religion and technical ability) while also being seen as an 'outsider' due to factors like education and position within academia.

Listening Without Judgement

It can be hard to withhold judgement! Zina often gives workshops in Hong Kong and one of her students flew from there to Australia (where she now works and lives) for a visit. Over lunch, he and his wife told her that their youngest son, who was ten and had gone to boarding school in the UK, had been crying on the phone every day saying that he hated it, was being picked on and racially abused, and really wanted to go home. Now Zina was raised, and still lives, in a cultural reality where she could not even contemplate sending any ten-year-old of hers that far away from home. Yet in no way does she question that this family's decision was made out of love and a desire to give their child the best. It's just that it is so far from her own reality and the way she has been socialized.

She had to make a conscious effort to suspend judgement and not snarl 'What were you thinking, sending him there in the first place?' People can sniff out judgement from a mile off, and if you do not make an effort to suspend or withhold it, you won't stand a chance at building trust and getting to the heart of an issue. Be conscious of both verbal and non-verbal cues here – what you say, how you say it, your facial expressions and your body language can all work to build trust or alienate the other.

Now it may seem as though issues of trust are more likely to be a factor in research that involves close interaction with the researched, for example, when conducting an **interview**. And while this is true, it is also worth thinking about how trust can be undermined or built in a survey. The words you use, the concepts you call on and the assumptions you make can all conspire to put respondents at ease or cause them to feel alienated.

Approaching Methods with Consistency

Once you have worked through issues related to the management of subjectivities and the building of trust to capture 'truth', the quest for integrity in knowledge production turns to questions of method. It is important to remember that, regardless of approach, researching is not a haphazard activity. Rather, it is an activity that needs to be approached with discipline, rigour and a level of standardization. If the goal is to have your research stand up to scrutiny and be taken as credible, it is important that readers are confident that your methods have been implemented in ways that best ensure consistency.

Often consistency in methods is referred to as reliability or the extent to which a measure, procedure or instrument provides the same result on repeated trials. A good example here is bathroom scales. If you were to jump on your scales ten times in a row and got the same results each time, the scales would be reliable. The scales could be wrong – they might always be 10 pounds heavy or 10 pounds light, but they would be reliable. A more complicated example might be trying to measure job satisfaction with a questionnaire. The questionnaire would only be reliable if results were not dependent on things like who administered the questionnaire, what kind of day the respondent was having, or whether or not it was a weekend.

The flipside of this is that people are complex and multifaceted. At any given time, for any given reason, they may only reveal part of themselves. Suppose you wanted to ask about stress – this is something that can, and often does, vary from day to day. So developing methodological tools that are 'reliable' might not be straightforward. Nevertheless, the process of data collection needs to be more than haphazard. In fact, it should meet the criteria of **dependability**. Methods need to be designed and developed in ways that are consistent, logical, systematic, well documented and designed to account for research subjectivities.

Box 4.4

Validity and Reliability – Isn't That the Main Game?

There are many who argue that validity and reliability are fundamental indicators of good research. Together they are seen as what defines scientific proof. When we have validity, we know that we are measuring what we intend to measure and that we have eliminated any other possible causal relationships. In other words, we have hit the target.

When we have reliability, we know that results are not just one-off. Results will be the same under repeated trials, given that circumstances stay constant. In other words, we hit the target over and over again.

When we have both validity and reliability, well then we have a situation where we are repeatedly not only hitting the target but hitting the bull's eye each and every time (see Figure 4.2).

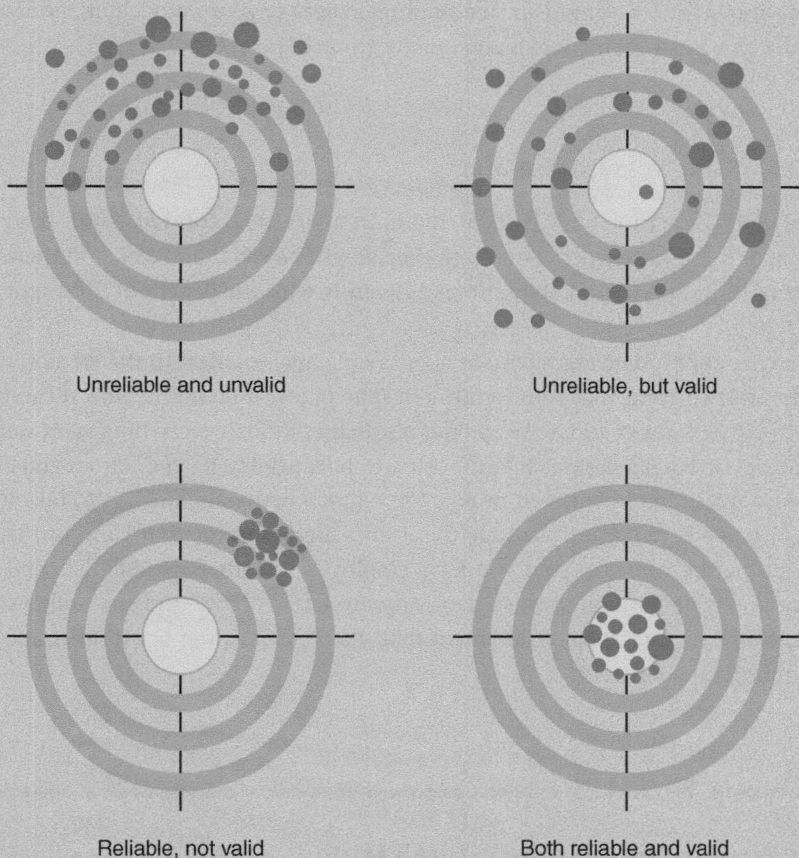

Figure 4.2 Validity and reliability

And this is undeniably a good thing. What is tricky, however, is when you demand validity and reliability as prerequisites to credibility and scientific truth. When we do this, we shut the door to research into the hard-to-pin-down reaches of the human/social world.

If you accept the possibility of multiple realities, varied perspectives, human variability and inconsistency, then it is essential to find indicators of good research that can work within this complex and multifaceted reality. This is why 'post-positivist' researchers call on authenticity (defined in Table 4.1, below) alongside validity and dependability (also defined in Table 4.1) alongside reliability.

Making Relevant and Appropriate Arguments

Assume you are at the point where you have some great data. You're pretty sure you have been able to manage your biases, got your respondents to open up, and employed data-collection tools and analysis strategies capable of holding up to a good level of scrutiny. The next step is to put forward some credible arguments. Now this will involve a few challenges we have already discussed: keeping a check on subjectivities and exploring multiple interpretations. But, as discussed below, it will also involve weighing up your findings in light of your study's limitations and being confident that you are speaking for an appropriate group of people.

Being True to Your Study's Limitations

Very few researchers get to conduct their studies in a way they consider ideal: there is rarely enough time or money; the cooperation of others might be less than ideal; and there could be a whole list of things they would have done differently with the benefit of hindsight. So what do you do?

Well, making appropriate arguments is about being able to attest to the credibility of your data and the trustworthiness of your results – in spite of any limitations. Now it can be tempting to downplay difficulties and write up your research as though everything went smoothly in a study that was optimally designed. But if you are challenged here, your ethics and credibility can come into question. As outlined in Box 4.5, a much better approach is to take it in three steps. The first step is to honestly outline the study's limitations or shortcomings. The second step is to outline the strategies that you have employed to gather credible data and generate trustworthy results because of, or in spite of, any limitations. The third step follows from the second and is a 'therefore' type of statement that offers justification or rationalization for the data and findings of your study.

Box 4.5

Being True to Your Study's Limitations

The following student excerpt is a good example of the three-step approach to outlining your study's limitations:

> While the original data-collection protocol was to survey a random sample of the population, preliminary investigation showed that the extent of this population is unknown. A directory of men who have experienced domestic abuse simply does not exist. It also became clear that many men who had experienced this type of abuse did not want to be approached [Step 1]. It was therefore decided to ask for volunteers through the use of flyers in counsellors' offices, and combine that with snowball sampling that asked the volunteers to pass on the request to anyone else they might know of who has experienced a similar situation [Step 2]. While there is no guarantee that the results from this sample will be representative of the greater population, this study, through the use of willing and open volunteers, does offer valuable insights to the phenomenon, and sheds much light on an under-explored area of domestic violence [Step 3].

Speaking for an Appropriate Group of People

Conclusions relevant to only a particular **sample** or only within a certain research setting can provide important knowledge for key stakeholders, but they do not allow findings to be applied to a broader **population** and thereby limit broader generation of new knowledge.

Broad applicability of findings is therefore a goal of many researchers. There is a desire to argue that findings extend beyond a particular sample or setting. But to do this, researchers need to ensure they are speaking for an appropriate group of people. Any sample used should be representative of a wider population, and large enough that they can be confident that their findings do reflect larger trends.

Meeting these criteria means that your findings are **generalizable**. The key (as discussed in Chapter 11) is ensuring both adequate and **broad representation**. And this is certainly possible in medium- to large-scale survey research. But what if your research project is centred on a particular **case**, or is designed to collect more in-depth qualitative data that will limit your sample size? Under these circumstances, you may not be able to argue generalizability. Yet broader applicability may still be a goal. If this is the case, your goal will be the indicator of **transferability** or highlighting 'lessons learned' that are likely to be applicable in alternative settings or populations. For example, the results of an in-depth **case study** in any one school will not be representative of all schools – but there will definitely be lessons learned that can illuminate relevant issues and provide rich learning within other school contexts. The key here is providing a detailed description of the research setting and methods so that applicability can be determined by those reading the research account.

Providing Accurate and Verifiable Research Accounts

Conducting research is a highly complex process. Without a doubt, it is hard to get it right. So it is the responsibility of the researcher to consciously minimize the possibility that results are false or misleading. To that end, research approaches are expected to be open and accountable. The physicist Richard Feynman (1997, p. 94) argues the need to 'report everything that you think might make it [your study] invalid – not only what you think is right about it. ... Details that could throw doubt on your interpretation must be given, if you know them.' The admission of shortcomings and limitations is encouraged and research is expected to be reproducible. In fact, codes of ethics often require researchers to keep their raw data for a period of five to seven years, thereby protecting themselves from accusations of fraud or misrepresentation.

Even though the price of fraudulence can be quite high (students shown to be acting fraudulently are often forced to withdraw from their degree programmes), misrepresentation and fraud are quite rampant. Researchers (and not just students) have been known to:

- blatantly fabricate data or falsify results;
- omit cases or fiddle with numbers in order to show 'significance';
- plagiarize passages from articles or books without crediting the original author(s);
- misrepresent authorship by using a ghost writer, taking full credit for authorship when more than one author was involved or naming a co-author who had no involvement with the study.

Verifiable accounts are therefore considered essential. As well as allowing others to attempt to replicate or reproduce findings, verifiable accounts help establish a study's credibility by making them 'auditable' (others can see exactly how findings were generated). It is difficult to blatantly fabricate data, falsify results, omit cases, fiddle with numbers, plagiarize and even misrepresent authorship, if your methods are out there for all to see.

Box 4.6

Managing Data for Integrity

The collection, storage and use of data is increasingly under scrutiny in a world where it feels like our every move is being tracked by tech giants. For example, the global movement for indigenous data sovereignty advocates for transparency and control over how data is used. As researchers, managing data has both political and practical implications. If the goal is research integrity, then we need data integrity. If you are sloppy with your data, things can be mislabelled, things can be lost, things can be entered incorrectly. When these things happen, research integrity is lost. This is where being pedantic is a good thing. Be organized, be systematic, be meticulous. Log everything. Being on top of your data at all times is the key to good data management.

Indicators and Checklist

A challenge for all research students is to become conversant with indicators of research integrity. Not only will you need to work towards such indicators in your own research, but also your ability to critically engage with relevant literature will be enhanced if you can assess the work of others in relation to relevant indicators. Table 4.1 provides a summary of the key issues above and offers a range of associated 'indicators' appropriate to different **modes** of research.

Table 4.1 Credibility indicators by issues and paradigm

'Positivist' indicators	'Post-positivist' indicators
Have subjectivities been acknowledged and managed?	
Objectivity – conclusions based on observable phenomena; not influenced by emotions, personal prejudices or subjectivities	*Neutrality* – subjectivities recognized and negotiated in a manner that attempts to avoid biasing results/ conclusions. Subjectivity with transparency – acceptance and disclosure of subjective positioning and how it might impact on the research process, including conclusions drawn
Has 'true essence' been captured?	
Validity – concerned with truth value, i.e. whether conclusions are 'correct'. Also considers whether methods, approaches and techniques actually relate to what is being explored	*Authenticity* – concerned with truth value while recognizing that multiple truths may exist. Also concerned with describing the deep structure of experience/phenomena in a manner that is 'true' to the experience

'Positivist' indicators	'Post-positivist' indicators
Are methods approached with consistency?	
Reliability – concerned with internal consistency, i.e. whether data/results collected, measured or generated are the same under repeated trials	*Dependability* – accepts that reliability in studies of the social may not be possible, but attests that methods are systematic, well documented and designed to account for research subjectivities
Are arguments relevant and appropriate?	
Generalizability – whether findings and/or conclusions from a sample, setting or group are directly applicable to a larger population, a different setting or to another group	*Transferability* – whether findings and/or conclusions from a sample, setting or group lead to lessons learned that may be germane to a larger population, a different setting or another group
Can the research be verified?	
Reproducibility – concerned with whether results/conclusions would be supported if the same methodology was used in a different study with the same/similar context	*Auditability* – accepts the importance of the research context and therefore seeks full explication of methods to allow others to see how and why the researchers arrived at their conclusions

I Have a Question!

Can Qualitative Research Ever Have the Same Credibility as Quantitative Research?

Phew ... tough question. And that's because there are a lot of researchers who would say no! They would argue that without a large enough sample, you cannot have **statistical significance**, and therefore no generalizability. And if that is their line of argument, they are correct. Qualitative research is not often generalizable. But is that the goal? Qualitative research argues that there is value in delving deep and in exploring meaning and understanding. And certainly, qualitative research, when judged appropriately, can meet rigorous standards of 'post-positivist' credibility. Qualitative research judged on quantitative criteria, however, will always fall short.

ETHICS: INTEGRITY AND THE 'RESEARCHED'

Absolutely central to research integrity is ethics. With power comes responsibility. As a researcher you have an explicit and fundamental responsibility towards the 'researched'. The dignity and well-being of respondents, both mentally and physically, is absolutely crucial. Understanding how this responsibility is best negotiated at legal, moral and ethical levels is a prerequisite for any potential researcher.

Legal Obligations

In a nutshell, researchers are not above the law. Some might like to be – but clearly, they are not. The laws of society stand in the world of research. If it is illegal for the general public, then it is illegal for researchers and research participants. Now for most researchers, the criterion of non-engagement in illegal activities is not too difficult to appreciate or meet. Most recognize the logic here. But a more common legal dilemma is faced by researchers who:

1. wish to study illegal activities; or
2. come across illegal activities in the course of their investigations.

For example, we have had students with interests in everything from cockfighting, to abuse of patients by hospital staff, to corporal punishment in private schools. And a dilemma that faces these student researchers is knowing whether they have an obligation to report any illegal activities they may come to know of in the course of their study. For example, suppose you were interviewing parents about stress and you discovered a case of child abuse. Do you maintain **confidentiality**, or are you obliged to report the abuse?

Well, the law here is quite ambiguous and can vary by both country and case. You may or may not be obliged to report illegal activities, but in most countries the courts can subpoena your data and files. Legal precedents suggest that researcher assurances of confidentiality do not hold up in court. As a researcher, you are not afforded the same rights as a lawyer, doctor or priest.

Our advice is to seek advice. There are two solid avenues here. The first is through your ethics committee. Hopefully, when you applied for ethics approval there was some consideration given to the possibility of such challenges coming up. The committee should have offered strategies and protocols for dealing with such circumstances prior to giving approval ... and it is important to follow such protocols. The second avenue is your supervisor. If you find yourself in a situation that you do not know how to handle, do turn to your supervisor for advice.

Moral Obligations

When we talk about morals, we are talking about rights and wrongs, societal norms and values. In research, this boils down to responsibility for the dignity and welfare of both individuals and cultural groups. Put simply, research should not be offensive, degrading, humiliating or dangerous. In fact, it should not be psychologically or physically damaging in any way.

Some moral considerations in the conduct of research include:

- Conscientiousness – This refers to a need to keep the interests of respondents or participants at the forefront in any decision-making processes related to the conduct of research. It is important to remember that researchers hold a certain position of power and being conscious of this power is essential in ensuring the well-being of those involved in your research project.
- Equity – Equitable research is concerned with the practice of asking only some segments of the population to participate in research, while other segments are immune from such requests. For example, prisoners, students, children and minorities may have

characteristics that make them targets for research studies. It is important that particular groups of individuals are not treated as, or made to feel like, 'guinea pigs'.

- Honesty – There is an expectation that researchers are open and honest and that details of the research process are made transparent. If some deception is required (e.g. to hide the purpose of the study so you can examine participants' natural reactions), you need a solid debriefing procedure where you explain what you did and why to participants afterwards.

Ethical Obligations

Ethics tend to be based on moral obligations, but put a professional spin on what is fair, just, right or wrong. Ethics refer to principles or rules of behaviour that act to dictate what is actually acceptable or allowed within a profession. Ethical guidelines for the conduct of research will vary by professional code, discipline area and institution, but generally cover the following areas:

- Ensuring respondents have given **informed consent** – Participants can only give 'informed consent' to be involved in a research study if they have full understanding of their requested involvement, including time commitment, type of activity, topics that will be covered, and all physical and emotional risks potentially involved. Informed consent implies that participants are:
    - competent – they have reasonable intellectual capacity and psychological maturity;
    - autonomous – they are making self-directed and self-determined choices;
    - involved voluntarily – they are not unaware, forced, pressured or duped;
    - aware of the right to discontinue – they are under no obligation (or pressure) to continue involvement;
    - not deceived – the nature of the study, any affiliations or professional standing, and the intended use of the study should be honest and open;
    - not coerced – positions of power should not be used to get individuals to participate;
    - not induced – while it may be acceptable to compensate individuals for their time and effort, an inducement should not compromise a potential participant's judgement.
- Ensuring no harm comes to respondents – This includes emotional or psychological harm as well as physical harm. Now physical harm is relatively easy to recognize, but risks of psychological harm can be hard to identify and difficult to predict. Whether it be resentment, anxiety, embarrassment or reliving unpleasant memories, psychological 'harm' can be unplanned and unintentional, yet commonplace. Keep in mind that as well as being ethically and morally unacceptable, risks of harm can give rise to legal issues. We are talking about lawsuits here. So even if your conscience or your professional ethics can justify your decisions, the potential for legal action may be enough to make you reassess your approach.
- Ensuring confidentiality and, if appropriate, **anonymity** – Confidentiality involves protecting the identity of those providing research data; all identifying data remains

solely with the researcher. Keep in mind that pseudonyms may not be enough to hide identity. If others can figure out who you are speaking about, or who is doing the speaking, you need to further mask identity or seek approval for disclosure. Anonymity goes a step beyond confidentiality and refers to protection against identification even from the researcher. Information, data and responses collected anonymously should not be identifiable with any particular respondent. A good example of this is 'anonymous' class evaluations where students should feel confident that there is no chance of damning feedback coming back to bite them. As well as masking identity, protection of confidentiality and anonymity should involve: secure storage of raw data; restricting access to the data; the need for permission for subsequent use of the data; and eventual destruction of raw data.

While such guidelines may seem straightforward, there's likely to be a trade-off between following such guidelines and the data you want to collect. Ethics, however, must always take precedence. Dilemmas do arise (see Box 4.7), so it is good to be prepared even if this means your design needs to go through a process of modification. Luckily, ethics committees have approval processes that can help you identify and work within the boundaries that define the conduct of ethical research.

Box 4.7

Ethical Dilemmas in Real-World Research

So what types of ethical dilemmas are you likely to face when doing research? Well, protocols in almost all universities make sure you have informed consent and that participants know what your research is about and what their involvement will entail. And thankfully, ethics protocols have immensely reduced the risk of physical harm. But in our experience, ethical pitfalls you might still face include:

1 Being insensitive to marginalized groups/respondents

If you are doing research as an outsider, it's essential to develop cultural knowledge and cultural sensitivity. Seek advice and input to make sure you don't unintentionally offend the people involved in your research.

2 Not ensuring confidentiality

You promise that responses will be confidential, but when reporting on key informant interviews, for example, you give away a person's workplace, department and position, such that tracing this individual becomes an easy feat.

3 Putting respondents in tense/conflict situations

We have seen this happen in many an ill-fated **focus group**. Tensions rise and if conflict is not well managed, it can get ugly. Even worse, if focus group members are from the same workplace, family or school, tension from the research process can spill into other parts of their lives. The advice here is never to do your first focus group (particularly on a subject likely to raise debate) on your own. Also avoid focus groups that centre on problems. Focus groups that focus on solutions are easier to manage.

4 Asking insensitive and potentially threatening questions

It can be hard to know what people are sensitive about. We know to be cautious when it comes to researching sexual assault, domestic violence or experiences of war. But we have seen hurt arise when people are asked about Facebook, dieting habits and procrastination. And this is where we really appreciate the scrutiny of an ethics committee. It means responsibility for unanticipated harm is not all ours.

5 Putting yourself in a situation where you (feel you) need to break confidences

Child abuse, dangerous work practices, fraud, theft: you may come across knowledge of any of this. Do you say, 'stuff the research process' and report it? Well, we certainly hope so in the case of child abuse. But what about petty theft? What about embezzled funds? What about serious breaches of occupational health and safety? What about minor breaches of occupational health and safety? Massive dilemma. But one you need not take on alone. Talk to your supervisor - refer it on to the ethics committee. Do not shoulder this burden by yourself.

6 Keeping yourself safe

We often focus on potential harms for research participants but it's also important to consider your own safety and well-being as a researcher. In some cases, there may be physical risks associated with fieldwork or data collection. And there are also psychological risks, for example, in listening to people talk about traumatic experiences you may also share. Having a plan for how you will deal with these challenges is important both for the progress and integrity of the research, and your own mental health and success as a researcher.

Ethical Case Studies

The ethical principles we've outline above are broadly applicable for most kinds of research. But how you specifically tackle each ethical challenge will depend on the practices and conventions associated with your chosen research approach/method. For example, evaluative, action-oriented and emancipatory strategies (covered in Chapter 10) often work collaboratively with communities or organizations which can impact on when and how decisions are made.

Nairn, K., Showden, C. R., Sligo, J., Mathews, K. R. and Kidman, J. (2020) 'Consent requires a relationship: rethinking group consent and its timing in ethnographic research', *International Journal of Social Research Methodology*, 23(6): 719-731. https://doi.org/10.1080/13645579.2020.1760562

Nairn and colleagues discuss the importance of building relationships before seeking consent and show that negotiated agreement is important to consider when working with groups in ethnographic research.

(Continued)

Farbotko, C. Watson, P. Kitara, T. and Stratford, E. (2023) 'Decolonising methodologies: Emergent learning in island research', *Geographical Research*, 61(1). https://doi.org/10.1111/1745-5871.12519

A research team of 'settler allies' and an indigenous knowledge holder talk about the messy and difficult realities of trying to do decolonial work and how a Tuvaluan concept - Fale Pili (treating a neighbour's problems as your own) - came to guide their attempts to ethically engage across cultures.

Datta, R. (2018) 'Decolonizing both researcher and research and its effectiveness in Indigenous research' *Research Ethics*, 14(2), 1-24. https://doi.org/10.1177/1747016117733296

Reflecting on case studies from 15 years of teaching and research with indigenous communities, Datta argues that decolonizing research is a way of both honouring participants' rights in research and empowering researchers. A broader political view of research and how we are trained as researchers is essential for ethical work when research following the status quo does harm to indigenous peoples.

Ethics Approval Processes

Commitment to the conduct of ethical research is simply not enough. Most universities and large bureaucratic institutions, such as hospitals or some government departments, require you to obtain official approval that will involve the development of an ethics proposal (see Chapter 5), including consent forms and information statements in order to undertake a study (see Box 4.9, below). This will require you to carefully examine all aspects of your study for ethical implications and work through all the logistics.

Now there are quite a few researchers who believe that getting ethics approval is simply a bureaucratic hurdle-jumping process designed to take up limited and precious time. But there are actually some good reasons to take the process seriously. An ethics committee is there to: ensure integrity in knowledge production; promote responsibility towards participants; and protect both the researcher and the granting institution from any potential legal ramifications that might arise from unethical research.

Getting ethical approval is a major milestone and one you want to schedule carefully. Some of Emma's students have been caught out by tight deadlines for committee meetings or protracted amendments that can severely slow or derail a project. Make sure to get advice from your supervisor to plan when and how to engage with your institution's ethics committee.

Most universities will have their own ethics protocols, but there is a move for greater standardization. The Economic and Social Research Council in the UK, for example, has developed the ESRC Framework for Research Ethics, a 51-page guide that sets out requirements for ethics approval for ESRC-funded research (see Box 4.8). It is often adopted by other UK funders as well. Australia has gone a step further with the development of a National Ethics Approval Form (NEAF) designed to assist researchers to complete standardized proposals for submission to various research committees (now adopted by most Australian universities). The goal is to increase the consistency, efficiency and quality of the review processes.

Box 4.8

Standardizing Ethics Applications

The UK Economic and Social Research Council (www.esrc.ac.uk/funding/guidance-for-applicants/research-ethics/useful-resources/) ethics requirement guide includes a flow-chart (Figure 4.3) to help researchers work through the key decision-making points in the approvals process.

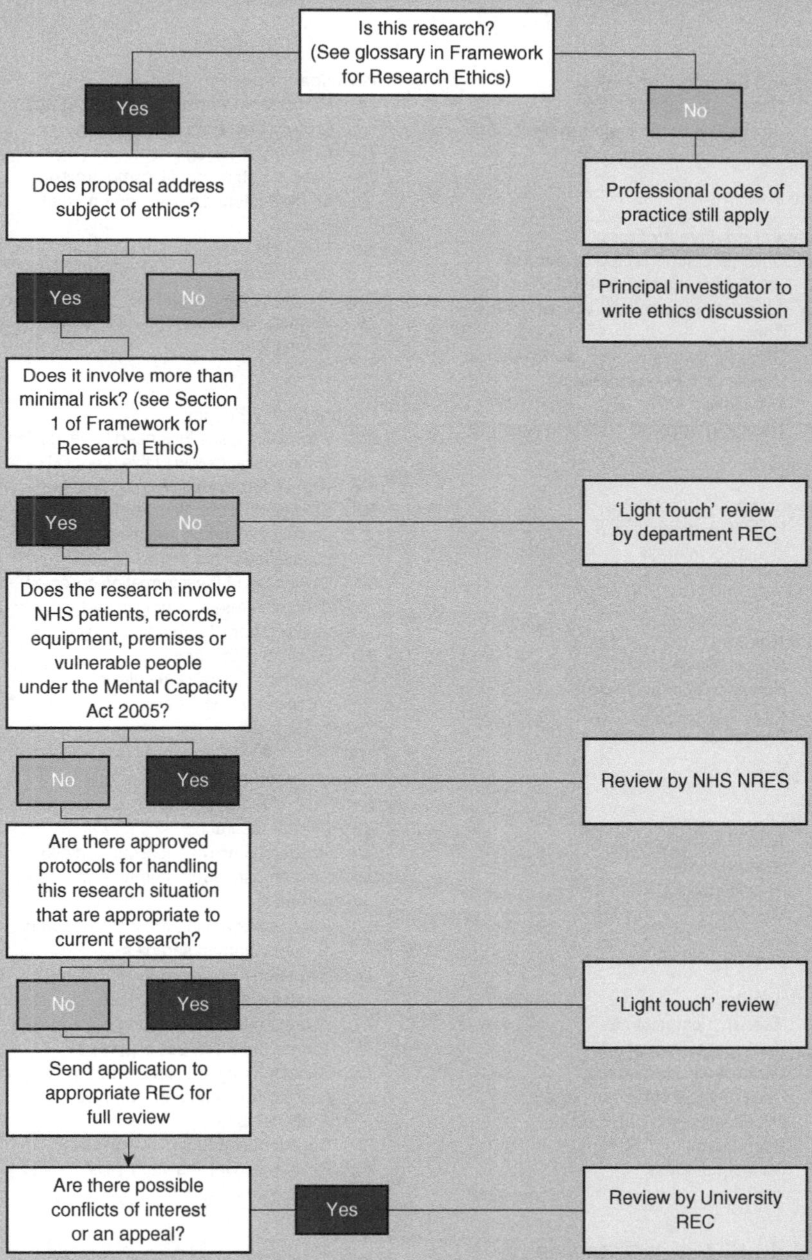

Figure 4.3 ESRC ethics flowchart

(Continued)

The National Ethics Application Form (NEAF)

Quick reference map:
This is a listing of all sections in NEAF. The sections you will be required to answer will depend on the type of research you are undertaking.

Administrative Sections

Section 1:

Title and Summary of Project
1.1 Title
1.2 Description of the project in plain language

Section 2:

Researchers/investigators
2.1 Chief researcher(s)/investigator(s)
2.2 Principal researcher(s)/investigator(s)
2.3 Associate researcher(s)/investigator(s)
2.4 Contact
2.5 Other personnel to the research project
2.6 Certification of researcher(s)/investigator(s)
2.7 Training of researcher(s)/investigator(s)

Section 3:

Resources
3.1 Project funding/support
3.2 Duality of interest

Section 4:

Prior Reviews
4.1 Ethical review
4.2 Research conducted overseas
4.3 Peer
4.4 Ethical review sections

Section 5:

Project
5.1 Type of research
5.2 Research plan
5.3 Benefits/risks
5.4 Monitoring

Section 6:

Participants
6.1 Research participants
6.2 Participant description
6.3 Participation experience
6.4 Relationships of researcher(s)/investigator(s) to participants
6.5 Recruitment
6.6 Consent process

Section 7:

Participant Specific
7.1 Participants whose primary language is other than English (LOTE)
7.2 Children or young people
7.3 People with a cognitive impairment, an intellectual disability or a mental illness
7.4 People in dependent or unequal relationships
7.5 People in other countries
7.6 Women who are pregnant and the human foetus

Section 8:

Confidentiality/Privacy
8.1 Do privacy guidelines need to be applied in the ethical review of this proposal?
8.2 Using information from participants
8.3 Storage of information about participants during and after completion of the project
8.4 Ownership of the information collected during the research project and resulting from the research project
8.5 Disposal of the information
8.6 Reporting individual results to participants and others

Section 9:

Project Specific
9.1 Type of research/trial
9.2 Clinical research
9.3 Research involving ionizing radiation
9.4 Research involving human embryos or gametes
9.5 Research involving the collection and/or use of human samples
9.6 Research involving genetic testing/genetic research
9.7 Research involving Aboriginal and Torres Strait Islander peoples
9.8 Research on workplace practices or possibly impacting on workplace relationships
9.9 Research conducted overseas
9.10 Research involving stem cells

Figure 4.4 NEAF reference map

Australia's National Ethics Application Form (developed by the National Health and Medical Research Council) - see www.neaf.gov.au/default.aspx - is quite detailed and often seen as onerous by student researchers. Good advice is to see the NEAF as more than an ethics application. Frame it up as an exceptional tool that forces you to take your project from vague ideas to a tangible research process. Figure 4.4 outlines the NEAF application.

Box 4.9

Ethics Application Addendums - Participant Information Statements and Consent Forms

Two commonly required documents that are addendums to almost all ethics applications are participant information statements and consent forms. Most ethics committees will have clear requirements, examples and/or templates on their websites and you would be well advised to refer to these. There are, however, key elements in these documents, as outlined below.

Participant Information Statement

1. A brief description of the aims and objectives of the study in lay terms, including what you expect to achieve.
2. Information on who is conducting the study, including person or team, institution, degree undertaken and supervisor.
3. What the study involves - interview, focus groups, video recording, etc. Also include locations, topics that will be covered, time required of participants and risks.
4. Right of the participant to withdraw at any time.
5. Assurances of confidentiality.
6. Benefits to participants.
7. Contact details for further information and to discuss any concerns.

Consent Form

1. Title of the project.
2. A permission statement, such as 'I, ..., give consent to my participation in the research project.'
3. Details of what participants are consenting to: 'In giving my consent I acknowledge that:
    - The procedures required for the project and the time involved have been explained to me.
    - I have read the Participant Information Statement and have been given the opportunity to discuss the information and my involvement in the project with the researcher/s.

(Continued)

- I understand that being in this study is completely voluntary - I am not under any obligation to consent.
- I understand that my involvement is strictly confidential. I understand that any research data gathered from the results of the study may be published; however, no information about me will be used in any way that is identifiable.
- I understand that I can withdraw from the study at any time, without affecting my relationship with the researcher(s) or the University of X.'

(See the online resources for more examples and templates.)

I Have a Question!

I Need to Get Started, and My Ethics Approval is Delayed! How Bad Can It Be to Start My Data Collection Before Final Approval?

It is absolutely fine if nothing goes wrong, but disastrous if it does. And when we say disastrous, we mean disastrous. By going rogue you can:

1. put participants at risk - for example, you may trigger an emotional response you are not ready for;
2. put yourself at risk - if someone were to complain about your conduct and your lack of approval comes to light, you can risk your project and candidature - you may also face a lawsuit with no protection from the university;
3. put the university at risk - both reputationally and legally.

Our advice? Follow up, but wait it out! And besides, we are pretty sure you have a literature review and methods section you could be working on until approval comes through.

Chapter Summary

- Responsibility and integrity should be paramount research considerations. This includes integrity in the production of knowledge, and integrity in dealing with research participants.
- Ethical and political awareness need to be a mainstream consideration in research. Power, politics and ethics must now be actively managed.
- Rather than selecting indicators strictly by paradigm, researchers are encouraged to consider underlying challenges and determine appropriate indicators by critically examining their methodological approaches. Challenges include: managing subjectivities; building trust; capturing truth; making relevant arguments; and providing accurate accounts.

- Integrity and the 'researched' refers to responsibility for the dignity and welfare of research participants. Such responsibilities can be legal, moral and ethical.
- Official ethics approval will ensure integrity, promote responsibility towards participants, and protect both the researcher and the granting institution from legal ramifications.

FIND YOUR NEXT STEP

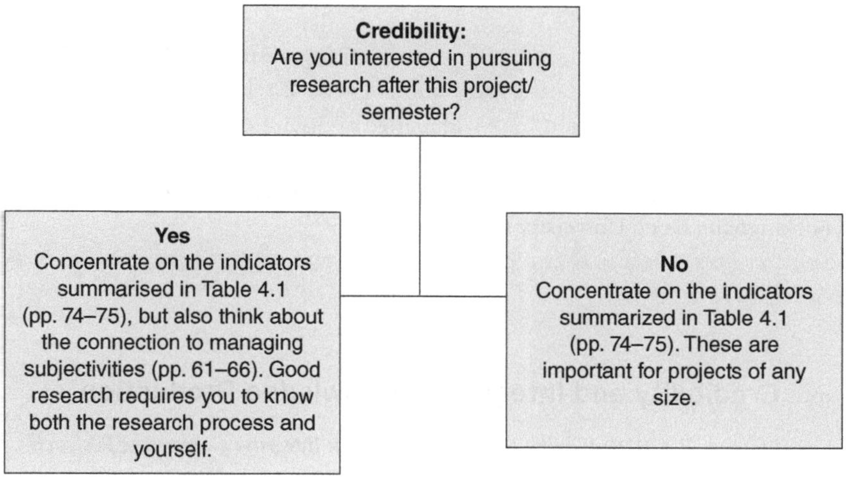

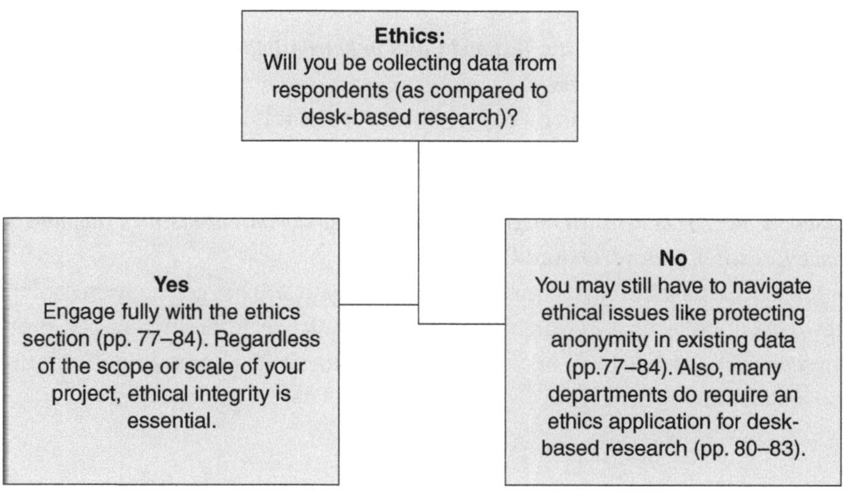

FURTHER READING

Power and Politics in Research

Smith, L. T. (2021). *Decolonizing Methodologies: Research and Indigenous Peoples*, 3rd edition. London: Zed Books.
A landmark text (first published in 1999) that highlights the intersections between imperialism and research. As well as important theorizing about research, it includes case studies of decolonizing work by indigenous researchers. Essential reading.

Connell, R. (2007). *Southern Theory: Social Science and the Global Dynamics of Knowledge*. Hoboken NJ: Wiley
'Southern' theories from Australia, Indigenous peoples, Latin America, India, Africa, Islam are often overlooked but offer important contributions to social science. Although theory-heavy, the writing is accessible and relevant for a wide range of disciplines.

Hood, S., Mayall, B. and Oliver, S. (eds) (1999) *Critical Issues in Social Research: Power and Prejudice*. Buckingham: Open University Press.
A good read that frames research as a political activity and explores the exercise of power as central to research integrity.

Credibility and Integrity in Knowledge Production

Bowden, J. and Green, P. (2019) *Playing the PhD Game with Integrity: Connecting Research, Professional Practice and Educational Context*. New York: Springer.
This book is set in the context of Australian PhD programmes but does point out commonalities and divergences with the UK, US and Europe. It'll certainly give you food for thought.

Macrina, F. L. (2014) *Scientific Integrity: Text and Cases in Responsible Conduct of Research*, 4th edition. Herndon, VA: ASM Press.
While this book covers all key topics, what we like most about it is the interactive case studies. Well worth a look.

Nichols-Casebolt, A. (2012) *Research Integrity and Responsible Conduct of Research (Building Social Work Research Capacity)*. Oxford: Oxford University Press.
While this book does draw heavily on social work examples, it still has good coverage of integrity as it relates to data collection; research ownership; conflict of interest; subjects' protection; research misconduct; authorship and publishing; mentor and mentee responsibilities; peer review; and collaborative science.

Ethics

Anderson, E. and Corneli, A. (2018) *100 Questions (and Answers) About Research Ethics*. Thousand Oaks, CA: Sage.
What a super-friendly format. Questions are logically grouped and answered in a practical manner.

Israel, M. (2014) *Research Ethics and Integrity for Social Scientists: Beyond Regulatory Compliance*, 2nd edition. London: Sage.
We think this is a good, comprehensive and accessible guide with relevant examples and case studies that takes a critical look at both ethics and the ethics approval process.

Oliver, P. (2010) *The Students' Guide to Research Ethics*, 2nd edition. Buckingham: Open University Press.
A very practical student focus here that will get you thinking about the ethical considerations you will need to take into account as you design and progress your project. Good links to further readings.

Resnik, D. (2018) *The Ethics of Research with Human Subjects: Protecting People, Advancing Science, Promoting Trust*. New York: Springer.
We like how this book frames ethics around the concept of trust. It makes ethics much deeper than something that is just rule-based. And trust, of course, is not only paramount to ethics, it's paramount to credibility.

Robinson-Pant, A. and Singal, N. (2016) *Researching Ethically across Cultures: Issues of Knowledge, Power and Voice*. Abingdon: Routledge.
Standard ethical procedures like informed consent also have a Western/Eurocentric bias that mean they don't always translate well in cross-cultural research. This book has theoretical and practical resources to help you ethically engage in research across cultures.

5

CRAFTING A RESEARCH PROPOSAL

Learning Objectives

- Role of the proposal
  - To understand how proposals highlight: the merits of the research question; the proposed methods; and the researcher
- Elements of the proposal
  - To become familiar with the key elements contained within a research proposal
- Writing a winning proposal
  - To understand the need to pedantically follow any prescribed proposal guidelines
  - To develop skills in purposeful writing
  - To appreciate the need to develop multiple drafts
- Obstacles and challenges
  - To understand and manage challenges that can arise when proposed research methods: do not fit proposal requirements; are emergent; or need to change direction

ROLE OF THE PROPOSAL

Let us read with method, and propose to ourselves an end to which our studies may point.

Edward Gibbon (1814)

When it comes to research, very few projects get off the ground without some sort of approval. It may be as straightforward as verbal approval from your lecturer, but it is equally likely to involve a formal approval process gained through an admissions board, an ethics committee or a funding body. And of course you may need approval from more than one of these.

This means you will need to develop a research proposal. Now many see the proposal as an opportunity to clarify thinking, bed down ideas and articulate thoughts in a way that will provide a study's outline as well as a blueprint for future action. And yes, a research proposal is all these things. But – and this is important – a proposal is not something you write for yourself. It is, without a doubt, a sales pitch. Your proposal is your opportunity, and sometimes your only opportunity, to sell your project and get your study off the ground.

So whether you are after admission to a university research programme, seeking ethics approval or looking for funding, the role of the proposal is to convince the powers that be that what you are proposing meets their requirements. Namely, that the research question, the proposed methods and the researcher all have merit. In other words, a committee will assess not only whether a project is useful and practicable, but also whether or not it thinks you as the proposer have the ability to carry the project out.

Now keep in mind that the weight given to various aspects of a proposal varies according to the type of committee you are addressing and the type of approval you are seeking. For example, a proposal written to get into a PhD programme really needs to sell your potential as a researcher. A proposal written for an ethics committee needs to focus on the relationship between methods and participants. A proposal to a funding body, however, would need to have a strong emphasis on practicalities of method and the benefits of potential outcomes.

Demonstrating the Merits of the Research Question

Essential to any successful proposal is your ability to sell the merits of your research question. Demonstrating merits will rely on two things. The first is that you are able to clearly and succinctly share your research topic and question (generally the work of the title, summary/abstract, aims/objectives, research question/hypothesis). The second thing is that you can demonstrate that your research question is worth answering; that is, your question is significant enough to warrant support either at the level of admission to a programme or via funding (generally the work of the introduction/background/rationale).

When it comes to a committee's assessment there are several possible scenarios:

1 The worth of the research question is self-evident (e.g. 'What are the most effective strategies for curbing binge drinking in under-18s?'), and you are able to argue the importance and significance of your question to the satisfaction of the assessors. So far so good.
2 The worth of the research question is, as above, self-evident, but you do a lousy job arguing the case and do not convince the assessors that you are capable of mounting what should be a straightforward argument. Major problem.
3 The worth of the research question is not self-evident (e.g. 'Do residents of the UK enjoy watching Big Brother more than US residents?'), but you are able to convincingly argue the case by citing evidence that attests to a real issue and what benefits there might be

in conducting research into this area. If you can do this (particularly for this question), that's impressive!

4 The worth of the research question is, as above, not self-evident, and you do little to help your case. Your arguments are weak, so assessors are left scratching their heads and quickly put your proposal into the reject pile.

The point here is that while the significance of the research question is important, what is actually being assessed is your ability to argue the significance. It is therefore crucial that your writing be tight, well structured and well referenced.

Demonstrating the Merits of the Proposed Methods

Once your assessors are convinced that your research question has merit, their focus will turn to methods. Here they are looking for several things:

1 Are the proposed methods clearly articulated? If your assessors cannot make sense of what you are proposing, your proposal has little chance of getting off the ground.
2 Are the proposed methods logical? In other words, do they make sense and do the assessors believe your approach can lead to credible data (generally the work of the methods section)?
3 Has the candidate considered the study's boundaries as well as any potential hurdles to effective data collection and analysis? Established assessors know that all research is constrained; your job here is to acknowledge this and show the credibility of your methods in spite of any limitations (generally the work of the methods and limitations/delimitations sections).
4 Are the proposed methods ethical? As discussed in Chapter 4, ethics are central to all research processes (and of course the main focus of an ethics proposal). Your proposal needs to show that the dignity and well-being of respondents, both mentally and physically, are fully protected (the work of the methods and ethical considerations sections).
5 Are the proposed methods practical/doable? It doesn't matter how logical and well considered your methods are if your assessors do not believe they can be implemented. You need to show that you have or can develop the necessary expertise; that you can gain access to required data; that your timeline is realistic; and that you will come within budget (the work of the methods section as well as, if required, the timeline and budget).

Basically, your methods section needs to convince readers that your approach is an efficient, effective and ethical way to get credible answers to your questions and that you are capable of pulling this off.

Demonstrating the Merits of the Researcher

Let's assume the assessors are happy with both your questions and your methods. The final issue is whether they think you are the right person for the job. Do they trust that you can pull this off? Do they believe you have the necessary background knowledge, at least some familiarity with the literature and writing skills commensurate to the task?

Now that's a lot of questions, and it would be great if your assessors could get to know you and get a real feel for what you are capable of. But that's not likely to happen. In fact, there is a good chance your proposal will be reviewed by people you have never met. So what do they use to assess your potential? Simply your proposal. Assessors will judge your ability to engage with the literature through your proposal's short literature review. They will assess your ability to carry out methods, based on the knowledge you show and how well you argue your methodological case. And they will assess your potential to write by the quality of writing in your proposal. It therefore pays to give close attention to detail and make your proposal one of the tightest pieces of writing you have ever attempted.

ELEMENTS OF THE PROPOSAL

Proposal requirements vary according to the role of the proposal and by institution. But generally you will be required to include some combination of the following:

- Title – Go for clear, concise and unambiguous. Your title should indicate the specific content and context of the problem you wish to explore in as succinct a way as possible.
- Summary/abstract – Proposals often require a project summary, usually with a very tight word count. The trick here is to briefly state the what, why and how of your project in a way that sells it in just a few sentences – and trust us, this can take quite a few drafts to get right.
- **Aims/objectives** – Most proposals have one overarching aim that captures what you hope to achieve through your project. A set of objectives, which are more specific goals, supports that aim. Aims and objectives are often articulated in bullet points and are generally 'to' statements: for example, to develop …; to identify …; to explore …; to measure …; to explain …; to describe …; to compare …; to determine …. In management literature you are likely to come across **'SMART' objectives** – SMART being an acronym for specific, measurable, achievable, relevant/results-focused/realistic and time-bound. The goal is to keep objectives from being airy-fairy or waffly; clearly articulating what you want to achieve aids your ability to work towards your goal.
- Research question/hypothesis – As discussed in Chapter 3, a well-articulated research question (or hypothesis) should define your investigation, set boundaries, provide direction and act as a frame of reference for assessing your work. Any committee reviewing your proposal will turn to your question in order to get an overall sense of your project. Take time to make sure your question/hypothesis is as well defined and as clearly articulated as possible.
- Introduction/background/rationale – The main job of this section is to introduce your topic and convince readers that the problem you want to address is significant and worth exploring and even funding. It should give some context to the problem and lead your readers to the conclusion that, yes, research into this area is absolutely essential if we really want to work towards situation improvement or problem resolution.
- Literature review – A formal 'literature review' (discussed in more depth in Chapter 6) is a specific piece of argumentative writing that engages with relevant scientific and academic research in order to create a space for your project. The role of the literature review is to

inform readers of developments in the field while establishing your own credibility as a 'player' capable of adding to this body of knowledge. This is a tough piece of writing with a very tight word count, so be prepared to run through a few drafts.

- Theoretical perspectives – This section asks you to situate your study in a conceptual or theoretical framework. The idea here is to articulate the theoretical perspective(s) that underpin and inform your ideas, and, in particular, to discuss how 'theory' relates to and/or directs your study.
- Methods – Some form of 'methods' will be required in all proposals. The goal here is to articulate your plan with enough clarity and detail to convince readers that your approach is practical and will lead to credible answers to the questions posed (see Chapter 7). Under the heading of methods you would generally articulate:
    - the approach/methodology – for example, if you are doing ethnography, action research or maybe a randomized controlled trial (see Chapters 8, 9 and 10);
    - how you will find respondents – this includes articulation of population and sample/**sampling** procedures (see Chapter 11);
    - data-collection method(s) – for example, **surveying**, interviewing and document analysis (see Chapters 12, 13 and 14);
    - methods of analysis – whether you will be doing statistical or **thematic analysis** and perhaps variants thereof (see Chapters 1 and 16).
- Limitations/delimitations – Limitations refer to conditions or design characteristics that may impact the generalizability and utility of findings, such as small sample size or restricted access to records. Keep in mind that most projects are limited by constraints such as time, resources, access or organizational issues. So it is much better to be open about 'flaws' than leave it to assessors who might be much more critical. **Delimitations** refer to a study's boundaries or how your study was deliberately narrowed by conscious exclusions and inclusions, e.g. limiting your study to children of a certain age only, or schools from one particular region. Now remember that your overarching goal here is to convince readers that your findings will be credible in spite of any limitations or delimitations. So the trick is to be open about your study's parameters without sounding defensive or apologetic. It is also worth articulating any strategies you will be using to ensure credibility despite limitations.
- Ethical considerations – Whenever you are working with human participants there will be ethical issues you need to consider (see Chapter 4). Now if this were an application for an ethics committee you would need to focus much of your proposal on ethical issues. But even if this were a proposal for admission, your readers would still need to be convinced that you have considered issues related to integrity in the production of knowledge and responsibility for the emotional, physical and intellectual well-being of your study participants.
- Timeline – This is simply superimposing a timeline on your methods, and is often done in a tabular or chart form. The committee reading your proposal will be looking to see that your plan is realistic and can conform to any overarching timeframes or deadlines.
- Budget/funding – This is a full account of costs and who will bear them. While not always a required section for ethics proposals or proposals for academic student research, it will certainly be a requirement for a funding body. Now it is definitely worth being

realistic – it's easy to underestimate costs. Wages, software, hardware, equipment, travel, transcription, administrative support, etc. can add up quite quickly, and running short of money mid-project is not a good option. But also keep in mind that if you are tendering for a commissioned project, it's a good idea to get a ballpark figure of the funding body's budget. This will put you in a position to design your methods accordingly and hopefully make you competitive.

- References – This can refer to two things. The first is citing references in the same way as you would in any other type of academic/professional writing. Believe it or not, it's often missed. The second is that some committees want a list of, say, 10 or 15 primary references that will inform your work. This information can help a committee assess your knowledge and give its members a clearer indication of the direction your study may take.

I Have a Question!

So Should I Put in All the Elements You Talk About, or Should I Just Stick with the Template They Have Given Me?

The template, definitely the template. The list above will give you some idea of what you might expect, and it will give you some guidance about what goes into each of these sections, but it should not override what you are directly asked to provide. Stick with the template, and its word counts. As discussed below, when it comes to proposals, being pedantic is a good thing.

WRITING A WINNING PROPOSAL

In our experience, when a person or a committee has the power to make major decisions about someone else's work/future, they like to wield that power, and they often wield it in very defined ways. When it comes to assessing research proposals, this translates into committees wanting what they want, the way they want it, when they want it. If you are the person writing the proposal, this means you need to be just as pedantic and make sure you follow all guidelines, write purposively and be prepared to work through several drafts. Box 5.1 takes you through a real-world example.

Box 5.1

Proposal Example

Here are a few sections from a longer funding proposal Zina and a colleague and submitted some time back. Their goal was to make sure the proposal met the funding body's specifications quite directly. Surprisingly, they did not ask for any background literature, so none was provided.

Project title: Great Speech: De-mystifying Powerful Presentations in the Public Sector

Project overview (150–250 words): We all know outstanding presentations and inspirational speakers when we hear them. We know because we are moved. We know because we want to tell others about it. We know because we feel inspired. Yet inspiring can be a difficult objective to reach. In spite of the abundance of advice, dry, tedious, uninspired presentations are often the norm – public sector presentations included. Change within the public sector, however, is generally reliant on cycles of advocacy; and such cycles often culminate in presentations. Reform is often reliant on influence, so the need to drive an idea and inspire an audience is undeniable. Knowing the best means for influencing an audience through an effective presentation is often challenging, particularly in an information age, where Google and Wikipedia now hold knowledge once the domain of experts.

The goal of this project is to offer recommendations for improved teaching and learning in the space of public sector presentations. Through an analysis of 70 of the best, most inspired presentations of the past decade, with particular reference to the public sector, this project will deconstruct the core elements that underlie truly inspirational presentations. The project will then analyse a cross-section of trans-Tasman public sector presentations in a bid to identify gaps in best practice and thus training needs.

Project objectives (100–200 words): The overarching aim of this research project is to offer clear recommendations for improved teaching and learning in the space of public sector presentations.

The objectives of this project are:

- to identify the core elements that make for highly effective, highly motivational presentations;
- to identify core elements and contextual issues of particular relevance to the public sector;
- to create a qualitative matrix for easy identification of core elements;
- to assess the effectiveness of presentations in the Australia/New Zealand public sector and identify gaps in effective Australia/New Zealand public sector presentations in order to develop and enhance teaching and learning development within this space.

Project benefits (100–200 words): Within the public sector, rarely is there an initiative, project, programme or policy reform that does not need to be championed. Advocacy is essential and presentations that fail to motivate can end the run of a potentially good reform. This project, with its goal of improving teaching and learning in the arena of public sector presentation, offers benefits to three stakeholder groups.

The trans-Tasman public sector will benefit via increased ability to influence the policy cycle. Improved presentations can lead to more engaged debate on key public administration issues and contribute to continuing reform in the public sector.

The funding institution will benefit through the development of resources for future teaching and applied learning/knowledge activities. The aim is to enhance leadership in public sector communication training, while supporting the development of best practice in government.

Students will benefit from increased skills, confidence and levels of influence.

(Continued)

Methodology – What research method(s) will your project use (50–150 words)? The methodology will rely on a two-phase qualitative approach reliant on both online and 'face-to-face' data.

Phase One – Analysis of 70 highly motivational presentations of the past decade. Population: Online presentations (in English) deemed highly motivational by media/speaking experts. Sampling Strategy: Targeted sampling designed to include a wide range of speaker demographics – with a minimum of 35 public sector presentations. Analysis: Development of a best-practice matrix through the use of **narrative analysis**, **content analysis** and **semiotics**.

Phase Two – Analysis of 30 public sector presentations in the trans-Tasman region. Population: Presentations at ANZSOG's annual conference as well as online presentations. Sampling Strategy: Random, cross-sectional. Analysis: Gap analysis via assessment of presentations against the matrix developed in Phase One. All presentations used in this phase will be de-identified and aggregated without identifying data. The aim is to identify common gaps in practice rather than critique individual presentations.

What is the rationale for using this method/these methods for this project (100–150 words)? The methodology for this project does not neatly fall within one particular approach, or even one particular paradigm, but rather represents a question-driven approach that utilizes both traditional social science methods as well as project management tools. Specifically, this project relies on: sampling strategies developed within the quantitative paradigm; data analysis methods such as content analysis, narrative analysis and semiotics drawn from the qualitative school; and a gap analysis more traditionally found in project management. Such mixed methodologies are often advocated for **applied research** not tied to paradigmatic traditions. The ability to draw from varied schools of thought as well as the ability to leverage the power of the Internet gives veracity to methods and allows for the development of context-driven methods. The particular methods to be employed in this project are those considered most likely to give credible results within the desired timeframe.

Following Guidelines

So how many words can you get away with when the application says the title needs to be no more than 20 words or that the abstract must be less than 150 words? Well, it is certainly not uncommon for applicants to try to stretch these limits – but we would advise against it. Some assessors can judge harshly when they think applicants cannot follow simple directions. Are they being too harsh? Maybe. But you need to realize that assessors often see the application as a test of whether you will be able to meet requirements when you actually start working on your project. It may seem a bit parochial, but if you cannot follow guidelines in a short application, your assessors might just ask what that says about your potential to complete.

The best advice here is to follow guidelines as close to the letter as possible. This means:

- constructing your proposal according to, or as close as possible to, the recommended sections/headings;
- keeping to all word limits;
- being absolutely meticulous about spelling and grammar;
- strictly adhering to deadlines.

Writing Purposively

It is important to recognize that a proposal should never be sloppy, rushed or thrown together at the last minute. It needs to be a highly polished and well-constructed piece of writing. Remember: the clarity of your thoughts, the veracity of your arguments and the quality of your writing will be used to judge your potential as a researcher.

Emma has reviewed a lot of proposals for her university's postgraduate committee. Although the projects differ, key aspects of a great proposal are the same. The following tips should help you craft a winning proposal:

- See if you can get access to a few successful proposals – If possible, seek out proposals that have gone through the committee you are applying to, or to as similar a committee as possible. The institution assessing your application may have proposals online. If they don't, then google 'research proposal example'. You can combine that with the level of study (PhD, undergraduate) and/or your broad area of study (business, sociology, policy). But keep in mind that not all proposals up on the Internet are good ones! You can also refer to the examples in the books cited at the end of the chapter.
- Find a voice – The convention here is third person; however, using 'I' to state what you will do is now more commonly accepted. Also remember to write in the future tense. A proposal is about what you will do, not what you are doing now, or have done in the past.
- 'Write tight' – Your writing needs to be concise and succinct, direct and straightforward. Avoid rambling and/or trying to show off by using unnecessary jargon.
- Write enough – Somewhat paradoxical to the above, you also need to make sure you write a sufficient amount for assessors to make judgements.
- Write for the 'non-expert' – Your proposal needs to be 'stand-alone' and be comprehensible to someone potentially outside your field.
- Do your homework – The last thing you want in a short formal proposal is 'mistakes'. Get your facts right, make sure you don't have gaping holes in your literature and make sure any references to theory and/or methods are accurate.
- Don't over-quote – Generally the writing expected is so tight that you probably won't have enough room for too many direct quotes. Keep the words and ideas yours, supported by the literature.
- Don't let the deadline sneak up on you – Plan on finishing early so that you have time to review and redraft. Remember: deadlines are often inflexible, and this is a case where you do not want to have to rush and let quality suffer.
- As discussed below, be prepared to draft and redraft.

Drafting and Redrafting

The best advice here is to leave yourself enough time to get feedback and redraft, if possible, more than once. Remember: even if your reader does not understand the details, the overarching arguments should make sense to the non-expert – so don't hesitate to ask a peer, parent, friend, etc. if they can follow the proposal and if it makes sense. But if you have access, we certainly recommend seeking the advice of someone who has experience in research and research proposals.

Chapter 17 offers detailed checklists for working towards final drafts, but to summarize here, your final draft should: follow set criteria; be logical; make your point with convincing arguments; contain sufficient information; use a consistent voice; avoid being repetitious; be clear and fluent; avoid waffling; avoid paragraph-long sentences; limit acronyms and jargon; strictly adhere to word counts; have exemplary spelling and grammar; avoid all typos; and be well formatted.

OBSTACLES AND CHALLENGES

So if you do all of the above, surely you are bound to impress? It should all be plain sailing, shouldn't it? Well, hopefully that will be the case. But there are a couple of sticky situations you may need to negotiate.

When Your Design Does Not Fit Proposal Requirements

If you have read this far, you know how important we think it is to give a committee what it asks for. But what if your research design simply does not fit in with the committee's requirements? Many of Emma's students face this challenge on qualitative projects where terms like hypothesis, variables, validity and reliability may not be appropriate to your study but may nonetheless be required 'sections' in your proposal.

Unfortunately, there can still be a bias towards the quantitative paradigm, the legacy of which can be reflected in proposal proformas and even committee expectations. If this is the case, we would suggest seeking the advice of someone who has worked with the committee to see how it tends to handle such dilemmas – each committee will have a different approach. If, however, you cannot get this insider information, or are told 'Just do the best you can', we would suggest remembering the bigger agenda of the proposal; that is, to demonstrate the merits of the research question, the merits of the proposed methods and the merits of the researcher. So, regardless of paradigm, you will need to show you are confident with the theoretical, conceptual and methodological landscape you are proposing to enter. To that end, write confidently, not aggressively nor apologetically. If the committee wants a hypothesis, yet it is not appropriate, you have the option of writing 'N/A' and giving justification for inappropriateness (see Chapter 3). If the committee wants you to list variables but your study is more exploratory, say so. If validity, reliability or generalizability is inappropriate, confidently talk about credibility indicators that are more appropriate (see Chapter 4). Any committee worth its weight will be able to spot a researcher who knows what they are talking about, even when it doesn't fit with the committee's expectations/jargon.

Critical Thinking Challenge 5

Eye on the Prize

You would think that the goal of crafting a research proposal is telling a committee about your research. But what it's really about is getting them to approve your research. This means it's time to think not just critically, but strategically. What's important to the committee? What do they need to see? What do they not want to see? What will give them faith in you and your research processes?

Take the time to put yourself in the position of a committee member and ask questions of people in the know. You're much more likely to be on target when you are taking the perspective of those you want to influence.

When Your Design Is Emergent

Another major dilemma is when you are proposing a study that will have evolving methods that cannot be fully articulated at the time proposal applications are required. This is particularly problematic for ethics proposals, which are used to protect the dignity and welfare of the 'researched' as well as protect the researcher and home institution from legal liability. These proposals often demand a full account of methods, which often includes appending things like surveys and interview schedules.

Once again 'qualitative' researchers who wish to use conversational/unstructured data-gathering techniques that are not fully predetermined will face a dilemma. Those undertaking action research can also struggle as their methodological protocols are based on stakeholder collaboration in multiple cycles (see Chapter 10). In fact, there are many research projects (including quantitative studies) in which methods are conducted in multiple phases, with each phase determined by what has happened previously. For example, **key informant** interviews may be used to inform survey design, or survey results may determine the questions used in in-depth interviewing.

The best strategy here is to be open and knowledgeable about your approach. Show that your design is not haphazard or ill considered. Show that even if you cannot articulate all the specifics, your required flexibility is planned, and you have a defined framework. Show the committee forethought. Offer, if possible, indicative questions. And finally, show that you can link your approach back to accepted methodological literature. If you can manage to make such arguments your chances of success will be greatly enhanced.

Of course, even if you are able to make such arguments there is the possibility that the committee will require further information. If this is the case, you can attempt to add more definition to your methodological plan. But if your overarching design makes this impossible and your committee is immovable, you will need (1) to see if it is possible to put in a supplementary application as your methods evolve; or (2) to talk to your supervisor about required methodological modifications.

When You Want to or Need to Change Direction/Method

Suppose you are all set to interview 15 CEOs, but, try as you might, you just can't get more than three to participate. Or suppose you plan on surveying 1,000 homeless people, but after much effort you only have 36 surveys returned. Or imagine that you have undertaken a much more comprehensive literature review than included in your proposal and you realize that the survey questions you originally proposed are way off target.

What do you do? Well, from a methodological standpoint, you improvise. You think about your question, talk to your supervisor and determine the most 'doable' way to get some credible data. But disappointingly, most students in this situation simply charge ahead and change their study protocols without further committee consultation. And while this may be the path of least resistance, it is not recommended. If your application represents a 'contract' to do a job for a funding body, for example, you need to inform it of shifts in your approach. Updating ethics applications is equally important. Not only do you want an outside committee to see that you will not threaten the dignity and well-being of the researched, but you also want to ensure that you have protected yourself and your institution from potential lawsuits.

I Have a Question!

What Do I Do If My Proposal Is Knocked Back?

That is a very difficult situation. One that often leads to an emotional response: anger, disappointment, feeling disheartened, etc. A knock-back is never easy, but it is particularly difficult when it is one that sees you having to 'reassess' where you are going. We think the best advice here is to take a deep breath and regroup. Once you have worked through the emotional side, it will be time to get information; to figure out where you went wrong, and what you need to do now. Read the feedback carefully, seek clarification, talk to others. The more you know, the better position you will be in to avoid pitfalls in the future.

Chapter Summary

- A research proposal offers an opportunity to clarify your thinking, bed down ideas and articulate thoughts in a way that will provide a blueprint for future action. It is also a means for 'selling' your project by articulating the merits of the research question and proposed methods.
- Proposals differ in requirements, but most will ask you to articulate some combination of the following: title; summary/abstract; aims/objectives; research question/hypothesis; introduction/background/rationale; literature review; theoretical perspectives; methods; limitations/delimitations; ethical considerations; timelines; budget/funding; and references.
- Writing a winning proposal requires you to closely follow your institution's guidelines and to write purposively. This involves good planning, knowing your subject, finding a voice, writing tightly yet sufficiently, writing for the non-expert and being prepared to redraft.
- Obstacles you may face include proposals that do not fit a committee's requirements and proposals with **emergent designs**. In both cases, being knowledgeable, confident and open will enhance your chances of success.
- Even though it may seem painful, if you want or need to change direction/method it is a good idea to keep your approval body informed.

FIND YOUR NEXT STEP

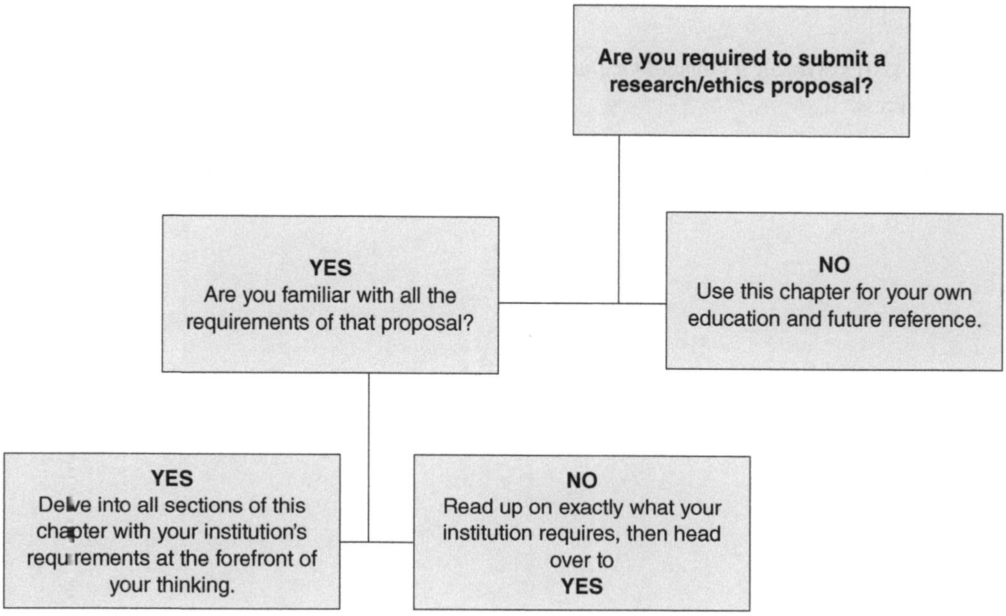

FURTHER READING

There are quite a few books that can help you navigate your way through proposal development, most of which give good examples. Have a look at:

Decuir-Gundy, J. and Schutz, P. (2016) *Developing a Mixed Methods Proposal: A Practical Guide for Beginning Researchers*. Thousand Oaks, CA: Sage.
We like that this book is specific to mixed methods. It can be a challenge to be clear and concise when working across two paradigms. This book gives you good guidance.

Krathwohl, D. R. and Smith, N. L. (2005) *How to Prepare a Dissertation Proposal: Suggestions for Students in Education and the Social and Behavioral Sciences*. Syracuse, NY: Syracuse University Press.
A good step-by-step guide that covers qualitative, quantitative and mixed methodology. They have great student examples to ground recommendations.

Locke, L. F., Spirduso, W. W. and Silverman, S. J. (2013) *Proposals That Work: A Guide for Planning Dissertations and Grant Proposals*. London: Sage.
A comprehensive guide for students undertaking a thesis or applying for a grant – easy to follow and offers a range of relevant examples.

O'Leary, Z. (2018a) *LQF: Research Proposals*. London: Sage.
Another book by one of your favourite authors! Like the research questions book, this is a very short graphic book designed to work you through the process of proposal development.

Punch, K. (2016) *Developing Effective Research Proposals*, 3rd edition. London: Sage.
Terrific guide that covers both qualitative and quantitative research. It takes you through the basics of a proposal, how to go about writing one and what it should look like when complete.

Terrell, S. (2015) *Writing a Proposal for Your Dissertation: Guidelines and Examples*. New York: Guilford Press.
This is a very comprehensive user-friendly work that incorporates several engaging pedagogical features. Good on theory and practice.

6

REVIEWING LITERATURE

Learning Objectives

- The importance of literature
  - To understand the critical nature of working with literature throughout the research process
  - To understand the ways in which literature can inform the research process
- Sourcing relevant literature
  - To become familiar with various types of literature and their role in illuminating your research project
  - To develop a range of skills for effectively sourcing appropriate literature
- Managing the literature
  - To be able to systematically assess the quality and relevance of located literature
  - To be able to critically annotate relevant sources
- Writing the formal 'literature review'
  - To understand the purpose of a formal literature review
  - To be able to determine appropriate literature review coverage
  - To become familiar with the steps involved in writing an effective literature review

THE IMPORTANCE OF LITERATURE

> Reading is not optional.
>
> Walter Dean Myers (2012)

There really is no way around it – reading is an essential part of the research process. Why? Because you cannot really engage in research from a platform of ignorance. When you are learning and your goal is to take on board knowledge that is already out there, it does not really matter if you know a little or a lot. The goal is self-education, which needs to, and should, start from wherever you are and attempt to take you to the next level.

Conducting research is a bit different. When you are conducting research, you are attempting to produce knowledge, knowledge that you hope others will learn from, act on and use towards situation improvement. And this demands responsibility. You need to know what you are talking about. The production of new knowledge is fundamentally dependent on past knowledge. Knowledge builds, and it is impossible for researchers to add to a body of literature if they are not conversant with it.

Yes, a lot of knowledge can come from experience – and we strongly advocate drawing on this. But even rich experience is likely to be seen as anecdotal if it is not set within a broader context. Reading is what gives you that broader context. It inspires, informs, educates and enlightens. It generates ideas, helps form significant questions and is instrumental in the process of research design. It is also central to writing up; a clear rationale supported by literature is essential, while a well-constructed literature review is an important criterion in establishing researcher credibility.

Working with literature, however, is often seen as an onerous task. The multiple purposes, the volume and variety, the difficulty in finding it and managing it, dealing with its inconsistencies, the need to formally review it, and, perhaps underpinning all of this, your own lack of knowledge, experience and proficiency can make working with literature somewhat daunting.

Figure 6.1 outlines the variety of tasks involved in working with literature, and explores processes that will help you understand it, source it, manage it and review it.

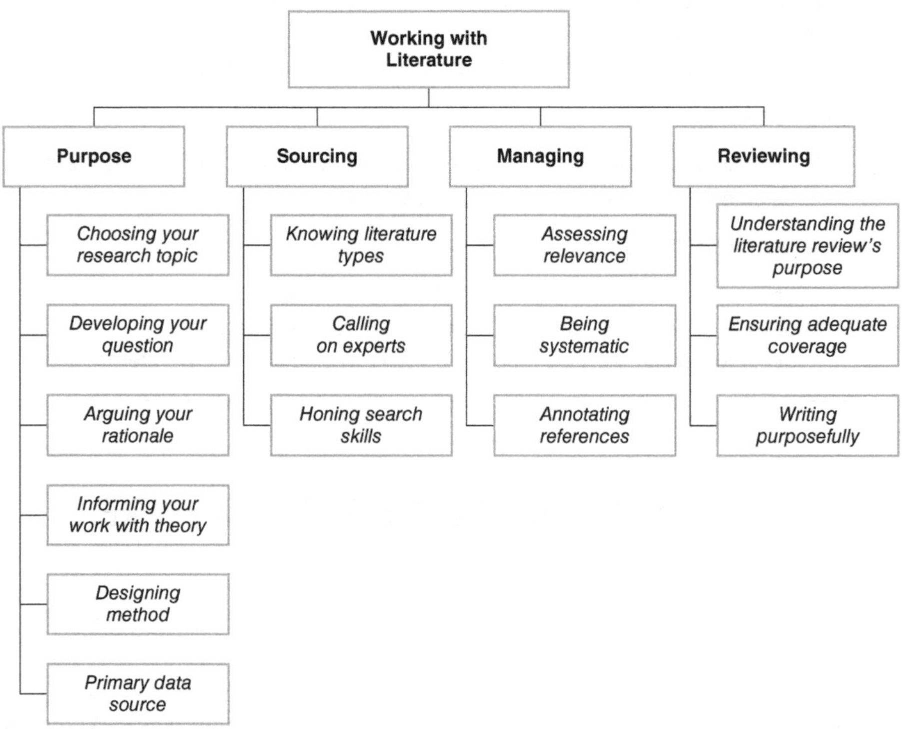

Figure 6.1 Working with literature

The Role of Literature

As shown in Figure 6.2, research requires engagement with literature at each and every stage of the process. A very early use for literature is in the exploration of a topic. Not many students, or even experienced researchers for that matter, know all they need to know about a particular topic, and reading can certainly help you get up to speed. This might involve delving into texts and media reports, as well as journal-based research studies that make up an area's scientific literature.

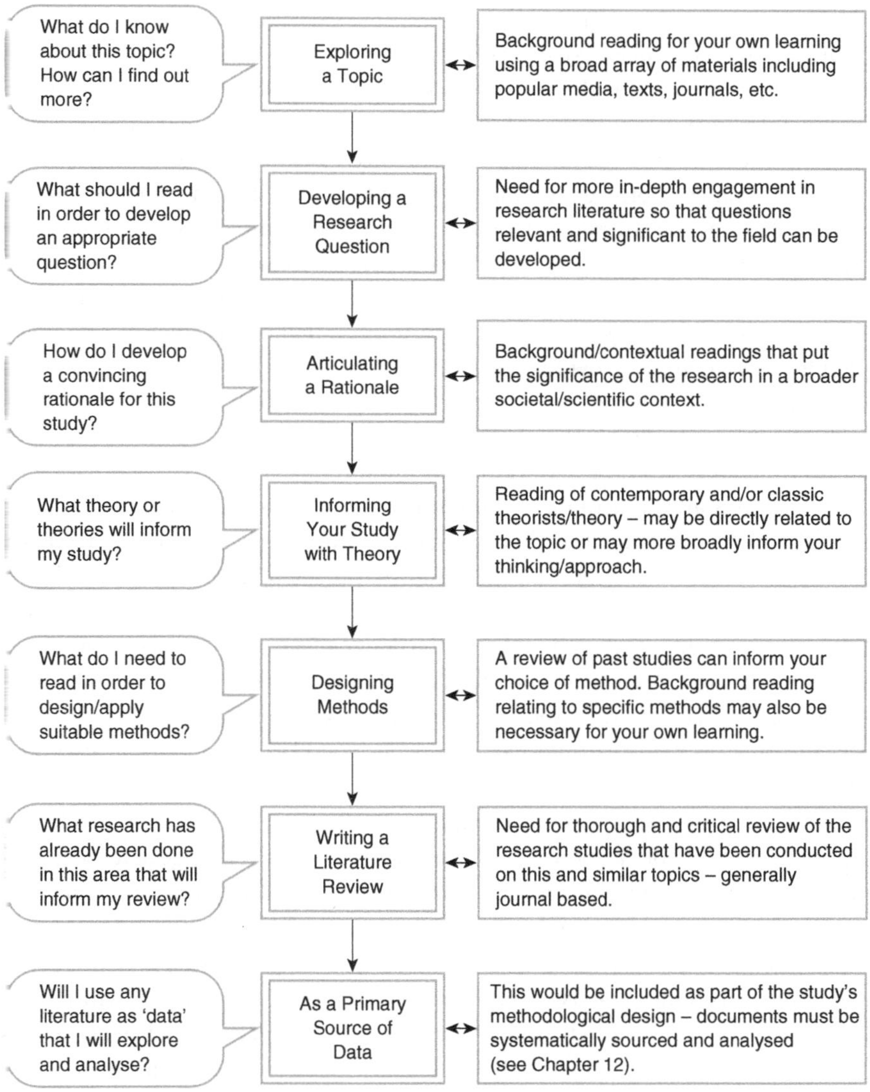

Figure 6.2 Literature and the research process

Literature is also essential in the *development of your research question*. As discussed in Chapter 3, a good place to look for guidance on the development of your research question is in literature. Popular media covering current debates, controversies and disputes around a particular issue can help generate questions of societal significance. Engagement with research literature can also be instrumental in the development of questions. Finding 'gaps', exploring questions that have not been adequately addressed and attempting to ask questions within a new context are all dependent on 'reading'.

Hand in hand with the development of your question is the *development of your rationale*. A well-articulated rationale is part and parcel of any research proposal and needs to suggest why time and money should be invested in addressing your particular research question. In order to do this, you need to draw on literature that can argue the societal and scientific significance of your study. This does not have to be academic literature and is often based on reported statistics, media coverage or company reports.

Literature is also used to *inform your study with theory*, and this *is* based on academic material. Theoretical reading can be difficult for students who perceive a large gap between research and theory – something not uncommon. For years, social 'scientists' engaged in research without strong links to theory, while social 'theorists' theorized without doing much research. This tendency to dichotomize, however, is diminishing and we are beginning to recognize the value of exploring quite tangible issues in relation to theory. For example, research that touches on issues of power, class and religion generally demands the exploration of theorists such as Weber, Marx and Durkheim. In fact, every discipline area (nursing, education, management, etc.), as well as broader areas of sociology and philosophy, rests on rich theory that can add both depth and credibility to your study. Now for some, theoretical reading is a passion and a joy – and therefore not problematic. But for others, it can be a laborious task. If you fall into the second category, it is important to discuss the issue of theory with your supervisor and clearly negotiate the extent to which it is expected to inform your work.

Designing method is also something well informed through reading. Reading can support the design of methods in a number of ways. It can: support learning related to relevant methodologies and methods; allow you to critically evaluate, and possibly adopt, methods considered 'standard' for exploring your particular research question; help you in assessing the need for alternative methodological approaches; and support you in the design of a study that might overcome methodological shortcomings prevalent in the literature. To appropriately design a study, collect the data and conduct analysis, you will need to engage with broad-ranging methods texts such as this one; books focusing on particular research approaches you plan to adopt (e.g. **ethnography**, action research or statistics); research articles on methods themselves; and journal articles that report on studies that use methods similar to those you plan to use. The recommended readings and bibliography in this book can be a great starting point for finding a range of relevant literature.

This next task, *writing a literature review*, is an obvious use of literature and what our mind jumps to when we think of the overlap between research and literature. A formal 'literature review' is a critical review of a body of knowledge, including findings, and theoretical and methodological contributions. It is a very specific piece of argumentative writing that acts to create a 'space' for your research study. It reviews past research and relies on articles published in well-established research journals and is usually a distinct and required section of any research write-up, including grant applications, research reports and journal articles. Virtually all student theses require a literature review that should be relevant, critical and comprehensive; in fact, the review should represent a level of engagement with the literature that indicates a readiness to contribute to the literature itself. The ins and outs of writing a good literature review are covered later in this chapter.

Finally, we can use literature *as a source of research data*. We generally think of data as something we purposefully generate (e.g. transcripts from interviews or the results of surveys). But as covered in Chapters 13 and 14, all types of literature can be used as primary sources of data. From **meta-analysis** of past studies, to content analysis of the media, to in-depth analysis of historical documents, literature can be used to do more than provide context, inform your study and argue the case. It can, in fact, be central to your analysis.

SOURCING RELEVANT LITERATURE

Unfortunately, recognizing the importance of literature and understanding its varied uses will not put it in your hands. You still need to find and access it. To do this efficiently, you need to be familiar with various categories of literature; be ready to call on experts and ask for help; understand the power of databases; and hone your search skills so that you are in a position to best utilize the library and the Internet.

Types of Literature

The array of literature you might find yourself delving into may be a fair bit broader than you first imagine. Because reading for research is something that informs all aspects of the research journey, almost any type of reading is fair game. For example, you are likely to call on:

- Discipline-based reference materials – It is easy for those who know the jargon of a particular discipline to forget that many of its terms are not a part of everyday language. If you are relatively new to a particular discipline, subject-specific reference books can help you navigate your way through the area's central terms, constructs and theories.
- Books – These might include introductory and advanced texts, anthologies, research reports, popular non-fiction and even fictional works that can provide background and context, or inform theory and method. When it comes to the formal literature review, however, the lengthy production time of books means that the most contemporary research is more likely to be found in journals than in books.
- Journal articles – These take you beyond background readings to readings providing rigorous research accounts. They are central to literature reviews because they are often targeted at 'academic' audiences; are generally peer reviewed, which means they have met at least some benchmark for credibility; and have specific areas of content and regularity of production, which means articles are likely to be both relevant and current. The array, specialization and accessibility of journal titles are ever increasing, and online access and digital inter-library loan schemes have made them highly accessible.
- Grey literature – This refers to both published and unpublished materials that do not have an International Standard Book Number (ISBN) or an International Standard Serial Number (ISSN), including conference papers, unpublished research theses, newspaper articles and pamphlets/brochures. Most researchers utilize some type of grey literature in the course of their study. Recent theses and conference papers can be

a valuable source of contemporary original work, while newspaper articles, pamphlets and brochures can be used for background and context – or in the process of document analysis (see Chapter 13).

- Official publications, statistics and archives – These materials can be a valuable source of background and contextual information, and often help shape a study's rationale. They can also be a terrific source of **primary data** in document analysis or a good source of secondary data in statistical analysis (see Chapter 13).
- Writing aids – These include bibliographic reference works, dictionaries, encyclopaedias, thesauruses, almanacs, yearbooks, books of quotes, etc. Such resources can offer significant support during the writing-up process and can be used to improve the linguistic style of your work; to add points of interest to the text; to check facts; and to reference those facts.

Calling on 'Experts'

One resource you do not want to overlook is your university librarian. Our first-year university students often grumble about the need for library orientations. But information technology is changing so fast that students and professional researchers alike need to update their skills on a regular basis. See your librarian! Not only are librarians experts on the latest database searching facilities, but they can often provide you with the training necessary to have you searching for books/articles in libraries all over the world. Many university librarians are designated to a particular academic area (social science, nursing, education, environment, etc.). These 'specialists' can introduce you to relevant databases, journals (both paper and electronic), bibliographies, abstracts, reviews, etc., specific to your area.

'Academics' can also be quite helpful in your search for relevant literature. Talk to supervisors, professors and lecturers. They often know the literature and are able to point you in the right direction; or can at least direct you to someone better acquainted with your topic who can give you the advice you need to make a start. Also, see if you can browse through their bookshelves. While any one academic's library is unlikely to cover all perspectives or be completely up to date, academics often hold key readings that can kick-start your search. Another possibility is to join an academic community such as Academia.edu or ResearchGate. These are the LinkedIns of academia – communities of scholars online, most of whom regularly update their pages with current research. This is a great place to get the latest research. You can search by topic or author and ask to be notified of current publications as they happen. Enrolment is free.

Finally, think about calling on experts in the field. Those working in your area have often had to source relevant literature. Often our students tell us that they are having difficulty finding literature and can only find one or two recent studies that relate to their research question. We tend to ask them, 'Well, who did these people cite? Who is in their reference list?' One relevant journal article should lead to several relevant readings. As well as relevant journal articles, have a look at master's and PhD theses. These works require comprehensive literature reviews and thorough bibliographies that can give you a huge head start when it comes to sourcing your readings. And don't forget that you can also turn to practitioners – those who actually work in the area often know the literature. Finally, try attending relevant conferences. It is quite likely that this will lead to a wealth of leads in your literature search.

Accessing Databases

Most library search engines allow you to search not only what their library holds – including the journals they subscribe to – but also the articles within these journals. You can search for all types of material, including print and electronic books, articles, journals, multimedia, theses, newspapers, e-repositories, etc. They are usually ranked by relevance and you can limit your search by criteria such as year, format and language.

Google Scholar allows you to search a range of scholarly materials and is best used with the advanced search option (hit the three dashes in the upper-left-hand corner for access) to limit by things like year of publication and name of journal (see Figure 6.3). If you are looking for journal articles, but you don't know the names of relevant journals, simply type 'journal' in the 'Publication' box. This will limit your search to journals with the word journal in the title (which is a good percentage) and will cut out a lot of extraneous hits. Although Google Scholar is openly available, we recommend logging on to your university website and accessing it through there. Doing this will allow you to access, without a fee, the full text of any articles that are in journals to which your university subscribes.

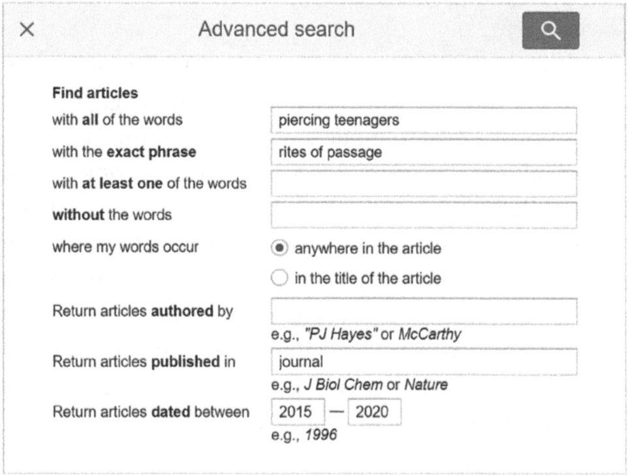

Figure 6.3 Google Scholar advanced search

Another option is to delve into discipline-related databases. While more inclusive search engines are ever improving, the vast array of databases out there warrants you having a deeper discipline-based look – you often find access to articles that simply do not show up with a generalized search engine. Academic databases may be divided by discipline, journal collection or both. A good place to start is the Web of Science or Web of Knowledge databases. For business or the social sciences, the SSCI database provides references and keyword searchable abstracts, with additional links to full text. Of particular use is the 'Cited Ref Search' to search for articles that cite an article you have found valuable. There are a few publishers who now offer full-text versions of articles in their journals through their own websites (i.e. without a library subscription). Cambridge University Press (Cambridge Journals Online) and Sage (Highwire) are two prominent examples. Databases allow you to search within relevant journals. Now there any many databases, and as shown at the very top of Figure 6.4, you can view the databases by title. But if you do not know the names of the relevant databases you can search by topic area. You simply click on the topic you're interested in, say 'Nutrition', and all the relevant databases that your library has access to are offered to you.

Honing Your Search Skills

You're likely familiar with searching the Internet in your everyday life but searching library databases or making the most of Google Scholar is a bit different from a regular Google search. The first step is to identify appropriate keywords. This means having short words or phrases for your topic, subtopics, variables, theories, theorists, methods, key concepts, etc. Once you've got this list you can get sophisticated with your searching.

Suppose you were interested in body piercing, particularly in teenagers. Your first keywords might be:

- body piercing (earrings, nose rings, etc.);
- teenagers (girls) (boys) (youth) (adolescents).

When you put these keywords into a search, there are a few things to be aware of. The first is to use quote marks if you have keywords that are phrases (e.g. "body piercing" and "nose ring"). The second is to consider how to input those keywords into a search engine. Truncation is a technique which will allow your search to include different word endings or spellings. For example, searching for child* will return child, childs, children, childrens, childhood in the results. (Although the symbols for truncation may vary across database.) Similarly, you can use wildcards to capture different spellings, e.g. wom*n will return both woman and women.

Once you've got your keywords, now it's time to combine. There are three basic functions (called Boolean operators) that you should be familiar with: the AND, the OR and the NOT.

You can use AND to combine multiple keywords. This will tell the database all search terms must be present in the results. Google automatically puts AND between search terms, but other databases don't necessarily. This is a good way to narrow your results. Make sure to use quote marks around phrases (i.e. "body piercing" rather than body piercing which becomes body AND piercing).

You can use OR to connect multiple related keywords which is a good way to broaden your results. For example, the search: "body piercing" AND ("girls" OR "boys") will return more results than "body piercing AND girls AND boys".

You can use NOT to exclude specific words from your search. This can be helpful to narrow your search or avoid concepts that may be implied by your keywords. For example, piercing NOT tattooing.

It's probably best to start with a basic AND search. This is likely to lead you to a mass of relevant literature that can be culled by adding additional variables you find particularly relevant or interesting (and will let you know which terms might need to be included/excluded in future searches). For example:

- rebellion;
- rites of passage.

Databases by Title

A - B - C - D - E - F - G - H - I - J - K - L - M - N - O - P - Q - R - S - T - U - V - W - X - Y - Z -

New - Trials - Alerting services - E-journals - E-books - For mobile devices

Databases by Subject

Aboriginal Studies
Accounting
Agricultural Science
Agricultural and Resource Economics
Agriculture – Plant Science
Ancient History
Anthropology
Arabic & Islamic Studies
Archaeology Architecture, Design and
Planning
Art history and theory
Asian Studies See also
Chinese Studies, Japanese Studies, and
Korean Studies
Australian Literature
Behavioural and Social Sciences in Health
Biochemistry and Microbiology
Biological Sciences
Business Information Systems
Business, International and Entrepreneurship
Business Law
Celtic Studies
Chemistry
Chinese Studies –English language and Chinese language
Classics
Coaching Psychology: – See Work and Organisational Studies Commercial Law – see Business Law Computer Science – see Information Technologies Curriculum Studies – see Education and Curriculum Studies
Dentistry
Development Studies
Digital Cultures

Econometrics & Business Statistics
Economics
Education
Engineering
English Literature and Language
Environmental Science
Exercise and Sports Science
Film Studies
Finance
French
Gender and Cultural Studies
Geosciences
Germanic Studies
Government & International Relations
Health Informatics
Hebrew, Biblical and Jewish Studies
History
History and Philosophy of Science
Human Resources – See Work and Organisational Studies
Image & online video databases
Indigenous Health Studies
Indian Sub-Continental Studies
Indonesian Studies
Industrial Relations
– See Work and Organisational Studies
Information Technologies
International Business/ Entrepreneurship
Italian Japanese Studies – English language and Japanese language
Korean Studies – English language
Labour History
– See Work and Organisational Studies
Law
Library Catalogues
Linguistics
Logistics see Transport/Logistics Management – See Work and Organisational Studies
Marketing

Mathematics and Statistics
Media and Communications
Medical Humanities
Medical Radiation Sciences
Medicine
Microscopy and
Microanalysis
Modern Greek
Museum Studies
Music
News Services
Nursing and Midwifery
Nutrition
Occupational Therapy
Organisational Behaviour – See Work and Organisational Studies Orthoptics
Peace and Conflict Studies
Performance Studies
Pharmacy
Philosophy
Physics & Astronomy Physiotherapy
Political Economy
Project Management
Psychology
Public Health
Religious Studies
Social Work & Policy Studies
Socio-Legal Studies
Sociology and Social Policy Spanish
Speech Pathology Statistics – See Mathematics and Statistics
Transport/Logistics
United States Studies
Urban Planning
Veterinary Science
Work and Organisational Studies

Figure 6.4 Electronic resources – databases

Using this process, you can add additional keywords (e.g. family background) or a particular theorist (e.g. Foucault) in order to narrow your search. You can also remove keywords to capture more literature – or swap keywords around to see what you come up with.

Figure 6.5 highlights the relevance of the generated literature based on key concepts and their interrelationships. Some areas of intersection may not yield much literature, but if you keep playing around with ideas, concepts and variables, you are bound to build a solid literature base.

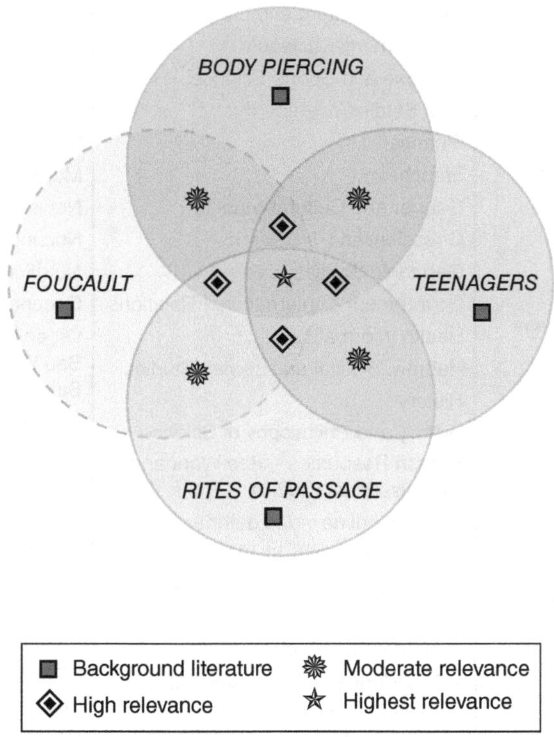

Figure 6.5 Intersecting areas of literature

I Have a Question!

My Supervisor Says I Need to Keep on Top of Literature Throughout My Project. Are There Any Tips for Finding Something New, Even When I've Been Through It All Before?

One important tip in the seemingly never-ending search for literature is to be true to where you are in the review process. In other words, the stage of your review process and the goals you have in looking at the literature. For example, at the start you are really engaged in explorative searching – just having a look at what might be out there; later you will move to more methodical searching – a more deliberate and refined search with well-considered key terms; from there you may move to more explicit searching - looking for particular articles that others have referenced; and finally you will move to monitoring - keeping abreast of any new research in your area.

Understanding Copyright

There is one more thing to watch out for in your search for literature – and that is **copyright**. When something is copyright protected, it means that the creator of an original work has exclusive rights to it (usually for a limited period of time). You cannot copy copyrighted material unless it falls under the rules of **fair dealing** (as it is referred to in Commonwealth countries) or **fair use** (in the US).

When it comes to study and non-commercial research in Australia, for example, under fair dealing, you can copy:

- 5% or one chapter of a book;
- one article from a journal or newspaper issue;
- one paper from a set of conference proceedings;
- one case from a volume of law reports;
- short literary pieces as long as they are less than 10 pages long;
- one (hard) copy of web material (unless otherwise indicated on the site).

In producing a thesis with photocopied material, you are allowed to make as many copies as needed for assessment as long as there is proper acknowledgement. Fair dealing and fair use have different exclusions and rules in different countries. It is well worth checking copyright laws for your country either with your institution or by googling them.

MANAGING THE LITERATURE

Students are often shocked at just how much literature might be relevant to a research project. In your searching, you are bound to gather a mound of readings, and finding a way to manage it will be essential. Making it manageable involves being able to quickly and efficiently assess relevance; systematically keep track of sources; and make relevant notes.

Assessing Relevance

You probably won't be able to read every word of every piece of relevant literature you have located, so being able to quickly and efficiently wade through your literature in order to assess relevance and 'get the gist' will save you a lot of time and frustration. If you are reading a journal article, look at the abstract or executive summary. This should give you a good sense of relevance. In a book, peruse the table of contents, the back-cover blurb and the introduction. Also have a look at chapter conclusions, as well as the overall conclusion. Within a few minutes you should be able to assess if a work is likely to be of value to your own research process.

One simple suggestion is to rank the relevance of readings using sticky notes. For example, if you are looking at literature related to three distinct concepts, you could use sticky notes (real or virtual) of three different colours, one for each concept, and then rank the overall work, or chapters within a work, with a 1 (minimally relevant), 2 (somewhat relevant) or 3 (highly relevant). It is amazing how much time this can save when you begin a more rigorous review of materials.

Assessing Quality

Just because a piece of literature is relevant, it doesn't mean it represents quality. There is a lot of rubbish out there online! It can be biased, full of personal agendas and sometimes simply inaccurate. Yes, you will do better if you turn to peer-reviewed journal articles. And this is generally what is expected in a literature review. But even with journal articles there is a need to assess quality. So how do you do this? Well there are several questions you can ask that relate back to the indicators of research credibility covered in Chapter 4 (Table 4.1).

As you read through the article ask yourself:

- Have researcher subjectivities been acknowledged and managed?
- Have they used logical methods that lead to valid and/or authentic truth?
- Are their methods approached with consistency?
- Are arguments relevant and appropriate?
- Can the research be audited/verified?

Now we realize that if you are new to research, you may find it a challenge to assess the work of 'real' researchers. But developing this skill is essential. As a researcher, you are contributing to a body of knowledge and you need to be able to assess the state of play within that body. Doing this necessarily involves critiquing what is out there. As your research skills develop, so too will your ability to assess the work of others.

Being Systematic

Nothing is worse than looking for a lost reference that you really need. It could be a quote with a missing page number, or a fact with no citation, or a perfect point that needs to go right there – if only you could remember where you read it. If you can incorporate each of your resources into a management system you will be saving yourself a lot of future heartache.

Keep and file copies of relevant books, articles, etc., and avoid lending out your 'only copies'. It's amazing how many books and articles never get returned, even when the borrower swears they will get it back to you by the end of the week. You also need to keep good citations. Now as common as it may be to see bad referencing, we refuse to believe that proper referencing is an intellectually difficult task. A pain in the neck – yes, but it really is not that hard to do right. You just need to be organized and diligent. Find out right from the start what your recommended referencing style is, get a style guide, and just get on with it. Rigorous referencing and appropriate filing can save you much grief in the future.

You may also want to consider using bibliographic file management software such as Mendeley, EndNote, RefWorks, Zotero or Citationsy. These programs can automatically format references in any number of styles (e.g. Harvard, APA, Vancouver), once basic bibliographic details are entered. Just one final point: be sure to back up anything and everything related to your project, including references. If there is one thing you can rely on, it's that computers cannot be relied on.

Annotating References

> Reading furnishes the mind only with materials of knowledge; it is thinking that makes what we read ours.
>
> John Locke (1824: 356)

It is definitely worth developing a systematic approach to note taking that allows for a methodical and organized review of materials from the first read. Many students will read materials without such a systematic approach, and later find they need to go back and reread the material – often when they are short of time and hard pressed to meet deadlines.

A good strategy here is to keep an **annotated bibliography** or a **systematic review** of all your significant literature that can remind you of the relevance, accuracy and quality of sources cited (see Box 6.1). This does not mean you need to take huge amounts of formal notes. Annotations are generally for your eyes only and are jotted down in order to minimize the time it takes to incorporate these works into your own. So while 'annotating' every single relevant reference may seem like a highly onerous task, you will be grateful for the annotations when you undertake a formal literature review, or when you need to call on the references while writing up.

Box 6.1

Annotating Systematically

Annotations vary in both content and length depending on the relevance of the reviewed work, but there are key elements worth noting:

Author and intended audience – The Internet is full of misinformation, uninformed opinion and less-than-credible research. Ask yourself: Who is doing the writing? What are their qualifications? Are they professionals, politicians, researchers or unknown? And who is the work written for? Is it for an academic audience, general public, constituents, clients? If the answers to these questions leave you feeling less than comfortable with the source, it is probably best to move on to more credible literature.

Summary – The aim here is to jot down key points that will help you research and write. You may be able to summarize a less relevant work in a sentence or two, while others will be much more instrumental to your own thinking and researching and require more in-depth coverage. Write what you think you will want to know later on and try not to fall into the trap

(Continued)

of trusting your memory. Annotations don't have to be formal. Doodles, mind maps, quotes, page numbers, etc. are all fair game - as is cutting, pasting and highlighting relevant bits of the abstract with notes in the margins.

Critical appraisal - We know the word 'critical' has a tendency to imply negativity - picking holes - but in academic reviewing the word 'critical' means informed and considered evaluation. As a potential researcher you need to be able to ask and answer the question 'What did I really think of that and why?' Is it new? Is it old? Is it cutting edge? Is it just a rehash? Are there fundamental flaws in the methodology? Are author biases coming through? Are the results credible? Also consider comparing and contrasting this work with others you have read. How does it 'sit' with the general literature?

Relevance - This is where you try to make the connection between what others have done and what you propose to do. Ask yourself how this work sits in relation to the study you plan to conduct. Is there anything in the work that turns a light bulb on in your head? How does the theory or ideology compare? What about the methods? Is there some flaw in the thinking/methods that makes you want to explore this area/topic/question from a different angle? Is there a quote, passage or section that really gets to the heart of what you are trying to do or say? Look to be inspired. Look to be surprised. Look to be appalled. Use this section to get the creative juices flowing.

WRITING THE FORMAL 'LITERATURE REVIEW'

As discussed at the beginning of the chapter, a literature review is a very specific piece of argumentative writing, based largely on a critical review of relevant journal articles, that acts to create a 'space' for your research. It is generally required in research projects, proposals, reports, journal articles and student theses. So it needs to be tackled – even if it is seen as a somewhat overwhelming task.

It is quite common to feel overwhelmed by the thought of doing a literature review. Indeed, the need to write a literature review can strike fear into the heart of even the most confident student. Not only do you need to engage with a body of literature, you also need to be able to compare, contrast, synthesize and make arguments with that literature in ways that indicate a readiness to contribute to the literature itself. And that is a big task, especially if it is your first rigorous attempt.

Just knowing how to start can be difficult – and not all supervisors know how to get you on your way. Most will know a good literature review when they read one, but more than a few will have difficulty articulating exactly how to go about constructing one. Understanding the literature review's purpose, coming to grips with the potential ways you can handle coverage and approaching the task methodically can go a long way in making the task manageable.

Purpose

You'd think that the purpose of a formal literature review should be simply to review the literature. But expectations of what a literature review is meant to achieve go far beyond a simple articulation of what previous researchers have done and found. The formal literature review is a purposeful argument that needs to:

1. Inform readers of developments in the field – Not only should a research study inform readers of your particular research question, but it should also inform them of the general topic. The inclusion of a strong literature review should provide readers with contextual learning through an up-to-date account and discussion of relevant theories, methods and research studies that make up a particular topic's body of literature.
2. Establish researcher credibility – Because researchers are responsible for the production of new knowledge, it is essential they show they are abreast of the field; are aware of relevant new developments; and are conversant with academic and scientific discourse and debate within their research area. The literature review allows researchers to establish credibility through rigorous and critical evaluation of relevant research works; a demonstrated understanding of key issues; and the ability to outline the relationship of their own work to the rest of the field.
3. Argue the need for, and relevance of, their study – The literature review needs to make an argument for a researcher's own research agenda. It needs to set the current study within the context of past research. The literature review has the potential to identify 'gaps' that show the appropriate and significant nature of a study's research questions. It can also justify methodological approaches by: critically evaluating methods that are generally accepted for and typical of this type of research; highlighting the limitations that might be common to past studies; and uncovering the possibly unwarranted assumptions that can underpin method.

Please note: a literature review is not a **document analysis**. It is, for the most part, an overview of research studies that have been conducted by past researchers. Document analysis is a form of indirect data analysis (see Chapter 13). If you want to explore things like policy documents, legislation and organizational protocols, in order to gather data and look for evidence, it should not be included in the literature review. If the exploration of documents is warranted as a credible approach to answering your research question, then our advice is to include it in the method, and report on it in your findings section.

Table 6.1 attempts to outline the purpose in a bit more depth by highlighting the broader, more self-educative reasons for reviewing the literature, and the corresponding purposes of the formal 'literature review'.

Table 6.1 Reviewing the literature versus the 'literature review'

Self-educative reasons for reviewing the literature	What the formal 'literature review' attempts to achieve
Inform yourself of what is happening in the field	Inform your audience of what is happening in the field
Form a foundation of topical and methodological knowledge and expertise	Establish your credibility as a knowledgeable and capable researcher
Develop skills in critical thinking/analysis	Argue the relevance and significance of your research question
Find potential gaps in the literature that may point to potential research questions	Provide the context for your own methodological approach
Critically evaluate common/typical methods	Argue the relevance and appropriateness of your approach
Facilitate the development of your own methodological approaches	

Coverage

Once you understand its purpose, the question you are likely to ask is 'What exactly needs to go into my literature review?' Well, the coverage in your literature review should be broad enough to: inform your readers of the nature of the discourse and debate current to your topic; establish your own credibility as a researcher abreast of the field; and demonstrate the need for, and relevance of, your own research. But the depth of the general body of literature, the arguments you are trying to make, and the level of the project/thesis will also determine what is both suitable and required. A one-semester undergraduate project may only demand engagement with 20 or so of the most relevant and recent articles, while a PhD thesis may require in excess of 250 articles and oblige you to dig into both theory and seminal works.

Options for coverage include: exhaustive coverage that cites all relevant literature; exhaustive coverage with only selective citation; representative coverage that discusses works that typify particular areas within the literature; coverage of seminal/pivotal works; a combination of the above.

Critical Thinking Challenge 6

The Politics of Citation

Whose voices are represented in your literature review? The 'canon' of scholarly works is dominated by white men. The intellectual traditions of indigenous peoples, oral cultures and marginalized groups are not well represented. It's important to consider who can access academia and whose ideas get widely circulated through citation and whose are overlooked.

Plagiarism

Everything is online. And that means a finished literature review can be as close as a few 'cut and paste' operations away. Don't do it! First, it is wrong: you are essentially stealing the work of others. Second, it can get you kicked out of your degree programme. Third, it simply does not lead to a good literature review. Yes, you can cut and paste and string together bits of abstracts. But there will be no arguments running through it. There will be no driving message. You need to write this as a custom piece: a piece that clearly argues the need for, and relevance of, your study. So what exactly constitutes plagiarism? Plagiarism is when the words, ideas or data of another person are not referenced and are therefore passed off as your own. This means you cannot:

- cut and paste ideas, phrases, paragraphs, diagrams or images without referencing the source;
- pay someone else to write for you;
- download a paper from an online source and submit it as your own;
- copy from another student's work without acknowledgement;

- mention a source in your bibliography but not reference it in the text;
- change the words of someone else's original idea without referencing it;
- quote from a speech or lecture without acknowledging the speaker.

I Have a Question

Can I Use ChatGPT to Write My Literature Review?

Using generative AI like ChatGPT is slightly more sophisticated than copying and pasting, but it is still a bad choice. For one, the information is often inaccurate. Chatbots trawl information available on the Internet but most academic research is restricted behind paywalls. ChatGPT sometimes invents references as a result. However, the strongest reason against using chatbots is that it avoids the necessary work of a literature review: you making choices and engaging with the ideas of others. Your research is part of an ongoing conversation and the literature review is your attempt to locate your work within it. That's an essential part of the task and one that can't and shouldn't be skipped.

Now we realize that asking you to do original work by referring to experts may seem like a contradiction. But the key is acknowledgement - in other words, appropriate referencing. You need to be diligent and even pedantic. Find out what referencing style is recommended in your faculty and follow guidelines that can be readily found online or from your institution.

Critical Thinking Challenge 7

Metaphors

There are different metaphors for engaging with the literature that may resonate with you. In a sense, you are moving from a consumer (a student who is learning) to a producer (a researcher who is contributing). What does taking this step mean? It may also feel like you are entering 'occupied territory' and cautiously figuring out who to include, who to exclude, how to critique those who have gone before. A slightly more encouraging metaphor, which Emma uses with her students, is to think of joining a conversation. What have people been talking about before you arrived, how does what you want to say build on what has gone before and take it in a new direction?

The Writing Process

There are students who are able to pull together an impressive literature review without too much guidance. They have a sense of the task and tackle it admirably. But we have to say this is the exception. Most students struggle and are looking for a clear way forward. So while the following is not the only process you can follow, it is one that will get you from A to B and help you go well beyond a 'he said, she said' report. Remember: the goal here is to inform, establish and argue. To do this, we suggest the following steps:

1 Make doing the literature review an ongoing process – Your literature review will inform your question, theory and methods, and your question, theory and methods will help set the parameters of your literature review. This is a cyclical process. A literature review is often a moving target that should evolve in both thinking and writing as your study develops.
2 Read quite a few good, relevant reviews – You need to have a sense of what a good literature review is before you are in a position to construct your own.
3 Identify the keywords for your study – For instance: (a) body piercing; (b) teenagers; (c) rites of passage.
4 Develop a list of synonyms or alternatives – For instance: (a) piercing, earrings, nose rings, body art, etc.; (b) teenagers, girls, boys, adolescents, young adults; (c) rites of passage, initiation, induction, observance.
5 Place the terms in a Venn diagram – As shown earlier in Figure 6.5.
6 Use a search engine – Look for appropriate databases and/or ask your librarian for guidance. Search using a combination of keywords and their synonyms/alternatives.
7 Compile citations with abstracts – Many of these will be available electronically.
8 Read abstracts and cull all irrelevant articles – Get rid of anything obviously off-topic and rank remaining readings by relevance.
9 Assess whether you need to dig deeper or focus your review – To focus in, you can add relevant keywords (see Figure 6.3) and/or look at studies conducted in the past, say, five or seven years. You can also think about limiting your review to selective or representative coverage. Expanding may mean limiting/modifying variables and/or increasing the time span. Remember that studies do not have to directly explore your particular research questions to be relevant, informative and useful.
10 Systematically log your relevant readings – Choices here are to manually construct a comprehensive bibliography or use bibliographic software such as ProCite, EndNote or Reference Manager.
11 Read and annotate each relevant article – As suggested earlier in the chapter, comment on author/audience, key points, critical comment and relevance.
12 Sort and organize your annotations – Look for themes, issues of concern, common shortcomings, etc. You may find that patterns begin to emerge, which can go a long way towards the development of your own arguments.
13 Develop a potential outline for your literature review – Consider what arguments will best convince readers that you are fully engaged with the relevant body of literature. Your structure can always be modified as your thinking evolves, but your main argument should relate to the need for your research study to be undertaken in the way you are proposing.
14 Write purposefully – You cannot write a formal 'literature review' without an agenda. Your audience should be able to readily identify the 'point' of each section of your review. If your audience do not know why you are telling them what you are telling them, you need to reconsider your approach (see Box 6.2). This is why tools like ChatGPT are a false economy – you need your own ideas and to write in your own voice.

15 Use the literature to back up your arguments – Rather than review, report or borrow the arguments of others, use the literature to help generate, and then support, your own arguments. That means each paragraph should make a point that is backed up by the literature.

For instance: within the context of climate change, the relationship between knowledge and behavioural change is contentious (the point you are trying to make). While several studies have shown that knowledge of climate change affects behaviour (Wong, 2002; Smith, 2007; Jones, 2008), a new study conducted by Burnie and Powis (2009) argues that knowledge has minimal impact on change and that practices of peers and neighbours are much more influential (the evidence that supports your point).This is a much more sophisticated approach than leading each paragraph by author, i.e. starting paragraphs with 'Wong (2002) found', 'Smith (2007) argues' and 'Jones (2008) states'.

16 Adopt an appropriate style and tone – The trick here is to avoid being too deferential, but also avoid being overcritical. Keep in mind that your goal is to engage, debate, argue, evolve your own ideas and contribute. If you think of yourself as a mere student, you might find it hard to be critical. On the other hand, if you attempt to establish credibility by showing you are able to pick holes in the work of others, you run the risk of being judgemental, hypercritical and unable to draw relevance and significance from the works reviewed.

17 Get plenty of feedback – Writing a literature review is not an easy task, and supervisors' expectations can vary widely. Don't wait until the last minute to begin the writing process or to get feedback. Be sure to pass a draft to your supervisor, or anyone else willing to read it, early on.

18 Be prepared to redraft – Whether you are a student or professional researcher, you are not likely to get away without a redraft or two (or three or four).

(See the online resources for a few examples of both good and bad literature reviews.)

Box 6.2

Writing Styles in the Literature Review

Descriptive writing - As the title implies this is all about describing - offering facts/information, saying what is - a large part of the literature review.

Analytical writing - Analytical writing takes descriptive writing a step further by organizing information into logical groupings. It also compares, contrasts and explores relationships. This is what begins to give your literature review some structure.

Critical writing - A natural next step when comparing works is to make judgements. You are now assessing works and ascribing value. You are engaged with the work and sharing what you think about it.

Persuasive or argumentative writing - Once you have your head around your critiques of the literature, you will need to organize these critiques so you are in a position to make arguments. In the case of the literature review you are arguing the place for your own research.

I Have a Question!

I Am Still Struggling. You Say to Use Arguments, but What Exactly Am I Arguing?

This is actually an easy one to answer. There are a lot of ways to get there, but in the end the argument driving every literature review is the same. You are working through the literature in a way that allows you to conclude ... therefore there is a need to conduct this study as I have proposed. You're arguing need. Where that need comes from depends on what you found as you became familiar with the body of literature surrounding your work. Perhaps you will argue that much of the literature is based on false assumptions, or that studies are not contextually relevant, or that they are methodologically flawed. Perhaps you will argue that the preponderance of quantitative studies has meant that a deep dive into a situation has not occurred, or that there has yet to be a comprehensive quantitative look at the situation. You may argue a number of these things, and of course you may have other insights. The bottom line is that as you review the literature you are not only reviewing what has been done, you are reviewing in a way that makes a space for your own research.

Chapter Summary

- Good research demands engagement with topical, methodological and theoretical literature. This will help you explore a topic, define a question, articulate a rationale, theoretically inform your study, develop appropriate design, write a formal literature review and sometimes be a source of primary data.
- Literature types include reference materials, books, journals, grey literature, official publications, archives and writing aids. To find appropriate material, you should call on the expertise of librarians, supervisors and other researchers.
- The ever-increasing availability of literature requires students to develop proficient keyword search skills for use in accessing a variety of electronic databases and search engines. You will also need to quickly cull vast amounts of written work for relevance and quality.
- Managing and annotating sources provides a record of relevant literature. It should include the citation, articulation of the author and audience, a short summary, critical commentary and notes on relevance that can remind you of the significance, accuracy and quality of the sources cited.
- The formal literature review is a very specific piece of argumentative writing designed to inform your readers of your topic, establish your credibility as a researcher and argue the need for, and relevance of, your work. Most find it a difficult task that takes patience, practice, drafts and redrafts.

FIND YOUR NEXT STEP

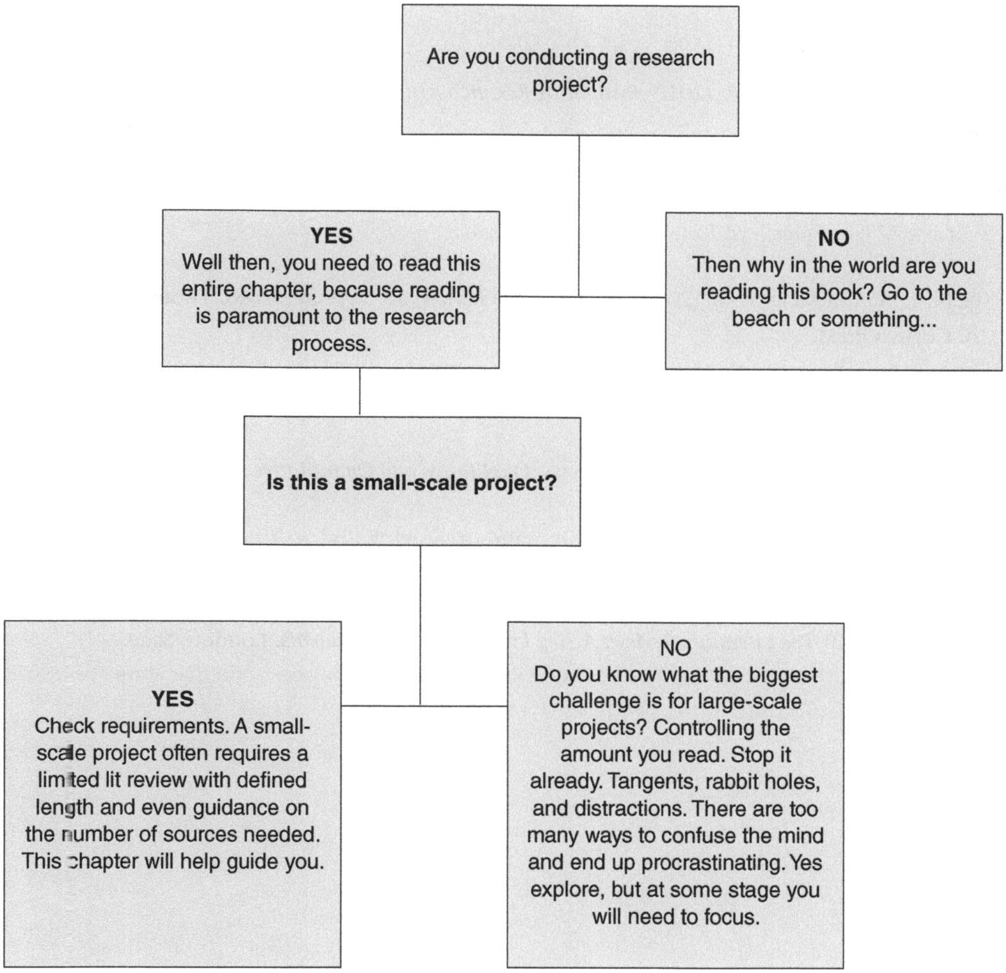

FURTHER READING

There are quite a few readings that can help you navigate your way through the complexities of working with research literature. You may find the following sources a good place to start:

Fink, A. (2019) *Conducting Research Literature Reviews: From the Internet to Paper*, 5th edition. Thousand Oaks, CA: Sage.
Good accessible guide that explains how literature reviews form the basis of arguments that justify the need for and significance of research and explain a study's findings. Terrific array of examples and exercises.

Galvan, J. L. and Galvan, M. (2017) *Writing Literature Reviews: A Guide for Students of the Social and Behavioral Sciences*, 6th edition. Glendale, CA: Pyrczak.
We like the way this book uses examples of real literature reviews to illustrate key points. Easy to follow.

Girden, E. and Kabacoff, R. (2010) *Evaluating Research Articles from Start to Finish*. Thousand Oaks, CA: Sage.
Critiquing someone else's research, particularly a professional's, can be a real challenge for the student researcher. The systematic approach to critique that the authors take here – as well as their use of examples – will make the task easier.

Machi, L. A. and McEvoy, B. (2016) *The Literature Review: Six Steps to Success*. Thousand Oaks, CA: Corwin Press.
The authors offer a simple six-step approach to: topic selection; literature searching; argument development; literature surveying; critical appraisal; and writing up. Highly useful.

Pan, M. L. (2017) *Preparing Literature Reviews: Qualitative and Quantitative Approaches*, 4th edition. Glendale, CA: Pyrczak.
Good guide for evaluating existing research and organizing and writing up a literature review. Useful exercises and good examples.

Ridley, D. (2012) *The Literature Review: A Step by Step Guide for Students*. London: Sage.
We really like this book. Its use of cases and examples to draw out best-practice works very well. Good coverage of online sources and lots of practical tips.

7

DESIGNING A RESEARCH PLAN

Learning Objectives

- Moving from questions to answers
    - To understand the need for methodological design to address your research question; to be within your capacity and interest; and to be practical and doable
    - To understand the need to determine appropriate methodology as well as appropriate methods of data collection
- Getting it right for the researcher
    - To be able to align research design with personal interest and skills
    - To be able to identify various researcher roles
- Pragmatics: making it doable
    - To be able to assess the practicality of your methodological plan
- It's all in the details
    - To be able to work through the fundamental design questions of who; where; when; how; what
    - To understand the challenges of emergent and flexible methodological design

MOVING FROM QUESTIONS TO ANSWERS

Methods and means cannot be separated from the ultimate aim.

Emma Goldman (1924)

When it comes to **methodological design**, it may sound incredibly obvious, but your goal is to come up with a plan that will allow you either to answer your well-articulated research question, or to test your skilfully constructed hypothesis. Now this clearly implies that methodological design requires a well-articulated research question or a skilfully constructed hypothesis, and this is true. As discussed in Chapter 3, a well-articulated question defines an investigation, sets boundaries, provides direction and acts as a frame of reference for assessing your work. In this way, your question acts as a blueprint for decision-making related to method. So if you think you are ready to move to methodological design, but you are still struggling to articulate your question clearly, you really need to go back and work on the question itself. If you don't know where you want to go, you simply can't determine a path for getting there.

Finding a Path

So let's talk about paths for a minute. Assuming you are pretty happy with your research question, the next step is figuring out how to best go about getting the answers; in other words, defining the elements of your methodological design. Figure 7.1 represents a common conception of how we move from questions to answers. The arrow represents the methodological design that will best get you from Q to A. The assumption here is that there is a correct or best design.

Figure 7.1 The path

Figure 7.2 offers an alternative representation of methodological possibilities. Here the assumption is that there might be numerous ways to move from questions to answers. Paths are varied and diverse, but they all have the potential to generate the data that can lead to credible answers. The trick is to travel down a methodological path that is appropriate for the question, the researcher and the context.

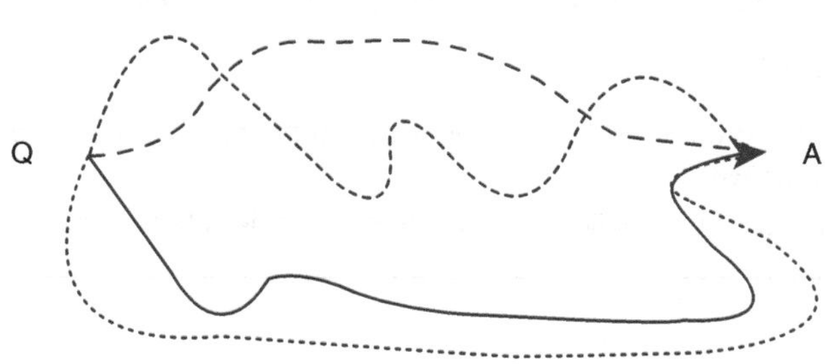

Figure 7.2 Multiple paths

Figure 7.3 works on the same 'multiple path' assumption as Figure 7.2 but reminds us that both who we are and what we do can influence how we see and what we find. Each methodological design has the potential to draw out answers from a somewhat different perspective. As Werner

Heisenberg, one of the twentieth-century physicists who founded the area of quantum mechanics, said: 'It is worth remembering that what we observe is not nature itself, but nature exposed to our method of questioning' (in Shulman and Asimov, 1988: 324).

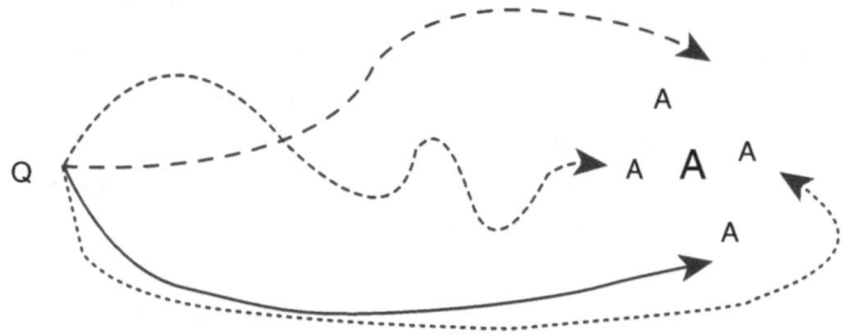

Figure 7.3 Paths and perspective

The significance of the progression of these models is in the increased responsibility they represent for the researcher. As you move from finding the path, to choosing from a range of potential paths, to reflexively considering the implications of the paths themselves, your need to consider issues associated with credibility increases. If you view the development of method in a manner similar to that in Figure 7.3, design becomes a real thinking game that requires you to make well-considered decisions that best ensure you are approaching your study in a manner that will lead to highly credible data and trustworthy results.

So what do you need to consider in your methodological decision-making? Well, as depicted in Figure 7.4, getting your methodological design on target requires that: your methodological design addresses your question; you have, or are willing to develop, the skills and interests needed to undertake your plan; and all the elements of your methodological design are doable.

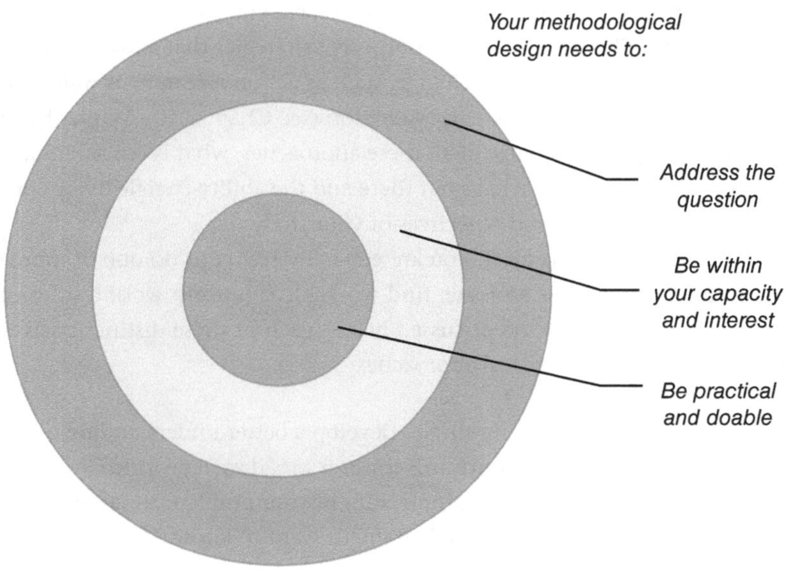

Figure 7.4 Getting your methodological design on target

Addressing Your Question

Unfortunately, there can be a real tendency for researchers, both new and established, to be quite wedded to particular methodological approaches. They might have it in their minds that they will do an ethnography or population study, or a survey or series of interviews, even before they have really engaged in a critical examination of what their question logically demands. But keep in mind that the goal in developing methodological approaches is working towards what is most appropriate for answering your question. It is important that you do not fall prey to the belief that one way of doing things is inherently better than another, or that it's okay to stay within your comfort zone. Methods need to fall from questions.

Now, as discussed in Chapter 3, this does not mean your question must be set in stone from its first articulation. Research is generally an ongoing and iterative process of development and redevelopment that may see questions shift at various stages throughout the research process. What needs to be stressed, however, is that in the end, there needs to be a goodness of fit between your final question and your methodological design. One, the other or both may evolve, but in the end, your question and your design (which will incorporate decision-making at both the level of methodology and methods) will need to have the tightest of relationships.

Working at the Level of Methodology

One of the most crucial factors involved in the selection of methodology is familiarization. You need to be aware of what is out there. As covered in Chapter 8, you can explore traditional quantitative strategies based on scientific, **hypothetico-deductive methods**, as well as any number of qualitative strategies designed to get you delving at a deeper level. You might also consider mixed-methodological approaches that will have you working across more than one strategy (see Chapter 9). There are also more purposive strategies that allow you to work simultaneously towards both knowledge and change, such as action research, as well as methodologies designed for both front- and back-end evaluation (see Chapter 10). While the ideal would be for you to have in-depth knowledge of all these approaches, what is crucial in undertaking a research project is familiarity with what's out there and the ability to reflexively consider these strategies in relation to the aims and objectives of your study.

Now when it comes to your project, you are generally trying to do one or more of the following: understand a problem or an issue; find workable solutions; work towards a solution; or evaluate success and/or failure. As discussed below, each of these distinct goals tends to be aligned with particular methodological approaches:

- Understanding a problem – Attempting to develop a better understanding of a problem situation might involve looking outwards towards broad societal attitudes and opinions, or inwards into the intricacies and complexities of your problem situation. Take, for example, the issue of workplace stress. You might want to know 'How common is stress in the workplace?' If this were your question, outward exploration – for example, a population study using a survey approach – might be called for. If, however, your interest was in understanding how a particular staff group react to stress, or what it feels like to live with workplace stress, you might look at more inwardly focused strategies that allow you to delve deeper into complexity – for example, ethnography or **phenomenology** (see Chapters 8 and 9).

- Finding workable solutions – The quest to find workable solutions might involve: assessing needs and visioning futures; locating potential programmes, interventions and/or services; or exploring the feasibility of particular change initiatives. For example, sticking with the issue of workplace stress, your goal might be to understand what can be done to reduce such stress. Specific questions might be: 'Is workplace stress a priority issue for employees?', 'What vision do employees have for a different workplace culture?', 'What programmes have been introduced in other settings to reduce stress?' or 'Will programme X be suitable/cost effective for my workplace?' Now these types of question are sometimes referred to as 'front-end analysis' and are common approaches in evaluative research. So if this is where your aims/objectives are pointing, you need to explore this area of literature (see Chapter 10).
- Working towards solutions – we are referring here to research goals that go beyond the production of knowledge, i.e. research that has the goal of change directly embedded in its research agenda. Now this might refer to improving practice, shifting systems or even working towards some level of fundamental or radical change. Suppose your goal was to collaborate with staff on a co-learning project that developed and implemented a stress reduction strategy. Whether you want to work on changing employee behaviours, workplace practices or the broader corporate culture, your desire to produce knowledge while actioning change is likely to lead you towards the literature related to 'action research' (see Chapter 10).
- Evaluating change – The goal here is to answer the question, 'Has a change initiative/programme been successful?' Now your interest in evaluation might be related to outcomes, such as 'Did programme X meet its objectives?' But it might also be related to a process, for example 'How and how well is programme X being implemented?' So if you wanted to evaluate a recently introduced stress reduction programme you might ask 'Has programme X reduced stress?' This question would lead you to literature related to 'outcome' or 'summative' evaluation. If, however, you wanted to ask 'What are the strengths, weaknesses, opportunities and threats related to the implementation of this programme?', you would need to explore the 'process' or 'formative' evaluation literature (see Chapter 10).

Figure 7.5 attempts to logically work you through the links between aims, questions and methodology. While neither definitive nor exhaustive, it will give you examples of sound connections and point you to areas that you may want to explore further. But also keep in mind that you always have the option of using a **mixed approach** – which may just help you answer your question in a more holistic fashion (see Chapter 9).

Working at the Level of Method

Once your broader methodological approaches are in line with your aims and objectives, you will need to go a step further and think about the actual methods best suited for collecting and analysing your data.

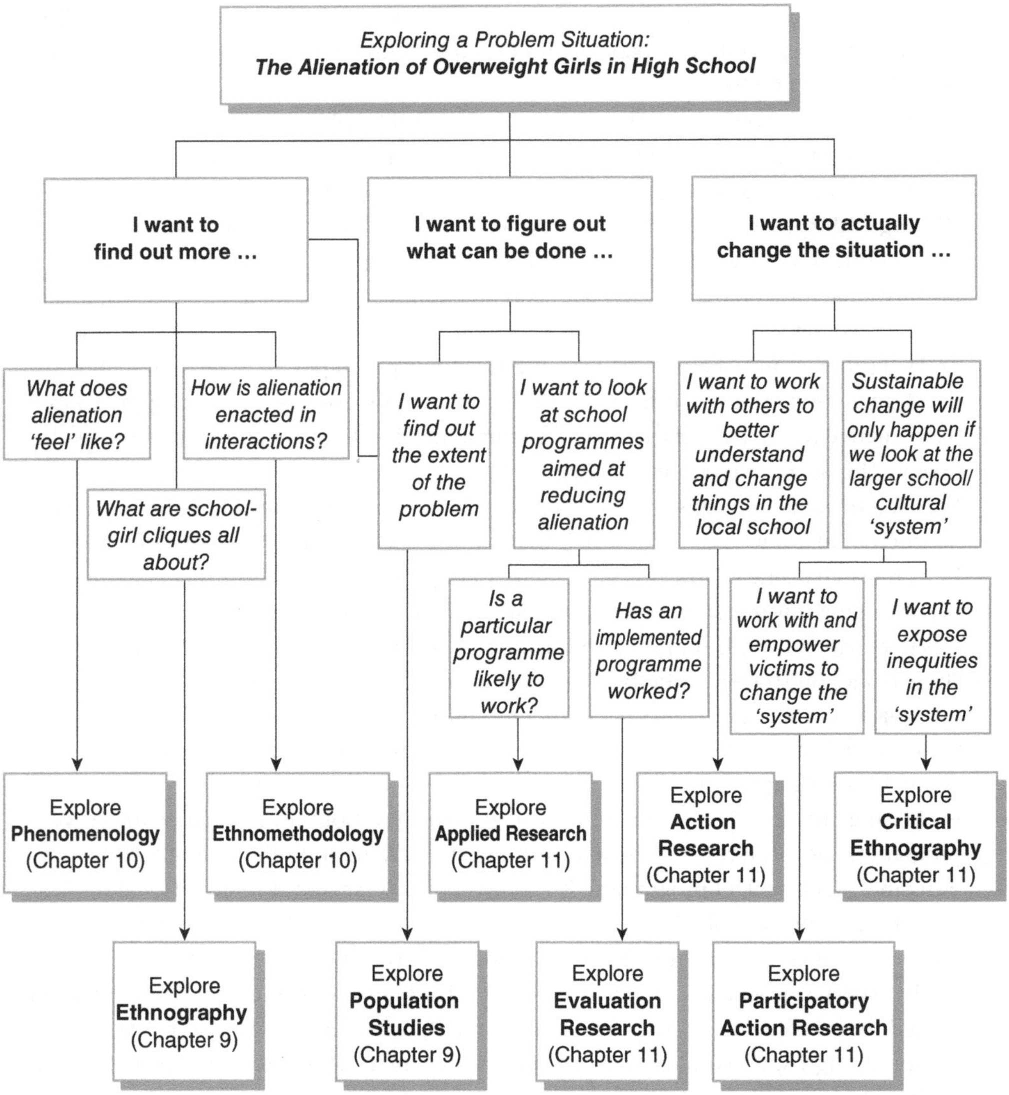

Figure 7.5 Exploring methodologies

Now decision-making related to methods is clearly question-driven. A well-articulated question should lead you to who you need to talk to and what you need to ask – and as an extension of this, what data-collection methods/tools you might use. For example, imagine you want to research the self-image of teenage girls. You can do one of two things. You can jump in and begin to design your study – after all, you have it in your mind that you will conduct 'interviews'. Or you can really think about what you want to know, go through some of the more relevant literature, work on the process of narrowing and clarifying, and maybe even work through a further articulation of your question before you attack the issue of methods.

In our experience, students who go for the jump-in approach and work from a topic rather than a question can really struggle. They often end up getting lost and confused. Things take a long time to fall into place (and sometimes never do), and students can end up with data they don't know how to use. Believe us, trying to retrofit a question to your data is not easy – and rarely works!

On the other hand, suppose you have been able to narrow your question to 'Do parents somehow teach their daughters that worth is dependent on external beauty?' Because you know what you want to know, deciding on the methods is only one small logical step away. For example, you can consider whether you want to get the perspective of parents, children or maybe counsellors. This then clearly points you to both the population and sample you will need to target in your data collection (see Chapter 11).

You can then consider the scale of research you wish to do – perhaps a large-scale survey that compares various socioeconomic or cultural groups; or perhaps you think conducting interviews or focus groups will draw out richer descriptions (see Chapter 12). You might also consider a less obtrusive measure like observation that will allow you to witness parent–daughter interactions at first hand (see Chapter 12). Perhaps you will consider doing a variety of the above.

No matter what the case, familiarity with the expectations related to methodology, as well as clarity and precision in your question, can readily lead to a range of methods that can be explored and considered on the basis of both their logic and practicality.

Critical Thinking Challenge 8

Perfect Alignment

The biggest challenge in designing methods is alignment. Do your methods align with your research question?

In order to assess:

1. Really think about what your research question is trying to determine.
2. What information do you see each of your methods getting for you?
3. How do your answers for 1 and 2 match up? Are they aligned?

If there are gaps, what do you need to do to close them? Change your methods? Add methods? Or modify your question?

GETTING IT RIGHT FOR THE RESEARCHER

There is often a desire to stay with what you know. But, as discussed above, questions should drive choice of both methodology and method. So it is important to check your own assumptions, biases and, dare we say, narrow-mindedness. Too many researchers are dismissive of what is outside their comfort zone and do not take the time to understand what each approach has to offer holistic knowledge production.

But even given this treatise on the importance of being open and willing to push at the boundaries of your comfort zone, it can be difficult to work with an approach that conflicts with your own epistemological framework. In fact, there is no sense undertaking a traditional 'quantitative' study if you hold a well-considered, strong critique of positivism/scientific method. Similarly, you will not be comfortable delving into the qualitative paradigm if you have a problem with the value of data not supported by statistics. You need to give real consideration to your own belief systems, as well as your willingness to develop new skills/interests and to take on particular research 'roles'.

Skills and Interests

Are you a people person, or do you like sitting behind a computer? Are you comfortable having intimate chats with strangers, or are you better at more distant and formal communication? Do you like working with words or would you rather play with numbers? Can you handle a level of emotional investment or do you want to be removed and always 'objective'? Can you be objective or will you struggle to keep your opinions to yourself? Do you loathe statistics or is 'loathe' not a strong enough word?!

Yes, you can develop new skills, and of course this is a worthwhile goal, but you really need to keep your timeline in mind. New skills are not always easy to master, and the number of new skills you would need to develop to be able to do it all is probably not practical. Have a good think about where your skills and interests lie. It would be silly to go down the path of large-scale surveys if you know you hate statistics and the thought of having to do it makes you break out in hives. On the other hand, even if you see the value of in-depth interviewing, without the right communication skills it might be a torturous route that ends up not doing justice to your research process. Not only do you need to consider your own comfort zone, you also need to think about how your skills, or lack thereof, might affect the quality of the data you collect. Remember that competence is not a luxury – it is a requirement.

Research Roles

There is no shortage of metaphors for the role of the researcher. From theorist to scientist, choreographer to change agent, the range of metaphors used to depict the researcher points to the diversity of possibilities for approaching your research project. Have a look at the following metaphors and consider which best suits you and your research process. Perhaps just as important, consider what roles might be uncomfortable or inappropriate for you and your methodological design. Also keep in mind that there is no need for these roles to be mutually exclusive, and of course there is nothing keeping you from creatively and strategically creating your own researcher role.

- Theorist – The 'philosopher' or 'thinker'. The theorist metaphor suggests a researcher who can analyse critically and think abstractly. Theorists are likely to draw on the work of other theorists and are interested in new ways of seeing. In explaining a particular phenomenon or situation, theorists often attempt to develop understandings that lie outside the dominant paradigm. The theorist can be comfortable with various methodological/methods approaches.
- Scientist – The 'objective expert'. The scientist metaphor suggests a researcher who works to a formula; is removed, precise, methodical, logical, highly trained; and is in control of the research process. Objectivity ensures that scientists do not have an undue influence

on the research process. The scientist is most comfortable with the 'quantitative' paradigm.

- Change agent – The 'emancipator' or 'activist'. The change agent metaphor suggests a researcher who not only acknowledges subjectivities but is working to better a situation based precisely on these subjectivities. There is often devotion to the research/change process and sensitivity to the words and actions of respondents. Change agents often work in participatory and collaborative ways. They are most suited to action research strategies.
- Bricoleur – The 'jack of all trades' or 'professional do-it-yourself person'. The bricoleur metaphor suggests a researcher who sees methods as emergent and dependent upon both question and context. The bricoleur will employ a variety of methodological tools and even create new ones as needed to solve a puzzle or find a solution (Denzin and Lincoln, 2007). The bricoleur is comfortable with a variety of methodological/methods options.
- Choreographer – The 'coordinator of a dance'. The choreographer metaphor suggests a researcher who begins with a foundation of key principles, has vision and tries not to have a limited view. The choreographer works by warming up or preparation, exploration and exercise, and finally illumination and formulation (Janesick, 2007). The choreographer is usually comfortable with 'qualitative' approaches.

PRAGMATICS: MAKING IT DOABLE

Assume your intended design addresses your research question. In fact, you are quite comfortable with the approach, and believe you have or can develop the skills and adopt the roles necessary to carry off your project. There is just one more question. Is it doable? Regardless of how appropriate your methodological design might be for you and your question, if you do not have ethics approval, or the resources, time or access necessary to accomplish the task, you will need to rethink your approach. The 'best' design is simply worthless if you are going to come up against impermeable barriers to implementation.

The following questions can help you assess the practicality of your methodological plan:

- Is your method ethical?/Is it likely to get required ethics approval? A clear criterion of any research design is that it is ethical; and ethicality is likely to be audited by an ethics committee. If a study calls for interaction with people, it will often require formal workplace and/or university approval. Chapter 4 talks about ethics in some detail, but to summarize, an ethical study takes responsibility for integrity in the production of knowledge and ensures that the mental, emotional and physical welfare of respondents is protected.
- Do you have the required access to data? A major challenge for researchers is gaining access to data. Whether you plan to explore documents, conduct interviews or surveys, or engage in observation, the best-laid plans are worthless if you cannot find a way to access people, places and/or records. It is about being realistic. Ask yourself how you will go about gaining access and whether your methods are truly feasible.
- Do you have a plan for data management? Getting the data is one thing, managing it properly is another. You'll need a plan for logging and entering your quantitative data. You will also need a plan for handling qualitative data, i.e. recordings and transcripts.

A good tip here is to enter everything as you go. Things can go missing if you procrastinate here. You may also need a plan for securely storing your data in order to ensure confidentiality.

- Is your timeframe realistic? Yes, ambitious is good, but ambitious yet realistic is much better. If you have not given yourself enough time to do what your methodological design demands, you are likely to be headed down a very frustrating and stressful path that might include missing deadlines; compromising your study by changing your methods mid-stream; doing a shoddy job with your original methods; compromising time that should be dedicated to other aspects of your job/life; or not completing your project at all.
- Do you have access to adequate resources? Doing research is not cheap, and university funding for student research projects generally ranges from non-existent to very limited. It is therefore extremely important to develop a realistic budget for your study. You are likely to be surprised at just how expensive your design might be. Surveys can be done cheaply online, but you might want to offer compensation to participants to increase the quality of responses. If you want to gather data from 300 respondents, even a small compensation can add up. Even a smaller number of in-depth interviews can also be expensive. Will you or your participants travel to meet in person; or do you have licences for video-conferencing software? A transcript for a one-hour interview can be over 50 pages long. If you plan on paying someone to type up a few of those, costs will add up really quickly. Books, computers, software, equipment, interpreters, translators, training, etc. all need to be realistically considered. Any project, no matter how worthy, will not be practicable, or in fact possible, if you cannot cover costs.

IT'S ALL IN THE DETAILS

Once you feel comfortable with your general research plan, it is time to get down to the nuts and bolts of that plan. This involves being able to answer fundamental questions related to the who, where, when, how and what of your approach. If you can answer these questions, you are well on your way to articulating a clearly defined research design.

Fundamental Questions

As they say, it's all in the details. It is amazing how well defined a methodological plan can become once you work through the basic questions outlined below.

Who:

- Who do you want to be able to speak about? In other words, what is your 'population', or the realm of applicability for your results? Are your findings limited to only those you spoke to, or do you want to be able to speak for a broader group? For example, are your findings applicable to the children you interviewed, children from Philadelphia, children from the USA, or children from the Western world? Or do your findings represent one rural community in Norway, or all rural communities in Scandinavia?

- Who do you plan to speak to/observe? It is quite rare to be able to speak to every single person you wish to speak about. If who you wish to speak about is your 'population', then those you will actually speak to are your 'sample'. The key is that your sample is either intrinsically interesting or representative of a broader population. Chapter 11 discusses the issue of sampling and population in depth.

Where:

- What is the physical domain of your sample? This relates to working out how far afield you need to go in order to carry out your methods. Will you need to travel to different geographic areas? Are there various sites you need to visit?
- Are settings relevant to the credibility of your methods? This involves considering how place can impact on method. For example, if you wanted to conduct job satisfaction interviews with construction workers, you would need to consider if an informal chat at the Friday night watering hole will generate data distinct from that gathered through informal on-site interviews.

When:

- How do your methods fit into your timeframe? There are plenty of students who underestimate just how long it takes to collect data, let alone analyse it, draw conclusions from it and finally produce a report. The question of 'when' needs to be framed in relation to your overall timeline.
- Is timing relevant to the credibility of your methods? If you were to conduct a survey or interview when it is most convenient for you, without considering how 'when' can affect your data, you could put your study's credibility at risk. For example, a face-to-face community survey conducted between 9 am and 5 pm is likely to lead to a large underrepresentation of workers. And if you conduct university subject evaluations on the same day as results are released, it is sure to affect your data.

How:

- How will you collect your data? This involves deciding on the methods and tools you will use to collect, gather and/or generate your data. Chapters 12 and 13 cover a range of fundamental methods such as observation, interviews, surveys and document analysis.
- How will you implement your methods? Once you decide on your methods, thinking about how you will implement those methods is an even deeper level of 'nitty-gritty'. For example, you will need to consider whether you will record your interviews or take notes; or whether your observations will involve living in a community for a year, or making a defined number of visits.

What:

- What will you look for/what will you ask? Depending on your methods, this might involve developing questionnaires, observation checklists and frameworks for document analysis. Do not do this alone; make sure you get advice and support. These tools are difficult things to get right, and it may take a few trials or pilots to really develop them to a point where you are comfortable with the data they generate (see Chapters 12 and 13).

Table 7.1 provides an example of this who, where, when, how, what framework for developing the nitty-gritty of your methodological design. It embeds the 'prerequisites' discussed at the start of the chapter (true to the question, right for the researcher and doable) to assess the appropriateness of those elements.

Table 7.1 Checklist for methodological design

'Do parents (mothers) teach their daughters that worth is dependent upon external beauty?'
A one-year research project

Photo 7.1 Beauty and worth

Source: Vanity Studios (www.vanitystudios.co.uk/family-photography)

Methods – 1st draft	Methods – 2nd draft
WHO	**WHO**
Speaking about: parents of girls in Ireland	**Speaking about:** mothers of young girls in Ireland
Speaking to/observing: 30 mothers of 2–5-year-old girls in Dublin	**Speaking to/observing:** observe 30 mothers of 2–5-year-old girls in Dublin, interview 10 mothers in two focus groups
✗ True to the question (not a tight match – mothers ≠ parents; Dublin ≠ Ireland – need to modify)	✓ True to the question (I will modify question to 'mother' rather than parent and try to make a case of Irish applicability through the literature)

Methods – 1st draft	Methods – 2nd draft
WHO	**WHO**
✓ Right for the researcher (I will enjoy working with the group)	✓ Right for the researcher (I will enjoy working with the group)
? Doable (I have access, but 30 interviews may be too many)	✓ Doable (10 in two groups is more realistic)
WHERE	**WHERE**
Domain: Dublin	**Domain:** Dublin
Setting: book room at university for interviews/ observations	**Setting:** observe and conduct focus group at playgroup
? True to the question (maybe I need a more natural setting)	✓ True to the question (more naturalistic observation)
✓ Right for the researcher (convenient)	✓ Right for the researcher (mothers live locally)
✓ Doable (can book room)	✓ Doable (I have checked with playgroup coordinator)
WHEN	**WHEN**
Timing: midday, midweek	**Timing:** during playgroup (4 weeks)
Timeframe: early May	**Timeframe:** March
? True to the question (mothers may be rushed/stressed – affect nap times, etc.)	✓ True to the question (already in mothers' weekly schedule)
✓ Right for the researcher (convenient)	✓ Right for the researcher (convenient)
? Doable (midday fine, may might not leave enough 'me time')	✓ Doable (March should fit the overall timeline)
HOW	**HOW**
Method: observation and individual interviews	**Method:** observation and focus group interviews
Use of method: will video mothers and children on four occasions and also video the interviews	**Use of method:** will use an observation checklist at playgroup and audio-record focus groups
? True to the question (lots of detail with video, but mothers may act differently if they feel under surveillance)	? True to the question (I think the checklist and recording will work, but I will need to trial the method before I really know – will pilot – may need to modify depending on pilot results)
? Right for the researcher (I have made videos before, but not analysed them – will need skill development)	✓ Right for the researcher (I have done some observation and group facilitating – but will work on developing skills)
× Need to modify (too many cameras needed to capture it all, a few mothers have said they do not feel comfortable being video recorded; 30 interviews may generate too much data)	✓ Doable (should be able to manage the data generated)

(Continued)

Table 7.1 (Continued)

Methods – 1st draft	Methods – 2nd draft
WHAT	**WHAT**
Questions: develop observation checklist and interview questions	**Questions:** develop observation checklist and focus group discussion topics
? Answers the question (I will need to get support in development and pilot the tools)	? Answers the question (I will need to get support in development and pilot the tools)
✓ Right for the researcher (these are skills I would like to build)	✓ Right for the researcher (these are skills I would like to build)
✓ Doable (I have support of supervisor/ methods lecturer in developing tools)	✓ Doable (I have support of supervisor/ methods lecturer in developing tools)

In this example, the use of the framework has led to significant modifications in the second draft that should make the quest for credibility much more achievable. Note that even in the second draft, there are a couple of question marks remaining. This highlights that beyond mere reflection, there is a need to pilot or trial certain aspects of your design before you can fully assess its appropriateness.

I Have a Question!

All This Seems Logical, but It Implies That You Have a Defined Plan. What Happens When Your Methodological Plan Evolves or Shifts?

This happens all the time. It can be out of unexpected circumstances or it might be part of the plan itself. In **grounded theory**, for example, 'emergent methodological design' is part and parcel of the approach. Researchers work inductively to generate theories strictly from the data. In the first phase of a grounded theory study a research question or topic is defined, a methodological protocol for initial data collection is implemented, data is coded and analysed, and theories subsequently generated. Any successive phases of the study are then emergent based on generated theories. This can involve re-examination of existing data, or the development and implementation of new methodological protocols for generating, coding and analysing additional data. In both cases, grounded theory researchers know that, from the planning phase of their study, much of their methodological protocol cannot be developed in advance, and is in fact dependent on what emerges from initial data. Grounded theory may be flexible, iterative and emergent, but it is never ill-defined, haphazard or ad hoc.

Action research methodology (see Chapter 10) is also highly emergent. The goal of action research is to work with stakeholders to generate knowledge in order to action change. Because this process works towards significant change for the stakeholders, they take on the role of co-researchers. The main 'researcher' becomes a facilitator of a team that will develop the methodological protocols necessary for the action research process. This is a highly participative and collaborative type of research for which defined methodological approaches are outside the full control of the lead researcher. Rather, the process is emergent and cyclical and is based on collaborative input from the stakeholder/researcher team.

But even when it is not a part of methodological design, it is important to remember that all designs need to incorporate some flexibility. Life is unpredictable and research is not any different. You can have a plan - but that won't stop circumstances from arising that you will need to respond to. Whether it is surveys that are not completed, a workplace that suddenly won't give you access, or a key informant who drops out of the picture, hurdles will arise, and if you want to get over them you will need to be flexible and ready to redesign at a moment's notice.

Chapter Summary

- There are often a number of ways to credibly move from questions to answers, with each path giving a different perspective.
- Getting your design on target requires that it addresses your question; that you have/can develop necessary skills and interests; and that your approach is doable.
- As a researcher you need to design methods that sit well with your own epistemological frameworks, interests and skills.
- The 'best' possible design is worthless if you cannot gain ethics approval; cannot access required data; cannot finish on time; or run out of funds.
- Getting down to the nuts and bolts of design involves being able to reflexively answer questions related to who, where, when, what and how. This involves forward planning, but there will be times when you will want to have flexibility.

FIND YOUR NEXT STEP

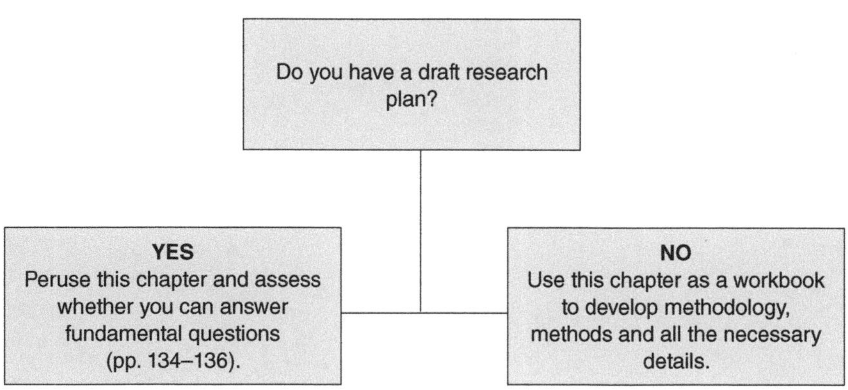

FURTHER READING

There are quite a few readings that can help you navigate your way through the complexities of designing methods. You may find the following sources a good place to start:

Creswell, D. and Creswell, J. W. (2022) *Research Design: Qualitative, Quantitative and Mixed Methods Approaches*, 6th edition. London: Sage.
It was terrific to see qualitative and quantitative design compared and contrasted when the first edition of this book came out. The addition of mixed methods makes this an even more essential read.

Leedy, P. D. and Ormond, J. E. (2018) *Practical Research: Planning and Design*, 12th edition. Englewood Cliffs, NJ: Prentice Hall.
We like the step-by-step approach that this book offers. It stresses the importance of design and gives excellent guidance through the research planning process.

Leavy, P. (2017) *Research Design: Quantitative, Qualitative, Mixed Methods, Arts-Based, and Community-Based Participatory Research Approaches*, 1st edition. New York: Guilford Press.
We like the novel and practical approach Leavy takes in this broad-ranging book. She offers a research template for each methodological approach and then gives you the knowledge and skills to fill it in.

8

UNDERSTANDING METHODOLOGIES

Quantitative and Qualitative Approaches

Learning Objectives

- Understanding quantitative and qualitative approaches to research
    - To understand the context of quantitative and qualitative research and the traditions they represent
- The quantitative tradition
    - To become familiar with scientific/hypothetico-deductive methods
    - To be able to design basic experiments and population studies
- The qualitative tradition
    - To understand how credibility manifests in qualitative research
    - To understand the key elements of ethnography, phenomenology, ethnomethodology and feminist research

UNDERSTANDING QUANTITATIVE AND QUALITATIVE APPROACHES TO RESEARCH

It would certainly be more straightforward if the production of knowledge was without contention, but what fun would that be? Engaging in debates around how we can best understand our world is a favourite pastime of many social scientists, with one of the most common debates being that which exists between what is labelled 'qualitative' and what is labelled 'quantitative'.

Now, 'quantitative' and 'qualitative' might be two of the most confusing words in methods language. Zina regularly gets asked if she is a quantitative or qualitative sociologist and Emma is often drawn into debates about the two. But these aren't appropriate descriptors for a researcher, or for that matter a methodology or method. It is much more useful to see these terms as simply adjectives for types of data and their corresponding modes of analysis: qualitative data, represented through words, pictures or icons analysed using thematic exploration; and quantitative data, represented through numbers and analysed using statistics.

'Quantitative' and 'qualitative', however, have come to represent a whole set of assumptions that can unfortunately dichotomize methods and limit the potential of researchers to build holistic understandings. **Quantitative research**, for example, is often characterized as an objective positivist search for singular truths that relies on hypotheses, variables and statistics, and is generally large scale, but without much depth. Qualitative research, on the other hand, rejects positivist 'rules' and works at accepting multiple realities through the study of a small number of in-depth cases. Such processes, however, can be accused of being subjective, value-laden, biased and sometimes ad hoc (Cavana et al., 2001; Creswell and Poth, 2024; Neuman, 2005); see Figure 8.1.

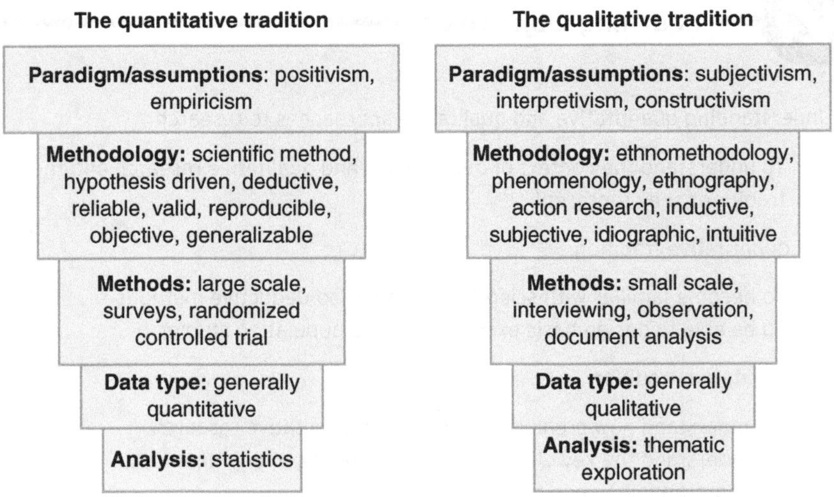

Figure 8.1 Assumptions related to the quantitative and qualitative traditions

While there's no doubt that quantitative and qualitative traditions represent a fundamental and important debate in the production of knowledge (see Chapter 1), there's also no doubt that the use of the terms 'quantitative' and 'qualitative', particularly in relation to methodology, can be confusing, divisive and limiting. In fact, these terms imply that designs that sit under the quantitative banner simply dismiss 'words', while those designs that sit under the qualitative banner do not have the time or space to deal with 'numbers'. This is simply untrue. After all, isn't quantitative data simply a coding system for qualitative concepts? And to think that you need to avoid counting or tallying in a qualitative study is ludicrous.

But these descriptors define the social science research landscape, so there is no question that understanding these traditions, the assumptions that underlie them, and the well-established and highly valuable research strategies they offer is extremely important.

I Have a Question!

Does This Mean I Have to Choose Between Quant. and Qual.?

Although you don't have to decide if you are a 'quantitative' or 'qualitative researcher', you will eventually need to decide on methodology, methods and types of data you will collect. And these choices should be determined by what will best answer your well-defined research question. Now this will be either quantitative approaches (which collect mostly quantitative data - but can collect qualitative as well - think of the open-ended questions in a survey); or it will be a qualitative approach that collects mostly qualitative data (but can collect quantitative as well - think of a survey embedded within a case study; or it could be a mixed-methodology approach that seeks to draw from both traditions/data types (see Chapter 9). The idea is to avoid being limited by paradigm, but to be directed by best practice.

THE QUANTITATIVE TRADITION

The quantitative tradition is based on a belief that the study of society is no different than the scientific study of any other element of our world – from particles to animals. The social sciences (note the word 'sciences') are subject to the same rules of engagement as, say, physics or biology. There is a strong belief in the scientific method, the need to test hypotheses, **deductive logic**, the need for objectivity and, as the name suggests, the value of quantification. There is an underlying belief in the power of numbers and their ability to represent the world with both vigour and accuracy.

In the social sciences what underpins the quantitative tradition are scientific or hypothetico-deductive methods, including experimental and **quasi-experimental design**. Such approaches attempt to follow the same rules and laws as are applied to the study of non-human objects. Quantitative social scientists also call on existing data and survey techniques in their quest to study and capture the reality of human populations. Each of these strategies is discussed here in turn.

Scientific/Hypothetico-Deductive Methods

The scientific standard for conduct of research goes something like this:

1 Engage with and adopt, adapt or generate a theory.
2 Drawing from the theory and using processes of deductive reasoning (the process of working down from theories to more specific examples), generate specific propositions or hypotheses.
3 Gather quantitative data, often through experimental design or, in the case of the social sciences, large-scale survey research.
4 Analyse the data using statistical processes.
5 Draw conclusions that may or may not support or reject your hypothesis.

This process acts as a scientific control mechanism and gives us the right to produce 'real' knowledge. It differentiates researchers from those who might say, 'Trust me, I just know', 'It came to me in a dream' or 'It was revealed to me by an angel'. By setting a standard, it also offers us protection from those who, in theory, accept the premise of scientific method, but might practise shoddy science tainted with personal biases, political agendas, sloppy procedures and/or flawed logic.

In the social sciences, this methodological approach also allows us to step away from our object of study and the societies we are necessarily a part of, and therefore maintain scientific objectivity. This then allows us to work towards traditional indicators of credibility such as validity, reliability, generalizability and **reproducibility** (see Chapter 4). In addition, the process of quantification allows us to tackle large populations and offers validity of results through the use of statistics and probability.

In the social sciences, the quantitative tradition goes back to the roots of the discipline and generally manifests in the methodologies of experimentation and population exploration through larger-scale, survey-based research.

Experimental Design

> The true method of knowledge is experiment.
>
> William Blake (1788)

Now you might not be able to define **experiment** but it is probably a term you are at least familiar with. After all, it's the mainstay of medical researchers, crime scene investigators and mad scientists alike – and would be a method of choice if your goals included: evaluating the effects of pharmaceutical drugs on disease; looking at the connection between suspect heights and bullet trajectories; or creating the perfect human–monster hybrid.

In the social sciences, you are unlikely to be working with cells, DNA, inanimate objects or laboratory animals. The likely object of your inquiry will be people in all their complexity. It's also unlikely that your experiments will take place in the controlled confines of a laboratory. Your research is likely to take place in less controlled settings, with all the attending challenges.

But even in the face of such challenges, experimentation offers tremendous potential in the social sciences. For example, suppose you were interested in exploring students who had difficulty engaging in learning. An experimental design would allow you to test a hypothesis, such as student attentiveness can be enhanced by group-oriented classroom layout, by manipulating classroom layout (the **independent variable**) to see how it affects student attentiveness (the **dependent variable**).

Or suppose you were interested in understanding the factors that affect sick leave. You might hypothesize that a lack of general fitness increases sick leave and design an experimental study that introduces a workplace exercise programme (independent variable) to see if the number of sick days taken decreases (dependent variable). Or if you were interested in high levels of domestic waste in a particular county or municipality, and hypothesize that there is a desire in the community to recycle, but implementation is difficult, you might 'experiment' by introducing free household recycle bins (independent variable) to see if this leads to a reduction in household waste levels (dependent variable).

Conducting an Experiment

A story on the radio a while back claimed that 'eating fish increases your IQ'. The story reported on the latest research that found that children who eat fish at least once a week have higher IQs than their non-fish-eating peers. Hence, the 'eat fish and get smart' headlines that led the story. But it turned out that the study looked at children's IQs and explored it in relation to a number of factors including diet, education, socioeconomic status, age of the parents, parental marital status and parental education level. And one of the correlations they found was between eating fish and IQ. As fish consumption rose, so too did intelligence – but then again you could also say that as IQ rose so did fish consumption. Does eating fish make you smart or do smart people eat more fish? Correlation is simply not cause and effect.

An intervening or confounding variable might also come into play. Maybe it's not the fish that makes you smart – maybe what is going on is that smart parents feed their children fish, and their child's IQ is determined by genetics.

Suppose you really want to get to the bottom of the great fish debate and you decide you want to determine cause and effect by conducting an experiment (after all, you've read that experiments really are the best way to work through this type of research problem). So how do you go about it?

Well, initial planning will involve lots of decision-making. As you work through your methodological design you will need to decide on your:

1 Dependent and independent variables – You will need to identify the main focus of your study or what you are trying to assess (the dependent variable), as well as the variable(s) you will manipulate in order to cause an effect (the independent variable(s)). In this case, you are hypothesizing that IQ depends on fish consumption, thereby making IQ the dependent variable and fish consumption the independent variable. This identification of variables by type is central to moving from correlation to cause and effect.

2 Assessment of change – In order to determine whether the manipulation of your independent variable has affected your dependent variable, you will need to be able to assess change. The most effective way to do this is through pre- and post-testing, which means collecting or having access to good baseline data and being able to collect

comparable data after the experimental intervention. In this case, assessing change is relatively straightforward and would involve administering standardized IQ tests (assuming, of course, that you believe in their efficacy).

3 Research setting – Consider whether you will be conducting your study in a controlled environment such as a laboratory or if you will use a natural setting. In this case a lab may give you total control, but, as is the case for many social science questions, it may not be practicable. In our scenario, other options include asking parents to vary diets at home, or to make arrangements with a day-care centre to change its weekly menu.
4 Number of participants – The number of participants you will use is also crucial. Think about how many participants will be necessary for you to make any conclusive or statistically significant judgements. For example, if you find a pattern in five children, is it enough? (Chapter 11 covers the basics of determining sample size.)
5 Number of groups – You will also have to decide if you will use a control group. In our fish example, using a **single group** would involve testing the IQ of all the children, feeding all of them fish a set number of times a week and testing them at some period thereafter to see what happens. With a control group you would test all of the children at the start, put half the children in a control group and the other half in a target group and only give fish to the children in the target group. You would then test both groups again at a later date and compare findings.
6 Assignment strategy – If you are using a control group you will need to determine how you will assign your groups. Will children be randomly selected for fish consumption or will you use different criteria for selection? While randomization will provide you with stronger cause and effect arguments, you might find it more practical to select children based, for example, on the days of the week they are in a day-care centre.
7 Number of variables – Will you test just one independent variable or will you test for others as well? For example, will you simply look at fish consumption or are there other aspects of the children's diet you will explore, such as vegetable intake?
8 Ethics – Consider whether you will need informed consent. In our fish consumption case, you will need parental consent. You will also need to consider if there are any advantages or potential threats to group members based on their inclusion in either a control or a target group. Now while there may not be high risks associated with eating or not eating fish, issues of equity represent a huge ethical dilemma in drug trials, treatment programmes and educational initiatives.
9 Control of the environment – Finally, you will need to consider how you will negotiate the balance between the practicalities of working in real-world situations and the need to control the environment. In other words, you need to consider how you can ensure your findings can be attributed to a true cause and effect relationship between your independent and dependent variables. Now the more controls you embed into your experimental design, the more convincing your arguments will be. But without such controls, arguments can be spurious:

   a Without a controlled environment it can be hard to ensure that the only variable that has been changed, shifted, manipulated or introduced is your particular independent variable. Other dietary changes, changes in sleep patterns, personal stress, etc. may be happening outside your experimental design.
   b Without adequate numbers it will be hard to show statistical significance or that results are more than coincidence.
   c Without a control group it is hard to ensure that there is not some other factor that might account for changes in your target or dependent variable – that improvements

in IQ scores cannot be attributed to things such as the additional attention that the children might be receiving, practice in taking IQ tests, or the coincidental commencement of a new educational programme.

d Without a random assignment strategy (which is often impractical in field-based research) you will need to argue that differences between the two groups are non-existent or at least minimal. In our case, if there is an innate difference in the learning abilities of the two groups, it will be impossible to attribute increased IQ to dietary habits.

The decisions you make will determine the 'type' of experiment you will conduct. The gold standard is the 'true' experimental design (often called a **randomized controlled trial**). In this type of design, independent variables are manipulated by the researcher; experiments are conducted under controlled circumstances; control groups are used; and there is random assignment to both control and target groups.

Unfortunately, random assignment may not always be possible in field situations. Suppose you did get agreement from a local preschool to trial a food programme. The school, however, will not allow random assignment (the school predicts chaos when some kids get chicken nuggets and others have to eat grilled flounder), so it asks you to run your trial on Mondays and Wednesdays. There is therefore a control group (which is good), but there is no random assignment (which is a problem if the groups are qualitatively different from each other – brighter children on these days, different teachers/carers, different cooks, etc.). When you have a control group but no random assignment, you have a quasi-experimental design, and while this is less than ideal, it is often a reality in social science field research.

Even more problematic is when you do not have access to any control group (so you have a single-group design). Suppose the preschool wants an all-or-nothing approach. Your only measure of success will be pre-/post-testing, which will not allow you to ensure that any change in the class is due to your programme and not any other factors.

Photo 8.1 Eat fish and get smart!

Source: Nazrul Islam on Pexels

Strengths and Challenges Associated with Experiments

There is definitely something appealing about saying 'I wonder what would happen if I were to ...?', and then being able to set up and assess the effects of that exact scenario. You would get to see it unfold for yourself. You would get to manipulate the environment and both witness and record the results. You would be in control.

Experiments, if well conducted, allow you to: assess cause and effect; compare groups; explore real actions and reactions and, if so designed, in real contexts; avoid reliance on respondents' memory or reactions to hypothetical situations; and generate both standardized quantifiable data and in-depth qualitative data.

Sounds pretty good. But as you might already suspect, there is no guarantee of smooth sailing. When studying individuals, often in a social context, it is hard to control for all influences that sit outside your experimental design. In social science experimentation you will need to consider: (1) if there is equity in your design (e.g. will the manipulation of your independent variable advantage or disadvantage any individuals/or groups?); (2) if your design will allow you to get informed consent from participants; (3) if participants will stay involved for the duration of the experiment; (4) if you can control for your own biases; and (5) if your design can control for extraneous, confounding or **intervening variables** (the things that affect your study that are not a part of your methodological design).

The Hawthorne studies, a series of classic workplace-based experiments conducted in the 1920s (Mayo, 1933; Roethlisberger and Dickson, 1939), offer an excellent example of social science experimentation and the challenges posed by real-world settings (see Box 9.1 in the next chapter).

EXPLORING A POPULATION

A central objective in social science research is to understand the make-up, or demographics, of a particular population and build an understanding of that population's knowledge, attitudes and practices on a particular topic or issue. In fact, this is one of the most common objectives in social science research.

Now without a doubt, the population that a social scientist might want to explore can be quite small and certainly studied in depth, often at a cultural level (see the discussion on ethnography later in the chapter), but what is more often referred to is larger-scale studies that attempt to understand broad populations – and it is precisely this scale that leads to the need for quantification and places this type of research squarely under the quantitative umbrella.

Conducting Studies of Populations

In the quantitative tradition, there are actually two broad methodological strategies that can help you understand a population: to capitalize on existing data or to generate your own primary data.

Capitalizing on Existing Data

We'd argue that it makes a lot of sense to at least consider/explore the possibility of working with existing data. Data is truly everywhere – with any number of organizations, individuals, students, research teams, professors, government and non-government agencies alike collecting, re-collecting and replicating data-collection processes (see Chapter 13). Resist falling into the trap of thinking that the only data you can use are data you generate. The data you find may not be in a form that directly answers your question, but therein lies the challenge. Remember: refining the wheel will often get you further than reinventing it. Box 8.1 gives an example of this type of study.

Box 8.1

Using Existing Data to Explore the Incidence of Food Poisoning in Palau

A few years ago, Zina was asked to be part of a team working on the development of Palau's National Environmental Health Action Plan. Before this invitation, she had barely even heard of Palau. As it turns out Palau is a speck in the middle of the Pacific Ocean, to the north of Indonesia. It is made up of over 300 limestone rock islands and has a population of about 20,000. Up until 1994 it was a US Protectorate, but it is now a new nation trying to stand on its own two feet. With its unparalleled snorkelling and diving, its economic future relies on building its tourism sector.

Quite early in the orientation, Zina and her colleague were told that food safety was one of the greatest challenges facing the Palauan Division of Environmental Health (DEH). There was a lot of anecdotal evidence suggesting high rates of food poisoning, particularly among tourists. But there were no real 'data' to support these concerns. They decided to prioritize designing a method for finding out more. They grappled with how to find out about the number of cases, severity of cases, who is affected, if there are seasonal variations and potential causes.

After working through a number of options (including surveying tourists), they decided to capitalize on existing records. The team was to go to every hospital, doctor and medical facility in the country and identify and explore records for all reported cases of food poisoning (which might sound bigger than it was - remember this is a nation whose total population is less than that of a small town). They did understand that this review of records would have its limitations: it would be a review of reported cases, not all cases; it would be reliant on getting access to records; and it was reliant on the accuracy and thoroughness of the records reviewed. Nonetheless, they believed that this was the most effective and cost-efficient method for collecting data that would allow the DEH to (1) generate a 'reported' food poisoning figure; (2) look at distribution by season, race, tourist versus local, etc.; (3) begin to look at recorded causes; (4) write more effective food safety policy; and finally (5) produce recommendations about systematic data collection within the medical sector.

(Continued)

Photo 8.2 Palau
Source: travelinsider on Flickr

Gathering Primary Data

Existing data and records directly related to your specific topic are not always available, or perhaps not available to you. So there will be plenty of times when the best strategy for exploring a population is to gather primary data; that is, to generate data from a population for the express purposes of your study. For the most part this involves survey processes, which are summarized here but discussed in much more depth in Chapter 12. Gathering this type of primary data involves:

- Defining the population from which you wish to ascertain information – For example, all people living in a particular community, state, country, cultural group, workplace or school district, or who have a common interest/trait (e.g. casual tennis players, people with muscular dystrophy).
- Assessing whether it is possible to gather information from every element of that population – This is rarely possible owing to the difficulty of identifying all population elements. For example, think of the difficulties associated with generating a list of all homeless people in the US or all Australian mothers suffering from postnatal depression. Additionally, even if all members of a population can be accounted for, the time and resources needed to access each element are almost always beyond our capability. One exception here is national censuses, which do invest the resources necessary to gather information from all members of their populations. If a **census** is impractical, however, you will need to move to the next step.
- Developing a sampling strategy with a goal of representativeness and generalizability – Your aim here is to gather information from enough people who represent the greater

population so that statistically significant conclusions about that population can be drawn.

- Adopting, adapting or generating a standardized instrument – Most often a survey questionnaire that can gather the information you require.
- Thoughtfully piloting and fine-tuning that instrument – This is essential in all survey processes.
- Implementing – Distributing and collecting the completed instrument.
- Using statistics to analyse the data – You will probably call on both descriptive and inferential statistics.

(See also Chapter 11 for more information on populations/sampling, Chapter 12 for surveying and Chapter 15 for quantitative analysis.)

Strengths and Challenges Associated with Studying Populations

While the desire to work with both pre-existing and generated data can offer much to the production of knowledge, there are always trade-offs between opportunities and challenges.

On the plus side, survey data: are generally derived from a large number of respondents; represent an even larger population; are confidential and anonymous; can generate standardized, quantifiable, empirical data; enable you to show statistical significance; and allow you to mathematically establish reliability, validity and generalizability.

There are, however, limitations inherent in the process. For example, it can be difficult to get an adequate response rate; the eventuating sample can be **skewed** and not representative; you are limited to what you have thought to ask; you do not have the opportunity to offer additional question clarification; it can be hard to assess respondent candour and honesty; and you cannot dig for more depth.

I Have a Question!

I Have Decided to Do a 'Natural' Experiment, but I Am Finding It Difficult to Control for All Variables or Find a Good Control Group. Will This Ruin the Credibility of My Study?

It really depends. There are definitely studies where there is small margin for error – drug trials for example. If you have anything less than a randomized controlled trial, your results will not be credible. You either meet exacting standards or you do not bother. There are other studies, however, where the trade-off between real-world setting and research precision allows you to produce valuable results despite methodological limitations. What is essential is making sure you (1) do everything you can to control for a messy environment, and (2) give a strong justification for why your methods, even with limitations, will produce credible and useful results.

THE QUALITATIVE TRADITION

> An existing paradigm has ceased to function adequately in the exploration of an aspect of nature to which that paradigm itself had previously led the way.
>
> Thomas Kuhn (2012)

If the quantitative tradition represents the study of the social premised on the tenets of positivism, particularly tried-and-true scientific, hypothetico-deductive methods, then the qualitative tradition might best be described as a critique of positivism as the reigning epistemology, and a recognition of the need for alternative ways to produce knowledge. The qualitative tradition therefore calls on inductive as well as deductive logic; appreciates subjectivities; accepts multiple perspectives and realities; recognizes the power of research over both participants and researchers; and does not necessarily shy away from political agendas. It also strongly argues the value of depth over quantity and works at delving into social complexities in order to truly explore and understand the interactions, processes, lived experiences and belief systems that are a part of individuals, institutions, cultural groups and even the everyday.

Delving into qualitative methodologies therefore means working in a world that accepts and even values: the search for holistic meaning, research conducted in natural settings, emergent methodological design, small numbers, **non-random sampling** strategies, rich qualitative data, inductive analysis, in-depth interpretation and even the possibility of negotiated outcomes that recognize the need for the researched to be party to a researcher's constructed meanings. The goal is to gain an intimate understanding of people, places, cultures and situations through rich engagement and even immersion in the reality being studied.

This section covers some of the key methodologies that social science researchers call on to understand a complex world. Ethnography is included as a classic anthropological method whose strength is in attempting to understand the world from the point of view of its participants (rather than searching for an 'objective' truth or premising the researcher's point of view). Phenomenology is included because of its recognition of the importance of lived experience and the impact of belief, regardless of truth. **Ethnomethodology** is included as an approach that looks quite closely at how meaning in the world is constructed by 'actors'. Finally, this section looks at **feminist methodology**, which developed, like the qualitative tradition, as a response to and critique of positivism (see Chapter 1) and, in the eyes of some feminists, patriarchal ways of knowing.

Now some student researchers will delve right into one of these qualitative methodologies and do, for example, an ethnographic or ethnomethodological study. But others will develop their own framework and, as appropriate to their research question, draw on some of the insights and strategies that are key to these various approaches to knowing – making their research that much richer.

It is also worth mentioning what's not in this section. Often found under qualitative methodology are grounded theory and case studies. Grounded theory is a methodology that seeks to generate theory through the analysis of data. Rather than begin with a hypothesis or hunch, grounded theory begins with data collection and progresses through to a step-by-step process for analysing data so that theory is generated. Its strength is in how it handles data – and we believe its processes of analysis can be of value in many types of 'qualitative' research. It is therefore taken up in much more depth in Chapter 16.

Case studies are also often labelled as a qualitative methodology. A case study is the study of elements of the social through comprehensive description and analysis of a single situation or case. We can understand arguments for calling it a methodology, but there are two reasons why we have not included case studies here. First, case studies can include a variety of data-collection methods, including, if the case is an organization or community, surveys. And of course surveys sit better under the quantitative paradigm. Second, the logic in selecting a case to study is similar to the logic of studying a population, a sample, a key informant. We argue that it makes sense to see a case as a unit of study. Case studies are therefore included in Chapter 11.

Credibility in Qualitative Studies

Because the 'rules' of science were born of the positivist/quantitative tradition, methodologies that sit under the qualitative umbrella are sometimes maligned for not reaching standards of credibility (see Chapter 4). But that does not mean that standards for credibility do not exist in the qualitative world. On the contrary, the rigour required of such studies is of the highest standard, and criteria appropriate to the task, as discussed in Chapter 4, have certainly been developed.

Debates over credibility, however, can arise when qualitative studies are inappropriately assessed according to positivist/quantitative criteria and, as might be expected, fall short of expectation. Many of Emma's students struggle with this challenge, but she reminds them that this is a matter of using the wrong criteria for the job. As discussed in Chapter 4, all studies, regardless of goals or even their paradigmatic positioning, need to consider whether: subjectivities have been managed; methods are approached with consistency; 'true essence' has been captured; findings have broad applicability; and, finally, whether research processes can be verified. Criteria for such assessment, however, are likely to be neutrality or transparent subjectivity rather than objectivity; dependability over reliability; authenticity over validity; transferability over generalizability; and auditability rather than reproducibility (see Chapter 4). Box 8.2 covers some of the strategies that 'qualitative' researchers use to reach appropriate standards of credibility.

Box 8.2

Strategies for Achieving Credibility in Qualitative Studies

Techniques that can be used to ensure thoroughness and rigour include:

- **Saturation** - Finishing collecting data only when additional data no longer adds richness to understanding or aids in building theories.
- **Crystallization** - Building a rich and diverse understanding of one single situation or phenomenon by seeing the world as multifaceted, and accepting that what we see depends on where we look, where the light is, etc.
- **Prolonged engagement** - Investment of time sufficient to learn the culture, understand context and/or build trust and rapport.
- **Persistent observation** - Looking for readings of a situation beyond an initial, possibly superficial, level.

(Continued)

- **Broad representation** - Representation wide enough to ensure that an institution, cultural group or phenomenon can be spoken about confidently.
- **Peer review** - External checking on the research process in which a colleague is asked to act as a 'devil's advocate' with regard to all aspects of methodology.

Techniques that can be used to obtain confirmation or verification include:

- **Triangulation** - Using more than one source of data to confirm the authenticity of each source.
- **Member checking** - Checking that interpretation of events, situations and phenomena gels with the interpretations of 'insiders'.
- **Full explication of method** - Providing readers with sufficient methodological detail so that studies are auditable and/or reproducible.

Ethnography

> Ethnography is something you have actively be aware of doing; it's not passive work. It takes considerable conscious effort to do it well.
>
> Leticia Supple (2013)

If you were to come to one of our houses for dinner and you were to reflect on that experience, you would probably do so in relation to what happens in your own home (e.g. 'we do that', 'that's different', 'how bizarre'). You would judge our families in relation to your own family or your own frame of reference.

Well, when it comes to studying cultural groups this is precisely what ethnography tries to avoid. Ethnography – which literally means 'culture writing' – explores a way of life from the point of view of its participants and tries to avoid assessing a culture using pre-existing frames of reference or from a particular worldview. The goal is to 'see' things the way group members do and grasp the meanings they use to understand and make sense of the world. In other words, ethnographers attempt to suspend judgement and understand the symbolic world in which people live in order to interpret meaning from within a culture.

To build this type of rich understanding, ethnographers tend to immerse themselves within a culture for a significant period of time. They participate, and then reflect on their lived conversations and observations. Whether it be foreign cultures, marginal cultures closer to home or even their own culture, ethnographers attempt to delve into cultural complexities in order to understand the world from the perspective of participants. Ethnographers attempt to explore how cultural understandings are shaped, and how group members make sense of their experiences. The goal is to go beyond an exploration of simply what is and begin to explore why it is (see Box 8.3).

The roots of ethnography stem from cultural anthropology, particularly the work of Clifford Geertz, who argued that building 'thick descriptions' is the only way we can uncover the underlying frameworks that produce both behaviour and meaning ([1973] 2017).

Now on the surface this may seem fairly straightforward, but a number of complexities become clear as you unpack the definition:

1 Ethnography is the study of cultural groups. This is significant because the term 'cultural' suggests that what binds the group is more than, say, genetics, biology or geography. 'Cultural' groups are bound together by social traditions and common patterns of beliefs and behaviours (e.g. ethnic groups, community groups or even workplace groups). Ethnographic studies are premised on the belief that how an individual processes the world is constructed and constrained by cultural experience. The study of cultural groups is thus the study of shared understandings as well as the symbolic aspects of behaviour that can uncover cultural or normative patterns. In other words, ethnography explores the methods, rules, roles and expectations that structure any given situation.
2 Ethnography explores a way of life from the point of view of its participants. Ethnography attempts to understand the symbolic world in which people live. The goal is to 'see' things the way group members do and grasp the meanings that they use to understand and make sense of the world. In other words, ethnographers attempt to interpret meanings from within a culture, or build what Geertz ([1973] 2017) refers to as 'thick descriptions'. This is significant because ethnography accepts multiple realities and requires cultural empathy. Rather than set understandings against a sometimes unrecognized Western worldview, ethnographers attempt to suspend judgement and understand from the perspective of the researched.
3 Ethnography involves a bid to understand, discover, describe and interpret. A somewhat common critique of ethnography is that it is merely descriptive. But generating 'thick descriptions' that build an understanding of the underlying frameworks that produce both behaviour and meaning is an act of discovery and interpretation as much as it is an act of description.

Box 8.3

Ethnographic Exemplar – 'Women on the Line'

In the late 1970s and early 1980s Miriam Glucksmann, working under the name Ruth Cavendish, conducted an ethnographic study of female factory workers, exploring their lives within the factory walls, how they juggled work and home responsibilities, and their views of life from the factory floor (Glucksmann, 2009). 'Ruth', as a participant observer, not only empathetically engaged with the women she studied, but actually made an attempt to live their reality. Through this experience she offered an insightful, vivid, empathetic and intimate narrative portrayal of the realities of the lives of women in an industrial world, a picture that could not have been painted through traditional social science techniques such as experimentation, surveys or interviews. For these and a host of other reasons, Cavendish's study is now considered not only a classic/pioneering ethnographic study, but also a classic study in economic sociology, the sociology of gender and the sociology of work.

(Continued)

Photo 8.3 On the line
Source: Tyne & Wear Archives & Museums on Flickr

Conducting an Ethnographic Study

Because ethnographic studies attempt to understand the reality of the researched, they generally rely on multiple data-collection strategies, involve the exploration of cultural groups within natural settings, and often require 'immersion' through prolonged engagement and persistent observation. The research process is flexible and emergent, and likely to evolve as lived realities within the cultural group are revealed. While ethnography is a methodology commonly used in anthropological studies, its principles can be used in a wide range of contexts.

The Range of Potential Cultural Groups

As discussed, a cultural group is defined by more than biology or geography. A cultural group needs to meet the prerequisite of a shared culture. It may be a foreign culture, or a culture closer to home (e.g. a migrant community or a boarding school). It is also possible to study a 'dominant' cultural group, which can be quite revealing because it is often dominance itself that causes privileged knowledge and governing ideologies to go unseen.

The selection of any particular cultural group will be driven by pragmatics, intrinsic interest, theory or any combination thereof. Pragmatics might involve research commitments, timely opportunities or accessibility. Cultural groups can also be selected to increase understanding, because they are unique and unfamiliar; misunderstood or misrepresented; marginal and unheard; or dominant, yet not reflexively explored. Finally, cultural groups can be selected on the basis of theory. For example, if the goal of a study is to understand how meaning is constructed, or to explore the interpretive and/or symbolic practices that define 'cultures', then the selection of a particular group might be made on the basis of being typical, atypical, extreme or rare.

Regardless of how a cultural group is selected, it is essential that an ethnographic researcher has a very high level of access within the group. The researcher must believe that it will be possible to build rapport and trust. Credible ethnographic studies require that researchers are able to get below the surface, break through the pleasantries, and observe cultural actors and actions that are not performed solely for the benefit of the researcher.

The Range of Potential Data Collection/Analysis Methods

The goal of the ethnographer is thick description and rich and reflexive interpretation, and few ethnographers would want to limit themselves to only one method of data collection. Data collection is therefore multi-method and often continues until **saturation**. While the data generated can include the quantitative, the preponderance of ethnographic data is likely to be qualitative so that the richness of the symbolic world can be fully described. Data-collection methods include:

- Observation – Participant observation is common to most ethnographic studies and tends to involve deep cultural immersion. Ethnographers attempt to build cultural empathy and 'live' the reality of the other. Ethnographers can also engage in non-participant techniques in order to generate more structured observations.
- Interviews – These are generally in depth and unstructured, and, in line with participant observation, often take the form of 'conversations'. Such 'interviews' can involve key informants and/or individuals who represent cross-sections of the cultural group – men, women, children, the elderly, new members, foundational members, etc.
- Document analysis – Sometimes a good way to understand the reality of the researched is to examine the texts that they themselves produce. Depending on the nature of the cultural group being explored, this might involve an examination of local newspapers, television and/or radio broadcasts. Or it may involve analysis of local art, the poetry and essays of schoolchildren, journals and diaries, and/or doctrine and dogma.
- Surveys – While surveys are often critiqued by those conducting ethnographies for being too reductionist, we do not believe they should be unilaterally dismissed as a potential data-gathering tool. While studies based solely on survey research would not qualify as ethnography, a survey instrument, such as a questionnaire, may be the best way to explore widely within a particular cultural group.

Strengths and Challenges Associated with Ethnography

Researchers are willing to immerse themselves in ethnographic studies because they believe they offer rich and in-depth exploration of the values, norms, symbols, beliefs and practices of cultural groups. This allows them to enter into a dialogue with existing theory and/or develop insights that can lead to the development of new theory. Ethnographers also recognize the importance of multiple worldviews as well as the value of building understandings from the perspective of the researched.

Some of the difficulties associated with ethnography are shared by a range of studies that involve 'immersion'. These include: gaining access and building trust; emotional costs; the potential for the researcher to have an effect on the researched; and the demands placed on those being studied.

But there are also concerns more specific to ethnography that need to be seriously considered and skilfully negotiated. First, ethnographers need to guard against 'homogenization' that can give minimal recognition to divergence within a particular group. Ethnographers also need to be aware of a somewhat paradoxical dilemma in representing the reality of others. Ethnography has an explicit goal of building and interpreting understandings from the perspective of the researched. However, it also accepts that descriptions are necessarily interpretive, and that the basis of interpretation is the filtering of observations and inputs through theoretical and analytic frameworks that are, of course, imbued with a researcher's own worldview. This then begs the question whether an outsider (particularly one from a very divergent culture) can ever truly know, describe and interpret the reality of being an insider.

How you manage this 'paradox' will depend on how you reflect on the above question, as well as your ability to mount arguments that will satisfy a sceptic's concerns over credibility. This will require you to reflexively consider and articulate: how you as a researcher have had an impact on the interpretive practices within your research; what strategies you have employed to seek thoroughness and confirmation (see Box 8.2); and the significance of your research findings to a particular body of knowledge.

Now it is extremely difficult to get ethics approval to immerse yourself in a culture. Joining a cult or a gang is not likely to be approved! But ethnography might be worth considering if you are already immersed within a new cultural group you wish to explore. For example, if you are living and studying overseas or have just been offered a job on a fishing boat. Or, as was the case for one of Zina's fellow graduate students who had a rough working-class background, you find yourself immersed in the bizarre ivory-tower world of academia.

Even more likely is that you draw on ethnographic understandings to make your research more empathetic and sensitive. Most interview and data analysis techniques can be greatly enhanced by making a concerted effort to understand that respondents may have cultural realities distinct from those of the researcher – and that this alternative reality needs to be validated and appreciated.

Phenomenology

Is it worth knowing what it feels like to win – or to lose? Is it worth understanding the lived experience of struggling with breast cancer? Is it worth knowing what it feels like to be at the bottom of the class? Now we're not talking about cause and effect. We're not asking why someone won or lost, or the implications of cancer, or why someone might struggle at school. We are strictly talking about 'phenomenon' or 'lived experience' – what it feels like for those subject to the experience.

Well, we think understanding lived experience is absolutely vital. Let us try to explain. One of the key premises of adult education is that you need to start where people are. And we have certainly found this to be the case – not only in our own teaching, but also in conflict mediation, change agency, situation improvement, counselling and problem resolution. If you want to be truly effective in getting people to move from A to B you need to start at A, and you can only do that if you understand and appreciate A. Not just intellectually, but emotionally.

If you want to know why athletes are willing to take steroids, you need to understand their lived reality of winning and losing. If you want to help someone through breast cancer, you need to know how they feel about their body, their self-esteem, their future. If you want to understand how you can help motivate struggling students, you need to know what it is really like for them at the bottom of the class.

This is the goal of a phenomenological study. Rather than ask what causes X, or what is X, phenomenology explores the lived experience of X. In fact, phenomenologists would argue that 'objective' knowing or truth should be 'bracketed' or put aside so that the focus can be on internal processes of consciousness. There is no need to worry about causes, truth value, reality or appearances. In a socially constructed, intersubjective world, our direct awareness is the only thing we can really know, since all knowing depends on individual perceptions (see Box 8.4, below).

Phenomena as an object of study may be somewhat new to you, so let's break down the basic elements in a phenomenological study and highlight the role each element plays in defining, understanding and researching phenomena:

1 Phenomenological studies are highly dependent on individuals. Individuals, either through interviews or their cultural products – what they write, paint, etc. – are used to draw out the experiences of a particular phenomenon. For example, refugees, athletes or leaders might be called upon to provide descriptions of the experience of displacement, victory and power, respectively. Individuals are therefore central to the conduct of phenomenological studies. But it is their descriptions of lived experience, rather than they themselves, that are the focus of phenomenology.
2 Phenomenological studies are also highly dependent on constructs. Constructs such as displacement, victory and power are central to the phenomenological experience being explored. In phenomenological studies, however, the 'reality' of the construct is not of concern and should, in fact, be 'bracketed' – explored as free as possible from what the world says it is supposed to be or supposed to mean. In phenomenology, a construct freed from its constructed meaning is often referred to as an 'object'.
3 Phenomena, which are the focus of phenomenology, actually sit at the intersection of people and objects, and centre on an individual's lived experience of these objects. Rather than ask what causes X, or what is X, phenomenology explores the experience of X. In other words, phenomenology is the study of the experience of the relationship between the individual and the object. It is the study of a phenomenon as it presents itself in an individual's direct awareness.

Conducting a Phenomenological Study

There are three basic elements in most methodological approaches in the social sciences. These are your participants, your data-collection methods and intended modes of analysis. And of course, the end product is your 'report'. Well, it does not quite work that way in phenomenology. The product of phenomenological studies is phenomenological descriptions; and gathering descriptions, making sense of those descriptions and writing up those descriptions are not necessarily discrete activities.

Producing Phenomenological Descriptions

The key outcome of phenomenological studies is rich phenomenological descriptions. In fact, the goal is to produce descriptions so full of lush imagery as to allow others to share in how a particular phenomenon is experienced.

The process of generating such descriptions generally involves sourcing people who have experienced a particular phenomenon and conducting one or more in-depth interviews with each participant. The number of respondents can vary – but given that there is likely to be more than one way to experience any particular phenomenon, you generally need to conduct a sufficient number of interviews to draw out variation. Interviewers often look for saturation, whereby additional interviews no longer add new perspectives.

The goal of the interviews, most often conducted as a 'conversation', is to draw out rich descriptions of lived experience. In other words, you want your respondents to tell you what a phenomenon feels like, what it reminds them of and how they would describe it. Respondents are then encouraged to further reflect on various aspects of their descriptions. This often involves digging below the surface of words to understand the meaning behind them. For example, the phenomenon of 'winning', first described as 'fantastic', might be further described as 'like being on top of the world' or 'I know I have worth'. In this way, the researcher and the researched create a narrative that is both descriptive and interpretive, and is often rich, poetic and full of metaphor.

In addition to, or instead of, conducting interviews, researchers can also explore pre-produced texts. Beautiful, rich phenomenological descriptions abound in letters, journals, books, movies, poetry and music. Take, for example, the phenomenon of 'going into battle'. Imagine the rich, candid and chilling descriptions you might be able to gather just from reading letters home.

A Second Cycle

Once you have generated (or located) your descriptions and you feel you have reached a point of saturation, the next step is synthesis. The goal here is to explore commonalities and divergences in the experience of the same phenomenon. You are looking for the range of experiences related to the phenomenon itself. This is generally done by cycling between the texts and eventuating themes in a bid to reduce unimportant dissimilarities and integrate the essential nature of various descriptions. In some of Zina's own research, for example, she found that giving up God showed itself in three 'types' of lived experiences – 'angry and resentful reaction'; 'gloomy and melancholic introspection'; and 'open spiritual exploration' (O'Leary, 2001b).

Box 8.4

Phenomenological Exemplar – Hospitality Workers' Career Choices in the Wake of COVID-19

The aim of the study 'Exploring hospitality workers' career choices in the wake of COVID-19: Insights from a phenomenological inquiry' (Liu-Lastres, Huang and Bao, 2023) is to understand the perspectives of hospitality workers (the individuals the study was dependent upon) on the experience of stress during the COVID-19 pandemic (the lived experience) and its impacts on their career decisions (the construct). Far from an academic knowledge-only exercise, objectives of this study included finding out how hospitality employees can best be supported. In order to accomplish this, Liu-Lastres and colleagues used a phenomenological approach that involved semi-structured interviews (phenomenological descriptions) with 31 current and former hospitality employees with first-hand experience working during the COVID-19 pandemic. Each conversation was iteratively explored (the second cycle of synthesis) with three themes identified (appraisal of COVID-19 induced stress; coping strategies; re-appraisals) that documented the interpretive process through which employees made sense of their career decisions.

Strengths and Challenges Associated with Phenomenology

We think the main strength of phenomenology is that it offers a way of exploring this thing called 'phenomena', something highly important in understanding our social world, yet often ignored in studies of the social. We tend to explore demographics, opinions, attitudes, beliefs and behaviours of people, and we study the ideas, ideologies and constructs that make up the social world, but the study of phenomena is marginalized and often goes undiscussed as a potential research strategy available to student researchers.

But just think about the value of being able to understand and describe lived experience. How much more insightful could change initiatives or problem resolution strategies be if we had this level of understanding? Take, for example, understanding and describing the lived experience of critical illness. This would be essential reading for anyone wishing to develop appropriate protocols for mental health workers dedicated to the critically ill. Or what about capturing the essence of what it is like to grow up in a war-torn country, a description that could be invaluable to building cultural empathy? And any study that explored stress would not be complete without understanding what it actually feels like.

Do not underestimate the power of phenomenological approaches in your own research. As social scientists, we tend to study what happens in the head, but many of the actions of the human world are driven by the heart. They are driven by feeling rather than by thinking. For example, if you are wanting to know why people do 'illogical' things like drink-driving or drug taking, or how people deal with difficult things like imprisonment or death of a child, it just might be worth asking more than 'why' and 'how'. It may be worth asking what it feels like.

As with anything worth doing, it's not necessarily easy. The literature on phenomenology tends to be thick and philosophical and does not offer a lot of clear guidance on actual 'methods'.

You probably won't get much advice from research texts either. Few texts cover the topic at all, and those that do, don't do it very well. The same goes for teaching and learning. In our 'training' as social scientists, phenomenology was not a method that was discussed, and when it was covered in Zina's philosophy classes, it was not done in a way that would help her in conducting a phenomenological study. The implication is that unless you have a supervisor or mentor experienced in phenomenology, 'doing' a phenomenological study will require you to get into the literature (some suggestions are offered at the end of the chapter).

Ethnomethodology

Throughout our day we interact – with our parents, friends, the checkout person at the grocery store. And we make judgements, sometimes consciously but mainly subconsciously, about how we should act and what we should say. And we generally do this without too much stress because we are socialized with appropriate 'methods' – rules, norms and patterns – that help us wade through such interaction.

Ethnomethodology is the study of everyday interactions and argues that individuals engage in interpretive work every time they interact with the world. In order to do this in a way that makes sense, they engage in what Garfinkel (1967), the father of ethnomethodology, refers to as the **documentary method**. This involves **indexicality** – selecting cues from a social interaction that conforms to a recognizable pattern – and then making sense of that interaction in terms of that pattern. We know this sounds confusing, but in practice it is pretty simple because it is something you do automatically every day. For example, if someone said, 'I couldn't help but notice you', you would take cues from the social interaction to find the likely pattern and formulate an appropriate response. So if you were in a nightclub with lots of single people, the pattern might be 'the pick-up' and you might reply with a disgusted 'Get lost, you loser', or a seductive 'Yeah ... I noticed you too'. The other party then has to subconsciously find the right pattern, in this case let's say 'rejection' or 'flirtation', and form the appropriate response. You then use that response to generate your next response, and so on until the interaction ends. In this way, the pattern is emergent, but is consistently used in its most recent formulation to interpret new elements of the interaction. But imagine if the same original line, 'I couldn't help but notice you', was said while you were pulled over in your car and the person saying it was in a police uniform. The interaction would immediately take a different form (see Box 8.5).

Box 8.5

Ethnomethodology Exemplar – 'Garfinkel's Agnes'

In his seminal 1967 work *Studies in Ethnomethodology*, Garfinkel attempted to capture the socially situated work whereby Agnes, a 19-year-old transgender woman, accomplished the daily task of being a woman. Garfinkel's goal was to unmask the taken-for-granted familiarity and everyday occurrence of being a woman. Having been raised as a man for the first 17 years of her life, Agnes offered a unique window for unmasking (and adopting) the generally taken-for-granted and unseen tasks associated with the daily work of being female. Garfinkel's work reveals the working of a 'natural attitude' towards sex and gender which Emma and her colleague have shown underlies contemporary transphobic rhetoric (Henderson and Tennent, in press). Ethnomethodology is a powerful tool to document how people produce the interactions that make up their everyday lives.

Conducting an Ethnomethodological Study

The goal of doing an ethnomethodological study is to draw out how individuals go about the interpretive work necessary to make sense and make meaning in everyday interactions. Approaches for drawing out meaning include **breaching experiments**, exploring the building of shared interpretation and exploring interpretive miscues.

Breaching Experiments

In breaching experiments (something Garfinkel often had his students attempt), the goal is to expose the rules of the everyday by breaking them and taking note of your own reactions as well as the reactions of others. In this way, what is taken for granted can become apparent (e.g. facing the back of a full elevator or speaking to your family as though you had just met them). Not only are you able to document the confusion, frustration, discomfort, etc. of those around you, but you can also reflect on how it feels to break taken-for-granted rules. Logically, facing the back of a full elevator should not be an exceedingly stressful task, but it can make some 'experimenters' exceptionally uncomfortable.

Exploring the Building of Shared Interpretations

Every cultural group has embedded communication practices that seem free and natural but are actually culturally constructed. And this cultural construction is largely hidden to those on the inside. Because they are surrounded by it and have a shared interpretation, it becomes the norm and other ways of interacting go unconsidered. Those on the outside of the cultural group, however, are better placed to see this construction.

Let's give you an example. When Zina first moved to Australia, she noticed that there was a certain way, quite standard, that an interview unfolded after a rugby match. It wasn't just the content, it was the words used, the tone and the phrasing. So, from an interviewer starting with 'Tough match out there' to the point where it ends with 'Well done and good luck for the rest of the season', the players interviewed, regardless of age, ethnicity or years on the field, all sounded very similar: 'Thanks, mate', 'The boys really put it out there', 'The boys should be proud', 'Full credit to the [insert opposing team's nickname, e.g. Doggies]', 'They made us work for it', 'No time to celebrate, mate', 'We need to put our heads down and get on with the rest of the season', 'Cheers, mate'. And when someone breaks these rules it is highly noticeable. An example ... after a big Australian rugby league game in June 2016 (State of Origin series), a footballer compared a hard-fought victory to losing his virginity. The quip was 'It was a bit like losing your virginity, it wasn't very nice but we got the job done'. A clear breach of the rules, which made the quip not just controversial, but newsworthy.

Contrast that to the 'rules' in other sports and in other countries. The way an American football player's interview happens is very different. Different again is that of an English cricketer. Rules that help structure interactions exist, but often go unseen.

As a strategy of ethnomethodology, exploring how we build shared interpretations involves collecting raw data that capture everyday interactions. These interactions are often specifically defined – interactions between doctor and patient, family members, friends, members of a particular cultural group or in this case interviewer and interviewee. Data is then captured by audio recording or, if analysis will go beyond speech, video recording. This data is then faithfully transcribed, often including hesitations, comments on tone, attitude, use of sarcastic pitch, non-verbal cues, etc. A method called **conversation analysis** then turns to a search for how the interaction is built collaboratively. The goal is to identify the 'rules' that underpin the interactions or how individuals manage action or conversation. This necessarily involves exploration of the context and how it is understood by actors. Context (or, as Garfinkel refers to it, the indexical nature) is essential because context means that the pattern of interaction is cued for this particular setting – in the case above, the post-game interview.

Exploring Interpretive Miscues

A final method that can be used to uncover the taken-for-granted nature of communication and interaction is the exploration of conflicts or miscues – essentially, when it simply doesn't go the way it is expected. It is easier to spot, deconstruct and understand the 'taken for granted' when it is exposed by those doing things that buck the norm. Zina's mother, who is Korean but has been living in the US since she was 20, was visiting her in Australia and provided a classic example at her daughter's first birthday party. She often behaves inappropriately, both because she doesn't care about convention and because she likes to get a laugh. A group of us were in the lounge room when she walked into a conversation about how cute one of the babies was. As she realized who they were talking about – and with a confused look on her face – she blurted out 'That baby! That baby ugly like a shit!' OK, maybe it was just a little true – and just maybe the same thoughts had crossed the mind of others (which could explain the raucous laughter that ensued). But everyone else in the room knew and respected the conventions – you simply don't say that about a baby, particularly when the baby's godparents and aunt are in the room (thankfully the parents had left – not that her mother knew that at the time). Her mother's unwillingness to buy into acceptable interpretive practice exposed cultural expectations. In fact, comedy often exposes acceptable interpretive practice by breaching it for a laugh. We don't always see patterns of interaction that are embedded as normal, but we can see them when they are breached because we react with something like surprise, laughter, shock, horror or anger.

Strengths and Challenges Associated with Ethnomethodology

Ethnomethodology has a lot to offer the study of the social, including recognition of the interpretive work of individuals, as well as methods for exploring that work. It explores how individuals make sense of, and make sense in, the social world, and recognizes that individuals are not passive in making meaning and establishing social order.

Ethnomethodology also recognizes that the actual process of interacting ('how' questions) is a worthy topic of investigation, and that the topic of verbal interactions ('what' questions) and the reason for interactions ('why' questions) are not the only types of question a social scientist can ask. It is also another way to study culture. Ethnomethodology can be used to explore how members of a particular cultural group make meaning and engage in interpretive work. This can offer much to our understanding of the nature of communication and social structure within a culture. Finally, ethnomethodology offers a way of investigating how particular types of interactions are performed. For example, how juries deliberate and draw conclusions, or how medical practitioners can best deliver bad news in ways that minimize negative reactions.

Ethnomethodology and conversation analysis (sometimes shortened to EMCA) have a long history of exploring human–computer interaction and how we use technologies in everyday life. Today, the question of how we interact online and across different digital technologies is of great interest to marketers, communication experts, community engagement specialists and social science researchers alike. How communication is performed and how organizations can engage with this new form of interpretive practice is a hot topic and bringing new relevance to ethnomethodology as a social science methodology.

As with any methodological approach that sits outside the mainstream, there are a number of issues that can make using its methods quite difficult. This includes the difficulty of getting experienced support and having to explain and justify your choice of methodology to those who may not know much about it.

Some also argue that because ethnomethodology does not explore the 'meaning' of utterances or actions, it does not help us understand fundamental social issues or important constructs such as race, class or gender. Some even say that the 'rules' ethnomethodology draws out are obvious and not very interesting. Others, however, argue that the interpretive work of ethnomethodology can help us understand how individuals produce, for example, racism or sexism.

Another misconception is that the analysis of interpretive works is limited to talk and the intricate exploration of transcribed verbal data (see Chapter 16). In fact, conversation analysis is a bit of a misnomer because the analysis includes non-verbal conduct like gaze, gesture, interaction with objects that can be just as, if not more, important to interaction.

Understanding Feminist Approaches

> The opening of public discourse to multiple voices and perspectives calls into question the very notion of a single standpoint from which a final overriding version of the world can be written.
>
> Dorothy Smith (1999: 68)

First things first. Is there such as a thing as feminist methodology? Well, if there was, it would be almost impossible to define, since feminist researchers call on any variety of methodological frameworks and methods to conduct their research. Just as there's no unified definition of feminism, there's no unified definition of feminist research.

However, there are some key aspects to a feminist perspective on research. The premise here is that traditional 'rules' of research are based on patriarchal and white/Eurocentric worldviews.

Feminist researchers argue that what we accept as general knowledge is actually white male knowledge – that is, knowledge underscored by racist and patriarchal values and beliefs that shape what research is and how it should be done. This bias pervades all aspects of the process from question development to the collection, interpretation and presentation of data. Most significant is that this bias tends to go unaddressed in mainstream research. So research protocols derived from one particular reality are accepted as the standard, proper and credible way to produce knowledge.

To resist and overcome these forms of bias, feminist research takes a critical stance towards existing methodological approaches. There is a need to unmask race and gender bias and work towards research that is informed by feminist theory and principles throughout all stages of the research process.

The feminist perspective argues that research:

- is always politically motivated;
- should be committed to the empowerment of women;
- should work towards changing social inequality;
- needs to represent human diversity, including marginalized voices;
- needs to recognize important differences between women and men, as well as among women themselves (according to race, class, ethnicity, religion, culture, sexual orientation, etc.);
- needs to acknowledge the power and position of the researcher;
- should lessen the distinction between researcher and researched;
- should accept and search for multiple, subjective and partial truths.

The feminist critique of traditional social science method, however, is not without its own critique. First, many argue that the premises above are not unique to feminist methodology and are central to many, if not most, qualitative frameworks. Second, feminist researchers have been accused of overlooking intersections between gender, race, class, (dis)ability and so on which can result in middle-class white bias. Critical scholars have pointed out that the underlying assumptions of research are not limited to patriarchy, but include racism, imperialism and capitalism. There is value in engaging with literature on feminist methodology – not necessarily to adopt it, but as a way of exposing the cultural biases embedded in the game of research. We are then in a better place to design a research approach free from the legacy of an inherently biased way of seeing the world.

Critical Thinking Challenge 9

The Great Divide

So what do you think?

Lots of approaches coming from various disciplines, worldviews and ideologies.

What do you make of it?

Do you think it is logical, historical, ridiculous, constructed, necessary, unnecessary? If you can engage at this level, you are definitely becoming a reflexive researcher.

I Have a Question!

I Find This Qualitative Stuff Really Interesting, but Just How Useful Are Phenomenological and Ethnomethodological Studies?

We know that if you are new to it, it can seem like qualitative studies are a bit out there, but they can add amazing insights to our understanding of the social world. And they can do this in very useful ways. A colleague at grad school, for example, used an ethnomethodological approach to understand how mediation sessions between parents battling for custody could be best structured to lead to positive outcomes. Another used a phenomenological approach to understand the experience of PTSD in returned servicemen, with a view towards improved health care.

Chapter Summary

- Quantitative and qualitative research traditions represent a fundamental debate in the production of knowledge, but the use of the terms 'quantitative' and 'qualitative', particularly in relation to methodology, can be confusing, divisive and limiting.
- The quantitative tradition is based on a belief that the study of society is no different than the scientific study of any other element of our world, and premises scientific method, deductive logic, objectivity and quantification. In the social sciences it often involves hypothesis testing through experimental design or the analysis of quantitative data.
- The qualitative tradition critiques the assumptions that underpin the quantitative tradition, and premises **inductive logic**, subjectivity, multiple truths, the political nature of research and the value of depth over quantity. Ethnography, phenomenology, ethnomethodology and feminist approaches are examples of qualitative methodology.
- Studies with mixed methodologies traverse traditional divides and employ quantitative and qualitative approaches in a single study. If well handled, they can capitalize on the best of both traditions while overcoming their shortcomings.
- Mixed approaches can be premised in the quantitative tradition with acceptance of qualitative data, the qualitative tradition with acceptance of quantitative data, or be driven by the questions themselves.

FURTHER READING

As you begin to narrow in on your approach, you will probably want to go a bit further in your reading. The following list is not comprehensive, but it does offer you a few good starting points.

FIND YOUR NEXT STEP

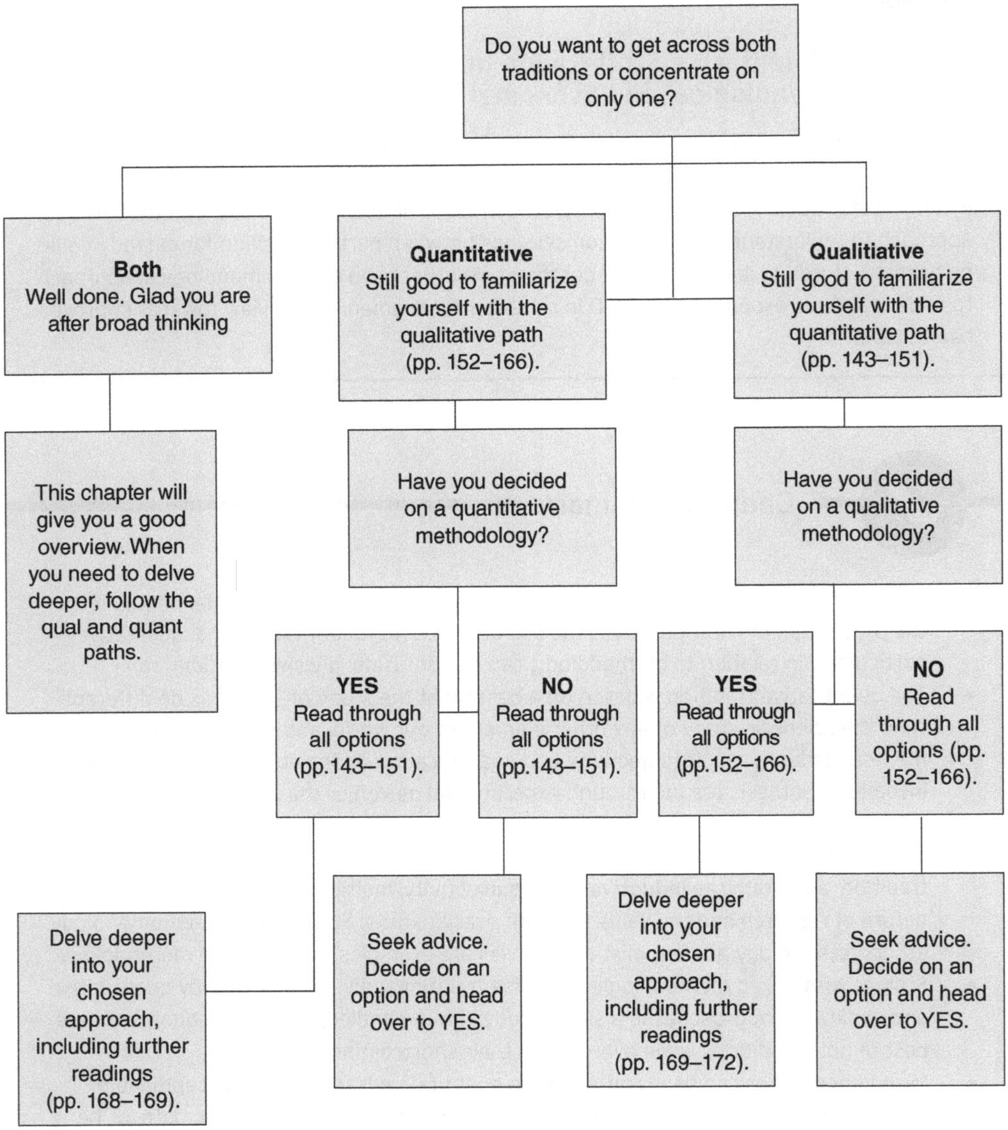

The Quantitative Tradition

Martin, W. and Bridgmon, K. (2018) *Quantitative and Statistical Research Methods: From Hypothesis to Results*. San Francisco, CA: Jossey-Bass.

This book aligns itself completely in the quantitative tradition. It approaches methods as a 'recipe' more than a thinking game, but it does offer all the knowledge you need to conduct this mode of research.

Kaplan, D. (ed.) (2014) *The SAGE Handbook of Quantitative Methodology for the Social Sciences.* Thousand Oaks, CA: Sage.
If you can only have one quantitative resource, this is not a bad choice. It covers an array of quantitative techniques as well as critiques of those techniques. Very comprehensive.

Hypothetico-Deductive Methods

Carey, S. S. (2011) *A Beginner's Guide to Scientific Method.* Belmont, CA: Wadsworth.
We think this is a very good introduction to the ways and means of scientific method. It will help you in both the design and assessment of research that uses experimentation.

Weakliem, D. (2016) *Hypothesis Testing and Model Selection in the Social Sciences.* New York: Guilford Press.
Probably not a beginner's book, but a good one if you need to get right into hypothesis testing and the challenge of modelling and in-depth statistical analysis.

Experimental Design

Coleman, R. (2018) *Designing Experiments for the Social Sciences: How to Plan, Create, and Execute Research Using Experiments.* Thousand Oaks, CA: Sage.
This in an accessible book that will help you think about the design of your social science experiments. It is step-by-step and offers clear examples.

Dunning, T. (2012) *Natural Experiments in the Social Sciences: A Design-Based Approach.* Cambridge: Cambridge University Press.
This is a comprehensive work that looks at the potential for experimental design to show cause and effect in the social world. The author does a good job of laying out the challenges of working in the real world and gives good guidance for achieving credibility.

The 'Qualitative' Tradition

Creswell, J. and Poth, C. (2024) *Qualitative Inquiry and Research Design: Choosing Among Five Approaches*, 5th edition. Thousand Oaks, CA: Sage.
Creswell is known for his clear writing, and this work is no exception. It outlines five qualitative methodological approaches, namely, narrative research, phenomenology, grounded theory, ethnography and case studies.

Denzin, N. K. and Lincoln, Y. S. (eds) (2017) *The SAGE Handbook of Qualitative Research.* Thousand Oaks, CA: Sage.
You'll see this handbook on the shelf of almost all 'qualitative' researchers – and with good reason. It is comprehensive, yet grounded, and covers most issues in qualitative research.

Marshall, C. and Rossman, G. B. (2015) *Designing Qualitative Research*, 6th edition. London: Sage.
A good guide to the basics of qualitative design. We particularly like the vignettes used to illustrate the methodological challenges researchers often face.

Braun, V. and Clarke, C. (2013) *Successful Qualitative Research: A Practical Guide for Beginners*. London: Sage.
An accessible introductory text, with a practical focus on how to do qualitative research. Helpful case studies and illustrations of real-life research studies as well as additional online resources.

Ethnography

Fetterman, D. (2019) *Ethnography: Step-by-Step*. London: Sage.
As the title indicates, this is a step-by-step guide that will help you make sense of ethnographic data. But perhaps more than the title indicates, it also delves into the theory and importance of ethnography as a way of researching.

Geertz, C. ([1973] 2017) *The Interpretation of Cultures*. New York: Basic Books.
Geertz is the man when it comes to ethnography and this seminal work really defined an approach that is still the standard for how we can best study and understand cultures.

Glucksmann, M. (2009) *Women on the Line*. Abingdon: Routledge.
See Box 8.3 above.

Madden, R. (2017) *Being Ethnographic: A Guide to the Theory and Practice of Ethnography*. London: Sage.
The immersion necessary in ethnographic studies creates a need for more than just a 'how to' guide. It creates the need for works that challenge you to look at how you fit into and influence your research processes. This book does it well.

Phenomenology

Berger, P. L. and Luckmann, T. (1967) *The Social Construction of Reality: A Treatise in the Sociology of Knowledge*. New York: Anchor.
A classic read that explored post-positivist thinking including phenomenology, relativism and constructionism before they were even defined. Not the easiest read, but a thought-provoking one.

Peoples, K. (2020) *How to Write a Phenomenological Dissertation: A Step-by-Step Guide*. London: Sage.
A solid translation of theory into methods. It offers students pathways for the conduct of a phenomenological study with some good practical elements.

Liu-Lastres, B., Huang, W. and Bao, H. (2023) 'Exploring hospitality workers' career choices in the wake of COVID-19: Insights from a phenomenological inquiry', *International Journal of Hospitality Management, 111*: 103485.
See Box 8.4 above.

Smith, J., Flowers, P. and Larkin, M. (2009) *Interpretative Phenomenological Analysis: Theory, Method and Research.* London: Sage.
It can be difficult to find books that concentrate on phenomenology as a methodology – rather than a philosophical theory – but this one does a pretty good job. Labelled interpretative phenomenological analysis, it covers the steps one can follow to produce phenomenological research.

van Manen, M. (2014) *Phenomenology of Practice: Meaning-Giving Methods in Phenomenological Research and Writing.* Abingdon: Routledge.
This is a really comprehensive book that moves between some of the philosophical traditions of phenomenology and its methods. If you really want to take on the challenge of understanding lived experience, this is worth reading.

Ethnomethodology

Francis, D. and Hester, S. (2004) *An Invitation to Ethnomethodology.* London: Sage.
The authors outline a research strategy referred to as observational sociology, which is based in ethnomethodology and conversation analysis. Its strength comes in the way the authors challenge readers to conduct observational sociology studies within their domains, starting with their family.

Garfinkel, H. (1967) *Studies in Ethnomethodology.* Englewood Cliffs, NJ: Prentice Hall.
The classic work from the father of ethnomethodology. In fact, it is this work that defines our understanding of this approach to knowing. Well worth a read.

Lynch, M. and Sharrock, W. (eds) (2009) *Ethnomethodology.* London: Sage.
A four-volume set that comprehensively looks at unmasking the hidden rules of practice that construct conversation and interaction. Some interesting insights for exploring social order and social change.

Ten Have, P. (2014) *Understanding Qualitative Research and Ethnomethodology.* London: Sage.
We think this book does a good job of exploring the relationship between more traditional qualitative methods and ethnomethodology, and it argues that ethnomethodological approaches can enhance what we know about our world.

Feminist Perspectives

Ackerly, B. and True, J. (2019) *Doing Feminist Research in Political and Social Science.* London: Red Globe Press.
We like the authors' focus on doing, while still engaging in the debates and challenges common to feminist approaches.

Kelly, M. and Gurr, B. (2019) *Feminist Research in Practice*. Lanham, MD: Rowman & Littlefield.
It takes critical awareness to truly execute feminist methodologies. This book keeps the need for this awareness at the fore, while still giving practical guidance.

Leavy, P. and Harris, A. (2018) *Contemporary Feminist Research from Theory to Practice*. New York: Guilford Press.
This book also bridges the gap between theory and practice. It premises building empathic understanding of diverse individuals.

Nagy Hesse-Biber, S. J. and Leavy, P. L. (eds) (2013) *Feminist Research Practice: A Primer*, 2nd edition. London: Sage.
This work offers a good range of feminist perspectives and draws on in-depth examples from ethnography, oral history, focus groups, content analysis, interviewing and survey research.

Sprague, J. (2016) *Feminist Methodologies for Critical Researchers: Bridging Differences*, 2nd edition. Lanham, MD: AltaMira Press.
Rather than align feminist methodology with the qualitative paradigm, this work argues that a critical stance can enhance all methods and that all methods, including surveys and experiments, are capable of making valuable contributions to knowledge.

Rhee, J. (2020). *Decolonial Feminist Research: Haunting, Rememory and Mothers*. Abingdon: Routledge.
A personal and profound work that explores what methodologies are available to notice and study a reality that exceeds and defies modern scientific ontology and intelligibility. As a Korean migrant to American and educational qualitative researcher, Rhee weaves her own perspectives and insights into these questions for research and life.

9

UNDERSTANDING METHODOLOGIES

Mixed Approaches

Learning Objectives

- Arguments for mixed methodology
  - To understand the value of capitalizing on quantitative and qualitative traditions
  - To understand the value of approaches that supersede paradigmatic divides
- Challenges and possibilities
  - To understand the challenges associated with mixed-methods studies and what it takes to overcome them
- Perspectives and strategies
  - To be familiar with options for integrating quantitative and qualitative studies/data
  - To be able to demonstrate credibility in mixed-methods studies
- Managing and analysing mixed data
  - To understand the cost/benefits of managing and analysing complex data

ARGUMENTS FOR MIXED METHODOLOGY

Endless variations and ideas arrive, sometimes just in time.

Cat Richards (2020)

The previous chapter explored quantitative and qualitative traditions by focusing on the premises of each tradition, as well as their tried-and-true approaches. But it is time to mix things up. It is time to ask if, why and when it is appropriate to traverse this traditional divide and employ quantitative and qualitative approaches in a single study, as well as how to go about it.

Mixed approaches are certainly becoming ever more common in social science research. Since the 1980s there has been a growing acceptance of research that traverses the traditional divide of quantitative and qualitative. There are two very good arguments for this. The first is that mixed approaches can overcome the shortcomings and biases inherent in each individual approach. The thinking here is that if a researcher has a paradigmatic preference, if they 'see' themselves as a quantitative or qualitative researcher, then they may be working under a set of assumptions that can narrow their worldview. Accordingly, their ways and means of understanding and exploring the world can be limited.

The second reason, certainly linked to the above, is that mixed approaches have the potential to be expansive. This can start with an openness to various ontologies and epistemologies (see Chapter 1), through to an open-minded approach to the selection of methods of data collection and analysis. This means that mixed-methods research can allow for methodological diversity, complementarity of approaches, and both inductive and deductive reasoning. Researchers can work to creatively develop question-driven approaches no longer limited by paradigm.

Although mixed approaches primarily refer to quantitative and qualitative, a different kind of mixed approach combines conventional Western research with indigenous philosophies or non-Eurocentric worldviews. For example, Botha (2011) argues that mixing methods allows for appropriate theoretical tools and ethical practices for indigenous research, while Martell et al. (2021) show that combining different paradigms as equals can develop a bicultural research framework.

Practically speaking, this allows mixed-methods research to:

- build a broader view by adding depth and insights to 'numbers' through inclusion of dialogue, narratives and pictures;
- add precision to 'words' through inclusion of numbers and statistics (which can make results more generalizable);
- use various research protocols in phased stages;
- facilitate the capture of varied perspectives;
- allow for triangulation.

CHALLENGES AND POSSIBILITIES

All this sounds exceedingly positive. And mixed methodologies certainly make sense; why not take advantage of both traditions and build as rich a picture as possible? This goal is certainly admirable and definitely worth exploring. But as with everything worthwhile, the advantages need to be balanced with an awareness of the obstacles and challenges.

For example, one thing you need to work through is whether or not you are likely to have issues with quantitative and qualitative paradigmatic assumptions that may be at odds with each other. There are definitely traditionalists out there who argue that the assumptions underlying quantitative and qualitative traditions do not allow for a mixed approach. The paradigms are at cross-purposes and cannot work in concert. Others, however, suggest that the logic that underpins various research paradigms is compatible and that methodological choice should always be based on what is useful in answering your question, regardless of any philosophical or paradigmatic assumptions. Ask yourself where you sit. Can you reconcile the traditions? Can you be open to the possibility of more than one way of seeing the world?

If you believe this openness, acceptance and appreciation around methodology is possible, you still need to consider whether you are willing to/have the time to learn about two distinct paradigms and their approaches to exploring the world. This includes the assumptions that underpin both traditions; the techniques they each employ in collecting and analysing data; and how to work towards appropriate criteria for credibility (i.e. understanding the difference between validity and authenticity, reliability and dependability, generalizability and transferability, etc.) and how these are best ensured (see Chapter 4).

Now learning 'about' something is one thing, but you also need to ask yourself if you are willing to practise the research skills associated with both paradigms. Can you become adept at collecting and analysing both quantitative and qualitative data? And this can be a challenge. Open-ended questions, for example, are often asked in 'quantitative' surveys, but rarely analysed to their full potential. Similarly, students who are more familiar with qualitative work, but wish to quantify some of their data, can let a fear of statistics limit their analysis.

Finally, you will need to consider the practicalities associated with using a mixed approach. You are likely to have limits on what you can achieve, so you will need to be mindful of over-ambitious design and the possibility that you are trying to do two projects instead of one.

So given these considerations, is a mixed-methodological approach something you should pursue? Well, as covered in Chapter 7, the main prerequisites in any research design are: (1) that your approach answers your question; (2) that it is right for you as a researcher; and that (3) your design is doable. Thus, deciding on the efficacy of any mixed-methodological approach comes down to the exploration of these criteria. Ask yourself:

1. Do I believe that a mixed approach is the best way to answer my research question? This is, by far, the most crucial question. If a mixed approach does not make sense or add anything to the well-considered research question you wish to answer, then there simply isn't an argument that justifies the use of a mixed-method approach. If, however, after thoughtful consideration, expert opinion and some good old-fashioned reading, you believe the answer is yes, a mixed-method approach is appropriate to the question, then ask:
2. Is this the right approach for me? Am I willing to learn about and develop the skills necessary to carry off more than one approach? Belief, dedication and skills are central to the conduct of credible research, so you need to be honest in your assessment. Talk to your supervisor and other researchers about the challenges of working across two traditions. If you are still up for it, ask:
3. Is this doable? Will a mixed approach be practical due to supervisory, time and/or financial constraints? Practicality must always be taken into account. If your supervisor is uncomfortable with your methods and/or does not feel experienced enough to supervise across both traditions, you will need to think about the issue of support. It will also be a real challenge if you run out of time and money. Deadlines always come up more quickly than you realize, and we know of very few students with unlimited funds.

The idea of the three questions above is to allow you to assess the efficacy of a mixed approach for answering your question, as well as to honestly assess how a mixed approach sits with your perspective on research – while always minding practicalities. After all, what we are after is the most appropriate approach in a real-world situation.

PERSPECTIVES AND STRATEGIES

Okay – you see this mixed-methods stuff as having real potential for your research, and you feel ready to jump in and start designing a study that can collect both qualitative and quantitative data. Well before you get going, it is worth knowing that there are a number of ways to think about and approach a mixed study – at both theoretical and operational levels.

Theoretical Perspectives

At a theoretical level, there are actually a number of ways to justify the choice of mixed methodology. In fact, if you are going to pursue mixed methods, it is good to consider your beliefs about mixed approaches and your justification for their adoption. One potential breakdown of these perspectives follows:

- Paradigm perspective – With this perspective you allow room for quantitative and qualitative traditions with a broad worldview. Historical distinctions such as quantitative and qualitative are seen as constructs that can be rewritten – and in fact should be rewritten, as more holistic knowledge of the world evolves.
- Methodology perspective – With this perspective paradigmatic assumptions are seen as real/distinct, but quantitative and qualitative traditions are both seen as valued. Methodologies and methods thus follow appropriate paradigm-based rules and are treated discretely. Both, however, should be incorporated in a single study in order to capitalize on complementary strengths.
- Research question perspective – With this perspective, methods are determined by the research question. It is logic that determines the appropriateness of a mixed approach, rather than any paradigm. This might also be called a non-paradigmatic stance where issues of design sit below explicit paradigmatic considerations. This is often the case in small-scale/applied research.
- Methods/data perspective – With this perspective mixed methods are a means for collecting and analysing both quantitative and qualitative data (number and words/ images) and as such are not inherently tied to issues of paradigms. Words and numbers would be a part of any and all paradigms.

Operational Perspectives

The theoretical perspectives discussed above will help you rationalize your choice of a mixed approach and help you develop arguments around the credibility of your methodological approach. But they only go so far in telling you how to go about your research – how to operationalize your mixed methodology. And there is definitely more than one way to attack a mixed study with each approach leading you to quite varied research designs and research strategies.

Quantitative Approach with Acceptance of Qualitative Data

Zina was once told (by a statistician) that mixed methodology was all about adding a bit of qualitative flesh to quantitative bones. The underlying premise here is, no surprise, that at the heart of a mixed approach is a belief in the quantitative. Researchers who think this way tend to accept the underlying assumptions of the quantitative tradition but are willing to accept that qualitative data might help 'flesh out' their study. And there are certainly benefits in this qualitative colour – both for depth of understanding and for construction of more powerful narratives – but qualitative data is generally seen as the second cousin.

The most common example here is designing a survey that asks a few open-ended questions that allow for further exploration within a closed question survey; for example, you survey your sample using yes/no, agree/disagree, **Likert scale** items and ranking scales – but then ask for further explanation that allows respondents to write out their responses. And while asking for more depth makes sense, the challenge for those ensconced in a quantitative paradigm who have decided to collect qualitative data is allowing the qualitative data to do the work that such data can/should. In fact, it is not uncommon for this type of qualitative survey data to be (1) quantified or (2) ignored.

The warning here is that even if using qualitative data as a supplement within a more quantitative study, there is still a need to engage with qualitative thinking/methods that allow that qualitative data to do their job effectively.

Qualitative Approach with Acceptance of Quantitative Data

It probably won't come as a surprise, but there are actually a few qualitative researchers out there who are a bit wary of numbers. Their predilection for quality over quantity has left them questioning whether working with quantities means a lack of quality. Luckily this position is softening, with more and more qualitative researchers accepting the power of numbers and recognizing that they can be capitalized on, even given the underlying assumptions of the qualitative tradition.

So how might this manifest? Well, one example might be an ethnographic study that embeds a small community survey; for example, you are exploring the local church community trying to get a feel for what it means to be a member of this church. In fact, you've joined the church and rented a small nearby apartment for a month. And while you are getting much from the lived experience, you decide to supplement your ethnographic research with a short community survey.

Another possibility is that you conduct a series of in-depth interviews and decide to quantitatively code the data for tallying/statistical analysis; for example, you decide to explore the church community through a series of 50 interviews. As you look for themes, you realize that with 50 respondents, it might be of value to produce a few pie charts or bar graphs to visually represent some of your findings.

You might also complement a case study with an examination of existing data; for example, you delve into the church community and engage in interviews and observation. But you also look at attendance figures and membership data that the church has kept over the last ten years.

The basic premise here is that in-depth exploration under a qualitative framework will best answer the research question, but that quantification, of at least some of the data, makes sense and can add to the analysis. Whether in the form of an embedded survey, quantifying what is traditionally seen as qualitative data or exploring existing data, quantitative data can add breadth to a study and may even work towards making it more representative. The warning, however, parallels that given in the previous section. Even if using quantitative data as a supplement to a more qualitative study, there is still a need to engage with quantitative thinking/methods that allow quantitative data to do their job effectively.

Phased Approach

A really interesting practice in mixed methods is using one method to build the efficacy of another. You might, for example, conduct a few key informant interviews at the start of a project in order to facilitate the development of a survey; for example, you interview a foreman and the head occupational health and safety officer of a mining company in order to determine the main issues that affect workplace stress so that you can produce a relevant employee survey. This is sometimes called an instrument design model – in this case, the final analysis will be quantitative, but the quantitative tool used to generate these results is reliant on qualitative methods.

On the flip side you might conduct key informant interviews after a survey to add depth to survey findings; for example, you conduct your survey on employee stress, analyse results and then have focus groups to discuss key issues arising from the analysis. This is sometimes referred to as an explanatory model. The phase two qualitative data is there to offer fuller and richer explication of the quantitative findings. Of course, there is also the possibility that new and unexpected findings will be uncovered through this type of process. The challenge is knowing how to integrate findings that do something other than validate and expand upon your survey results – a difficult, but rewarding situation.

Triangulation Approach

The thinking behind the triangulation approach is that confirmation of any particular data source occurs through comparison and validation of a different data source. So rather than being reliant on survey data alone, or solely interview data, or only data from a document analysis, studies designed under a triangulation banner, by design, gather various types of data to look for corroboration that improves the overall robustness and credibility of a study.

Under the banner of a triangulation approach, gathering quantitative and qualitative data need not happen simultaneously. Data collection is not phased; one process does not rely on another. In fact, data-collection processes are designed to be independent of each other. Data is analysed separately with integration occurring through discussion of commonalities and divergences. The challenge occurs when varied sources of divergent data point to different results, and triangulation does not occur. In this case, researchers need to reflexively consider both methodological design and the robustness of potential findings.

Question-Driven Approach

This is a direct operationalization of the theoretical position discussed above. The question-driven approach involves putting questions before paradigm, and premises neither the quantitative nor the qualitative tradition. It simply asks what strategies are most likely to get the credible data needed to answer the research question; and sees researchers adopting whatever array of strategies they think can accomplish the task, regardless of paradigm.

As required by the research question, this can include any of the quantitative, qualitative or phased approaches discussed above. It might also involve a study that is looking for both in-depth understanding and broader representation; for example, a project on the experience of bullying in a local high school that asks what it feels like (suited to phenomenological approaches) and how common it is (suited to survey research).

Another possibility is a study that targets two groups of respondents that require different approaches; for example, a study exploring workplace culture that targets general employees (suited to survey research) and upper-level management (suited to key informant interviews). In Zina's work, she finds this a very common driver of mixed-methods approaches. She generally works with students doing applied research in organizational settings. Students need to develop a work-based research question that can be answered in a matter of weeks or months. It is recommended that research questions be tight and highly useful to their organization. Because of the work-based nature of their project, a good percentage of students want to understand how individuals within an organization feel about a new challenge, new practice, new policy, impending threat, etc. And for many that means engaging with a variety of stakeholder groups and needing an array of strategies to accomplish this. Interviews, focus groups and surveys often become part of the same methodological plan – simply because it is deemed to be the best/most efficient way to gather the necessary data.

We are advocates of the question-driven perspective. And that is because we value both the quantitative and qualitative traditions and understand the strengths and shortcomings of each. So we are open to anything from classic quantitative and qualitative approaches to quite eclectic multi-method approaches. The criteria for design is simply what will gather the most credible data possible (see Box 9.1). As well, we believe that even when selecting from the approaches listed above, a key criterion should be whether an approach will best answer your question in a practicable way. This makes the question-driven approach compatible with the reflective decision-making you will need to make about all the other approaches.

Box 9.1

Mixed-Methodology Exemplar – 'The Hawthorne Studies'

Between 1924 and 1932 a series of experiments were conducted at the Hawthorne Plant of the Western Electric Company on factors (such as lighting, breaks, hours of work) that might impact on productivity (Mayo, 1933; Roethlisberger and Dickson, 1939). To the surprise of the researchers, outputs generally increased anytime a variable was manipulated, even when this was counterintuitive or the manipulation was simply to change the variable back to how it was originally. The act of changing a variable, in any way, increased productivity.

(Continued)

Such confounded findings (the phenomenon of behaviour changing simply by being observed, now known as the Hawthorne effect) led to the development of a mixed-methodological approach designed to offer a more holistic understanding of factors related to productivity. From 1928 to 1932, researchers interviewed about 21,000 employees at the Hawthorne Plant on issues such as worker attitudes, morale, home life, upbringing, diet and other habits. They also engaged in observation, closely monitoring the daily activities of one particular work group. The original experimental methods were thus complemented by more qualitative strategies.

Photo 9.1 Hawthorne plant. 'Women in the Relay Assembly Test Room', ca. 1930

Western Electric Company Hawthorne Studies Collection © 2007 President and Fellows of Harvard College; all rights reserved

MANAGING AND ANALYSING MIXED DATA

The best ideas emerge when very different perspectives meet.

Frans Johansson (2011)

You are going to end up with two or more sources of data (from your mixed approaches), likely to include two types of data (both quantitative and qualitative). That is an awful lot to take on, because you have to manage these data and then you're going to have to analyse them. This means you need to plan.

You will need to design a plan for logging and entering your quantitative data. If you have more than one source of quantitative data, you will need to decide if you will manage and analyse each source separately or if you will combine them into a single database and analyse them together. If you take the second option of combining the sources, you will still need to identify the source of the data to keep yourself open to the possibility of delineating the sources in the future.

Qualitative data also need to be meticulously managed. Now keep in mind, you may have more than one source of qualitative data. For example, if you have interview data, you're likely to have digital recordings. You need to decide how you will label, save and store these. And then there is the possibility of transcriptions. If you decide to transcribe your interviews, you will need to develop a system for labelling, saving and storing them for analysis. You may also have notes on each interview. These too will need systematic management.

Another source of qualitative data might be documents. These documents need to be managed and organized as well. You also need to decide how you will log culled sections of the documents. Finally, you'll need to decide whether you will combine your interview and document data and do a singular analysis or whether you'll analyse them separately.

Decisions, decisions, decisions ... and a massive need for systematic organization. But this also brings up another issue, and that is doability. What is the scope and scale of your project? How long do you have to complete? Mixed approaches are fabulous for giving us broad views and triangulated findings, but they demand much more of your time. In the quest for credibility, you do not want to take on more than what is feasible. To do so can cast a shadow on the validity of your findings.

Now let's not forget about analysis. When it comes to actually analysing data derived from mixed approaches, this is always done by data type. So for quantitative data, you would follow the advice given in Chapter 15. Analysing qualitative data is addressed in Chapter 16.

Critical Thinking Challenge 10

A Cost-Benefit of Mixed Methods

As with most things in life, there tends to be a trade-off. While there are definite benefits to taking a mixed approach, it doesn't come without costs. For this critical thinking challenge, we'd like you to analyse both the cost and benefits of undertaking mixed methods. We've put a few headings in Table 9.1 to get you started, but there may be things you'd like to add. Filling this table out will not only help you determine the value of taking on a mixed approach, it'll also help you work through some of the challenges you're likely to face.

Table 9.1 Template for doing a cost-benefit analysis of a mixed-methods approach

MIXED METHODS	
COSTS	**BENEFITS**
Time	Quality
Resources	Triangulation
Skill development	Breadth
Timeline	Credibility
$$	Broad skills
Depth	

I Have a Question!

I Know That There Are Qualitative Data Analysis Programs and, Of Course, Stats Programs but Is There Anything Specifically Designed for Mixed-Methods Studies?

We'll talk about this in the analysis chapters, but yes, there actually are specific mixed-methods analysis programs. Product developers are starting to recognize the need. At least two qualitative products are now integrating quantitative data into their functionality. MAXQDA, www.maxqda.com/products/maxqda/mixed-methods-functions, allows you to import and export quantitative data to and from stats packages like SPSS. QDA Miner, http://provalisresearch.com/products/qualitative-data-analysis-software, also allows for the integration of quantitative data, While QDA Miner is qualitative tool, it does offer integration with SimStat, http://provalisresearch.com/products/simstat, a statistical data analysis tool, and WordStat, http://provalisresearch.com/products/content-analysis-software, a quantitative content analysis and text mining tool. Another good option is Dedoose, www.dedoose.com. Dedoose markets itself as the only truly mixed-methods analysis tool. It is a cross-platform tool that allows you to work with data from a variety of sources including text, audio, video, Word documents, Excel spreadsheets, Access databases, SurveyMonkey, etc. This type of program would be particularly useful if your mixed-methods approach finds you combining various data types prior to analysis.

CREDIBILITY IN MIXED-METHODS RESEARCH

We want to end this chapter with a quick note on appropriate credibility criteria for mixed-methods studies. Now, while the advice in Chapter 4 is all relevant here, it is worth pointing out challenges particular to mixed approaches. Basically, the challenges associated with mixed methods centre on the need to be very clear on what you are trying to achieve, and thus what credibility indicators are appropriate for your work.

The indicators that are most expected and accepted in quantitative work are: objectivity, validity, reliability, generalizability and reproducibility. These are not only the gold standard for quantitative research but are often seen as the gold standard for all research. So what happens when you incorporate qualitative research into a basically quantitative study, and you are no longer working with **representative samples**, or even a single verifiable truth? How do you credibly weave in post-positivist indicators such as neutrality, authenticity, dependability, transferability and auditability; and is it even appropriate to do so?

And what happens if you are arguing a more post-positivist, qualitative framework and you suddenly want to argue the importance of a representative sample? Can you work between the two sets of assumptions that drive these paradigms in a way that allows your research to be seen as credible?

Well, we think it can be done; and would suggest it be done method by method. The steps you might want to include are: (1) make sure your use of a mixed approach is warranted; (2) ensure that each method you employ will add important/insightful data to your research; (3) make sure you are engaged in best practice for that particular method; (4) show how your best-practice approach meets the credibility indicators appropriate to your particular research method. As long as the question that each method is trying to explore is well matched and you can show rigour in your processes, you should be able to make sound arguments for using indicators that span the quantitative/qualitative divide.

Chapter Summary

- Studies with mixed methodologies traverse traditional divides and employ quantitative and qualitative approaches in a single study. If well handled, they can capitalize on the best of both traditions while overcoming their shortcomings.
- Challenges associated with mixed-methods studies include being familiar with the presumptions of both traditions, developing skills in their respective data-collection/analysis protocols, as well as managing the time and fiscal constraints of working across two traditions.
- There are several ways to frame mixed-method approaches. Mixed approaches can be integrated at the level of paradigm, methodology, research question or method.
- Mixed approaches can be premised in the quantitative tradition with acceptance of qualitative data, the qualitative tradition with acceptance of quantitative data, be based on phases of qualitative and quantitative methods, work towards triangulation or be driven by research questions themselves.

FIND YOUR NEXT STEP

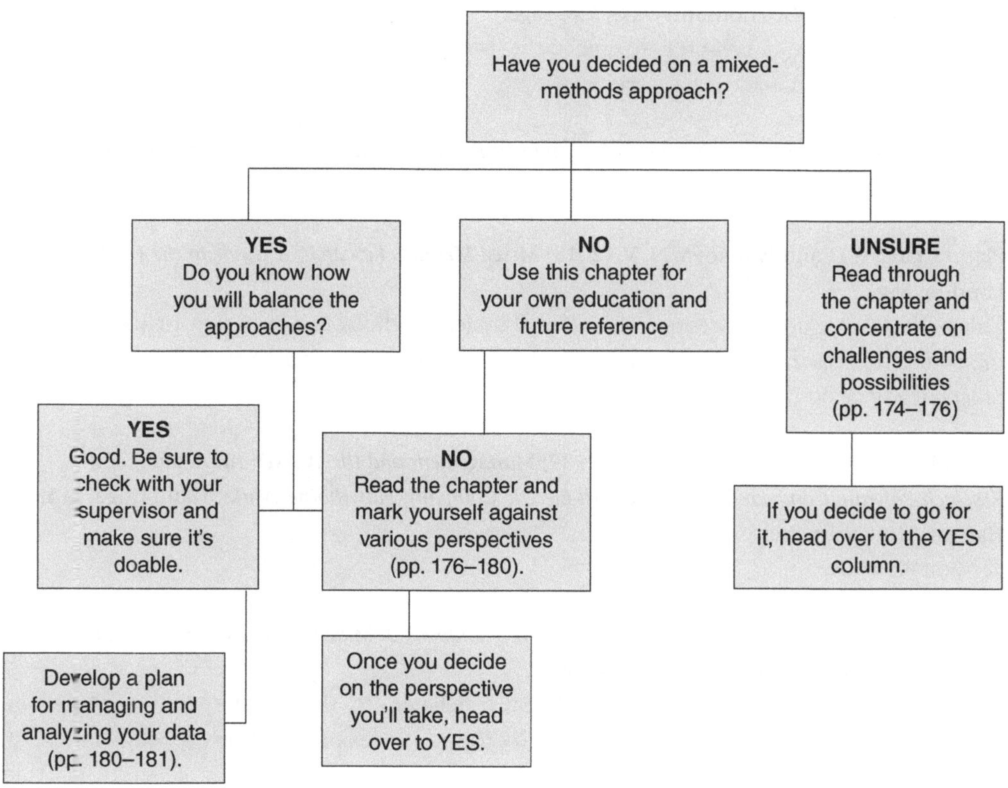

FURTHER READING

If you are enticed by a mixed-methods approach, you may want to delve into some more specialist readings. The following list offers some more recent work in the 'mixed' area.

Mixed Methodology

Creswell, D. and Creswell, J. W. (2023) *Research Design: Qualitative, Quantitative and Mixed Methods Approaches*, 6th edition. London: Sage.
We like that this book is very user-friendly, avoids jargon and offers clear guidance. A great place to start your exploration of methodological considerations.

Creswell, J. W. (2021) *A Concise Introduction to Mixed Methods Research*, 2nd edition. London: Sage.
By design, mixed methods draws from two approaches for which you may already have readings. If this is the case, an overview such as this gives you the logic that you need to effectively combine quantitative and qualitative approaches.

Creswell, J. W. and Plano Clark, V. L. (2017) *Designing and Conducting Mixed Methods Research*. London: Sage.
A great step-by-step guide that offers six different approaches to mixed-method design. The use of published mixed-method studies as examples adds to the work.

Fetters, M. (2019) *The Mixed Methods Research Workbook: Activities for Designing, Implementing, and Publishing Projects*. Thousand Oaks, CA: Sage.
We love a workbook – a great way to embed the learning through doing. Perfect if you are stuck and not sure how to make it happen.

Mayo, E. (1933) *The Human Problems of an Industrial Civilization*. New York: Viking Press.
See Box 9.1 above.

Plano Clark, V. L. and Ivankova, N. V. (2015) *Mixed Methods Research: A Guide to the Field*. London: Sage.
This book takes a deeper theoretical dive into mixed methods in a way that helps you frame mixed methods as more than drawing from two different paradigms. This is complemented by practical advice on how to action these methods.

Roethlisberger, F. J. and Dickson, W. J. (1939) *Management and the Worker: An Account of a Research Program Conducted by the Western Electric Company, Hawthorne Works*. Cambridge, MA: Harvard University Press.
See Box 9.1 above.

Tashakkori, A. and Teddlie, C. (eds) (2010) *SAGE Handbook of Mixed Methods in Social and Behavioral Research*. Thousand Oaks, CA: Sage.
This is a comprehensive handbook that really delves into the debates and controversies surrounding mixed-methods approaches. Good specific examples from a wide range of disciplines.

Mixed Approaches for Decolonizing Research

Botha L. (2011) 'Mixing methods as a process towards indigenous methodologies', *International Journal of Social Research Methodology*, 14(4): 313–325. https://doi.org/10.1080/13645579.2010.516644

A theoretical discussion and exemplar of Botha's own research that mixes conventional qualitative methods with indigenous research. Also helpful to read alongside Chapter 10.

Martel, R., Shepherd, M. and Goodyear-Smith, F. (2021) 'He awa whiria—a "braided river": an indigenous Māori approach to mixed methods research', *Journal of Mixed Methods Research*, 16(1): 17–33. https://doi.org/10.1177/1558689820984028.

A clear example of bicultural mixed-methods research from New Zealand that uses the metaphor of a braided river as a way of connecting paradigms as equals. Helpful diagrams that connect some of the 'ologies' from Chapter 1 with practical examples.

10

UNDERSTANDING METHODOLOGIES

Evaluative, Action-Oriented and Emancipatory Strategies

Learning Objectives

- Research that attempts to drive change
    - To understand various research agendas and their relationship to change
- Evaluative research
    - To understand the goals and methods of outcome evaluation
    - To understand the goals and methods of process evaluation
    - To be aware of the politics inherent in evaluative research
    - To be able to negotiate the real-world challenges of evaluative research
- Action research
    - To understand the scope and key elements of action research
    - To be aware of the challenges associated with action research
- Emancipatory research
    - To understand the goals and agendas of emancipatory research
    - To understand the basics of participatory action research and critical ethnography

RESEARCH THAT ATTEMPTS TO DRIVE CHANGE

The purpose of man is in action, not thought.

Thomas Carlyle (1833–4)

Chapters 8 and 9 explored methodology paradigmatically – that is, they explored approaches to research according to various traditions. But the structure of Chapter 10 is somewhat different. In this chapter, methodologies are discussed by goals rather than a particular paradigmatic positioning. We look at methodologies according to objectives, in particular change-oriented objectives.

Now you may be thinking, all research is about the potential for change, isn't it? Shouldn't research lead to problem resolution, situation improvement or progress? Well, as shown in Figure 10.1, the goals of research can be placed on a continuum from knowledge to change. At one end is basic or 'pure' research that attempts to produce knowledge in order to better understand the world. At the other end of the continuum is research that is conducted for the purpose of radical change to dominant structures. Those two ends of the continuum may seem worlds apart, but we would argue they are not diametrically opposed.

As far as the pursuit of pure research is concerned, we cannot think of too many 'ivory tower' researchers who conduct their research without some practical purpose in mind. In fact, all research proposals demand a rationale that highlights the scientific or social significance of the research questions posed. In this type of research, however, applying findings is not part of the researcher's agenda. For those involved in applied/evaluative research, change is more closely tied to a project's objectives. Knowledge production is, in fact, driven by the immediate need for information that can facilitate practical, effective, evidence-based decision-making. Action research takes this a step further – and rather than expect change because of research, it actually demands change through research processes. Finally, **emancipatory research** attacks change at the most fundamental levels, and includes liberation and self-determination in its agenda.

All researchers want their research to be useful, at least at some level, in the real world. The question is whether that usefulness involves the production of knowledge that may eventually lead to change, or whether change itself will be a direct product of the research process. Regardless, it is well worth seeing research as a political endeavour.

EVALUATIVE RESEARCH

If there is one thing we are not short of it is initiatives. In order to improve a situation, we are willing to try new things: new products, new practices, new policies, new legislation, new interventions, new programmes, new strategies, new structures, new routines, new procedures, new curricula, etc., etc. But how successful are our endeavours? Did whatever we try do whatever it was supposed to do? Have we been able to make some contribution towards positive change? Have we been able to alleviate a problem situation? Answering these types of questions is the goal of evaluative research.

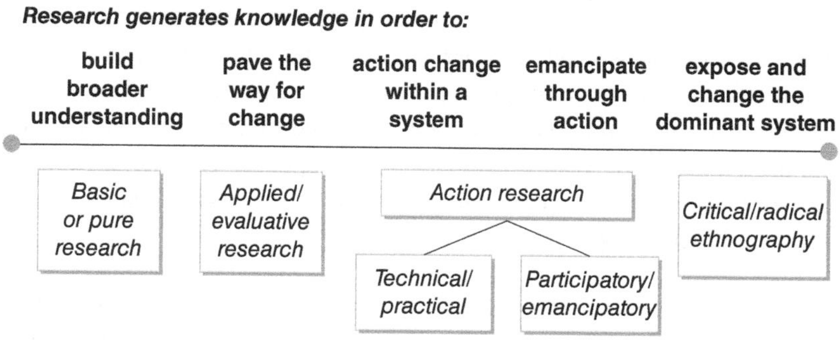

Figure 10.1 From knowledge to change - the goals of research

The need for evaluative studies is ever increasing. A well-conducted evaluation is now a key strategy for supplying decision-makers with the data they need for rational, informed, evidence-based decision-making. In fact, change intervention proposals increasingly require evaluative components so that assessment is embedded into the management of change from conception.

Evaluative studies basically attempt to determine whether an initiative should be continued as is, modified, expanded or scrapped, and do this by asking various stakeholder groups two types of questions. The first is related to outcomes; for example, did a particular initiative meet its objectives? The second is related to process; for example, how successful was a particular initiative's implementation and how might it be improved?

Summative/Outcome Evaluation

Summative evaluation, also referred to as outcome evaluation, aims to provide data and information related to the effectiveness of the change strategy in question (that goals, aims and objectives have been met) and its efficiency (that the effects justify the costs). The idea here is to investigate whether an initiative is responsible for outcomes that would not have occurred if it were not for the initiative, and this should include both intended and unintended effects. Now in the real world, the financial bottom line is almost always a factor, so many outcome evaluations also include data related to cost-effectiveness, often in the form of a cost–benefit analysis.

The results of outcome evaluations are expected to inform decision-making related to programme funding, continuation, termination, expansion and reduction. While findings are often case-specific, results can be of interest to any number of stakeholder groups and, depending on the nature of the change intervention, might be of interest to the wider population as well.

Methods Appropriate to Summative Evaluation

So what exactly is involved in the conduct of an evaluative study? Well, rather than be defined by any particular methods, an evaluative study is distinguished by its evaluative goals, and it is these goals that determine the appropriate approach. In summative evaluation, the main goal is to find out if an initiative worked. In other words, whether it met its objectives. As shown in Table 10.1, initiatives often have multiple objectives that are likely to vary for each stakeholder group. As an evaluator exploring outcomes, you will need to determine whether success is to be measured from the perspective of the provider, the recipients, the wider community or all of these. You need to determine which outcome objectives are to be explored and whose perspectives you seek. Your methods will then vary accordingly.

- Provider perspective – When designing methods, there are two general ways to find out if providers believe an initiative is a success. This first is to ask. Interviews and focus groups (see Chapter 12) allow you to talk to those responsible for design, delivery and implementation, as well as those with a higher level of organizational responsibility. The second method is to look at documentary evidence (see Chapter 13). This is particularly relevant for questions that focus on cost-effectiveness, or anywhere that evidence of success is likely to be in the 'records'.
- Recipient perspective – This is where you really get down to brass tacks and see if the initiative's change-oriented outcome objectives have been met. Many (including Zina) would argue that the best way to do this is through experimental or quasi-experimental designs (see Chapter 8) that allow for comparison across groups and time. There are three possibilities here:
    - Case/control design – To see whether an initiative has made a difference for a target group, you can use a control group to compare those who have undergone an initiative with those who have not.
    - Before/after design – Sometimes called 'time series analysis', this approach allows for comparison of the same group of individuals before and after an initiative is implemented.
    - Case/control – before/after design – This allows for even more definitive results by combining the two methods above.

Table 10.1 Evaluative methods

	Provider perspective	**Recipient perspective**	**Wider perspective**
Outcome			
Did it work?	Was it cost-effective/ beneficial to the provider?	Was there a real change in the target group?	Did it meet a wider community need?
	Potential methods:	Potential methods:	Potential methods:
	Document review Key informant Interviews Focus groups	Experimentation/quasi-experimentation using control groups or before/after data Exploration of post group only by survey/interview	Surveys Focus groups

	Provider perspective	Recipient perspective	Wider perspective
Process			
How could it be improved?	What were the strengths/weaknesses? How could the process be made more efficient/effective for the organization?	What were the strengths/weaknesses? How could the process be made more efficient/effective for those it is intended to benefit?	What were the strengths/weaknesses? How could the process be made more efficient/effective for the community?
	Potential methods:	Potential methods:	Potential methods:
	Interviews with key organizational stakeholders Focus groups Observation Document review	Surveys Focus groups Interviews	Surveys Focus groups Interviews (often key informants/stakeholders)

All three of these approaches require forward planning and, as discussed at the end of this section, this is not always possible. The alternative is to evaluate perceptions of change, rather than change itself, by surveying or interviewing recipients after implementation (see Chapter 12). The goal here is to see if recipients believe that change has occurred.

- Wider community perspective – Initiatives often include objectives related to stakeholder groups that are not direct recipients. For example, a school initiative to curtail bullying may include an objective related to decreasing parent/community anxiety. Or a health-care initiative may include an objective related to improving an organization's reputation in the community. The methods of choice here are surveys and focus groups (Chapter 12). And while such approaches generally ask community members to report on their perceptions and recent changes in those perceptions, the collection of similar data prior to the initiative will allow you to engage in direct comparison.

Formative/Process Evaluation

Formative evaluation, also referred to as **process evaluation**, aims to provide data and information that will aid further development of a particular change initiative. Such studies investigate an initiative's delivery and ask how, and how well, it is being implemented. These studies can assess strengths, weaknesses, opportunities and threats, and often work to assess the factors acting to facilitate and/or block successful implementation.

The results derived from process evaluations are expected to inform decision-making related to programme improvement, modification and management. And while these studies also tend to be case-specific, 'transferable' findings will allow other organizations interested in the use of any similar initiatives to apply 'lessons learned' (see Chapter 4).

Methods Appropriate to Formative Evaluation

As highlighted in Table 10.1, the main objective in formative or process evaluation is to assess an initiative's strengths and weaknesses and ask how the process could be made more efficient and effective. Stakeholder perspectives again play an important role here since providers, recipients and the wider community are likely to have quite varied opinions on what did and did not work so well. Design of methods is, therefore, highly dependent on working out precisely what you want to know and whose perspective you seek:

- Provider perspective – The methods you use here will be highly dependent on the complexity and diversity of the groups responsible for provision. For example, at one end of the spectrum you might be asked to evaluate a classroom initiative driven by a particular teacher. In this case, an in-depth interview would make most sense (see Chapter 12). At the other end of the spectrum, you might be evaluating a new government health-care policy whose design, development and implementation have involved individuals working at various levels of government and private industry. With this level of complexity you might need to call on multiple methods – interviews, focus groups and even surveys – to gather the data you require (see Chapter 12). There might also be value in direct observation of the process or in a document review that finds you trolling through and examining records and minutes related to the process being explored (see Chapter 13).
- Recipient perspective – Just because management thinks something went well doesn't mean recipients will think the same. Good process evaluations will go beyond the provider perspective and seek recipient opinions on strengths, weaknesses and potential modifications. As with providers, target groups also vary in size and complexity, and you might find yourself calling on a variety of methods, including interviews, focus groups and surveys, to gather the data you require (see Chapter 12).
- Wider community perspective – The first question you need to ask here is 'Do you or your "client" want wider community opinion?' You might not feel that the wider community is a relevant stakeholder, or that broader community groups have the prerequisite knowledge for providing an informed opinion. On the other hand, the initiative under review might have far-reaching implications that affect the community or might be related to a problem where the community sees itself as a key stakeholder; for example, an initiative aiming to stop neighbourhood graffiti. In this situation, canvassing wider opinion on an initiative's strengths and weaknesses may be of value. The methods most likely to be called upon here are surveys, focus groups and possibly key informant interviews (see Chapter 12).

The Politics of Evaluative Research

> It is important for scientists to be aware of what our discoveries mean, socially and politically. It's a noble goal that science should be apolitical, acultural, and asocial, but it can't be, because it's done by people who are all those things.
>
> Mae Jemison (2001)

It is said that all research is political, but none more so than evaluative research. It would be naive to pretend otherwise. Vested interests are everywhere and the pressure for researchers to find 'success' can be high.

So how do you begin to negotiate and balance the sometimes divergent political and scientific goals of evaluative research? The first step is to understand researcher–researched realities and relationships. For example, those seeking to have initiatives evaluated do not always have the same goals. Yes, some want honest and open feedback, but others might be after validation of what they have done, while others might just be doing what they need to do to meet funding requirements. And of course, some may be after a combination of these.

The same is true of researchers, whether insiders or outsiders; not all evaluative researchers operate with the same style, skills or goals. For example, some see themselves as objective researchers whose clear and unwavering objective is credible findings regardless of political context. Others operate at a more political level and are highly in tune with government/organization/political funding realities, and perhaps their own ongoing consultancy opportunities. There are others who tend to be overcritical and need to show their intelligence by picking holes in the work of others. Finally, there are those who see themselves as facilitators or even mentors who are there to help.

When Zina first began doing evaluative research she came across and learnt from all of these styles and assumed that my way forward would be as an objective researcher. But she soon realized that the political end of evaluative research cannot be ignored and that the key to real-world evaluation is flexibility. Now her main grounding objective, which is tied to her own professional ethics, is to produce credible and useful findings. But how those findings are presented, what is emphasized and what is sometimes best left unsaid are undeniably influenced by both politics and context.

Table 10.2 looks at the intersection of researcher–researched goals in terms of researcher credibility and researcher–researched relationships. While the matrix does not capture all possibilities, it does provide some insights into the realities of evaluative research and the skills required to work effectively in such a politically charged environment.

Table 10.2 Relationships in evaluative research

Clients who seek ... **Evaluators whose style tends to be that of ...**	**Honest feedback**	**Validation**	**To meet funding requirements**
The critic			
Credibility: can be difficult to build trust, thereby influencing data/findings. Findings tend to overemphasize the negative and not point out the positive	While the clients may appreciate knowing their initiative's shortcomings, they can be left feeling deflated and undervalued by the critic	This relationship spells trouble. Clients are likely to be demoralized, disheartened and even angry. Critics are likely to burn their bridges here	Those who do not appreciate the value of evaluation are likely to be further put off by the critic. There is a good chance here of weakening trust and building resentment

(Continued)

Table 10.2 (Continued)

Clients who seek ... Evaluators whose style tends to be that of ...	**Honest feedback**	**Validation**	**To meet funding requirements**
The unbiased scientist			
Credibility: best odds of credible data/findings, particularly if the approach is one that attempts to build trust while collecting unbiased data	A good match, but still no harm in the 'scientist' honing political skills. Even those who want honest feedback appreciate diplomacy	While findings might be fair, how they are accepted and acted upon by those seeking validation often depends on a researcher's sensitivity and communication skills	Relationships tend to be enhanced by supportive findings and a researcher's interpersonal skills – communication skills can be instrumental in 'selling' the value of evaluation
The facilitator/mentor			
Credibility: likely to result in credible findings if the initiative is a success. There can be a tendency to gloss over shortcomings and emphasize the positive. Can lead to thorough process-related recommendations	While relationships are generally positive, clients can be frustrated if they feel they are not getting the feedback/hard data they need for effective decision-making	This is actually a good match that can leave clients feeling their work is valued. Good chance that process-related recommendations will be taken up	Mentors might be able to build trust and instil the value of evaluation. But if clients remain cynical, they may not put a high value on the mentor's recommendations
The politician			
Credibility: findings need to be explored in light of the political context – there is a need to read between the lines. Findings may support the agenda of those commissioning the research	Generally not too problematic as long as expectations are clear. Researcher and client objectives should be made explicit and negotiated so that they are not at cross-purposes	If politician and client goals are the same (i.e. validation), the relationship is likely to be good, even if feedback is uncritical. If, however, goals are at cross-purposes, client satisfaction can be low	This tends to be a good match because goals are usually aligned with a particular agenda. Levels of critical feedback should be discussed and negotiated

Zina has worked with quite a few evaluators and she thinks the best ones are politically astute but always work under a code of professional ethics and integrity. Some will adapt their style depending on the client and context, while others will stay true to a certain way of working. But almost all good evaluators understand the need to negotiate clear expectations that meet both client and researcher needs and goals with integrity.

I Have a Question!

How Should I Go About Writing Up an Evaluation When the Results Aren't so Good?

Carefully! It is worth thinking through your goals as someone doing evaluative research. Zina's are to:

1 conduct a rigorous study;
2 produce credible findings and sound conclusions;
3 make well-considered recommendations;
4 have those recommendations taken up by the organization;
5 possibly be engaged as an evaluator in the future (might as well put that on the table).

So first and foremost you need to conduct your study in ways that ensure research integrity and credibility and that will take care of points 1 and 2 above (see Chapter 4). Where it gets interesting is points 3 and 4 - making well-considered recommendations that the organization will take up. Now this goal is different from offering recommendations. Getting an organization to act means using some political nous. So say your most difficult finding is 'Initiative X did not meet four of six goals' and your recommendation is 'it should not be continued'. Yes, you can go out and say that, but the reality is that sometimes the same people who have engaged you to do the evaluation are invested in the very project you are evaluating. So what do you do?

Well you never fudge the results - but you can make them more palatable. So you might say something like, 'Given the fiscal constraints and challenges in staffing [whatever reasons you found for the lack of success], it is not surprising that Initiative X struggled to meet some of their goals. While goals X1 and X2 were achieved, the initiative did fall short in relation to goals Y1, Y2 [etc.].' Your recommendation might be, 'For this project to meet indicators of success it would require a large investment of funds and at least one dedicated staff member. The organization will need to balance this against competing needs of projects shown to produce results in a more cost-effective manner.' In the end, rather than telling the organization what to do (no one likes to be told what to do), you are laying it out and letting the organization make the hard call.

This type of writing takes practice, but it is well worth it. And not just for you (a combination of credible research and political nous should help you reach point 5 - be re-engaged in the future), it is also valuable for the organization. There is no use doing applied research that shuts your audience down and does not lead to change.

Negotiating Real-World Challenges of Evaluative Research

Political realities are not the only challenge to the production of credible data in evaluative research. Evaluations tend to be conducted within messy and chaotic real-world settings, and you will need to skilfully negotiate this level of complexity if you want to produce solid, valuable results.

Now in an ideal world, all initiatives to be evaluated would be well established with clear and measurable aims and objectives. But rarely is this the case. You often need to find ways to work around circumstances that are less than ideal. Such situations include the following.

When the Decision to Evaluate Comes after Initial Implementation

It would be terrific if the need to evaluate was a recognized part of project planning from conception. You would then have all the options. Early planning would allow you to design comparative studies such as randomized controlled trials, quasi-experiments with control groups, or before and after designs (see Chapter 8). But there are plenty of circumstances where you will need to undertake evaluations where the evaluative planning was but an afterthought – thereby limiting your methodological options.

The key here is remembering that evaluative studies, particularly those studies related to outcomes, are all about comparison. And by far the best way to compare is by using at least two data sets. Effective evaluations are based on either before and after data (data collected before the initiative that can be compared with data collected after the initiative), or case/control data (data collected from two groups, one that has undergone the initiative and one that has not).

Without the aid of forward planning you will need to consider if either of these options is available to you. In other words, you will need to determine whether you will be able to collect solid relevant baseline data, or whether you will be able to find a comparable control group. If you can, rigorous evaluation is not too problematic. But if baseline data or a comparable control group is not available, you are left with the following methodological options:

1. Do a 'post-group only' study in which you ask stakeholders about the effects (on knowledge, attitude and/or practice) of the initiative under review. While generally not as strong as truly comparative methods, this approach can still have value. The key here is clear expectations. Your clients need to be aware of your methodological constraints and how they might affect findings.
2. Limit your study to process evaluation that centres on stakeholders' reflections on an initiative's design, delivery and implementation.

When Objectives are not Clearly Articulated or are not Readily Measurable

If you want to know if an initiative has achieved its goals, then you clearly need to know two things: what those goals were/are; and how they might be measured. Now by far the best objectives are those that are 'SMART': specific, measurable, achievable, relevant and time-bound. If your initiative has been developed with such objectives in mind, in terms of methodological design, you are half-way there. By definition, your objectives are measurable – so you just need to go out and measure. But for initiatives where objectives are not clearly articulated, or are not measurable, you have to do a bit more work. Since you simply cannot evaluate non-existent or waffly objectives, you will need to:

- work with stakeholders to clearly draw out and articulate the initiative's objectives – this may involve working through '**programme logic**' (see below);
- decide which objectives will be prioritized for evaluation;
- determine and agree on how these objectives can be operationalized (e.g. designing a method that can measure 'the joy of reading in children' is much more difficult than designing a method that can measure 'an increase in recreational reading of third graders by 50% by the end of the year').

When the Initiative Has Not Been Going Long Enough to Expect Results

It is not unusual for the timeframe given for evaluation to be shorter than that needed for an initiative to produce its intended results. For example, in health-promotion campaigns, goals are often related to disease alleviation, such as reducing the incidence of lung cancer or type-2 diabetes. But such effects are hard to attribute to a particular campaign and may not be seen for several years.

A common strategy used by evaluators facing this situation is to negotiate short- to medium-term outcomes that can be measured within the timeframe available and correlated to the expected long-term outcomes. For example, success might be measured by increased awareness; for example, increased community knowledge about the dangers of smoking or increased awareness of the impact of carbohydrates on insulin. Success might also be measured by changes in behaviour, such as reducing the number of cigarettes smoked or decreasing levels of sugar consumption.

When Effects Are Difficult to Measure/Difficult to Attribute to the Initiative

Suppose you were asked to evaluate a high school sex education programme that has a clear and central goal of increasing abstinence. To evaluate this programme, not only would you need to collect sensitive data from young people (who may not feel comfortable exposing their beliefs/practices), but you would also need to design a research protocol that could control for any other factors that are known to have an effect on abstinence, such as parents, peers and the media. Remember: you are not just looking for a correlation here. You are actually trying to establish cause and effect, and your methods need to control for any other factors that might be causal to any perceived change or difference. Controlling for extraneous factors is the only way to be able to attribute results to the programme itself.

Table 10.3 Evaluation in an ideal world

Evaluation in an ideal world would mean ...	Unfortunately, in the real world ...
Politics	
Full stakeholder cooperation	Cooperation can be hard to obtain. Programme initiators may not want to invest time and resources, and they may resent feeling judged
True desire for unbiased results	Not everyone will want a candid assessment of their initiatives. Some will, but others will be looking to meet requirements, or simply receive validation
No pressure from vested interests	Whether overt or subtle, pressure to find success can come across loud and clear
Direction	
Clear client directives	A need to evaluate might be recognized, but there is often little consensus on the exact nature of the evaluation to be undertaken
Realistic expectations	Expectations are often unrealistic – especially when initiative effects can be: (1) difficult to measure; (2) difficult to attribute to the initiative under study
The initiative	
Evaluation planned from the initiative's onset	The decision to evaluate often comes after implementation, which means solid baseline data and/or comparable control groups can be hard to find

(Continued)

Table 10.3 (Continued)

Evaluation in an ideal world would mean ...	**Unfortunately, in the real world ...**
Clear and measurable aims and objectives	Objectives can be (1) implicit and not clearly articulated and/or (2) not measurable
Well-established, mature initiatives	Interventions rarely show immediate success, yet they can be subject to deadlines that might come before you would expect to see any real change
Resources	
Adequate time and funding to undertake the study	As in any study, time and resources can be in short supply
Researchers with insider knowledge, political nous and outsider objectivity	There is almost always a need to balance political and research agendas

The lesson here is that before taking on an evaluative research study, you need to clearly consider, articulate and negotiate what is, and what is not, possible. In the real world it can be difficult, if not impossible, to control for all extraneous variables that may affect change (see Table 10.3). Remember: it is much better to have your methodology critiqued before you undertake a study, rather than after it has been completed!

ACTION RESEARCH

In most research approaches, contributions are limited to the production of knowledge. Even in applied/evaluative research where the goal is to have research knowledge become key in evidence-based decision-making, any actual change comes after the completion of research processes. But what if you want to do more than produce knowledge? What if your goals are to go beyond evidence and recommendations? What if your research goals include doing, shifting, changing or implementing? Enter action research.

The term 'action research' was coined by Kurt Lewin (1946) and represented quite a departure from 'objective' scientific method that viewed implementation as discrete from research processes. Under this traditional framework, responsibility for what happened as a consequence of the production of knowledge was not generally part of a researcher's agenda.

Researchers, however, began to recognize that: (1) the knowledge produced through research should be used for change; and (2) researching change should lead to knowledge. The appeal of a research strategy that could link these two goals while embedding elements of evaluation and learning was quite high, particularly in the fields of organizational behaviour and education, where continuous improvement was, and still is, a primary goal.

Action research also offered a departure from the notion of 'researcher' as expert and the 'researched' as passive recipients of scientific knowledge. It therefore had great appeal among community development workers who saw value in a collaborative research approach that could empower stakeholders to improve their own practice, circumstances and environments (see Box 10.1, below).

The Scope of Action Research

Action research, as it developed through the disciplines of organizational behaviour, education and community development, has travelled down a number of divergent paths, each with its own priorities and emphases. Common across their divergences, however, is a desire for real and immediate change that involves the engagement and involvement of stakeholders as collaborators or co-researchers; prolonged involvement in learning cycles; the production of rigorous, credible knowledge; and the actioning of tangible change.

The nature of the potential change can involve anything from improved practice to shifted programmes, policies and systems as discussed below, through to more radical 'cultural' shifts that include empowering the marginalized (discussed under emancipatory research). While the goals of any one action research proposal may sit neatly in any one of these categories, it is not uncommon for action research studies to work simultaneously across a number of goals.

Improving Practice

Action research can be an effective way of empowering stakeholders to improve their own professional practice. Rather than mandates that come down from on high, or knowledge that comes from outside experts, action research, which is expressly designed to improve professional practice, recognizes that various stakeholders can contribute to their own learning and development. Action research recognizes the professional nature of stakeholders and their ability to conduct meaningful research. In doing so, it helps break down the divide between stakeholders and the 'academic elite' and brings research into day-to-day professional practice.

Improving practice through action research is quite common in the educational sector where teachers are encouraged to work in ways that develop their own skills and practice. In recent years, however, there has been an increase in action research studies in health care and nursing, where the desire for professional recognition, autonomy and respect for learned/local knowledge is high.

Shifting Systems

Sometimes the action you want to pursue begins and ends with developing your own professional practice, but at other times you may want to work at the organizational level. Beyond practice, you may be interested in working within an organizational setting to improve procedures or programmes. In fact, findings from an action research study aimed at developing professional practice can contribute to the development of effective policy.

We cannot think of any organization that could not be improved in some way or another. Inefficient systems, ineffective management and outdated policy provide action research opportunities for those working in and with businesses, government and non-government agencies, community groups, etc. But while action research has been around for the better part of 60 years and can offer much to the management of organizational change, it is not generally a core management strategy. The action research literature certainly addresses organizational change, but the change-management literature rarely tackles action research.

Nevertheless, terms such as learning, education, facilitation, participation, negotiation and collaboration that are core in action research are also core in change-management speak. This is particularly so in organizations that have recognized the value of on-the-ground knowledge, as well as the role of engagement and ownership in working towards effective and sustainable change. Action research as a strategy for driving workplace-based change can be highly effective in securing stakeholder support. It can also get a wide range of staff working together towards a common goal; provide a systematic and well-established approach to sustainable change; provide a framework for the conduct of research; and embed the concept of research into management practice. It can also be a step along the way in the development of a learning organization.

Key Elements of Action Research

Because action research is quite distinct from traditional research strategies, working through its key elements is well worth the time. Understanding the benefits and challenges of this mode of research is an essential preliminary step in determining the appropriateness of action research for any particular context.

Addresses Real-World Problems

Action research is grounded in real problems and real-life situations. It generally begins with the identification of practical problems in a specific real-world context. It then attempts to understand those problems and to seek and implement solutions within that context. Action research is often used in workplaces and rural communities where the ownership of change is a high priority or where the goal is to improve professional practice. It is also considered an effective strategy when there is a strong desire to transform both theory and practice.

Pursues Action and Knowledge

Action research rejects the two-stage process of 'knowledge first, change second', and suggests that they are highly integrated. Action research practitioners believe that enacting change should not just be seen as the end product of knowledge; rather it should be valued as a source of knowledge itself. And we are not talking here about anecdotal knowledge. The knowledge produced from an action research study needs to be credible and must be collected and analysed with as much rigour as it would be in any other research strategy.

Action is also a clear and immediate goal in every action research project. Whether it be developing skills, changing programmes and policies, or working towards more radical change, action research works towards situation improvement based in practice, and avoids the problem of needing to work towards change after knowledge is produced.

Participation

The notion of research as the domain of the expert is rejected, with action research calling for participation of, and collaboration between, researchers, practitioners and any other interested stakeholders. It minimizes the distinction between the researcher and the researched and places high value on local knowledge. The premise is that without key stakeholders as part of the research process, outsiders are limited in their ability to build rich and subtle understandings – or implement sustainable change. Contrary to many research paradigms, action research works with, rather than on or for, the 'researched', and is therefore often seen as embodying democratic or decolonial principles. The key is that those who will be affected by the research and action are not acted upon.

The nature and level of participation and collaboration are varied and based on: the action research approach adopted; the particular context of the situation being studied; and the goals of the various stakeholders. This might find different stakeholders involved in any or all stages and cycles of the process. As for individuals driving the research process, in addition to taking on the role of lead researcher, at various points throughout the project, they might also have to act as planner, leader, catalyser, facilitator, teacher, designer, listener, observer, synthesizer and/or reporter.

Cycles of Learning and Action

Action research is a cyclical process that takes shape as knowledge emerges. The premise here is that you learn, you do, you reflect, you learn how to do better, you do it better, you learn from that, do it better still, and so on. You work through a series of continuous improvement cycles that converge towards better situation understanding and improved action. Action research can therefore be seen as an experiential learning approach to change. The goal is to continuously refine methods, data and interpretation in light of the understanding developed in the earlier cycles.

The cycles themselves can be defined in numerous ways. But, as shown in Figure 10.2, they generally involve some variation on observation, reflection, planning and action.

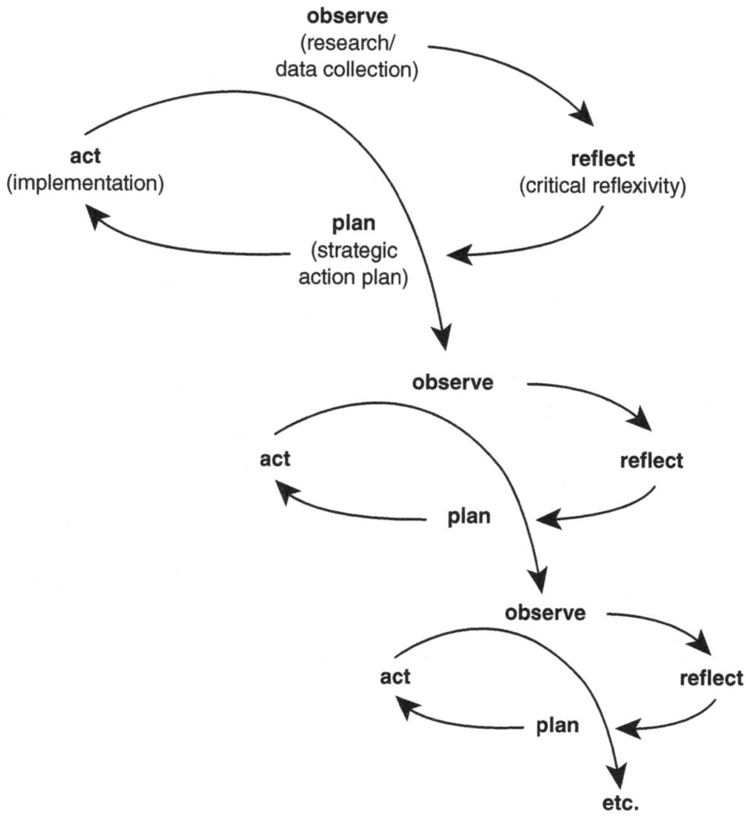

Figure 10.2 Cycles in action research

The exact nature of the steps in each part of the cycle is emergent and developed collaboratively with stakeholders who form the research team. Research for the 'observation' part of the cycle is likely to be set within a particular case, and is likely to involve a variety of approaches, methodologies and methods in a bid to gather data and generate knowledge. The 'reflection' part of the cycle can be informal and introspective or can be quite formal and share many elements with formative evaluations, as discussed earlier. The steps related to 'planning' and 'action', however, are likely to go beyond reflection and research, and may require practitioners to delve into the literature on strategic planning and change management.

Box 10.1

Action-Research Exemplar – 'Improving Indigenous Completion Rates'

The empowerment of research participants is always paramount in action research and is therefore a highly effective methodology for the engagement of traditionally marginalized groups. In the action-research study Improving Indigenous Completion Rates in Mainstream TAFE (Balatti et al., 2004), the authors attempt to address the practical problem of high indigenous student dropout rates in Australian technical and further education (TAFE) through a participatory, cyclical process designed to generate knowledge and enact change. To that end, research processes involved the forming and facilitating of four teams of 7–10 people drawn from a range of stakeholder groups including students, administration, support officers, managers and community members, plus a facilitator and a cultural adviser. Each group then worked on a distinct problem, recording their processes and attempting to both generate new knowledge and influence change (such as new organizational arrangements, new learning initiatives and new forms of delivery) through their activities.

Photo 10.1 Indigenous cohort graduation

Courtesy University Archives, Arizona State University Libraries

Challenges Associated with Action Research

Yes, action research can produce knowledge and change in empowering ways. But anyone who has ever facilitated the process can tell you that it is far from easy. The participatory, cyclical and multi-goaled nature of action research can make it a difficult process to navigate. And while a team approach means you will not have full control, you are still likely to be the one responsible for overall management. So you will be the one responsible for keeping the team to tight timelines and budgets. Being practical and realistic is, therefore, critical to the success of any action research project. In short, the project must be manageable.

Some of the issues you will need to negotiate as an action researcher include:

- Facilitating rather than directing – Because of its participatory nature, the ultimate direction of the project is not fully in your hands. Decisions made about the project's direction and its probable outcomes should be collective.
- Managing the scope – Action research projects can get very big very quickly. New researchers can be surprised to find that a rigorously conducted needs assessment or the conduct of an evaluative study within just one action research cycle can be a large research project in its own right.
- Ensuring rigour in methods – While continuous improvement strategies can rely on anecdotal evidence and general reflections, action research demands a higher degree of rigour. Perhaps the best advice is to identify the key research questions within each action research cycle and treat each of these as a small research study in its own right. While these studies will certainly need tight, realistic boundaries, they still need to be conducted so that they meet indicators of good research – validity, authenticity, reliability, consistency, etc. (see Chapter 4).
- Managing the pace – Getting stakeholders together, getting consensus and actioning real change can be slow, particularly in multiple cycles. Action research takes time and tends to work best when embedded in day-to-day practice.
- Keeping momentum – In a long-term project, many things can go astray. Key stakeholders may come and go, change initiatives may not get off the ground and the conduct of rigorous research may become overwhelming. And while this is the nature of action research, realistic planning, acceptance of the unexpected and being prepared to be flexible can help keep the momentum going.
- Managing people – Facilitating collaboration is not easy. Some stakeholders may feel unheard, ignored and/or marginalized; some may be overbearing and pompous; others may be pushing their own agenda. As a facilitator, you will need to call on negotiation, facilitation and, potentially, conflict-resolution skills.
- Acting ethically – Researchers carry the burden of ethical responsibility for both the production of knowledge and for the welfare of the researched (see Chapter 4). In action research, the involvement of stakeholders in the research team, combined with the agenda of actioning change, make for very high levels of participant involvement. Protecting the welfare of these participants is paramount.
- Needing a range of skills – In addition to being a competent researcher, the action researcher must also be a consummate organizer, effective communicator, skilled negotiator, conflict resolution specialist, well-organized time manager, strategic

planner, efficient documenter and willing to get their 'hands dirty' as an on-the-ground implementer – all of which might require the development of specialist skills.

- Ownership – Finally, the researcher needs to negotiate ownership of research outcomes, which may include rights to publish and issues of authorship.

When it comes to knowledge and change, action research attempts to let you have your cake and eat it too (which actually makes sense – after all, what good is a cake you can't eat?). It also allows you to work with others in empowering ways. And, while action research can be quite challenging, for individuals and organizations whose goals match those of action research, it can be a challenge well worth taking up.

EMANCIPATORY RESEARCH

> The philosophers have only interpreted the world in various ways; the point, however, is to change it.
>
> Karl Marx (1845)

It is one thing to want to improve skills and practice, or to endeavour to change how things are done in a workplace, school or community, but what if you believe that the only path to sustainable change is through fundamental transformation of larger social systems? What if you believe that it will take more than working within the system, and that at the heart of the social issue or social problem is injustice or inequity in the system itself – the repressive school system, the authoritative nature of the workplace or the hierarchical structures of the community? Or underpinning even this, the underlying ideologies of capitalism, patriarchy, colonisation or globalization?

To strive for **critical emancipation** is to expose these underlying ideologies in a bid to liberate those oppressed by them, which requires the following: **criticality**; **radical views**; and **emancipatory goals**.

Critical emancipation thus refers to fundamental or revolutionary changes in current thinking, practices, conditions or institutions that can free people from the constraints of dominant social structures that often limit self-development and self-determination. For those whose research includes goals of critical emancipation, research is likely to proceed on the assumption that if social problems arise from a system, they are unlikely to be solved within that system. Critical emancipatory research necessarily delves into the underfelt of social systems. It is laden with political purpose and does not claim to be value-free. It seeks transformation of society such that individuals are liberated and empowered towards action that opens up possibilities for improved situations.

Now in its radical extreme this might mean exploring the disempowerment and injustice created by industrialized societies; investigating the economic impacts of mass globalization; or exposing the patriarchal structures that act to disadvantage women. For smaller-scale research projects, however, the application might be as 'ordinary' as exploring workplace stress, bullying in the playground or low self-esteem in young girls. The 'critical' end of such studies comes from exploring the ideologies that create systems in which: workplace stress becomes an expected product of well-entrenched practices of authority, power and control; low self-esteem in girls can be seen as 'ordinary' given the cultural emphasis on the body image of women in the public eye; and bullying in the playground can be seen as quite reasonable given the legitimization of power through other forms of aggression readily accessible to youth (movies, video games, sport, etc.). This criticality is then applied to emancipation through the production of knowledge that exposes repressive ideologies and opens up possibilities.

In the social sciences, these critical emancipatory goals have led to variations on ethnographic and action research. 'Participatory' action research has an explicit goal of emancipation through action, while 'critical' ethnography seeks to change existing social systems by exposing their dominant and repressive ideologies (see Box 10.3, below, for examples).

Participatory Action Research

Participatory action research (PAR), sometimes referred to as emancipatory action research or 'southern' participatory action research (which comes from the notion of working in developing countries often in the southern hemisphere), falls under the action research umbrella. It has goals of emancipation but maintains the action research dedication to cycles of knowledge and action that produce on-the-ground change. Now action research can certainly have emancipatory goals, but PAR makes these goals much more explicit. It works in participatory ways that value local knowledge and attempts to empower communities to expose and liberate themselves from repressive systems and ideologies. PAR is often found in international development research that strives towards social transformation of the 'marginalized' through advocacy and action.

The goal of PAR is to pursue action and knowledge in an integrated fashion through a cyclical and participatory process. It attempts to facilitate exploration and unmasking of the ways that dominant ideologies and systems shape and constrain thinking and action, and works towards interventions that can liberate the marginalized from those forces that contribute to poverty, oppression, repression and/or injustice. PAR relies on the same basic tenets as action research, but with a more specific emancipatory agenda:

- It addresses practical problems – As with action research, PAR works with real problems in order to produce knowledge and action directly useful to stakeholders. This often involves the empowerment of the 'marginalized' as they act to construct their own knowing and attempt to create and action their own strategic plan for emancipation.
- It generates knowledge – PAR attempts to challenge not only things within the system, but also the system itself. It attempts to unmask the political aspects of knowledge production that often sees knowledge as an instrument of power and control.
- It enacts change – As is common to all action research processes, PAR goes beyond knowledge generation and incorporates change into its immediate goals. In PAR, these goals are directly related to emancipation and liberation by changing inequitable power relations.
- It is participatory – PAR works with the researched, rather than on or for them. It recognizes that the knowledge and experience of the 'marginalized' should be respected and valued, and that attempts to capitalize on capabilities and cultural practices are often ignored. PAR also attempts to work towards 'conscientization' (Freire, 1970) or awakening of the oppressed, and acts to strengthen their capacity to generate knowledge and

action from their own perspectives and in their own interests. Methods used to generate knowledge and action are broad, eclectic and emergent, and need not be limited to traditional Western ways of researching. Song, poetry, art, drama and storytelling might emerge as appropriate ways to draw out and generate knowledge.

- It relies on a cyclical process – As with all forms of action research, PAR converges towards better situation understanding and improved action implementation through cycles of observation, reflection, planning and action.

Critical Ethnography

Ethnography can be defined as 'the exploration of cultural groups in a bid to understand, describe and interpret a way of life from the point of view of its participants'. **Critical ethnography**, also referred to as radical ethnography, adds a political agenda of exposing inequitable, unjust or repressive influences that are acting on 'marginalized' cultural groups, in a bid to offer avenues for positive change.

There is thus an assumption that the dominant or existing system is indeed repressive or unjust and needs to be exposed. Critical ethnography attempts to expose the political nature of knowledge and unmask the dominant forces that shape our view of the world. By critical examination of worldviews, ideology and power, critical ethnography attempts to contextualize the current situation in a larger socio-historic framework that offers, and encourages others to engage in, critical reflection. The goal is to work towards conscientization, empowerment and liberation of the 'marginalized'.

While traditional ethnographic techniques can – and many would argue should – consider how interpretations are influenced by dominant paradigms, critical ethnographers have an explicit goal of understanding and interpreting situations from both within and outside the dominant framework. By naming and then distancing themselves from cultural assumptions in a bid to work through a series of alternative conceptions, critical ethnographers expose dominant paradigms. The goal is to present alternative and potentially more liberating realities (see Box 10.2).

Clearly, the highly political goals of critical ethnography link exposure of the dominant system to emancipation – to bring about change is a defined objective. According to Thomas (1993), ethnography as action can be seen in its ability to:

- change the cognitive functioning of researchers;
- offer a 'voice' to the marginalized;
- instigate interactions with others that raise social awareness;
- create networks of those with common goals;
- become a starting point for legislative and/or policy reform.

Box 10.2

A Journey Towards Critical Ethnography

A student of Zina's conducted an ethnographic study of first-year university students who were subjected to hazing or bastardization. The study attempted to understand the reality of bastardization from the perspective of the 'victims'. Through observations, interviews and document analysis, the student wanted to be able to give a thick description and interpretation of both the phenomenon of bastardization and the culture in which it thrived. As she progressed in this work, she realized that understanding the culture and how it might shift could not be done without a critical examination of the forces that allow this culture to continue and in fact flourish. She thus found herself immersed in exploration of the socio-historic context of the campus in a bid to expose and deconstruct notions of patriarchy, myth, aggression, mateship, cultures of silence, power and control. In the end, her work had shifted to a strongly critical study that attempted to expose the broader social systems that had created a particular cultural reality.

Photo 10.2 Hazing

Source: Roberto Herrera Pellizzari on Flickr

Box 10.3

Examples of Emancipatory Research

Markussen, U. (2017) 'Towards an Arctic awakening: Neocolonialism, sustainable development, emancipatory research, collective action, and Arctic regional policymaking', in K. Latola and H. Savela (eds), *The Interconnected Arctic – UArctic Congress 2016*. Springer Polar Sciences. Cham: Springer. https://doi.org/10.1007/978-3-319-57532-2_31

This chapter recommends a form of regional policymaking based on collective action and emancipatory research to meet the needs of Arctic people. Evidence-based policy making is essential to tackle challenges like climate change, but not all kinds of evidence are treated equally. For example, Arctic Indigenous peoples have thousands of years of experience of climate which must be integrated into effective policy.

(Continued)

Caxaj, C. S. (2015) 'Indigenous storytelling and participatory action research: Allies toward decolonization? Reflections from the Peoples' International Health Tribunal', *Global Qualitative Nursing Research*, 20(2), DOI: 10.1177/2333393615580764

Caxaj spent four months in a rural Guatemalan community and developed the Peoples' International Health Tribunal as a community-driven knowledge translation activity. This study reports on how the tribunal highlighted Indigenous voices, local experiences, and community justice and pushed back on Western framings of community health concerns.

Stoudt, B. G., Fox, M. and Fine, M. (2012) 'Contesting privilege with critical participatory action research', *Journal of Social Issues*, 68(1): 178–93.

This study is based on a collaborative research project with New York City urban youth. The project explored experiences of both justice and injustice faced by urban youth when interacting with public institutions. The authors analyse the historic and unacknowledged role of privilege and the developmental support it affords relatively advantaged youth. In true PAR style, the authors analyse privilege not only for understanding, but also as a potential platform for activist solidarity.

Fitzpatrick, K. (2011) 'Stop playing up! Physical education, racialization and resistance', *Ethnography*, 12(2): 174–97.

This year-long ethnographic study explored the place of physical education in the lives of youth in one multi-ethnic school in an area of South Auckland, New Zealand, known for poverty, crime and cultural diversity. The critically of this study is seen in the approach the author takes to understanding both the positive aspects of physical education (relationship building, play and critical resistance), but also the negative, politically fraught space of self and societal judgements of the body in relation to race and gender.

Issues in Emancipatory Research

There is a level of debate around the intertwining of research goals and political agendas – basically this is because it flies in the face of one of the most well-entrenched 'positivist' rules of research, namely objectivity. It is easy to be accused of confusing social activism with research and an associated inability to manage subjectivities. And although both critical ethnography and PAR sit under a 'post-positivist' umbrella, they nevertheless suffer from this critique and are accused of confusing social activism with research. For those wanting to conduct such studies it will be important to clearly outline your methodological protocols, and call on literature that legitimizes, and acknowledges the importance of, critical agendas in research. Luckily, the proliferation and acceptance of post-positivist methodologies make this task ever easier. For example, the increasing recognition of decolonising methodologies (Smith, 2022) provides a rigorous standpoint from which to contest and respond a single yardstick for evaluating research.

This said, there is still a need to manage subjectivities. It is one thing to have and work towards a political agenda, but it is another to have it bias the interpretation and analysis of your research. Political agendas may be acceptable, but to have them colour your perception in unrecognized ways will put a question mark over research credibility.

Another, perhaps more problematic, critique is the risk of dedicated and motivated researchers imposing their political agenda on the 'marginalized'. Are problems necessarily problems if they are not recognized as such by those being researched? Is it the researcher's right to stir this up, even if the goal is liberation and emancipation? Is 'conscientization' always justified? Within a particular culture, a problem identified by Western researchers might not be viewed as a problem by those supposedly affected by it. A huge responsibility in emancipatory research is thus negotiating political agendas that can 'arise from', 'be assigned to' or 'be imposed on' the researched.

Critical Thinking Challenge 11

Driving Change

Do you see driving change as a researcher's role?

There is often a gap between researchers (those who produce knowledge) and change agents (those who drive change). Do you think it's appropriate, as a researcher, to do both? What do you think are the benefits and what do you see as the biggest challenges/obstacles?

I Have a Question!

I Am Really Interested in Doing Research That Can Drive Change – but There Are so Many Options. How Do I Choose?

Yes, there are a lot of options. If you want to do change-oriented research, figure out first what you want to change. What is the issue and what do you want to happen/what change do you want to see? Then ask yourself about the nature of that change in relation to your research. Do you want to offer recommendations for change? Then think about applied/evaluative research. Do you want to do research on how change happens as a part of your research practice? Then look at action research. Do you want true liberation and emancipation for a particular group? Then consider emancipatory research. And while the options here can be really exciting, you will need to temper this with a good hard look at practicalities like funding, supervisory support and timeframes.

Chapter Summary

- When it comes to methodologies dedicated to enacting change, applied research including evaluation seeks to offer recommendations for change; action research embeds change directly into its research processes; while emancipatory research attacks change at fundamental levels including liberation and self-determination.
- Evaluative research is undertaken to determine the value of some initiative such as a programme or policy and covers both implementation and outcomes. It is a highly political, real-world endeavour that calls on a variety of methods.

(Continued)

- Action research is dedicated to the integrated production of knowledge and implementation of change. Its goal is to empower stakeholders to be involved in their own learning and development through a participatory and collaborative approach.
- Participatory action research is explicit in its agenda of empowerment and radical change. Its goal is to help community groups construct their own knowing in order to create and action their own plan for a better future.
- Critical ethnography attempts to expose dominant systems in the interest of the 'marginalized'. Change comes from the voice offered to the oppressed, as well as the starting point it offers for action at individual, legislative and policy levels.

FIND YOUR NEXT STEP

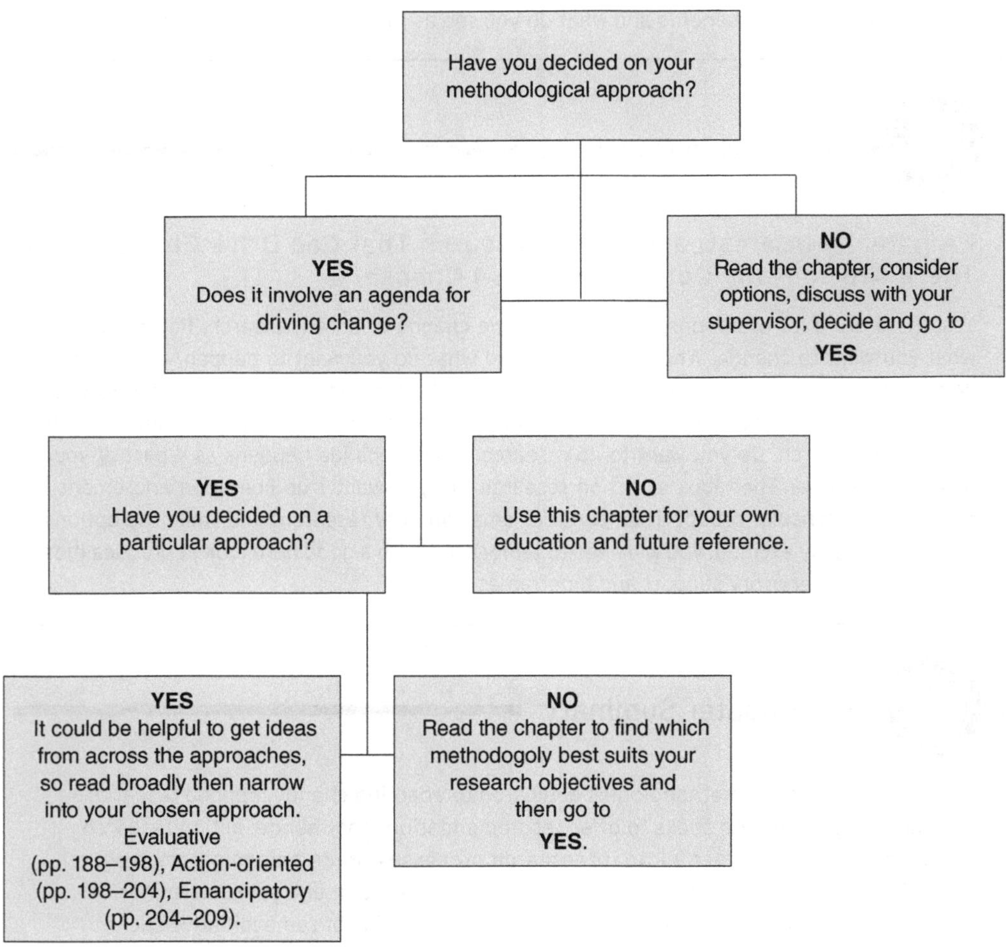

FURTHER READING

While most students determine their projects with the ultimate goal of change in mind, the majority do not give much consideration to research strategies that see change as a more instrumental goal of the research process itself. We hope this chapter has inspired you to consider at least some approaches that link knowledge and action. If so, have a look at some of the readings listed below. They represent a large range of possibilities for linking research and change.

Evaluative Research

Linfield, J. and Posavac, E. (2018) *Program Evaluation: Methods and Case Studies*. Abingdon: Routledge.
We like the case-study approach the authors take here. It allows them to offer theory, models, practical techniques as well as reflections from actual cases.

Mertens, D. M. and Wilson, A. (2018) *Program Evaluation Theory and Practice*. New York: Guilford Press.
A comprehensive guide that covers a range of approaches including mixed methods and online strategies. We like the practical checklists and activities the authors offer.

Newcomer, K. E., Hatry, H. P. and Wholey, J. S. (eds) (2015) *Handbook of Practical Program Evaluation*, 4th edition. San Francisco, CA: Jossey-Bass.
An interesting array of essays here. Together, they make for quite a comprehensive reference work for anyone involved in the evaluation of programmes run in the public sector. We particularly like the common-sense approach to cost-effective, yet credible, evaluation design.

Rossi, P. H., Lipsey, M. W. and Henry, G. T. (2019) *Evaluation: A Systematic Approach*. Thousand Oaks, CA: Sage.
Great 'how to' guide that covers a wide variety of approaches. Strengths of the work are the breadth of examples used and coverage of the political context of evaluation.

Royse, D., Thyer, B. A. and Padgett, D. K. (2016) *Program Evaluation: An Introduction to an Evidence Based Approach*. Boston: Cengage Learning.
As the title indicates, this is a solid, practical introduction. We find it clear, easy to follow and quite applied. Not a bad place to start.

Action Research

Balatti J., Gargano, I., Goldman, M., Wood, G. and Woodlock, J. (2004) *Improving Indigenous Completion Rates in Mainstream TAFE – An Action Research Approach*. Leabrook, South Australia: NCEAR.
See Box 10.1 above.

Coghlan, D. (2019) *Doing Action Research in Your Own Organization.* London: Sage.
As well as covering the intricacies of action research, this book also delves into the political and ethical challenges of working as a researcher and change agent within your own organization. We strongly recommend this for anyone attempting action research in their own workplace.

Herr, K. G. and Anderson, G. L. (2014) *The Action Research Dissertation: A Guide for Students and Faculty*, 2nd edition. London: Sage.
The authors use the term 'road map' and we think it is appropriate. This is a very practical, step-by-step 'how to' guide that will accompany you through the action research process. We particularly appreciate the authors' acknowledgement of the resistance that action researchers can face in the academic world, and the strategies they offer for overcoming such challenges.

McNiff, J. (2017) *All You Need to Know About Action Research.* London: Sage.
Another good, step-by-step 'how to' guide that is quite accessible. We think the case studies the author uses to draw out their points work well. A good starting point.

Reason, P. and Bradbury, H. (2007) *Handbook of Action Research.* London: Sage.
This is a very useful set of essays that really delves into the debates, controversies and potential of action research. It offers several exemplars that show the range of possibilities for social change through action research.

Stringer, E. (2013) *Action Research.* London: Sage.
This is an accessible work that offers a simple look, think and act framework. This may seem simplistic, but it is a way of organizing the challenges that the conduct of action research is likely to bring up.

Emancipatory Research

Brown, S. G. and Dobrin, S. I. (eds) (2004) *Ethnography Unbound: From Theory Shock to Critical Praxis.* Albany, NY: State University of New York Press.
This is still a great way to immerse yourself in the world of critical ethnography and the debates that surround this contentious approach to knowing. A terrific read for those interested in critical and radical change through research.

Chevalier, J. M. and Buckles, D. J. (2019) *Participatory Action Research: Theory and Methods for Engaged Inquiry.* Abingdon: Routledge.
This is a highly comprehensive treatise on PAR that gives practical tools and techniques designed to ensure authentic understanding, while empowering the 'researched'. A terrific book if you want to delve into the ins and outs of this type of emancipatory research.

Fine, M. (2017) *Just Research in Contentious Times: Widening the Methodological Imagination.* New York: Teachers College Press.
This is more than a book on methods. It is the author's reflections on a 30-year journey of using research as a tool for impacting on policy and practice for the betterment of

community. In doing so, she covers not only appropriate research methods, but the challenges of responsible emancipatory research.

Fitzpatrick, K. (2011) 'Stop playing up! Physical education, racialization and resistance', *Ethnography*, 12(2): 174–97.
See Box 10.3 above.

Freire, P. (1970) *Pedagogy of the Oppressed*. New York: Herder & Herder.
About as classic as you can get, Freire's groundbreaking work has aided the empowerment of marginalized people throughout the world. A must-read for anyone interested in radical transformation through empowered practices.

Kemmis, S., McTaggart, R. and Nixon, R. (2014) *The Action Research Planner: Doing Critical Participatory Action Research*. New York: Springer.
Through the use of five extended examples, the authors draw out the lessons learned, and in doing so offer guidance on the key success factors needed when undertaking this type of emancipatory research.

Madison, D. S. (2019) *Critical Ethnography: Method, Ethics, and Performance*. London: Sage.
We think this work does a good job of traversing the divide between the sociological theories that underpin critical ethnography and the practical research methods and techniques that a student researcher would need to know. Worth a look.

Stoudt, B. G., Fox, M. and Fine, M. (2012) 'Contesting privilege with critical participatory action research', *Journal of Social Issues*, 68(1): 178–93.
See Box 10.3 above.

Silva, C. M. da, Sauerbronn, F. F. and Thiollent, M. (2022) 'Decolonial studies, non-extractive methods, and participatory action research in accounting', *Revista De Administração Contemporânea*, 26(4): e210014. https://doi.org/10.1590/1982-7849rac2022210014.en
Accounting might not be the discipline you think of when you think of decolonizing studies, but this article discusses the importance and relevance of participatory action research for understanding financial capitalism in the Global South.

Bertilsdotter Rosqvist, H. Kourti, M., Jackson-Perry, D., Brownlow, C., Fletcher, K., Bendelman, D. and O'Dell, L. (2019) 'Doing it differently: Emancipatory autism studies within a neurodiverse academic space', *Disability & Society*, 34(7–8): 1082–1101. DOI: 10.1080/09687599.2019.1603102
This co-authored article is a demonstration of the strengths of partnership between autistic and non-autistic people as researchers and participants. A reflection on parts of the research process not often discussed in published research.

11

IDENTIFYING AND SELECTING SAMPLES, INFORMANTS AND CASES

Learning Objectives

- Where does the answer lie?
    - To understand the critical nature of identifying where your answers are likely to be found
- Samples: selecting elements of a population
    - To understand the opportunities of working with a sample
    - To be able to develop both random and non-random sampling strategies
- Key informants: working with experts and insiders
    - To understand the opportunities and challenges of working with key informants
    - To be able to develop strategies for selecting informants
- Cases: delving into detail
    - To understand the value of case studies
    - To understand the importance of targeted case selection

WHERE DOES THE ANSWER LIE?

If the research process is all about getting your research question answered, then it is probably a good idea to think about where the answer to your question lies. Let's think about this for a minute. In most 'quantitative' models of social science research, what we are after is answers that are held by some population. We want to know what the 'masses' do, think or feel. In this scenario, answers rest with a broad segment of society. In fact, one of the main reasons we work with quantitative data is because we want to reach such a broad sector of society that gathering qualitative data would not be feasible.

In 'qualitative' models of research, however, the opposite tends to be true. Because we want to preserve powerful text and rich narrative, we tend to target answers that are held by the 'few' rather than the 'many'. Answers may still sit with a broad sector of society or within a population, but they might also be held by experts and insiders or even within the experiences of a particular individual.

And it is not just people who hold answers. Answers might be held within the practices of a setting or a case, such as a school or workplace. Or they may be held in documents, videos, social media, existing databases, past research, websites. In an information age, many answers are out there just waiting for us to find and make sense of them.

No matter what the scenario, it is absolutely crucial to figure out where the answers lie and how you will open up opportunities to gather that information. And because answers can lie just about anywhere, you may need to employ several strategies for finding them. Seeking broad representation (sampling a population where that population could be anything from people to websites) may be most appropriate. But working with those in the know (by selecting key informants) and delving into the experiences of an individual or a setting (by defining an appropriate case) might be better suited to some qualitative approaches. And of course, as covered in the previous two chapters, there are plenty of research questions and research designs that will require you to use more than one strategy.

There are, not surprisingly, plenty of challenges. Whether you decide to work with samples, key informants, cases or a combination of these, the issue of credibility is paramount. With individuals you will be seeking those who are appropriate, representative, open, honest, knowledgeable, have good memories, are not afraid to expose themselves and do not feel a need to present themselves in any particular light. This can be true of what is produced by individuals as well. Biases, subjectivities, propaganda, etc. can also exist in the secondary data you are seeking to explore. At times you will need to be systematic. You may decide that what is most appropriate is a defined sampling strategy that can generate a representative sample. At other times, you will need to be strategic. You may decide to turn to where you know you have an 'in' and can call on pre-existing relationships. You will need to be aware of the complexities of working with others in a bid to fulfil your own research agenda. Whether you decide to work with samples, informants or cases, there will be plenty of issues and challenges you will need to work through.

SAMPLES: SELECTING ELEMENTS OF A POPULATION

Often the goal in social science research is to understand a population. In other words, to get a representative picture of what a particular group of people really do and really think or what existing documents really represent.

The ultimate in population research is to be able to ask everyone/explore everything – in other words, to be able to gather data from every element within a population. But with the exception of in-depth research into very small, defined and accessible populations, or the conduct of a census, which is a survey of every element within a population, the goal of asking everyone just isn't practical. Your study will probably involve a population that you cannot reach in its entirety; it will either be too large or have elements that you simply cannot identify or access.

Yet our inability to access every element of a population does little to suppress our desire to understand and represent it. For example, in our day-to-day lives we might talk about a chain of restaurants or a race of people, but rarely do we do this on the basis of a 'full data set'. We are unlikely to have eaten at every McDonald's, or to have chatted with every Asian person. So what do we do? We gather information from a 'few' in order to capture the thoughts, knowledge, attitudes, feelings and/or beliefs of the 'many'.

There are parallels in social science research. Rarely do we speak to everyone we wish to speak about, so we sample, investigate, conclude and attempt to argue the broader applicability of our findings. The trick, however, is being able to apply our findings in a credible manner.

Opportunities in Working with a Sample

So why would you choose to work with a sample? Well, samples can make the research process manageable. They allow you to explore groups of people, organizations, events and existing material that you simply could not access in their totality. Whether your population is too large, too widely dispersed, too difficult to locate or too hard to access, sampling can provide you with a window for exploring an unwieldy population.

Sampling can also be used to represent a population with some level of 'confidence'. Certain sampling strategies actually allow you to calculate the statistical probability that your findings are representative of a greater population. Sampling is therefore key to making research affordable and, if done with integrity, also credible.

Sample Selection

In the real world, we would not taste a spoonful of spaghetti sauce to determine if the entire pot needs more salt without stirring first. We recognize that generalization requires appropriate, representative and unbiased sampling.

The same is true in selecting a research sample. Far from a haphazard activity, sampling is a process that is always strategic, and sometimes mathematical. The goal is to select a sample that is: (1) broad enough to allow you to speak about a parent population; (2) large enough to allow you to conduct the desired analysis; and (3) small enough to be manageable. In studies with goals of generalizability, this will involve using the most practical procedures possible for gathering a sample that best 'represents' a larger population. At other times, however, the nature of the research question may make representativeness impossible to assess or inappropriate. In these cases, researchers will still strategically select their samples, but in ways that best serve their stated research goals.

Meeting these goals will require you to think through a number of sampling issues, including the need to: define your population; construct a **sample frame**; determine appropriate sample size; and select a suitable sampling strategy.

Defining Your Population

It is important to have a very clear and well-defined population in mind before you do any sampling. This means you will need to go into your study knowing the total class of 'elements' you want to be able to speak about. Suppose you want to present findings that will be representative of 13- to 18-year-olds in the UK. Your population here is made up of individuals (the most common type of population in social/applied science research) with a particular set of defining characteristics, in this case both age (13–18) and geography (in the UK). Keep in mind that in a study of individuals you might have used other defining characteristics, such as gender, marital status or race.

And, of course, populations don't always need to be made up of individuals. Depending on the nature of your question, 'elements' of your population might be households, workplaces, documents, websites or even events. For example, your population might be hospital emergency rooms across Sweden. In this case, it is a particular type of organizational setting that makes up the population. Defining characteristics include both geography (across Sweden) and type of setting (hospital emergency room). Other possibilities for defining 'organizations' might include number of employees, years of operation, and public or private. An example of a population made up of events might be professional soccer matches held in Barcelona in 2023. Defining characteristics here are type of activity (professional soccer matches), geography (Barcelona) and time period (2023).

Constructing a Sample Frame

A sample frame is a list that includes every member of the population from which a sample is to be taken; it is essential to all sampling processes. Now ideally, a sample frame would match your target population, but this is rarely the case. Being able to define your population does not guarantee you will have access to every element within it. There are plenty of times when you just cannot get the full 'list'. Listing all homeless people in Washington, DC, for example, would be impossible. That kind of list simply does not exist and cannot be generated with any accuracy.

The key here is to make strategic decisions that ensure your sampling frame is as close to the target population as possible, and to be ready to argue the relevance of your frame despite any discrepancies.

Determining Sample Size

Once you have come up with the best possible sampling frame, you will need to figure out how many elements from within that frame should be in your sample. And the answer to the question 'how many?' is 'it depends'. There are no hard-and-fast rules. Sample size is highly dependent on the shape and form of the data you wish to collect, and the goals of your analysis.

Statistical analysis of quantitative data, for example, will require a minimum number. Statistics and the ability to work with probabilities rest on adequate and appropriate sample size. On the other hand, the in-depth nature of qualitative data will generally limit sample size; you simply cannot collect that type of data from thousands. But fortunately you don't have to. **Qualitative data analysis** strategies are not generally dependent on large numbers.

The following guidelines might help you work through the intricacies of determining appropriate sample size:

- Working with quantitative data/analysis – When working with quantified data, the basic rule of thumb is to attempt to get as large a sample as possible within time and expense constraints. The larger the sample, the more likely it is to be representative, and hence generalizable. Minimum numbers are determined by the level of statistical analysis you wish to do:
    - Minimal statistical analysis – Because statistical analysis is based on probability, the most basic statistical analysis requires a minimum of about 30 respondents; anything smaller and it can be difficult to show statistical significance, particularly if findings are widely distributed. Keep in mind that, with small samples, you will need to argue representativeness.
    - Intermediate statistical analysis – As you move to more sophisticated analysis, the use of any 'subdivisions' will require approximately 25 cases in each category. For example, you may have a sample of 500 members of a particular community, but only 263 women. Out of this, there are 62 mothers with children under 18, and only 20 mothers with children under 5. Statistical analysis of mothers with children under 5 would be difficult. Similarly, if you want to show significance in multivariate analysis (the analysis of simultaneous relationships among several variables), you will need at least 10 cases for each variable you wish to explore.
    - Advanced statistical analysis – If you want to represent a known population with a defined level of confidence, you can actually calculate the required size using the following formula:

$$n = [K \times S)/E]^2$$

    in which K is the desired **confidence level**, S is the sample **standard deviation** and E is the required level of precision. Personally, we prefer not to work with formulae unless we have to, so we tend to use a 'sample size calculator' where the only things we need to know are: the population size; the **confidence interval** (the range you will accept above and below the **mean**, say ± 5%); and the confidence level (how sure you want to be that your findings are more than coincidental, generally 95% or 99%) – see Chapter 15. Table 11.1 was generated with a calculator from www.surveysystem.com/sscalc.htm and gives you some idea of the required sample size for more commonly used confidence levels. Note that as the population increases, shifts in sample size do not increase that dramatically. What does require a significantly increased sample size, however, is a desire for higher levels of confidence.

- Working with qualitative data – Many researchers who collect qualitative data in order to understand populations are not looking for representativeness. Their goal is often rich understanding that may come from the few rather than the many. Such studies are reliant on the ability of the researcher to argue the 'relativeness' of any sample (even a single case) to a broader context. For those who want to collect qualitative data from a sample that does represent a target population, the challenge is to be able to do this in-depth collection from a large enough sample size. There are two strategies you can call on here. The first is to **hand-pick** a limited sample using criteria chosen to ensure representativeness. For example, selecting your sample based on a clearly defined population profile, i.e. individuals with, for example, the average age, income and education of the population you are studying. Rather than relying on numbers, you will need to argue logically that your sample captures all the various elements/characteristics of your population. The second strategy is to select a sample large enough to allow for minimal statistical analysis. This will give you the option of quantitatively summarizing some of your findings in order to make more mathematical generalizations about your population.

- Working with both quantitative and qualitative data – If you are working with both data types, you will find that the nature of collecting qualitative data will limit your sample size. However, any planned statistical analysis will require a minimum number of cases. The best advice is look at Table 11.1 to determine the minimum size necessary for any statistical analysis you wish to do, then consider the practicalities of collecting and analysing qualitative data from this sample. Unless you have unlimited time and money, there will usually be some trade-off between the collection of rich, in-depth qualitative data and the level of statistical analysis that might be possible.

Table 11.1 Required sample size

Population	95% ± 5% CI	99% ± 5% CI	99% ± 1% CI
30	28	29	Insufficient
100	80	87	99
500	217	286	485
1,000	278	400	943
5,000	357	588	3,845
10,000	370	624	6,247
50,000	381	657	12,486
100,000	383	661	14,267
1,000,000	384	665	16,369

Keep in mind that all the advice above needs to be checked against the criterion of doability. Large samples are likely to mean less error, but they also mean more money and more time. But this does not mean you can simply reduce sample size and forget about generalizability. On the contrary, the credibility of your research needs to be paramount in all methodological considerations. What doability does highlight, however, is the need for credible research to be designed with practicalities firmly in mind.

Employing a Sampling Strategy

Once you have defined your population, constructed a sample frame and determined appropriate sample size, it is time to adopt a strategy for gathering your sample. There are two main ways to go about this. The first is to use a strategy for random selection. The second is to use a strategy that aims to strategically select your sample in a non-random fashion. The best method will depend on a number of factors, including the nature of your question, the make-up of your population, the type of data you wish to collect and your intended modes of analysis.

Random Samples

Random samples rely on random selection, or the process by which each element in a population has an equal chance of being selected for inclusion in a sample; for example, by drawing names out of a hat, or using computer-generated random numbers. The idea here is that if you have an adequate sample frame and a large enough sample size, random selection will allow you to: control for researcher bias; represent a population; and generalize findings to that population. An example is Nielsen Ratings, which monitor a small percentage of TV viewers' habits but generalize back to the entire population. Random samples are therefore seen as the gold standard in social science research.

At the technical end, the logic of random samples is based on the **central limit theorem**. This posits that a random sample of observations for any distribution with a finite mean and finite **variance** will have a mean that follows a normal distribution. This allows researchers to conduct quite sophisticated analysis in the form of **inferential statistics** (see Chapter 15). Random sampling, however, demands that (1) all elements of a population are known and accessible, and that (2) all elements are equally likely to agree to be part of a sample.

If this is not the case, two types of error can occur:

1 **Coverage error** – This is when your sample frame is deficient and does not adequately represent your target population. For example, while every name in the hat has an equal chance of being drawn, if your name belongs in the hat but wasn't put in there, you have a coverage error. This is a common problem in telephone surveys of households as many people do not have landline phones. Surveys reliant on email addresses have a similar problem as not everyone has an email address. It is therefore important to consider whether your sample frame is complete and how you can give a voice to any sector of the population that might miss inclusion.
2 **Non-response bias** – This is when those who agree to be in a sample are intrinsically different from those who decline. Non-response is not problematic if the characteristics of those who accept and those who decline are basically the same. But that is not often the case. For example, in customer satisfaction surveys, it might be that those who agree to participate have an axe to grind. Or you may want to offer an inducement that appeals to those with a particular need for, or interest in, what is being offered. In both cases your eventuating sample will not be representative of your population and you will need to come up with strategies that will ensure broad representation.

True (or simple) random samples are actually quite difficult to generate in real-world research, but, as shown in Table 11.2, there are several sampling strategies that attempt to approximate a **simple random sample**.

Non-Random Samples

Non-random samples are just that – samples that are not drawn in a random fashion. Now there are some quantitative researchers who view non-random samples as inferior because they cannot be statistically assessed for representativeness. For these researchers, 'non-random' implies samples that are gathered through strategies seen as second best or last resort.

Table 11.2 Random sampling

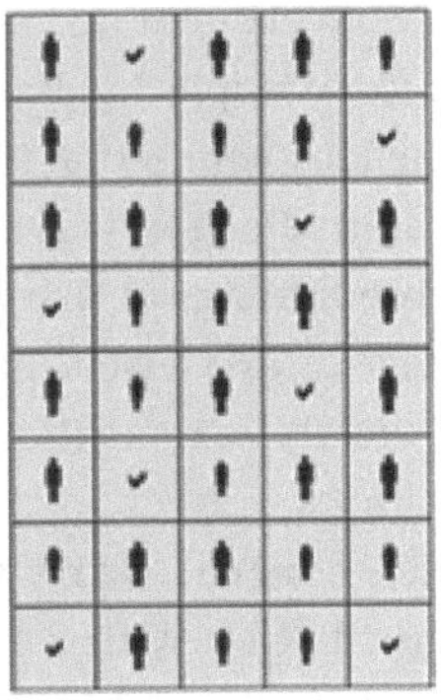	**Simple random sampling** Involves identifying all elements of a population, listing those elements and randomly selecting from the list All elements have an equal chance of inclusion Considered 'fair', and allows for generalization Rarely used in practice because the process of identifying, listing and randomly selecting elements is often unfeasible Resulting samples may not capture enough elements of particular subgroups you are interested in studying
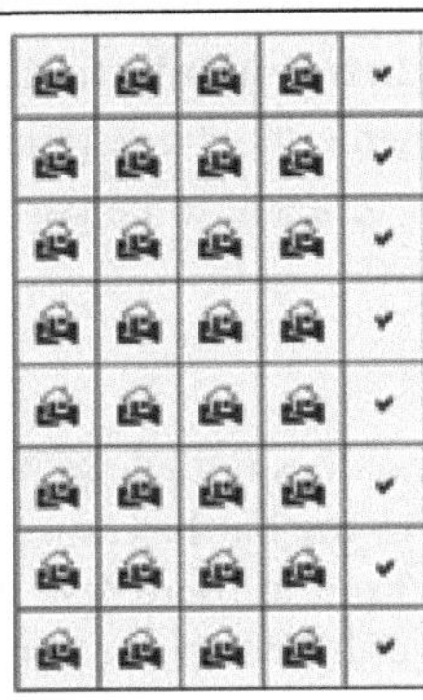	**Systematic sampling** Involves selecting every nth case within a defined population. For example, going to every 10th house or selecting every 20th person on a list Easier to do than devising methods for random selection Offers a close approximation of random sampling as long as elements are not in a particular order. For example, you would not have a random approximation if you were to go to every 10th house, which just happened to always be a detached home on the corner, in a neighbourhood with lots of duplexes
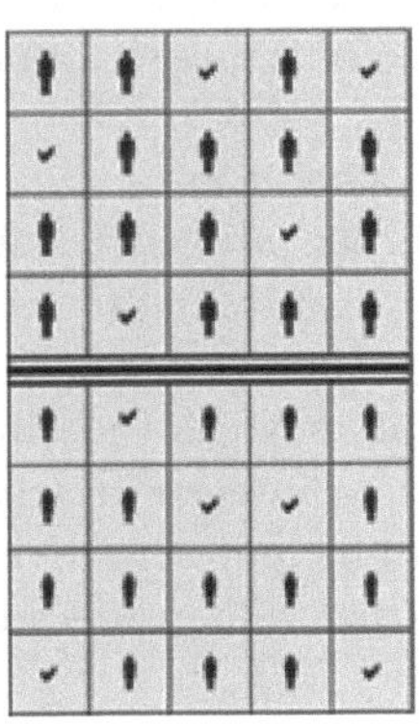	**Stratified sampling** Involves dividing your population into various subgroups and taking a random sample within each one Ensures your sample represents key subgroups of the population, e.g. males and females Representation of the subgroups can be proportionate or disproportionate. For example, if you wanted to sample 100 nurses with a population of 80% females and 20% males, a proportionate stratified sample would be made up of 80 females and 20 males. In a disproportionate stratified sample you would use a ratio different from the population, e.g. 50 males and 50 females Stratification can be used in conjunction with systematic as well as random sampling
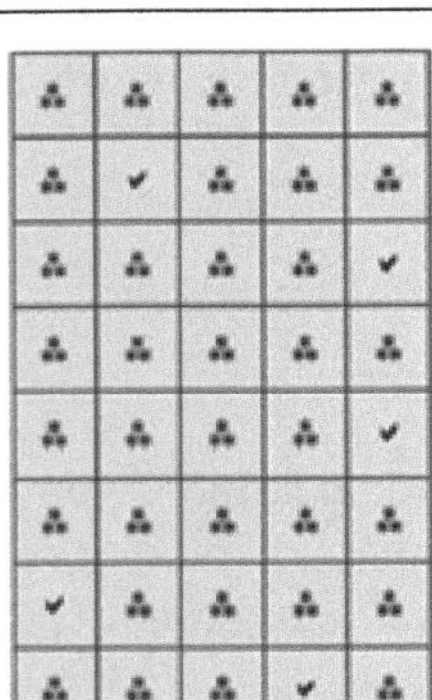	**Cluster sampling** Involves surveying within whole clusters of the population Clusters can include schools, hospitals, regions, etc. Clusters are sampled so that individuals within them can be surveyed/interviewed. The thinking here is that the best way to find high school students is through high schools; the best way to find hospital patients is through hospitals

	Often conducted in multiple stages. For example, if your population is hospital patients in China you would use a random sampling strategy to select regions across China, then use a sampling strategy to select a number of hospitals within these regions, before employing another sampling strategy to select your final patients from these selected hospitals
	Full population lists are not required, and eventuating samples can be geographically contained

There is growing recognition, however, that there is no longer a need to 'apologize' for these types of samples. Researchers using non-random samples may be involved in studies that are not working towards representativeness or generalizability. They may be selecting their sample for other defined purposes common in qualitative research. For example, they may be looking to include deviant, extreme, unique, unfamiliar, misunderstood, misrepresented, marginalized or unheard elements of a population. This is why non-random samples are sometimes called 'purposive' or 'theoretical' samples.

There is also growing recognition that non-random samples can credibly represent populations if: (1) selection is done with the goal of representativeness in mind; and (2) strategies are used to ensure samples match population characteristics. When working with populations that are hard to define and/or access (e.g. homeless women or sports people who have used steroids) non-random strategies may be the best option. There is, however, an added burden of responsibility in ensuring that eventuating samples are not biased. Specifically, researchers who are after representativeness need to be aware of **unwitting bias** and **erroneous assumptions**.

- Unwitting bias – This is the tendency to unwittingly act in ways that confirm what you might already suspect, something that can be quite easy to do when you are hand-picking your sample. For example, you may want to conduct a focus group that can help evaluate an initiative you have started in your workplace; unless you make a conscious decision to do otherwise, it is just too easy to stack the deck in your favour. Or in a study of sexually active teenagers, you may be drawn to those whose experiences tend to reinforce your belief that, say, parental conflict is related to sexual promiscuity. You unwittingly seek out teenagers whose history matches your preconceived notions. In both cases, any generalization will not be credible.
- Erroneous assumptions – This refers to sample selection premised on incorrect assumptions. Suppose you want to study Jewish women living in Detroit and you decide to go to Detroit's synagogues to look for volunteers. The problem is that you have assumed all Jewish women go to a synagogue. You might also make erroneous assumptions about the characteristics of 'elements' within your sample. Say, for example, you want to study teenage 'angst' and you select what you believe are extreme cases of angst. If your assumptions are incorrect and what you see as extreme is actually quite average, the generalizations you make will not be valid.

In order to control for such biases, it is worth brainstorming your assumptions and expectations as they relate to both your research questions and your sample. This will put you in a strong position to work towards the development of an appropriate sampling strategy.

Table 11.3 highlights a range of non-random sampling strategies. While they can be used to build representative samples, these strategies can also be called upon in studies that do not rely on representativeness; for example, when the goal is to build knowledge by working with cases and/or key informants.

Table 11.3 Non-random sampling

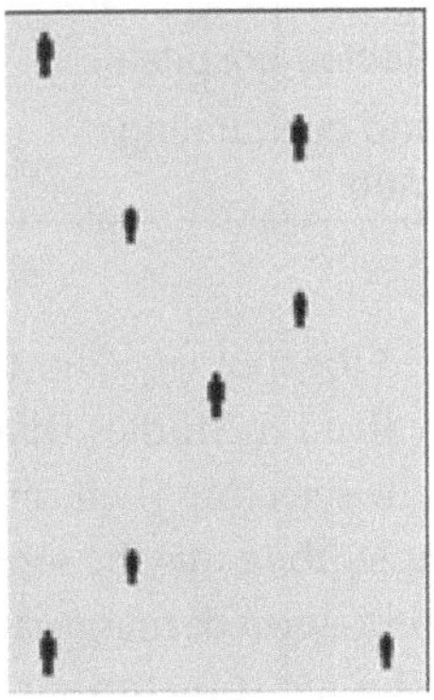	**Hand-picked sampling** Involves the selection of a sample with a particular purpose in mind Representativeness will depend on the researcher's ability to select cases that meet particular criteria such as typicality, wide variance, 'expertise' Other options include the selection of critical, extreme, deviant or politically important cases. While not likely to be representative, the selection of such cases allows researchers to study intrinsically interesting cases, or enhance learning by exploring the limits or boundaries of a situation or phenomenon
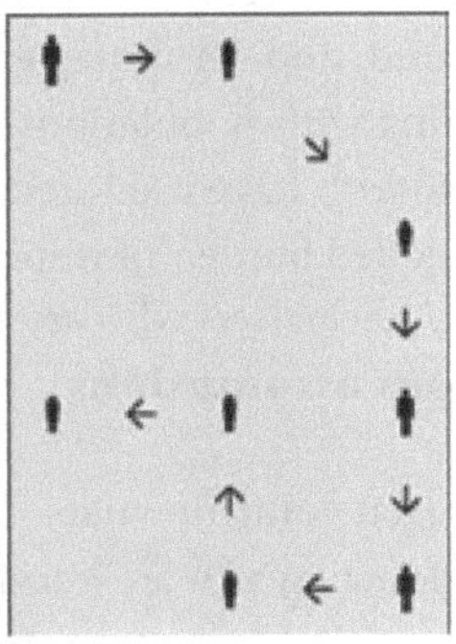	**Snowball sampling** Involves building a sample through referrals Once an initial respondent is identified, you ask him or her to identify others who meet the study criteria. Each of those individuals is then asked for further recommendations Often used when working with populations that are not easily identified or accessed. For example, a population of homeless persons can be hard to identify, but by using referrals a sample can build quite quickly Snowballing does not guarantee representativeness. An option here is to develop a population profile from the literature, and assess representativeness by comparing your sample with your profile
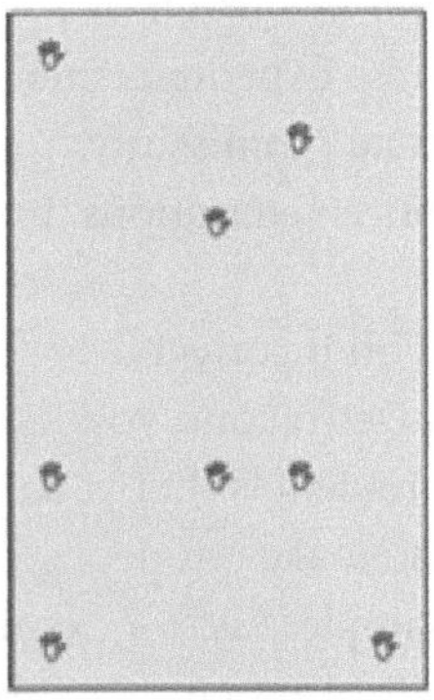	**Volunteer sampling** Involves selecting a sample by asking for volunteers. For example, putting an ad in the newspaper or going to local organizations such as schools or community groups While convenient, it is not likely to be representative. The characteristics of those who volunteer are likely to be quite distinct from those who do not Arguments for representativeness will rely on strategies used to minimize the difference between volunteers and the rest of the population
	**A note on 'convenience' sampling** In the course of your reading, you may have come across something referred to as 'convenience' sampling: that is, selecting a sample in a manner convenient to the researcher. In fact, non-random sampling is sometimes referred to in this way. But keep in mind that convenience sampling has no place in credible research.

	There needs to be more to a sampling strategy than just convenience. Limited time and resources may see convenience as one factor in sample selection. But convenience should not be the main criterion or descriptor of a sampling strategy. Regardless of type, all sampling strategies need to work towards the ultimate goal of research credibility

I Have a Question!

I Am Interested in How University Courses on Sexuality Differ in the US and Europe, and My Supervisor Suggested That I Do This by Comparing the Curricula of Relevant Courses. Should I Use a Sample, and Can I Use the Same Strategies as You Would for People?

Whether you need to sample will depend on the size of the population (how many courses there are), the depth of analysis you wish to do, the goals of your research and the time that you have to do it. So, say there are over 1,000 courses, you want to look at the syllabi of all relevant subjects, you want to compare the US and Europe, and time is limited. You are likely to need to sample. And yes, you can take much from the strategies above. Because you want to compare, non-random sampling would make sense, probably stratified random sampling. The logic here is the same. The major difference being the nature of your population. In an information age, this is ever more common. As our ability to access and sample the products of people increases, the need to survey them directly has actually decreased.

KEY INFORMANTS: WORKING WITH EXPERTS AND INSIDERS

There is no doubt that social science research has a bias towards samples, particularly representative samples. Because we can make arguments about generalizability, we think this is where we need to go in order to gather credible data. But the goal in rigorous research is to determine the best possible means for credible data collection, and, depending on your question, this might just mean working with key informants rather than samples.

Working with key informants means attempting to gather some insider or expert knowledge that goes beyond the private experiences, beliefs and knowledge base of the individual you are talking to. Your goal is to find out what this individual believes 'others' think, or how 'others' behave, or what this individual thinks the realities of a particular situation might be. Working with key informants means you believe the answers to your research questions lie with select individuals who have specialized knowledge and know what's going on.

But then again, who really knows what's going on? Take Zina's workplace as an example. If you were investigating her little academic world, you should not bother asking her anything, she is just not in the know. Instead, you could talk to her Head of School or the Dean – but then again they may end up giving you the party line; when you work at that level, you are sometimes forced to call on rhetoric. Wait, here is an idea: you should talk to Joycee from administration. She is an institution unto herself, and if anyone knows what's going on, she's the one. While she does not have official 'power', she does have knowledge – which, of course, is a form of power in its own right.

This type of scenario tends to be the case in almost any institution, organization or community group you might want to explore. There tend to be people 'in the know'. Whether through a position of power or some less official means, some people have a knack for knowing what's really going on. So it is not unusual for 'experts' or 'insiders' to be precisely the right people to help you answer your research questions.

Opportunities in Working with Key Informants

There is nothing like having an inside track or an expert at your fingertips. In fact, key informants can be instrumental in giving you access to a world you might have otherwise tried to understand while being locked on the outside. The insights you can gather from one key informant can be instrumental not only to the data you collect, but to how you process that data, and how you might make sense of your own experiences as well as the experiences of others.

Now this does not mean that all your data should come from key informants. Informants may end up being just one resource in your bid to build understandings – but they can do this in several ways. Key informants can:

- Be instrumental to preliminary phases of an investigation – Key informants can be called upon by researchers to build their own contextual knowledge. They might also be used to help generate relevant interview questions or be called on to aid in the construction or review of a survey instrument.
- Be used to triangulate or confirm the accuracy of gathered/generated data – Data from interviews with key informants can be used to confirm the authenticity of other data sources such as data gathered by survey, observation or document review. Key informants might also be called upon in a less formal way to overview data to confirm credibility, or to explore researcher interpretations for misunderstandings, misinterpretations or unrecognized bias.
- Be used to generate primary data – In-depth interviews with key informants can also be a primary source of qualitative data in their own right.

Informant Selection

There are six distinct challenges you need to face before you can work with key informants. The first is to identify the type of informant you are after. It is important to recognize that key informants do not need to be foremost experts. There are a number of characteristics that might make someone useful to your research processes. Depending on your research question and context, any or all of the following might have something to offer:

- Experts – The well-respected who sit at the top of their field.
- Insiders – Those who sit on the inside of an organization, culture or community and who are willing to share the realities of that environment.

- The highly experienced – Perhaps not deemed an expert, but someone with a rich depth of experience related to what you are exploring.
- A leader – This might be at a formal or informal level.
- The observant – Individuals in an organization or community who have a reputation for knowing who's who and what's what.
- The gossip – Similar to the observant but enjoys passing on observations (and sometimes rumours); it will pay to make sure your information here is accurate.
- Those with secondary experience – For example, if exploring the problem of youth suicide, in addition to youth you might look to certain counsellors, teachers or parents to provide relevant insights.
- Stool pigeons – Individuals who want to be classic police-type 'informants'; you will need to be wary of both overt and hidden agendas!
- The 'ex' – This might include someone who is disenfranchised, alienated, recovered, converted, retrenched, fired or retired.

The second challenge is to identify individuals who have the characteristics associated with that type. It makes sense to ask around or try a snowball technique in which you generate a list of informants through a referral process (see Table 11.3). One person in the know is likely to lead you to a host of others.

The third challenge is to confirm the status of those identified. Do they really have the expertise, experiences or insider knowledge that will inform your study in a credible way? The advice here is to seek confirmation by looking for things like a long record of involvement, direct personal experiences and detailed comments from potential informants that show internal consistency. You are after more than just broad generalizations.

The fourth challenge is related to your ability to gather open and honest information from your informants. Key informants must be accessible and willing to share information. If they have the knowledge you are after, but are not willing to share it, they will not be of any use to your study. Building trust (see Chapter 4) will be essential.

The fifth challenge is to look for and recognize informant subjectivities. All respondents will have a particular worldview and some will have a real agenda operating. Some may want to be listened to, some may have an axe to grind, some may like the sound of their own voice, some may think they know a lot more than they do, and some may think their particular take on an experience is how the world should or does respond to the same experience (sounds like a family reunion!). You will need to develop and build a strong relationship with your key informants, not only so they can open up to you, but so you are in a position to know how to best treat the data they provide.

The final challenge is related to ethics. If you look at the list of informant types above and think about their motivation, it should be pretty obvious that ethics and integrity need to come into play when selecting and working with key informants. In addition to the challenge of managing bias – both yours and theirs – you will need to think about your power as a researcher. You have to remember that key informants can be put, and can put themselves, in very vulnerable positions. It is your responsibility to respect their needs at all times.

Table 11.4 highlights some of the ethical issues you will need to negotiate when selecting and working with key informants.

Table 11.4 Key informants: opportunities and ethical dilemmas

Opportunities	Ethical dilemmas
Building relationships of trust to enhance flow of information	Having informants become too emotionally invested Developing friendships that are one way Making promises you cannot or do not intend to keep
Gaining the ability to avoid or skirt around official channels and protocols	Putting informants in an unethical position Acting unethically in regard to the organization you might be exploring
Being able to get your hands on confidential information	Asking for, expecting or accepting illegal/unethical conduct from your informants Acting unethically, and possibly illegally, in regard to the organization you might be exploring
Being able to really dig into the emotional aspects of a topic	Asking your informant to make a large emotional investment Having your informant relate private and personal details of others Asking your informants to relive their own unpleasant memories

I Have a Question!

What If You Have the Perfect Key Informant, but After Interviewing Them, You Get a Sense That They Aren't Telling You What's Really Going On. What Do You Do?

Trust your gut here. If you sense that credibility is an issue, do not just accept your informant at face value, no matter how good they seem on paper. Think about triangulation - can you confirm information through another source? Can you gather some background information to see if there is an agenda at play? Can you talk to someone else in the know and see if there is divergence, and even explore why? Remember the goal of your research is authenticity that will allow you to offer credible findings and sound recommendations. You cannot do that if you do not believe in your data.

CASES: DELVING INTO DETAIL

When it comes to respondents, how many is really enough: 100, 200, 1,500? Well, these are the kinds of numbers we think of when we think of samples/respondents. Even in qualitative research we are looking at 10, 20, 30 interviews. But what about one or two? Can one or two ever be enough? Can it ever be more than thin? When Zina was a student, a professor once told her that if she were to do a PhD that surveyed 1,500 people, he might expect her to generate between 1,500 and 3,000 pages of data. He then asked her how much data she thought he would expect from a single case study of one individual. She really had no idea and guessed 200–300 pages. He told her, 'No, 1,500–3,000 pages, same as the survey.'

In other words, he was telling her there is no shortcut. A case study is all about depth; it requires you to dig, and to dig deep. You need to delve into detail, dig into context and really get a handle on the rich experiences of the individual, event, community group or organization you want to explore. The goal is to get underneath what is generally possible in, for example, large-scale survey research.

If you think the answer to your research question might require this type of in-depth exploration, then legitimate, valid and worthwhile answers might just be held by or within a particular **case** or in a **case study**.

The use of cases in social science project research is more common than you might realize. Researchers often limit their methodological design to a particular context in a bid to maximize both relevance and practicality. At the practical end, cases are often located in one site, which means travel is minimized, access is enhanced and costs are reduced. But more importantly, it allows for the building of holistic understandings through prolonged engagement and the development of rapport and trust within a clearly defined and highly relevant context.

Prolonged engagement and immersion (common elements of case studies) can, however, involve their own costs. First, the required level of access can be difficult to negotiate. Second, because case studies draw from only one or even a few, the demands on that one or few, particularly when they are individuals, can be quite high. Third, researchers can come to have an effect on the researched and vice versa. Finally, immersion can come with emotional costs for all parties involved.

Now if you decide to tackle a case study, you may come across an academic who just won't give the time of day to any study not deemed to be representative or generalizable. But if you can clearly articulate your goals and show how your study contributes to a particular body of knowledge, you are more likely to establish credibility and worth. Cases can:

- Have an intrinsic value – Cases might be extremely relevant, politically 'hot', unique, interesting or even misunderstood; for example, exploring a cult undergoing close media scrutiny. They might also be important within and to a particular organization/community.
- Be used to debunk a theory – One case can show that what is commonly accepted might, in fact, be wrong; for example, societal assumptions related to violence in prison can be called into question through in-depth case exploration that attempts to understand the phenomenon from a prisoner's perspective.
- Bring new variables to light – Exploratory case studies can often bring new understandings to the fore; for example, in-depth exploration of a particular hospital emergency room might uncover new staff stressors yet to be identified in the literature.
- Provide supportive evidence for a theory – Case studies can be used to triangulate other data collection methods or to provide support for a theory; for example, a particular organization might be explored as a lived example of a twenty-first-century learning organization.
- Be used collectively to form the basis of a theory – A number of cases may be used to inductively generate new understandings; for example, finding empowerment as a common theme in the ability to recover from the stress of divorce might be the basis of new insights.

Case studies can also allow researchers to breach the quantitative–qualitative divide (see Chapter 9). In a case study of an organization, for example, strategies for data collection could easily include both survey research and in-depth interviewing. And that is worth stressing. Case studies allow for multiple methods that are determined by both the nature of the research question and the type of cases with which you're working. It is a wonderful site for using a range of data-collection methods (see Chapters 12 and 13).

Case Selection

If you think your research question can be illuminated by delving into cases, you will need to turn your attention to the process of case selection. Now if you already have a case in mind, and your research is designed around and for that case, then case selection has already occurred. But if you do need to select a case/cases there are two distinct processes involved. The first is to define your case, or to set the boundaries that will give meaning and characterization to the class of 'elements' you wish to explore. The second involves selecting an individual case or series of cases that meet your definition and sit within your case boundaries.

To define a case, you need to set clear and distinctive characteristics. Perhaps the broadest and easiest distinction here is to decide if your cases will be made up of individuals, institutions, events, cultural groups, etc. Will you be looking at people, places or things? Once this is determined, more specific criteria can be applied. For example, if your cases will be made up of individuals, you might turn to characteristics such as employment status, gender or race to narrow the case description. If you are looking at institutions, you might look at function (factory, hospital, school, etc.), location or size. Cultural groups (groups bound together by social traditions and common patterns of beliefs and behaviours) can be further defined by things like geography, social networks or shared hardships. Finally, for events, defining characteristics will be the nature of the event as well as things like timeframe, geography and size.

As shown in Figure 11.1, the possibilities are wide open. The only criteria are that your boundaries are clear, and you are able to argue the importance of case exploration within those boundaries.

Once your class of cases has been defined, your boundaries are clear and you know precisely what it is that you are trying to delve into, you will need to select the right case (or cases) from the range of possibilities. Now depending on your goals, you may decide to delve into only one case, or you may want to compare and contrast two or more cases. You might also decide to analyse a number of cases in order to make broader generalizations.

After determining the appropriate number of cases to be explored, the selection of any particular case or cases is generally done through a strategic process, with researchers often hand-picking cases with a particular purpose in mind. Factors that will influence case selection include:

- Pragmatics – There is nothing wrong with being practical. Pragmatics can involve commitments such as being commissioned/sponsored to study a particular case. They might also involve timely opportunities that see you take advantage of current events and work at being in the right place at the right time; for example, studying a community recovering from a flood event, or exploring a recent sports-related riot. Pragmatics can also involve accessibility where you take advantage of access that might normally be hard to get; for example, exploring a case that has connections to your own workplace, or delving into a case involving an individual with whom you have an existing relationship based on mutual trust and respect.

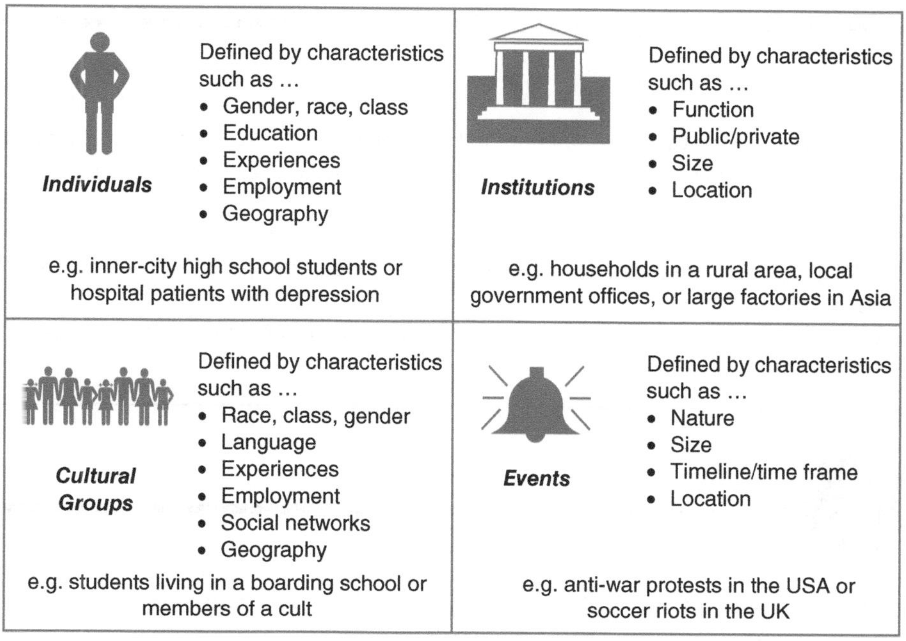

Figure 11.1 Defining a case

- Purposiveness – Researchers will often select cases they hope will enable them to make particular arguments. For example, if the purpose is to argue representativeness, you may select a case considered 'typical'. 'Extreme' or 'atypical' instances may be chosen in order to debunk a theory or highlight deviations from the norm, while wide variance in cases might be used to build new understandings and generate theory. The section on non-random sampling earlier in this chapter provides strategies that can be used in purposive case selection.
- Intrinsic interest – Researchers might also select a particular case because it is interesting in its own right. It might be relevant, unique, unfamiliar, misunderstood, misrepresented, marginalized, unheard, politically hot or the focus of current media attention. In this situation, the challenge is to argue the inherent worth and value of a particular case.

It is worth keeping in mind that a prerequisite for all case selection should be access. It is absolutely essential that researchers who wish to delve into cases will be able to reach required people and data. When working with individuals, your ability to generate rich data will depend on building high levels of trust and rapport. In an organizational setting, you may need to gain high-level access to relevant records and documents or be allowed broad access to an array of individuals associated with a case. In fact, organizational case studies may require you to seek respondents from within the case itself. This can see you searching for both key informants and samples, as discussed earlier in the chapter. No matter what the situation, the holistic understanding and rich detail demanded in case studies will require you to have access to what is going on 'inside'.

Critical Thinking Challenge 12

Who Holds the Answer?

Think of yourself as an investigator. You want to know something. You seek answers. But to find these answers, you need to know where they lie and, of course, answers can lie in more than one place (even if you don't have the time to dig them all up).

So where do you think the answer to your question lies? Can you find and access the right people? Will they be willing to talk to you? Will they be honest with you? Will you be able to look in alternative places?

We sometimes go from research questions to data collection without enough consideration of these questions that sit in the middle.

I Have a Question!

I Thought Case Studies Sit Under Qualitative Methodologies. Why Are You Covering It in This Chapter?

You are right; case studies are often classed as a qualitative methodology, and if you are reading other methods books (as if you would), you might find them covered in such a chapter. This is because they imply an in-depth approach to research that follows qualitative traditions. But cases are also an object of study similar to that of a population or key informant. Yes, cases may be more complex and imply qualitative methodological approaches/methods (although case studies on organizations or communities can involve surveys), but for us, they're still a site of investigation, hence the decision to treat cases in this chapter. But even given a variance in how case studies are classified, a big divergence in understanding should not be inferred. More likely it is simply a difference of opinion on where and how they should be presented. The goal of reflexive research into cases, regardless of how it is labelled, is likely the same. As researchers, we are after in-depth, sensitive, appropriate, insightful studies that lead to credible findings and an ability to add to a knowledge base.

Chapter Summary

- Knowing who might hold the answer to your questions or where the answers lie, whether it be populations, key informants, cases or a combination of these, and how you will open up opportunities to gather information from them, is fundamental to collecting credible data.
- Within a respondent type you will need to face the challenge of locating and accessing respondents who are appropriate, representative, open, honest, knowledgeable, have good memories, are not afraid to expose themselves and do not feel a need to present themselves in any particular light.

- Sampling allows us to gather information from a 'few' in order to capture the thoughts, knowledge, attitudes, feelings and/or beliefs of the 'many'. Random sampling aims to generate a representative sample, while non-random sampling allows respondents to be hand-picked, or found through snowball techniques or by volunteering.
- Key informants can be a valuable source of information in project research. They can be used in preliminary phases of an investigation; to triangulate and confirm data; or as a primary source of data per se. Informants can include experts, the experienced, leaders, the observant, gossips, those with secondary experience, insiders, stool pigeons and 'ex'es.
- Studying elements of the social through comprehensive description and analysis of a single situation or case is called a case study. While not necessarily representative, cases can add to new knowledge through their ability to debunk theory, generate theory and support existing theory.

FIND YOUR NEXT STEP

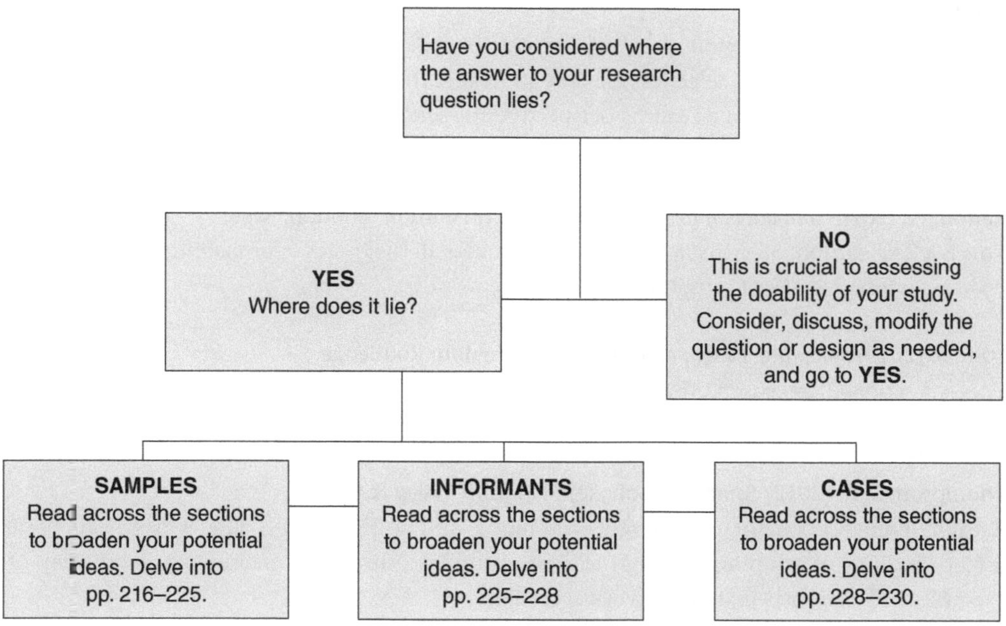

FURTHER READING

While there is plenty of literature that can help you in your quest to work with both samples and cases, it is much more difficult to find literature that deals directly with key informants. You can, however, extrapolate quite a bit from readings on both 'non-random' sampling and case selection.

Samples and Sampling

Blair, E. and Blair, J. (2014) *Applied Survey Sampling*. London: Sage.
This book covers the basics and the complexities of gathering a survey sample. It not only covers standard procedures but also challenges associated with low response rates, online surveys, cell-phone use and the emergence of Big Data.

Boeri, M. and Rashi, S. (eds) (2019) *Inside Ethnography: Researchers Reflect on the Challenges of Reaching Hidden Populations*. Los Angeles: University of California Press.
We sometimes forget to question the accessibility of populations. But we need to if we want to get a sense of hidden populations. Using a qualitative perspective, this work reflects on the challenge of research that involves marginalized and hidden populations.

Daniel, J. (2011) *Sampling Essentials: Practical Guidelines for Making Sampling Choices*. London: Sage.
A good non-technical guide that will help you make appropriate sampling choices without the need to delve into formulae or statistics. A good starting point for students.

Emmel, N. (2013) *Sampling and Choosing Cases in Qualitative Research: A Realistic Approach*. London: Sage.
The gold standard in sampling is 'representativeness'. But what do you do in small-scale qualitative research where selection must be strategic? This book takes you through the ins and outs of case selection from a realist's perspective showing how non-random selection can lead to credible research outcomes.

Kalton, G. (2020) *Introduction to Survey Sampling*, 2nd edition. London: Sage.
This is a 2nd edition, 35 years in the making. It covers all the basics of probability sampling, but now includes coverage of sampling in our online world.

Lohr, S. (2019) *Sampling: Design and Analysis*. Abingdon: Routledge.
This is a more advanced text that delves right into the complexity of sampling. Best suited for graduate students, particularly those working with statistical analysis software.

Thompson, S. K. (2012) *Sampling*. Hoboken, NJ: John Wiley & Sons.
Great reference book for obtaining, interpreting and using sample data. Goes from basic understandings of sampling through to more complex estimation methods. A good array of exercises and examples makes the work accessible.

Wu, C. and Thompson, M. (2020) *Sampling Theory and Practice*. New York: Springer.
This is a very comprehensive new work that tackles basic sampling theory, current research trends and challenges. Could be a one-stop shop.

Cases/Case Studies

The readings offered here all have sections on case selection, but they also provide guidance on appropriate methods. No need to limit yourself. As you develop your approach and decide if you will be interviewing, surveying, observing and/or exploring documents, be sure to refer to the following texts and their recommended readings.

Thomas, G. (2021). *How to Do Your Case Study*, 3rd edition. Sage.
A friendly writing style and a strong coverage of theory and practice for doing case study research.

Gerring, J. (2016) *Case Study Research: Principles and Practices*. Cambridge: Cambridge University Press.
A good section here on case selection. We also like the acknowledgement and coverage of various approaches that can be incorporated into case studies, including experiments, ethnography, observations, interviews and surveys.

Hancock, D. R. and Algozzine, R. (2016) *Doing Case Study Research: A Practical Guide for Beginning Researchers*. New York: Teachers College Press.
From developing a rationale to reviewing the literature, designing a study, interviewing, observing, analysing and writing up, this book will take you step-by-step through the conduct of a case study. A good starting point for someone embarking on this research strategy.

Stake, R. E. (1995) *The Art of Case Study Research*. Thousand Oaks, CA: Sage.
A classic in the making, this book draws from a range of qualitative approaches in its exploration of the case study. The use of an actual case to explore key lessons in case study design and conduct works extremely well. Definitely worth a look.

Swanborn, P. (2010) *Case Study Research: What, Why and How?* Thousand Oaks, CA: Sage.
The strength of this work is the way it brings together and discusses various standards of case study research. It will help you make informed decisions and appropriately situate your research.

Yin, R. K. (2017) *Case Study Research: Design and Methods*. Thousand Oaks, CA: Sage.
We like how comprehensive this book is. It offers over 50 case studies drawn from a wide range of disciplines. Good coverage of quantitative, qualitative and mixed-methods approaches. Delving into this work will definitely give you a good feel for case study research.

12

PRIMARY DATA

Surveys, Interviews and Observation

Learning Objectives

- The opportunities and challenges of collecting primary data
  - To understand the importance of primary data in research studies
- Surveying
  - To understand the nature of surveying and when it is most appropriate to undertake
  - To be able to construct and pilot a robust survey instrument
- Interviewing
  - To understand the nature of interviewing and when it is most appropriate to undertake
  - To be able to effectively plan and conduct an interview
- Observation
  - To understand the nature of observation and when it is most appropriate to undertake
  - To be able to effectively plan and conduct an observational study

THE OPPORTUNITIES AND CHALLENGES OF COLLECTING PRIMARY DATA

Primary data is data collected by researchers expressly for their research purposes – it is data that does not exist independent of the research process. Primary data is current, created by the researcher and, most importantly, it is targeted to specific issues the researcher is exploring.

The most common way to collect primary data is through surveys and interviews. These methods put you, as the researcher, in charge. Not only do you get to ask what you want, when you want, you also get to ask it how you want – you get to choose the wording, the order, the **prompts**, the **probes**. Observation studies are similar in that you set up the protocols for data collection – you decide what you will observe, when you will observe it, what you will record as 'data'. In all three approaches, data collection is directed with some precision towards your research question, hypothesis, aims and objectives, and this has real appeal. The data collected is in fact custom-built for your research project.

But there are some challenges associated with the collection of primary data. For one, it is a lot of work. Whether it be surveys, interviews or observation studies, it is not easy to design your own research protocols. Survey instruments are notoriously difficult to get right. Getting through a series of interviews and thoughtfully analysing them can be an exercise in frustration. And observation studies can be complex and leave you with a pile of messy data.

Primary data collection is also time-consuming, often expensive and doesn't always go to plan. Getting enough survey respondents within your timeframe, racing around different parts of the city or state to conduct an interview, and the prolonged engagement that observation sometimes demands – all those need to be factored into the research design decision-making process.

If you can overcome these challenges, however, there can be great rewards. You have data expressly generated for your own research purposes, and this will surely give you insights not available if you had used a pre-existing data set.

So what do you need to know in order to get the most from these methods?

SURVEYING

You are probably all too familiar with surveys and surveying. Zina hates to admit it, but when she was an undergraduate at Rutgers University, she actually worked for a market research company. Yes, she was one of those highly annoying people who called in the middle of dinner and asked if you would mind 'answering just a few short questions that should only take a couple of moments of your time'. As the French author de Certeau (2002) said, 'surveys are everywhere'. Market research, political polling, customer service feedback, evaluations, opinion polls, social science research – when we want to know what the masses are thinking, we survey.

Options and Possibilities

You may think all surveys are the same, but they're not. In fact, in order to determine which approach best suits you and your research agenda, you will need to work through several key features in Table 12.1. The survey approach you adopt will be dependent upon whether you

Table 12.1 Survey issues and types

Do you plan to sample or ask everyone in your population?	
Census: a survey that does not rely on a sample. In other words, a survey that covers every single person in a defined population	The US Census is a good example. A smaller-scale census might be all the students in a particular school
Cross-sectional surveys: surveys that use a sample or cross-section of respondents. The goal is to be able to represent your target population and generalize findings back to that population	Most surveys fall under this category, e.g. a community survey that targets only one in ten households but aims to represent the entire community
Will your survey simply describe or attempt to explain?	
Descriptive surveys: the goal is to get a snapshot or to describe your respondents by gathering: demographic information, e.g. age, socio-economic status and gender; personal information/behaviours, e.g. voting patterns or use of illegal drugs; and attitudinal information, e.g. attitudes towards multinational corporations, abortion or health care costs	A classic example here is political polling, which attempts to describe voters and voter intentions
Will your survey simply describe or attempt to explain?	
Explanatory surveys: the goal is to build complex understandings that go beyond description or even correlation. The aim is to figure out why things might be the way they are; in other words, determine cause and effect	An Australian newspaper recently conducted a survey that collected data describing attitudes to the Iraq conflict as well as data used to establish what might shape and form those attitudes, e.g. personal experience, familial attitudes and political leanings
Will you survey over a period of time and, if so, do you want to explore changing times or changing people?	
Trend surveys: a trend survey asks the same cross-section (similar groups of respondents) the same questions at two or more points in time. The goal here is to see if classifications of individuals change over time	An example here is a three-phase survey conducted over a 20-year period (1989, 1999, 2009) that asks newlyweds their attitudes towards marriage. The goal is to assess if attitudes of newlyweds now are the same as attitudes of newlyweds in the late 1980s and 1990s
Panel study: a panel study involves asking the same (not similar) sample of respondents the same questions at two or more points in time. The goal here is to see if individuals themselves change over time	Using the example above, if you had surveyed newlyweds in 1989, you would survey these same individuals in 1999 (10 years after their marriage) and again in 2009 in order to assess attitudinal shifts as individuals get older
How do you plan to administer your survey?	
Face-to-face surveys: *Pros*: good response rate, allow rapport and trust to be established, can motivate respondents, allow for clarification, prompting, probing and the reading of non-verbal cues *Cons:* can be lengthy and expensive, limit geographical range, do not assure anonymity or confidentiality, and require surveyor training	One example here is the mall or supermarket survey where you are stopped by someone with a clipboard ready to ask you a series of questions
Telephone surveys: *Pros*: relatively inexpensive, allow wide geographic coverage, offer some assurance of anonymity and confidentiality, and allow for some clarification, prompting, probing *Cons:* response rate can be low, it is easy to catch people at a bad time, respondents can hang up on you if they've had enough and you are limited to surveying only those with a telephone	In market research the telephone tends to be the mode of choice – but as more and more individuals get annoyed by this, it becomes harder for social science researchers to get individuals to participate over the phone
Self-administered mail/e-mail/online surveys: *Pros:* can offer confidentiality/anonymity, allow wide geographic coverage, and give respondents the opportunity to answer in their own time *Cons:* response rates can be very low, do not allow for clarification, and the snail mail version can end up being costly	These can include snail mail, e-mail and online surveys. Online e-mail can save you thousands in printing and postage costs, but you are limited to surveying within online populations. Additionally, the proliferation of spam mail means that unless your respondents know you, your survey may not even be looked at

want to: sample a range of respondents or target everyone in your population; describe or explain; capture a moment, changing times or changing people; administer face-to-face, or by mail, email or phone.

Issues and Complexities

When it comes to the collection of credible data, there are no easy answers. There will always be trade-offs between opportunities and challenges, and this is certainly true when it comes to surveying. While surveys can offer much to the production of knowledge, their reputation for being a relatively simple, straightforward and inexpensive approach is not really deserved – they can be a thorny and exasperating process, particularly if you want to do it right.

On the upside, surveys can: reach a large number of respondents; represent an even larger population; allow for comparisons; generate standardized, quantifiable, empirical data; generate qualitative data through the use of open-ended questions; be confidential and even anonymous.

On the downside, constructing and administering a survey that has the potential to generate credible and generalizable data is truly difficult. As you probably realize, there are a lot of badly designed surveys out there that aren't worth the paper they are printed on, yet the data they generate are reported as truth and used in all kinds of decision-making processes. Challenges associated with surveying include: capturing the quantifiable data you require; gathering in-depth data; getting a representative sample to respond; getting anyone at all to respond; needing proficiency in statistical analysis; only getting answers to the questions you have thought to ask; going back to your respondents if more data is required.

The Survey Process

Conducting a good survey is a process that involves several steps. Surveys require you to: plan your attack; develop your survey instrument; pilot your approach; make necessary modifications; administer; and manage/analyse your data. Boxes 12.1–12.4 break this down and outline the steps involved in surveying. You should find these boxes helpful as both guides and checklists.

Planning

Without a doubt, the success of your survey will hinge on the thought you put into your planning processes. A good survey does not just happen. It is planned. There are a range of crucial considerations necessary before you even begin the task of survey construction, from knowing your target population and how your sampling approach will represent that population, through to issues of access and ethics, consideration of who you are in terms of both biases and skills, and of course being clear about the data you seek and how you will prepare for the unexpected.

Box 12.1 takes you through the essential steps in planning a survey.

Box 12.1

Planning a Good Survey – Consideration of 'Who', 'Where', 'When', 'How' and 'What'

The main planning points to consider are:

1. Population and sample/respondent/participants – Who you plan to speak about (population) and gather data from (sample) (see Chapter 11).
2. Access – How you will reach your sample. This includes considering any language or cultural barriers that might limit access, as well as where and how you will seek respondents.
3. Your biases – Recognizing and controlling for subjectivities in ways that can best ensure the credibility of any survey instrument you use.
4. Your skills – How you might develop the skills/resources needed to carry out your survey, e.g. proficiency in using survey software and conducting statistical analysis.
5. Ethics/ethics approval – Consideration of any ethical dilemmas inherent in your project and getting appropriate ethics approval.
6. Data – Thinking through the aspects of your research question that can be answered through a questionnaire. Also considering if the shape and form of the data you will collect will be compatible with intended modes of analysis.
7. Details – Distribution, reminders, response rates and data management.
8. Contingencies – The unexpected, the unplanned and the unfortunate. This means having a back-up plan ready if response rates are low.

Developing Your Questionnaire

What a fantastic challenge – but not an easy one. Novices tend to think they can simply whack together a few questions tied to their research question, do a section on demographics, and that's it. But it is not so easy: there are only about a dozen traps and pitfalls along the way! To really do questionnaire construction properly you need to think about whether you can capitalize on any existing questionnaires, and if not, how you can move your concepts to variables; how to best draft your questions; what response categories will best capture the data you want; and allow for the right statistical analysis, review, rewrite, layout and offering of clear instruction. Emma once worked on a project surveying academics across 30 countries. There were pre-existing questions, but it took almost as much work to adapt the questions to the local context as it would have to start from scratch!

Piloting and Modification

You're thinking 'Yes! This questionnaire is looking good – time to send it out.' Well, hold on there. Not so quick. We guarantee you that you have fallen into at least some of the more common survey traps and pitfalls. And the best way to find this out? Pilot. It is essential that you have a run-through and that you get the feedback you need, not only in terms of the respondents' experience, but also in terms of the quality of the data you've collected and how amenable it is to statistical analysis. From there a round or two of modification and you'll be getting close. Box 12.2 takes you through the steps in piloting and modifying your survey.

Box 12.2

Piloting and Modifying Your Survey

Good planning and development are essential - but not sufficient. The only way really to know if something is going to work is to give it a try.

1 Have a run-through - Pilot your process with a group of respondents whose background is similar to those in your 'sample'.
2 Reflect - Reflect on the piloting process and note any difficulties you encounter. Also review your data and note any difficulties in making sense of your completed surveys.
3 Seek feedback - Get feedback from the pilot group in relation to the effectiveness of the cover letter, the overall layout and design, the usefulness of the instructions, the question wording and the length of time it took to complete the questionnaire.
4 Trial your statistics package - Attempt to create variables, code the pilot responses and then enter them into a statistical program to see if you are likely to encounter any issues when you input your main data.
5 Make modifications - This will be based on your reflections, the feedback from your pilot group, as well as the quality of the data generated.
6 Back to the start? - If the need for modification is substantial, you may need to revisit your planning, development and piloting process. This may involve a return to the ethics committee.

Survey Administration and Analysis

Woo hoo! Finally! You can now get down to the business of administering your questionnaire, collecting your data and making sense of it all. And yes, whether face-to-face, snail mail, email or online, it is time to get your survey out to your respondent group. But just remember that this is only half of the story – and the easy half of the story at that. The other half is getting your respondents to complete it. And then of course is the meaning making – statistical analysis and making sense of those statistics. Unless your data is effectively managed and thoughtfully analysed, all your hard work will be wasted. Box 12.3 takes you through the steps in survey administration and analysis.

There is a good chance you'll be considering administering your survey online in some form – emailing people directly, advertising on social media, or recruiting respondents from crowdsourcing platforms like Amazon's Mechanical Turk. Online surveys have low administration costs and data is automatically entered into a database – no manual data entry required – with basic statistical analysis also something that can happen 'automatically'. But consider whether you will be able to reach your targeted response group. First, is all of your population online? If not, who is missing? Do you attempt to capture them, and, if so, how?

Second, will people be bothered to fill in your questionnaire? The Internet is awash with surveys and you might get low response rates, incomplete surveys, or even worse, bots completing your survey rather than real people! Third, there are important ethical considerations to platforms like Mechanical Turk that pay workers (limited) compensation for completing surveys.

Without a representative sample and adequate response rate, you're likely to encounter non-response bias, where those who participate in your survey are qualitatively different from those who don't, thereby leaving you with results that cannot be generalized back to your population.

Box 12.3

Survey Administration and Analysis

Most researchers want to get to this point as quickly as possible, and some are willing to short-cut some of the steps above, but this is a sure-fire way to get into trouble.

1. Administration - Time to distribute your questionnaires. Think creatively about how you will distribute/advertise your survey to reach the people you are after. One of Emma's students printed out flyers with a QR code to the online survey and left these in lecture theatres and places where students gather on campus.
2. Low-response-rate plan - Put this into action if not enough data has been gathered by your deadline.
3. Organize/collate your data as soon as possible - When the time comes to work with your data, nothing is worse than a big mess. Be systematic and organized, use a database if appropriate and enter data expediently.
4. Analysis - Time to see what your data yield. Most survey data will be analysed statistically (see Chapter 15), but you will need to engage in thematic analysis for any open-ended questions (see Chapter 16).

The Survey Instrument

Students often underestimate the difficulty of constructing a good survey instrument. The best advice is to take it in steps, pilot and get lots of feedback. It is almost impossible to get a questionnaire right the first time around. As discussed below, developing a questionnaire will require you to: (1) operationalize your concepts; (2) formulate your questions; (3) decide on response categories; (4) provide background information and clear instructions; (5) decide on organization and length; and finally, (6) create an aesthetically pleasing layout and design. All of this needs to be done in conjunction with several stages of piloting and redevelopment.

Concept Operationalization

Operationalizing concepts refers to turning abstract concepts into measurable variables. Suppose you wanted to conduct a survey that could help you determine if old-fashioned parenting was a cause of teenage rebellion. Your abstract concepts would be 'old-fashioned parenting' and 'teenage rebellion'. Operationalizing these concepts means not only defining them, but also developing indicators so that you can determine whether your survey respondents are the products of some level of old-fashioned parenting and whether they should be considered rebellious and to what extent.

This is an area where a lot of projects fall short. Students want to capture concepts, but they don't put enough effort into exploring the literature and searching for measures that have proven to be both valid and reliable (validated measures). Concepts such as self-esteem, anger, angst and poverty, for example, have been studied by countless researchers who have developed various scales, items and indicators that can capture these concepts with credibility. This is definitely a situation where you do not want to reinvent the wheel. Remember: your goal is to add to a body of knowledge, and drawing on what other researchers have done is an important part of the process.

Valid and reliable indicators for various concepts, however, cannot always be located in the literature. A student of Zina's, for example, has set out to determine levels of environmental citizenship in Australian adults. Standard, valid, reliable indicators of environmental citizenship, however, have yet to be established. Now if she manages to capture this, not only will she make a contribution to the literature by offering an understanding of Australians' levels of environmental citizenship, but she will also be offering a range of indicators that can be used in measuring this concept.

One of the most common ways to operationalize a concept is to have a scale that allows you to place respondents along a continuum for some variable of interest. Suppose you wanted to understand high school students' attitudes towards online learning – your goal might be to give them a rating that indicates where they fall, from least to most positive. Three options are Likert, **Guttman** and **Thurstone scales**.

For each type of scale, development begins by generating a large set of items (as many as 100) that reflect the concept you are interested in. A good idea is brainstorming with a knowledgeable group. If you were to do this for items related to high-school students' attitudes towards online learning you might come up with a list of items including the following:

1 I think online learning is better than face-to-face instruction.
2 I am comfortable using zoom with my teachers.
3 I do not want to speak up in a zoom classroom.
4 I think online learning is the way of the future.
5 I think my school adapted well to online learning during the pandemic.
6 And so on ... (up to 100 items).

For all three scales, the next step is to have experts give opinions on how relevant each statement is to the concept. Now it is important to realize that you are not interested in whether the experts personally agree with each statement – you just want to understand whether they think it is relevant.

Each scale has its own way of gathering expert opinion on relevance – which leads to the three distinct scales, as follows:

- Likert – To rate relevance, experts use five-point scales such as 1 = strongly unfavourable to the concept, 2 = somewhat unfavourable to the concept, 3 = undecided, 4 = somewhat favourable to the concept, 5 = strongly favourable to the concept. The researcher then uses a statistics package to compute correlations between all pairs of items, and keeps items with the highest correlations with the total score across all items (high levels of correlation show that experts are in agreement on these particular items). The goal is to come up with 10–15 reliable items.

  - Administering the scale involves asking respondents to rate each of the chosen 10–15 items on a four- to nine-point response scale. A five-point scale, for instance, might consist of 1 = strongly disagree, 2 = disagree, 3 = undecided, 4 = agree, 5 = strongly agree. Scales with an odd number of points offer a neutral midpoint, while even-number scales omit the neutral midpoint and force the respondents to take sides. To get the overall rating, individual item scores are summed.

- Guttman – Experts give a yes for each statement that is favourable towards the concept and a no for each that is not. The researcher then constructs a table that shows respondents' answers on all items and sorts this into a matrix so that respondents who agree with more statements are listed at the top and those agreeing with fewer are at the bottom. The goal is to come up with a set of items that are ordered so that a respondent who agrees with any specific question in the list will also agree with all previous questions. So, if the respondent scores a 3, it should mean that he or she agreed with the first three statements. If the respondent scores a 7, it should mean he or she agreed with the first seven. The object is to find a set of items (done through scalogram analysis) that perfectly matches this pattern.

  - Administering the scale involves asking respondents to check items they agree with. Each item has a scale value associated with it (obtained from the scalogram analysis), and to get the overall rating you simply add the scale values of every item respondents checked.

- Thurstone – Experts rate each item from 1 to 11, where 1 is extremely unfavourable towards the concept and 11 is extremely favourable towards the concept. The researcher then computes the **median** and **inter-quartile** ranges for each item and selects the statements that are at equal intervals across the range of medians and have a small range (this shows most agreement between experts). The goal is to come up with a yardstick for measuring where people sit on a continuum. Items with higher medians should indicate a more favourable attitude towards the concept.

  - Administering the scale involves asking participants to agree or disagree with each statement. To get the overall rating you average the medians of all the items that the respondents agreed with.

Question Formulation

There is certainly more than one way to ask the same question. In fact, the possibilities are almost endless. The dilemma here is that subtle (or not so subtle) differences can affect your data. Box 12.4 offers a distillation of the most fundamental rules related to question wording. The aim is to help you avoid the pitfalls of leading, offending or confusing your respondents.

Box 12.4

Questions to Avoid

Good questions should be unambiguous, inoffensive and unbiased - something easier said than done. It is easy to fall into the trap of constructing questions that are:

Poorly Worded

- Complex terms and language - There are plenty of people who are hippopotomonstrosesquipedaliophobic (scared of big words). If these words are not necessary, don't use them. Polysyllabic linguistic terminology can act to obscure connotations ... big words can be confusing.
- Ambiguous questions - Frames of reference can be highly divergent, so writing an ambiguous question is easy. For example, consider the questions 'How big is your family?' and 'Do you use drugs?' Families can be nuclear or extended; for children of separated parents, they may include two households. Similarly, 'drugs' is an ambiguous term. Some respondents will only consider illegal drugs, while others may include prescription drugs. And, of course, it would be impossible to know whether alcohol or cigarettes were also considered.
- Double negatives - Like many people, we have a hard time with double negatives. Take the following agree/disagree statement: 'You are not satisfied with your job.' To state that you are satisfied, you would have to choose 'disagree', which can be quite confusing.
- Double-barrelled questions - This is when you ask for only one response to a question with more than one issue. For example, 'Do you consider the president to be an honest and effective leader?' Respondents may think yes, effective - but no, definitely not honest.

Biased, Leading or Loaded

- Ring-true statements - These are statements that are easy to agree with simply because they tend to 'ring true'. Some good examples here are agree/disagree statements like 'You really can't rely on people these days' and 'Times may be tough, but there are generally people around you can count on'. Both of these somewhat opposite statements are likely to get a high percentage of 'agrees' because they tend to sound reasonable.
- Hard-to-disagree-with statements - These are statements where your respondents are likely to think 'Yes that's true, but ...'. They are not, however, given a chance to elaborate and are forced to agree or disagree. For example, 'It is good for young children if their mothers stay at home through the week'.
- Leading questions - Leading respondents in a particular direction can be done unintentionally, or intentionally for political purposes. Consider how the wording of these agree/disagree statements might affect responses: 'Protecting defenceless endangered species from inhumane slaughter is something the government should take seriously' versus 'The protection of biodiversity should be a government priority'; 'Mothers have the right to murder an unborn child' versus 'Women should be able to make choices about their own bodies'.

Problematic for the Respondent

- Recall-dependent questions - These are questions that rely on memory. For example, 'How many relationships have you had?' Without boundaries such as level of significance or timeframe, this question can be easy to answer 'incorrectly'.

- Offensive questions – If respondents take offence to a question or a series of questions, not only are they likely to skip them, but they may stop answering there. Offensive questions can range from 'What did you do to make your husband leave you?' to 'How much money do you earn?'
- Questions with assumed knowledge – Don't assume your respondents know about, or are familiar with, the same things as you. Take, for example, the agree/disagree statement 'Marxist theory has no place in twenty-first-century politics'. You should not be surprised when the response here is 'What kind of academic crap is this?!'
- Questions with unwarranted assumptions – Respondents are likely to be at a loss when it comes to answering a question that contains an assumption they do not agree with. For example, the question 'What was the most enjoyable part of your hospital stay?' assumes that the respondents enjoyed something about their hospitalization.
- Questions with socially desirable responses – This is more likely to be an issue in face-to-face surveying. For example, a respondent may be uncomfortable disagreeing with the statement 'Do you think women serving in the armed forces should have the same rights and responsibilities as their male colleagues?', especially if the interviewer is female.
- Questions about mundane or hard to measure things – some things are so everyday we do them without thinking which makes it problematic to get an accurate response. For example, 'How long do you spend on social media each day?' is not only subject to social desirability (most of us spend longer than we think we ought to) but also accuracy problems. Unless you track your social media usage already, you probably don't have an accurate sense of precisely how long you've been scrolling (let alone that it might vary day to day!).

Working within these guidelines is a start, but unlikely to be enough. Once you have drafted your questions, run them past an experienced researcher. They are likely to pick up things you have missed. You can also trial your questions with your peers. They will certainly be able to tell you if you managed to confuse, offend or lead them in any way. Finally, once you have made modifications based on feedback received, you will need to run a pilot study. The idea here is to distribute your survey to a small group of individuals whose characteristics match those of your sample and then thoroughly debrief with them. Remember: in the end it is not what you think, or even what your supervisor or peers think that counts; the only opinion that really matters will be that of your eventual respondents.

Response Categories

As if making your questions as precise and unproblematic as possible was not enough, a good survey and good survey data are equally dependent on the response categories you use. And there are a lot of things to consider here. First, response categories will influence the data you collect. For example, if you add an 'I'm not sure' option to a controversial yes/no question, it will affect your findings. Second, different types of response categories generate data with different types of **measurement scales**, and data with different measurement scales demand quite distinct statistical treatment. In fact, understanding the difference between **nominal**, ordinal, interval and **ratio** data (as discussed in Chapter 15) will definitely facilitate the process of survey construction, particularly determining response categories. But until you actually have some data to play with, the relationship between data types and survey construction might seem quite abstract.

This makes conducting your first survey a real challenge. So, we come back to the need for a good pilot study. A pilot study will allow you not only to assess your questions and response categories from the perspective of your respondents, but also to generate a small data set that you can enter into a database and work with statistically. This really is the best way to see how your data-collection protocols, including response category determination (whether open or closed), will impact on your analysis.

Open Responses

With open responses respondents are asked to provide answers using their own words. They can offer any information or express any opinion they wish, although the amount of space provided for an answer will generally limit the response. The data provided can be rich and candid, but can also be difficult to code and analyse.

Closed Responses

With closed responses, respondents are asked to choose from a range of predetermined responses. The data here is generally easy to code and statistically analyse. Closed-response categories come in many forms, each with their associated issues.

Yes/No or Agree/Disagree

Do you drink alcohol? Yes/No

'Drinking is bad for your health' Agree/Disagree

While it can be easy to work with 'binomial' data (or data with only two potential responses), you need to consider whether respondents will be comfortable with only two choices. For example, in the first question a respondent might be thinking 'Not really (I only drink when I go out, which is hardly ever)', or for the second question, 'It depends on how much you're talking about'. A potential strategy is to offer a 'don't know' or 'no opinion' option, but this allows for a lot of 'fence sitting'. This is also a place where politics and your own subjectivity need to be considered. For example, many surveys present 'male' and 'female' for respondents to choose from, which conveys an assumption of a gender binary. Different ways of asking the question can be more inclusive, but come with their own issues of interpretation and analysis.

Fill in the Blank

How much do you weigh? ____________________

Even a simple question like this (assuming your respondents know the answer and are willing to tell you) can lead to messy data. Will respondents write 90 kg, 198 lb or 14 stone? Of course you can convert these answers to one system, but that is not going to be possible if they just put 9C.

Choosing from a List

What would you drink most often?

Beer Wine Spirits Mixed drinks Cocktails

There is an assumption here that there will not be any 'ties'; you need to consider what you will do if more than one option is circled. You also need to make sure all options are covered (options are collectively exhaustive) and do not overlap (are mutually exclusive). A potential strategy is to offer an 'Other' or 'Other: __________' option.

Ordering Options

Please place the following drinks in order of preference:

Beer Wine Spirits Mixed drinks Cocktails

These questions tend to be quite difficult for respondents, particularly if lists are long. It is worth remembering that if respondents get frustrated trying to answer, they are likely to leave the question blank, leave it half-finished or just write anything at all.

Interval Response Scale

'It is normal for teenagers to binge drink.'

1	2	3	4	5
Strongly disagree	Disagree	Unsure	Agree	Strongly agree

Interval response scales – often referred to as Likert scales – offer a range of responses, generally ranging from something like 'Strongly disagree' to 'Strongly agree'. In this type of scale, you will need to consider: the number of points you will use; whether you will force the respondent to take sides by using an even number of responses; and whether you think your respondents are likely to 'get on a roll' and keep circling a particular number.

Information and Instructions

A survey instrument is not complete without some level of background information that can give credibility to your study and make your respondents feel like they are a part of something. In your background information, it is a good idea to include: the sponsoring organization/university; the survey's purpose; assurances of anonymity/confidentiality; and a 'thank you' for time/assistance. This information can be included at the start of the survey, or as a cover letter.

Also crucial are instructions. What might be self-evident to you may not be so obvious to your respondents. Instructions should introduce each section of the survey, give clear and specific directions for each question type, provide examples and be easy to distinguish from actual survey questions. In fact, we would suggest using a distinct font – try changing the style, size, boldness, italics, underlining, etc. It may take a couple of drafts to get your instructions as clear and helpful as possible. Be sure you seek advice and feedback from other researchers, peers and your pilot group.

Organization and Length

Once you are comfortable with all the various elements of your survey, you will need to put it together in a logical format that is neither too long nor too short: too short, and you won't get all the data you need; too long, and your survey might be tossed away, returned incomplete or filled in at random. People might not mind spending a few minutes answering your questions, but ask for much more and they may not be bothered to help you out. Appropriate length is another aspect of your survey you can assess in your pilot run. Be sure to ask your trial respondents what they thought of the overall length and the time it took to complete the survey.

In terms of logical organization, there are a few schools of thought. Some suggest that you start with demographics in order to 'warm up' your respondents. Others, however, suggest that you start with your topical questions and finish off with questions related to demographic information. What is right for your survey will depend a lot on the nature of both your questions and your respondents. In fact, you may want to pilot two different versions of your questionnaire if you are unsure how it should be laid out.

There is one consistent piece of advice, however, and that is to avoid starting your survey with questions that might be considered threatening, awkward, insulting, difficult, etc. It is really important to ease your respondents into your survey and save any sensitive questions for near the end.

Layout and Design

You would think that all of the intense intellectual work that has gone into operationalizing your concepts, writing clear and unambiguous questions with appropriate, well-thought-out response categories, accompanied by clear instructions and organized into a sensitive, logical and manageable form would be enough to ensure a 'good' survey. Not quite. Aesthetics count!

If your survey looks unprofessional, respondents will be less likely to complete it and the potential for mistakes increases if questions are cluttered, cramped, or unclear. So the effort here is well worthwhile. There are many online tools that offer terrific flexibility in how questions can be displayed – things like check boxes and pull-down and pop-up menus are easy to incorporate.

Online Survey Software

If your research question warrants an online approach and you have worked through the challenges of adequate and representative response, there are some fantastic survey development and administration tools online. Most have limited free versions – with more sophisticated elements reserved for those willing to pay. A few choices worth a look include:

- SurveyMonkey (www.surveymonkey.com);
- SurveyGizmo (www.surveygizmo.com);

- Qualtrics (www.qualtrics.com);
- QuestionPro (www.questionpro.com);
- Typeform (www.typeform.com);
- Zoho (www.zoho.com);
- Ask Nicely (www.asknicely.com);
- Nextiva Surveys (www.nextiva.com);
- Survey Sparrow (www.surveysparrow.com).

Keep in mind, however, that programs come and go, so it is worth looking on the Internet to see what the latest and greatest might be. Things to look for in a good program include the ability to:

- manipulate the look and feel of the survey – look for high flexibility and customization;
- segment users – allows you to split your respondent groups for discrete analysis;
- converse – allows your survey to flow like a conversation;
- use skip logic – that means those who answer 'no' to question 9 should be able to skip to question 13;
- pipe – pull answers from one part of a survey into another – so if your respondent says she went to Jefferson High School, that name is inserted into future relevant questions such as, 'How enjoyable was your time at Jefferson High School?';
- randomize – automatically randomize question order within selected sections;
- question-morph – ability to change the format of a question, for example from open-ended to multiple choice;
- integrate with an existing website – allow for having your survey on its own page or integrated into an existing site;
- analyse data – most offer simple summary descriptive statistics, but others offer complex inferential statistics.

I Have a Question!

I Had No Idea That Conducting a Survey Was so Complicated. Should I Give Up?

No! Don't give up, but do think strategically. And that means two things. First, be totally aware of all the ins and outs of surveys. We have not shied away from letting you know how challenging it can be: from conceptualization, to design, to administration, to data collection and analysis. Being aware means that you can be prepared and have contingency plans ready. Second, think about possibilities for adopting, adapting and piggy backing. Can you adopt a survey already designed and validated that you can simply plug into your research processes? Can you adapt a survey that almost meets your needs, which means you can concentrate more on refinements and adaptations? Can you attach survey questions to data-collection protocols already happening? Can you make your survey part of an existing survey already going out to say, customers, students or community members? You will still need to work through all issues of design, but administration is taken care of. Being prepared and strategic cannot be stressed enough.

INTERVIEWING

Listen, be a good listener. You don't have to fill space. Just sit there and listen.

Ed Bradley (2004)

Interviewing: the 'art of asking' or the 'art of listening'? There is no doubt that asking and listening are both crucial to the interview process, but we tend to spend a much greater proportion of our time working on getting our questions and questioning right. When it comes to the listening end of things, we barely give it a mention. Well, according to Bradley, you don't always need to fill the space. Unfortunately, there are quite a few researchers who would rather talk than listen. Remember: your job is to talk only enough to facilitate someone else's ability to answer. It is your interviewees' voice that you are seeking, and it is their voice that needs to be drawn out.

Options and Possibilities

What pops into your mind when you think 'interview'? Perhaps you conjure up an image of a job interview – that formal scenario where the interviewee has to get dressed up, do the firm handshake, make a formal presentation of self, all the while feeling quite nervous, while the interviewer sits behind a big desk, holds all the cards and wields all the power. It is not surprising to find that it is this image that new researchers subconsciously take with them into the research world; they tend to think this is how research interviews should unfold. But they do not have to. Research interviews can be formal – but, as covered in Table 12.2, there are actually quite a few options that might better suit your research agenda.

Table 12.2 Interview issues and types

Will you conduct your interview in a formal manner or will it be more relaxed?	
Formal: the interviewer attempts to be removed from the interviewee and maintains an objective stance. This is often done within a formal setting	This can be likened to the classic job interview. While it allows interviewers a high level of control, it can limit interviewee comfort and possibly free flow of information
Informal: bends or ignores rules and roles associated with formal interviewing in order to establish rapport, gain trust and open up lines of communication. The style is casual and relaxed in order to minimize any gulf between the interviewer and the interviewee	Settings are not limited to an office and might occur over a beer at a bar or while having a cup of coffee at the local preschool. The idea is to do what you can to get your interviewee chatting comfortably. Informal interviews are often unstructured, but this varies with the style, comfort zone and goals of the researcher
Will your interviews be highly structured or more free flowing?	
Structured: use of pre-established questions, in a predetermined order, with a standard mode of delivery. Prompts and probes are also predetermined and used under defined circumstances. Interviewers often call on a formal style to help them stay on track	Best suited for interviews where standardized data is a goal. Inexperienced interviewers generally feel most comfortable with this high level of structure

Will your interviews be highly structured or more free flowing?	
Semi-structured: use of a flexible structure. Interviewers can start with a defined questioning plan but will shift in order to follow the natural flow of conversation. Interviewers may also deviate from the plan to pursue interesting tangents	The advantage here is being able to come away with all the data you intended but also interesting and unexpected data that emerges. This style of interviewing can take a bit of practice
Unstructured: attempts to draw out information, attitudes, opinions and beliefs around particular themes, ideas and issues without predetermined questions. The goal is to draw out rich and informative conversation. Often used in conjunction with an informal structure	Most interviewees enjoy this type of interview because it allows them to talk and really express their ideas in a way not dictated by the interviewer. Interviewer challenges here are to avoid leading the conversation and to keep it focused enough to get the data needed
Will you interview one person at a time, or will you attempt to tackle a group?	
One-to-one: an interaction between an interviewer and a single interviewee. This allows the researcher control over the process and the interviewee the freedom to express his or her thoughts. It can also involve an additional person such as a translator or note taker	One-to-one interviews are generally face-to-face, but can also be done over the telephone in order to increase geographical range or capture a difficult-to-catch respondent. The lack of non-verbal cues in telephone interviews, however, can be a challenge
Multiple: interviewing more than one person at a time. This can be done in a formal structured way that attempts to capture the independent thoughts of each individual or may involve a more open process that allows respondents to interact and influence each other's opinions	Not only can a group interview save time and money, but it can also really get people talking (which can influence data – something you will need to consider/manage). Group interviews can, however, leave some members feeling unheard or marginalized. Group interviews can be difficult to follow, so most interviewers attempt to preserve raw data by tape-recording
Focus group: a type of group interview with around 4–12 people. It is more a discussion than a strict question/answer process. The interviewer acts as a facilitator or moderator and there is an express goal of interaction within a nurturing environment (see 'Excuse me, I have a question' at the end of this section)	The goal is to use rich discussion to draw out depth of opinion that might not arise from direct questioning. Added bonuses are high efficiency and lower costs
Will you interview face-to-face or online?	
Face-to-Face: As the name implies, this involves two people in the same location.	This is the traditional form of interviewing that allows you to build rapport, read body language and get a sense of someone's energy.
Online: Increasing bandwidth and a growing need/desire to work from home, particularly post-COVID-19, have made online interviewing ever more common.	Conferencing apps are popping up every day. Beyond Skype, there's now Zoom meetings, Google Meet, GoToMeeting, WEbX, BigBlueButton, and BlueJeans just to name a few. The challenge here is being able to build trust and rapport over a screen. As the world gets used to this mode of communication, this may get easier. In the meantime, take a few minutes at the start of your interview to establish a strong rapport.

Issues and Complexities

What could be better than getting out there and actually talking to real people, asking them what they really think, finding out at first-hand how they genuinely feel? Well, interviews allow all of this, but like any other data-collection method, the opportunities are balanced by a series of challenges. Interviews allow you to develop rapport and trust; provide you with rich, in-depth qualitative data; allow for non-verbal as well as verbal data; are flexible enough to allow you to explore tangents; are structured enough to generate standardized, quantifiable data.

Now many of these 'pros' are the result of the human element in interviewing – but so too are the 'cons'. The closer you become to your respondents and the closer they become to you, the bigger the challenge you will face in managing the process.

One major challenge, for example, is gaining access to interviewees in an ethical manner. Consider how you can use, but not abuse power. Can you:

- use official channels and protocols, and not avoid or skirt around them;
- establish points of contact, but not go around or above the appropriate person's head;
- use gatekeepers and insiders, without asking them to act unethically or to go behind management's back;
- build rapport without ingratiating yourself to the point of becoming sycophantic;
- leave doors open without becoming a nuisance;
- offer something back without making promises you cannot or do not intend to keep?

You also need to think about all the ways in which you can make a good impression that will keep doors open. And this means doing your homework. Be prepared to talk about your research. The ability to clearly articulate the rationale, aims, objectives and methods of your project can be instrumental in getting the right doors opened. Also consider preparing a brief outline of your project. Certain individuals or organizations may want to have a document they can consider and/or present to gatekeepers. A letter of introduction can also help you professionally answer questions like 'Who are you and where are you from?' Finally, find out about appropriate protocols. Sometimes the contacts that are most willing to help do not have the authority to authorize access. Finding out about appropriate protocols can help avoid awkward situations.

Good impressions also require professionalism. Always be respectful. Choose the right time for your approach, be prompt, dress appropriately and be modest in your initial requests. It also pays to plan for the unexpected. Very rarely does the research process run smoothly, especially when you are dealing with individuals – be prepared for glitches. Resist the urge to lead your respondents and be sure to facilitate honest and open responses. Also suspend judgement – if respondents feel judged, ashamed or offended, it is difficult to gather credible data. You will also need to consider how attributes such as race, gender, ethnicity, class and age of interviewer and interviewee alike might affect the interview process.

And make sure you leave doors open – many researchers swear they have collected all the data they are going to need, but later wish they could go back and ask just a few more questions. One good strategy here is to offer something back. Don't disappear. Let your contacts know how things are progressing and/or send a note of thanks. Even better, make results available. It is quite natural to have a sense of curiosity about studies of which you are a part; the results of your study can be quite valued by those who have facilitated your research.

And if the more political and management issues above are not enough, you will also need to watch for communication miscues. As shown in Box 12.5, moving from questions to answers is anything but a straightforward process. Misunderstandings and misinterpretation are all too common.

Box 12.5

It's Just Q&A, Isn't It?

	From A to K	Getting lost along the way ...
The Interviewer	A formulates a question	A to B: Your thoughts and words do not always match up.
	B asks the question	B to C: Respondents can simply mishear. Accents, language difficulties and interpreters can make this quite common.
The Respondent	C hears the question	C to D: Respondents don't always share the same understandings as the interviewer.
	D interprets the meaning	D to E: Respondents can intentionally filter/hide/lie or simply forget.
	E considers a response	E to F: Again, words do not always capture thoughts.
	F articulates an answer	F to G: Interviewers also have the potential to mishear. If taping, make sure audio is of adequate quality.
	G hears the response	G to H: The more 'foreign' the culture, the more potential for divergent interpretation.
The Interviewer	H interprets the meaning	H to I: Note taking is not easy. You can miss significant information. You can also lose data in the transcription process.
	I takes notes J synthesizes/analyses	I to J: Judgements/interpretations need to be made by the interviewer. J to K: The interviewer reports back understandings as truth!
	K reports	

The Interview Process

As with surveying, conducting a 'good' interview is a process that requires a lot more steps than you may realize. Interviewing involves the need to: plan for all contingencies; prepare an interview schedule and data-recording system; run a trial and modify the process as appropriate; conduct the interviews; and, finally, analyse the data. Boxes 12.7–12.10 will take you through key steps and can be used as both guides and checklists.

Planning

So exactly how much planning needs to go into an interview? Don't you just show up and ask a few questions? If only it were that easy. As well as being clear on all the details of the interview process, you need to remember that there are two key players who need to be considered. The first is your interviewee. You need to thoughtfully decide on who you will be interviewing. The second key player is you, the interviewer. This is a role that needs to be reflexively considered. You need to recognize that you do have power as an interviewer and that you can influence the responses of your interviewee. If you do not work up a plan for neutralizing this influence, you can jeopardize the integrity of your results. Box 12.6 takes you through the essential steps in planning a successful interview.

Box 12.6

Planning – Consideration of 'Who', 'Where', 'When', 'How' and 'What'

The success of your interview will hinge upon the forethought you have put into the planning process.

1 Population and sample/respondent/participants – Who you plan to speak about (population) and gather data from (sample) (see Chapter 11).
2 Access – The first step in an interview is, as discussed above, gaining access in an ethical way.
3 Your role – How will you present yourself? How will you strike a balance between formality and rapport? Is your interview style or research goal better suited to officiousness or informality? What tone of voice will you use? Will you joke around? Also consider body language. Reading non-verbal cues (while your interviewee is reading yours) is worth thinking about. Are you both making eye contact, looking down, looking around, picking your nails, coming across aggressively or looking relaxed?
4 Your biases – Recognizing and controlling for subjectivities in ways that can best ensure the credibility of any survey instrument you use. A good idea is to brainstorm preconceived ideas/expectations as well as alternatives.
5 Ethics approval – Consideration of any ethical dilemmas inherent in your project, and getting appropriate ethics approval.
6 Data – Exactly what it is you want to elicit from your respondents (e.g. memories, descriptions, feelings, thoughts, opinions).
7 Details – Appointments, timing (travel time, interview time, wait-around time), location, recording methods, etc.
8 Potential cultural/language barriers – Familiarizing yourself with, and planning for, any potential language and/or cultural issues. Find and trial a good translator if necessary.
9 Contingencies – The unexpected, the unplanned and the unfortunate. This means developing a contingency plan in case key interviews fall through.

Developing Your Interview Schedule and Recording System

Now that you have planned all the preliminary details, it is time to delve into the 'What' and 'How' of the interview process. What will you ask? How will you ask it? What order will you ask it in? How will you encourage better depth and breadth in responses? How will you record the information provided? What checks will you have on credibility? All of these things will influence the quality of responses you can elicit from your interviewee. Box 12.7 takes you through what needs to be considered in developing your interview schedule.

Box 12.7

Developing an Interview Schedule/Recording System

No matter what style of interview you intend to conduct, you will need to have a game plan ready to go.

1. Draft questions and/or themes - For a structured interview this will involve drafting and redrafting your questions. For a less-structured and more conversational interview, you will need to think about the themes you want to cover and whether you will put any boundaries on potential conversation.
2. Review - Carefully read each question and consider whether your questions might be confusing, leading, offensive or problematic for your interviewees (see Box 12.5).
3. Rewrite questions - Run them past a few peers/supervisors for their assessment. Repeat this step as many times as necessary to get each question as right as possible.
4. Order questions - Put questions in an order that will be logical and ease respondents into your interview.
5. Prepare additional information - Consider and develop any instructions, prompts or probes you feel are appropriate to the interview.
6. Decide on recording methods - If note taking, consider/develop a form that can aid this process. If audio or video recording, be sure to acquire and become familiar with the equipment (discussed more fully in the next section - 'Conducting the Interview').
7. Train any note takers/translators - If using note takers or translators you will want to work as a team, which is likely to involve some trial and error.

Piloting and Modification

Things will inevitably go wrong. Emma once conducted an interview (with someone who had very strong views about the initiative in question) only to get back to the office and realize the recorder had run out of battery! Piloting might not have prevented this, but it gives you an idea of the challenges you need to manage. Box 12.8 takes you through the steps in piloting and modifying your interview processes.

I Have a Question!

I've Heard of Piloting a Survey, but Not Really Piloting an Interview. Is This Really Necessary?

In a word, yes. Remember that you, as interviewer, have a tremendous amount of control and influence over the direction of the interview and the potential content direction, feel and tone of what is said. So you need to check yourself. As with surveying, it is essential that you have a run-through and take note of the interviewees' reflections on the process as well as your own reflections. Only then will you be in a position to modify your processes in ways that maximize the potential authenticity of your data.

Box 12.8

Piloting and Modification

Good planning and development are essential - but not sufficient. Interviewing is a skill that takes practice, and giving your process a run-through can be invaluable. You can then review and refine until you are comfortable with the process and data collected.

1. Have a run-through - A mock interview can boost confidence and highlight potential issues.
2. Reflect - Note any difficulties you encountered, such as access, time taken, question clarity, structure, introductory information, instructions, prompts, pacing, comfort zones, recording/note taking, roles, objectivity, conversational flow, ambiguities and cultural issues.
3. Seek feedback - Get feedback from the interviewees on the issues above and anything else they wish to discuss.
4. Review notes/transcribe data - Make sure you can make sense of notes and that transcription (if a goal) is doable. You may be surprised at how labour- and time-intensive transcription tends to be.
5. Make modifications - This will be based on your own reflections, feedback from your interviewee, as well as the quality of the data generated.
6. Back to the start? - If the need for modification is substantial, you may need to revisit your planning, development and piloting process. This may involve a return to the ethics committee.

Conducting and Analysing Your Interview

Okay – all the preliminaries are done. Processes have been developed, trialled and modified. Time to get out there and talk to some people. But wait, there is still a bit more to consider before you get right into the heart of the matter. You still need to get set up, go through your purpose and ethics, establish rapport, ease into the main themes, manage the whole process – including your influence within the process, and finally wind things up. Then of course is the analysis – the real challenge of working across one or more interviews to draw out themes both expected and unexpected. Box 12.9 will take you through the steps in interview conduct and analysis.

Box 12.9

Conducting and Analysing Your Interview

Finally, you get to talk to someone! While covered more fully in the next section, conducting your interview involves the need to:

1. Take care of preliminaries – Make appointments early (people can put you off for months) and arrive early for your interview so that you have time to set up and check any equipment.
2. Make your interviewee as comfortable as possible – Establish rapport, introduce the study and discuss 'ethics'.
3. Ease into main questions/themes – It is easy to offend when you jump straight into controversial areas, so ease your way into things.
4. Keep a balance – Manage the process and work between keeping on track and/or exploring interesting tangents as appropriate to your interview goals.
5. Wind down and close the interview – Make sure you show your gratitude and attempt to keep the door open for future interaction.
6. Organize/collate your data as soon as possible – When the time comes to work with your data, nothing is worse than a partially forgotten conversation or illegible notes. Be systematic and organized.
7. Thematic analysis – It's time to see what your data yield. Most interview data will be analysed thematically (see Chapter 16), but if you have 30 or more interviews you may want to engage in some level of statistical analysis (see Chapter 15).

Conducting the Interview

> It's no use of talking unless people understand what you say.
>
> Zora Neale Hurston (1942)

'Intimidating': We do not think there is a better word to describe what it feels like to conduct your first interview. No matter how prepared you think you are, you are still likely to feel nervous at the beginning, and to wish you had done things differently at the end.

When you start to prepare, you will probably spend a lot of time thinking about what to ask and how to say it, and this is important. But even more important are your listening skills. Perhaps the golden rule of interviewing is to listen more than talk.

The main game is facilitating an interviewee's ability to answer. To do this with confidence you will need to: take care of preliminaries; ease respondents into the interview; ask questions that facilitate answers; effectively manage the process; and wind down at the right time – all the while being true to your role.

Take Care of Preliminaries

Quite a few things need to come together before you are in a position to ask your first question. Asking good questions is preceded by: making appointments early – allow for travel time, interview time and wait-around time; arriving on time – building rapport can be a real challenge if you keep someone waiting, and if you miss an appointment altogether you may not get a second chance; setting up and checking any recording equipment – you can do this in advance or, if done efficiently, when you first arrive for your interview; establishing rapport – this includes introductions, handshakes, small talk and expressions of appreciation; introducing the study – this includes reviewing who you are, the purpose of the study, why involvement is important and approximately how long the interview will take; explaining ethics – this can involve assurances of confidentiality, the right to decline to answer any particular questions and the right to end the interview upon request.

Ease Your Respondents into the Interview

As with surveying, it is important to ease your way into the main questions and themes. If you start off with a 'sensitive' question or one that might be considered threatening, you may find yourself facing an uphill battle for the remainder of the interview. In fact, it can be easy to get an interviewee off-side, so it is well worth considering how you might handle such a situation.

Ask Questions that Facilitate Answers and Be Ready to Capture Those Answers

If you ask a yes/no question, you should expect a yes/no answer. Try to ask questions that open up conversations and draw out rich responses. Questions should create possibilities, open up options, dig below the surface and lower defences. Remember your job is to facilitate an interviewee's ability to answer – much more than it is to ask questions.

Capturing answers can be done in a number of ways, and you may need to trial a couple of recording methods in order to assess what is best for you and your research process. In most cases you will be responsible for both conducting an interview and capturing responses. Under some circumstances, however, you may use a note taker, which can allow you to focus and engage more fully in listening and directing your interview, or even a translator (see Box 12.10). But as well as considering resource implications, you will need to carefully consider whether a third party is likely to have an effect on the respondent and the interview process.

- Video recording – The potential here is for the capture of raw data at its best. Not only do you preserve words, tone and intonation, you get the added bonus of being able to record visual cues. However, it is more intrusive; is prone to more technical difficulties; and can generate data that are hard to analyse.
- Audio recording – This is highly recommended because it preserves raw data for review at a later date. It therefore allows you to focus on the question/answer process at hand, while allowing you to re-engage at your convenience. The disadvantages of recording are: its inability to capture non-verbal cues; the enormous time and financial cost of

transcribing data (a half-hour interview can generate up to 30 transcription pages); and the unease it can cause for the interviewee – a good thing to remember here is that if you sense wariness you can offer to stop recording and just take notes.

- Post-interview data dump – This is a method of choice for Zina and involves dumping your thoughts and impressions into a digital recorder right after an interview. It is a great supplement to note taking and can be helpful even after a recorded interview.
  Your impressions of an interview can be a valuable source of data in their own right. And while you think you might remember your insights, it is easy to lose them a few interviews later.
- Note taking – This can range from highly structured to open and interpretive. Highly structured note taking often utilizes a form that can be filled in as the interviewee speaks. It may even include a list of codes for common responses (this can allow for statistical analysis if enough interviews are conducted). At the other end of the spectrum is unstructured note taking that may take the form of a concept map or involve jotting down interpretive ideas during or even after an interview. Remember that if you are going to take notes during an interview, be sure you practise talking, listening and note taking simultaneously – and that you can read your own writing. You also need to keep in mind that note taking is actually a preliminary form of analysis (you are making decisions about what to record). You may want to consider taking notes in conjunction with audio or video recording.

Box 12.10

Lost in Translation

If you are speaking to an interviewee in a language that is not your or their first language, all of the challenges above can be even harder. It's important to pilot and modify in the planning stage and take the time you both need in the interview to get things right.

If you and your interviewee(s) don't share a language, you may need a translator which can affect your ability to collect credible data. You will need to consider whether:

1. your translator is experienced – be sure to trial and/or seek references;
2. your translator will translate for you and the interviewee on the spot or will conduct the interview in the interviewee's native language and translate for you at a later time;
3. you would like to capture a literal translation or whether you want your translator to use some discretion and judgement in conveying meaning;
4. you can (and how you can) manage the overall process, including establishing rapport, keeping on time, exploring tangents, keeping respondents focused, etc., all through a translator.

There are no rights and wrongs here. It is the context of your particular research question that will determine the best course of action, and you may need to trial a couple of processes before you know which way to go.

Manage the Process

Conducting an interview is quite a complicated management task because you are actually doing three things at once. The first is questioning, prompting and probing in ways that will help you gather the richest possible data. The second is actively listening to, and making sense of, what your interviewee is saying. The third is managing the overall process so that you know how much time has passed, how much time is left, how much you still need to cover and how you might move it all forward.

Moving the interview forward might involve the use of prompts (giving the interviewee some ideas that might jog a response) and probes (comments and questions that help you dig for more, such as 'tell me more', 'really' or 'why?'). Sometimes probes can be an inquisitive look or a few moments of silence. You will also need to consider the balance between keeping on track and exploring interesting tangents. If you are conducting a structured interview and have a limited amount of time, you will want to make sure you are keeping your interview on track and moving at a good pace. If your interview is less structured, you may find yourself wanting to explore interesting tangents as they develop. The trick here is to be mindful of the time and be sure you end the interview with the full range of data you aimed to gather.

Wind Down/Close

Winding down involves questions that 'round off' an interview and ask respondents if there is anything else they would like to cover, contribute or clarify. The interview then ends by thanking your interviewees for their contribution and their time, and asking them if it might be possible to contact them again if you need to ask any further questions, or need to clarify any points. It is also good practice to offer something back (e.g. a copy of your completed report).

Be True to Your Role

It is easy to get swept up in your interview – after all, you are probably highly interested in the topic and full of your own informed opinions. But this needs to stay in check. Remember: before anything else, and regardless of the style of interview you conduct, you are a researcher whose primary objective is credible data. Even if your goals are highly change-oriented and even emancipatory (see Chapter 10), your desire for change should not leave a question mark over your interpretive work.

Online Interviews

We are living in a post-COVID-19 world that has pushed technology's adoption and acceptance of online communication along at an exponential rate. This has absolutely expanded the possibility of conducting interviews and focus groups online. And this is a fantastic thing. Online interviewing allows you to expand your geographic boundaries – interviewing someone overseas is no longer an issue. In fact, a single focus group can have participants from all over the globe. You can also reach individuals who have traditionally been difficult to interview face-to-face, for example drug dealers or those who live in dangerous places. And, of course, it can save a bundle in travel costs.

There are, however, trade-offs that need to be considered. If you are conducting an online interview using, for example, instant messaging or a webcam, you are actually engaged in a computer-mediated relationship. As such, you will need to consider how you will: ensure that participants have access to the needed technology – computer, webcam, high-speed Internet, programs such as Skype, Zoom, Google Meet, GoToMeeting, WEbX, BigBlueButton and BlueJeans just to name a few; ensure participants have the technical competence/motivation to get it all working properly (think of the aged here); if using instant messaging, ensure that participants can type/write well; establish rapport and trust; achieve long-term commitment, if necessary; control for interruptions.

Remember: a key factor in a good interview or focus group is ease. Respondents need to feel at ease For those who are used to the dark arts of web communication – instant messaging, Skyping or web-based conferences calls – this will be second nature, so you probably won't be adding technological pressures to the interview process. But for those new or unpractised in web-based communication, tackling something so new can add a layer of 'dis'ease to the interview. And this is enough to have an effect on the entire interview process.

But it is worth pursuing. As the speed of the Internet increases, the use of webcams rises and communication/conference technology further develops, online interviewing will grow exponentially. This will massively expand research possibilities, including the types of questions researchers can ask and answer.

I Have a Question!

How Different Is Running Focus Groups from Interviewing More Than One Person at a Time?

It is actually quite different. When you are simultaneously conducting multiple interviews, you are not looking for respondents to bounce off of each other. It is more a matter of expediency – you are saving time. This tends to work best with formal interviews. But keep in mind that it does very much limit a more free-flowing discussion. The agenda for focus groups is quite different. With a focus group you are trying to encourage the development of thoughts and ideas that participants may not even have in their minds at the start of the group. The goal here is to facilitate discussion amongst participants that can lead to consolidated, better, or even new ideas. There are different challenges here – should the focus group consist of strangers or people who know each other? Emma has facilitated focus groups with high school students in friend groups and analysed data from focus groups made up of strangers. As you might imagine, the conversational dynamics are quite different! Focus groups can be good for exploratory research, research on sensitive topics, and to brainstorm solutions. A focus group that is working on 'what is wrong' can disintegrate into a mass of tension and even aggression. You might also find yourself circling around complaints for too long. Facilitators need to be quite skilled to be able to manage this.

Critical Thinking Challenge 13

What You Don't Know Can Hurt You

If you're conducting a survey or series of interviews, you'll have things you want to ask. And this is what will get answered, analysed and reported in findings and conclusions. But what about the things you didn't think to ask? Think about things that are important but didn't make it into your survey or interview schedule. Think about the implications here. What will this do to your findings and conclusions? What will it do to your study's credibility?

OBSERVATION

> When we observe, we are forced to pay attention. We have to move from passive absorption to active awareness.
>
> Maria Konnikova (2013)

Observation is sometimes overlooked as a potential primary data-collection method; surveying and interviewing tend to corner the social science research market. But Emma does a lot of observational research and can give you many good reasons for thinking about conducting an observational study. First, there are times when you need to 'see it for yourself' – having it explained to you is just not the same. Second, the gulf between what people say they do and what they actually do can be far and wide. Third, data collected through observation generally take place in the real world, not a constructed research world. You are out there in the field, in the heart of the action.

Observation invites you to take it all in – to see, hear, smell, feel and even taste your environment. It allows you to get a sense of a reality and work through the complexities of social interactions.

Options and Possibilities

The options for observation are incredibly broad and range from studies that are highly removed and structured to those that are highly involved and messy. For example, at the structured end, you might be talking about a psychologist holding a clipboard and watching a series of interactions from behind a one-way mirror. At the messy end, it might be an anthropologist who has lived in a remote village in Papua New Guinea for the past 15 years and is dedicated to understanding the reality of this village from the perspective of the observed.

On the surface, there may appear to be few similarities between these types of observations. In fact, these extremes are often treated as two distinct methods of data collection derived from diverse paradigms and disciplines. But when you get down to brass tacks you will find that these two extremes do sit on a continuum. Table 12.3 covers the key issues you will need to negotiate in order to determine how your own observation processes should best unfold. Now while the observation types covered in this table can be combined in any number of ways, Figure 12.1 delves into four major strands of observation that combine candid and covert strategies with varying levels of participation.

Table 12.3 Observation issues and types

As an observer will you attempt to be removed or immersed? In other words, will you become a participant in the environment you are studying?	
Non-participant: researchers do not become, nor aim to become, an integral part of the system or community they are observing. The observer is physically present but attempts to be unobtrusive. Non-participant observation tends to occur over a fixed time period and is often highly structured	Examples here include watching interactions through a one-way mirror, sitting in the corner of a room observing a meeting or watching how pedestrians cross a dangerous intersection
Participant: researchers are, or become, part of the team, community or cultural group they are observing. The goal is to preserve the natural setting and to gain cultural empathy by experiencing phenomena and events from the perspective of the observed. Participant observation is often aligned with a less structured, often ethnographic, process	Observers may be outsiders who attempt to become insiders (a researcher joins a cult) or they can be insiders who decide to study their own group (a member of a workforce, community or church). In both cases, participant observation can involve large emotional and time commitments
Note: Participant and non-participant roles are not necessarily discrete and often overlap, which can cause difficulties for the researcher. For example, when non-participant observers begin to participate, they can influence and contaminate their research settings. On the other hand, observation is still the goal of the 'participant', and the more immersed the participant becomes, the harder it may be to maintain the role of researcher	
Will you conduct your observations in a covert fashion, or will you offer full disclosure?	
Candid: researchers offer full disclosure of the nature of their study; the role the observations will play in their research; and what they might expect to find through the observation process. Full disclosure is often an ethics requirement	It is hard to act naturally when you know you are being watched – even more so when you know you are being 'studied', so building trust and making sure participants are comfortable with candid/open processes is essential
Covert researchers do not disclose the nature of their study to those they are observing; they may not even disclose that they are undertaking a study at all. It can be difficult to get ethics approval for covert studies since they breach the core ethical principle of informed consent	Covert studies overcome the issue of participants struggling to act naturally by allowing researchers to 'spy' and observe unfeigned behaviours – but this can be unethical
Will you use highly structured or unstructured observation techniques?	
Structured: researchers use predetermined criteria related to people, events, practices, issues, behaviours, actions, situations and phenomena to collect data in a highly systematic fashion	Checklists or observation schedules are prepared inadvance, and researchers attempt to be objective, neutral and removed in order to minimize personal interactions
Semi-structured: observers use, but are not limited to, predetermined criteria	Observation schedules or checklists are used to organize observations, but observers also attempt to record the unplanned and/or the unexpected
Unstructured: observers attempt to observe and record data without predetermined criteria	Observers can record all observations and later search for emergent patterns, or they make judgement calls on the relevance of initial observations and attempt to focus any subsequent observations

Issues and Complexities

It is easy to think that conducting an observation study will be straightforward – you just need to 'observe' and take note of what is happening in a given situation or context. But it is important to recognize observation as a systematic data-collection method. It can be challenging to take something done on a daily basis and convert it into a rigorous **research tool**. But if done with rigour, observation allows you to: explore what people actually do, and not just what they say they do; take it in for yourself, often in the field; collect both rich, in-depth qualitative data and standardized, quantifiable data; collect non-verbal as well as verbal data.

Observation studies, however, do require you to consider continually and negotiate how your inherent biases – your history, interests, experiences and expectations – can colour observations. As highlighted in Figure 12.2, a world exists but we cannot capture all of it – our

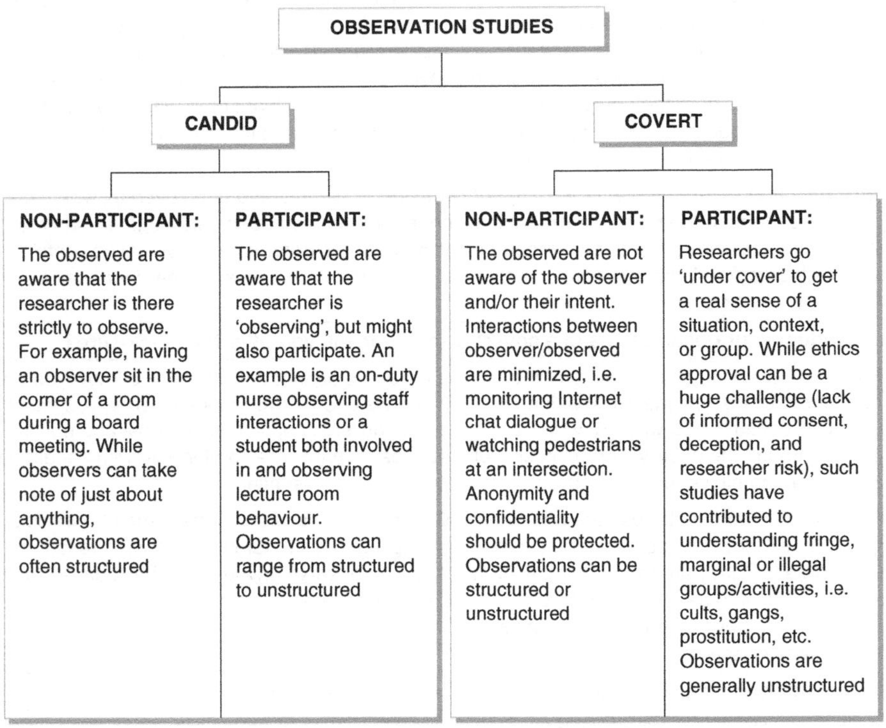

Figure 12.1 Four major strands of observation studies

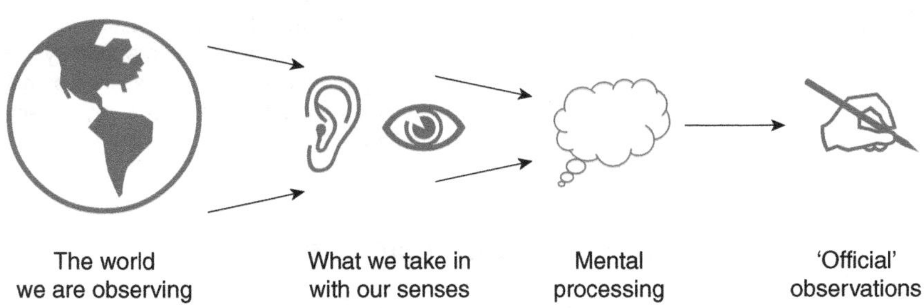

Figure 12.2 Filtering observations

understandings are narrowed by what we can manage to take in through our senses. Sensory input is then filtered and processed by a brain that has been socialized into thinking and understanding through very structured, defined and indeed limited frameworks. Finally, our constructed understandings are condensed into our official observations.

This puts a lot of responsibility for the generation of credible data squarely on the thought processes of the researcher and highlights the need for observational studies to be systematically planned and, if possible, confirmed through the use of other methods.

The other thing you need to consider is how you will manage your relationship with study participants. For example, people don't always act the same when they know they are being observed. You will need to consider whether you can expect natural behaviours from those who know they are being watched. But being covert in your observations has its own dilemmas, and you will need to have a plan you can put into place if your covert study suddenly becomes exposed. And what if, as a non-participant, you cannot help yourself and start to participate? Or what if you get too immersed in the culture you are studying and begin to have second thoughts about your research role? These can be huge challenges and may require you to rethink your methodological design.

Of course the paradox here is that the more entwined you become with the researched, the richer and more meaningful the data you might generate. But this entwining can also make it a much more difficult process to navigate. The key will be your ability to think through such issues, to plan with care and to exercise considered flexibility.

The Observation Process

Even though we make casual observations on a daily basis, observing as a social science method definitely requires planning. You will need to plan for all issues and contingencies; observe all aspects of the situation and record observations; review the process and refine as appropriate; and, finally, analyse the data. Boxes 12.13–12.15 outline the steps involved in observation. As was the case for surveying and interviewing, you should find these boxes helpful as both guides and checklists.

Planning

Do you know why planning is so crucial in observational studies? It is because most of us do not have well-defined distinctions within our minds between general observation and observation as a research method. We observe things, people and places every day – but not with the rigour demanded of it as an approach to the collection of credible, valid, authentic data. For this to occur there is a need to really think through a variety of issues, including: the type of observation (candid or covert, participant or non-participant); who and/or what you will be observing and for how long; how you will capture data; the role you will take; how you will navigate all the messy ethical issues associated with watching or participating with others; and how you will deal with the unexpected. Box 12.11 takes you through the essential steps in planning a successful observational study. Look back at Box 12.6 – planning an interview – as there is some overlap when thinking about populations/sampling and your biases.

Box 12.11

Planning – Consideration of 'Who', 'Where', 'When', 'How' and 'What'

The success of your observation study will hinge on the thought you put into the planning process.

1. Consider the type of observation study – Do your goals and context lend themselves to an observation study that is candid or covert, participant or non-participant, structured or unstructured, and of what duration?
2. Access – Realistically consider access/acceptance to the group/situation/activities you wish to observe. That is, are there any potential language and/or cultural issues likely to affect the process? Can you get past 'gatekeepers'? Will you be welcome? Will you be able to build trust?
3. Your skills – How you might develop the skills/resources needed to carry out your observations.
4. Presentation of self – The role you will take and how involved you will be.
5. Credibility – Consider strategies for ensuring credibility (see Chapter 8, Box 8.2).
6. Tools – Prepare an observation schedule/checklist or, if unstructured, consider any relevant themes to explore.
7. Details – What timeframe will you be working towards? Will you observe on one occasion, multiple occasions, or will your study involve prolonged engagement? How will you record your data?
8. Ethics approval – For participant studies, you will need to consider whether immersion will have a physical, mental or emotional toll on the observed and/or the observer. For example, observers may find themselves immersed in a dangerous situation; they may feel pressured to become involved in immoral/illegal activities; or they may feel stressed when they need to leave the setting and report findings. Issues related to covert studies include justifying and getting approval for a study where there is a lack of informed consent. While some ethics committees are loath to do this under any circumstances, others will consider such studies if the researcher can give convincing assurances related to the physical, mental and emotional welfare of the observed and observer; protection of confidentiality; and perceived societal benefits.
9. Contingencies – The unexpected, the unplanned and the unfortunate. This means having a back-up plan ready to go if your original plan does not pan out.

Observing, Recording and Preliminary Analysis

Once all preliminaries are in order, you can actually go out there and begin to observe. There are several types of observation studies. There are those that are covert and those that are candid, those that are participatory and those that are more removed (Figure 12.1). This means that the protocols you adopt will need to meet the goals you have set for your study. It also means that you will need not only to observe the object of your observation, but also to keep close tabs on yourself. So take notes on what you observe, but also what you experience. This is essential for reflecting on your observation processes as you begin your data collection; in fact, it is part of your analysis. Box 12.12 takes you through the essential steps in observing and recording observations.

Box 12.12

Observing, Recording and Preliminary Analysis

Rigour and reflection in both observation and recording are key to successful data analysis in observational studies. To do this you need to:

1 Ease into the observation situation - If structured and candid, this will be similar to the opening stages of an interview where you need to be on time, set up and check any equipment, introduce the study and establish rapport. If your study involves greater immersion into a culture, the early stages will require you to sit back, listen, attempt to gain trust and then establish rapport.
2 Be ready for a range of sensory input - Use all your senses, and possibly your intuition, to gather data.
3 Invest time - Because you will not be directing the process, you need to be prepared to invest significant time in your observations.
4 Look for saturation - Try to ensure your observations no longer yield new knowledge before ending the process.
5 Record your observations as soon as possible - Observations need to be recorded in a timely manner. If using schedules, they should be filled in while observations occur. If you are more immersed in your research context, you may want to record your observations when removed from the situation either on data sheets or in a journal. Your record may also include photographs and video/audio recordings.
6 Analysis - Data collected by observation can be quantitative (through the use of checklists; see Chapter 15) or can be much more qualitative (through the use of journaling or photography; see Chapter 16). Remember: analysis should work towards addressing your research questions in insightful ways.

Reviewing, Refining and Continued Analysis

In observational studies, particularly those with prolonged engagement, reviewing and refining protocols are central to credibility. This reflection is crucial because in observational studies the judgements that are made about what and how something is recorded are a form of analysis in their own right. If you are not a reflective practitioner and you do not keep refining as you go, you risk your data being tainted with bias, and your analysis being full of your own subjectivities. In fact, as a check on subjectivities, observation often requires you to confirm your insights with the insights and knowledge of others. Box 12.13 takes you through the steps in reflectively refining your observation protocols.

Box 12.13

Reviewing, Refining and Continued Analysis

The ability to reflectively refine your observational studies is essential. You will need to:

1 Review the process - Note any difficulties encountered; for example, access, time taken, engagement, cultural 'ignorance', comfort zones, recording/note taking, roles, objectivity/subjectivity.

(Continued)

2. Review your observation records – Note any difficulties you might encounter in making sense of your record.
3. Confirm – Check with an insider; ask another observer to compare notes; or triangulate your observational data with other data types.
4. Make modifications – Based on: your own review of the process; any confirmation strategies you have attempted; and the quality of the data generated.
5. Keep reviewing and refining – Observation takes practice; keep refining until you are comfortable with the process and the data collected.
6. Major issues? – If there are major issues, you will need to openly discuss them with your supervisor and consider modifications.
7. Continued analysis – Whether data is quantitative (see Chapter 15) or qualitative (see Chapter 16), keep moving between your observations, your theories, your research questions, your aims and objectives, and the checks on subjectivity you have adopted.

Receiving, Reflecting, Recording and Authenticating

As highlighted above, a common feature of all observation studies is that they attempt to document what people actually do, rather than what they say they do; observational studies rely on actual behaviour. There are no tools used to generate particular responses from the observed. There are no questions. It is simply the observed doing what they do, and observers taking that in, noting it and making sense of it. While the perceived advantage here is genuineness, the disadvantage is how complicated it can be for researchers to work through the process of receiving, reflecting, recording and authenticating their observations.

Receiving

When it is time to begin your observations, the exact protocol you will use will be highly dependent on the type of observation study you plan to conduct. Most observation processes, however, begin by attempting to build rapport and gain trust. The idea is to try to make the observed feel as comfortable as possible – comfortable enough to carry on as if you were not even there.

The next step is opening your eyes, ears and mind to all that is going on around you. What do you see, what do you hear, what do you sense? We tend to be a visual society, so it is important to make sure you are taking it in through your full range of senses. And this can take time. Because you are not directing the process, you need to be prepared to make a significant investment in order to get the data you need. In fact, unless your design sees you observing for a predetermined period of time, it pays to look for saturation (the point at which your observations no longer yield new knowledge) before ending the process.

Keep in mind that we do not all take in or perceive the world in the same way. Some of us are tuned into the bigger picture, while some of us concentrate on separate components. Some like to take in the world by looking around, some like to listen. Others understand best by moving, doing and touching. So when it comes to observation, it is quite likely that two observers in the same situation will take things on board in quite different ways. Acknowledging this is important. If your observations are structured, an observation schedule that requires information to be gathered through a variety of senses can ensure you don't miss any potential sources of data. In a less structured study, the key will be your ability to critically reflect on your data-collection processes and make any necessary modifications.

Reflecting

While not always conducted as a 'pilot', there is still a need to review, reflect on and modify your observation methods. Such modifications are generally based on difficulties you encountered in your initial observation work; for example, difficulties with access, timing, cultural 'ignorance', comfort zones, recording/note taking, roles and objectivity. It also pays to review your observation records and assess if they make sense, and are logical, rich and complete.

Also look for bias. It is exceptionally difficult for researchers, particularly those who choose to immerse themselves within the research setting, to be objective. Our worldviews are embedded within us. We carry with us the biases and prejudices of both our attributes and our socialization. They are a part of how we understand and make sense of the world, and how we might go about observing it. And as discussed in Chapter 4, if we do not recognize and attempt to negotiate our subjectivities, our research will be imprinted with our own biases and assumptions. This can lead to observations that: are interpreted through the perspective of the observer, rather than the observed; are insensitive to race, class, culture or gender; have difficulty hearing marginalized voices; tend to dichotomize what is seen; and do not respect the power of language.

Remember: it is quite easy to see the things you expect to see and hear the things you want to hear. It's like when you get a new car and you suddenly see that model everywhere you go. The cars were always there – you just never noticed them before. And we know that much of the feedback we give students is positive, but every bit of (constructive!) criticism seems to loom ten times larger in their brains. Before you go out in the field, it is well worth consciously brainstorming your own expectations. You can then brainstorm a range of alternatives, so that you are less likely to observe and reflect on your observations in ways that confirm what you already suspect.

Recording

There are actually two quite different strategies for recording observations. The first involves the capture of raw data by such means as photography, audio and/or video recording. This allows observations to be preserved in a raw form so that they can be reviewed and used at a later date. These methods, however, demand the use of equipment and can be considered intrusive. The second strategy is note taking or journaling. These methods can capture anything from descriptive and formal accounts of space, actors, acts and events to much more interpretive narrative accounts that include goals, feelings and underlying stories. The form also varies and can range from coded schedules and quantitative tallying to qualitative pictures, concept maps and jotted ideas.

The recording method (or methods) you will need to adopt will vary depending on the level of participation, openness and structure in your observational processes. For candid studies, the use of an observation schedule that you fill in as observations occur might be appropriate, as would the use of photography and audio and/or video recording. For studies that involve high levels of immersion and are perhaps covert, you might want to note, journal, doodle or map your observations when you are removed from your observational setting and have some privacy. Your circumstances may also see you looking to employ a combination of the above. Regardless of the methods you choose to adopt, it is important to record your data in as systematic a fashion as possible. After all, these are data you will need to analyse in the future.

Authenticating

It can be hard to assess whether you have been able to control for your biases and generate credible data by reflection alone. There are, however, a number of strategies that can be used to ensure thoroughness in data collection and confirm the authenticity of reflections. Thoroughness can be achieved through broad representation, prolonged engagement, persistence, **crystallization**, saturation, peer/supervisor review of your process and full explication of method. Strategies for confirmation include informant/member checking and triangulation (see Box 8.2, p. 153).

I Have a Question!

How Does Observation Work for Online Behaviour?

The same ethical dilemmas and decisions present themselves as for in-person observation. It is difficult, for example, to get permission for a covert study. So, getting permission to observe what happens on, say, Chatroulette.com without the express permission of those you are observing is unlikely to get approval. But there are other possibilities where you might be able to disclose your research intent. Say, for example, you wanted to observe virtual reality online gaming behaviours. You may be able to negotiate some sort of permission to gather data while watching a game unfold - perhaps you will do this as a participant observer or just an outside observer.

Chapter Summary

- Primary data is current, created by the researcher and targeted to researcher needs, but collecting it can be demanding, time-consuming and expensive.
- While you can use a pre-existing data set, designing and conducting your own study will give you rich insights beyond what might be contained in captured data.
- Surveying involves gathering information from respondents related to their characteristics, attributes, how they live, opinions, etc. through administration of a questionnaire. It has the potential to reach a large number of respondents, generate standardized, quantifiable, empirical data (as well as some qualitative data), and offers confidentiality/anonymity.

- Interviewing involves researchers seeking open-ended answers to any number of questions, topic areas or themes. It can generate standardized, quantifiable data, but is more often used to capture in-depth qualitative data.
- Observation relies on researchers' ability to gather data through their senses and allows them to document actual behaviour rather than responses related to behaviour.

FIND YOUR NEXT STEP

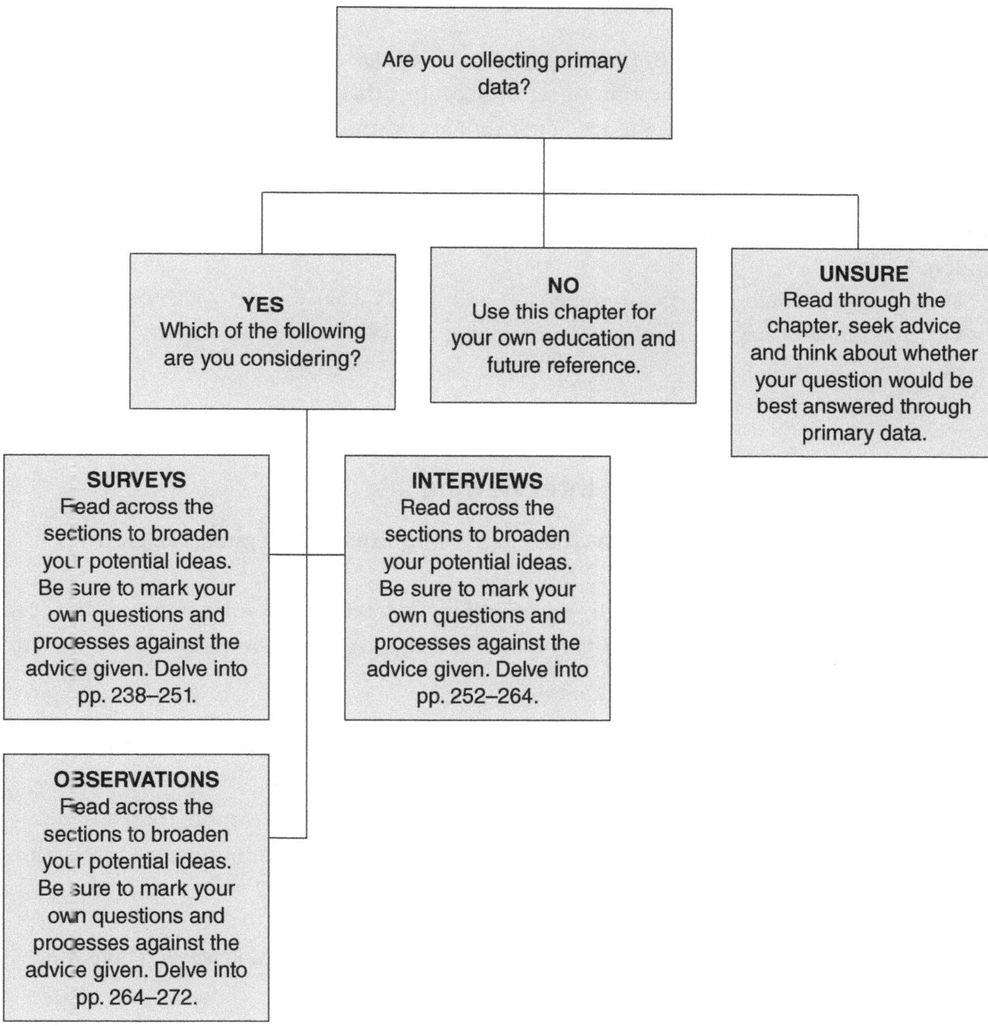

FURTHER READING

Surveying

Aarons, H. (2020). *A Practical Introduction to Survey Design: A Beginner's Guide*. Thousand Oaks, CA: Sage.

Clear steps to follow and lots of real-life examples of good and bad survey data. A great starting point.

Fink, A. (2016) *How to Conduct Surveys: A Step-by-Step Guide*. Thousand Oaks, CA: Sage.
This book will help you both evaluate surveys (something that is necessary, given that the quality of published survey work is not always assured) and develop your own credible survey instruments. Good, clear, accessible read.

Fowler, F. J., Jr (2013) *Survey Research Methods*. London: Sage.
We like the depth here. This work will help you consider how survey construction and administration can affect credibility. Also has good coverage of Internet survey approaches and the impact of mobile phones on survey research.

Robinson, S. B. and Firth, K. (2018) *Designing Quality Survey Questions*. Thousand Oaks, CA: Sage.
It is much easier to ask a bad question or set of questions than you might realize. Follow the advice in this book and you have a much better shot at constructing a tool that will get you the credible answers you seek.

Wolf, C., Joye, D., Smith, T. and Fu Y. (eds) (2016) *The SAGE Handbook of Survey Methodology*. London: Sage.
At 740 pages, you would expect comprehensive and that is what you get. With contributions from a wide range of experts from across the globe, this book covers all the ins and outs of survey methodology.

Interviewing

Bogner, A., Littig, B. and Menz, W. (eds) (2009) *Interviewing Experts*. Basingstoke: Palgrave Macmillan.
This is a great find. In applied research, key informant interviews are quite standard, but it is hard to find expert advice. This book offers it. If you are going down this path, it is well worth a look.

Gubrium, J. F., Holstein, J. A., Marvasti, A. B. and McKinney, K. D. (eds) (2012) *The SAGE Handbook of Interview Research: The Complexity of the Craft*. London: Sage.
Very comprehensive. We like the acknowledgement of the interview as more than a one-way data-gathering technique. Good recognition of the interview as a communicative interaction and the effect this has on research processes.

Krueger, R. and Casey M. (2014) *Focus Groups: A Practical Guide for Applied Research*. Thousand Oaks, CA: Sage.
Facilitating focus groups takes a different skill set than that needed for conducting interviews. If this is a method you will pursue, it is well worth diving into a specialist book that covers all the ins and outs, such as this one.

Kvale, S. and Brinkman, S. (2014) *InterViews: Learning the Craft of Qualitative Research Interviewing*, 3rd edition. London: Sage.
This book looks at interviewing from the perspective of various approaches within the qualitative paradigm, including narrative, discursive, relational, linguistic and conversational practice. If interviewing within a qualitative methodology, this is a good book to have.

Rubin, H. J. and Rubin, I. S. (2011) *Qualitative Interviewing: The Art of Hearing Data*. Thousand Oaks, CA: Sage.
A good description of the interview process, including the importance and opportunities of interviewing as a data-gathering technique. The authors' experience comes through.

Seidman, I. (2019) *Interviewing as Qualitative Research: A Guide for Researchers in Education and the Social Sciences*, 5th edition. New York: Teachers College Press.
This book in now in its 5th edition and has proven itself a user-friendly step-by-step guide that will take you through both the basics and complexities of interviewing as a data-gathering technique.

Observation

DeWalt, K. M. and DeWalt, B. R. (2010) *Participant Observation: A Guide for Fieldwork*. Lanham, MD: AltaMira Press.
If you are going to engage in any type of participant observation you really need to explore the literature and get a sense of the opportunities and responsibilities associated with this approach to research. This is a terrific place to start that exploration.

Gillham, B. (2008) *Observation Techniques: Structured to Unstructured*. London: Continuum International.
We think this is still a good all-rounder that covers the ins and outs and options associated with observation studies.

Jorgensen, D. (2020) *Principles, Approaches and Issues in Participant Observation*. Abingdon: Routledge.
This work does not skimp on theory. It approaches participant observation as much more than a data-collection method and sets it in the context of philosophical paradigms of knowing. This work is appropriate for anyone wanting to delve deeper into participant observation as an epistemology.

Lofland, J., Snow, D. A., Anderson, L. and Lofland, L. H. (2005) *Analyzing Social Settings: A Guide to Qualitative Observation and Analysis*, 4th edition. Belmont, CA: Wadsworth.
Originally published in 1971, this is a good reference guide for anyone observing social settings. Good array of examples and applications.

Rosenbaum, P. R. (2020) *Observational Studies*. New York: Springer.
This book takes a more quantitative/statistical approach to observation studies. The use of real-world examples helps in understanding how observations can be quantified and appropriately analysed.

13

SECONDARY DATA

Learning Objectives

- What is secondary data?
  - To become familiar with the benefits and challenges of working with secondary data
  - To become familiar with various types of secondary data
- Working with existing data
  - To be able to analyse various types of 'texts'
  - To be able to analyse existing data sets/databases
- Analysing previous studies
  - To be able to synthesize both qualitative and quantitative findings of existing studies

WHAT IS SECONDARY DATA?

Can't reinvent the wheel. But you can put your own spin on it.

Lauren Beukes (2013)

Secondary data is situational. It is data that exists independently of a research project. It is the data that can be found in documents, and in the findings of past research – none of which was created by the researcher for the express purpose of their research project. It is existing data that researchers simply gather and analyse.

Secondary data was once seen as well … secondary. That is because access was limited. We generally had to go to the source or to a specific library to get these types of resources. But the online world has certainly opened up the possibilities here, which definitely makes it worth exploring.

Benefits and Challenges of Working with Secondary Data

Benefits

There are some real advantages in exploring secondary data. First of all, it is everywhere – and answers to your question may not require a new data-collection protocol. And that is a massive advantage. Existing data also allows you to: explore what people have actually produced; collect rich, in-depth qualitative data and standardized, quantifiable data – as well as both verbal and non-verbal data; and eliminate the need for physical access to research participants – which can reduce costs as well as minimize stress for both researchers and research participants. It can therefore save you time, energy and money.

Moreover, it provides an objective buffer between the researcher and the researched. Primary research such as interviewing, surveying and even observation studies are driven by the researcher, who undoubtedly has an impact on the reality of the situations, events or people being explored; researchers and researching have an influence on social environments. However, with existing data, there is no researcher interaction, so the possibility of tainting data with bias is removed. These kinds of data pass what Edward Potter (1996, p. 135) called the 'dead social scientist test' – that the situation 'would have taken place in the form that it did had the researcher not been born or if the researcher had got run over on the way to the university that morning'.

It can also eliminate worries related to: building trust; getting people to act naturally; role playing; and figuring out how attributes such as race, gender, ethnicity, class and the ages of the researcher and the researched might confound data collection. Finally, secondary data overcomes the expectation that 'real' research demands interviews and surveys.

Challenges – Bias

Hopefully the above benefits have piqued your interest in exploring data that is traditionally underutilized. But there are challenges associated with pre-existing data (see Box 13.1). Pre-existing data requires you to: work through data not expressly generated to answer your particular research question(s); make sure your own biases do not colour your interpretations and understandings; avoid taking records out of context; protect the needs of uninformed respondents, i.e. protection of privacy, anonymity and/or confidentiality; question a text's origin/agenda – remember that some sources are, by their nature, subjective, i.e. media coverage, personal communication or 'party line' material with an express political agenda, and even authoritative texts with an explicit goal of unbiased knowledge can be tainted by subjectivities.

Finally, older data sets may suffer from bias inherent in the classification and coding systems that may not be immediately obvious. For instance, a longitudinal study of individual time use over the last 50 years suggests that leisure time is increasing, particularly for women. However, embedded in this conclusion is that time spent child-rearing is categorized as leisure time. Nonetheless, the trade-offs involved with existing data are worth exploring, but it does require an observant researcher.

Challenges - Data Management

It's easy to recognize the need for good data management when you are collecting primary data, but you also need these tight protocols when you are working with secondary data. In fact it is crucial, given that the data often comes from multiple sources and presents in a variety of shapes and sizes.

The best bet here is stages. Stage one is to sort and store the data by source; make sure your filing system is clear, well defined and accurately coded. As you begin to work through the data, you will want to manage like sources together. You have now entered stage two. Grouping sources can happen by topics covered and/or by data type. Stage three takes this a step further and involves extracting like data from each source in preparation for possibly combining into one database. Keeping track of your data through these stages is essential! An Excel spreadsheet is a good idea here (or even a dedicated notebook if you are old school).

Box 13.1

Credibility in Secondary Data

Secondary data needs to be explored in terms of relevance, currency and methodological issues. Since it is data that has generally been collected for an alternative purpose, it may not be as relevant or current as primary data. Moreover, you may not be aware of methodological flaws in any previous collection methods. So assessment is crucial. You need to be able to assess if the pre-existing data is unbiased, complete and accurate. As a first step, ask yourself questions that can be answered by the research study itself:

- Credentials - What is the authority of the author? What are the author's qualifications or credentials?
- Motive/intention - Affiliation or sponsorship. What organization are they associated with? Is there a link to a contact number or email address associated with that organization? A link to an association does not necessarily mean that the organization has approved the content.
- Recognized authority - Does the author have publications in scholarly or professional publications? These publications are often peer-reviewed by other experts, meaning that mistakes are caught and usually ruthlessly exterminated by a community of scholars.
- Objectivity - Are there clues to author bias? Are they promoting a product?
- Methods - Are methods well designed and reviewed? Is there broad representation? Does it explore multiple sources of data?
- Verifiability - Does the author provide a complete list of works cited? If so, who do they reference and are they experts in their field?
- Currency - Is the web information current? Are links missing or broken? Poor web maintenance may mean the site has been abandoned and it may be difficult to determine if information presented is current.

More broadly, you can also look outside the work by seeking peer/expert review (what are others saying about this source of information?) and, if possible, checking and comparing notes with an insider or other researcher.

Types of Secondary Data

Evidence of where we have been and what we have done is absolutely everywhere. We document it in a million ways, we research it, report on it, log it, video it, journal it, blog it, legislate it, develop policy on it, leave our fingerprints on it, draw it, photograph it, write poetry about it, capture it in song, send postcards, write letters, send emails and texts, post about it on social media, etc. The physical traces of this activity literally surround us. The challenge is making sense of it.

Now in this chapter, we are referring to data that, while often found on the Internet, still exists independently of it (Internet-generated data is covered in Chapter 14). This can refer to almost any human/social artefact and covers a huge array of data types that might be derived from an organization, an individual or perhaps a family. Your text might also be located on the web, on the television, at the movies, at a school, or at a museum or park. It may be in the public domain, or it might be private. It may be held by other researchers, local government, national government or international agencies. And getting your hands on it may involve searching the Internet, but it may also involve writing away for it, going to the library, making a personal appeal or going into the field. Types of existing data include:

- Official data and records – While you may have to work at getting access, it may be worth exploring:
    - International data held by organizations such as the United Nations, the World Bank or the World Health Organization.
    - National data held by many federal or national governments and government departments, e.g. national census data.
    - Local government data such as state of environment reports, community surveys, water-quality data, land registry information, etc.
    - Non-governmental organization data collected through commissioned or self-conducted research studies.
    - University data, which is abundant and covers just about every research problem ever studied.
    - Archival data such as records of births, deaths, marriages, etc.
    - Legislation including local ordinances, state and federal regulations/laws.
- Policy documents from both the public and private sectors.
- Organizational communication, documents and records – Official communication that includes, but is not limited to: websites; press releases; catalogues, pamphlets and brochures; meeting agendas and minutes; inter- and intra-office memos; safety records; sales figures; human-resource records; client records (these might be students, patients, constituents, parishioners, etc., depending on organization type).
- Personal communications, documents and records – Personal and often private communications that include, but are not limited to: emails; letters; journals, diaries and memoirs; texts; sketches and drawings; poetry and stories; photographs and videos; medical records; educational records; household records, e.g. cheque-book stubs, bills, insurance documents.

- The media/contemporary entertainment – Data here is often examined in relation to questions of content or portrayal; for example, the content of personal ads, how often male characters are shown crying, or how often sexual assault has made the national news over the past two years. Data can come from: newspaper or magazine columns/articles/advertisements; news programmes and current affairs shows; TV dramas, sitcoms and reality shows; commercials; music videos; biographies and autobiographies.
- The arts – The arts have captured and recorded the human spirit and condition over the ages in every corner of the globe, making them perfect for comparing across both culture and time. Societal attitudes are well captured in: paintings, drawings and sketches; photography; music; plays and films.
- Social artefacts – These include any product of social beings. Examples of social products or social traces are extremely broad-ranging and can include things like: garbage; graffiti; children's games; rites and rituals; jokes; T-shirt slogans; tools; crafts; videos (YouTube has created a huge and accessible database here).

Given this diversity, the key to success is being prepared. You will need to know well in advance where your data sources are located; who the gatekeepers might be; how to best approach them; whether or not you will need to use a sampling strategy; and whether the collection of sensitive or private data will require ethics approval.

WORKING WITH EXISTING DATA

Existing data can come in many forms, but is organized here as: (1) contemporary documents (defined quite broadly), best explored through a process of document analysis; (2) historical documents, best explored through **historical analysis**; (3) artefacts, best explored with **cultural artefact analysis**; and (4) data sets, best explored through secondary analysis.

Textual/Document Analysis

Often the answers to research questions are held in documents, perhaps letters, journals, policy documents and reports. The method we use for analysing such documents is aptly named document analysis. But we might also be interested in forms of communication such as videos, TV shows, radio broadcasts, even websites. In this case, rather than refer to these as documents, we use a slightly more generic term 'texts' and engage in **textual analysis**. The logic for both these approaches, however, is quite similar. They both involve exploring various forms of text as a source of research data. Similarly, Emma does research with audio recordings of calls recorded by organizations using the method of conversation analysis.

Before jumping into analysis, however, the issue of bias is worth a mention. In document/textual analysis, pre-existing texts need to be thoughtfully considered in relation to subjectivity. The credibility of the data you generate will, in part, be dependent on recognition of the bias/purpose of the author/creator (see Box 13.1). It may be tempting to treat the printed word as the truth but, if you do, you will need to ask whose truth. A second source of bias lies with you as the researcher. As with any method, how you read and draw from the documents will be coloured by your own reality. You will need to consider your biases, your skills, what exactly you are looking for and how you will ensure credibility for data you did not yourself collect.

Because document analysis does not involve document production, the steps involved differ somewhat from other methods of data collection. In order to carry out textual analysis you need to: plan for all contingencies; gather your 'texts', review their credibility and interrogate their witting and **unwitting evidence**; and finally, reflect, refine your process and analyse your data. Boxes 13.2–13.4 provide the steps/checklists for the process of textual analysis.

Planning

Did you know that even when exploring texts, just like when working with human respondents, you need to consider population, sample and access? In other words, you will need to think about what range of documents you are considering as your pool of potential works; which ones you will you actually look at; and how you plan to get your hands on them. And just like other methods that deal with human participants, you also need to consider your biases; your skills; what exactly you are looking for; how you will ensure credibility when you did not collect the data yourself; and how you will plan for the unexpected. One of Emma's students investigated personality language in job advertisements posted on an online site. Job ads are a type of document that are publicly available for a limited time before they disappear. This meant important consideration was needed of which period to sample from as well as how many and which kinds of ads would be sufficient for the sample. Box 13.2 takes you through the essential steps in planning textual/document analysis.

Box 13.2

Planning – Consideration of 'Who', 'Where', 'When', 'How' and 'What'

The success of your analysis will hinge upon the thought you have put into the planning process.

1. Population and sample/respondents/participants – In textual analysis this involves creating a list of 'texts' you wish to explore and understanding who they will speak for. If the breadth of texts you wish to explore is overly wide, you will need to develop an appropriate sampling strategy (see Chapter 11).
2. Access – How you will locate and access texts. You will also need to consider any language or cultural barriers that might keep you from fully drawing from your texts.
3. Your biases – Recognizing and controlling for subjectivities in ways that can best ensure you explore 'texts' with an open mind.
4. Your skills – How you might develop the skills/resources needed to carry out your analysis.
5. Credibility – Consider strategies for ensuring credibility (see Boxes 8.2 and 13.1).
6. Data – Knowing exactly what it is you are looking for or trying to find in your texts.

7 Ethics/ethics approval - Consideration of any ethical dilemmas inherent in your project, and getting appropriate ethics approval; i.e. seeking approval to explore texts that might be classified, in confidence, sensitive or private.
8 Contingencies - The unexpected, the unplanned and the unfortunate. This means having a back-up plan ready to go if your original plan does not pan out.

Gathering, Reviewing and Interrogating Texts

So how do you get a text to talk? Once you locate, acquire and assess the credibility of your texts, you will be ready to 'extract' the data. Now the first step is to ask yourself questions about the text. This refers to questions related to the author/creator, audience, circumstances of production, type, whether it is a typical or exceptional example, the style, tone, agenda, political purpose, whether it contains facts, opinions or both; basically any background information related to the document. This is sometimes called the latent content or 'unwitting' evidence. Answers to these questions may lie within the text itself (e.g. type, tone and style), or may require further investigation (e.g. information about the author or the document's genre).

The next step involves exploration of the 'witting' evidence or the content within the document. There are a couple of ways you can do this. The first is by using an 'interview technique', while the second involves noting occurrences, a method akin to formal structured observation (Box 13.3 will take you through the steps of thorough document interrogation), but first, the interview technique is as follows:

- The interview – In 'interviewing' your documents, you are, in a sense, treating each document as a respondent who can provide you with information relevant to your inquiry. The questions you ask will be dependent on the nature of your inquiry and on the document type. As with an interview, you will need to determine what it is you want to know, and whether your document can provide you with the answers. You then need to 'ask' each question and highlight the passages in the document that provide the answer. Organizing your responses can be done by using a colour-coded highlighting system, or you can turn to qualitative data-management programs such as Lumivero's NVivo, MAXQDA or ATLAS.ti to help you with document indexing.
- Noting occurrences – Noting occurrences is a process that quantifies the use of particular words, phrases and concepts within a given document. As in formal structured observations, the researcher determines what is being 'looked for' and notes the amount, the frequency and often the context of the occurrence. For example, say you wanted to trace the growth of climate change as a point of reference in federal legislation. You would first determine what legislative documents you would want to explore and ensure you have access. Noting occurrences would consist of a search for the phrase 'climate change' and other related terms you feel are relevant.
- Automated text analysis – This is discussed more thoroughly in Chapter 14, p. 309, but suffice it to say that if your texts are Internet-based and expansive, you'll need an automated process. Automated text analysis uses algorithms to do the work we once did manually.

Box 13.3

Gathering, Reviewing and Interrogating 'Texts'

To start the process of interrogating texts you need to:

1. Gather relevant texts - Most of the texts outlined above can be collected, but a few will require you to go out in the field; for example, you may want to look at graffiti, museum exhibits or waste in situ.
2. Organize - For collected texts, you will want to develop and employ an organization and management scheme.
3. Copy - Make copies of original text for the purpose of annotation.
4. Confirm authenticity - Assess the authenticity and credibility of the text.
5. Explore the text's agenda - Review the text and consider any inherent biases.
6. Explore background information - Extract background information on author/creator, audience, purpose and style, as is appropriate to the text being explored.
7. Ask questions about the text - Who produced it? What did they produce it for? What were the circumstances of production? When, where and why was it produced? What type of data is it? Basically, you want to explore any background information that is available (sometimes called the latent content or unwitting evidence).
8. Explore content - This will vary by the type of text and, as discussed in the next section, can involve qualitative and quantitative processes. The key to success here is outlining what you plan to extract from the text well in advance.

Reflecting, Refining and Analysing

Any time you take on the challenge of collecting data in a new way, you will start off as a novice and need to go on a learning journey before you can become a competent researcher, and perhaps someday even an expert. And while you may read all about the approach, you are unlikely to get your head around it until you get your hands dirty. And for us this means reflection. As with any method, good textual analysis requires you to reflect, refine and improve as you go. You may also need to be flexible. Because the documents you will be exploring were not written for your express research purpose, each will need a critical eye that can uncover and discover what you are looking for, and maybe even relevant information you did not know you were looking for. Once you develop this skill, analysis can be a rich endeavour. Box 13.4 takes you through the steps of reflecting, refining and analysing, while Box 13.5, below, takes you through a relevant example.

Box 13.4

Reflecting, Refining and Analysing

1. Learn and improve as you go - View analysis as an iterative and ongoing process.
2. Review the process - Reflect on any difficulties associated with gathering the texts, reviewing the sources and exploring the content.

3 Review your notes - Reflect on any difficulties you might encounter in making sense of your record.
4 Make modifications - Based on your own review of the process and the quality of the data generated.
5 Keep reviewing and refining - Keep refining until you are comfortable with the process and data collected.
6 Major issues? - If there are major issues you will need to openly discuss them with your supervisor and consider modifications.
7 Analysis - Data collected in textual analysis can be quantitative (through various modes of tallying and more in-depth statistical analysis; see Chapter 15) or can be much more qualitative (through deeper reflective processes; see Chapter 16). Remember: analysis should work towards addressing your research questions in insightful ways.

Historical Analysis

Historical analysis is a specific form of textual analysis that can include any and all forms of 'text' covered above, and generally involves all the steps covered in Boxes 13.2–13.4. The main point of distinction, however, is that historical analysis has a quite defined purpose of establishing facts and drawing conclusions about the past. While this goal may seem straightforward, it is actually a multi-pronged goal that involves: (1) ascertaining what actually happened – sometimes the myth or the legend is not based on facts, or at least a full array of facts; (2) ascertaining why it happened – historical analysis goes beyond 'what' and asks about multiple realities, circumstances, context and conditions – there is an attempt to understand situated complexity; (3) understanding implications – historians believe the past is the key to unlocking the future; historical analysis therefore attempts to link analysis of the past to present conditions and future possibilities.

To accomplish these goals, researchers turn to a wide variety of sources that may be primary (e.g. the testimony of those who were witness to events, or social bookkeeping, which refers to records that survived from the past) or secondary (accounts of the past that were not generated within the historical period being explored, namely someone else's account/analysis of the past).

The challenges here are: (1) ensuring the authenticity and credibility of the resources used; (2) gathering enough data for an account to be considered complete; and (3) finding trends and patterns among what might be disparate and contradictory evidence.

Analysis of Cultural Artefacts

When we interact with the world, we leave our mark. Evidence of where we have been and what we have been up to is everywhere. And as any crime scene investigator will tell you, through this evidence we reveal something about ourselves.

Beyond the written word, evidence of our interactions includes the wear and tear we cause as well as the things we leave behind. In the world of social science research, we refer to these as measures of erosion and accretion:

- Erosion – Explores wear and tear. In a crime scene this might mean looking at footprints or skid marks. In the world of social science we might look at how worn seats are to determine where people most prefer to sit on the train, or determining patient reading preferences by examining the condition of waiting-room magazines.
- Accretion – Explores what people leave behind. For example, if we go back to the crime scene, we might look for DNA or a dropped matchbook. In the social science world we attempt to determine if staff are conforming with waste disposal policy by looking through hospital garbage bins or we might study toilet-door graffiti to examine attitudes to promiscuity.

This type of exploration often goes unconsidered by project students, but it can offer huge insight in certain types of research. Historical research, for example, might be illuminated by exploration of artefacts such as dwellings, tools and art – in fact, just about anything that sheds light on the social condition of the period being explored. Cross-cultural studies can also be enhanced through this type of exploration. Comparing children's games or the marriage ceremonies of different cultures, for example, can be extremely enlightening.

In fact you could argue that understanding any culture can be enhanced by exploring its physical evidence or its 'tracks'. One contemporary example here is 'carbon footprinting', or the estimate of the carbon produced by an individual, household or business (and thus its contribution to global warming). This measure of accretion has actually become newsworthy and a part of everyday discourse.

Box 13.5

Document and Textual Analysis Examples

Halabi, S., Smith, W., Collins, J., Baker, D. and Bedford, J. (2013) 'A document analysis of HIV/AIDS education interventions in Ghana', *Health Education Journal*, 72(4): 486–500.

This document analysis involved using a snowball sampling procedure to gather 24 curricula – seven school-based, 15 adult-based and two multi-purpose curricula of prevention programmes – and explore them for informational accuracy. Each curriculum was coded independently by two reviewers, who noted specific lines, sections or images of the curriculum which were problematic. Findings included factual errors; omitted information; oversimplified facts; promotion of fear-based abstinence; confusing condom information; a presentation of infection as a women's problem; and misrepresentation of individual risk.

Sofalvi, A. (2011) 'Health education films of the silent era: A historical analysis', *International Electronic Journal of Health Education*, 14: 135–41.

This historical/textual analysis explored 11 health education films produced in the silent film era as well as published reviews of these films. The films of this era dealt with tuberculosis, hookworms, breastfeeding, traffic safety, dental care and children's health. The authors set the films in their socio-historic context and argue that such works are important historical resources for health education specialists.

Wales, E. and Brewer, B. (1976) 'Graffiti in the 1970s', *Journal of Social Psychology*, 99(1): 115–23.

This classic artefact analysis explored graffiti from male and female restrooms in four high schools selected to represent different socioeconomic and racial populations. The graffiti were sorted by three independent judges into 16 content categories. The researchers found that 88% of graffiti was produced by females, with content being predominantly romantic. Students from higher socioeconomic backgrounds wrote less romantic and more erotic material than those from lower socioeconomic backgrounds. The authors suggest that this may be an effect of an increased emphasis on female sexuality and freedom of expression.

Secondary Data Analysis

Data collection is such an entrenched part of research processes that we sometimes forget that the data we seek may have already been collected – censuses, large-scale surveys and organizational records can all potentially hold the answers to research questions. Capitalizing on these data sets makes sense. Using secondary data allows you to 'skip' data-collection processes and all the stress, cost and time they involve. It can also allow you to work with samples that might otherwise have been inaccessible, or samples much larger than you would have been able to generate on your own. But remember: secondary data is only as good as its collection processes – and you have no control over these.

Now perhaps the most crucial step in secondary analysis is knowing exactly what you are looking for – that is, having a clearly articulated research question and knowing what types of data might answer that question. When it comes to secondary analysis, this can actually be more difficult than you might realize. When you are working with an existing data set, you skip the process of design, including working through decisions about population, samples, questions, response categories, etc. You also do not get to explore data as it comes in. And both of these processes offer tremendous opportunity for conceptual work. In secondary analysis, you need to consciously think through such issues, even if design and preliminary data were done by others. Only then will you be in a position to assess the relevance of an existing data set to your research question.

The basic steps of secondary analysis are covered in Box 13.6.

Box 13.6

Steps in Secondary Analysis

1. Determining your research question - As indicated above, knowing exactly what you are looking for.
2. Locating data - Knowing what is out there and whether you can gain access to it. A quick Internet search, possibly with the help of a librarian, will reveal a wealth of options.

(Continued)

3 Gaining access to the data - Knowing where it is does not ensure you will gain access to it. You made may need to seek permission. Being ready to share your agenda, and the benefits of your research can help here.
4 Evaluating relevance of the data - Considering things like the data's original purpose, when it was collected, the population, sampling strategy/sample, data-collection protocols, operationalization of concepts, questions asked and form/shape of the data.
5 Assessing credibility of the data - Establishing the credentials of the original researchers, searching for full explication of methods including any problems encountered, determining how consistent the data is with data from other sources, discovering whether the data has been used in any credible published research.
6 Analysis - This will generally involve a range of statistical processes (see Chapter 15).

An example here might be as follows. Step 1, determine your research question: 'How has religious affiliation in Canada changed over the past 30 years?' Step 2: determine what data sets, including possibly the census, might have this information. Step 3: explore relevance by exploring how the question is asked; if there is any bias or assumption in how it is asked; and if it has been asked in the same way over the 30-year period you wish to explore. Step 4: assess credibility: in the case of the census, methods should be well documented. Step 5: analyse by exploring trends in affiliation and how this might vary by demographic characteristics such as geographic region, age, socioeconomic status, gender and education.

I Have a Question!

Just How Helpful Are Online Databases and the Datasets They Might Have?

Online databases can offer a wealth of information including census information, demographic statistics, conflict data and economic development indicators. This research is useful for nearly every field of inquiry including business, social sciences, health, education and STEM (science, technology, engineering and mathematical) fields. Some comprehensive national and international databases worth exploring include: the World Bank http://data.worldbank.org; the United Nations https://data.un.org; US federal statistics data.gov; the Australia Bureau of Statistics www.abs.gov.au; UK government data www.data.gov.uk; and Gapminder www.gapminder.org. A quick Google search using your discipline of interest will uncover many more.

Critical Thinking Challenge 14

Is It Out There?

Changes in the research landscape generally follow the waves of change that mark the information age. We are now surrounded by a sea of data. What are you looking for? Any chance it is out there? (We'd be surprised if at least some of it wasn't.) Where is it? Do you think it is credible? Accessible? Useful? Should you be pursuing it? Can it be your main source of data, or is it likely to be supplementary?

ANALYSING PREVIOUS STUDIES

Finally, in the existing data stakes, we need to talk about exploring existing research studies – of which there are plenty! Research abounds: there are over three million new journal articles produced every year. And a solid research question is one that asks whether there any definitive results we can draw on from a range of similar studies. This is necessary because research findings can often conflict and there is a real need to collate findings to see if anything definitive can be found.

There are two strategies for working with existing studies and their data: systematic review and meta-analysis. Systematic reviews are used to assess and synthesize a range of studies to determine more conclusive results. Meta-analysis is a subset of systematic analysis and involves running combined data sets through analysis to synthesize or confirm results. So let's start with systematic reviews.

Systematic Reviews

So is a systematic review (sometimes called an **integrative review**) just a literature review? In a word, no. A literature review is a critical review of a body of knowledge, including findings and theoretical and methodological contributions. It is an overview of a body of literature. A systematic review goes beyond this and attempts to determine the validity of individual studies and synthesize the results of these in order to find some 'truth'. The goal is to offer a thorough yet condensed view on the evidence in a particular area.

Systematic reviews are most common in the area of medicine, in particular, randomized controlled clinical trials. But they are of value anywhere a rigorous assessment of validity and truth within a particular area of study will aid understanding and decision-making. In fact, systematic reviews are increasingly used to inform policy and practice decisions. And while systematic reviews are well suited to quantitative studies, they can also be applied to studies that sit under the qualitative paradigm. Systematic reviews offer:

- a transparent, verifiable and replicable approach;
- minimization of bias and error;
- conclusions of higher validity and reliability;
- a comprehensive picture of a research area that can be quickly disseminated to researchers, practitioners and policy-makers;
- context for interpreting the results of a new study.

The basic steps of a systematic review are:

1. Formulate the research question – Like any research process, a clear, unambiguous research question will help set the direction for your study. For example, 'What types of health promotion campaign have been most effective in reducing smoking rates of Australian teenagers?' or 'Does school leadership make a difference to educational standards?'
2. Develop and use an explicit, reproducible methodology – Key to systematic reviews are that bias is minimized and that methods are transparent and reproducible.
3. Develop and use clear inclusion/exclusion criteria – The array of literature out there is vast. Determining clear selection criteria for inclusion is essential.

4 Develop and use an explicit search strategy – It is important to identify all studies that meet the eligibility criteria set in point 3. The search for studies needs to be extensive and should draw on multiple databases.
5 Critically assess the validity of the findings in included studies – This is likely to involve critical appraisal guides and quality checklists that cover participant recruitment, data-collection methods and modes of analysis. Assessment is often conducted by two or more reviewers who know both the topic area and commonly used methods.
6 Analysis of findings across the studies – This can involve analysis, comparison and synthesis of results using methodological criteria. This is often the case for qualitative studies. Quantitative studies generally attempt to use statistical methods to explore differences between studies and combine their effects (see meta-analysis below). If divergences are found, the source of the divergence is analysed.
7 Synthesis and interpretation of results – Synthesized results need to be interpreted in light of both the limitations of the review and the studies it contains. An example here might be the inclusion of only studies reported in English. This level of transparency allows readers to assess the credibility of the review and the applicability of findings.

Now with all the methodological safeguards in place, systematic reviews should be bullet-proof. But varying degrees of quality and even divergent results of supposed replicable methods have been found. The reality of real-world research means that there are likely to be differing opinions on what constitutes quality, and how to deal with results from various research traditions, plus limited resources and varying levels of research skills and experience. It is worth remembering that systematic reviews are only as good as the ability of researchers to follow protocols.

Box 13.7 overviews three centres dedicated to the advancement of systematic reviews.

Box 13.7

Centres Dedicated to Advancing Systematic Reviews

The Cochrane Collaboration (www.cochrane.org)

> The Cochrane Collaboration is an international network of more than 37,000 dedicated people from over 130 countries. We work together to help health care providers, policy-makers, patients, their advocates and carers, make well-informed decisions about health care, by preparing, updating and promoting the accessibility of Cochrane Reviews – over 5,000 so far, published online in the Cochrane Database of Systematic Reviews.

Concentrating on the area of health care, the Cochrane Collaboration site offers systematic-review training links, an extensive library and vast review resources, including the world's largest collection of randomized controlled trial records.

The EPPI Centre (eppi.ioe.ac.uk)

> The Evidence for Policy and Practice Information and Co-ordinating Centre (EPPI-Centre) is part of the Social Science Research Unit at the Institute of Education, University of London. Since 1993, we have been at the forefront of carrying out systematic reviews and developing review methods in social science and public policy. We are dedicated to making reliable research findings accessible to the people who need them, whether they are making policy, practice or personal decisions.

The EPPI-Centre site offers a series of links to systematic review training, tools, methods and databases. It also has a library of over 200 reviews in education and in public health and participative research.

The Campbell Collaboration (www.campbellcollaboration.org)

> The Campbell Collaboration is an international research network that produces systematic reviews of the effects of social interventions. The Campbell Collaboration ... helps people make well-informed decisions by preparing, maintaining and disseminating systematic reviews in education, crime and justice, and social welfare.

The Campbell Collaboration site offers a library of over 300 reviews as well as a resource centre with policy documents, guidelines, review templates, useful links and video tutorials.

Meta-Analysis

So what exactly is the difference between a systematic review and a meta-analysis?

Well, a systematic review – as indicated above – locates, critically appraises and synthesizes the findings and results of credible studies by using transparent reproducible methods. Meta-analysis is simply one of those transparent reproducible methods. In fact, it is the gold standard of systematic review methods. This is because it implies that studies under review are quantitative (which, particularly in medical research, is seen as being more objective than qualitative studies), highly comparable and treated statistically, thereby minimizing bias. Meta-analysis, if carried out within a rigorous systematic review, should offer an unbiased synthesis of empirical data. The goal is a more statistically robust analysis than that which could be achieved with a single study with a single set of assumptions and conditions.

As compared to single studies, meta-analysis offers:

- more statistical power;
- more confidence in results;
- possible explanations of variance;
- greater ability to apply findings to the general population.

On the downside, meta-analysis can:

- be costly, as it can be a time-consuming challenge to find 'combinable' studies;
- require advanced statistical techniques;
- be tainted by publication bias (studies with results that fit a particular agenda are more likely to be published).

Since meta-analysis is a subset (but not a requirement) of systematic reviews, the basic steps are similar. Therefore, only point 6 is expanded upon. For more on the other points see systematic reviews above.

1 Formulate the research question.
2 Develop and use an explicit, reproducible methodology (this step was done when meta-analysis was originally decided upon).

3 Develop and use clear inclusion/exclusion criteria.
4 Develop and use an explicit search strategy.
5 Critically assess the validity of the findings in included studies.
6 Analysis of findings across the studies – Statistical analysis would involve decisions related to:
   a the dependent and independent variables under review;
   b how studies will be weighted according to sample size;
   c how to conduct sensitivity analysis (the extent to which study results stay the same, given different approaches to aggregating data);
7 Synthesis and interpretation of results.

Box 13.8 offers brief summaries of systematic reviews that used meta-analysis as their methodological approach towards synthesis.

Box 13.8

Meta-Analysis Examples

It's quite easy to search databases for meta-analyses, since the term 'meta-analysis' is often included in the article title. Here is a very brief summary of three studies that show a diversity of topic and approach.

Jeynes, W. H. (2005) 'A meta-analysis of the relation of parental involvement to urban elementary school student academic achievement', *Urban Education*, 40(3): 237–69.

This meta-analysis synthesized 41 studies that explored the relationship between parental involvement and the academic achievement of urban elementary school children. The statistical analysis sought to determine the effect of parental involvement overall and subcategories of involvement. The analysis showed a significant relationship between parental involvement and academic achievement. This relationship was found to hold for both white and minority children and also for males and females.

Doucouliagos, H. and Ulubaşoğlu, M. A. (2008) 'Democracy and economic growth: A meta-analysis', *American Journal of Political Science*, *52*(1): 61–83.

This meta-analysis synthesized 84 studies on democracy and growth using meta-regression analysis. The analysis found that democracy does not have a direct impact on economic growth. It did find, however, that democracy has significant and positive indirect effects on economic growth through higher human capital, lower inflation, lower political instability and higher levels of economic freedom. Larger governments and less free international trade were also found to be associated with democracy.

Ferguson, S. S. (2008) 'Nicotine patch therapy prior to quitting smoking: A meta-analysis', *Addiction*, *103*(4): 557–63.

This meta-analysis synthesized four pre-cessation patch treatments in order to evaluate the incremental efficacy of starting nicotine patch treatment prior to quitting compared to the current regimen of starting patch treatment on the target quit day. Patch treatment prior to quitting was found to double the odds of quitting. Co-treatment with mecamylamine did not modify these effects.

I Have a Question!

I Was Just Going to Collect Primary Data. I had No Idea There Were So Many Options for Secondary Data. Does This Mean I Need to Add It to My Study?

When Zina first started teaching methods and supervising students, it was all about primary data. In fact, a study wasn't a study if primary data wasn't collected. Secondary data was, well, secondary. But times have changed. There is just too much data out there to reinvent the wheel if an existing wheel is pretty good and serves the purpose. So do you need to collect secondary data? Well, you may or may not end up making such data a part of your study, but you absolutely need to consider it, and look for it. We *always* ask our students if there is any data out there we can use. And if it can help answer the research question, secondary data definitely needs to be considered as a potential research approach.

FIND YOUR NEXT STEP

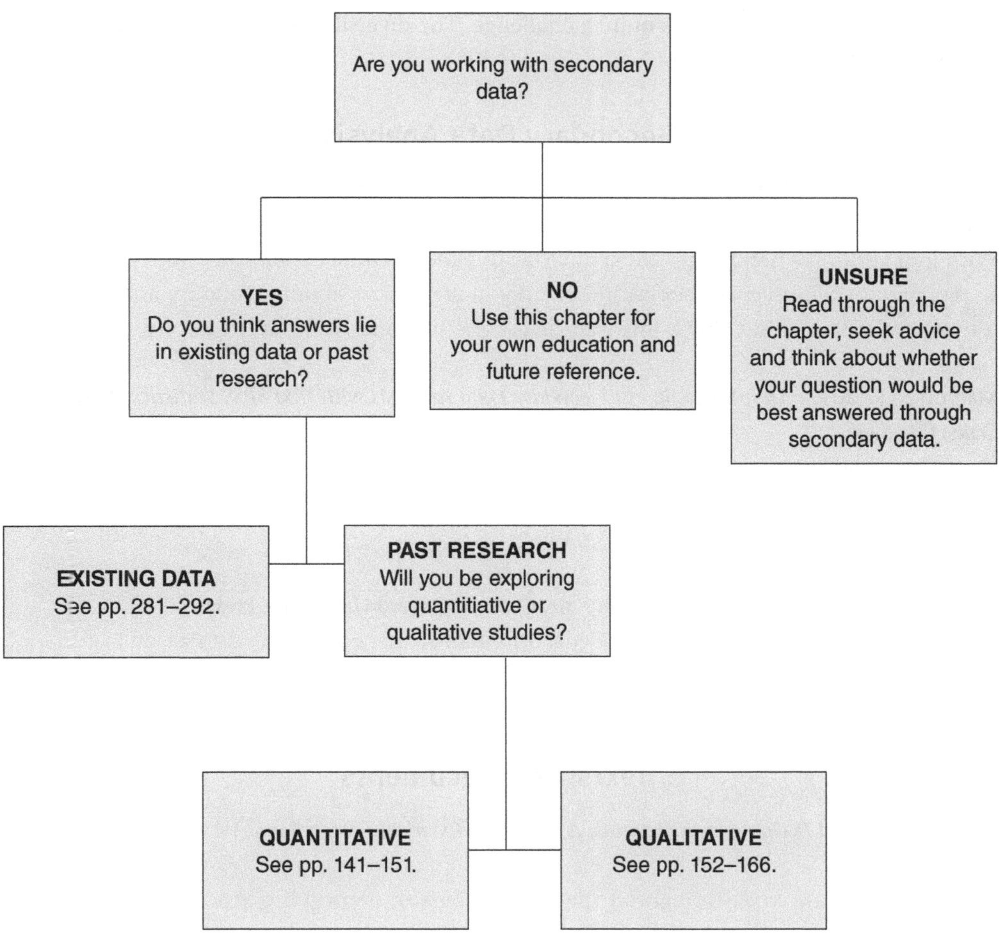

Chapter Summary

- Secondary data is existing data that can be found in documents, databases and in past research, none of which was created by the researcher for their research purposes.
- Working with secondary data can save time and resources as well as eliminate researcher bias/influence. But because secondary data will have been collected for another purpose it may lack relevance, lack currency and be tainted with methodological flaws.
- Traces of social activity literally surround us. Reports, legislation, policy, diaries and journals, articles, videos, blogs, photographs, poetry, songs, letters and Facebook posts are all documents or broader 'texts' that can be explored through research processes.
- There is a good chance that your research question has already been explored. You can offer overarching analysis of existing studies by using systematic reviews and meta-analysis.

FURTHER READING

Working with secondary data is quite a challenge. The diversity of data types is only matched by diversity of methods.

Secondary Data Analysis

Bulmer, M., Sturgis, P. and Allum, N. (eds) (2009) *The Secondary Analysis of Survey Data*. London: Sage.
With four volumes, 1,600 pages and a price tag of 1,080 US dollars, this is not one you are going to pick up at the university bookstore. But if you are serious about secondary analysis, as the ultimate reference guide, this is just waiting for you to come visit it at the library.

MacInnes, J. (2017) *An Introduction to Secondary Data Analysis with IBM SPSS Statistics*. Thousand Oaks, CA: Sage.
There are two things you need to know when doing secondary analysis: the logic of design and how to actually conduct the analysis using a program. This book gives you both and is the right choice if you are going down the SPSS path.

Vartanian, T. (2010) *Secondary Data Analysis*. Oxford: Oxford University Press.
We like the way this starts by having students consider whether a secondary data set, and which one, is right for their project. Good coverage of how to download, merge and analyse secondary data.

'Texts' and Documents

Brundage, A. (2017) *Going to the Sources: A Guide to Historical Research and Writing*. Chichester: Wiley-Blackwell.
This book will take you through all the ins and outs of identifying, finding and evaluating credible texts and other forms of data that can illuminate historical periods of interest.

Halabi, S., Smith, W., Collins, J., Baker, D. and Bedford, J. (2013) 'A document analysis of HIV/AIDS education interventions in Ghana', *Health Education Journal*, *72*(4): 486–500.
See Box 13.5.

Prior, L. (ed.) (2011) *Using Documents and Records in Social Research*. London: Sage.
We love how the author sells the value of documents in social research. By using examples drawn from criminology, health, education, organizational research, science and technology, she highlights the value that documents can bring to our understanding of the social.

Rapley, T. (2018) *Doing Conversation, Discourse and Document Analysis*. London: Sage.
We think this is a good introduction to the challenges and promise of collecting and analysing conversations and documents. Clear and easy to understand.

Sofalvi, A. (2011) 'Health education films of the silent era: A historical analysis', *International Electronic Journal of Health Education*, *14*: 135–41.
See Box 13.5.

Wales, E. and Brewer, B. (1976) 'Graffiti in the 1970s', *Journal of Social Psychology*, *99*(1): 115–23.
See Box 13.5.

Webb, E. J., Campbell, D. T., Schwartz, R. D. and Sechrest, L. ([1966] 2015) *Unobtrusive Measures: Nonreactive Research in the Social Sciences*. London: Sage.
This book is a classic and really opened our eyes to research that looks at traces of human activity and how this can supplement more traditional research data. Terrific illustrations help make arguments undeniable.

Previous Studies

Cooper, H., Hedges, L. and Valentine, J. (eds) (2019) *The Handbook of Research Synthesis and Meta-Analysis*. Thousand Oaks, CA: Sage.
When Sage puts out a 'handbook' you can rest assured that it is broad reaching, thought-provoking and comprehensive, but also expensive. So, if this is not in your library, request it.

Cooper, H. M. (2016) *Research Synthesis and Meta-Analysis: A Step-by-Step Approach*. Thousand Oaks, CA: Sage.
Good advice here for systematic reviews and meta-analyses across the social, behavioural and medical sciences. A clear seven-step process to follow and lots of grounded examples.

Doucouliagos, H. and Ulubaşoğlu, M. A. (2008) 'Democracy and economic growth: A meta-analysis', *American Journal of Political Science*, *52*(1): 61–83.
See Box 13.8.

Elsbach, K. and van Knippenberg, D. (2020) 'Creating high impact literature reviews: An argument for "integrative reviews"', *Journal of Management Studies*, *57*(6): 1277–89.
A robust argument for the evolution of the literature review into a source of data; in other words, an integrative review (another name for systematic reviews).

Gough, D., Oliver, S. and Thomas, J. (eds) (2017) *An Introduction to Systematic Reviews.* London: Sage.
We like this book. It is short and accessible and covers qualitative approaches such as meta-ethnography and statistical approaches such as meta-analysis. A good, user-friendly introduction.

Higgins, J. P. T. and Green, S. (2019) *Cochrane Handbook for Systematic Reviews of Interventions.* New York: Wiley-Interscience.
The Cochrane Collaboration (see Box 13.7) is a world leader in the conduct of systematic reviews, particularly in the area of health. This handbook outlines the methodological protocols required for doing a Cochrane review, but can be easily applied to systematic reviews of all kinds.

Jeynes, W. H. (2005) 'A meta-analysis of the relation of parental involvement to urban elementary school student academic achievement', *Urban Education, 40*(3): 237–69.
See Box 13.8.

Linnenluecke, M., Marrone, M. and Singh, A. (2019) 'Conducting systematic literature reviews and bibliometric analyses', *Australian Journal of Management, 45*: 175–94.
This work also argues the need to take advantage of the data opportunities of systematic reviews and offers defined steps to ensure a process that has methodological rigour.

Schwarzer, G., Carpenter, J. and Rücker, G. (2015) *Meta-Analysis with R.* New York: Springer.
R software is powerful and free, so naturally it is gaining popularity with social science researchers. If you are undertaking meta-analysis and want to explore using R, this book will give you all the ins and outs through detailed examples and data sets available online.

14

ONLINE-GENERATED DATA

Learning Objectives

- Data stored online vs online-generated data
  - To become familiar with the benefits and challenges of working with online-generated data
  - To become familiar with various types of online-generated data
- Finding and assessing online-generated data
  - To understand the challenges of searching for online-generated data
  - To be able to critically interrogate and assess online-generated data
- Working with online-generated data
  - To understand the value of the Internet as a way of capturing moments in time
  - To understand the value of web mining, data scraping and automated textual analysis
  - To understand approaches studying online communities

DATA STORED ONLINE VS ONLINE-GENERATED DATA

There are actually two distinct ways we can think of online data. The first is the online data that simply sit on the Internet. In this case, think of the Internet as a massive library or repository. Almost every bit of paper that every organization, government agency, NGO, researcher, etc. produces also (and sometimes, only) exists online. Digital photographs, records, databases and government files are available at your fingertips. You may not even realize how extraordinary this is. If you are under 30, you probably never knew, and if you are over 30 you are likely to have forgotten, what it was like before everything we wanted to know was right there. BI (before Internet), if you wanted to know the lyrics of a song, and you didn't have the album cover or the CD case, you had to ask a friend. BI, we visited actual buildings called libraries, and searched through rows and rows of index cards to locate books made of real paper organized by the Dewey Decimal System. BI, the news was delivered to us by a kid on a bike who threw rolled-up sheets of paper at us.

And aside from accumulating the vast sum of all human knowledge, the Internet is also an archive of itself. Copies of websites are preserved at specific moments in time. This means that web pages are preserved as they existed in 1997 or 2006. Think of it as a virtual time machine, where the dancing animated clip art of the 1990s comes alive. Websites that would otherwise be overwritten, updated or deleted are forever preserved.

This makes the Internet a researcher's best friend and is, in fact, the main resource for the secondary data we talked about in Chapter 13.

But that is still not online-generated data. Online-generated data is a different beast. It is data that is produced by the Internet or only exists because of the Internet. We are talking here about websites, feeds, blogs, posts, videos and tweets that are proliferating at an unfathomable pace. It is also the data we generate as we live out our lives online; i.e. the evidence of our net-based communities. This is the data that would cease to exist if the Internet was abolished. A frightening thought, given that we live more of our lives online, removed from the physical spaces that once defined us.

For researchers, this is relatively new territory, and is territory that is shifting and expanding at a rate with which we can barely keep up. But as our world shifts in this direction, we need to keep pushing the boundaries of social science research, which is why this chapter is dedicated to exploring online-generated data.

Benefits and Challenges of Working with Online-Generated Data

> Today's emerging research methodologies are intertwined with multi-sensory input devices creating new possibilities for cross content validation.
>
> Mitra Cline (2019)

Benefits

The social world, for many of us, centres around Instagram, Facebook, TikTok, Tinder and other apps that are yet to hit the market. And since this is where social interactions are happening, we need methods for studying them. The same goes for the workplace. As companies and departments move further online, our analyses need to follow. Government is similar. Think about tweet-happy presidents, for example. If we are not ready to analyse this new form of communication, we will miss out on a massive source of global influence. So working with online data has benefits, including a better understanding of our contemporary world, but beyond beneficial, it is now essential.

Challenges

The biggest challenge of working with online-generated data is how fast things change. There is exponential growth, not only in the amount of data but in the types and sources. The Internet is a tremendous resource, but it can be a virtual rabbit hole that you can emerge from with nothing credible in hand. Remember the programmer's mantra: GIGO (Garbage In, Garbage Out). Well, the Internet is full of garbage. So the ability to assess websites is foundational to Internet research. And even if you find credible sites, it does not ensure valid, reliable, accurate and representative information. The Internet is full of the good (credible, authentic, valid, reliable information), the bad (incorrect, erroneous, inaccurate, false information) and the ugly (misleading, deceptive, bogus, counterfeit, fake information). So, it is imperative that you are able to wade through it with a critical eye (see Chapter 13, Box 13.1, p. 279).

We also have to analyse unprecedented large-scale data. By definition, we are talking about data that is so large that our traditional social science methods don't cut it. And then there are the ethical issues surrounding data protection. Data storage and data management have always been a researcher's concern, but as we start to work with such large databases, the challenge becomes even more complex. The European Union has the General Data Protection Regulation that protects privacy through principles of lawfulness, fairness and transparency; purpose limitation; data minimization; accuracy; storage limitation; integrity and confidentiality; and accountability. These are sound principles whether or not you're in the EU.

So how do we, as researchers, not only cope with, but take advantage of, this new world order? How do we design studies that take advantage of Big Data? How do we wade through the challenges posed by a world where every actor is producing data without mediation, controls or gatekeepers? And how can we begin to understand communities that only exist in a virtual space? How do we immerse ourselves in something we cannot touch? How do we keep pace with technology and the impact it has on how we interact and communicate?

We wish we had all the answers – but the answers keep moving and are certainly moving faster than the pace of book publishing. The best we can do is simply highlight the opportunities and challenges associated with this space and outline the approaches we are adopting and adapting in an attempt to keep up and build understandings.

Types of Online-Generated Data

According to Forbes, as of March 2024 there are 5.35 billion Internet users and 201.8 million live websites. Every single minute, we:

- share 65,972 photos and videos on Instagram;
- watch 625 million videos on TikTok;
- submit over 5.9 million queries to Google;
- swipe on Tinder 1.1 million times;
- send 2.34 million emails;
- post 350,000 tweets on Twitter/X;
- share 2.43 million snaps on Snapchat;
- post 510,000 comments, 293,000 statuses, and 240,000 photos on Facebook.

In three to five years' time, these figures will be but a fraction of what they are now. And, of course, there will be new forums for data creation that we can't even fathom – that's **Big Data**.

Big Data

The sheer volume of online-generated data is why this type of data is called Big Data. In fact, the data it produces is so massive that traditional data-processing applications are insufficient. This is the world of the Internet. Big Data causes big headaches. But it does have big potential, as the trends Big Data can track can be significant. The Australian Tax Office, for example, is using the analysis of Big Data to understand trends in tax evasion. Big Data is also being used for things like understanding sexual preferences (what types of porn people are watching, and not just saying they are watching) and political affiliations, political leanings and political activism. In fact, applications are unlimited and ever-broadening.

There are several important subsets of Big Data that are useful for social science research. Please keep in mind that those we decided to cover below are not collectively exhaustive or mutually exclusive. In other words, they may not cover everything and there are definite overlaps – but are chosen for their usefulness to social science research.

Social Data

Social data is data that individuals knowingly and voluntarily share; examples include tweets, posts and videos shared on Twitter, Instagram, Facebook, Tumblr, TikTok and YouTube. The unprecedented use of these media means that most social data is Big Data.

One of the great things about social data is how massive and current it is. It has the ability to give us both a snapshot of now and a look into the future. Understanding travel plans, outbreaks of viruses, political opinion, cyber bullying, dating, responses to social disasters and, in fact, anything that an Internet community is currently discussing represents the potential to draw on an extremely large pool of data. This, of course, saves you the time and cost associated with commissioning studies that rely on the collection of primary data.

Social data means variety, volume and velocity. There is ease of access to user content and ample evidence of network ties. Topics and data are virtually limitless and it is easy to create event timelines.

There are, however, significant challenges. For one, we can become bamboozled by the amount of data and forget that we don't have a representative sample. And we are not just talking about a lack of representativeness within a narrowly defined population. We are also talking about the ability to misrepresent a global population. If, for example, international policy decisions are to be influenced by social data, then developing countries with limited computer and Internet access will not be in a strong position to engage in informed decision-making.

Privacy is another major issue. Is something public just because it is shared online? There is a real blurring of public and private spheres. There are mounting concerns around the world about what social media companies (and others) are doing with our data and using this data for research means wading into that debate. Additionally, the ability of Internet data to be traced means that researchers are not in a position to ensure anonymity. On the flip side, it can be equally difficult to verify the identity of research participants, if there is a need to ensure credibility.

The sheer volume of the data and velocity of change also pose massive challenges for researchers. Traditional research methods were never designed for what the Internet is now delivering and certainly not for what it will be delivering in the future. Our processes of funding, design and conduct, writing up and publishing research studies are undeniably slow. Data collected in one year may not be published in a study for two to three years – and by that time it will likely be outdated. Platforms like Facebook and Twitter (as it was then called) used to offer researchers free access to API (application programming interface) tools for data collection. Many of those tools are now paywalled or unavailable. Likewise, the popular platforms of today may be superseded by the newest app or social media site, so if you have developed highly specific technical skills these may no longer been adaptable. User-generated social data is also inherently flawed. We may want to track followers, likes and views but these can all be bought. Fake traffic is a reality. If there is a financial incentive to falsify such data, it will happen. We also have to look at the interests of Google, which is there to sell advertising and make money. Yes, it may be tracking what we do, but through its tracking and targeted ad placements, it also influences what we do. Google has vested interests that have an influence on data.

Machine Data

As more of our appliances become 'smart', more of the rhythms of our daily lives become data points. Use a smartphone as your alarm? What time you woke up is recorded. Read online? Then what you are reading (and how long) is being recorded. Use a public transport card? Where you're travelling to and from is recorded. Use Google Maps? Your every move can be followed. Use a credit card? What you bought, and where you bought it is logged. Use a smart TV or a streaming service? Viewing habits now tracked. And that's before you voluntarily put things on Instagram, Facebook or TikTok. We are leaving traces (or digital exhaust) everywhere.

This data is not being collected for academic research. Primarily, it's big tech companies who use data to increase profits. The way this data is collected (often without consent; or with pages of terms and conditions no one really reads) and how it is used raises major ethical issues. Beyond individual privacy concerns, developments like the indigenous data sovereignty movement point to global ethical concerns (Rainie et al., 2019).

Nonetheless, there is remarkable potential for academic research here. From looking at past behaviours, to exploring current trends, to making future predictions, this type of data can be invaluable in many applications. But you will still need to think about data quality and security. As with social data, you need to consider whether the data is valid, complete and representative.

Real-Time Data

This type of data tells you what is going on right here and now. Sometimes this is convenient – Google Maps giving you real-time updates on traffic, accidents and speed traps. And sometimes it's freaky – when you get an ad on your phone because you're near a shop that sells that exact product. This data is delayed only by the speed of transfer. Data that can be used just as well for marketing as for disaster management.

As with all types of Big Data, data quality and data security need to be managed.

Transactional Data

This type of data is often associated with the business world and is useful for its marketing potential. In short, it is data derived from daily transactions such as invoices, payment orders, storage records and delivery receipts. It is often seen to have limited use in social science research. But when we broaden this type out from its business roots just a little, such data can be quite useful in the political/social sphere. If we include transactions such as newsletter sign-ups, donations, feedback and event registrations, then the application for understanding things like activism, campaigning, philanthropy, etc. become quite interesting. The same caveats on data quality and security apply.

Analytic Data

Analytic data is actually a broad term for computational analysis of data which can be descriptive (what happened), predictive (what might happen) or prescriptive (what should happen). When we hear the term, however, we often think of website performance and associated statistics. And while this is just one application, this itself can be helpful to researchers. A common research question for government departments is how to optimize website performance. With analytics, this can be as detailed as producing mouse-move and click-move heat maps that show you exactly how your website is being used/misused. As our systems become more robust and data quality improves, analytics will be increasingly used in sectors such as education where it can explore student performance and predict things like graduation and dropout rates (see Box 14.2, below).

FINDING AND ASSESSING ONLINE-GENERATED DATA

Finding the Data

In the first edition of this book, Zina had to cover online searching in depth. It was quite new and we were just moving from card catalogues (some retro trivia for you to look up if you haven't heard of these) to computer searches. But online searching is now an everyday activity with search engines becoming ever more intuitive. So what can we tell you? Well, first and foremost, be very clear on what it is you want to know. Your research question should be crystal clear. You should also know it off the top of your head. You'd be surprised at how many students ask questions about their research methods but cannot articulate their question.

Once your question is at the forefront of your mind, you need to be just as clear on what aspects of the question you want to answer through your online search. Only when you have that clarity can you choose the right terms. We cover the basics of online searching in Chapter 6, pp. 109–110, but you can take this a step further by honing your skills.

Box 14.1

Refining Your Online Search

- Put the tilde operator ~ before your search term to return results that include synonyms.
- Use the term 'or' to search for either of two terms.
- Use the minus - sign to identify terms you don't want in your results.
- Put quotation marks around words " " to search for that exact phrase.
- Use the wildcard operator * - Google calls it the 'fill in the blank' operator.
- Start your search with 'site:' - this limits your search to specific sites or types of site (.org, .edu).
- Add 'filetype:' and the three-letter file abbreviation to limit your search to only that type of file, e.g. PDF or PPT.
- Use the Google Goggles app and take a photo instead of typing a search.
- Add a zip code/postcode to the end of a search to get local offerings.
- Use 'related:' to find similar sites. For example, 'related:www.youtube.com' can be used to find sites similar to YouTube.

Assessing the Data

Now that you've found the data, let's talk about assessing it. We've already referred you to Chapter 13, Box 13.1, which covers credibility in secondary data, but is there anything specific to online-generated data? Well, the answer is yes. With online-generated data you are dealing with data that do not have professional gatekeepers to monitor content. Remember that Big Data is generally not intended for collection, let alone analysis. There are therefore often issues with:

- Consistency – This can arise from errors in data entry; changes in how data is produced over time; synonyms, abbreviations and acronyms; varying frames of reference; different formats, i.e. text vs voice, photo vs video; differences in semantics and coding.
- Provenance – This is the source of the data and whether it is credible. Think here of all the controversy over foreign election interference on Facebook, or reviews that are purchased.
- Accuracy/truthfulness – This can come from data entry errors, data integration errors and system errors. But it can also come from the tendency for people to forget or misrepresent.
- Completeness – On the data management side, this includes errors in collection, storage and processing. On the human side, it can mean the tendency to only show one side of things (don't we all look like we have rich lives on Facebook or Instagram?).
- Objectivity/subjectivity – The conflation of fact and opinion. It can be difficult to discern between the two.

- Privacy – When you are dealing with such vast amounts of data it can be difficult, if not impossible, to get permission for data use.

What do we do about this? Well, each case is situation specific, so the best advice is to be aware of potential issues and then critically assess whether the data you collect will, nonetheless, be useful in answering your questions. If you know you have poor data quality, you need a sound basis for determining whether and how the data can be used.

Critical Thinking Challenge 15

Social Data, Not Just for Your Amusement

Think about the social media platform that you're most familiar with. Given all the data-related issues of consistency, provenance, accuracy, completeness, objectivity and privacy, are there any questions you could ask of this medium that could be credibly answered?

If you're thinking of Facebook, what questions could your friends' status updates actually answer? If you're thinking of Instagram, what meta-narrative could you construct from the photographs? If you're thinking about TikTok, what do these short videos tell you about how we're connecting? Can you come up with any questions? Are the questions relevant? Significant? Do you think there's value in conducting this type of research given all the limitations?

I Have a Question!

Are There Tips Specific to Website Credibility That I Should Think About?

One idea is to deconstruct the web address. Web addresses, or URLs, provide one of the most obvious hints about the origin of information and thus its credibility. For instance, if there is a tilde (~) in the URL, the website is probably a personal web page or blog and should be used only with extreme caution. Domain names matter as well. You might find the following table useful.

Suffix	Use	Credibility
.com .net	Most common, commercial or personal site	Low
.org	Traditionally a non-profit organization, whose purpose is advocacy, so there may be rich information on specific issues, but also a particular bias. Note that .org is becoming increasingly common as a generic domain extension	Low to medium
.edu	Educational institution. Sites using this domain extension range from primary through postgraduate. Students affiliated with a university may also receive web space with an .edu domain suffix, so check whether individual pages are by faculty or students in the department	Medium

Suffix	Use	Credibility
.mil	Military. Good luck getting past the glossy recruitment page without some clearance credentials. Depending on the branch, there may be useful reports or study findings on the public pages	Medium
.gov	Government websites, usually at the federal level. Information typically includes official statistics, department portals and judicial rulings	High

WORKING WITH ONLINE-GENERATED DATA

Given all the challenges of working with online-generated data, what research approaches can help you wade through masses of messy, less than trustworthy data; and what strategies can you call on to ensure credibility of results?

Well, such strategies are ever-developing. What is interesting, however, is that methodological developments in this space are not necessarily being led by academics. Market researchers and advertising agencies have driven the growth of the private sector as they recognize the profits that can come from data mining. Companies like Sisense, Domo, IBM Congos, Rapid Miner and Oracle Data Mining all offer 'business insight' through Big Data analytics, while companies like Datasift and Gnip allow clients to get answers to their questions from social media in real time. The focus here is generally business-based, but when used to track political opinion, emergent health issues and influential people, we can begin to see overlaps into traditional academic areas of health, social science and political science.

Big Data methods are becoming ever more common in academia (Box 14.2 gives examples of academic big/social data studies). Common methods (and those covered in the rest of this chapter) include moment capture, **web mining**, **data scraping** and automated textual analysis. Also covered are online ethnography and **netnography**, which explore the data produced by online communities.

Box 14.2

Studies Using Big/Social Data

Academic research in this area is still playing catch-up. Facebook first opened up site data to suicide research in 2013 (Lopatto, 2013). Facebook allowed researchers at the suicide prevention group SAVE.org access to individuals' posts in the days leading up to their suicides. Researchers could explore changes in content, tone, type of language being used, intervals between posts, etc. to gather information on pre-suicidal cues.

Since this study, more and more research has been conducted on social media, but issues of privacy have made it difficult for it to become standard practice. For example, in the Facebook study mentioned above, the goal of better identifying suicide warning signs was highly admirable, but many felt that privacy was breached since there was no informed consent.

(Continued)

Two less controversial examples follow:

Leetaru, K. H. (2012) 'A Big Data approach to the humanities, arts and social sciences: Wikipedia's view of the world through supercomputing', *Research Trends*, 30 September.

In this study, Wikipedia's world history content is explored and visualized through spatial, temporal and emotional data mining. Using Big Data content-mining approaches, more than 80 million locations and 42 million dates between AD 1000 and 2012 were explored. The author explores the challenges and opportunities facing Big Data analysis in the humanities, arts and social sciences, including computational approaches, data acquisition workflow, data storage, metadata construction and translating text into knowledge.

Viloria, A., Naveda, A., Palma, H., Núñez, W. and Núñez, L. (2020) 'Using Big Data to determine potential dropouts in higher education', *Journal of Physics: Conference Series, 1432*(1): 012077.

The authors use statistical learning techniques (with de-identified data), to predict possible dropouts based on their demographic and academic characteristics. The authors discuss the importance of degree progression as a key predictive factor as well as discussing the logic behind their choice of methods.

Capturing a Moment

An interesting application of online-generated data is the 'Internet preserved for posterity'. Since 1996, the Wayback Machine has archived more than 450 billion web pages and saved for posterity two petabytes of data (1 petabyte = 1,000 terabytes = 1,000,000 gigabytes). This type of data can be extremely useful for analysing the impact of significant events, movements and/or technologies. How has financial regulation changed after 9/11 or the Global Financial Crisis? Open-source Internet archives hold back-ups of specific websites, saved periodically over the last two decades. The best part is that these web pages are not a static screen shot, but rather a back-up version of the page, meaning some links can still be accessed within them. Two of the best sources for Internet time travel include:

- Wayback Machine – The Wayback Machine, from the Internet Archive, lets you see a particular website's development over time, http://archive.org/web/web.php.
- Library of Congress Web Archives – The Library of Congress Web Archives project has archived sites relating to significant events, such as the 9/11 attacks, US elections and the Iraq War, http://lcweb2.loc.gov/diglib/lcwa/html/lcwa-home.html.

While the Wayback Machine may appear to be a quirky tool, opportunities for original research abound (see Box 14.3). These archived web pages could be used for anything from auditing a company's marketing strategy (to determine consistency of brand image and message through their website over time) to researching information about local community agendas. Archived websites from the Wayback Machine have even been used as evidence in commercial court cases (such as patent litigation) or to unravel mysteries. Just as detectives can learn a lot from your trash, you too can learn from the discarded remnants of the Internet.

Internet archives like the Wayback Machine are particularly handy for triangulation. For instance, say you have data from a couple of sources (perhaps literature, or interviews) that suggests an early marketing strategy of X product was unabashedly sexist. By looking at the board members listed for the company in that year, you may find that there is no female representation.

If you use online archive tools as part of triangulation, be aware that not everything on the Internet has been archived. The web existed before 1996 – when the Wayback archive began – and since then, various pages may have been excluded. An absence of a website from the archive does not prove that it did not exist at that time. Moreover, more sites have sought to exclude archiving. In fact, anyone can use a robots.txt file on the server to exclude the Internet Archive's web crawler. As a result, far too many pages have already implemented this impediment to archiving.

Box 14.3

Internet Sleuthing

The Wayback Machine is a non-profit web crawler that archives old versions of Internet pages. In 2014, it preserved this social media posting: 'In the vicinity of Torez, we just downed a plane, an AN-26. It is lying somewhere in the Progress Mine. We have issued warnings not to fly in our airspace. We have video confirming. The bird fell on a waste heap. Residential areas were not hit. Civilians were not injured.'

Only minutes later, international news broke that a Malaysian Airlines commercial flight MH17 had been downed over Ukraine killing all 298 people on board. Could this be the same plane? Page administrators for the group responsible for the social media posting seemed to think so. When news of the civilian airliner disaster broke, the group tried to delete their post. They could not, however, remove the screen grab from the Internet Archive. 'Here's why we exist', the Wayback Machine wrote on Facebook, with links to earlier versions of the Facebook page. 'A Ukrainian Separatist boasted his pro-Russian Group shot down a Ukrainian plane on his website. When it turned out to be #MH17 #MalaysiaAirlines he erased it, but our Wayback Machine captured the page for history.'

The Internet Archive and others like it are powerful testaments for a new wave of pro-transparency bots and tools, all of them dedicated to leveraging technology to expose how governments, politicians and other powerful figures can manipulate the digital landscape. 'Important work', one commenter wrote on the Internet Archive page. 'Without it, we're in Orwell's 1984.'

Web Mining

Web mining is the process of discovering patterns in web-based large data sets involving methods that call on artificial intelligence, machine learning, statistics and database systems. When it comes to the web, there are actually three distinct things you can mine for: web usage, which looks at users' history and tell us what people are looking at on the Internet; web content, which extracts and integrates data from web page contents; and web structure, which analyses the connection structure of a website by exploring hyperlinks. Because of structural diversity and ever-expanding sources, it is getting more and more difficult to mine effectively.

Large language models like ChatGPT and other artificial intelligence systems can autonomously extract and organize web-based information, opening up new possibilities (as well as pitfalls) for research.

The benefits here include information that can aid targeted marketing. Government agencies are also using this technology to identify criminal activities and even classify threats of terrorism. In the public sector, web mining can help pinpoint public perceptions and needs. In health care, it can uncover disease outbreaks as well as health fears.

As a research strategy, however, there are methodological concerns related to data quality and representativeness that need to be approached with transparency; as well as concerns related to ethics. Mining usage, for example, is an invasion of privacy. There are plenty of places we go on the web that we might not want others to know about, and the process of de-individualization is not foolproof. Ethics committees are developing and redeveloping their policies as academic research becomes ever more common in this space.

Data Scraping

Data scraping is a process that allows you to move data from a website into a spreadsheet or file saved onto your local computer. One of the best features of data scraping is the ability to trawl through and grab unstructured data from diverse locations and put it into one place so that it can become structured, standardized and ready for analysis. Not only can this be done one-off, it can also be dynamic with updates constantly made to your spreadsheet from the latest version of data from your target website/s. While data scraping is generally used for text, new image recognition software is putting image scraping squarely on the horizon. As with other Big Data tools, privacy is a major concern.

Data scraping can be done directly with Excel. The video How to Extract Data from ANY Website to Excel (https://youtu.be/noqkJciAfWE) will give you basic instructions. If you are working large scale across a variety of sites, a dedicated scraping tool may be more effective. Tools worth exploring include Data Scraper (Chrome plugin), WebHarvy and import.io. However, when using third-party tools be wary that you may be getting a particular snapshot of the data rather than the full dataset.

Automated Text Analysis

Automated text analysis is pretty self-explanatory. It is an automated computer process for textual analysis (see Chapter 13, pp. 281–285) that extracts and classifies information you deem relevant from documents, such as texts, tweets, emails, posts, etc. Software like R and AI tools like ChatGPT are common ways to do this.

It works by using algorithms that are created from examples of tagged text. Text can be tagged on the basis of sentiment, topic, etc., extraction, excerpt and keyword extraction, and clustering (similar sets of words).

The algorithms then differentiate, sort and associate text and can even go as far as making predictions. Algorithms can be based on:

- Word frequency – Listing the most frequently occurring words or concepts in a given text.
- Collocation – Identifies words that commonly appear close to each other.
- Concordance – Identifies the context of words (how the word is being used).

This can be applied to whole documents or to subsections such as chapters, sections, paragraphs or even sentences.

A major advantage here over manual text analysis is the volume of text that can be processed and the ability to do this work 24/7.

I Have a Question!

Do I Need to Know How to Code to Access Online Data?

If you already have some skill in coding, that will definitely help you out when it comes to online-generated data. But it's not a requirement. If you have the skills, you can create your own tool to scrape websites to generate data pretty easily (although there are ethical or legal limitations here!) But there are also lots of tools out there that can help you collect, organize, and analyse online-generated data and new ones are being developed all the time. These tools vary from no-code, low-code and coding level applications. Consider your level of proficiency and what level of detail is actually required for your research project.

EXPLORING ONLINE COMMUNITIES

Let's take a well-deserved break from Big Data and talk about online communities. So what exactly constitutes an online community and how can we explore it?

A regular old community, you know, back in the day, was a geographically bound group of individuals – a neighbourhood, a village or a local church group. People within the community got together in a social setting and communicated face-to-face. Communities offered individuals shared points of reference, support, a bit of gossip, friendship, belonging, as well as norms, judgement and even social sanctions.

Online communities can offer similar social 'benefits', but they are not geographically bound. Physical social settings like town squares, local parks or church grounds are replaced by chatrooms, newsgroups, emails, bulletin boards, newsfeeds/dashboards, forums and virtual worlds. This means individuals within online communities can be located just about anywhere and that proximity is no longer the main commonality. Online communities can form over any type of shared interest. So whether it be Facebook, the Metaverse, a dating site, a learning environment or a gaming world, there are new virtual sites of human interaction that make up a growing part of our social world. And with ever-improving innovations in online communication, online communities are likely to grow and take on new dimensions.

How do we best study this phenomenon? When it comes to communities, the first methodology any social science researcher, particularly an anthropologist, will think of, is ethnography. Now ethnography, as covered in Chapter 8, involves exploration of a cultural group in a bid to understand, discover, describe and interpret a way of life from the point of view of its participants. It involves participant observation, prolonged engagement and rich immersion in the group you are exploring. The question is whether this approach can be, or should be, adapted for the online world.

Those who advocate this adoption and adaptation often refer to online ethnography. But there are those who believe that online communities are inherently different in nature from real-world communities, and that the traditional methods of ethnography are not suited to the online world. The term 'netnography' was introduced as an alternative that recognizes the unique nature of online communities and the need for standardized approaches to their study. For examples, see Box 14.4.

In practice, online ethnography and netnography can be very similar. Proponents of netnography, however, argue that it is worth defining a new approach for a new form of 'community'. They argue that this is necessary because online communities are:

- a non-physical environment in which social cues can be missing;
- somewhere in between private and public;
- easier to join, making access less problematic;
- a place where social interactions are captured and archived, creating an unprecedented database.

Regardless of nomenclature, there are standard means and ways of doing online ethnographic and netnographic studies. These generally include:

1 Working through ethics – You are unlikely to get ethics approval for participant observation without full disclosure. And this might be a stumbling block – your agenda might not be appreciated by all members. But it is unclear what constitutes informed consent, exactly who you need consent from and how often you need to remind them who you are. This is a new and contentious space for ethics committees.
2 Gaining access to and acceptance in the online communities you wish to explore – This involves both understanding how the community works and participating in forums, blogs, bulletin boards, chats, instant messaging, game worlds and whatever else ties the community together.
3 Collecting data – This is both what is captured in downloads of forums, blogs, bulletin boards, chats, instant messages, etc. (some of the Big Data techniques we talked about above), and what is reflected by the researcher in their journaling (a classic ethnographic approach). The goal is rich understandings based on prolonged engagement.
4 Analysing data – This is more than just data mining for content. Ethnographic approaches require the cultural context likely to come from prolonged engagement and immersion. This is particularly important online where visual and social cues are often limited.

Box 14.4

Ethnographic Research on Online Communities

Underwood, M. (2017) 'Exploring the social lives of image and performance enhancing drugs: An online ethnography of the Zyzz fandom of recreational body builders', *International Journal of Drug Policy, 39*: 78-85.

This study explores the use of image and performance enhancing drugs in the world of recreational body building. Ethnographic techniques were used to understand a large international online community of recreational body builders who idolized Zyzz, a Russian-born Australian body builder and an alleged user of performance-enhancing drugs.

Cappellini, B. and Yen, D. (2016) 'A space of one's own: Spatial and identity liminality in an online community of mothers', *The Journal of Marketing Management, 32*(13/14): 1260-83.

Using netnographic and ethnographic techniques which involved thorough investigations of posts, this study investigates the online community of 11 Taiwanese women living in the UK and how they negotiate mothering at a collective level.

Chapter Summary

- Online-generated data is an ever-growing space that includes a number of types of Big Data such as social data, **machine data**, **real-time data**, **transactional data** and analytic data.
- Searching for online-generated data is similar to any web-based search, the real trick is the ability to assess the credibility of the data in terms of consistency, provenance, accuracy, completeness, objectivity and ethics.
- Working with online data can involve using the web to capture moments in time, or using a variety of approaches for extracting and analysing Big Data including web mining, data scraping and automated text analysis.
- There are both practical and ethical considerations for using online-generated data for research
- Virtual or online communities also offer a new form of ethnographic studies that attempt to understand the lived realities of those participating in such online groups.

FIND YOUR NEXT STEP

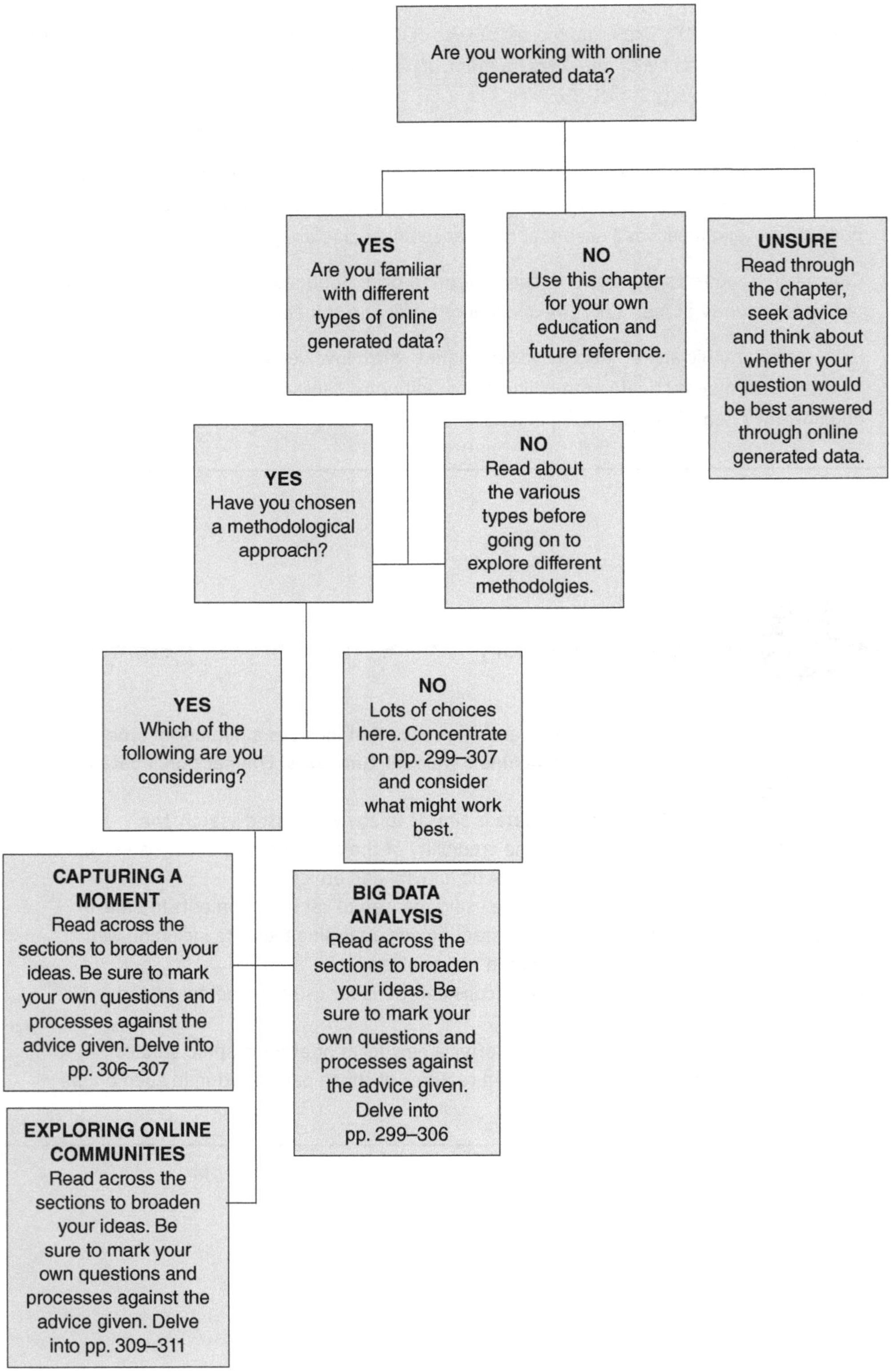

FURTHER READING

The following readings will open up this world to you, but keep in mind that methods related to online data are ever-evolving. It is well worth having a look online for what the current state of play might be.

Rainie, S. C., Kukutai, T., Walter, M. Figueroa-Rodríguez, O. L., Walker, J. and Axelsson, P. (2019) 'Issues in open data: Indigenous data sovereignty', in T. Davies, S. Walker, M. Rubinstein and F. Perini (eds), *The State of Open Data: Histories and Horizons* (pp. 300–19). Cape Town and Ottawa: African and International Development Research Centre.
This clear and concise chapter (from a great book on Open Data) offers an overview of indigenous data sovereignty and the challenges the movement poses to current approaches to data ownership, licensing, and use. Good reading for all.

Analysis of Online-Generated Data

Foster, I., Ghani, R., Jarmin, R., Kreuter, F. and Lane, J. (eds) (2016) *Big Data and Social Science: A Practical Guide to Methods and Tools*. New York: Chapman & Hall.
With so many Big Data books concentrating on business/marketing applications, this is a terrific find for the social science researcher with a plethora of expert advice.

Hill, C., Biemer, P., Buskirk, T., Japec, L., Kirchner, A., Kolenikov, S. and Lyberg, L. (eds) (2020) *Big Data Meets Survey Science: A Collection of Innovative Methods*. Hoboken, NJ: John Wiley & Sons.
With 800 pages from an array of researchers at the forefront of the field, this work will offer you all the latest insights, tools and strategies linking Big Data with traditional social science protocols.

Aragon, C., Guga, S., Kogan, M., Muller, M. & Neff, G. (2022). *Human-Centred Data Science: An Introduction*. Cambridge, MA: MIT Press.
Bias and inequality go hand-in-hand with big datasets. This book has a brief and accessible overview of data science techniques that can help address these issues. Practical guidelines and real-world case studies

Holmes, D. (2018) *Big Data: A Very Short Introduction*. Oxford: Oxford University Press.
A good place to start. Big Data cover so much, but at 144 pages,this book will do what it says and give the novice a pretty clear understanding of the landscape.

Kettl, D. (2017) *Little Bites of Big Data for Public Policy*. Thousand Oaks, CA: Sage.
We like the practical, end-goal focus of this book – the betterment of public policy. This work has a strong problem-based focus and helps readers strategically use the data they need to make strong credible arguments.

McNamara, D. S., Graesser, A. C., McCarthy, P. M. and Cai, Z. (2020) *Coh-Metrix: Automated Evaluation of Text and Discourse*. Cambridge: Cambridge University Press.
This work explores Coh-Metrix, one of the more powerful and most used automated textual analysis programs. We like that the first half covers theory, while the second half is extremely practical.

Myatt, G. J. and Johnson, W. P. (2014) *Making Sense of Data: A Practical Guide to Exploratory Data Analysis and Data Mining*. New York: Wiley-Interscience.
A practical approach to working with existing data sets. Good, logical coverage of key issues and excellent step-by-step coverage of the things you need to do to get existing data working for you.

Russell, M. and Klassen, M. (2019) *Mining the Social Web: Data Mining Facebook, Twitter, LinkedIn, Google+, GitHub, and More*. Sebastopol, CA: O'Reilly Media.
This work will help you get your head around the social web and give you some strategies for analysing its content. This is an ever-changing landscape, so make sure you look for the latest edition.

Online Ethnography

Caliandro, A. (2018) 'Digital methods for ethnography: Analytical concepts for ethnographers exploring social media environments', *Journal of Contemporary Ethnography*, *47*(5): 551–78.
Not only do online ethnographers need to deal with new settings for lived experience, they also need to adopt a new set of tools for understanding this landscape. This work will help you navigate some of this terrain.

Cappellini, B. and Yen, D. (2016) 'A space of one's own: Spatial and identity liminality in an online community of mothers', *The Journal of Marketing Management*, *32*(13/14): 1260–83.
See discussion in Box 14.4.

Hine, C. (2015) *Ethnography for the Internet: Embedded, Embodied and Everyday*. Abingdon: Routledge.
We like that Hine uses a range of examples to show how the techniques of ethnography can be applied to various realms of the online world. It covers both foundational principles and defined strategies.

Kozinets, R. V. (2019) *Netnography: The Essential Guide to Qualitative Social Media Research*. London: Sage.
For anyone wanting to undertake an online ethnographic study, this book is worth a read. It is one of the more thorough attempts at redefining ethnography for virtual communities and sets out clear protocols for ethical exploration of this space.

Lopatto, E. (2013) 'Facebook opens up site data to suicide research', *Bloomberg News*, 27 January.
See discussion in Box 14.2.

Przybylski, L. (2020) *Hybrid Ethnography: Online, Offline, and in Between*. London: Sage.
Maybe it doesn't have to be one way or the other. This book looks at combining traditional and online ethnographic ways of knowing to offer a robust methodological approach to understanding social groups that have an online presence.

Underwood, M. (2017) 'Exploring the social lives of image and performance enhancing drugs: An online ethnography of the Zyzz fandom of recreational body builders', *International Journal of Drug Policy*, *39*: 78–85.
See discussion in Box 14.4.

15

ANALYSING QUANTITATIVE DATA

Learning Objectives

- Moving from raw data to significant findings
    - To understand the importance of maintaining a sense of the overall project while analysing data
- Managing data and defining variables
    - To be able to meticulously manage quantitative data
    - To be able to identify distinct variable types
- Descriptive statistics
    - To be able to use appropriate statistics to describe a data set
- Inferential statistics
    - To understand what types of questions are suitable for inferential statistics
    - To be able to select appropriate statistical tests
- Presenting quantitative data
    - To be able to appropriately represent quantitative data through tables, charts, graphs and infographics

MOVING FROM RAW DATA TO SIGNIFICANT FINDINGS

All meanings, we know, depend on the key of interpretation.

Mary Ann Evans (under the pseudonym George Eliot) (1876)

It's easy to fall into the trap of thinking the major hurdle in your research project is data collection. And yes, as covered in the previous chapters, gathering credible data is certainly a challenge – but so too is making sense of the data. That intimidating mound of data you have managed to collect cannot really tell you anything until you have gone through a systematic process of interrogation and interpretation. In fact, just as English novelist George Eliot states, the key to meaning is 'interpretation'.

Managing the Project

We think one of the most important challenges in interpreting quantitative data is staying on top of it the whole way through your analysis. Alvin Toffler is reputed to have once said, 'You can use all the data you can get, but you still have to distrust it and use your own intelligence and judgement.' In fact, there can be a real temptation to relinquish control of the data to your computer – and without a doubt, there are ever more powerful and user-friendly statistics programs that can help you manage and analyse your data. But it is important to remember that there is no substitute for the insight, acumen and common sense you need to manage the process. Computer programs might be able to facilitate analysis and do the 'tasks', but it is the researcher who needs to work strategically, creatively and intuitively to get a 'feel' for the data, to cycle between that data and existing theory, and to follow the hunches that can lead to significant findings – both expected and unexpected. Researchers cannot afford to get lost in a swarm of numbers and lose sense of what they are trying to accomplish. Keeping a keen sense of their overall project is imperative.

Figure 15.1 depicts analysis as a process that is much more comprehensive and complex than simply plugging numbers into a computer. Reflexive analysis involves staying as close to the data as possible – from initial collection right through to the drawing of final conclusions. It is a process that requires you to: manage and organize your raw data; systematically code and enter your data; engage in statistical analysis; interpret meaning; uncover and discover findings; and, finally, draw relevant conclusions, all the while keeping an overall sense of the project that has you consistently moving between your data and your research questions, aims and objectives, theoretical underpinnings and methodological constraints.

It is important to remember that even the most sophisticated analysis is worthless if you are struggling to grasp the implications of your findings to your overall project. To do this you need to conduct your analysis in a critical, reflexive and iterative fashion that cycles between your data and your overarching frameworks. Rather than hand your thinking over to a computer program, the process of analysis should see you persistently interrogating the data, and the findings that emerge from that data. Stay engaged. It's not that hard to produce an amazing array of 'findings', but not know what it all means. Box 15.1 runs through a series of questions you should ask before and during data interrogation. The questions are designed to help you keep your eye on the bigger picture.

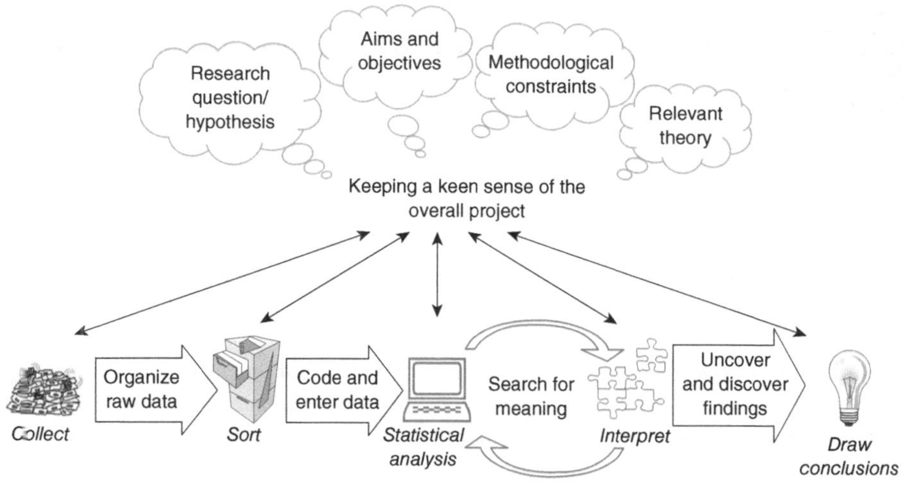

Figure 15.1 The process of reflective analysis

Box 15.1

Questions for Keeping the Bigger Picture in Mind

Questions related to your own expectations:

- What do I expect to find, i.e. will my hypothesis be borne out?
- What don't I expect to find, and how can I look for it?
- Can my findings be interpreted in alternative ways? What are the implications?

Questions related to the research question, aims and objectives:

- How should I treat my data in order to best address my research questions?
- How do my findings relate to my research questions, aims and objectives?

Questions related to theory:

- Are my findings confirming my theories? How? Why? Why not?
- Does my theory inform/help to explain my findings? In what ways?
- Can my unexpected findings link with alternative theories?

Questions related to methods:

- Have my methods of data collection and/or analysis coloured my results? If so, in what ways?
- How might my methodological shortcomings be affecting my findings?

I Have a Question!

I Plan on Using an Online Survey Tool Like SurveyMonkey, and I Think They Do All the Stats Stuff for You. Do I Need to Read the Rest of the Chapter?

That is totally up to you. You won't be the first person to avoid stats! But we will give you a few reasons to press on.

1 SurveyMonkey will give you basic descriptive statistics, but you need a 'Gold' package for anything inferential, and even then, it is limited. If you don't know what you don't know, you won't be able to assess if what they do is adequate or appropriate.
2 You just might change your mind as you get into things and want to be more hands-on with your data.
3 Even if you never do a quantitative study again, it is still worth knowing the language of statistics. That way you are better placed to understand the findings of quantitative studies conducted by others.

Doing Statistical Analysis

It was not long ago that 'doing' statistics meant working with formulae, but you no longer need to master formulae. Doing statistics in the twenty-first century is more about your ability to use statistical software than your ability to calculate means, modes, medians and standard deviations – and look up p-values printed on the inside back cover of statistics books.

Okay, we admit these programs do demand a basic understanding of the language and logic of statistics. But focusing on formulae is like trying to learn to ride a bike by being taught how to build one. Sure, being able to perform the mechanics can help you understand the logic of application (and there are many excellent resources that can help you build that knowledge), but if your primary goal, like most students tackling a project, is to be able to undertake relatively straightforward statistical analysis your needs will include understanding:

1 how to manage your data;
2 the nature of variables;
3 the role and function of both descriptive and inferential statistics;
4 appropriate use of statistical tests;
5 effective data presentation.

While this chapter will do its best to help you through the above, you are well advised to supplement your reading with some hands-on practice (even if this is simply playing with the mock data sets provided in statistics programs). Very few students can get their heads around statistics without getting into some data – so success depends on getting your hands dirty by working with relevant statistical programs. For this type of knowledge 'to stick', it needs to be applied.

The other piece of advice is to ask for help. When you get deeper into the mysteries of statistics, particularly inferential statistics and **multivariate analysis**, it becomes hard for even experienced researchers to know the best way forward. If your analysis is likely to reach this level of sophistication, it is worth seeking the help of a statistics specialist. In fact in many universities, doctoral candidates doing high-level statistics are not only allowed, but also sometimes encouraged, to have their data analysed by an expert. But even if you are outsourcing (which generally requires funding), there is no getting around the need to know the basics. You will still need to run your own preliminary analysis, direct the higher-level outsourced analysis, understand and interpret results, and be knowledgeable enough to ask critical questions.

MANAGING DATA AND DEFINING VARIABLES

It is critical to effectively and efficiently manage your data so you can build a workable database. Data can build up pretty quickly, and you might be surprised by the amount you have managed to collect. The challenge is employing a rigorous and systematic approach to data management that will allow you to build or create a data set that can be managed and utilized throughout the process of analysis. There are five steps that are essential to effectively managing your data.

1 Familiarize Yourself with Appropriate Software

Familiarizing yourself with appropriate software involves accessing programs and arranging necessary training. Most universities have licences that allow students access to certain software, and many universities provide relevant short courses. Programs themselves generally contain comprehensive tutorials complete with mock data sets. Programs you are likely to come across include:

- IBM SPSS statistics – sophisticated and user-friendly (www.spss.com);
- SAS – often an institutional standard, but some feel it is not as user-friendly as SPSS (www.sas.com);
- Minitab – more introductory, good for learners and small data sets (www.minitab.com);
- Excel – while not a dedicated statistics program, it can handle the basics and is readily available on most PCs (Microsoft Office product);
- RStudio – free software environment for statistical computing and graphics (www.rstudio.com);
- JMP – powerful statistics and dynamic graphics;
- Stata – powerful stats, good tutorials and excellent model building (www.stata.com);
- Jamovi – free and open source software that integrates with R.

2 Keep a Record of Your Data

Data can come from a number of sources at various stages throughout the research process, so it is well worth keeping a record of your data as it is collected. You can do this manually in a notebook or log it into a program such as Excel. Keep in mind that original data should be kept for a reasonable period of time (5–7 years). This can be for ethical purposes as well as the need to be able to trace results back to original sources.

3 Screen Your Data for Any Potential Problems

Data screening is a preliminary check to see if your data is accurate and complete. You're likely to have some missing data, but you don't want it to the extent where it's affecting your analysis. If done early enough, you can uncover potential problems not picked up in your pilot and make improvements to your data-collection protocols. There's nothing worse than discovering too late that you have a systemic issue.

4 Enter the Data

There are actually two steps involved in data entry. The first is to define your variables. Figure 15.2 shows an SPSS Variable View window, which requires you to input variable information such as name, measurement type, labels, values, etc.

The second step is to systematically enter your data into a database. While your data can be entered as it comes in or after it has been collected in its entirety, other than for the purpose of a trial run, full analysis does not take place until after data entry is complete. Figure 15.3 shows an SPSS data entry screen.

It's worth noting that if you use an online survey tool, such as SurveyMonkey, your data is uploaded automatically.

5 Clean the Data

Cleaning the data involves combing through it to make sure any entry errors are found, and that the data set looks in order. When entering quantified data it is easy to make mistakes – particularly if you're moving fast. It is essential that you go through your data to make sure it is as accurate as possible.

Understanding Variables – Cause and Effect

A key way to differentiate variables is through cause and effect. This means being able to clearly identify and distinguish your dependent and independent variables.

While understanding the theoretical difference between dependent and independent variables is not too difficult, being able to readily identify each type comes with practice. One way of doing this is simply to ask what depends on what: achievement depends on parental influence; so achievement is dependent making parental influence independent; income depends on gender, so income is dependent, making gender independent.

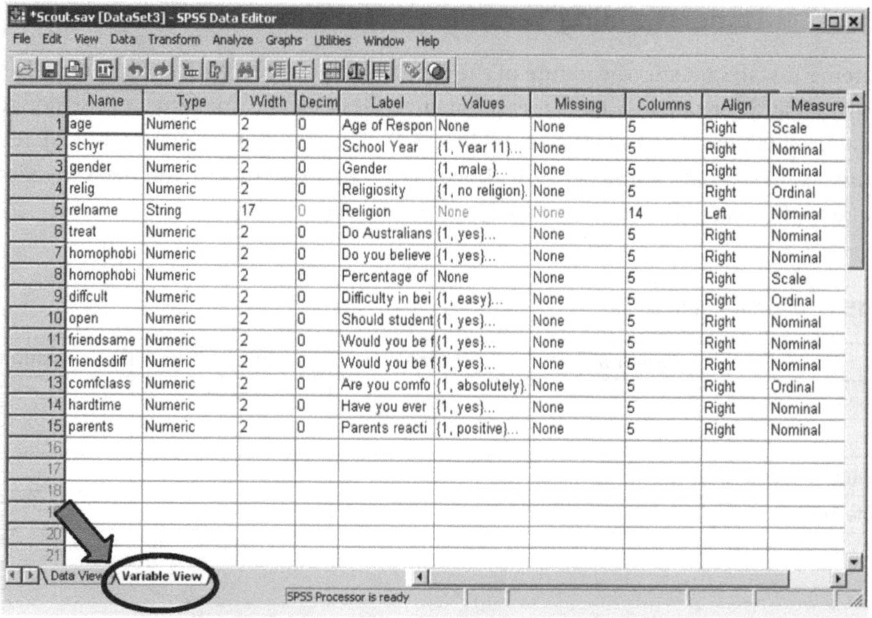

	Name	Type	Width	Decim	Label	Values	Missing	Columns	Align	Measure
1	age	Numeric	2	0	Age of Respon	None	None	5	Right	Scale
2	schyr	Numeric	2	0	School Year	{1, Year 11}...	None	5	Right	Nominal
3	gender	Numeric	2	0	Gender	{1, male }...	None	5	Right	Nominal
4	relig	Numeric	2	0	Religiosity	{1, no religion}.	None	5	Right	Ordinal
5	relname	String	17	0	Religion	None	None	14	Left	Nominal
6	treat	Numeric	2	0	Do Australians	{1, yes}...	None	5	Right	Nominal
7	homophobi	Numeric	2	0	Do you believe	{1, yes}...	None	5	Right	Nominal
8	homophobi	Numeric	2	0	Percentage of	None	None	5	Right	Scale
9	diffcult	Numeric	2	0	Difficulty in bei	{1, easy}...	None	5	Right	Ordinal
10	open	Numeric	2	0	Should student	{1, yes}...	None	5	Right	Nominal
11	friendsame	Numeric	2	0	Would you be f	{1, yes}...	None	5	Right	Nominal
12	friendsdiff	Numeric	2	0	Would you be f	{1, yes}...	None	5	Right	Nominal
13	comfclass	Numeric	2	0	Are you comfo	{1, absolutely}.	None	5	Right	Ordinal
14	hardtime	Numeric	2	0	Have you ever	{1, yes}...	None	5	Right	Nominal
15	parents	Numeric	2	0	Parents reacti	{1, positive}...	None	5	Right	Nominal

Figure 15.2 IBM SPSS Statistics Variable View

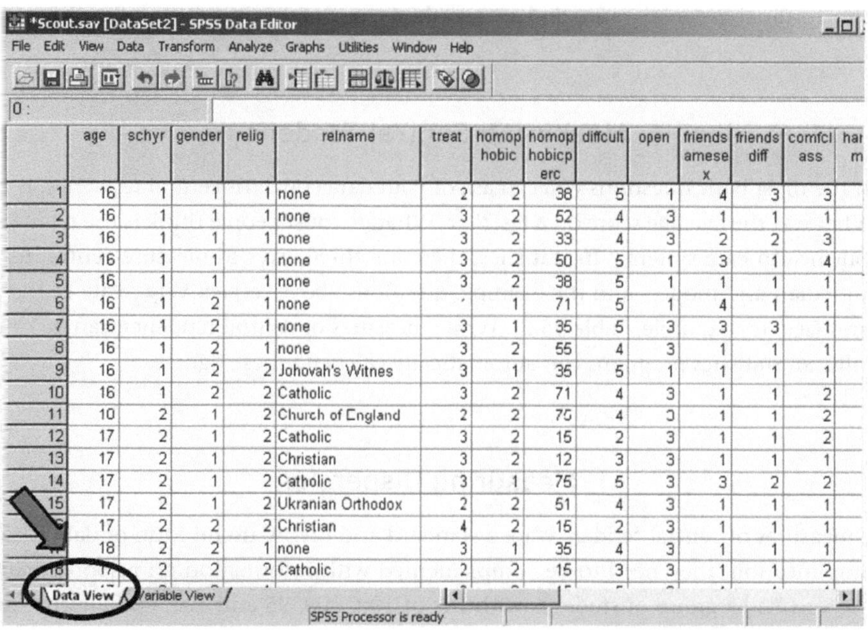

	age	schyr	gender	relig	relname	treat	homophobic	homophobicperc	diffcult	open	friendsamesex	friendsdiff	comfclass
1	16	1	1	1	none	2	2	38	5	1	4	3	3
2	16	1	1	1	none	3	2	52	4	3	1	1	1
3	16	1	1	1	none	3	2	33	4	3	2	2	3
4	16	1	1	1	none	3	2	50	5	1	3	1	4
5	16	1	1	1	none	3	2	38	5	1	1	1	1
6	16	1	2	1	none	[illegible]	1	71	5	1	4	1	1
7	16	1	2	1	none	3	1	35	5	3	3	3	1
8	16	1	2	1	none	3	2	55	4	3	1	1	1
9	16	1	2	2	Johovah's Witnes	3	1	35	5	1	1	1	1
10	16	1	2	2	Catholic	3	2	71	4	3	1	1	2
11	10	2	1	2	Church of England	2	2	75	4	3	1	1	2
12	17	2	1	2	Catholic	3	2	15	2	3	1	1	2
13	17	2	1	2	Christian	3	2	12	3	3	1	1	1
14	17	2	1	2	Catholic	3	1	75	5	3	3	2	2
15	17	2	1	2	Ukranian Orthodox	2	2	51	4	3	1	1	1
[illegible]	17	2	2	2	Christian	4	2	15	2	3	1	1	1
[illegible]	18	2	2	1	none	3	1	35	4	3	1	1	1
18	17	2	2	2	Catholic	2	2	15	3	3	1	1	2

Figure 15.3 IBM SPSS Statistics Data View

Understanding Variables – Measurement Scales

Measurement scales refer to the nature of the differences you are trying to capture within a particular variable. There are four basic measurement scales that become respectively more precise: nominal, ordinal, interval and ratio (see Table 15.1). The precision of each is directly related to the statistical tests that can be performed on them. The more precise the measurement scale, the more sophisticated the statistical analysis you can do.

Table 15.1 Measurement scales

	Nominal	Ordinal	Interval	Ratio
Classifies	✓	✓	✓	✓
Orders		✓	✓	✓
Equidistant units			✓	✓
Absolute zero				✓

DESCRIPTIVE STATISTICS

As the name implies, **descriptive statistics** are used to describe the basic features of a data set and are key to summarizing variables. The goal is to present quantitative descriptions in a manageable and intelligible form. More specifically, descriptive statistics provide measures of **central tendency**, **dispersion** and distribution shape. Such measures vary by data type (nominal, ordinal, interval, ratio) and are standard calculations in statistics programs.

Measuring Central Tendency

One of the most basic questions you can ask of your data concerns central tendency. For example: 'What was the average score on a test?' or 'What do most people think is the main problem with our health care system?' In statistics, there are three ways to measure central tendency: mean, median and mode – and the example questions above respectively relate to these three measures (see, for example, Table 15.2). While measures of central tendency can be calculated manually, all statistics programs can automatically calculate these figures.

Measuring Dispersion

While measures of central tendency are a standard and highly useful form of data description and simplification, they need to be complemented with information on response variability. Suppose you had a group of students with IQs of 100, 100, 95 and 105, and another group of students with IQs of 60, 140, 65 and 135. Then the central tendency, in this case the mean, of both groups would be 100. Dispersion around the mean, however, will require you to design the curriculum and engage learning with each group quite differently. There are several ways to understand dispersion, which are appropriate for different variable types. As with central tendency, statistics programs can automatically generate these figures (Table 15.3).

Measuring the Shape of the Data

To understand a data set fully, central tendency and dispersion need to be considered in light of the shape of the data, or how the data is distributed. As shown in Figure 15.4, a **normal curve** is 'bell-shaped'; the distribution of the data is symmetrical, with the mean, median and mode all coinciding at the highest point of the curve. If the distribution of the data is not symmetrical, it is considered skewed. In skewed data the mean, median and mode fall at different points.

Table 15.2 Central tendency for 'age of participants'

Data related to age of participants in a local youth group	
Raw data	12, 12, 10, 9, 12, 15, 11, 12, 11, 11, 15, 16, 17, 12, 13, 13, 14, 11, 10, 9, 9, 8, 13, 14, 12, 14, 15, 13, 13, 10, 9, 13, 14, 13, 9
N (no. of cases)	35
Mean (average)	12.11
Median (midpoint)	12
Mode (most common value)	13

Note: Figures generated with SPSS

Table 15.3 Dispersion for 'age of participants'

Data related to age of participants in a local youth group	
Raw data	12, 12, 10, 9, 12, 15, 11, 12, 11, 11, 15, 16, 17, 12, 13, 13, 14, 11, 10, 9, 9, 8, 13, 14, 12, 14, 15, 13, 13, 10, 9, 13, 14, 13, 9
N (no. of cases)	35
Range (spread of the data)	8 to 17 = 9
Inter-quartile range (spread between 25th and 75th percentiles)	10 to 14 = 4
Variance (spread around the mean)	4.93
Standard deviation (square root of variance)	2.22

Note: Figures generated with SPSS

Kurtosis characterizes how peaked or flat a distribution is, compared with 'normal'. Positive kurtosis indicates a relatively peaked distribution, while negative kurtosis indicates a flatter distribution.

The significance in understanding the shape of a distribution is in the statistical inferences that can be drawn. As shown in Figure 15.5, a normal distribution is subject to a particular set of rules regarding the significance of a standard deviation, namely that:

- 68.3% of cases will fall within one standard deviation of the mean;
- 95.4% of cases will fall within two standard deviations of the mean;
- 99.7% of cases will fall within three standard deviations of the mean.

So if we had a normal curve for the sample data relating to 'age of participants' (mean = 12.11, s.d. = 2.22; see Tables 15.2 and 15.3), 68.3% of participants would fall between the ages of 9.89 and 14.33 (12.11 − 2.22 and 12.11 + 2.22). Table 15.4 shows the actual curve, skewness and kurtosis of our sample data set.

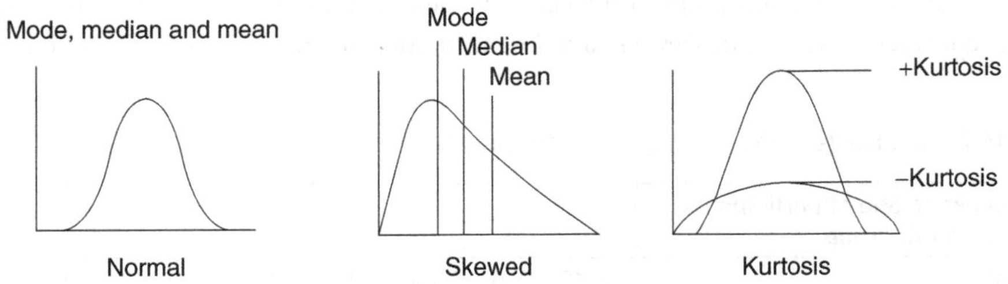

Figure 15.4 Shape of the data

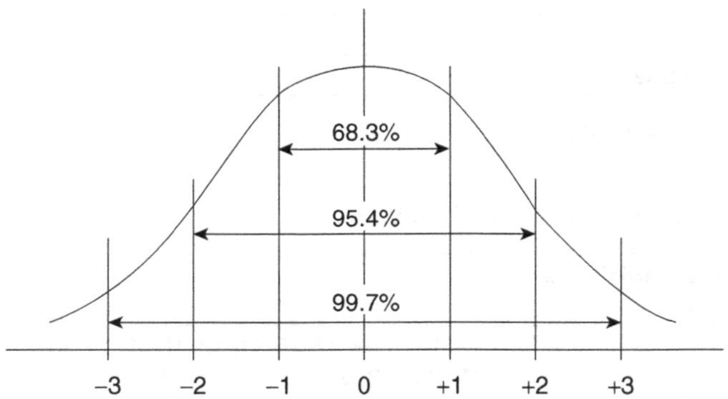

Figure 15.5 Areas under the normal curve

These rules of the normal curve allow for the use of quite powerful statistical tests and are generally used with interval and ratio data (sometimes called parametric tests). For data that do not follow the assumptions of a normal curve (nominal and ordinal data), the researcher needs to call on **non-parametric statistical tests** in making inferences.

INFERENTIAL STATISTICS

While the goal of descriptive statistics is to describe and summarize the characteristics of your sample, the goal of inferential statistics is to draw conclusions that extend beyond your immediate data/sample. For example, inferential statistics can be used to test various hypotheses about the relationship between different variables or, perhaps more importantly, to allow you to estimate characteristics of a population from sample data. In other words, inferential statistics allow you to generalize.

Table 15.4 Shape of the data for 'age of participants'

Data related to age of participants in a local youth group	
Raw data	12, 12, 10, 9, 12, 15, 11, 12, 11, 11, 15, 16, 17, 12, 13, 13, 14, 11, 10, 9, 9, 8, 13, 14, 12, 14, 15, 13, 13, 10, 9, 13, 14, 13, 9
N (no. of cases)	35
Histogram (distribution)	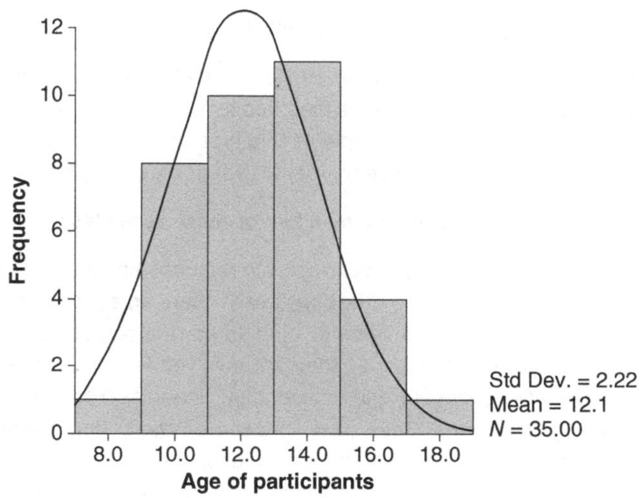
Skewness (symmetricality)	0.070
Kurtosis (flatness)	–0.562

Note: Figures and histogram generated with SPSS

Questions Suitable for Inferential Statistics

So exactly what can inferential statistics tell us? Well, inferential statistics, as shown in Box 15.2, can help us interrogate our data at a number of levels.

Box 15.2

Questions for Interrogating Quantitative Data Using Inferential Statistics

How do participants in my study compare to a larger population?

These types of question compare a sample with a population. Suppose you are conducting a study of students doing a particular university course. You might ask if the percentages of males or females in your sample, or their average age, or their interests are statistically similar to university students across the country. To answer such questions you will need access to population data for this larger range of students.

(Continued)

Are there differences between two or more groups of respondents?

Questions that compare two or more groups are very common and are often referred to as 'between subjects'. To stick with a student theme, you might ask if male and female students are likely to have similar interests; or whether students of different ethnic backgrounds are likely to do different courses; or whether students studying at different campuses have different grade point averages.

Have my respondents changed over time?

These types of questions involve before and after data with either the same group of respondents or respondents who are matched by similar characteristics. They are often referred to as 'within subject'. An example of this type of question might be 'Have final-year students' study habits changed since their first year at university?'

Is there a relationship between two or more variables?

These types of questions can look for relationships and correlations, or cause and effect. Examples of relationship questions are 'Is there an association between time spent studying and satisfaction with university?' and 'Is there a correlation between students' gender and the extracurricular activities they are involved in?' Questions looking for cause and effect differentiate dependent and independent variables. For example, 'Does satisfaction depend on study time?' and 'Does stress depend on the course taken?' Cause-and-effect relationships can also look to more than one independent variable to explain variation in the dependent variable (multivariate analysis). For example, 'Does satisfaction with university course depend on a combination of length of study habits, age and career aspirations?'

Statistical Significance

As discussed, the goal of inferential statistics is to be able to generalize beyond a sample. But because the data is still limited to a sample, it is impossible to say with 100% conviction that any generalization is without the potential for error. What inferential statistics do allow you to do, however, is assess the probability that an observed difference is more than a fluke or chance finding and is, in fact, statistically significant.

Statistical significance generally refers to a 'p-value', which assesses the actual probability that your findings are more than coincidence. Conventional p-values are 0.05, 0.01 and 0.001, which tell you that the probability that your findings have occurred by chance is 5/100, 1/100 or 1/1,000 respectively. Basically, the lower the p-value, the more confident that researchers can be that findings are genuine. Keep in mind that researchers do not usually accept findings that have a p-value greater than 0.05 because the probability that findings are coincidental or caused by sampling error is too great.

Understanding and Selecting the Right Statistical Test

There is a baffling array of statistical tests out there that can help you answer the types of questions highlighted in Box 15.2. And while it is important to understand the underlying logic that drives the most common statistical tests (see Table 15.5), programs such as SPSS and SAS are capable of running such tests without your needing to know the technicalities of their mathematical operations. The problem of knowing which test is right for your particular application, however, still remains. Luckily, you can turn to a number of test selectors now available on the Internet (see Bill Trochim's test selector at www.socialresearchmethods.net/kb/index.htm) and through programs such as MODSTAT and SPSS.

Table 15.5 Selecting statistical tests

Univariate	**Bi-/multivariate**		
	Nominal	**Ordinal**	**Interval/Ratio (Assumption of normality – if not normal use ordinal tests)**
Nominal			
2-point scale, e.g. gender: 1 = female, 2 = male	Compare two or more groups: **chi-squared**	Compare two groups: **Mann–Whitney** Three or more groups: **Kruskal–Wallis**	Compare two or more groups: **ANOVA followed by *t*-test**
3-point scale, e.g. religion: 1 = Catholic, 2 = Protestant, 3 = Jewish Central tendency: **mode** Dispersion: **frequency**	Compare within same group over time: 2 pts: **McNemar's test** 3+ pts: **Cochran's Q**	Compare within same group over two times: 2 pts: **Wilcoxon signed-rank test** 3+ pts: **Cochran's Q** Three or more times (2+ pts): **Friedman's test**	Compare within same group over times (2+ pts): **ANOVA followed by *t*-test**
Compare sample with population: **chi-squared**	Relationship with other variables: yes/no: **chi-squared**	Relationship with other variables: yes/no: **chi-squared** Relationship strength:	Relationship with other variables: yes/no: **Pearson's product moment correlation** Relationship strength: ***F*-test**
Nominal			
	Relationship strength: 2 pts: **phi** 3+ pts: **lambda**	2+ pts: **lambda**	With two or more independent and one dependent variables: **MANOVA** 2+ dependent variables and 3+ groups: **multiple regression** or **path analysis**
Ordinal			
TV viewing, order of preference: 1 = sitcoms, 2 = dramas, 3 = movies, 4 = news, 5 = reality TV or Likert scale: 1 = strongly disagree, 2 = disagree, 3 = neutral, etc. Central tendency: **median** Dispersion: **inter-quartile range**		Small sample, < 10: **Kendall's tau** Larger sample: **Spearman's rho**	**Jaspen's coefficient of multiserial correlation** With the interval/ratio variable as dependent: **ANOVA**

(Continued)

Table 15.5 (Continued)

Compare sample with population: **Kolmogorov–Smirnov**		With one variable as dependent: **Somer's *d***	
Interval/ratio			
Interval, e.g. IQ score Ratio, e.g. real numbers, age, height, weight Central tendency: **mean** Dispersion: **standard deviation** Compare sample with population: ***t*-test**			Relationship with other variables – no dependent/independent distinction: **Pearson's product moment correlation** With one independent and one dependent variable: **Pearson's linear correlation** With two or more independent and one dependent variables: **multiple regression** With two or more independent and two or more dependent variables: **canonical correlation**

But even with the aid of such selectors (including the tabular one in Table 15.5), you still need to know the nature of your variables (independent/dependent), scales of measurement (nominal, ordinal, interval, ratio), distribution shape (normal or skewed), the types of questions you want to ask and the types of conclusions you are trying to draw.

The glossary explains the distinction between **univariate** (one variable), **bivariate** (two variable) and multivariate (three or more variable) analysis, while Table 15.5 covers common tests for undertaking such analyses. Table 15.5 can be read down the first column for univariate data (the column provides an example of the data type, its measure of central tendency, dispersion and appropriate tests for comparing this type of variable with a population). It can also be read as a grid for exploring the relationship between two or more variables. Once you know what tests to conduct, your statistical software will be able to run the analysis and assess statistical significance.

Critical Thinking Challenge 16

Stats or Story?

You now have your stats, your facts and your figures but you know what? It's going to come down to story: to narrative.

As you analyse your data, think about the story that your stats are trying to tell you. And think about how you will use these stats to help weave a narrative for your audience.

Your stats will give you the significance of correlations, but you will need to construct a storyline to make these significant findings logical, consistent and compelling.

PRESENTING QUANTITATIVE DATA

When it comes to presenting quantitative data, there can be a real temptation to offer graphs, charts and tables for every single variable in your study. But it is important to resist this temptation and actively determine what is most important in your work. Your findings need to tell a story related to your aims, objectives and research questions.

Now when it comes to how your data should be presented, we think there is one golden rule: your presentation should not be hard work for the reader. Most people's eyes glaze over when it comes to statistics, so your data should not be hard to decipher. You should not need to be a statistician to understand it. Your challenge is to present your data graphically and verbally so that meanings are clear. Any graphs and tables you present should ease the task for the reader. So while you need to include adequate information, you do not want to go into information overload.

Using Graphs

As they say, a picture is worth a thousand words, so a good graph can go a long way in communicating your findings. Emma teaches her undergraduate students to recognize graphs as a powerful form of visual communication that can (mis)represent findings. It's important to understand basic principles of different kinds of graphs so you can identify which is right for your data and to represent your findings truthfully.

In order to run you through the most commonly used graphs in quantitative analysis, we mocked up a four-variable data set in SPSS using a hypothetical example of survey data from 60 students (30 males and 30 females) about to graduate from high school (Table 15.6).

'Plans after graduation' is a nominal variable, so bar and pie graphs tend to work well (see Figures 15.6 and 15.7). The line graph, however, does not work because it is better suited to showing change over time – which is not what we are trying to do.

Table 15.6 Mocked-up four-variable data set

Gender **1 = Female** **2 = male**	**Grade point average (out of a possible 4)**	**Plans after graduation** **1 = vocational/ technical training** **2 = university** **3 = workforce** **4 = travel** **5 = undecided** **6 = other**	**Importance of university** **1 = not at all important, to 7 = essential**
1	3.10	2	7
2	2.60	3	2
1	1.30	3	2
2	3.60	5	6
2	1.50	1	1

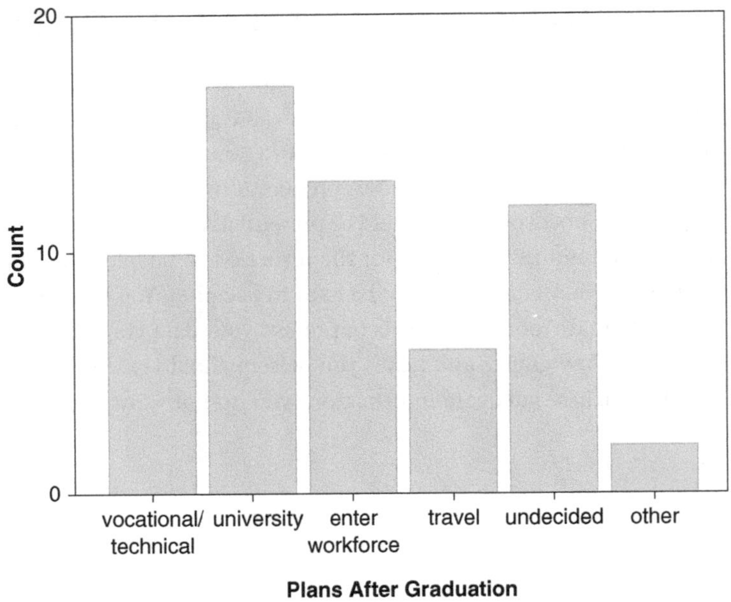

Figure 15.6 A bar graph

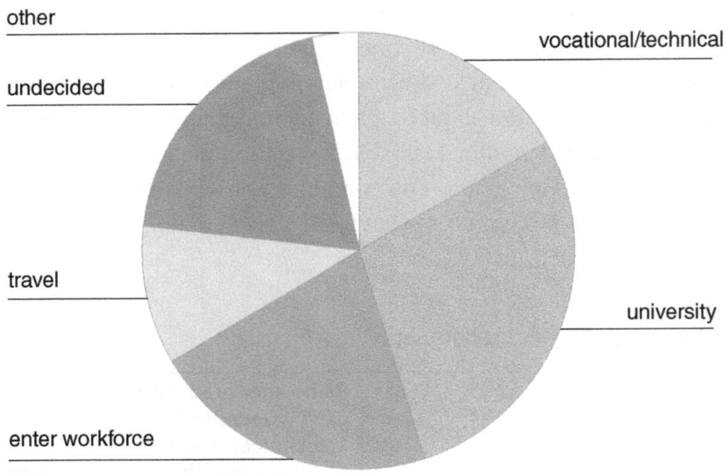

Figure 15.7 A pie graph

A line graph would be better suited for data that showed something like changes in a student's grade point average (GPA) over their high school career (GPA would sit on one axis and year of study on the other; see Figure 15.8).

A clustered bar graph allows you to compare the distribution of a nominal variable for two or more groups. In the example in Figure 15.9, 'plans after graduation' is compared by gender.

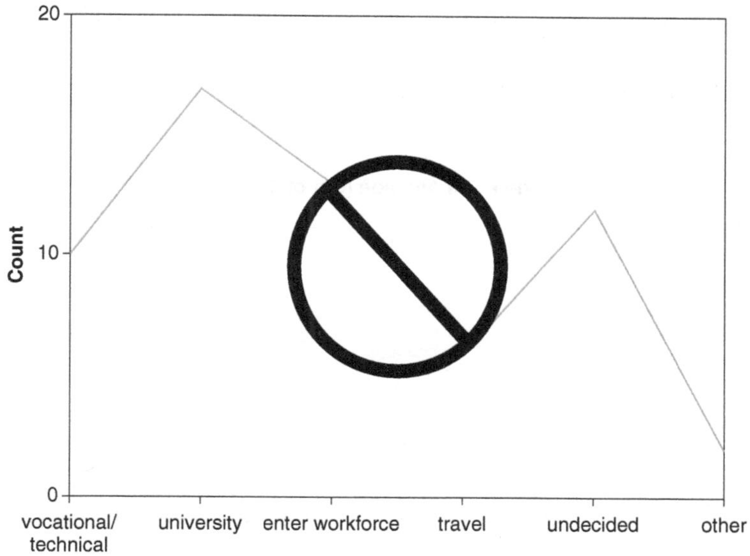

Figure 15.8 A line graph

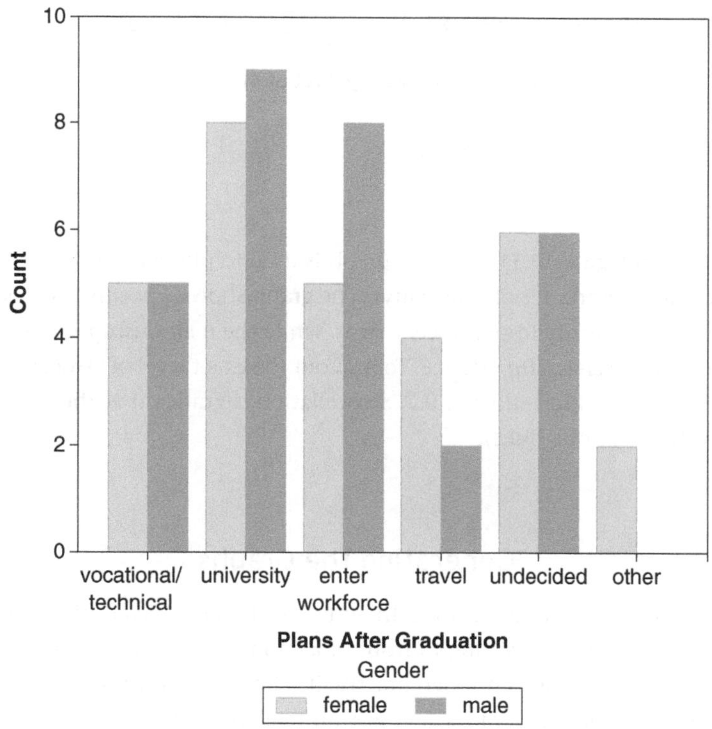

Figure 15.9 A clustered bar graph

A **histogram** is appropriate for showing the distribution of interval and ratio data. In Figure 15.10 we can see the distribution of GPA (a ratio variable), complete with mean, standard deviation, and the plotting of a normal curve.

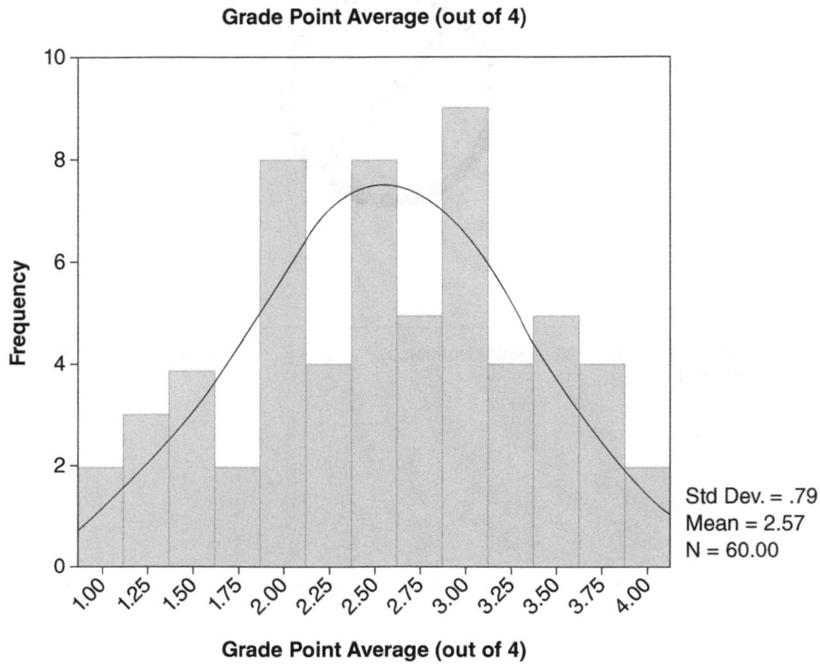

Figure 15.10 A histogram with normal curve

In the example in Figure 15.11, a scatter graph is used to plot a ratio variable (GPA) against an ordinal variable (importance of university). The graph shows a positive correlation between GPA and perceived university importance; that is, while the relationship is not perfect, as GPA goes up so too does perceived importance. To find out the exact level of association you can run a Pearson's correlation, which shows a 0.773 correlation, significant at the 0.01 level (you are 99% sure the pattern is not a fluke).

Generating the Graphs

OK – so how do you go about generating these types of graphs? Well, there are two ways to go about this and both involve sitting in front of a computer. The first is to have someone in the know show you what to do, and then practise it. The second is to sit down by yourself and have a play with a stats program. Most have great interactive online tutorials that can take you through the process from A to Z. While reading can give you familiarity, the best way to learn this kind of stuff is by doing.

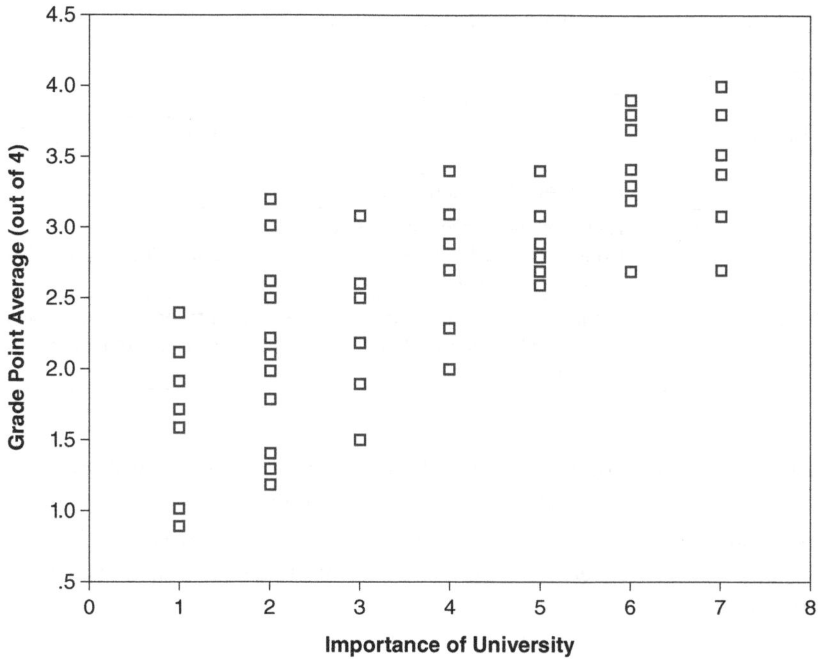

Figure 15.11 A scatter graph

Generating Tables

The idea here is to present complexity with simplicity. Tables are generally more complex than graphs because they attempt to summarize the relationship between a number of variables (multivariate analysis). And because this summary can involve multiple statistical operations, statistics programs rarely spit tables out in a ready-to-use form. Now you can use an automatic table generator (you can find these on the Internet – one example is TableMaker at www.bagism.com/tablemaker), and this can certainly help, but the chances are you will still need to do some manual manipulation. The challenge here is walking the line between enough and too much information.

Your tables should not: (1) give your readers a headache; (2) make their eyes glaze over; or (3) make them even more confused. While your tables should not stand alone (you will need to walk your readers through them), they should be something that the non-specialist can engage with and learn from. Your tables will be most effective if: you can provide clear and adequate information; you do not assume too much knowledge; and you keep them as simple as possible. Below are three examples taken from a study Zina did some time ago on the process of giving up religion.

Table 15.7 simply outlines the criteria Zina used to classify three distinct processes of religious disaffiliation and the percentage of her sample (n = 80) that fell into these categories. While this information is pretty self-explanatory and could have been presented in a non-tabular form, Zina thought the table allowed readers to get a quick sense of the distinctions she was trying to make.

Table 15.7 Classification of disaffiliation journey and distribution

Type of disaffiliation journey	Classification criteria
Angry rebellion 30%	A tone of: weariness; anger; irritated disgust, perhaps not with life, but at least with God or religion A journey of reaction or rebellion
Discontented doubt 29%	Empty, melancholic, depressive intellectualism Confused detachment wherein religion becomes deconstructed to the point of irreconcilable doubt and emptiness
Open exploration 41%	Without a reactionary basis, or a confused intellectualism. A willingness to expand the realms of spiritual possibility beyond immediate experience and frames of reference

Table 15.8 is a bit more complex because it looks at the frequency distribution (cross-tabulation) of these three types of disaffiliation journey by both gender and religion. It also shows, through chi-squared statistics, that religion is significant; i.e. the distribution is not even. You cannot assume that your readers will know what this means, so it is up to you to walk them through your table.

Table 15.8 Frequency distributions for demographic variables by type of journey

	Rebellion	Doubt	Exploration
Gender			
Female	50.0	45.8	46.9
Male	50.0	54.2	53.1
	100.0	100.0	100.0
Religion			
Protestant	29.2*	50.0	46.9
Catholic	70.8*	50.0	53.1
	100.0	100.0	100.0

* One-way ANOVA $p < 0.05$.

As shown in this table, those having gone through each of the three disaffiliation journeys are as likely to be male as female. The results for religion, however, are somewhat more interesting. Catholics and Protestants both tend to go through journeys of discontented doubt and open exploration in similar proportions. Those whose journeys are more rebellious in nature, however, are somewhat more likely to have a Catholic heritage.

Table 15.9 is even more complex, because it attempts to compare certain characteristics of the three disaffiliation journeys. In other words, Zina wants to show if there is a statistically significant distinction between the types of journey in relation to: how old individuals were when they first doubted their faith; how long the process took; whether it was still ongoing at the time of interview; and how intense the process was. The complexity of the table meant Zina definitely had to walk readers through it.

Table 15.9 Mean scores and significance for profile variables by type of journey

	Rebellion	Doubt	Exploration	Reb-Dbt	Reb-Expl	Dbt-Expl
Age first doubt	20.88	19.58	16.94		*	
Process length	4.42	10.83	5.62	*		*
Process ongoing	0.08	0.35	0.15	*		*
Intensity	0.70	0.42	0.32	*	*	

*Chi-squared test of significance $p < 0.05$. All numbers expressed as percentages.

The figures in this table point to varying and distinct patterns of disaffiliation for each type of journey. Those on a rebellious path generally complete an intense and relatively short journey away from faith. For those whose journey is marked by discontented doubts, however, the process is quite lengthy, lasting an average of almost 11 years, with one-third still in the process of moving away from religion at the time of interview. The journey for this discontented group, however, is not as intense as that of the rebellious contingent. Those whose journey out of faith is characterized by open exploration, on the other hand, go through a relatively short and often finalized process of disaffiliation that begins earlier in life. The process of disaffiliation is not generally seen as intense.

A Final Word

Good tables do take time to construct, and if you struggle at the high end of word processing, creating tables can be extraordinarily frustrating. But if you can manage to create tables that are well constructed and well explained, they can be an exceedingly important and effective communication tool.

I Have a Question!

Help! There Is So Much Information Here and, to Be Honest, Most of It Is Going Over My Head. Is This a Lost Cause?

We both think the hardest thing we are asked to do is teach statistics in a lecture room (or in a chapter). That's because no matter how much you know, or how well you teach, stats is one of those things that is hard to get your head around unless you are sitting at a computer working with it. It is Greek to most people. Well, literally – they actually use some Greek. So we would not even consider it a lost cause until you have sat down with some data, in front of the most recent user-friendly stats program, with someone in the know. This will bring all the abstract concepts into the real world – and we think you will be surprised at, not just how well you absorb it all, but how exciting it is to see your data tell you things.

FIND YOUR NEXT STEP

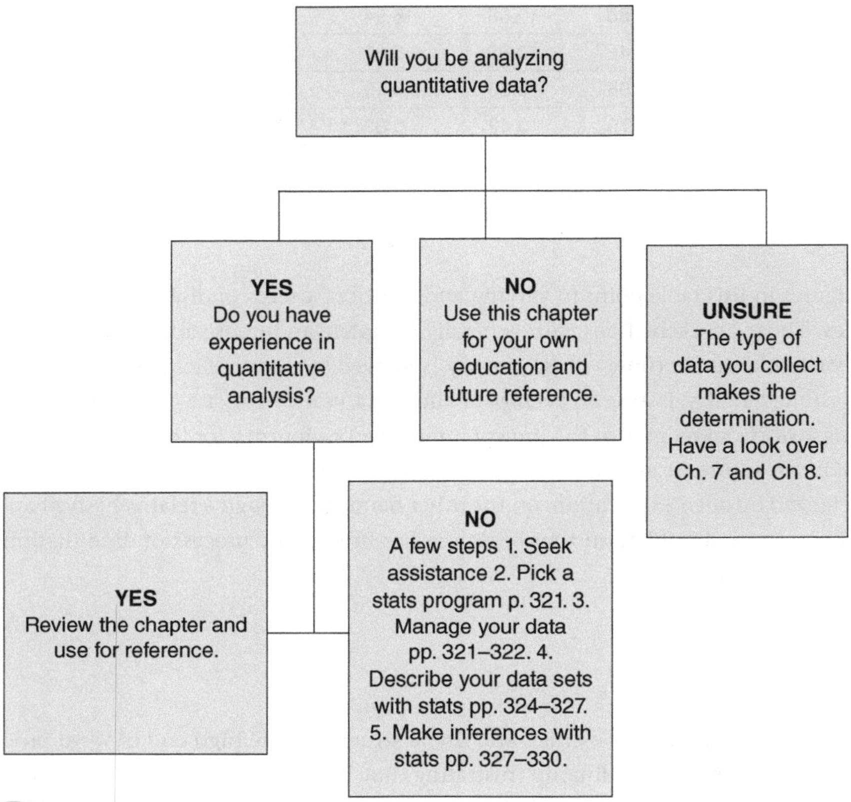

Chapter Summary

- Data interpretation is a major hurdle in any research study. Effective data analysis involves: managing your data; engaging in the actual process of analysis; and effectively presenting your data.
- Data management involves: familiarizing yourself with appropriate software; systematically logging in and screening your data; entering the data into a program; and 'cleaning' your data. It also means being able to distinguish variables' cause and effect (dependent or independent) and their measurement scales (nominal, ordinal, interval and ratio).
- Descriptive statistics are used to summarize the basic features of a data set through measures of central tendency (mean, mode and median), dispersion (range, **quartiles**, variance and standard deviation) and distribution (skewness and kurtosis).
- Inferential statistics allow researchers to assess their ability to draw conclusions that extend beyond the immediate data. For example, if a sample represents the population; if there are differences between two or more groups; if there are changes over time; or if there is a relationship between two or more variables.
- Presenting quantitative data often involves the production of graphs and tables. These need to be (1) selectively generated so that they make relevant arguments, and (2) informative yet simple so that they aid the reader's understanding.

FURTHER READING

General Social Science Statistics

Jackson, S. L. (2015) *Research Methods and Statistics: A Critical Thinking Approach*. Belmont, CA: Wadsworth.
We like that this book works at integrating the logic of research methods and statistics. Rather than just applying mathematical approaches to a study, this work will help you think about statistical analysis as an integral part of making meaning.

Rumsey, D. (2019) *Statistic Essentials for Dummies*. Hoboken, NJ: John Wiley & Sons.
So is a 'For Dummies' guide appropriate? Well, we appreciate them. They tend to be clear, user-friendly and full of examples – and they're written by academics. Deborah Rumsey is a Fellow of the American Statistical Association and a professor at the Ohio State University. If you want an introduction to statistics, this is not a bad place to start.

Tokunaga, H. (2018) *Fundamental Statistics for the Social and Behavioral Sciences*. Thousand Oaks, CA: Sage.
We like the way statistics is set in the context of the research process. Concepts are clearly explained and grounded through real-world examples.

Program-Specific

Field, A. and Miles, J. (2024) *Discovering Statistics Using IBM SPSS Statistics*, 6th edition. London: Sage.
If you need to use SAS, but don't feel you have the prerequisite statistics knowledge, let alone SAS program knowledge, this is a terrific find. From basic principles to in-depth analysis, the authors ground all learning in the SAS program.

Harris, J. (2020) *Statistics with R: Solving Problems Using Real-World Data*. Thousand Oaks, CA: Sage.
R is free statistical software – so a guide to its use is going to be mighty handy. This one is super-comprehensive (almost 800 pages) and uses clear examples and available data sets.

Salkind, N. J. (2021) *Statistics for People Who (Think They) Hate Statistics: Using Microsoft Excel*, 5th edition. London: Sage.
We can't say we're fans of using Excel for statistics. We would generally recommend a program like SPSS. But Excel is already on most students' computers, the stats pack is free and there is likely to be a familiarity with its spreadsheets. So it makes sense to recommend a reading here. The user-friendly nature of this work makes it a very good choice.

Wagner, W. E. (2019) *Using IBM® SPSS® Statistics for Research Methods and Social Science Statistics*. Thousand Oaks, CA: Sage.
Yes, SPSS has tutorials, but sometimes they just aren't enough. If you are feeling lost, or want to avoid feeling lost, this is a good choice. It will take you through the basics on to more sophisticated SPSS analysis.

16

ANALYSING QUALITATIVE DATA

Learning Objectives

- The promise of qualitative data
  - To understand the value of qualitative analysis
  - To become familiar with, and understand the value of, qualitative data analysis (QDA) software
- The logic of QDA
  - To understand how inductive and deductive reasoning work together in QDA
- The methods of QDA
  - To be able to move from raw data to theoretically meaningful understanding
  - To understand the basic steps of QDA
- Specific QDA strategies
  - To become familiar with various discipline-based QDA strategies
- Presenting qualitative data
  - To be able to appropriately represent qualitative data including the incorporation of direct quotes

THE PROMISE OF QUALITATIVE DATA

> Not everything that can be counted counts, and not everything that counts can be counted.
>
> William Bruce Cameron (1963)

The quote above is often mistakenly attributed to Einstein, who you may think of as an archetypal scientist. Yet even scientists recognize the limitations of quantification. When we say social science, health science or applied science, the words social, health and applied are the adjectives we use to describe a type of science. Our research traditions reflect this. Methods for research conduct and reporting are undeniably born of a science tradition – a tradition where objectivity rules and report writing is based on fact and, let's face it, is usually dry. But let's suspend this for a moment and think about what we aim to achieve. What we actually want to accomplish through research is to contribute to evidence-based decision-making, to influence change – and to do this we must influence others. And while no one is denying the power of solid credible research – such research is essential – it may be time to stop denying the power that is generated when we share our stories, our challenges and our passions. This is the power of qualitative data. It is the power to share the human condition in ways that simply cannot happen with statistical analysis of quantified experiences.

Yes, quantitative data and the use of statistics are a clearly defined and effective way of reducing and summarizing data. But statistics rely on the reduction of meaning to numbers. And when meanings are intricate and complex (which is often the case), reduction can be incredibly difficult. There can be a loss of 'richness' associated with the process.

This concern has led to the development of a plethora of qualitative data analysis (QDA) approaches that aim to create new understandings by exploring and interpreting complex data from sources such as interviews, group discussions, observation, journals and archival documents, without the aid of quantification. But the literature related to these approaches is quite thick and wading through it in order to find appropriate and effective strategies can be a real challenge. Many students end up: (1) spending a huge amount of time attempting to work through the vast array of approaches and associated literature; (2) haphazardly selecting one method that may or may not be appropriate to their project; (3) conducting their analysis without any well-defined methodological protocols; or (4) doing a combination of these.

So while we know there is inherent power in words and images, the challenge is working through options for managing and analysing qualitative data that best preserve richness yet crystallize meaning. We think the best way to go about this is to become familiar with both the logic and methods that underpin most QDA strategies. Once this foundation is set, working through more specific, specialist strategies becomes much easier.

Managing Your Project

In the methods literature, we tend to dichotomize quantitative and qualitative analysis. But when it comes right down to it, the logic underlying them is very similar. As shown in Figure 16.1, the process of reflective qualitative analysis requires researchers to: (1) organize their raw data; (2) enter and code that data; (3) search for meaning through thematic analysis; (4) interpret meaning; and (5) draw conclusions – all the while keeping the bigger picture, i.e. research questions, aims and objectives, methodological constraints and theory, clearly in mind. While this is very much in line with quantitative analysis, the main points of difference are the use of thematic (rather than statistical) analysis, and a closer, more entwined relationship between entering and coding data, data analysis and interpretation. Rather than being three distinct, ordered steps, qualitative analysis demands a more organic process that sees these three steps all influencing each other and working in overlapping cycles.

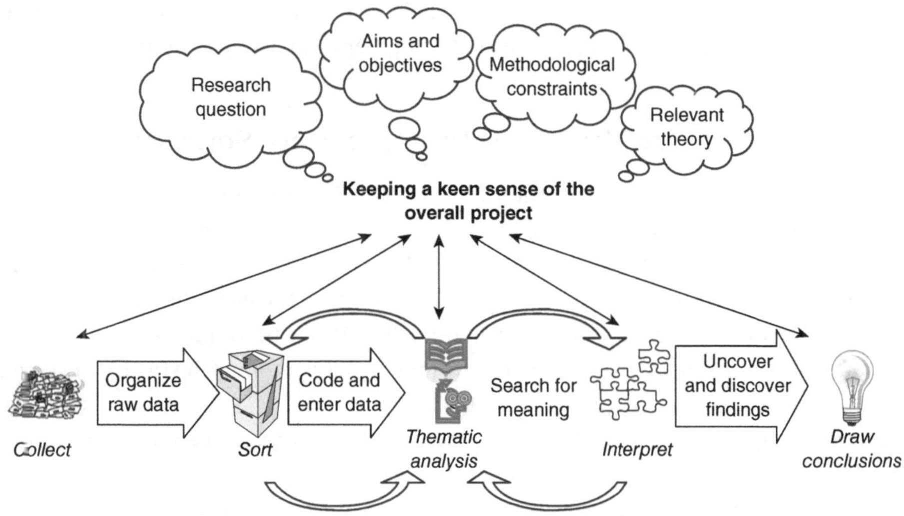

Figure 16.1 The process of reflective analysis

As with quantitative analysis, it is easy to get lost in the detail and lose focus. It is therefore extremely important to keep asking yourself questions that can help you maintain an overarching perspective. As fully articulated in Box 15.1 in the previous chapter, this means asking yourself questions related to:

1 Your own expectations – Both what you expect and do not expect to find.
2 Research questions, aims and objectives – How you can work with your data so that they help you achieve your project's stated goals.
3 Theory – How your data confirm your theories, how theory can help explain your data and whether your data is pointing to alternative theories.
4 Methods – How the methods employed might affect results.

Managing Your Data

In the world of qualitative analysis, raw data can be extremely messy. You might be facing a host of digital recordings, a mound of interview transcripts, a research journal (which can range from highly organized to highly disorganized), scribbled notes, highlighted documents, photographs, video recordings, mind maps – in fact the array is almost endless. And there is no doubt that a mound of messy data is extremely intimidating, especially if you are new to qualitative analysis.

The best advice is to be systematic. No matter how reflexive and iterative you intend your analysis to be, you still need to approach the management of your data with methodical rigour. And that starts with methodical data management. It is worth noting, however, that it is almost impossible to 'manage' qualitative data without engaging in some level of analysis. The process of organizing your data (e.g. deciding how you will group the data) will see you engaging with your data and making decisions that will have an effect on analysis, and should therefore be recognized as a part of analysis. Nonetheless, qualitative data, whether analysed manually or with the help of a software package, need to be effectively organized. The following steps will help you in that task.

Familiarize Yourself with Appropriate Software

There is definitely some debate as to the necessity for all research students to use specialist software for QDA, but it is certainly worth becoming familiar with available tools. QDA programs can store, code, index, map, classify, notate, find, tally, enumerate, explore, graph, etc. Basically, they can: (1) do all the things you can do manually, but more efficiently; and (2) do things that manual handling of a large data set simply will not allow. While becoming proficient in the use of such software can mean an investment in time (and possibly money), if you are working with a large data set you are likely to get that time back.

Talk to your supervisor/lecturer to find out what programs might be most appropriate for your goals and data and explore trial programmes and training courses if necessary. NVivo is one popular tool with accessible training courses online (see Figure 16.2).

Programs worth exploring include:

- NVivo, from Lumivero ((formerly QSR) https://lumivero.com/), The Ethnograph (www.qualisresearch.com), QDA Miner (www.provalisresearch.com) – used for indexing, searching and theorizing text;
- MAXQDA (www.maxqda.com), ATLAS.ti (www.atlasti.com) – can be used for images as well as words;
- Concordance (www.cloud9.com), HAMLET (www.hamlet.co.uk), DICTION (www.dictionsoftware.com) – popular for content analysis;
- CLAN (www.talkbank.org) – popular for conversation analysis;
- Raven's Eye (www.ravens-eye.net), Dedoose (www.dedoose.com) – good for big online data sets;
- QIQQA (www.qiqqa.com) – analyses PDFs.

As with quantitative software, most universities have licences that allow students access to certain qualitative programs. Universities may also provide relevant short courses.

Log in Your Data

It is rare that qualitative data come in at the same time, or in the same form, and can end up being a lot messier than a pile of questionnaires, so it is wise to keep track of your qualitative data as it is collected. It is well worth noting the respondents/source, data-collection procedures, collection dates and any commonly used shorthand.

Organize Your Data Sources

This involves grouping like sources, making any necessary copies and conducting an initial cull of any notes, observations, etc. not relevant to the analysis. As well as organizing, this process

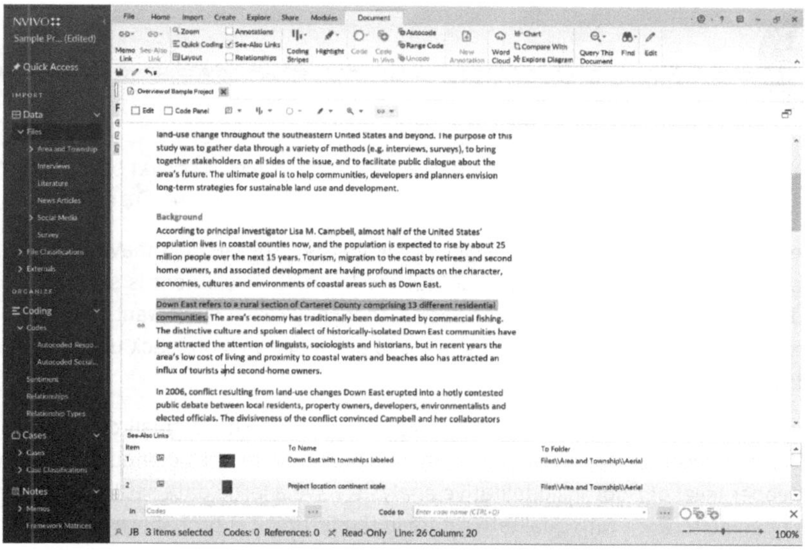

Figure 16.2 NVivo screen shot

Source: NVivo qualitative data analysis software; QSR International Pty Ltd. Version 10, 2012

allows you to screen your data. If done early, you can uncover potential problems not picked up in your pilot and make improvements to any ongoing data-collection protocols.

Read Through and Take Overarching Notes

It is extremely important to get a feel for qualitative data. This means reading through your data as it comes in and taking a variety of notes that will help you decide on the best way to sort and categorize the data you have collected. This is where data management and data analysis become highly blurred since any notes related to emerging themes are analysis.

Prepare Data for Analysis

If using a specialist QDA program, you will need to transcribe/scan your data so that it is ready to be entered into the program. If you plan on manually analysing your qualitative data, you may still need to go through this step so that you can print out your interviews, photographs, etc. You need to be able to actually put your hands on your data.

Enter Data/Get Analysis Tools Prepared

If you are using QDA software, you will need to enter your data into the program. If you are manually handling your data, you won't need to 'enter' your data, but you will need to arm yourself with qualitative analysis tools such as index cards, whiteboards, sticky notes and highlighters. In both cases, analysis tends to be ongoing and often begins before all the data has been collected/entered.

I Have a Question!

If QDA Programs Are so Efficient and Effective, Why Aren't They Used More Often by Researchers Working with Qualitative Data?

Well, there are three answers here: (1) lack of familiarity - researchers may not be aware of the programs, let alone what they can do; (2) the learning investment is seen as too large and/or difficult; (3) they may realize, or decide, that they really don't want to do that much with their qualitative data. They may just want to use it sparingly to back up a more quantitative study.

There are definitely pros and cons here. If you're working with a small data set and you cannot see any more QDA in your future, manual handling might be enough. But if you're after a deeper level of rigorous qualitative analysis, have a large data set to manage or see yourself needing to work with qualitative data in the future, it is probably worth battling the learning curve.

THE LOGIC OF QDA

Whether you are working with qualitative or quantitative data, the main game of any form of analysis is to move from raw data to meaningful understanding. In quantitative methods, this is done through statistical tests of coded data that assess the significance of findings; coding the data is preliminary to any analyses and interpretation. In qualitative analysis, understandings are built by a more tangled and creative process of uncovering and discovering themes that run through the raw data, and by interpreting the implication of those themes in relation to your research questions.

Balancing Creativity and Focus

There is no doubt that good qualitative analysis demands a degree of openness, a high level of curiosity and a willingness to accept fluidity. Qualitative analysis demands that you think your way through analysis and work your data so that it yields significant meaning. And such meaning may not be handed to you on a silver platter. As Isaac Asimov once said, 'The most exciting phrase to hear in science, the one that heralds new discoveries, is not "Eureka!" (I found it!) but "That's funny …".'

At the same time, however, we are not talking about airy-fairy metaphysical exploration. We are talking about research, with all the protocols and rigour thereof. As shown in Box 16.1, there is a real need for researchers to actively work between creativity and rigour. Creativity needs to be managed. You never want the cost of creativity to be credibility.

Box 16.1

Balancing Creativity and Rigour

- Think outside the box ... yet stay squarely on target.
- Be original, innovative and imaginative ... yet know where you want to go.
- Use your intuition ... but be able to share the logic of that intuition.
- Be fluid and flexible ... yet deliberate and methodical.
- Be inspired, imaginative and ingenious ... yet realistic and practical.

Moving Between Inductive and Deductive Reasoning

Moving from raw data, such as transcripts, pictures, notes, journals, videos and documents, to meaningful understanding is a process reliant on the generation/exploration of relevant themes; and these themes can either be discovered (through inductive reasoning) or uncovered (through deductive reasoning). So what do we mean by this?

Well, you may decide to explore your data inductively from the ground up. In other words, you may want to explore your data without a predetermined theme or theory in mind. Your aim might be to discover themes and eventuating theory by allowing them to emerge from the data. This is often referred to as the production of grounded theory or 'theory that was derived from data systematically gathered and analysed through the research process' (Corbin and Strauss, 2015: 12).

In order to generate grounded theory, researchers engage in a rigorous and iterative process of data collection and 'constant comparative' analysis that finds raw data brought to increasingly higher levels of abstraction until theory is generated. This method of theory generation (which shares the same name as its product – grounded theory) has embedded within it very well-defined and clearly articulated techniques for data analysis (see readings at the end of the chapter). And it is precisely this clear articulation of grounded theory techniques that has seen them become central to many QDA strategies.

Students who only engage with grounded theory literature, however, can fall prey to the false assumption that QDA is always inductive. But this need not be the case. Discovering themes is not the only QDA option. You may, for example, have predetermined (a priori) themes or theory in mind – they might have come from engagement with the literature; your prior experiences; the nature of your research question; or from insights you had while collecting your data. In this case, you are trying to uncover data deductively. You are mining your data for predetermined categories of exploration in order to support 'theory'. Rather than theory emerging from raw data, theory generation depends on progressive verification.

As shown in Figure 16.3, another likely possibility is that you will end up engaging in cycles of inductive and deductive reasoning. For example, you may design your study so that theory can emerge through inductive, ground-up processes, but as those theories begin to emerge from the data, it is likely that you will move towards a process of deductive confirmation. In this

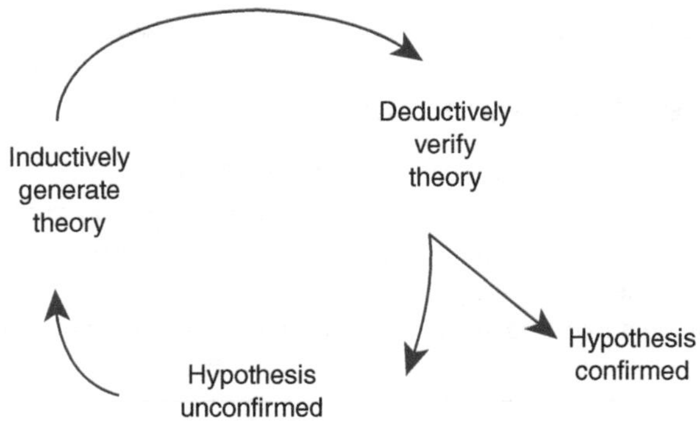

Figure 16.3 Cycles of inductive and deductive reasoning

case, theory generation depends on ongoing verification. On the other hand, the credibility of those testing hypotheses through deductive verification can depend on their willingness to acknowledge the unexpected that just might arise from their data. Researchers need to be able to generate alternative explanations inductively.

THE METHODS OF QDA

When it comes to QDA, the most important thing to recognize is the pressing need for ongoing rich engagement with the documents, transcripts, images and texts that make up your raw data. This will involve lots of reading and rereading that needs to start right from the point of data collection and continue through processes of data management, data analysis and even the drawing of conclusions. As articulated more fully below and drawn out even further in Box 16.2, analysis then involves: (1) identifying biases and noting overall impressions; (2) reducing (an evil word we know, but an essential step in moving from messy raw data to rich understanding), organizing and coding your data; (3) searching for patterns and interconnections; (4) mapping and building themes; (5) building and verifying theories; and (6) drawing conclusions.

There are two important things to note here. The first is that while the goal is to move from raw data to rich theoretical understanding, this process is far from linear. Qualitative data demands cycles of iterative analysis. The discovery of anything interesting will take you back to an earlier step including rereading, reviewing and re-engaging. The second thing to note is related to the notion of reduction. Students can get a bit worried when we tell them that part of the process is 'reducing'. They think this is antithetical to QDA's goal of preserving richness.

Well, richness is important, but qualitative analysis involves more than just preserving richness. Good qualitative analysis actually requires you to build it. Put it this way: raw data may be rich, but it is also messy and not publishable. If publishing in a journal, for example, you need to move from up to 1,000 or more pages of raw data to a ten-page article, and this necessarily involves processes of reduction that make the data manageable and understandable. But you will also want to make the data meaningful. So after processes of reduction, you will want to find interconnections, develop themes and build theories. As shown in Figure 16.4, getting to the point of meaningful understanding means abstracting your data back outwards so that it tells a full and powerful story that is in rich dialogue with theory.

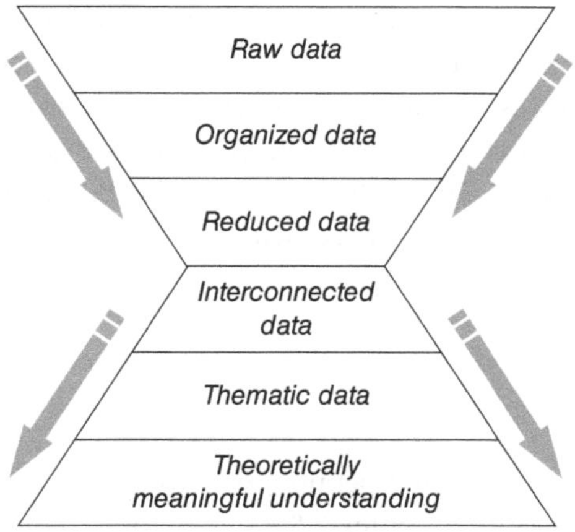

Figure 16.4 Working with qualitative data: drilling in and abstracting out

Identifying Biases and Noting Impressions

Because it is difficult to completely separate the process of data collection from analysis (you simply do not have the ability to constrain all thinking processes while engaged in listening to people's stories), you tend to analyse as you go. But this can be hazardous, since interpretations are always entwined with a researcher's biases, prejudices, worldviews and paradigms – both recognized and unrecognized, conscious and subconscious.

Because of these biases, a good way to start your analysis is to list as many of your assumptions and preconceived notions as possible. You need conscious recognition of biases if you are to engage in analysis that manages subjectivities. Think about what you expect to find as well as what you don't expect. And be completely ready to be surprised by what you didn't even think to expect! Not only will this help mediate bias, it will also help you elicit potential categories for exploration.

The second step is to engage in careful reading of all collected data, with 'general impression' notes recorded throughout the reading process. The objective here is to get an overall feel for the data and begin a process of holistically looking at disparate sources of data as an overarching story. As well as various topics, this might involve identifying feelings and emotions. If you were exploring experiences of divorce, for example, anger, frustration and hurt would be as important as division of property or custody arrangements.

Reducing and Coding into Themes

The next stage of analysis is to undertake a 'line-by-line' examination of all data sources. This involves systematic drilling into the raw data in order to build up categories of understanding. The idea is to reduce your data and sort it into various themes. If you are doing your analysis manually, a good approach is to make multiple copies of transcripts that you can highlight, cut and stack into relevant piles and play around with as your analysis progresses. You can also do something similar by replaying section of videos and taking, organizing and reorganizing notes. If you are using QDA software, your program will allow you to undertake a comparable process electronically.

As discussed above, this can be highly disconcerting. Suddenly your rich data is sorted and stacked into what may seem like superficial heaps. But remind yourself that this is just one stage in your analysis – and that this is a stage you can revisit as your insights grow.

What you are looking for in this line-by-line exploration are categories and themes, but this might be alluded to in several ways; that is, through the words that are used; the concepts that are discussed; the linguistic devices that are called upon; and the non-verbal cues noted by the researcher.

Exploring Words

Words can be explored through their repetition, or through exploration of their context and usage (sometimes called keywords in context). Specific cultural connotations of particular words can also be important. Patton (2001) refers to this as 'indigenous categories', while Corbin and Strauss (2015) refer to it as 'in vivo' coding. When working with words, researchers often systematically search a text to find all instances of a particular word (or phrase), making note of its context/meaning. Several software packages such as DICTION or Concordance can quickly and efficiently identify and tally the use of particular words and even present such findings in a quantitative manner.

Exploring Concepts

To explore concepts, researchers generally engage in line-by-line or paragraph-by-paragraph reading of transcripts, engaging in what grounded theory proponents refer to as 'constant comparison'. In other words, concepts and meaning are explored in each text and then compared with previously analysed texts to draw out both similarities and disparities. Thematic analysis (Braun and Clarke, 2022) is one of the most popular qualitative data analytic techniques. The concepts you explore can arise from the literature, your research question, intuition or prior experiences. Concepts may also be derived from 'standard' social science categories of exploration (e.g. power, race, class, gender). To find these you read through your text and deductively uncover the themes. The other option is to look for concepts to emerge inductively from your data without any preconceived notions (the practice of grounded theory). With predetermined categories, researchers need to be wary of 'fitting' their data to their expectations, and not being able to see alternative explanations. However, purely inductive methods are also subject to bias since unacknowledged subjectivities can impact on the themes that emerge from the data. As discussed above, working towards meaningful understanding often involves both inductive and deductive processes.

Exploring Linguistic Devices

Metaphors, analogies and even proverbs are often explored because of their ability to bring richness, imagery and empathetic understanding to words. These devices often organize thoughts and facilitate understanding by building connections between speakers and an audience. Once you start searching for such linguistic devices, you will find they abound in both the spoken and written word. Qualitative data analysts often use these rich metaphorical descriptions to categorize divergent meanings of particular concepts.

Exploring Non-Verbal Cues

One of the difficulties in moving from raw data to rich meaning is what is lost in the process. And certainly the tendency in qualitative data collection and analysis is to concentrate on words rather than the tone and emotive feeling behind the words, the body language that accompanies the words, or even words not spoken. Yet this world of the non-verbal can be central to thematic exploration. If your raw data, notes or transcripts contain non-verbal cues, it can lend significant meaning to content and themes: exploration of tone, volume, pitch and pace of speech; the tendency for hearty or nervous laughter; the range of facial expressions and body language; and shifts in any or all of these can be central in a bid for meaningful understanding. Conversation analysis is one such approach that Emma uses to study verbal and non-verbal actions in social interaction.

Looking for Patterns and Interconnections

Once your texts have been explored for relevant themes, the quest for meaningful understanding moves to an exploration of the relationship between and among various themes. For example, you may look to see if the use of certain words and/or concepts is correlated with the use of other words and/or concepts. Or you may explore whether certain words/concepts are associated with a particular range of non-verbal cues or emotive states. You may also look to see if there is a connection between the use of particular metaphors and non-verbal cues. And, of course, you may want to explore how individuals with particular characteristics vary on any of these dimensions.

Interconnectivities are assumed to be both diverse and complex, and can point to the relationship between conditions and consequences, or how the experiences of the individual relate to more global themes.

Mapping and Building Themes

As your range of patterns and interconnections grows, it is worth 'mapping' your data. Technically, when deductively uncovering data related to a priori themes, the map would be predetermined. However, when inductively discovering themes using a grounded theory approach, the map would be built as you work through your data. In practice, however, the distinction is unlikely to be that clear, and you will probably rely on both strategies to build the richest map possible (see Braun and Clarke, 2022).

Figure 16.5 offers a map exploring poor self-image in young girls built through both inductive and deductive processes. That is, some initial ideas were noted, but other concepts were added and linked as data immersion occurred. It is worth noting that this type of mind map can be easily converted to a 'tree structure' that forms the basis of analysis in many QDA software programs (see Figure 16.6).

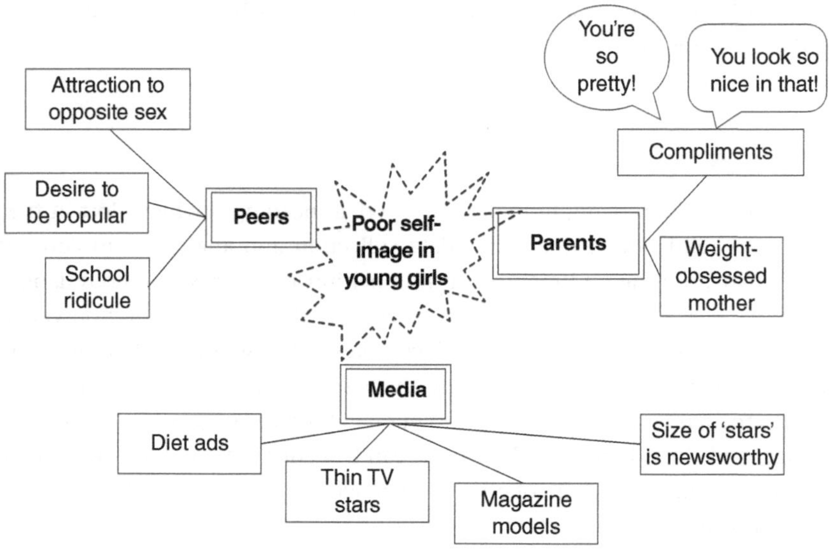

Figure 16.5 Mapping your themes

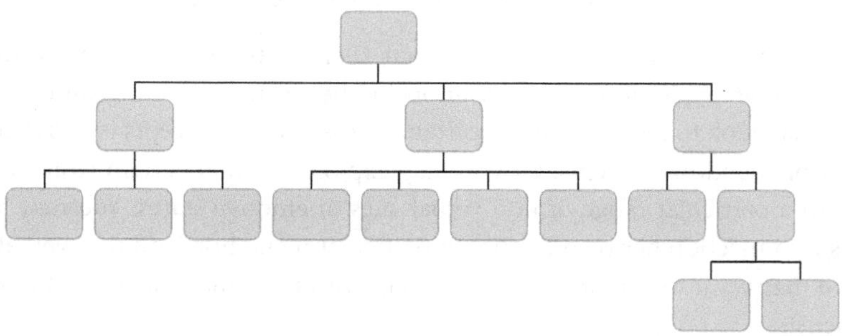

Figure 16.6 QDA 'tree structure'

At this stage, it is also a good idea to turn back to the literature, both past research studies and broader theoretical writings, and see how they might inform your data given the categories of understanding that have begun to emerge. This simultaneous engagement with the text and existing literature allows you to build much greater depth of understanding. Not only are you able to explore the content of your data, but also how and why that content is related to theory.

This then moves your data from piles sorted under simple categories of reduction to understandings that sit under much more meaningful themes. Mapping becomes an exercise that involves engaging themes in a dialogue and juxtaposing the themes (as well as the tensions among the themes) with relevant research and theoretically oriented literature. Reductive processes have thus expanded back out at a much more sophisticated level.

Developing Theory

While your analysis may culminate with thematic mapping, the conceptualization and abstraction involved can become quite advanced and can go from model building to theory building.

In other words, rich mapping is likely to spur new ideas – that 'Hey, you know what might be going on here' moment. It is quite exciting when you suddenly realize you are not just taking from the literature, but that you are ready to contribute back.

Drawing Conclusions

Drawing conclusions is your opportunity to pull together all the significant/important findings of your study and consider why and how they are significant/important. It is about clearly summarizing what your data reveals and linking this back to your project's main questions, aims and objectives. Your findings will need to be considered in relation to both current literature and your study's methodological constraints, and should clearly point to your overarching arguments. Remember: clarity is important, but do not force-fit your findings to portray a world without ambiguity and complexity.

In addition to summary, you can also consider sharing your findings, insights and ideas in the form of an original framework or model. Such devices not only add clarity to your reporting, but also help you establish your credibility as a researcher able to make original contributions back to the literature.

Box 16.2 takes you through the steps involved in effective QDA through a working example.

Box 16.2

QDA Steps – Number 1 Music Videos

We thought it would be a good idea to take you through a brief example of how the steps outlined above might unfold in practice. So let's look at music videos. For the purpose of this exercise imagine you want to undertake a study that explores the Number 1 music videos of the past three years in order to find any common elements. Analysis of the 37 Number 1 hits of this period might unfold as follows.

Step 1: Identifying Biases/Noting Overall Impressions

We all have them. You might, for example, think that music videos objectify women, that they have shallow lyrics and that country music videos are the most inane. Performing this step fully is extremely important. If you do not acknowledge preconceived notions and actively work to neutralize them, you are likely to find exactly what you expect to find!

The next step is to watch all 37 videos and take notes of overall impressions, perhaps related to content, lyrics, dancers, movement, emotions, style (these categories may derive from your own interests, insights or the literature).

Step 2: Reducing and Coding into Themes

This involves watching each video in turn and noting everything you possibly can related to the categories you noted/generated in step 1 (a deductive process) as well as any other categories you

(Continued)

uncover along the way (an inductive process). When it comes to lyrics for video 1, for example, you might find themes of cheating, heartbreak and trust. In this way, you build both categories and subcategories that are likely to expand as you work your way through each video.

Step 3: Searching for Patterns and Interconnections

You are likely to have overlapping themes across your 37 videos - so this step asks you to search for commonalities and divergences. For example, you may find that the video with the most explicit content comes from videos featuring bands rather than female artists, or that the dancers feature most heavily in country videos.

Step 4: Mapping and Building Themes

One small section of a preliminary map might be as follows (Figure 16.7):

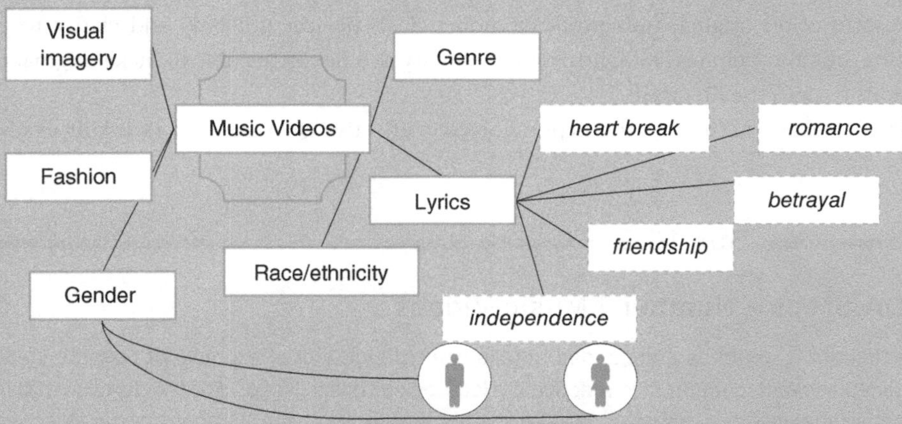

Figure 16.7 A section of a preliminary map

From here you would: (1) continue mapping all the main themes (genre, gender, etc.); (2) create even more subcategories as appropriate (e.g. under independence you might put males/females); and (3) map various interconnections. Don't forget to call on the literature in doing these tasks.

Now if you did not have clear boundaries on your study at the outset, you will probably come to realize that doing qualitative analysis of all aspects of music videos is a huge task that may not be manageable - so you may decide to narrow in on one or two particular interesting areas, for example gender. Remember: it is much better to do a really rigorous job on a smaller scale than a bad job on a larger scale.

Step 5: Building and Verifying Theories

This is your 'Hey, you know what might be going on here' moment that will hopefully dawn on you as you watch your videos for the 103rd time and play around with your maps for the 72nd time. Who knows? You may just come up with a mind-blowing theory that sets the music industry on fire.

Step 6: Drawing Conclusions

You are likely to find out much more through the processes than you could possibly share, so you will need to decide what is most significant/important and link this back to your project's main questions, aims and objectives in the most compelling and credible way. As shown in Figure 16.8, one way to graphically support a conclusion is through a word map.

Figure 16.8 Music video word map

QDA studies abound. A few that give a good explication of methods and cover a range of strategies and topics are offered in Box 16.3.

Box 16.3

Studies Using QDA and Thematic Analysis

Borrell, J. (2008) 'Thematic analysis identifying concepts of problem gambling agency: With preliminary exploration of discourses in selected industry and research documents', *Journal of Gambling Issues, 22*: 195–218.

This study thematically explores annual reports and papers from research bodies, noting instances where agency was indicated in relation to both gambling and problem gambling. The thematic analysis went beyond semantic content in a bid to examine the underlying ideas, assumptions, conceptualizations and ideologies.

Bischof, G. H., Warnaar, B. L., Barajas, M. S. and Dhaliwal, H. K. (2011) 'Thematic analysis of the experiences of wives who stay with husbands who transition male-to-female', *Michigan Family Review, 15*(1): 16–33.

This qualitative study analysed 14 cases of the wives of transgender women. Thematic analysis was used to identify and organize key themes in the experiences of wives who stayed with

(Continued)

partners undergoing gender transition. Themes clustered in three main areas: intrapersonal, couple relationship, and family and social relationships.

Pehlke II, T. A., Hennon, C. B., Radina, M. E. and Kuvalanka, K. A. (2009) 'Does father still know best? An inductive thematic analysis of popular TV sitcoms', *Fathering*, 7(2): 114–39.

In this study 12 programmes from the six major networks were recorded and analysed for themes related to father involvement. Inductive thematic analysis led to the identification of three themes: various ways fathers interact with children (spending quality time, emotion-based behaviours and teaching life lessons); how fathers of varying racial/ethnic groups and socioeconomic status are depicted; and negative messages regarding fathering (foolish or immature behaviours and being the butt of family members' jokes).

Bryne, D. (2022) 'A worked example of Braun and Clarke's approach to reflexive thematic analysis', *Quality & Quantity*, *56*: 1391–412.

This one is a bit 'meta'. Reflexive thematic analysis is both a widely used method and a common target of confusion. This study explores health and well-being educators' attitudes and provides a clear step-by-step approach of how to do a reflexive thematic analysis.

Critical Thinking Challenge 17

Qualitative 'Bias-Controlled' Reduction

There can be a tendency to think of reduction as a quantitative strategy not appropriate for qualitative data. But reduce you must. You have to go from what might amount to thousands of pages of raw data to very succinct findings and messaging without the aid of a statistical program. This means you must control for your own biases.

Ask yourself: What do I expect to find? What do I know will not be there? What am I absolutely sure of?

You need to put all of that aside if you want unbiased qualitative analysis. Trust me, with qualitative analysis, if you're not controlling your biases, you will find exactly what you're looking for.

SPECIFIC QDA STRATEGIES

Up to this point, we have been treating QDA as a homogeneous approach with underlying logic and methods, and we have not really discussed the distinct disciplinary and paradigmatic approaches that do exist. But as mentioned at the start of this chapter, a number of distinct approaches have developed over the past decades. Each has its own particular goals, theory and methods – and each will have varying levels of applicability to your own research. Now while we would certainly recommend delving into the approaches that resonate with you, it is worth keeping in mind that you don't have to adopt just one approach. It is possible to draw insights from various strategies in a bid to evolve an approach that best cycles between your data and your own research agenda.

The definitions you'll find in the glossary are not designed to be comprehensive enough to make you an expert on any particular branch of QDA, but they do provide a comparative summary of some of the more commonly used strategies. We cover **content analysis, discourse analysis, narrative analysis, conversation analysis, semiotics, hermentuics, grounded theory, visual analysis**. You can explore these strategies further by delving into the readings offered at the end of the chapter.

PRESENTING QUALITATIVE DATA

Not many books adequately cover the presentation of qualitative data, but they should. Students often struggle with the task and end up falling back on what they are most familiar with, or what they can find in their methods books (which are often quantitatively biased). Not only is quantitative report writing a little, well, dry, it can also result in students misapplying techniques for presenting their data. For example, students working on a qualitative project may only have three cases, five documents, or eight interviews, and they can end up with some pseudo-quantitative analysis and presentation that includes pie charts, bar graphs and percentages. They may say 50% feel ... and 25% think ..., when they are talking about a total of only four people.

This simply isn't where the power of qualitative data lies. The power of qualitative data is in the actual words and images themselves – so our advice is to use them. If the goal is the rich use of words, then avoid inappropriate quantification and preserve/capitalize on language. The best way to preserve and capitalize on words and images is through storytelling. What you need here is a clear message, argument or storyline, and to selectively use your words and/or images in a way that gives weight to that story. The qualitative data you present should be pointed and powerful enough to draw your readers in. If you've collected it, use it, share it and be true to the experiences you have captured. You may be surprised at how powerful your 'reporting' can become.

An example is probably the best way to get this across. Let's go back to Zina's own study on religious disaffiliation. Now for this study, she actually conducted in-depth interviews with 80 'apostates' (those who had given up religious faith), so she was able to effectively quantify and present the data in tabular form (see the end of Chapter 15). But while this quantification definitely makes for a nice summary, it is the words and stories of the apostates themselves that are most compelling (see Box 16.4).

Box 16.4

An Example of Qualitative Data Presentation

This example centres on the individuals whose processes of religious disaffiliation are best represented not by angry rebellion or open exploration, but by 'discontented doubts'. In Zina's research such individuals were labelled 'egoistic apostates', one of three types of apostate identified through the research (apostates being individuals who have given up religious faith).

(Continued)

The Egoistic Apostate

The Common Road

Egoistic apostates have a difficult time reconciling religion with the condition of the world or the condition of themselves. Processes of disaffiliation are inscribed with introspection, negative self-reflection and an emptiness that leads to a sense of disenchantment with God, religion and – at times – with the self. Apostasy tends to be an intense intellectual exercise in confusion and detachment. The following narrative captures the essence of egoistic disaffiliation:

> I was starting to have a really hard time; I think it was in year eight. My parents were fighting a fair bit, and ... God didn't seem to want to help. My life at times has not been easy ... I have been depressed, I have had some mighty lows and as a youth it was during these lows that I really doubted God. It's hard to believe in anything when you do not believe in yourself and I wanted to turn to God, but he didn't reach out. I often felt that God was not there for me ... It made me wonder whether he existed at all; I used to think about that all the time. Was he there? Did he just not care about me? (Interview No. 13)

Quite telling in this egoistic passage is a clearly articulated sense of disenchantment with both God and religion. The statements 'God did not seem to want to help' and 'he didn't reach out' show both disenchantment with familial religion and painful internalization of God's rejection of a personal relationship. Focus is placed on the self, and there is clear indication of the emptiness associated with religious doubts.

For egoistic apostates, the process of disaffiliation tends to be an introspective journey of doubt and questioning arising from a very personalized sense of disappointment. The hallmark of the egoistic journey is a meditative and intellectual focus accompanied by a sense of alienated loss. The following narrative further illustrates the point:

> I was sort of isolated as a child, I lived in a safe cocoon of ignorance, I didn't think that my parents really ... that I really ever felt that what they did or thought was right, but I didn't really know why. When I went to uni and met a few people that made me question things for the first time. All the inconsistencies that go along with the Church. I had never really looked at religion objectively; I don't even think I looked at it at all. Anyway, it's depressing. I mean you just have to look at the opulence of the Church as compared to that of the poor who they say they want to help, and you, ah, realize that there may be a problem with the idea of God. I really ... I had a hard time with that revelation; I mean I just think that, well that nothing makes sense. I just don't know. (Interview No. 67)

This passage clearly shows a sense of disenchantment with the notion of God and religion. The 'inconsistencies' of the Church leave this egoistic apostate with an internalized sense of disenchantment. The hypocrisy perceived in the Church leads to a loss of religion that is quite mournful. The statement 'I really ... I had a hard time with that' shows a sense of lost confusion that is difficult to resolve; God and religion are thoughtfully considered to the point of vulnerable uncertainty.

Divergent Paths

While lost and confused introspection is a common theme in egoistic journeys away from faith, the journey can still take somewhat divergent paths. For example, the depressed introspection that marks the egoistic respondent's journey can be associated with reactionary pain and anger:

> I was 16 when I started to doubt the traditional Church and a traditional God. There is just so much suffering in the world. How could there be a God who would allow so many people to die and so many children to suffer? ... How could we make sense of the world if there is a God who is such a strong father, yet such an absolute bastard? God made no sense. Either he is mean and vindictive or there is no God. I myself think that there is no male God. No religion that I have ever heard of really captures the essence of this world. I was completely disenchanted with religion, and with what it tries to give me ... the more I looked, the more I realized that the Christian faiths were all bastions of greed and oppression. It is such a waste, on both a personal and social level. That's why I became an atheist. (Interview No. 38)

For this respondent, egoistic disenchantment is the result of a resentful recognition of 'suffering in the world'. The perceived 'greed and oppression' of Christianity leads to both anger and alienation. For example, words such as 'mean', 'vindictive' and 'bastard' point to angry reactionism, while an egoistic sense of personalized alienation and emptiness is pointed to by the phrases 'It is such a waste' and 'I was completely disenchanted'. This respondent thus presents a simultaneous sense of mourning and anger.

Anger, however, is not the only construct associated with egoistic apostasy. Many egoistic journeys actually have a strong rational and logical component. In this case, disenchantment is coupled with a rational reflection on familial faith. The following narrative is indicative:

> I can't remember what exactly started me on the path, but I think that it is just all the problems in the world. Holy wars always spun me out. King Arthur and all that. I mean, Holy War, isn't that an oxymoron? Anyway, I think I just gave up the notion of God, God first. There can be no God in this world, and then, I mean look at it. Old people handing money to preachers over the phone and people still going to war. I don't get it, never will; how can you not have some serious question of both religion and God, how can you not let it get to you? I mean I really let that worry me ... once I gave up on God, well then you can start to really see religion for what it is ... it is a mess. Yeah, it may be hard, but once you think about it logically, what else can you do but let religion go? (Interview No. 68)

For this respondent, the egoistic, emotive components of the process appear to be tempered with a sense of logic. Egoism is present, particularly at the start of the apostatic journey. This egoism, however, has been negotiated with a less emotive plea to the intellect; that is, to 'think about it logically'.

Concluding Remarks

A journey in which both God and religion are examined and deconstructed on a personal level with a relatively acute sense of disenchantment, loss, confusion and emptiness may best characterize egoistic apostasy. From this common ground, however, the journey can take various paths, including journeys tainted with angry reactionism, and journeys that incorporate a sense of rationality and logic.

I Have a Question!

Is It Really That Bad to Tally up and Quantify Qualitative Data? I Just Did Interviews with Ten People - Are You Saying Not to use Pie Charts or Bar Graphs?

Graphs are not a good fit for qualitative data. Think about a pie chart - the inference is that the percentage of people who do something or think something is important. So say 70% of the people you interviewed think Las Vegas is tacky. What does that mean? Are you trying to say that 70% of some population think that? Well there aren't very many populations of interest where seven people will be representative of anything. So you really need to think about why you are telling us this. That the data is there isn't a good enough reason. Get to the heart of what your interviews were really seeking to explore. If it is only general opinions, we would question your research methods. But if you were going for depth, say interviewing people who regularly go to Vegas about how they deal with particular temptations, talk about that. 'How' questions are particularly interesting in qualitative work and lend themselves well to the type of write-up offered in Box 16.4 above.

Chapter Summary

- Qualitative data analysis (QDA) creates new understandings through critical and reflexive exploration and interpretation of complex data from sources such as interviews, group discussions, observation, journals and archival documents, without the aid of quantification.
- The logic of QDA involves balancing creativity and focus while inductively uncovering and deductively discovering themes that run through raw data. It is a process that demands researchers stay close to their data.
- QDA generally involves: identifying biases and noting impressions; reducing, organizing and coding; searching for patterns and interconnections; mapping and building themes; building and verifying theories; and drawing conclusions.
- There are a number of paradigm/discipline-based strategies for QDA including: content, discourse, narrative and conversation analysis; semiotics; **hermeneutics**; and grounded theory. **Visual analysis** intersects with all of these and reminds researchers of the importance of images.
- Effective presentation of qualitative data can give your report writing real power. The challenge is to create a clear storyline and selectively use your words and/or images to give weight to your story.

FIND YOUR NEXT STEP

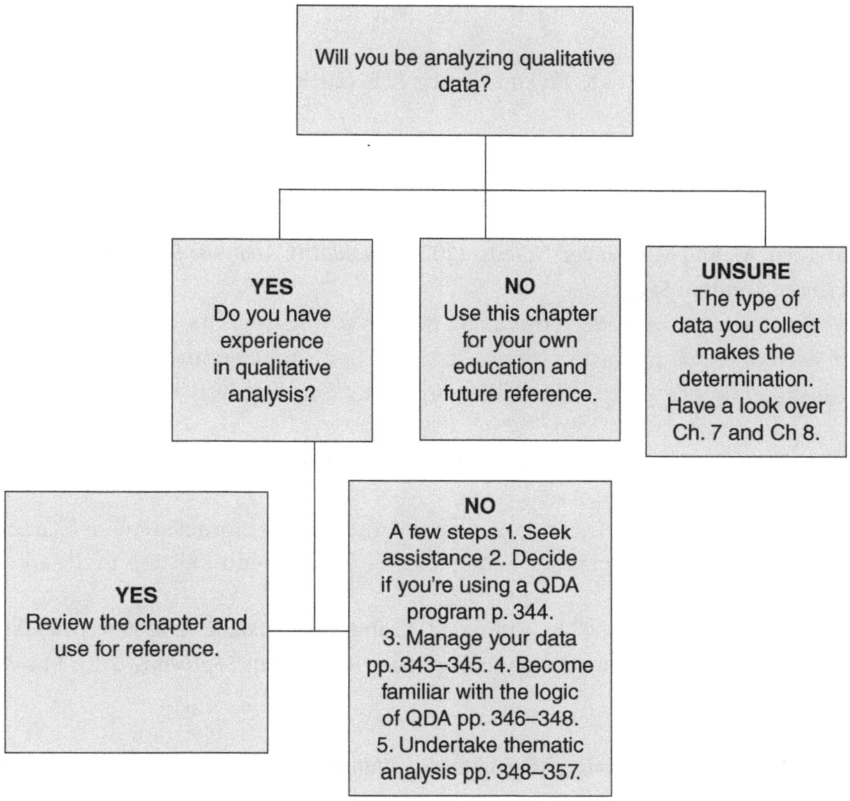

FURTHER READING

General Qualitative Analysis

Bazeley, P. (2021) *Qualitative Data Analysis: Practical Strategies*, 2nd edition. London: Sage.
This is a good overarching introduction to QDA. It is clear and accessible and takes you through all the necessary stages of analysis. Good use of examples from a range of disciplines.

Bischof, G. H., Warnaar, B. L., Barajas, M. S. and Dhaliwal, H. K. (2011) 'Thematic analysis of the experiences of wives who stay with husbands who transition male-to-female', *Michigan Family Review*, *15*(1): 16–33.
See Box 16.3 above.

Borrell, J. (2008) 'Thematic analysis identifying concepts of problem gambling agency: With preliminary exploration of discourses in selected industry and research documents', *Journal of Gambling Issues*, *22*: 195–218.
See Box 16.3 above.

Braun, V. and Clarke, V. (2022) *Thematic Analysis: A Practical Guide*. Sage: London.
A clear, easy-to-follow practical guide by the academics who developed thematic analysis, a widely used method for qualitative data analysis.

Guest, G. S., MacQueen, K. M. and Namey, E. E. (2018) *Applied Thematic Analysis*. Thousand Oaks, CA: Sage.
A guide like this is essential if you are attempting to analyse qualitative data. This one offers a grounded step-by-step approach that is both systematic and rigorous. Worth a look.

Järvinen, M. and Mik-Meyer, N. (eds) (2020) *Qualitative Analysis: Eight Approaches for the Social Sciences*. London: Sage.
We like the way this work is structured. It offers two chapters (one theoretical and one practical) on each of eight approaches (symbolic interactionism, phenomenology, hermeneutics, critical realism, grounded theory, narrative analysis, discourse analysis and actor network theory).

Miles, M. B., Huberman, M. and Saldana, J. (2019) *Qualitative Data Analysis: A Methods Sourcebook*. London: Sage.
This is a classic text on QDA that will take you through five distinct methods of analysis: exploring, describing, ordering, explaining and predicting. A terrific introduction to the art of QDA.

Pehlke II, T. A., Hennon, C. B., Radina, M. E. and Kuvalanka, K. A. (2009) 'Does father still know best? An inductive thematic analysis of popular TV sitcoms', *Fathering*, *7*(2): 114–39.
See Box 16.3 above.

Saldana, J. (2021) *The Coding Manual for Qualitative Researchers*, 4th edition. London: Sage.
One of the main techniques of QDA, particularly from the school of grounded theory, is coding data. This work offers 35 different techniques for doing so, with the breadth making it applicable to all types of qualitative analysis.

Silverman, D. (2024) *Interpreting Qualitative Data*, 7th edition. London: Sage.
This book is a modern classic in this area and covers some data-collection strategies as well as various strategies for analysis. Great use of worked examples.

Wertz, F., Charmaz, K., McMullen, L., Josselson, R., Anderson, R. and McSpadden, E. (2011) *Five Ways of Doing Qualitative Analysis: Phenomenological Psychology, Grounded Theory, Discourse Analysis, Narrative Research, and Intuitive Inquiry*. New York: Guilford Press.
It is hard to find one book that compares, contrasts and covers the techniques of a variety of QDA strategies – but this one does. We particularly like the way they use one narrative explored in five ways.

Content Analysis

Krippendorf, K. (2018) *Content Analysis: An Introduction to its Methodology*. London: Sage.
As well as offering a step-by-step process, this work also offers strong arguments for the relevance of content analysis to understanding today's markets, political preferences and emergent ideas.

Neuendorf, K. (2016) *The Content Analysis Guidebook*. Thousand Oaks, CA: Sage.
The author uses a good range of disciplines to offer a step-by-step guide to analysis. We particularly like her use of flow charts.

Discourse Analysis

Gee, J P. (2014) *An Introduction to Discourse Analysis: Theory and Method*. Abingdon: Routledge.
When it comes to discourse analysis you need a bit of theory to go with your methods. Understanding the socio-historical context of 'talk' when you are immersed in that very socio-historical period is not easy. This is an accessible work that can help you overcome common challenges.

Wodak, R. and Meyer, M. (eds) (2015) *Methods of Critical Discourse Analysis*. London: Sage.
This edited volume brings together a range of researchers who share their sometimes diverse approaches to discourse analysis. Good use of examples drawn from a range of contemporary issues.

Narrative Analysis

Clandinin, D. J. (2013) *Engaging in Narrative Inquiry*. Abingdon: Routledge.
Written by one of the experts in the field, this book offers a clear articulation of method. The critique of real cases helps to ground messages.

Holstein, J. A. and Gubrium, J. F. (eds) (2011) *Varieties of Narrative Analysis*. London: Sage.
An edited volume worth exploring. This comprehensive work has quite a practical focus and covers a variety of approaches used by the contributors to analyse stories and storytelling.

Kim, J. (2015) *Understanding Narrative Inquiry: The Crafting and Analysis of Stories as Research*. Thousand Oaks, CA: Sage.
We like the pedagogy that Kim uses in this work. She moves from theory to methodological practice by deconstructing six extracts from actual studies.

Conversation Analysis

Sidnell, J. (2010) *Conversation Analysis: An Introduction*. Chichester: Wiley-Blackwell.
A terrific introductory student guide that covers the history, methods and techniques of conversation analysis with real-life examples and step-by-step explanations.

Sidnell, J. and Stivers, T. (eds) (2014) *The Handbook of Conversation Analysis*. Chichester: Wiley-Blackwell.
An impressive list of contributors offers a comprehensive overview of not only conversation analysis, but also discourse analysis, linguistic anthropology, interpersonal communication, discursive psychology and sociolinguistics. A somewhat advanced book that covers a wide range of topics and disciplines.

Semiotics

Chandler, D. (2017) *Semiotics: The Basics*. Abingdon: Routledge.
Quite clear, concise and relatively jargon-free. Covers the basics, including what signs are, and how we can analyse and embed them in textual analysis. Not a bad choice.

Hall, S. (2012) *This Means This, This Means That: A User's Guide to Semiotics*. London: Laurence King.
As an introductory guide, we really like the non-theoretical way this book demystifies semiotics – an area of study that is sometimes presented in overly complex and philosophical ways. Very helpful visual examples.

Hermeneutics

Dibley, L., Dickerson, S., Duffy, M. and Vandermause, R. (2020) *Doing Hermeneutic Phenomenological Research: A Practical Guide*. Thousand Oaks, CA: Sage.
This book does a terrific job of integrating the theoretical and the practical. It is accessible (which is not always the case for methods arising from philosophical tenets) and offer a nice step-by-step guide for designing method.

Laing, C., Moules, N., McCaffrey, G. and Field, J. (2015) *Conducting Hermeneutic Research: From Philosophy to Practice*. New York: Peter Lang.
This book starts with an understanding and history of hermeneutics, but quickly moves on to the conduct of hermeneutical studies in a logical and practical way.

Grounded Theory

Bryant, A. and Charmaz. K. (eds) (2019) *The SAGE Handbook of Current Developments in Grounded Theory*. London: Sage.
This is an edited volume that brings together leading researchers and practitioners from around the globe, who together cover all the theory, all the techniques, and all the debates that surround this incredibly popular approach to analysing qualitative data.

Corbin, J. and Strauss, A. (2015) *Basics of Qualitative Research: Techniques and Procedures for Developing Grounded Theory*. London: Sage.
This is probably the most popular explication of grounded theory methods around. It is highly practical and offers a clearly defined approach to the inductive analysis of qualitative data and subsequent theory building. Essential for anyone undertaking grounded theory.

Glaser, B. and Strauss, A. (1967) *Discovery of Grounded Theory*. Chicago: Aldine.
A classic. The discovery of theory from data is a major contribution to the qualitative paradigm. You should not do a grounded theory study without at least a quick read of this work. Still highly applicable today.

Visual Analysis

Banks, M. and Zeitlyn, D. (2015) *Visual Methods in Social Research.* London: Sage.
Drawing from an anthropological tradition, this book covers all the basics of visual analysis and makes it relevant across various disciplines. This work also gives good coverage of digital media – a massive new source of visual imagery.

Pauwels, L. and Mannay, D. (eds) (2020) *The SAGE Handbook of Visual Research Methods.* London: Sage.
This comprehensive handbook (almost 800 pages) is an edited volume from a broad range of contributors who cover all key aspects and contemporary issues related to visual analysis.

Rose, G. (2016) *Visual Methodologies: An Introduction to Researching with Visual Materials.* London: Sage.
Documents and texts … texts and documents – well, what about photos, sketches, maps and videos? What about all the online images, think Instagram or TikTok? If you are interested in incorporating more visual forms of representation into your analysis, then this book is worth a look.

QDA Programs

Beekhuyzen, J. and Bazeley, P. (2025) *Qualitative Data Analysis with NVivo.* London: Sage.
NVivo is an extremely helpful program for anyone embarking on large-scale qualitative analysis, particularly those using a grounded theory approach. But it is worth getting some help in understanding the ins and outs of the program. When Zina was doing her PhD, Pat Bazeley was the one who taught her how to do qualitative analysis with NUD*IST (a precursor of NVivo). It's good to see her teaching expertise in print.

Friese, S. (2019) *Qualitative Data Analysis with ATLAS.ti.* Thousand Oaks, CA: Sage.
ATLAS.ti is a QDA program that will help you organize and analyse text and images. This book offers a clear step-by-step guide to using this program. Good array of exercises and examples.

Kuckartz, U. and Rädiker, S. (2019) *Analyzing Qualitative Data with MAXQDA: Text, Audio, and Video.* New York: Springer.
MAXQDA can handle mixed media as well as data from mixed-methods approaches. If you are using this program, you'<tab/>ll find this step-by-step book very comprehensive.

Lewins, A. and Silver, C. (2014) *Using Software in Qualitative Research: A Step-by-Step Guide.* London: Sage.
This book offers a nice overview of computer assisted qualitative data analysis (CAQDAS) packages that can aid your analysis. It is designed to help you choose the right program and understand how to get the most out of it once selected. With this type of work, it is always worth looking for the latest edition.

Salmona, M., Lieber, E. and Kaczynski, D. (2019) *Qualitative and Mixed Methods Data Analysis Using Dedoose: A Practical Approach for Research Across the Social Sciences*. London: Sage.
Dedoose is a program that allows you to weave different types of data together with cool visualizations. This is the right book to help you navigate this powerful web-based research tool.

17

THE CHALLENGE OF WRITING UP

Learning objectives

- The writing challenge
  - To appreciate writing for the challenge it can be
  - To understand the research write-up as a communication exercise
- The writing process
  - To be able to construct a convincing narrative
  - To understand the requirements of each section of a research report
  - To appreciate the necessity of drafting and redrafting your work

THE WRITING CHALLENGE

> I always write a good first line, but I have trouble in writing the others.
>
> Molière (1659)

We have not come across many students who consider writing up an easy process. In fact, writing up is almost always approached with a sense of apprehension and wariness. And in many ways, this is justified. For one thing, this could well be the biggest single piece of academic writing you have ever attempted. Second, there are major consequences attached to the quality of your write-up – research is often judged not by what you did, but by your ability to report on what you did. Finally, you probably are not too practised in the art of writing research reports. This is likely to be new terrain.

So we know there is a good chance you wish this whole research thing could happen without the need to write it up. But that is not the reality. This is something you have to tackle.

Luckily there are quite a few practical strategies for negotiating the writing process in a way that improves the overall quality of the project and makes the task less daunting. If you can (1) make a start, (2) see writing as part and parcel of the research journey rather than just an account of that journey, (3) craft a good story that engages others in your research and (4) accept the need to draft and redraft, you can produce and submit a research account that will impress examiners and maybe even make a real contribution back to the literature.

Box 17.1

On Writing

Writing is easy. You just sit down at the typewriter, open up a vein and bleed it out drop by drop.

Walter 'Red' Smith (1949)

First forget inspiration. Habit is more dependable. Habit will sustain you whether you're inspired or not.

Octavia E. Butler (1995)

The road to hell is paved with works-in-progress.

Philip Roth (1979)

No pen, no ink, no table, no room, no time, no quiet, no inclination.

James Joyce (1906)

Putting words on paper regularly is part of the necessary discipline of writing.

Pearl Cleage (2011)

I was working on the proof of one of my poems all the morning, and took out a comma. In the afternoon I put it back again.

Oscar Wilde (1884)

Writing ... a combination of ditch-digging, mountain-climbing, treadmill and childbirth.

Edna Ferber (1939)

Being a good writer is 3% talent, 97% not being distracted by the Internet.

Anonymous

Research Write-Ups – An Exercise in Communication

If there were only one piece of advice we could give to someone tackling a writing project, it would be to view writing as an exercise in communication. Now you may think the ultimate goal in writing up your project is simply reporting on what you did and what you found, but there is much more to it than this. The ultimate goal is to explain, illuminate and share your research with others. You need your readers to understand your research journey and appreciate its consequences. This is especially important if you want to counter the notion of the 'ivory tower' and have your research read and used by others.

When you view writing as a communication process you recognize that good writing demands consideration of your readers. It is worth remembering that very few people (yourself probably included) have the ability to sit through a monotonous monologue or stay engaged with dry and turgid writing – they need to be mentally, intellectually and/or emotionally involved. For an audience to appreciate what you have to say, you need to engage their thinking, predict their questions and respond to their inquiries. They may not be able to respond iteratively, but it is their response that gauges your success.

Knowing and Engaging Your Audience

A major factor in effective research communication is the ability to connect with your readers, and this starts with knowing who they are:

- Who am I writing for? – When it comes to academic work, you are generally writing for your professors and supervisors, but if your writing will be more broadly disseminated (community leaders, community members, managers, politicians and practitioners), you need to consider who they are and the agendas they may have. Good writing demands that you keep your readers at the forefront of your mind.
- What do they know? – In most forms of writing, the challenge is starting where readers are, not over or under their heads. This means considering what your readers are likely to know about your topic, as well as what they know about research processes. You need to 'add value' to what people already know without losing them in the process. The challenge in student writing is somewhat different. In this case, your readers are likely to know as much as or even more about your topic than you do – and are likely to be charged with the responsibility of judging your work. The trick here is not being the 'expert' but tackling your writing in a way that impresses your readers with your engagement, logic and insights.
- What are their expectations? – The expectation of academics, assessors or examiners is not that you will blow them away with your incredible knowledge (although that would be nice!), but that you are able to show thoughtful engagement with relevant literature and logically sound research processes. The other thing they will definitely expect is polished work. You simply cannot impress with spelling mistakes, typos and missing references.

Finding an Appropriate Structure and Style

One of the biggest challenges in writing up a research report is knowing how best to organize it. This will be determined by a number of factors, including the advice of your supervisor, your own sense of comfort and, perhaps most importantly, the paradigm you are working under. Studies that sit under the positivist umbrella, for example a study with a quantitative methodology, generally use a traditional format and formal style. But with a more qualitative methodology, there is some debate on how to best capture what you have done and find a voice that best reflects that paradigm. The traditional academic style comes with a long colonial history of prioritizing the written word over other forms of knowledge and emancipatory and critical work often draws on creative formats. For example, Shawn Wilson (2008) uses different fonts to distinguish the 'academic' style from personal narratives addressed to her sons which highlights the importance of relationality in indigenous research methods.

The Traditional Academic Format

When it comes to research reports, there is certainly a traditional structure that is recognized, accepted, expected and often advocated. This is the 'introduction, literature review, methods, findings, discussion, conclusion' format that dominates the literature. And it is quite easy to see why so many researchers adopt this approach. Not only does it tend to be expected, but it also answers readers' questions in a sequence quite natural to the flow of a normal conversation. As shown in Table 17.1, project-related questions and their respective answers can easily structure a report or thesis that readily falls into a traditional format.

Table 17.1 The standard conversation

The questions	The answers that structure the chapters/sections of the conventional report
So tell me what your research is about?	Title Abstract Introduction Research question(s) Hypothesis (as appropriate)
And why did you choose this particular topic/question?	Introduction Rationale
What do you hope to achieve?	Introduction Aims and objectives
I really don't know much about this; can you fill me in?	Background Literature review (recent literature and prior research) Theory (current and seminal as appropriate) Context (social, cultural, historic and geographic)
How exactly did you go about doing your research?	Research design/approach Methodological approach (framework) Methods (techniques/procedures) Limitations
And what did you find out?	Findings/results/emergent story Text, tables, graphs, charts, themes, quotes, etc. Discussion Analysis, interpretation and meaning of findings
How would you explain the relevance/importance of what you have done?	Conclusion Implications Significance Recommendations (particularly important in applied research)

While this format may not be appropriate for all approaches to research, it is a format that undeniably limits the work readers need to do to make sense of your write-up, and therefore your research – something that should never be underestimated, regardless of whether your goal is examination, publication or broad dissemination. It is also a format that does allow some flexibility. For example, the voice you adopt and the emphasis you place on each section will vary in accordance with the specifics of your projects.

Alternative Academic Formats

Depending on the nature of the paradigm you are working under, your comfort zone, your research topic, your methods and your readers, you might decide that an alternative structure will best get your message across. Alternative structures for writing up your research report can be based on:

- Chronology – Describing how the events within your research project unfolded over time.
- Theory building – Describing how theory was inductively generated and allowing that theory to build throughout your report.
- Findings first – Providing readers with your conclusions up front, and then describing how you got there.

Any one of these formats, a combination of them, or in fact something completely original might be better suited to your project than the traditional structure. But it is crucial that you consider whether your readers will be familiar with and/or accepting of something considered alternative.

There are two cases where the 'risks' of alternative formats are minimized, and perhaps even rewarded. The first is when you are using a format that is accepted as appropriate for your particular paradigmatic, disciplinary or methodological approach; for example, the use of a 'theory-building structure' for studies that have adopted a grounded theory approach, or perhaps a 'chronological structure' for a case study exploring change.

The second is when you know (or can confidently assume) that your readers are likely to be open to a more creative structure. If your write-up is to be assessed, consider whether your examiner(s) are likely to be open to the alternative, having perhaps written, or having had students who have written, in alternative ways. If they are firmly planted in the positivist tradition, you may want to reconsider your approach or, if possible, your examiner. If your goal is to have your research published, the key will be to find a journal for which the alternative is quite standard. Journals from North America and Britain dominate the field, and often only accept publications in English, although there are newer journals that are open to more creative and critical approaches (Trahar et al., 2019). If you decide to buck the system and go with a structure that is new to your readers, you need to take great care that the logic of that structure becomes self-evident as your readers progress through your account. You cannot afford for them to get 'lost' as you take them through your research project. In fact, it is absolutely crucial that your readers do not end up scratching their heads and questioning the credibility of your entire research project just because they are unfamiliar or uncomfortable with the way you have chosen to write it up.

Applied Research Formats

What if your research report is not academic in nature and is going to be a deliverable for an agency, department or business? Well, in this case, you really only have one pressing goal: the uptake of recommendations.

Academic reports sometimes conclude with recommendations, but they are not paramount or even required. In fact, sometimes the only recommendation is to conduct more research. But in an applied research report, recommendations are the end goal. The body of the report can be seen as an extended justification that acts to support the logic and credibility of the recommendations. In fact, sections which are critical in academic outputs (such as the literature review and methods sections) may even be minimal or relegated to the appendix. Table 17.2 summarizes some of the distinctions between academic and applied reports, while Box 17.2 offers tips for writing up an applied report.

Table 17.2 Differences between academic and applied outputs

	Academic Report	**Applied Report**
Summary	Abstract	Executive Summary
Main point	Thesis Argument	Recommendation Action Plans
Purpose	Inform	Persuade
Content	Theory Generation Theory Testing	Problem Solving Action Oriented
Audience	Experts	Generalists
Dissemination	Publishing	Circulation
Readership	Limited	Typically larger (including general public)

Box 17.2

Tips for Writing an Applied Report

1. Read examples of applied reports. Consulting firms such as McKinsey and Co, Deloitte, Boston Consulting Group offer plenty of high-quality examples.
2. Leave enough time for writing up. Reports, while short, still take time to produce.
3. Favour short and punchy sentences over extremely complex sentence structures.
4. Limit theories. Organizations care more about practicalities.
5. Ruthlessly edit for conciseness. A short report is a good report.
6. Make the document easy to read and navigate.
7. Have a colleague or manager review your work.

Of course, there are some deliverables that bridge the gap. Consultancy work is often produced by academic researchers commissioned by government agencies and private industry. These outputs tend to follow a report-based structure, while drawing heavily on academic rigour and research conventions. Other forms of research dissemination such as op-eds or community presentations may take a hybrid form of informing, illuminating and recommending certain courses of action. The best advice here is to be driven by audience consideration. If you have two very distinct audiences, i.e. academics and professionals, you may even want to have two separate deliverables.

So how can you best balance credibility and impact? Consider being:

- Problem-focused – Applied reports tend to centre around problems and explore the dimensions and impact of a particular issue. The scope is limited and practical.
- Analysis-driven – Possible solutions for any given problem are diverse and involve trade-offs. Applied reports analyse different options, taking into account the impact and feasibility of alternative policies by looking at the potential costs, benefits and impacts for different stakeholder groups.
- Evidence-based – To convince decision-makers, ideas must be demonstrably well-founded. Evidence could involve primary data, case comparisons, and/or effects of inactions or policies taken in other contexts/environments on this issue.
- Action-oriented. The goal is to persuade a decision-maker to address a specific issue and implement the recommendation devised. To be practical and actionable, recommendations should also demonstrate contextual awareness, and link to win–win outcomes.

I Have a Question!

Is There a Difference Between an Abstract and an Executive Summary?

Yes there is. An abstract is a brief synopsis (200 words or so) of your report that includes the question, methods and a summary of findings. It is designed to give an overview of the entire research process. The executive summary is designed for a different purpose, the uptake of recommendations, so recommendations take centre stage. The problem situation is linked to the recommendations with just a brief overview of anything else. The executive summary also tends to be longer (500–750 words).

THE WRITING PROCESS

Traditionally, research has been a three-step process: (1) write and submit a research proposal; (2) conduct the research; (3) write up the report. And while fewer and fewer academics advocate this process, it is a process whose legacy seems to linger in the practice of many supervisors and their students. For the inexperienced researcher, however, this can be perilous. For many, 'writing' can be a huge obstacle. If you leave it until the end, you risk writer's block, which can lead to inevitable delays and even put completion at risk.

Writing as You Go

More commonly advised (if not entirely practised) is to approach writing as a process central to every stage of the research journey. Writing should be considered an activity that progresses as your research progresses. For example, if you formulate even your earliest ideas in written form, you will have begun to produce notes for the first draft of your 'introduction' and 'methods'; and annotating your sources can lead to preliminary drafts of your 'literature review'. These sections can then be redrafted as you go through the process of data collection. Similarly, preliminary analysis, note taking and writing throughout data collection will provide you with a good start on 'findings'. Keep in mind that writing actually helps you think through what you're doing and will give you useful insight.

Keep in mind that even if you are a procrastinator and you are not that keen on writing as you go, it is a highly attractive option compared with facing the daunting prospect of having to start your writing from scratch when you complete your data collection and analysis. Writing is a skill; a skill that needs to be practised. The more you write and the sooner you write the easier it will become. We strongly suggest writing as you go and to avoid leaving it all until the very end. If you can force yourself to see writing as part and parcel of the research process rather than just an account of that process, you will never have to face what looks like an insurmountable obstacle.

Writing as Analysis

As well as a head start on report production, 'writing as you go' can actually be part of analysis. Very few people can formulate finalized ideas in their heads without committing them to paper. Ideas almost always evolve as you write, and in this way each draft of your writing will drive the evolution of your ideas. Writing, for example, can be central to the construction and interpretation of meaning. It can move you from the production of specific descriptive understandings, through to broader synthesis, and on to crafting significant, relevant, logical and coherent storylines. In fact, Emma finds writing and rewriting is the key to bringing storylines into focus.

Now while this is true for all types of research (it is virtually impossible to evolve ideas if they stay planted in the realm of the mind), it is particularly relevant to research that sits under post-positivist (subjectivist, interpretivist or constructivist) paradigms that demand iterative engagement with narrative, discourse and/or text. As you work through each draft, understandings evolve and your analysis goes one step deeper.

Constructing Your 'Story'

So why are we using the word 'story'? Well, because good stories grab reader interest, hold that interest, have a strong plot, take readers on a journey and lead them to logical, yet sometimes surprising, conclusions. The other implication of stories is that people simply won't read them if they are boring, tedious, long-winded and pretentious. Your write-up needs to report on your research, but it should do more than that: it should unfold, it should engage and it should tell an interesting story. Now as the author of that 'story', there are a number of things you need to do:

1. Think of your research account as a 'conversation' – we realize conversations are two-way, but you can apply this even in writing. You may not be there to see or hear a response, but you should be trying to engage your readers as if they are listening. In fact, if you can give relevant information, predict questions and respond to them, your writing will become 'interactive'. Remember that readers who feel involved are the most engaged.
2. Become familiar with the craft – Very few authors are not avid readers. One of the most effective things you can do is find 'good' examples of what you intend to write. As you read through your literature, take note of not just content, but also structure and style. Also have a look at theses or reports that have been well received. These examples may not be prototypes, but they can certainly give you some sense of the shape of your end product.
3. Find a voice – There is likely to be a tension between 'engaging storytelling' and 'take-me-seriously reporting'. How to best negotiate this tension will depend on you, your goals and your readers' expectations. The more you know about these elements, the better placed you will be to find an effective voice. Now the general rule of thumb is to avoid use of first person so that your research does not appear to be tainted with personal bias and subjectivities. But even within the positivist paradigm, this convention is relaxing (i.e. using the first person to give personal opinion will not be well received but doing so to report factually on things you did is now more commonly accepted). Objectivity is no longer seen as reliant upon masking a researcher's role. Under post-positivist paradigms, recognition of the researcher role is paramount so there aren't really any hard-and-fast rules against use of the first person. In fact, many 'qualitative' researchers use a highly reflexive first-person voice to outline their personal story, agendas, biases, etc. very early in their report/thesis. This, however, can leave some struggling to negotiate formality, as they move between a relaxed conversation and a logical and comprehensive research account. The key is a confident and consistent style that will be deemed appropriate to your project.
4. Develop your structure – Decide on a structure and work up an appropriate outline for your write-up early on. The more you know about where you want to go, the easier it will be to set a course that can help you get there. Remember that your structure can always be modified as your thinking evolves.
5. Craft the storyline – Whether you opt for a traditional or alternative structure, your report will need to take your readers through a clear, coherent, and hopefully compelling storyline with a beginning, a middle and an end. It needs to engage your readers, pique their interest and take them through your research journey in a way that unfolds the story and logically leads to your conclusion. A good idea is to use Table 17.1 as a checklist that can help you assess if your storyline will logically answer the questions readers are likely to ask. Some good tips for beginning this process include: writing a creative working title; constructing one or more draft outlines; and writing a one-page abstract (a task many researchers find exceptionally difficult, but extremely focusing).
6. Be ready to make convincing arguments – It is essential that you write purposefully. The quality and credibility of your write-up is largely dependent on your ability to construct logical and convincing arguments. Whether we are talking about your study's rationale, a review of the literature or the presentation of methods, findings and conclusions, the process of research demands more than simple summary and reporting. It is a process reliant on the ability of the author to convince, reason and argue a case – as well, of course, as your ability to back up your arguments with appropriate data and references.

7 Write/construct your first draft – You can think about it, and you can keep thinking about it, and you can think about it some more, but it will not happen unless you do it. If you have constructed writing as part of the research process rather than its product, the bones of your first draft will be there for you to put together and flesh out. If, however, you have followed the 'write-up after' approach, you will need to gather your notes and put it all down on paper. Regardless of approach, students generally find they need more time than they initially thought to write up that first draft.
8 Get appropriate feedback – Reader expectations can vary widely, so do not wait until the last minute to find out that your approach is inappropriate. Be sure to pass a draft of your write-up to someone who either has some experience in research or has some insights into reader expectations.
9 Be prepared to redraft – This should be an expectation. In fact, as discussed below, very few people can get away with submitting a second draft or even third draft, let alone a first.

Critical Thinking Challenge 18

Writing as Strategy

In order to write effectively, you need to be strategic.

Think about what you want to achieve through your research report. Is it: a grade, to inform, to influence, to get published, to get into a degree programme? Now think about who you need to reach? Is it a professor, a committee, a board, a community, a manager, an editor?

Once you know the what and the who you can start to think strategically about how; how to structure and how to construct a convincing story so that you can achieve your goal.

DEVELOPING EACH SECTION/CHAPTER

Let's get specific and talk about the writing needs within each section/chapter of your project write-up. Now we have decided to focus on the 'traditional' format, since it is the one most projects will adopt/adapt and the sections within it are likely to show up in some form even if you choose an alternative structure. As for the length of your document – well, regardless of whether the expectation is 20 or 350 pages, the expected sections are basically the same. Obviously, the depth will vary dramatically, but the actual structure and guidelines for effective construction vary very little.

The Front End

In Chapter 5, we went through each section expected in a research proposal. Now when it comes to the front end of your project write-up, you can draw on this work to build various sections expected in your final write-up:

- Title – don't work on this again until you have written up your entire project. At that stage you can take a look at the clear, concise and unambiguous title you constructed for your proposal and see if it still fits or if it can be reworked to better match your project.

- Summary/abstract – Abstracts are so condensed that they are hard to get right. But they are extremely informative to your processes. If you wrote one for your proposal, have a look at it now. If your learning is as rich as it should have been over the course of your research, you are likely to want to do a complete rewrite. There are four key 'moves' you need to make in an abstract: 1) *locate* your work in the bigger picture/problem, 2) *focus* on what part of that problem your research addresses, 3) *report* what you did and found, 4) *argue* why it matters (Kamler and Thomson, 2014). Have a go at this before you write the discussion and conclusion so you can think through your argument. And then go over it again at the very end so that it completely and utterly matches your work from aims and objectives through to methods, findings, discussion and conclusions.
- Research question/hypothesis – Given the emphasis in this book on the importance of a well-defined research question, we are hoping this is something that has been very close to you throughout your research project. Now is your last chance to really nail the articulation of what you attempted to find out.
- Introduction/rationale – If you wrote this up for your proposal, you will now need to revisit, strengthen and expand it. Keep in mind that, as highlighted in Chapter 5, the main job of this section is to introduce your topic and convince readers that the problem you want to address is significant and worth exploring (which is why a few existing statistics related to the extent/depth of the problem can be effective). This section should give some context to the problem (and in a more humanities-oriented write-up even some indication of your relationship to the problem), and lead your readers to a 'therefore' conclusion that sets up your aims and objectives. The trick is to write purposefully.
- Aims/objectives – If you are writing these for the first time, have a look at the advice in Chapter 5. If you have already articulated these, this is your opportunity to make sure you have a good fit between what you set out to do and what you eventually did. You may need to rewrite completely (particularly if your project took a turn in an unexpected direction) or simply refine and tighten.
- Overview of the study – A common convention in a thesis write-up is to give a brief and straightforward overview of each thesis chapter. This is usually done in one or two paragraphs per chapter and can cover not only content, but also purpose and argument. Paragraphs are likely to start with: Chapter One introduces … Chapter Two discusses … The purpose of the chapter is twofold … Chapter Three outlines … The chapter goes on to argue …
- Literature review – Hopefully, you will come to the final write-up stage with a draft literature review in hand. If not, start now! And follow the fairly detailed advice in Chapter 6. If you have a draft, review it, add any new research, and try to find and tighten lines of argument. Remember that the goal here is to review past research in order to show a place for your own research processes. Depending on the nature of your project, as well as covering past research, your literature review may have a section that situates your study in a conceptual or theoretical framework.
- Background – This is a fairly straightforward chapter/section that offers the reader contextual information about your research setting, culture, political arena, etc. For example, if your study were on the threats of tourism to the traditional culture of Palau, you would need to offer your readers context regarding Palau's geography; tourism

potential, history and culture; as well as tourism trends. Remember to include only what a reader needs in order to work through your thesis. If it is not essential, don't include it.

The Research Design Section

The research design section of your thesis is really the crux of your report. It is what defines your project as a true research study. It is how credibility will be judged – both the credibility of your project and your credibility as a social scientist.

- Methodology – Most research design sections of social science and certainly humanities write-ups will demand you engage with methodology, or the overarching framework you have used to situate your study within the paradigm(s) of science. Now this section can be quite theoretical and have you delving into the debates on paradigm outlined in Chapter 1. At this level, methodology situates understandings of truth, objectivity and the construction of knowledge, and the researcher might be integral to the discussion. This is also where you situate your study in terms of 'qualitative' and 'quantitative' approaches such as action research, experimental design and phenomenology.
- Methods – All research design sections include methods, comprising: information on how you found respondents (population and sample/sampling procedures); data-collection methods (e.g. surveying, interviewing and document analysis); and methods of analysis (e.g. statistical or thematic analysis). These sections are relatively straightforward reports of what you did (as compared with your proposal, which is what you were going to do).
- Limitations/delimitations – As discussed in Chapter 5, you will need to clearly articulate all factors that have had an impact on your research processes and results. While it is crucial that you offer full disclosure here, try to avoid being overly apologetic. You need to offer strong justification for what you did and why your data is credible in spite of any constraints.
- Ethical considerations/approval procedures – Finally, you will need to review: all ethical considerations; the processes you adopted in order to ensure the emotional, physical and intellectual well-being of your study participants; and the approval processes you may have gone through. Again this is a relatively straightforward reporting-type section.

The Back End

There are actually three ways you can handle the findings and discussion sections/chapters. The first is to offer one (or more) findings sections followed by one (or more) discussion sections. This means you present all the findings first, with all the discussion to follow. The second approach is thematic organization with findings and discussion related to one particular theme found within one section/chapter. This is repeated for as many strategic themes as you might have. The third approach is again thematic, but with less distinction between findings and discussion. These types of chapters are generally found in more humanities-oriented projects and are highly thematic in their organization.

- Findings – Findings are the presentation of the answers you have found to your key questions. They are not raw data or the full abstraction of your data back to theory. Rather, this is a summative description of data that you find most significant. It is therefore important to resist the temptation to summarize the answer to every question you asked in your research processes. What you need to present is what is most key, interesting, educative, informative and which best makes the case regarding your research question/hypothesis. But avoid doing too much with this information. Abstraction generally waits until the discussion section. The presentation of quantitative and qualitative data is covered in Chapters 15 and 16, respectively.
- Discussion – This is where you get to make something of your data. The structure here is almost always thematic and tied to the storylines that have emerged from your data. It is your opportunity to take what you discovered in your findings and argue their implications and significance. So while the findings section may be fairly straightforward reporting, the discussion section/chapter is made up of purposeful arguments – arguments that emerge from your findings and show that you have met your aims and objectives. To do this well, you are likely to find yourself working iteratively with both your data and the literature. In the case of qualitative data, the discussion section is often combined with findings.
- Conclusion – Drawing conclusions is all about clearly summarizing what your research processes have revealed and linking this back to your project's main questions, aims and objectives in the most compelling and credible way. This is generally a tight section/chapter (and should be, given the work your 'discussion' has done). You do not tend to introduce new material in the conclusion other than the possibility of an original framework or model. This would be appropriate if you've begun to conceptualize a bigger picture in a fairly sophisticated manner.
- Recommendations – In social science research, recommendations are often limited to 'recommendations for future research' – made on the basis of need for further verification due to the limitations and delimitations of the study; the next logical step in understanding an issue; or the identification of an existing gap in the literature. Such recommendations are generally included in the conclusion. In applied science research, however, recommendations are an essential part of the back end of a report and often warrant their own section. Such recommendations should be clearly linked to findings; highly applied; and practicable. Consider grouping these by ease of implementation in terms of timeframe, cost, difficulty and stakeholder involvement.
- References – Perfection! Nothing less is expected or accepted. Take the time to do this right – it's a good time to be anal.

FROM FIRST TO FINAL DRAFT

You don't start out writing good stuff. You start out writing crap and thinking it's good stuff, and then gradually you get better at it.

Octavia E. Butler (2000)

Whether you decide to write in a way that is formal or casual, traditional or alternative, dry or emotive, there is a common denominator. Regardless of format, style or voice, your final work needs to be highly polished and unarguably professional – you cannot afford to come across as an amateur. Your authority can be enhanced or destroyed not only by the quality of your research, but also by its presentation. And we honestly do not know anyone who can accomplish this without working through a number of drafts. Bottom line? Be ready (1) to seek and take advice and (2) to draft, redraft and redraft again.

Seeking and Using Feedback

There really is no way around it. If you want to move from a first to a final draft, you need to take the sometimes uncomfortable step of seeking quality feedback. Now you might think this would be a straightforward process, but that is not always the case. A PhD candidate of Zina's, for example, once submitted a preliminary draft of a chapter to a co-supervisor for comment. After a nervous wait of over two months, we found that the eventuating comments were all related to minor editing – spelling, grammar and even proper margins for quotes. And while that might be really helpful for a final draft, it was completely useless at the first-draft stage where ideas, concepts and logic were the things that needed to be reviewed.

This really brings home the need to ask the right people for advice, and to be specific in your requests. You need to know where you are in the process and to ask for comments related to your current needs. A good strategy here is to ask your readers to comment on the same questions you need to ask yourself as you work through various drafts of your document (see questions in the next section). If it is a first draft, you will probably want advice on overall ideas, arguments, logic and structure, while later stages will see you seeking suggestions for consistency, coherence, readability and, finally, copy-editing.

This means that you may not always go to the same person for advice. One professor Zina works with, for example, is excellent at broadening ideas, but is extremely sloppy. He could edit a children's picture book. Others will be great at the nitty-gritty detail but will not be able to engage with the bigger picture. Now while the advice of your supervisor(s) can be invaluable, so too can the advice of colleagues, peers and family. In fact, at some stage, it is worth asking a non-specialist to read your work to see if the logic makes sense to them – because it should. And don't forget to try to get a sense of timeframe. It can take some readers months to get back to you.

Now knowing who to ask and what to ask is one thing but being willing to hand over what you have written is another. What if your secret fears of not being good enough are validated? Handing over is always exposing, but keep in mind that fears of incompetence are often a crisis of confidence – not a lack of ability. And besides, it is better to find out if you are off track early than wait until you have invested a huge amount of time in an iffy direction. Many of Emma's students struggle with the desire to wait until the draft is 'perfect' before they give it to her to read. Not only is perfect a myth (all writing can always be made better), this anxiety often means you delay getting feedback that's essential to know if you are on the right track. Spending weeks rewriting a paragraph only to have your supervisor tell you to cut it is not the most efficient use of time!

OK, suppose you have managed to ask the right person the right questions and you get your draft back. If you are lucky, it is full of constructive, relevant and thought-provoking comments.

You should be happy – not only has someone put in a lot of time and effort, but they have provided you with a road map for moving forward. But, of course, you're human. So instead of being happy, you are devastated. In fact, you may feel insulted, frustrated and even incompetent. You are not alone here. Although what we want might be praise, what we really need – like it or not – is criticality. Validation simply doesn't move you forward. You need to accept advice and not take criticism personally. If you do, writing up will become an emotional minefield.

So now that you have the advice, what do you do with it? Well, unreflexive incorporation is just as bad as blanket dismissal. You need to mentally take the feedback on board, consider it in light of the source and work through the implications that the advice has for what you are trying to say. And, of course, this is particularly important if you find yourself getting conflicting advice. Talk to your supervisor/lecturer, but remember that it is your work, and you are the one who must make the final call.

Drafting and Redrafting

There is no doubt that the journey from first draft to submission can be long and challenging. In fact, contrary to the desire of just about every fibre in your body, you may find that your final document does not retain much from that first draft. The irony, of course, is that you could not get to that final draft without that first draft and all the drafts in between.

Now as you work through various drafts, you will be tightening up different aspects of your writing (see Box 17.3). But you can approach this in any number of ways. Some like to work sentence by sentence in a slow and diligent fashion, while others do not want to break a stream of consciousness – they try to get new ideas down on paper all at once, to be cleaned up later on. As long as you find a process that works for you, there is nothing wrong with developing your own approach. It is the end result that counts.

Box 17.3 offers a number of checklists for helping you get to a quality end product. While it may seem somewhat tedious, almost all good writers do go through some variation of this process.

Box 17.3

Checklists for the Redrafting Process

Reworking the First Draft

It would be nice if your first draft were it. But it rarely works that way. When you step back and take stock, you are likely to find that the process of writing itself has evolved your ideas, and that your thoughts have moved beyond what you initially managed to capture on paper. As you work through your first draft ask yourself:

- Is this making sense? Does the logic flow? Do I need to alter the structure?
- Am I using a 'voice' I am comfortable with?
- Do I need to incorporate more material/ideas – or are sections really repetitive?

(Continued)

- Am I happy with my overall argument, and is it coming through?
- Does each chapter or section have a clear and obvious point or argument?
- Have I sought and responded to feedback?

Reworking the Second Draft

Once you are happy with the overall ideas, arguments, logic and structure, it is time to fine-tune your arguments and strive for coherence and consistency. In doing this, ask yourself:

- How can I make my points and arguments clearer? Do I 'waffle on' at any point? Am I using lots of jargon and acronyms? Should I incorporate some/more examples?
- Do I want to include some/more diagrams, photos, maps, etc.?
- Is the structure coherent? Are there clear and logical links between chapters/sections?
- Is there consistency within and between chapters/sections? Do I appear to contradict myself at any point? Is my voice used consistently throughout the work?
- Is the length on target?
- Have I sought and responded to feedback?

Moving Towards the Penultimate Draft

Being ready to move towards a penultimate draft implies that you are reasonably happy with the construction and logic of the arguments running through your document. Attention can now be turned to fluency, clarity and overall readability. Ask yourself:

- Are there ways I can further increase clarity? Are my terms used consistently? Have I got rid of unnecessary jargon?
- Are there ways I can make this read more fluently? Can I break up my longer sentences? Can I rework my one-sentence paragraphs?
- Are there ways I can make this more engaging? Can I limit the use of the passive voice? Do I come across as apologetic? Are my arguments strong and convincing?
- Am I sure I have protected the confidentiality of my respondents/participants?
- Have I guarded against any potential accusations of plagiarism? Have I checked and double-checked my sources, both in the text and in the references or bibliography?
- Have I written and edited any preliminary and end pages, namely title page, table of contents, list of figures, acknowledgements, abstract, preface, appendices and references?
- Have I thoroughly checked my spelling and grammar?
- Have I done a word count?
- Have I sought and responded to feedback?

Producing the Final Draft

You would think that if you did all the above, your final document would be done. Not quite; you now need to do a final edit. If it is a large work and you can fund it, you might want to consider using a copy-editor. It is amazing what editorial slip-ups someone with specialist skills can find, even after you have combed through your own work a dozen times. Some things you may want to ask prior to submission are:

- Have I looked for typos of all sorts?
- Have I triple-checked spelling (especially those things that spell checkers cannot pick

up, like typing 'form' instead of 'from')?

- Have I checked my line spacing, fonts, margins, etc.?
- Have I numbered all pages, including preliminary and end pages, sequentially? Have I made sure they are all in the proper order?
- Have I checked through the final document to make sure there were no printing glitches?

Box 17.4

Zina's Tips on Writing

I like the way you write – it sounds easy and natural. I'm just not a good writer. Any tips?

Yep, what I write may sound easy and natural by the time it gets to you, but that is not how it starts out. Each chapter takes about four or five attempts just to find a start I am happy with (and that's just the first couple of paragraphs). Once I am comfortable with the start, I rewrite it sentence by sentence until I feel like it is pretty good. Only then do I move on to the next section. The next time I sit down to write, I reread that first bit and work through it a couple more times. Only at this stage do I feel like it is beginning to sound easy and natural, so I move on. This painstakingly slow process is repeated throughout the entire chapter until I get through it all. When a full draft of the chapter is finished, I review it again, make more modifications, and, when happy, give it to a reader who is tough, but whose opinion I respect. Undoubtedly, they will have comments, and I will take them into consideration and modify the text as I see fit. Now when the entire book is complete, I will look at all the chapters in context to make sure the whole thing nests together well. Again, more modification is guaranteed. I will then do a copy-edit and send it off to my publisher. Done? Not quite ... from there editors will help me with more reviews (and possible modifications), professional copy-editing, layout and design, and final proofing – and this is what you will eventually see. Tips?! Tenacity and drafts, and more tenacity and more drafts!

Chapter Summary

- Because your write-up is a considerable piece of work with major consequences attached to its quality, writing can be intimidating. There are, however, practical strategies that can improve the quality of your work and make the task less daunting.
- To write effectively you need to know your audience. Good writing evokes a conversation with the reader. Readers need to be engaged, and the best way to do that is to know their demographics and understand their agendas.
- Effective report writing will require you to decide on structure, craft a compelling storyline, and write purposively. Work towards your report being logical, concise and compelling.
- You won't be able to avoid the need to draft, redraft and redraft again.

The goals of logical, concise and compelling will demand it.

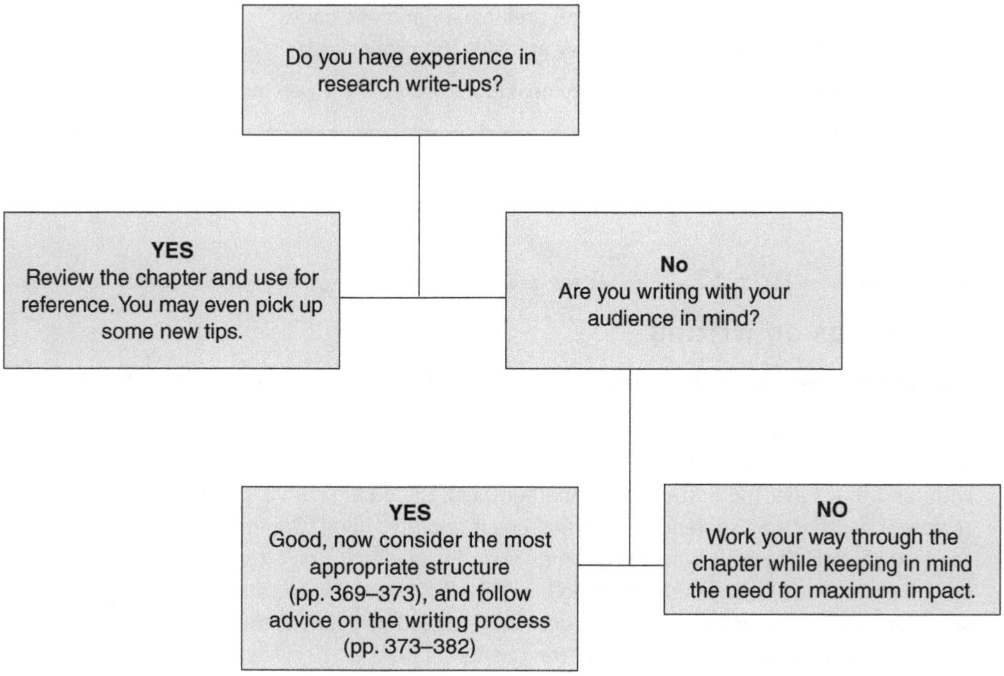

FIND YOUR NEXT STEP

FURTHER READING

There are three types of reading we would recommend to those in the final stages of writing up a project. The first is the internal documents produced by your university. Subject/course outlines, style guides and manuals produced by and for your institution or programme will not only provide you with hard and fast criteria, but also likely steer you in directions that meet with more general expectations. The second is readings that act as examples. If you know what 'product' you are trying to produce, finding a few effective examples can offer a world of learning. Finally, the third type of reading (recommendations below) is related to managing the actual writing process.

Hammond, M. (2022). *Writing a Postgraduate Thesis or Dissertation: Tools for Success*. Routledge

Study Skills Series. Abingdon: Routledge.
Peeling back the layers on the *process* of writing, this book focuses on what different sections of the thesis/dissertation are trying to achieve.

Sundström, M. (2020) *How Not to Write a Thesis or Dissertation: A Guide to Success through Failure.* Cheltenham: Edward Elgar.
Funny, witty and accessible, this book will have you chuckling as well as taking away some helpful ideas.

Booth, W. C., Colomb, G. C. and Williams, J. M. (2016) *The Craft of Research.* Chicago: University of Chicago Press.
A bestseller with clear guidance on good writing. Terrific for clarifying how building a strong argument helps readers accept your claims. Get a copy of this.

Holliday, A. (2016) *Doing and Writing Qualitative Research.* London: Sage.
This book will take you through the conceptualization process associated with doing a thesis, but from the perspective of writing. This is particularly important in qualitative research, where writing itself can act as analysis.

Joyner, R. L., Rouse, W. A. and Glatthorn, A. A. (2018) *Writing the Winning Thesis or Dissertation: A Step-by-Step Guide.* Thousand Oaks, CA: Corwin Press.
We think this book will help take away some of the anxiety that tends to accompany a major thesis write-up. This book is step-by-step and practical. It should help you see some light at the end of the tunnel.

Pyrczak, F. and Bruce, R. R. (2014) *Writing Empirical Research Reports: A Basic Guide for Students of the Social and Behavioral Sciences.* Glendale, CA: Pyrczak.
We like the simple, straightforward guidelines that are offered here. It outlines each expected section of an empirical report and helps you structure needed arguments. It will give you a handle on required structure.

Wolcott, H. F. (2009) *Writing Up Qualitative Research.* London: Sage.
Qualitative report writing is an art in itself. This book is highly accessible and user-friendly. The grounded examples will give you plenty of ideas for best presenting qualitative work.

Sword, H. (2023). *Writing with Pleasure.* Princeton, NJ: Princeton University Press.
For too many people, writing (particularly academic writing) can be dry, stressful, and dull. Based on her own research with hundreds of writers, Helen Sword offers inspiration and practical tips to help you find the joy in writing.

18

FINAL HURDLES

Learning Objectives

- To appreciate the need for your work to have exposure
- To understand the importance of dissemination planning
- The secret to presenting with impact
- To understand the key steps and elements in a persuasive presentation
- To understand the importance of targeting your audience
- To appreciate the importance of bringing your best self to your presentation
- Transitioning from student to professional
- To accept and appreciate the value of networking
- To understand how you can leverage research skills in the job market

DISSEMINATING YOUR RESEARCH

> It is of great importance that the general public be given the opportunity to experience, consciously and intelligently, the efforts and results of scientific research. Restricting the body of knowledge to a small group deadens the philosophical spirit of a people and leads to spiritual poverty.
>
> Albert Einstein (1948)

A tremendous amount of effort goes into the conduct of rigorous and credible research. So the last thing you want to do is go through the whole research process and not capitalize on your achievements. But this can actually be the rule rather than the exception. An unbelievable amount of research ends up as nothing more than a thesis/report sitting somewhere on a shelf. True, as a student researcher your immediate goal may be a grade or even a degree, but do not forget that the ultimate goal of research is to contribute to a body of knowledge, and your findings cannot add to a body of knowledge if they are not disseminated. For too long, academia has been an 'ivory tower' that few people have access to. However, there are increasing expectations that researchers take active steps to transfer knowledge (to participants, communities, and beyond) so that research can have real-world impact. Unfortunately, conducting a research project, even if it is done well, in no way assures wide dissemination. Take, for example, the PhD thesis, probably the most prestigious piece of academic research writing there is. Sadly, it can also be the most poorly disseminated. Most theses are read by the author, a reviewer or editor, the supervisor or supervisory panel and examiners. At the high end, that is about seven or eight people – not a lot of dissemination for a work that usually takes more than three or four years. Now this does not mean that research dissemination will not happen, but it does remind us that we need to take defined steps to facilitate it. Sure, by the time you finish up your research project, you may just be feeling over it. But fight that feeling. It is worth sharing what you've found.

Dissemination Planning

If you want something to happen, it is worth having a plan. When it comes to dissemination, this means thinking about your:

- Objective – This is what you want the dissemination of your report to achieve, i.e. to raise awareness, improve understanding, engage others, change practice, promote yourself. Setting your objective is a first step in deciding on audience, messaging, format, timing and channels for dissemination.
- Audience – Work out who your various audience groups might be. This can include stakeholders. Try to keep this group in the loop throughout your project, so they are waiting for your results. Audience may also include secondary groups that might benefit from using your research. Think about where this group looks for and receives information. Don't forget to disseminate to research participants who fed into your project; they have a vested interest. Also think about anyone who might be able to amplify your message and act as catalysts for dissemination.
- Messaging – This is what you will share in order to meet your objective. It is good practice to keep messaging clear, factual, simple and easy to understand. Language and tone should be appropriate for the target audience, generally non-technical and jargon-free. Messages should also be tailored to the audience and relevant to the receiver. The best messages are also actionable: the audience, if interested, should know next steps.
- Format – Deliverables should be appropriate to the audience. You are not limited to a report here, you may also deliver an action plan, a pamphlet, a video piece, a web page or anything else that might best deliver your message.
- Timing – Generally, we wait until research is complete, but you might want to share preliminary findings. You can also think about critical time points, the agenda and timeline of the target audience, outside influences and upcoming opportunities, e.g. a conference.
- Resources – Do you need to bring in some help? Your supervisor and others in your department, as well as other stakeholders, may have dissemination ideas you haven't considered.
- Channels – Think about a broad array of options here and which are most likely to find your target audience. Options include: presentations, blogs, posts, podcasts, social media, press releases, websites, conferences, newspapers, TV and radio broadcasts, workshops, newsletters, flyers and electronic databases such as: Academia.edu, ResearchGate.net, Figshare.com, ProQuest.com and journals (see Box 18.1 for more on academic publishing).

We want to take a minute to dive a bit deeper into conferences. They are, after all, a crucial stepping-stone for many in the move from student to professional. There are three good reasons for attending conferences. The first is to expose yourself to an incredible array of cutting-edge research and researchers in your field. Not only do you get to hear about their work, you get to converse and chat about what they/you are doing. The web has really made the search for relevant conferences quite easy. You are likely to be amazed at the depth and breadth of topics being discussed and researched. The second reason is to network. Whether you plan to pursue a job or a higher degree, knowing who's out there and having an opportunity to meet them can be invaluable to your future. The third reason is that they can be a good time. Making and catching up with friends; exploring new regions of the state, country or world; getting away – when you put it all together, it is an experience not to be missed.

Box 18.1

Academic Publishing

If you have undertaken a major project and you aspire to an academic career, you might want to (should) consider publishing. In fact, if you are pursuing a PhD, it is worth publishing as you go. You know what they say ... 'publish or perish'. You won't get far if you don't keep up with the journal publication train.

The ultimate in publication is a single-authored work in an international refereed journal. And this is a worthwhile goal. But it is one that can be quite difficult to achieve for the inexperienced researcher. An option here is co-authorship (often with a supervisor), which can give you expert advice and put more weight behind your submission. Be sure to openly discuss issues of primary authorship.

Many of the writing tips from the previous chapter apply, but you will probably need to condense, and sometimes drastically. The key here is to preserve logic – arguments need to be front and centre.

When it comes time to get published, some good tips are to:

1. Find academic journals directly suited to your area of expertise – Most journals describe their focus and scope on their website. The closer your work is to their core agenda, the better the likelihood of acceptance.
2. Review submission guidelines and stick to them – This means modifying your article so that it pedantically follows required formatting, word length and referencing system.
3. Write a professional cover letter that includes all relevant information, including contact details.
4. Share how your contribution sits within the wider scholarly landscape.
5. If you are asked to recommend reviewers, do not pass on this. Take up the opportunity. Your supervisor is likely to be a good source for contacts here.
6. Breathe deeply when your reviews come in – If you feel gutted, step away and reread later. We guarantee that it's not as bad as you thought on first read.
7. Revise and respond to reviewers' points when you resubmit – If you are rejected, see it as an opportunity to get more feedback, rewrite and try again. The 'revise and resubmit' is one of the most common verdicts so you are not alone in this.

THE SECRET TO PRESENTING WITH IMPACT

Do you need to present your research? Should you present your research? Do you want to present your research? Well in our experience, the answers are: maybe, yes and, ah, no.

You may be required to present your research as part of a unit or degree requirements. You may even need to do an oral defence (an oral examination in which you will be required to defend your thesis to an audience of experts). As far as whether you should present, well, we're going with yes for a few reasons: to get you/your work exposed to academia (think conference); to get you/your work exposed to a community (think presentation to an agency, department, local community, company); and to get experience in presenting. Presentations can be made:

- Within the university system – It can be within a class, as part of a seminar series or as part of a postgraduate group.
- At conferences – Conference presentations can give you and your work a heightened profile. Not only do they allow you to disseminate your work, but they also give you experience and confidence in this type of forum, help you generate new research ideas and, of course, allow you even more opportunities when it comes to networking.
- To various stakeholder groups – If your study is relevant to a community group, local government authority or particular workplace, it is well worth sharing your findings. As well as getting your research out there, networking is again a bonus.

The most common format is 'the talk' or spoken presentation, but academic posters that visually present your research are also common at conferences and research showcases. The challenge here is to visually present your research in a clear and compelling way. You may have a chance to stand alongside your poster and discuss, but this is primarily an exercise in visual communication. Check out the open source #betterposter templates online for some inspiration (or see Hall, 2020).

We do recognize that as far as wanting to present, many of you would rather face a rabid dog, but we're here to tell you it is worth it. Think of it as a bridge that you need to traverse on the way from student to professional. And the more practice you get, the more comfortable you will become with one of the realities of most professions: the dreaded presentation. So let's get to it.

Presenting for Impact and Influence

It may be tempting to prepare your presentation by plopping the main points of your research report straight into a PowerPoint and then reading through these points one by one. But, please, just say no. Jam-packing as much of your study as you can into a seemingly unending series of slides will cause your audience a great deal of unnecessary pain. They tune out, nothing is heard and you lose the opportunity to make an impact. Trust us, you can do better than this.

Dry, tedious, uninspired presentations need not be the norm. After all, we all know outstanding presentations when we hear them. We need to emulate these presenters. Research presentations are about sharing information for a purpose. So, there is a need to drive your presentation and motivate your audience to action. Sure, you can tell your audience what you did and what you found. But if you expect them to be inherently interested in you and your work, you're likely to be disappointed. You need to do the work to motivate an audience, to involve them, to influence them. This is the true value of presenting – to influence others. Telling is level one, getting them to know something is level two and getting them to do something is level three.

Now if you accept this premise, the standard process for developing a presentation falls short (see Box 18.2). When you are attempting to motivate an audience to action, you need to rethink what you know about presenting.

Box 18.2

Presenting: From Old and Tired to New and Improved

The standard process for developing a presentation:

Step 1: Figure out what your main point is, e.g. the message that you want to get across.

Step 2: Decide on supporting points that will assist you in delivering that main message.

Step 3: Gather research that will help you develop those supporting points.

Step 4: Write a talk based on the above and transpose key points to PowerPoint or go straight to PowerPoint, capturing all the key bits of information/data.

Step 5: Support your presentation with graphs, charts and graphics.

Step 6: Revise until you think you have something logical.

Step 7: Get out your stopwatch and practise until you sound professional within your allotted time.

Just say no. Whether explicit or implicit, this is the process we tend to turn to - it's what we've been taught. It's our go-to at university. It's the norm. But is it effective?

Well, if the goal of your presentation is to simply impart information, then this might suffice. But we would argue that when you are presenting research, you should be doing much more than delivering information. You should be working in the arena of influence, so we need to shelve these old school ideas and try the new seven!

The new steps! (steps that keep the audience at the fore):

Step 1: Decide on your audience-related objective. This is what you want your audience to do, feel or think differently about based on your presentation.

Step 2: Find out what you can about the audience (if you're trying to convince your audience of something, you need to know who they are and where they are in relation to your agenda).

Step 3: Decide on the messages that will help you move your audience from where they are to where you want them to be.

Step 4: Consider all the strategies and media that will help along this journey (data images, graphics, videos, stories, etc.).

Step 5: Develop your presentation. In a research context, this is likely to be PowerPoint but there are also other good options like Prezi, Google Slides and Canva.

Step 6: Consider how you will present yourself. When you're after influence, your presentation becomes as much about you and your ability to persuade as it does about the particulars of the message.

Step 7: Practise. But rather than practise speaking, practise talking, conversing, convincing, all while being your most relatable self.

A Shift in Focus

Rather than telling your audience about your research, a much more strategic goal is to motivate them to do something because of your research. It is this seemingly small, yet critical, shift that will lead your presentation down a completely different path. You will automatically (and quite intuitively) move towards best practice. For example, most of us know that best practice involves things like not having too many words on a slide, not having too many slides, making good eye contact, having good vocal performance and being passionate. But when you are giving out information – this is not intuitive. We tend to dispassionately read and/or memorize; it actually makes sense for the task. Now think about being influential. Best practice makes sense!

And don't fall into the trap of thinking that you will sound knowledgeable if you cram as much as is humanly possible into a 10-minute presentation and rush through it all without showing any personality. That's not how it works. A powerful presentation is not about showing people how much you know, it's about what your audience walks away with.

Without a doubt, you need to know your stuff. You shouldn't be presenting if you don't know what you are talking about. Knowledge gives you credibility and confidence. But ... here is the kicker ... you do not need to tell them everything you know! Let your knowledge show through your ability to extract essential, compelling elements. Let it show through your confidence. Let it show through your ability to strategically engage and motivate.

The Importance of Audience

Just as they are important in writing up, knowing and engaging your audience are key to successful presentations. You need to think about what you want from your audience, based on your presentation. This should be more than your audience knowing the ins and outs of your research. Consider whether you want your audience to be motivated, give you a great grade, hire you, uptake recommendations or be a change agent. If you can articulate this type of audience-related goal, it will absolutely impact on how you structure and deliver your presentation. You have no choice but to go from reporting to motivating; to getting your audience from point A to point B.

Speaking of point A, have you ever heard the saying 'You need to start where people are'? Well, it's a truism. Hitting the mark of where your audience is puts you in a position to move them to where you want them to go. So, as with writing up, think about the audience. Who are they? What interests them? Why are they there?

Remember, a single audience can be diverse. The key is still getting a sense of that audience. You may decide to direct your pitch to a particular segment of your audience. This is often the case for student presentations. Peers, who have a certain set of expectations, might make up the bulk of the audience; but you may want to direct your presentation to assessors – which makes sense. Keep in mind, however, that even in this situation, engaging the main audience is important, and can be quite impressive to assessors.

Elements of Best Practice

So, let's say you are with us and you want to motivate your audience to action. What do you need to do? Well it's not hit them with 103 densely worded slides delivered in a monotone voice. PowerPoint is just a tool. You, the presenter, need to be the star of the show. Think of your slides as notes that keep you on-message. They are not a substitute for your persuasion, insights and adaptability.

Second, less is more when it comes to the number of slides. Some speakers appear to be in competition for how many slides they can squeeze in before the buzzer (or people fall asleep/leave). Don't let this be you. Craft a few polished slides and spend time on and between each one. A good rule of thumb is to use no more than one or two slides per minute. This means that a 15-minute presentation should have no more than 15 slides. And don't try to cram in everything – your font needs to be legible from a distance. In fact, limiting words on your slide is a good idea. Compelling images are much more effective in a bid to be persuasive.

So that is what not to do. Here are some things you should be doing:

Storytelling

Without a doubt, the best presenters know how to tell a story. They tell a tale, they build anticipation, they shoot for 'a-ha' moments, they use anecdotes and they are not afraid of weaving in appropriate bits of emotion. Story does not have to be intimidating. Start by mapping out an overall journey. Try starting at the end point. This is where you want your audience to be when you're done. Then go back to the start. This is where they are now. Now think of three main points: (1) what can I say to hook them in – to get them listening? (2) what can I say to start bringing them along? (3) what can I say to seal the deal?

Sharing Anecdotes

You might be surprised to know that one of the biggest commonalities across great speakers is their use of anecdotes. This is because anecdotes draw the listener in. They create connection and relatability, and they lessen the distance between the speaker and the audience. Now some may say that anecdotes are not right for research presentations, but they are. They tell the audience how you became interested in your topic; the biggest challenge you faced; how you came across that great insight. True, it may not be standard practice at a conference – but it is best practice. We need to up our presentation game.

Offering Compelling Data

Story should be your overarching framework, but data rules, especially in a research presentation. Use your data to drive interest, not just impart information. Yes, information is critical but unless you are strategic with it, data as information will not only fail to engage, it can actually disengage an audience. Your data needs to do work. So think about using your data purposively. In fact, don't think of it as just data, think about your data as a tool that can drive engagement and drive change.

Using Audio-Visual Aids Strategically

Your audio-visual aids should support you, not replace you. Use slides strategically and think about incorporating video as well. It's also important to consider the accessibility of your slides. If you use Microsoft, there are built-in features under the Accessibility Checker, while considering basic elements of slide design and colour contrast are good places to start. Also think about animating yourself – move around and keep the focus on you, not your slides. Hiding behind a podium makes you nothing more than a talking head.

Showing Passion

The best way to convince someone of something is to be genuine. Share your passion, share your conviction, share your excitement. In short, share your belief. Make sure those you want to influence know why this is something worth acting upon.

Here are two truisms:

> You cannot expect people to care about your topic more than they perceive you to care. You need to take the lead.
>
> When you are in the business of influence, you want people to follow. This makes your perceived ability to lead as, or more important, than the message.

Using Vocal Performance

Be sure to use the full capacity of your voice. It is an instrument that can show passion and emotion. It cues your audience into how they should feel. In fact, it is the soundtrack to your presentation. So, vary your pace, tone, pitch, cadence and volume – good vocal performance is engaging!

Competently Answering Audience Questions

It is important to recognize that questioning is not often an adversarial process. Rather, a question is a continuation of a conversation. Be happy that your audience is interested enough to want to continue the dialogue. The worst-case scenario is not a room full of questions, but a room full of silence. Questions typically fall into four categories:

1. Clarification – What year are those data from? Does your recommendation require any ongoing costs? These can often be met with a quick piece of data and a credible source.
2. Analysis – How did you decide between the alternative recommendations? How do we know the problem of x is caused by z? These often require a longer response that shows your true engagement with the project.
3. Gaps – Did you consider x? I would have considered x, you should consider x. These questions/comments tend to arise from genuine interest (and sometimes a need to look intelligent). We'd suggest answering these honestly and openly.
4. Hostility – You'll be happy to know that hostile questions are actually quite rare. Brush these off as well as you can and move on. Remember these types of questions are a reflection of the asker (even to those in the audience), so don't take it personally and try not to let them get to you.

The Importance of You

Here's a fact. People are motivated by people. We tend to forget this and think that people are motivated by ideas. But it is people who are influential. It is people who motivate. It is people who inspire an audience to action. It's a speaker's passion, their conviction, their humour, their warmth, etc. that is remembered. And that means you count. Your presentation needs to have your stamp on it, you need to 'show up'.

But what if you are a nervous presenter and you think: 'It's just not me', 'I can't do it', 'I'm too nervous', 'I'm too shy', 'I'm an introvert', 'I freak out', 'I will never be a confident presenter.'

Well, trust us, it can get better. Here is what we know about great presenters. They tend to be gregarious, sharp, extroverted, passionate and funny. Does that sound like you? If so, great. You have a good head start at being an awesome presenter. If not, that's okay. It doesn't sound like most of the students we work with either. So, what do you do? Should you try to become an extrovert, tell endless jokes? No. If you try to be outgoing and you are naturally shy, you'll just get more nervous. If you tell jokes and it's not something you are comfortable with, you will flop.

But here is something else we know about great presenters. There are plenty who do not match the gregarious, sharp, extroverted, passionate and funny profile. So, what exactly is it about them that makes them influential/inspirational?

It is simply that they bring their best forward, no matter what their best is. If they are naturally sincere, they show their sincerity. If they are care a lot, they show that they are caring. Wise, then they show their wisdom. Empathetic, then they show that. No matter what it is, they allow their best to shine through.

So, what is your best-self characteristic? Think about what your best friend, your partner or your parents would say is your best quality. What is the thing they appreciate most when they talk one-on-one with you? Would they say you are you authoritative, sincere, sarcastic, warm, erudite, passionate, trustworthy, friendly, happy?

Once you identify this characteristic, you need to trust; trust that this part of yourself is what you need to be an influential presenter. Challenge yourself to present in such a way that your audience can see this quality reflected in the presentation. Lead with it. Why lead with nerves, when you have so much more to offer?

Don't be afraid to be the centre of your show. Don't let your audio-visuals overwhelm you. You do not want to be a talking head behind a podium. Step out, step up. Draw focus to yourself and hold your audience's attention. You, showing and sharing your best self, should always hold an audience's attention better than a set of PowerPoint slides. The TED Talks offered in Box 18.3 are well worth a look – pay attention to style and try to identify what makes these presenters so compelling.

Box 18.3

Great TED Talks (www.ted.com)

Catherine Price (2022) 'Why having fun is the secret to a healthier life'

Luis von Ahn (2023) 'How to make learning as addictive as social media'

Julia Dhar (2021) 'How to have constructive conversations'

Amy Cuddy (2012) 'Your body language may shape who you are'

Susan Cain (2012) 'The power of introverts'

William Stephen (2015) 'A talk about nothing'

Hans Rosling (2006) 'The best stats you've ever seen'

Julian Treasure (2014) 'How to speak so that people will want to listen'

Mat Walk (2019) 'Sleep is your superpower'

I Have a Question!

I Get Super-Anxious When I Have to Give a Presentation. Any Ideas for Overcoming This?

One strategy that we find really works well for students is the Q&A approach. Nervous presenters are almost always better at Q&A than they are in their main presentation. They relax and talk much more confidently about what they know ... rather than what they rehearsed. If this sounds like you, take advantage of it. Structure your slides as if they were Q&A. Try labelling each slide with a question and offer just a few dot points of things that you want to cover or maybe a visual that will answer that question. And then talk. So instead of heading your slide 'Rationale', head it 'Why is this research question significant?'; instead of 'Method', head it 'How did I collect my data?' Then answer the question as you would if someone asked you it while you were having dinner together. You know the information, so try changing the context in your head! You may revert to more traditional headings in your final draft - but the idea of simply answering questions in a logical order should make it much less anxiety-producing.

TRANSITIONING FROM STUDENT TO PROFESSIONAL

Next steps are not easy ... particularly if it involves the move from student to professional, but we bet you are further along than you might realize. The conduct of research develops a bevy of skills that you can leverage in your hunt for the perfect job. You just need to pull it together in a way that highlights your assets and sells you as a stellar potential hire. Some strategies for doing this include becoming a consummate networker and being able to leverage your research skills in the job market.

Networking

Networking, put simply, is making connections with others within your school, your organization, the industry and beyond. The term networking can sound a little off-putting and corporate, but this is about building relationships. It's something that can be invaluable to your career path, and it's something that you can't start too early. Many research students, however, are too buried in their project to even realize that they need to be making inroads. Others know they need to do this but aren't sure how to make connections. Graduation rolls around and they do not have a professional network or plan for career advancement.

So, take the time to do this. Networking is incredibly important in getting a job. Competition can be immense and knowing someone on the inside can be indispensable. You can get the ball rolling by:

- Recognizing that networking is not just about what you can get but equally about what you can give. This means you need to think about what you can offer, even if it's just your respect and admiration.

- Learning to recognize and take advantage of opportunities. This can happen before, during and after things like meetings, conference proceedings, dinners and events. Be willing and ready to introduce yourself to people. Also, join the alumni networks available to you. These can be an amazing resource in both the short and long term.
- Be ready to tell people a bit about yourself; even more importantly, give them the opportunity to talk about themselves. That's what people enjoy! Ask them how they got where they are in their professional lives. It's a little old school, but consider having a business card you can exchange. If the conversation is going well, you may even ask them if they have an interest in being your mentor.
- Follow up and stay engaged! A quick message on LinkedIn or an email is worth sending. You can also use LinkedIn to grow your network. It's well worth building a profile and joining in/contributing to relevant discussion groups.

Critical Thinking Challenge 19

What Energy Are You Radiating?

Zina used to run the internship programme at the Sydney University Business School and one of the things she was asked by students was, 'How can you become that person who others want to help?'

Sure, as students it is easy to have 'resting apathy face', but when you are trying to connect and network, you really need to be putting out good energy at every turn. So ask yourself, 'What message am I giving off when I speak; when I am at my desk; when I am getting lunch; when I meet new people?' Are you that person that others want to see succeed? Are you generous with your positive energy? Radiating positive energy can get you further than you might ever imagine.

Leveraging Your Research Skills in the Job Market

Too busy being a student to have developed the skills you need to make you highly competitive in the job market? Nope, not true. Think about the skill sets you developed through the conduct of your research that are valuable to potential employers. And we're not just talking about your new topical knowledge in water recycling or Internet bullying or delivering public value in times of fiscal restraint. And by all means, this knowledge is something you should sell. But you should also consider how your research processes have enhanced your broader skill set, for example:

- your experience in problem identification;
- your ability to engage in problem-based learning;
- your ability to commission research and evaluative studies;
- your ability to read and interpret evidence;
- your experience in contributing evidence to evidence-based decision-making;
- your exceptional listening skills;
- your ability to manage and complete a complex project on time;

- your logical and cogent writing skills;
- your ability to impactfully present with confidence.

It is well worth brainstorming all the challenges you've overcome as you've tackled your research project. Each challenge points to the development of skills likely to be highly valued by a potential employer.

You have also developed technical skills, and some of them are likely to be at a quite advanced level. If you used Excel in your quantitative analysis, for example, you are likely to be beyond a basic user. If you can create a spreadsheet, do simple calculations and filter results, you're a basic user. If you can use more complex formulae and create or modify macro commands, you're probably an intermediate user. If you can utilize advanced functions (If, VLOOKUP, IS), manage macros, work with Pivot tables and dabble in basic programming in VBA, you're an advanced or expert user. It's worth listing a few of these details to identify what experience you've had that would be valuable to an organization. These are all skills you can highlight in a CV, but they are also skills you can think about leveraging in a job interview.

The following are common interview questions that are perfect for telling the tale of your research journey:

- Tell me a bit about yourself. You as the investigator/problem solver/researcher.
- What projects did you work on? Think research project.
- Give me an example of a time you influenced a group. When you got the green light for your research project!
- What accomplishments have given you the greatest satisfaction? When you were able to submit your completed research report/when your research project recommendations were taken up by the organization.
- Tell me about a time you demonstrated leadership. Think about challenging decisions related to your project.
- Tell me about a time you were a team player. Perfect if your project utilized a team.
- Tell me about a time you overcame a challenge at work. All research processes have their challenges!
- What experiences/skills do you feel are particularly useful to our organization? Do your homework on the organization and make appropriate linkages.
- Where and when have you ever struggled to succeed? To be honest, juggling a research project and all other work and life commitments is a struggle for most.

THE FINAL WORD

> Everything has to come to an end, sometime.
>
> L. Frank Baum, The Marvelous Land of Oz (1904)

And that includes this chapter, this book and most likely the research project you have been working on. So congratulations. You have gone from a consumer to a producer of knowledge. We hope you are proud of your accomplishments and we hope that you may have even enjoyed the journey (even if just in parts).

Whether you are destined for more research, more study or the job market, we wish you well.

Chapter Summary

- The ultimate goal of any research project is to add to a body of knowledge. Once your project is complete, it is worth thinking about broader dissemination, including attending conferences, giving presentations, and writing and submitting papers.
- Oral presentations are your opportunity not only to share your work, but also to get others excited about the possibilities that arise from your research. It is well worth creating a presentation that will motivate your audience.
- It is difficult to make your way in a professional community without people on your side. Networking is critical to future success.
- Conducting a research project offers you more learning than you probably realize. You have just completed a challenging journey of discovery - discovery about the social world, but also discovery about yourself. It is worth reflecting and capitalizing on this.
- Employers are looking for people who can deliver professional reports, presentations and projects. The key is to demonstrate these skills clearly on your CV/résumé and leverage them in an interview.

FIND YOUR NEXT STEP

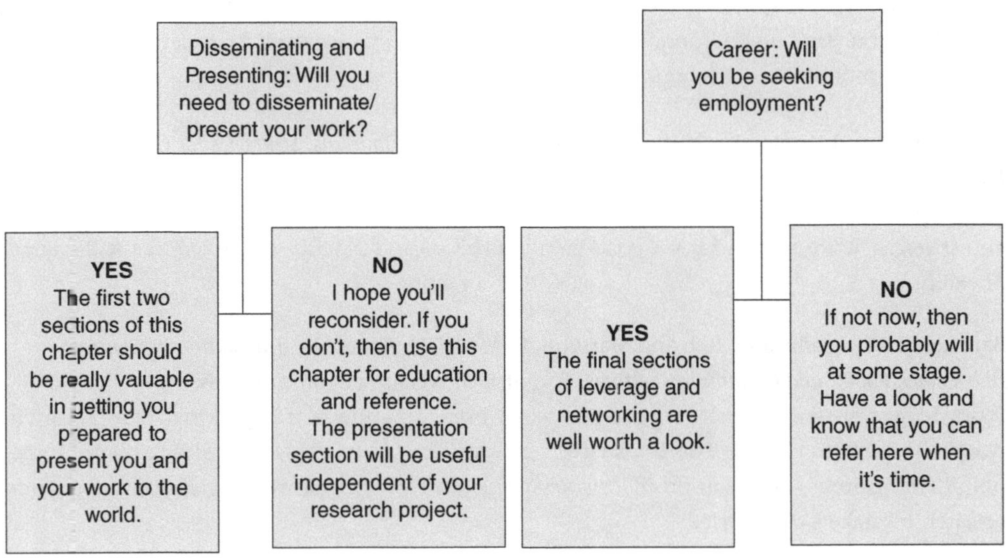

FURTHER READING

Disseminating

Belcher, W. (2019) *Writing Your Journal Article in Twelve Weeks: A Guide to Academic Publishing Success*. Chicago: University of Chicago Press.
The strength of this work is Belcher's ability to break down a complex process into small doable steps set within a defined timeframe.

Brownson, R., Colditz, G. and Proctor, E. (eds) (2017) *Dissemination and Implementation Research in Health: Translating Science to Practice*. Oxford: Oxford University Press.
While the context here is health, the strategies offered are widely applicable and important for anyone wanting to maximize the impact of their research.

Hartley, J. (2008) *Academic Writing and Publishing: A Practical Handbook*. Abingdon: Routledge.
A practical guide that will take you through all relevant publishing steps. Good examples offered here.

Rankin, J. (2018) *Sharing Your Education Expertise with the World*. Abingdon: Routledge.
This book is very comprehensive – as if you took the basic guidance given in this chapter and expanded it to 300-plus pages! We particularly like the section on how to multiply your impact.

Rocco, T. and Hatcher, T. (2011) *The Handbook of Scholarly Writing and Publishing*. San Francisco, CA: Jossey-Bass.
Getting published is quite a process. Not only do you need to have completed a significant study that you write up appropriately and convincingly, you also need to understand how the publishing game works. This book gives good coverage of relevant challenges.

Thomson, P. and Kamler, B. (2012) *Writing for Peer Reviewed Journals: Strategies for Getting Published*. Abingdon: Routledge.
This is quite a comprehensive guide that goes beyond simple steps and delves into the dilemmas and struggles writers often face. A good blend of theory and practice grounded in a wide range of examples.

Banister, E. M., Leadbeater, B. J. and Marsahll, E. A. (2011). *Knowledge Translation in Context: Indigenous, Policy, and Community Settings*. Toronto: University of Toronto Press.
'Knowledge transfer' is something of a buzzword, but is an important way to make sure research reaches those who need it. This book covers case studies of knowledge transfer in community, policy, Indigenous, and non-profit organizations, and is essential reading if you want your research to make a difference.

Presenting

Altman, R. (2019) *Why Most PowerPoint Presentations Suck*. Seattle, WA: CreateSpace.
A shared pet peeve of ours are bad PowerPoint presentations – so this title intrigued us. Since PowerPoint will be with us for quite a while, it is well worth figuring out how to use it effectively.

Donovan, J. (2013) *How to Deliver a TED Talk: Secrets of the World's Most Inspiring Presentations.* Seattle, WA: CreateSpace.
To be able to give an outstanding TED Talk is worth aspiring to. If you are unfamiliar with TED Talks, check out Box 18.3 or google the 'Top 10 TED Talks', and be ready to be impressed. Inspiring stuff. This book will offer you some guidelines for improving just about any presentation.

Evergreen, S. (2017) *Presenting Data Effectively: Communicating Your Findings for Maximum Impact.* Thousand Oaks, CA: Sage.
Great advice here that will help you present data with impact. It will help your data-based reports, slideshows, dashboards, posters and data visualizations become more engaging and powerful.

O'Leary, Z. (2019) *LQF: Presenting Your Research.* London: Sage.
That's Zina again with another quick guide She has been teaching in this space for a while, and she's very good at helping people draw out main messages and present with confidence and impact.

Transitioning

Basalla, S. and Debelius, M. (2014) *'So What Are You Going to Do with That?': Finding Careers Outside Academia.* Chicago: University of Chicago Press.
We just love the title. Too many of us can relate. But we tend to be ill-prepared and/or unrealistic. The authors do a great job of bridging the disconnect between students' career dreams and the realities they will find in the actual job market.

Kelsky, K. (2015) *The Professor Is In: The Essential Guide to Turning Your Ph.D. into a Job.* New York: Three Rivers Press.
Great practical advice here. Everything from publishing, securing grants, writing up your CV, to handling interviews. Well worth a read.

Martin, G. (2018) *Welcome to the Professional World: Success Principles for Entering the Workforce.* San Diego, CA: Cognella Academic Publishing.
A bit basic, but only if you already know it. So, if you are feeling quite lost, have a look. This work covers basic ins and outs as well as dos and don'ts.

Wickre, K. (2018) *Taking the Work Out of Networking: An Introvert's Guide to Making Connections That Count.* New York: Gallery Books.
Networking might be painful, but it can be done. And introverts can even leverage their ability to connect at deeper levels. Reading this may just help you get the skills and confidence you need to connect.

Zack, D. (2019) *Networking for People Who Hate Networking: A Field Guide for Introverts, the Overwhelmed, and the Underconnected.* Oakland, CA: Berrett-Koehler Publishers.
When running the internship programme for the Sydney University Business School, Zina certainly came across students who were introverted, overwhelmed and, therefore, under connected. If this is you, grab this book. It will help.

GLOSSARY

Action research Research strategies that tackle real-world problems in participatory and collaborative ways in order to produce action and knowledge in an integrated fashion through a cyclical process. In action research, process, outcome and application are inextricably linked.

Aim What you hope to achieve through your research project – generally a restatement of the research question.

Analytic data Data derived from the systemic computational analysis of data or statistics.

Annotated bibliography A list of citations with a brief descriptive and evaluative paragraph indicating the relevance, accuracy and quality of the cited sources.

Anonymity Protection against identification even from the researcher.

Applied research Research that has an express goal of going beyond knowledge production towards situation improvement.

Auditability Full explication of methods that allows others to see how and why the researchers arrived at their conclusions.

Authenticity Concerned with describing the deep structure of experiences and phenomena in a manner that is 'true' to the experience.

Automated text analysis Computer-based assistance for the conduct of textual and document analysis of online sources. The use of computer algorithms to analyse various forms of online text.

Axiology The nature of ethical behaviour – the nature of values and their role in research.

Basic research Research driven by a desire to expand knowledge rather than a desire for situation improvement.

Big Data Information/data sets so large and complex that they cannot be analysed using traditional databases or data processing applications.

Bivariate analysis A statistical analysis of the relationship between two variables. Bivariate analysis assesses relationships between two variables; for example, whether there is a relationship between education level and television viewing habits, or between gender and income. As covered in Table 15.5, the range of tests that are used to explore such relationships is quite extensive and varies by variable type. The most common tests are cross-tabulations (chi-squared, used for two nominal variables), ANOVA (used for one nominal and one ratio variable) and correlations (used for two ratio variables).

Breaching experiments Exposing the rules of the everyday by breaking them and taking note of your own reactions as well as the reactions of others.

Broad representation Representation wide enough to ensure that a targeted institution, cultural group or phenomenon can be spoken about confidently.

Case A site or a particular instance or entity that can be defined by identifiable boundaries.

Case study A method of studying elements of our social fabric through comprehensive description and analysis of a single situation or case; for example, a detailed study of an individual, setting, group, episode or event. Case study research can refer to single and multiple case studies.

Census A survey that does not rely on a sample. Every element within a defined population is included in the study.

Central limit theorem A random sample of observations for any distribution with a finite mean and finite variance will have a mean that follows a normal distribution. Thus, samples will be approximately equal to the mean of the population.

Central tendency Measures indicate the middle or the centre of a distribution: mean, median and mode.

Cluster sampling A sampling strategy that surveys whole clusters within a population; clusters can include things like regions, government departments and shopping complexes.

Confidence interval A range of possible values for an unknown number – computed in such a way as to have a specified probability of including the unknown number.

Confidence level The degree of certainty that a statistical prediction is accurate.

Confidentiality Protecting the identity of those providing research data; all identifying data remain solely with the researcher.

Content analysis To interpret meaning in speech. Can involve linguistic 'quantification' where words and 'text' are units of analysis that are tallied. Can also refer to thematic analysis through coding. Taken up in studies where occurrence is assumed to indicate important trends. For example, analysing the newsworthiness of a particular topic, or looking at an individual's subconscious references to a particular concept.

Conversation analysis To understand the structure and action of conversation. Painstakingly transcribed conversations are explored for structural organization of speech. Turn-taking between speakers and sequential ordering of utterances are of particular importance in understanding conversation. Often taken up in ethnomethodological studies that look at how individuals create meaning through dialogue.

Copyright A legal concept, enacted by most governments, giving the creator of an original work exclusive rights to it, usually for a limited time.

Correlation A statistical technique that can show whether, and how strongly, pairs of variables are related.

Coverage error When your sample frame is deficient and does not adequately represent your target population.

Credibility The quality, capability or power to elicit belief.

Critical emancipation Fundamental or revolutionary changes in current thinking, practices, conditions or institutions that can free people from the constraints of dominant social structures that often limit self-development and self-determination.

Critical ethnography As well as exploring cultural groups from the point of view of its participants, critical or radical ethnography attempts to expose inequitable, unjust or repressive influences that act on 'marginalized' groups, in a bid to offer avenues for positive change.

Criticality Challenging taken-for-granted ways of knowing. Asking not only what it is, but why it is, who benefits and what alternative possibilities there might be.

Cross-sectional surveys Surveys that use a sample or cross-section of respondents. The goal is to be able to represent your target population and generalize findings back to that population.

Crystallization The process of developing a rich and diverse understanding of a situation or phenomenon by seeing the world in all its complexity.

Cultural artefact analysis Collection, review, interrogation and analysis of various human-made objects to ascertain information about the culture of the objects' creator(s) and users.

Data scraping The process of moving data from a website to a local spreadsheet or local file.

Deductive logic Using an overarching principle to draw a conclusion about a specific individual fact or event. In qualitative analysis this means having some ideas or theories in mind and searching your data for potential confirmation of these.

Delimitations A study's boundaries; for example, conscious exclusions in your defined population.

Dependability That methods are systematic, well-documented and designed to account for research subjectivities.

Dependent variables The things you are trying to study or what you are trying to measure. For example, you might be interested in knowing what factors cause chronic headaches, a strong income stream or levels of achievement in secondary school – headaches, income and achievement would all be dependent variables.

Descriptive statistics Summary characteristics of distributions, such as shape, central tendency and dispersion.

Descriptive survey A survey that aims to describe your sample by gathering information on demographics, knowledge and attitudes.

Discourse analysis To interpret language as it is situated in a socio-historic context. Rather than focus on simply what is said, discourse analysis explores language as it constitutes and embodies a socio-historic context tied to power and knowledge. Analysis necessarily involves data exploration that is 'critical'; in other words, it challenges the dominant ideology. Taken up in studies where 'text' is assumed to have real political power and influence on social consciousness.

Dispersion How spread out individual measurements are from a central measure.

Document analysis A research tool for collecting, reviewing, interrogating and analysing various forms of written 'text' as a primary source of research data.

Documentary method Selecting cues from a social interaction that conforms to a recognizable pattern, then making sense of that interaction in terms of that pattern.

Emancipatory goals To work towards transformative change.

Emancipatory research Research that exposes underlying ideologies in order to liberate those oppressed by them.

Emergent design A research design in which full protocols develop as the research process progresses.

Empiricism A stance on knowledge (epistemology) that asserts all knowledge is limited to what can be observed through the senses. The cornerstone of scientific method.

Epistemology The nature of knowledge – how can we come to have legitimate knowledge of the world and what are the rules for knowing? Our personal epistemology points to how we come to understand the world; for example, how I came to believe in God, how I came to understand love or how I adopted the morals I have.

Erroneous assumptions Presumptions (about a population) that turn out to be false. This can lead to samples that do not accurately reflect a population.

Ethics Refers to a professional 'code of practice' designed to protect the researched from an unethical process, and in turn protect the researcher from legal liabilities. Key ethical considerations include informed consent, causing no harm and a right to privacy.

Ethnography The study of cultural groups in a bid to understand, describe and interpret a way of life from the point of view of its participants.

Ethnomethodology The study of the methods that individuals use to accomplish their daily actions and make sense of their social world. Ethnomethodological focus is on uncovering the 'rules' that direct ordinary life. It is not interested in whether what is said or done is right or wrong, true or false. In fact, ethnomethodology ignores the question of 'what' altogether and concentrates on 'how' interactions are performed.

Evaluative research Research that attempts to determine the value of some initiative. Evaluative research identifies an initiative's consequences as well as opportunities for modification and improvement.

Experiment A rigorous and controlled search for cause and effect. Researchers vary an independent variable (something they believe is a key determinant in their study) in order to see if it has an impact on their dependent variable (the main object of their inquiry). In other words, you manipulate X to see if it has an effect on Y.

Explanatory surveys Surveys that aim to explore why things might be the way they are; in other words, to determine cause and effect.

Fair dealing/fair use Limitation and exception to the exclusive right granted by copyright law to the author of a creative work.

Feminist methodology The conduct of research from a feminist perspective. While the approaches are varied, common characteristics include a critical perspective, overcoming patriarchal biases, working towards social change, empowering marginalized voices, as well as acknowledging the position of the researcher.

Focus group A planned and guided discussion among a group of participants for the purpose of examining a specific issue or set of issues.

Formative evaluation Also referred to as process evaluation, it investigates an initiative's delivery and provides data and information that can aid further development of a particular change initiative.

Generalizability Whether findings and/or conclusions from a sample, setting or group are directly applicable to a larger population, a different setting or another group.

Grounded theory To generate theory directly from data. Highly inductive (analytic induction). Use of 'constant comparative method' to explore each data source in relation to those previously analysed. Taken up by researchers who believe it is important to cast aside all preconceived notions and simply let the data tell the story.

Guttman scaling A scale that orders statements about a particular topic according to favourability, such that if you agree with the fourth statement it implies you agreed with the previous three. For example: (1) 'Pet dogs should be allowed in the back yard'; (2) 'Pet dogs should be allowed in the house'; (3) 'Pet dogs should be allowed in the bedroom'; and (4) 'Pet dogs should sleep on the bed'.

Hand-picked sampling Involves the selection of a sample with a particular purpose in mind, such as typicality, wide variance or 'expertise'.

Hermeneutics To interpret text in a dialogic fashion. Involves moving in and out of text using a 'hermeneutic spiral', or a process that cycles in on richer understandings by altering viewpoints. Focus on alternative perspectives – global versus detailed, conventional versus critical, etc. Often used in the study of literature, including historical documents, novels, lyrics, art works and theatre. Taken up when there is an assumption that meaning is a product of the relationship between author and audience.

Histogram A graph that uses vertical bars of different heights to represent the distribution of data.

Historical analysis Collection, review, interrogation and analysis of various forms of data in order to establish facts and draw conclusions about past events.

Hypothesis Logical conjecture (hunch or educated guess) about the nature of relationships between two or more variables expressed in the form of a testable statement.

Hypothetico-deductive methods Scientific method in which a general hypothesis is tested by deducing predictions that are then experimentally tested.

Independent variables The things that might be causing an effect on the things you are trying to understand. For example, reading might cause headaches; gender may have a role in determining income; parental influence may impact on levels of achievement. The independent variables here are reading, gender and parental influence.

Indexicality The contextual nature of behaviour and talk, in particular the cues that conform to a recognizable pattern that we use to make meaning.

Inductive logic Using specific individual facts to draw an overall conclusion, principle or theory. In qualitative analysis this means letting your raw data tell the story and building theory through your observations and analysis.

Inferential statistics Statistical measures used to make inferences about a population based on samples drawn from that population.

Informed consent Full disclosure of a research participant's requested involvement in a study, including time commitment, type of activity, topics that will be covered, and all physical and emotional risks potentially involved.

Integrative review Another name for a systematic review.

Inter-quartile The two inner quartiles of a quartile range – often used as a measure of dispersion because it eliminates outliers.

Interval A measurement scale that orders data and uses equidistant units to measure difference. This scale does not, however, have an absolute zero. For example, the year 2016 occurs 51 years after the year 1965, but time did not begin in CE1. IQ is also considered an interval scale even though there is some debate over whether points on the scale can be considered equidistant.

Intervening variable A variable that modifies the original relationship between the independent and the dependent variables but isn't readily observable. For example, you find a correlation between singing to your baby and calming her down. Singing creates calm. The intervening variable, however, may be undivided attention – undivided attention leads to calm, so just using a song recording does not have the full, desired effect.

Interview A method of data collection that involves researchers seeking open-ended answers related to a number of questions, topic areas and/or themes.

Key informants Individuals whose role or experiences result in them having relevant information or knowledge they are willing to share with a researcher.

Kurtosis Indicates how peaked or flat a distribution is, compared with 'normal'. Positive kurtosis indicates a relatively peaked distribution, while negative kurtosis indicates a flatter distribution.

Likert scaling A scale that asks respondents to select a position on a continuum from, say, 'strongly disagree' to 'strongly agree'. There are typically five to seven points on the continuum.

Limitations Design characteristics or constraints that may have an impact on the generalizability and utility of findings; for example, small sample size or restricted access to records.

Literature review A critical and purposive review of a body of knowledge including findings and theoretical and methodological contributions.

Machine data Data automatically generated by computer processes, capable of tracking everyday activity.

Mean The mathematical average. To calculate the mean, you add the values for each case and then divide by the number of cases. Because the mean is a mathematical calculation, it is used to measure central tendency for interval and ratio data and cannot be used for nominal or ordinal data where numbers are used as 'codes'. For example, it makes no sense to average the 1s, 2s and 3s that might be assigned to Christians, Buddhists and Muslims.

Measurement scales Ways of capturing the differences within variables: categorizing (nominal variables); ranking (ordinal variables); distance between points (interval variables); and distance between points with an absolute zero (ratio variables).

Median The midpoint of a range. To find the median you simply arrange values in ascending (or descending) order and find the middle value. This measure is generally used in ordinal data and has the advantage of negating the impact of extreme values (e.g. one extreme salary of $3 million will push mean income levels up – but it will not affect the midpoint). Of course, this can also be a limitation given that extreme values can be significant to a study.

Member checking Checking that interpretation of events, situations and phenomena gels with the interpretations of 'insiders'.

Meta-analysis Statistical analysis and synthesis of the results of two or more primary studies that address the same hypothesis in the same way – common in systematic reviews.

Methodological design The plan for conducting your research project that includes methodology, methods and research tools.

Methodology Overarching, macro-level frameworks that offer principles of reasoning associated with particular paradigmatic assumptions that legitimate various schools of research. Methodologies provide both the strategies and grounding for the conduct of a study. Examples here include scientific method, ethnography and action research (see Chapters 8, 9 and 10).

Methods The actual micro-level techniques used to collect and analyse data. Methods of data collection include interviewing, surveying, observation and unobtrusive methods (see Chapters 12 and 13), while methods of analysis comprise quantitative strategies (i.e. statistics) and qualitative strategies (i.e. thematic exploration) (see Chapters 14 and 15).

Mixed approach Incorporating quantitative and qualitative paradigms, approaches, concepts, methods and/or techniques in a single study.

Mixed methodology An approach to research that utilizes both qualitative and quantitative data. Both types of data are valued independently of ontological or epistemological assumptions.

Mode The most common value or values noted for a variable. Since nominal data is categorical and cannot be manipulated mathematically, it relies on mode as its measure of central tendency.

Multi-stage cluster sampling Surveying within whole clusters of a population that is done in several stages. For example, if your population was Australian high school students, you would (1) use a sampling strategy to select regions across Australia, then (2) use a sampling strategy to select a number of high schools within these regions, before (3) employing an additional sampling strategy to select students from within those schools.

Multivariate analysis A statistical analysis that explores the relationship between three or more variables and allows researchers to search for cause and effect, build models and test theories. With multivariate analysis researchers can not only explore if a dependent variable is dependent on two or more independent variables (i.e. income is dependent on both gender and educational attainment), but also acknowledge the relationship between the dependent variables (i.e. the relationship between gender and educational attainment). Some of the methods used in multivariate analysis are factor analysis, elaboration, structural equation modelling, MANOVA, multiple regression, canonical correlation and path analysis. It is worth noting that statistics specialists are often called on at this level of analysis.

Narrative analysis To interpret the 'stories' of individuals. Data collection and interpretation are often iterative, with focus on story building. Metaphors seen as important. Taken up in studies where there is a belief that it is helpful to draw out an individual's story. Usually involving a small sample and often called on in phenomenological research.

Netnography Attempts to understand the unique nature of computer-mediated online communities through agreed-upon standardized approaches to observing and participating in websites, blogs, discussion boards and social networking.

Neutrality Subjectivities are recognized and negotiated in a manner that attempts to avoid biasing results/conclusions.

Nominal A measurement scale in which numbers are arbitrarily assigned to represent categories. Since they are arbitrary and have no numerical significance, they cannot be used to perform mathematical calculations. For example, the variable 'plans after graduation' is also nominal, with numerical values arbitrarily assigned as 1 = vocational/technical training, 2 = university, 3 = workforce, 4 = travel abroad, 5 = undecided and 6 = other. In nominal measurement, codes should not overlap (they should be mutually exclusive) and together should cover all possibilities (be collectively exhaustive). The main function of nominal data is to allow researchers to tally responses in order to understand population distributions.

Non-parametric tests Statistical tests for data in which there is no assumption that the relevant population falls under a normal distribution.

Non-random sampling Processes in which the chance or probability of any particular case being selected in a sample is not known.

Non-response bias The effect caused when those who agree to be in a sample are intrinsically different from those who decline.

Normal curve A 'bell-shaped' distribution of data that is symmetrical, with the mean, median and mode all coinciding at the highest point of the curve.

Objectives These summarize what is to be achieved by the study including what you will do and for what purpose(s). Objectives work best if they are explicit, concrete and closely connected to your research question.

Objectivity That conclusions are based on observable phenomena and are not influenced by emotions, personal prejudices or subjectivities.

Observation A systematic method of data collection that relies on a researcher's ability to gather data through his or her senses.

Online ethnography Attempts to understand online communities based on classic anthropological assumptions. Individual researchers adopt methodological approaches that generally involve observing and participating in websites, blogs, discussion boards and social networking.

Online-generated data The vast array of qualitative and quantitative data that are produced on or by the Internet.

Ontology The study of what exists and how it can be understood and categorized. Our personal ontology points to what we think is 'real', what we think 'exists'; for example, the nature of our soul, God, love and morals. It is the nature of reality.

Operationalizing concepts Turning abstract concepts into measurable variables.

Ordinal A measurement scale that orders categories in some meaningful way. Magnitudes of difference, however, are not indicated. For example, socioeconomic status can be classed as lower, middle or upper class. Lower class may denote less status than the other two classes, but the amount of the difference is not defined. Other examples are air travel (economy, business, first class), and items where respondents are asked to rank-order selected choices (biggest environmental challenges facing developed countries). Likert-type scales, in which respondents are asked to select a response on a point scale (e.g. 'I enjoy going to work': 1 = strongly disagree, 2 = disagree, 3 = neutral, 4 = agree, 5 = strongly agree), are ordinal since a precise difference in magnitude cannot be determined. Many researchers, however, treat Likert scales as interval because doing so allows them to perform more precise statistical tests. In most small-scale studies this is not generally viewed as problematic.

Outcome evaluation Also referred to as summative evaluation. Aims to provide data and information related to the effectiveness and efficiency of the change strategy in question.

Panel study Involves asking the same (not similar) sample of respondents the same questions at two or more points in time in order to ascertain if individuals change over time.

Paradigm Assumptions about how things work; a *worldview*. Research paradigms are common beliefs shared among researchers about how problems can be understood and addressed.

Parametric tests Statistical tests for data in which there is an assumption that the relevant population falls under a normal distribution.

Participant observation Researchers are, or become, part of the team, community or cultural group they are observing.

Participatory action research Research that has emancipatory goals, but under the rubric of action research in which cycles of knowledge and action are used to produce on-the-ground change. Sometimes referred to as emancipatory action research or 'southern' participatory action research.

Peer review External check on the research process in which a colleague is asked to act as a 'devil's advocate' in regard to all aspects of methodology and research conduct.

Persistent observation To look for deep readings of a situation beyond an initial, sometimes superficial, level.

Phenomenology The study of phenomena as they present themselves in individuals' direct awareness and experience. Perception, rather than socio-historic context or even the supposed 'reality' of an object, is the focus of investigation.

Plagiarism When the words, ideas or data of another person are not referenced, and are passed off as your own.

Population Who you want to speak about. The total membership of a defined class of people, objects or events.

Positivism A stance on knowledge (epistemology), that all true knowledge is scientific and is best pursued by scientific method.

Post-positivism The view that understanding the world means an acceptance of chaos, complexity, the unknown, incompleteness, plurality, fragmentation, multiple realities and the construction of meaning.

Primary data Data that researchers collect expressly for their research purposes.

Process evaluation Also referred to as formative evaluation, this investigates an initiative's delivery and provides data and information that can aid further development of a particular change initiative.

Programme logic A planning, communication and evaluation model/tool that articulates the details of an initiative, its objectives and how success will be measured.

Prolonged engagement Investment of time sufficient to learn the culture, understand context and/or build trust and rapport.

Prompts and probes Techniques used to facilitate an interview. Prompts are cues or reminders you give your interviewee to help them answer. Probes are additional focusing questions used to get your interviewee to go deeper.

Qualitative approach An approach to research highly reliant on qualitative data (words, images, experiences and observations that are not quantified). Often tied to a set of assumptions related to relativism, social constructionism and subjectivism.

Qualitative data Data represented through words, pictures, symbols, videos or icons.

Qualitative data analysis Processes for moving from qualitative data to understanding and interpretation of people and situations under investigation.

Qualitative research paradigm An approach to understanding and studying the world that rejects positivist 'rules' and works at interpreting the world through multiple lenses.

Quantitative approach An approach to research highly reliant on quantified data (numerical data as well as concepts we code with numbers). Often tied to a set of assumptions related to realism, empiricism and positivism.

Quantitative data Data represented through numbers and analysed using statistics.

Quantitative research paradigm An approach to understanding and studying the world that is characterized by an objective positivist search for singular truths reliant on hypotheses, variables and statistics.

Quartile This involves subdividing your range into four equal parts or 'quartiles' and is a commonly used measure of dispersion for ordinal data, or data whose central tendency is measured by a median. Quartiles allow researchers to compare the various quarters or present the inner 50% as a dispersion measure. This is known as the inter-quartile range.

Quasi-experimental design An experiment that does not randomly assign subjects to control and target groups.

Radical views Advocating fundamental or revolutionary changes in current practices, conditions, institutions or ideologies.

Random sampling Process by which each element in a population has an equal chance of being selected for inclusion in a sample.

Randomized controlled trial An experiment conducted under controlled circumstances in which control groups are used and there is random assignment to control and target groups.

Range A measure of dispersion calculated by subtracting the lowest value from the highest value. This is the simplest way to calculate dispersion. For example, if your respondents varied in age from 8 to 17, the range would be 9 years. While this measure is easy to calculate, it is dependent on extreme values alone, and ignores intermediate values.

Ratio A measurement scale where each point on the scale is equidistant, and there is an absolute zero. Because ratio data is 'real' numbers, like age, height and distance, all basic mathematical operations can be performed.

Real-time data Sometimes called dynamic data; they are data that are delivered immediately upon collection.

Realism A stance on reality (ontology) that asserts the external world exists independently of perception. In other words, the truth is out there whether we can see and understand it or not.

Reflexivity Examining your own beliefs, judgements and practices and how they impact your research

Relativism A view of reality (ontology) that rejects universals. There is no singular 'true' reality that exists for everyone, but multiple subjective realities. Things like truth, morals and culture can only be understood in relation to their own socio-historic context.

Reliability Concerned with internal consistency; i.e. whether data/results collected, measured or generated are the same under repeated trials.

Representative sample A sample that adequately represents the research population in terms of characteristics such as age, gender, race, socioeconomic status and education.

Reproducibility Concerned with whether results/conclusions would be supported if the same methodology was used in a different study with the same/similar context.

Research The systematic study of materials and sources in order to establish facts and reach new conclusions.

Research tools The devices used in the collection of research data, such as questionnaires, observation checklists and interview schedules (see Chapters 12 and 13).

Respondents Individuals who agree to provide data for your research project.

Sample Who you actually speak to. The subset of a population included in a research study.

Sample frame A list that includes every member of the population from which a sample is to be drawn.

Sampling The process of selecting elements of a population for inclusion in a research study. Many samples attempt to be representative: that is, the sample distribution and characteristics allow findings to be generalized back to the relevant population.

Saturation When collecting data no longer adds additional understanding or aids in building theories.

Scientific method Systematic approach to theory building that involves repeated trials of observation, hypothesis formation, hypothesis testing and evaluation.

Secondary data Data that is not generated for the research process; it exists regardless of a researcher's questioning, prompting and probing.

Secondary data analysis Collection, review, interrogation and analysis of existing data sets in order to answer questions not previously or adequately addressed.

Semiotics To interpret the meanings behind signs and symbols. Involves identification of 'cognitive domains' – or the learning skills and mental processes used to make meaning. Attempts to deconstruct specific meanings in order to reconstruct understanding. Taken up in linguistics and humanities – social researchers using semiotics often attempt to understand how signs are created and used to affect social consciousness.

Sensitivity analysis The extent to which study results stay the same given adjustments to the way data is handled.

Simple random sampling A sampling process in which every element of the population has an equal chance of being selected.

Single group design A research design in which a single group is observed before and after an intervention. There is no control group.

Skewed A distribution of data that is not symmetrical. In skewed data, the mean, median and mode fall at different points.

SMART objectives Objectives that are *s*pecific, *m*easurable, *a*chievable, *r*elevant and *t*ime-bound.

Snowball sampling Building a sample through a series of referrals. For example, asking initial participants to nominate other potential participants who then nominate further participants.

Social constructionism A view of knowledge (epistemology) in which meaning is constructed by human beings as they interact and engage in interpretation.

Social data Data that individuals knowingly and voluntarily share online, such as posts, tweets, photos and videos.

Stakeholders Individuals and groups that affect and/or are affected by an organization and its activities.

Standard deviation (s.d.) This is the square root of the variance and is the basis of many commonly used statistical tests for interval and ratio data.

Statistical significance Generally refers to a '*p*-value'. It assesses the probability that your findings are more than coincidence.

Stratified sampling Dividing your population into various subgroups and taking a random sample from within each one.

Subjectivism Emphasizes the subjective elements in experience and accepts that personal experiences are the foundation for factual knowledge.

Subjectivity That conclusions are influenced by an individual's experiences, opinions, impressions, beliefs and feelings rather than observable phenomena.

Summative evaluation Also referred to as outcome evaluation, this aims to provide data and information related to the effectiveness and efficiency of the change strategy in question.

Surveying The process of collecting data through a questionnaire that asks individuals the same questions related to their characteristics, attributes, how they live, and/or their opinions.

Systematic reviews An overview of primary studies on a particular topic that relies on transparent reproducible methods to locate, critically appraise and synthesize the findings and results of credible studies.

Systematic sampling Selecting every *n*th case within a defined population. For example, going to every 10th house or selecting every 20th person on a list.

Textual analysis Exploration of traces of social activity including documents as well as blogs, videos, photographs, posts, memes, poetry, songs, tweets, etc.

Thematic analysis Involves searching through data to inductively identify interconnections and patterns. Patterns are then analysed and explored as potential themes. As themes solidify, the next level of abstraction hopes to build theory.

Thurstone scaling A scale that asks respondents to agree or disagree with different statements about a particular construct. Each statement carries a weighting (between 1 and 11) assigned by a panel of experts.

Transactional data Data that indicate a transfer, agreement or exchange between an organization and/or individuals.

Transferability Whether findings and/or conclusions from a sample, setting or group lead to lessons learned that may be germane to a larger population, a different setting or another group.

Trend surveys A survey that asks a particular cross-section of a population the same questions at two or more points in time. While the cross-section stays the same, the individuals typically change each time.

Triangulation Using more than one source of data to confirm the authenticity of each source.

Univariate analysis A statistical analysis of one variable at a time. It consists of measures such as central tendency, dispersion and distribution. While univariate analysis does not look at correlation, cause and effect or modelling, this type of analysis is a cornerstone of a descriptive study and is an essential preliminary stage in all types and levels of statistical analysis.

Unwitting bias The tendency to unintentionally act in ways that confirm what you might already suspect.

Unwitting evidence The background information related to a document, such as author/creator, audience, circumstances of production, text type, style, tone, agenda, political purpose, etc.

Validity Concerned with truth value, for example whether conclusions are 'correct'. Also considers whether methods, approaches and techniques actually relate to what is being explored.

Variables Constructs that have more than one value; variables can be 'hard' (e.g. gender, height, income) or 'soft' (e.g. self-esteem, worth, political opinion).

Variance This measure uses all values to calculate the spread around the mean and is actually the 'average of the squared differences from the mean'. Variance needs to be calculated from interval and ratio data and gives a good indication of dispersion. It is much more common, however, for researchers to use and present the square root of the variance, which is known as the standard deviation.

Visual analysis To interpret still and moving images. Can involve the logic of all of the strategies above, the point of difference being the analysis of images rather than words. Can also involve gathering people's opinions on, and reactions to, particular images, clips, art work, etc. When photographs are used this is called photo elicitation. Taken up by researchers who argue the importance of images to full social understanding – something increasingly recognized in our world with its Facebook, YouTube, TV and DVDs.

Volunteer sampling Involves selecting a sample by asking for volunteers; for example, putting an ad in the newspaper or going to local organizations.

Web mining The process of discovering patterns in large web-based data sets. Methods include content analysis, artificial intelligence, machine learning, statistics and database systems.

Witting evidence Information that the original author/creator of a text wanted to share with his/her audience.

REFERENCES

Ackerly, B. and True, J. (2019) *Doing Feminist Research in Political and Social Science*. London: Red Globe Press.

Altman, R. (2019) *Why Most PowerPoint Presentations Suck*. Seattle, WA: CreateSpace.

Alvesson, M. and Sandberg, J. (2024) *Constructing Research Questions: Doing Interesting Research*, 2nd edition. London: Sage.

Anderson, E. and Corneli, A. (2018) *100 Questions (and Answers) About Research Ethics*. Thousand Oaks, CA: Sage.

Balatti, J., Gargano, I., Goldman, M., Wood, G. and Woodlock, J. (2004) *Improving Indigenous Completion Rates in Mainstream TAFE – An Action Research Approach*. Leabrook, South Australia: NCEAR.

Banks, M. and Zeitlyn, D. (2015) *Visual Methods in Social Research*. London: Sage.

Basalla, S. and Debelius, M. (2014) *'So What Are You Going to Do with That?': Finding Careers Outside Academia*. Chicago: University of Chicago Press.

Baum, L. F. (1904) *The Marvelous Land of Oz: Being an Account of the Further Adventures of the Scarecrow and the Tin Woodman*. Chicago: Reilly & Britton.

Bazeley, P. (2021) *Qualitative Data Analysis: Practical Strategies*, 2nd edition. London: Sage.

Beekhuyzen, J. and Bazeley, P. (2025) *Qualitative Data Analysis with NVivo*. London: Sage.

Belcher, W. (2019) *Writing Your Journal Article in Twelve Weeks: A Guide to Academic Publishing Success*. Chicago: University of Chicago Press.

Berger, P. L. and Luckmann, T. (1967) *The Social Construction of Reality: A Treatise in the Sociology of Knowledge*. New York: Anchor.

Beukes, L. (2013) *The Shining Girls*. Cape Town: Random House Struik.

Bischof, G. H., Warnaar, B. L., Barajas, M. S. and Dhaliwal, H. K. (2011) 'Thematic analysis of the experiences of wives who stay with husbands who transition male-to-female', *Michigan Family Review*, *15*(1): 16–33.

Blaikie, N. and Priest, J. (2017) *Social Research: Paradigms in Action*. Cambridge: Polity Press.

Blair, E. and Blair, J. (2014) *Applied Survey Sampling*. London: Sage.

Blake, W. (1788) *All Religions Are One*.

Boeri, M. and Rashi, S. (eds) (2019) *Inside Ethnography: Researchers Reflect on the Challenges of Reaching Hidden Populations*. Los Angeles: University of California Press.

Boghossian, P. A. and Coliva, A. (2019) *Fear of Knowledge: Against Relativism and Constructivism*. Abingdon: Routledge.

Bogner, A., Littig, B. and Menz, W. (eds) (2009) *Interviewing Experts*. Basingstoke: Palgrave Macmillan.

Booth, W. C., Colomb, G. C. and Williams, J. M. (2016) *The Craft of Research*. Chicago: University of Chicago Press.

Borrell, J. (2008) 'Thematic analysis identifying concepts of problem gambling agency: With preliminary exploration of discourses in selected industry and research documents', *Journal of Gambling Issues*, *22*: 195–218.

Botha, L. (2011). 'Mixing methods as a process towards indigenous methodologies', *International Journal of Social Research Methodology*, *4*: 313–25.

Bowden, J. and Green, P. (2019) *Playing the PhD Game with Integrity: Connecting Research, Professional Practice and Educational Context*. New York: Springer.

Bradley, E. (2004) 'Interview with Ed Bradley', *Larry King Live*, CNN. 8 February. Transcript available at: http://transcripts.cnn.com/TRANSCRIPTS/0402/08/lkl.00.html

Braun, V. & Clarke, V. (2022). *Thematic Analysis: A Practical Guide*. Sage.

Brown, M.E., Dueñas, A.N. A Medical Science Educator's Guide to Selecting a Research Paradigm: Building a Basis for Better Research. Med.Sci.Educ. 30, 545–553 (2020). https://doi.org/10.1007/s40670-019-00898-9 image on pg. 546

Brown, S. G. and Dobrin, S. I. (eds) (2004) *Ethnography Unbound: From Theory Shock to Critical Praxis*. Albany, NY: State University of New York Press.

Brownson, R., Colditz, G. and Proctor, E. (eds) (2017) *Dissemination and Implementation Research in Health: Translating Science to Practice*. Oxford: Oxford University Press.

Brundage, A. (2017) *Going to the Sources: A Guide to Historical Research and Writing*. Chichester: Wiley-Blackwell.

Bryant, A. and Charmaz, K. (eds) (2019) *The SAGE Handbook of Grounded Theory*. London: Sage.

Bryman, A. (2021) *Social Research Methods*, 6th edition. Oxford: Oxford University Press.

Bulmer, M., Sturgis, P. and Allum, N. (eds) (2009) *The Secondary Analysis of Survey Data*. London: Sage.

Burr, V. (2015) *Social Constructionism*, 3rd edition. New York: Psychology Press.

Butler, O. E. (1995) *Bloodchild: And Other Stories*. New York: Four Walls Eight Windows/Seven Stories Press.

Butler, O. E. (2000) 'Interview with David Zindell', *Locus*, *44*(6, Issue 473), June.

Caliandro, A. (2018) 'Digital methods for ethnography: Analytical concepts for ethnographers exploring social media environments', *Journal of Contemporary Ethnography*, *47*(5): 551–78.

Cameron, W. B. (1963) *Informal Sociology: A Casual Introduction to Sociological Thinking*. New York: Random House.

Cappellini, B. and Yen, D. (2016) 'A space of one's own: Spatial and identity liminality in an online community of mothers', *The Journal of Marketing Management*, *32*(13/14): 1260–83.

Carey, S. S. (2011) *A Beginner's Guide to Scientific Method*. Belmont, CA: Wadsworth.

Carlyle, T. (1833–4) *Sartor Resartus: The Life and Opinions of Herr Teufelsdröckh*. London: Fraser's Magazine for Town and Country.

Cavana, R. L., Delahaye, B. L. and Sekaran, U. (2001) *Applied Business Research: Qualitative and Quantitative Methods*. New York: John Wiley & Sons.

Chakravartty, A. (2010) *A Metaphysics for Scientific Realism: Knowing the Unobservable*. Cambridge: Cambridge University Press.

Chandler, D. (2017) *Semiotics: The Basics*. Abingdon: Routledge.

Chevalier, J. M. and Buckles, D. J. (2019) *Participatory Action Research: Theory and Methods for Engaged Inquiry*. Abingdon: Routledge.

Clandinin, D. J. (2013) *Engaging in Narrative Inquiry*. Abingdon: Routledge.

Cleage, P. (2011) 'Emory University creativity conversations: Pearl Cleage and Rosemary Magee', 22 September.

Cline, M. (2019) 'Quotes from research design: Qualitative, quantitative, and mixed method approaches'. Retrieved from: https://mitracline.com/2019/05/01/quotes-from-research-design-qualitative%E2%80%8B-quantitative-and-mixed-method-approaches/

Coates, T. (2018) *We Were Eight Years in Power: An American Tragedy*. New York: Penguin Random House.

Coghlan, D. (2019) *Doing Action Research in Your Own Organization*. London: Sage.

Coleman, R. (2018) *Designing Experiments for the Social Sciences: How to Plan, Create, and Execute Research Using Experiments*. Thousand Oaks, CA: Sage.

Conee, E. and Sider, T. (2015) *Riddles of Existence: A Guided Tour of Metaphysics*, 2nd edition. Oxford: Oxford University Press.

Cooper, H. M. (2016) *Research Synthesis and Meta-Analysis: A Step-by-Step Approach*. Thousand Oaks, CA: Sage.

Cooper, H.M., Hedges, L. and Valentine, J. (eds) (2019) *The Handbook of Research Synthesis and Meta-Analysis*. Thousand Oaks, CA: Sage.

Corbin, J. and Strauss, A. (2015) *Basics of Qualitative Research: Techniques and Procedures for Developing Grounded Theory*. London: Sage.

Creswell, D. and Creswell, J. W. (2022) *Research Design: Qualitative, Quantitative and Mixed Methods Approaches*, 6th edition. London: Sage.

Creswell, J. W. (2021) *A Concise Introduction to Mixed Methods Research*, 2nd edition. London: Sage.

Creswell, J. W. and Plano Clark, V. L. (2017) *Designing and Conducting Mixed Methods Research*. London: Sage.

Creswell, J. W. and Poth, C. (2024) *Qualitative Inquiry and Research Design: Choosing Among Five Approaches*, 6th edition. Thousand Oaks, CA: Sage.

Daniel, J. (2011) *Sampling Essentials: Practical Guidelines for Making Sampling Choices*. London: Sage.

de Certeau, M. (2002) *The Practice of Everyday Life*. Berkeley, CA: University of California Press.

Decuir-Gundy, J. and Schutz, P. (2016) *Developing a Mixed Methods Proposal: A Practical Guide for Beginning Researchers*. Thousand Oaks, CA: Sage.

Denzin, N. K. and Lincoln, Y. S. (eds) (2007) *The SAGE Handbook of Qualitative Research*. Thousand Oaks, CA: Sage.

Denzin, N. K. and Lincoln, Y. S. (eds) (2017) *Strategies of Qualitative Inquiry*. Thousand Oaks, CA: Sage.

Denzin, N. K. and Lincoln, Y. S. (eds) (2017) *The SAGE Handbook of Qualitative Research*. Thousand Oaks, CA: Sage.

DeWalt, K. M. and DeWalt, B. R. (2010) *Participant Observation: A Guide for Fieldwork*. Lanham, MD: AltaMira Press.

Dibley, L., Dickerson, S., Duffy, M. and Vandermause, R. (2020) *Doing Hermeneutic Phenomenological Research: A Practical Guide*. Thousand Oaks, CA: Sage.

Donovan, J. (2013) *How to Deliver a TED Talk: Secrets of the World's Most Inspiring Presentations*. Seattle, WA: CreateSpace.

Doucouliagos, H. and Ulubaşoğlu, A. M. (2008) 'Democracy and economic growth: A meta-analysis', *American Journal of Political Science*, *52*(1): 61–83.

Dunning, T. (2012) *Natural Experiments in the Social Sciences: A Design-Based Approach*. Cambridge: Cambridge University Press.

Effingham, N. (2013) *An Introduction to Ontology*. Cambridge: Polity Press.

Einstein, A. (1948) 'Foreword', in L. Barnett (2005) *The Universe and Dr Einstein*. New York: Dover Publications Inc.

Elsbach, K. and van Knippenberg, D. (2020) 'Creating high impact literature reviews: An argument for "integrative reviews"', *Journal of Management Studies*, *57*(6): 1277–89.

Emmel, N. (2013) *Sampling and Choosing Cases in Qualitative Research: A Realistic Approach.* London: Sage.

Evans, M. A. (George Eliot) (1876) *Daniel Deronda.* London: William Blackwood & Sons.

Evergreen, S. (2017) *Presenting Data Effectively: Communicating Your Findings for Maximum Impact.* Thousand Oaks, CA: Sage.

Ferber, E. (1939) *A Peculiar Treasure.* York: Doubleday, Doran & Company.

Ferguson, S. S. (2008) 'Nicotine patch therapy prior to quitting smoking: A meta-analysis', *Addiction, 103*(4): 557–63.

Fetterman, D. (2019) *Ethnography: Step-by-Step.* London: Sage.

Fetters, M. (2019) *The Mixed Methods Research Workbook: Activities for Designing, Implementing, and Publishing Projects.* Thousand Oaks, CA: Sage.

Feynman, R. (1997) *Surely You're Joking, Mr. Feynman!* New York: W. W. Norton.

Field, A. and Miles, J. (2024) *Discovering Statistics Using IBM SPSS Statistics*, 6th edition. London: Sage.

Fine, M. (2017) *Just Research in Contentious Times: Widening the Methodological Imagination.* New York: Teachers College Press.

Fink, A. (2016) *How to Conduct Surveys: A Step-by-Step Guide.* Thousand Oaks, CA: Sage.

Fink, A. (2019) *Conducting Research Literature Reviews: From the Internet to Paper*, 5th edition. Thousand Oaks, CA: Sage.

Finkelde, D. and Livingston, P. (eds) (2020) *Idealism, Relativism and Realism: New Essays on Objectivity Beyond the Analytic-Continental Divide.* Berlin: De Gruyter.

Fitzpatrick, K. (2011) 'Stop playing up! Physical education, racialization and resistance', *Ethnography, 12*(2): 174–97.

Foster, I., Ghani, R., Jarmin, R., Kreuter, F. and Lane, J. (eds) (2016) *Big Data and Social Science: A Practical Guide to Methods and Tools.* New York: Chapman & Hall.

Fowler, F. J., Jr (2013) *Survey Research Methods.* London: Sage.

Francis, D. and Hester, S. (2004) *An Invitation to Ethnomethodology.* London: Sage.

Freire, P. (1970) *Pedagogy of the Oppressed.* New York: Herder & Herder.

Friese, S. (2019) *Qualitative Data Analysis with ATLAS.ti.* Thousand Oaks, CA: Sage.

Galvan, J. L. and Galvan, M. C. (2017) *Writing Literature Reviews: A Guide for Students of the Social and Behavioral Sciences*, 7th edition. Glendale, CA: Pyrczak.

Garfinkel, H. (1967) *Studies in Ethnomethodology.* Englewood Cliffs, NJ: Prentice Hall.

Gee, J. P. (2014) *An Introduction to Discourse Analysis: Theory and Method.* Abingdon: Routledge.

Geertz, C. ([1973] 2017) *The Interpretation of Cultures.* New York: Basic Books.

Gerring, J. (2016) *Case Study Research: Principles and Practices.* Cambridge: Cambridge University Press.

Gibbon, E. (1814) *The Miscellaneous Works of Edward Gibbon*, 2nd edition. London: John Murray.

Gillham, B. (2008) *Observation Techniques: Structured to Unstructured.* London: Continuum International.

Girden, E. and Kabacoff, R. (2010) *Evaluating Research Articles from Start to Finish.* Thousand Oaks, CA: Sage.

Glaser, B. and Strauss, A. (1967) *Discovery of Grounded Theory.* Chicago: Aldine.

Glucksmann, M. (2009) *Women on the Line.* Abingdon: Routledge.

Goldman, A. and McGrath, M. (2014) *Epistemology: A Contemporary Introduction.* Oxford: Oxford University Press.

Goldman, E. (1924) *My Further Disillusionment with Russia*. New York: Doubleday, Page & Company.

Gough, D., Oliver, S. and Thomas, J. (eds) (2017) *An Introduction to Systematic Reviews*. London: Sage.

Gubrium, J. F., Holstein, J. A., Marvasti, A. B. and McKinney, K. D. (eds) (2012) *The SAGE Handbook of Interview Research: The Complexity of the Craft*. London: Sage.

Guest, G. S., MacQueen, K. M. and Namey, E. E. (2018) *Applied Thematic Analysis*. Thousand Oaks, CA: Sage.

Halabi, S., Smith, W., Collins, J., Baker, D. and Bedford, J. (2013) 'A document analysis of HIV/AIDS education interventions in Ghana', *Health Education Journal, 72*(4): 486–500.

Hall, C. and Longman, J. (2016) *The Postgraduate's Companion*. London: Sage.

Hall, C. (2020, Feb 28). 'Fixing academic posters: The #BetterPoster approach'. Astrobites. Retrieved from: https://astrobites.org/2020/02/28/fixing-academic-posters-the-betterposter-approach/

Hall, S. (2012) *This Means This, This Means That: A User's Guide to Semiotics*. London: Laurence King.

Hancock, D. R. and Algozzine, R. (2016) *Doing Case Study Research: A Practical Guide for Beginning Researchers*. New York: Teachers College Press.

Harris, J. (2020) *Statistics with R: Solving Problems Using Real-World Data*. Thousand Oaks, CA: Sage.

Hartley, J. (2008) *Academic Writing and Publishing: A Practical Handbook*. Abingdon: Routledge.

Henderson, E. & Tennent, E. (in press). Sex, gender, and bodied: Transmisogyny and Garfinkel's status degradation ceremony. *Symbolic Interaction*.

Herr, K. G. and Anderson, G. L. (2014) *The Action Research Dissertation: A Guide for Students and Faculty*, 2nd edition. London: Sage.

Higgins, J. P. T. and Green, S. (2019) *Cochrane Handbook for Systematic Reviews of Interventions*. New York: Wiley-Interscience.

Hill, C., Biemer, P., Buskirk, T., Japec, L., Kirchner, A., Kolenikov, S. and Lyberg, L. (eds) (2020) *Big Data Meets Survey Science: A Collection of Innovative Methods*. Hoboken, NJ: John Wiley & Sons.

Hine, C. M. (2015) *Ethnography for the Internet: Embedded, Embodied and Everyday*. Abingdon: Routledge.

Hjelm, T. (2014) *Social Constructionisms: Approaches to the Study of the Human World*. London: Red Globe Press.

Hoffmann, B. and Dukas, H. (1972) *Albert Einstein: Creator and Rebel*. New York: Viking Press.

Holliday, A. (2016) *Doing and Writing Qualitative Research*. London: Sage.

Holmes, D. (2018) *Big Data: A Very Short Introduction*. Oxford: Oxford University Press.

Holstein, J. A. and Gubrium, J. F. (eds) (2011) *Varieties of Narrative Analysis*. London: Sage.

Hood, S., Mayall, B. and Oliver, S. (eds) (1999) *Critical Issues in Social Research: Power and Prejudice*. Buckingham: Open University Press.

Hurston, Z. N. (1942) *Dust Tracks on a Road: An Autobiography*. London: Hutchinson & Co.

International Labour Organization (2016) 'Facts on safe work'. Geneva: ILO. Retrieved from: www.ilo.org/wcmsp5/groups/public/—dgreports/—dcomm/documents/publication/wcms_067574.pdf

Israel, M. (2014) *Research Ethics and Integrity for Social Scientists: Beyond Regulatory Compliance*, 2nd edition. London: Sage.

Jackson, S. L. (2015) *Research Methods and Statistics: A Critical Thinking Approach*. Belmont, CA: Wadsworth.

Janesick, V. (2007) 'The dance of qualitative research design: Metaphor, methodolatry, and meaning', in N. K. Denzin and Y. S. Lincoln (eds), *Strategies of Qualitative Inquiry*, pp. 35–55. Thousand Oaks, CA: Sage.

Järvinen, M. and Mik-Meyer, N. (eds) (2020) *Qualitative Analysis: Eight Approaches for the Social Sciences*. London: Sage.

Jemison, M. (2001) *Find Where The Wind Goes: Moments From My Life*. New York: Scholastic Press.

Jeynes, W. H. (2005) 'A meta-analysis of the relation of parental involvement to urban elementary school student academic achievement', *Urban Education*, *40*(3): 237–69.

Johansson, F. (2011) 'Chick-fil-A® Leadercast® Voices of change', speech.

Jorgensen, D. (2020) *Principles, Approaches and Issues in Participant Observation*. Abingdon: Routledge.

Joyce, J. (1906), quoted in P. Hartshorn (1997) *James Joyce and Trieste*. Westport, CT: Greenwood Press.

Joyner, R. L., Rouse, W. A. and Glatthorn, A. A. (2018) *Writing the Winning Thesis or Dissertation: A Step-by-Step Guide*. Thousand Oaks, CA: Corwin Press.

Kalton, G. (2020) *Introduction to Survey Sampling*. London: Sage.

Kamler, B. and Thomson, P. (2014) *Helping Doctoral Students Write: Pedagogies for Supervision*, 2nd edition. Abingdon: Routledge

Kaplan, D. (ed.) (2014) *The SAGE Handbook of Quantitative Methodology for the Social Sciences*. Thousand Oaks, CA: Sage.

Kelly, M. and Gurr, B. (2019) *Feminist Research in Practice*. Lanham, MD: Rowman & Littlefield.

Kelsky, K. (2015) *The Professor Is In: The Essential Guide to Turning Your Ph.D. into a Job*. New York: Three Rivers Press.

Kemmis, S., McTaggart, R. and Nixon, R. (2014) *The Action Research Planner: Doing Critical Participatory Action Research*. New York: Springer.

Kettl, D. (2017) *Little Bites of Big Data for Public Policy*. Thousand Oaks, CA: Sage.

Killman, L. (2013) *Research Terminology Simplified: Paradigms, Axiology, Ontology, Epistemology and Methodology*. Sudbury, ON: Author.

Kim, J. (2015) *Understanding Narrative Inquiry: The Crafting and Analysis of Stories as Research*. Thousand Oaks, CA: Sage.

King, S. (2010) *On Writing: A Memoir of the Craft*. London: Hodder & Stoughton.

Kolb, D. A. (1984) *Experiential Learning: Experience as the Source of Learning and Development*. Englewood Cliffs, NJ: Prentice Hall.

Konnikova, M. (2013) *Mastermind: How to Think Like Sherlock Holmes*. Edinburgh: Canongate Books.

Kozinets, R. V. (2019) *Netnography: The Essential Guide to Qualitative Social Media Research*. London: Sage.

Krathwohl, D. R. and Smith, N. L. (2005) *How to Prepare a Dissertation Proposal: Suggestions for Students in Education and the Social and Behavioral Sciences*. Syracuse, NY: Syracuse University Press.

Krippendorf, K. (2018) *Content Analysis: An Introduction to its Methodology*. London: Sage.

Krueger, R. and Casey, M. (2014) *Focus Groups: A Practical Guide for Applied Research*. Thousand Oak, CA: Sage.

Kuckartz, U. and Rädiker, S. (2019) *Analyzing Qualitative Data with MAXQDA: Text, Audio, and Video*. New York: Springer.

Kuhn, T. S. (2012) *The Structure of Scientific Revolutions. 50th Anniversary*, 4th edition. Chicago: University of Chicago Press.

Kvale, S. and Brinkman, S. (2014) *InterViews: Learning the Craft of Qualitative Research Interviewing*. London: Sage.

Laing, C., Moules, N., McCaffrey, G. and Field, J. (2015) *Conducting Hermeneutic Research: From Philosophy to Practice*. New York: Peter Lang.

Leavy, P. (2017) *Research Design: Quantitative, Qualitative, Mixed Methods, Arts-Based, and Community-Based Participatory Research Approaches*, 1st edition. New York: Guilford Press.

Leavy, P. and Harris, A. (2018) *Contemporary Feminist Research from Theory to Practice*. New York: Guilford Press.

Leedy, P. D. and Ormond, J. E. (2018) *Practical Research: Planning and Design*, 12th edition. Englewood Cliffs, NJ: Prentice Hall.

Leetaru, K. H. (2012) 'A Big Data approach to the humanities, arts, and social sciences: Wikipedia's view of the world through supercomputing', *Research Trends*, 30 September.

Letherby, G., Scott, J. and Williams, M. (2012) *Objectivity and Subjectivity in Social Research*. London: Sage.

Lévi-Strauss, C. (1964) *The Raw and the Cooked*. Paris: Plon.

Lewin, K. (1946) 'Action research and the minority problems', *Journal of Social Issues, 2*: 34–6.

Lewins, A. and Silver, C. (2014) *Using Software in Qualitative Research: A Step-by-Step Guide*. London: Sage.

Linfield, J. and Posavac, E. (2018) *Program Evaluation: Methods and Case Studies*. Abingdon: Routledge.

Linnenluecke, M., Marrone, M. and Singh, A. (2019) 'Conducting systematic literature reviews and bibliometric analyses', *Australian Journal of Management, 45*: 175–94.

Liu-Lastres, B., Huang, W., & Bao, H. (2023) 'Exploring hospitality workers' career choices in the wake of COVID-19: Insights from a phenomenological inquiry', *International Journal of Hospitality Management, 111*: 103485.

Locke, J. (1824) *The Works of John Locke*. London: C. and J. Rivington.

Locke, L. F., Spirduso, W. W. and Silverman, S. J. (2013) *Proposals That Work: A Guide for Planning Dissertations and Grant Proposals*. London: Sage.

Lofland, J., Snow, D. A., Anderson, L. and Lofland, L. H. (2005) *Analyzing Social Settings: A Guide to Qualitative Observation and Analysis*, 4th edition. Belmont, CA: Wadsworth.

Lohr, S. (2019) *Sampling: Design and Analysis*. Abingdon: Routledge.

Lopatto, E. (2013) 'Facebook opens up site data to suicide research', *Bloomberg News*, 27 January.

Lynch, M. and Sharrock, W. (eds) (2009) *Ethnomethodology*. London: Sage.

Machi, L. A. and McEvoy, B. (2016) *The Literature Review: Six Steps to Success*. Thousand Oaks, CA: Corwin Press.

MacInnes, J. (2017) *An Introduction to Secondary Data Analysis with IBM SPSS Statistics*. Thousand Oaks, CA: Sage.

Macrina, F. L. (2014) *Scientific Integrity: Text and Cases in Responsible Conduct of Research*, 4th edition. Herndon, VA: ASM Press.

Madden, R. (2017) *Being Ethnographic: A Guide to the Theory and Practice of Ethnography*. London: Sage.

Madison, D. S. (2019) *Critical Ethnography: Method, Ethics, and Performance*. London: Sage.

Marshall, C. and Rossman, G. B. (2015) *Designing Qualitative Research*, 6th edition. London: Sage.

Martell, E., Shepherd, M. & Goodyear-Smith, F. (2021) '*He awa whiria*—A "braided river": An Indigenous Māori approach to mixed methods research', *Journal of Mixed Methods Research, 16*: 17–33.

Martin, G. (2018) *Welcome to the Professional World: Success Principles for Entering the Workforce*. San Diego, CA: Cognella Academic Publishing.

Martin, R. (2010) *Epistemology: A Beginner's Guide*. London: Oneworld Publications.

Martin, W. and Bridgmon, K. (2018) *Quantitative and Statistical Research Methods: From Hypothesis to Results*. San Francisco, CA: Jossey-Bass

Marx, K. ([1845] 1932) *The German Ideology*. Moscow: Marx–Engels Institute.

Mayo, E. (1933) *The Human Problems of an Industrial Civilization*. New York: Viking Press.

McNamara, D. S., Graesser, A. C., McCarthy, P. M. and Cai, Z. (2020) *Coh-Metrix: Automated Evaluation of Text and Discourse*. Cambridge: Cambridge University Press.

McNiff, J. (2017) *All You Need to Know About Action Research*. London: Sage.

Mertens, D. M. and Wilson, A. (2018) *Program Evaluation Theory and Practice*. New York: Guilford Press.

Miles, M. B., Huberman, M. and Saldana, J. (2019) *Qualitative Data Analysis: A Methods Sourcebook*. London: Sage.

Molière (1659) *The Precious Ridicules*, Act I, sc. Xi.

Myatt, G. J. and Johnson, W. P. (2014) *Making Sense of Data: A Practical Guide to Exploratory Data Analysis and Data Mining*. New York: Wiley-Interscience.

Myers, W. D. (2012) 'Reading is not optional: An interview with Walter Dean Myers', *Pen America*, 19 March. Retrieved from: https://pen.org/reading-is-not-optional-an-interview-with-walter-dean-myers/

Nagy Hesse-Biber, S. J. and Leavy, P. L. (eds) (2013) *Feminist Research Practice: A Primer*, 2nd edition. London: Sage.

Neuendorf, K. (2016) *The Content Analysis Guidebook*. Thousand Oaks, CA: Sage.

Neuman, W. L. (2005) *Social Research Methods: Qualitative and Quantitative Approaches*. Boston: Allyn & Bacon.

Newcomer, K. E., Hatry, H. P. and Wholey, J. S. (eds) (2015) *Handbook of Practical Program Evaluation*, 4th edition. San Francisco, CA: Jossey-Bass.

Nichols-Casebolt, A. (2012) *Research Integrity and Responsible Conduct of Research*. Oxford: Oxford University Press.

O'Leary, Z. (2001) *Reaction, Introspection and Exploration: Diversity in Journeys out of Faith*. Kew, VIC: Christian Research Association.

O'Leary, Z. (2007) *The Social Science Jargon Buster*. London: Sage.

O'Leary, Z. (2018a) *LQF: Research Proposals*. London: Sage.

O'Leary, Z. (2018b) *LQF: Research Questions*. London: Sage.

O'Leary, Z. (2019) *LQF: Presenting Your Research*. London: Sage.

Oliver, P. (2010) *The Students' Guide to Research Ethics*, 2nd edition. Buckingham: Open University Press.

Oxford English Dictionary (2012) Oxford: Oxford University Press.

Pan, M. L. (2017) *Preparing Literature Reviews: Qualitative and Quantitative Approaches*, 4th edition. Glendale, CA: Pyrczak.

Patton, M. Q. (2001) *Qualitative Research and Evaluation Methods*. Thousand Oaks, CA: Sage.

Pauwels, L. and Mannay, D. (eds) (2020) *The SAGE Handbook of Visual Research Methods*. London: Sage.

Pehlke II, T. A., Hennon, C. B., Radina, M. E. and Kuvalanka, K. A. (2009) 'Does Father still know best? An inductive thematic analysis of popular TV sitcoms', *Fathering*, *7*(2): 114–39.
Peoples, K. (2020) *How to Write a Phenomenological Dissertation: A Step-by-Step Guide*. London: Sage.
Plano Clark, V. L. and Ivankova, N. V. (2015) *Mixed Methods Research: A Guide to the Field*. London: Sage.
Potter, J. (1996) 'Discourse analysis and constructionist approaches: theoretical background', in J. Richardson (ed.), *Handbook of Qualitative Research Methods for Psychology and the Social Sciences*, pp. 125–40. Leicester: BPS Books.
Prior, L. (ed.) (2011) *Using Documents and Records in Social Research*. London: Sage.
Przybylski, L. (2020) *Hybrid Ethnography: Online, Offline, and In Between*. London: Sage.
Punch, K. (2016) *Developing Effective Research Proposals*, 3rd edition. London: Sage.
Pyrczak, F. and Bruce, R. R. (2014) *Writing Empirical Research Reports: A Basic Guide for Students of the Social and Behavioral Sciences*. Glendale, CA: Pyrczak.
Rainie, S. C., Kukutai, T., Walter, M., Figueroa-Rodríguez, O., L., Walker, J. and Axelsson, P. (2019). 'Indigenous data sovereignty', in T. Davies, S. Walker, M. Rubinstein and F. Perini (eds), *The State of Open Data: Histories and Horizons*, pp. 300–19. Cape Town and Ottawa: African Minds and International Development Research Centre.
Rankin, J. (2018) *Sharing Your Education Expertise with the World*. Abingdon: Routledge.
Rapley, T. (2018) *Doing Conversation, Discourse and Document Analysis*. London: Sage.
Reason, P. and Bradbury, H. (2007) *Handbook of Action Research*. London: Sage.
Resnik, D. (2018) *The Ethics of Research with Human Subjects: Protecting People, Advancing Science, Promoting Trust*. New York: Springer.
Richards, C. (2020) Interview (pers. comm.*)*, 18 October, Cleveland, OH.
Ridley, D. (2012) *The Literature Review: A Step by Step Guide for Students*. London: Sage.
Roberts, C. and Hyatt, L. (2018) *The Dissertation Journey: A Practical and Comprehensive Guide to Planning, Writing, and Defending Your Dissertation*. Thousand Oaks, CA: Corwin Press.
Robinson, D. (2013) *Introducing Empiricism*. New York: Totem Books.
Robinson, S. B. and Firth, K. (2018) *Designing Quality Survey Questions*. Thousand Oaks, CA: Sage.
Robson, C. (2016) *Real World Research*. Oxford: Blackwell.
Rocco, T. and Hatcher, T. (2011) *The Handbook of Scholarly Writing and Publishing*. San Francisco, CA: Jossey-Bass.
Roethlisberger, F. J. and Dickson, W. J. (1939) *Management and the Worker: An Account of a Research Program Conducted by the Western Electric Company, Hawthorne Works*. Cambridge, MA: Harvard University Press.
Rose, G. (2016) *Visual Methodologies: An Introduction to Researching with Visual Materials*. London: Sage.
Rosenbaum, P. R. (2020) *Observational Studies*. New York: Springer.
Rossi, P. H., Lipsey, M. W. and Henry, G. T. (2019) *Evaluation: A Systematic Approach*. Thousand Oaks, CA: Sage.
Roth, P. (1979) 'Works in progress', *The New York Times Book Review*, 15 July.
Roy, A. (2004) The 2004 Sydney Peace Prize Lecture. Seymour Theatre Centre, University of Sydney.
Royse, D., Thyer, B. A. and Padgett, D. K. (2016) *Program Evaluation: An Introduction to an Evidence Based Approach*. Boston: Cengage Learning.
Rubin, H. J. and Rubin, I. S. (2011) *Qualitative Interviewing: The Art of Hearing Data*. Thousand Oaks, CA: Sage.

Rumsey, D. (2019) *Statistic Essentials for Dummies*. Hoboken, NJ: John Wiley & Sons.

Russell, M. and Klassen, M. (2019) *Mining the Social Web: Data Mining Facebook, Twitter, LinkedIn, Google+, GitHub, and More*. Sebastopol, CA: O'Reilly Media.

Saldana, J. (2021) *The Coding Manual for Qualitative Researchers*, 4th edition. London: Sage.

Salkind, N. J. (2021) *Statistics for People Who (Think They) Hate Statistics: Using Microsoft Excel*, 5th edition. London: Sage.

Salmona, M., Lieber, E. and Kaczynski, D. (2019) *Qualitative and Mixed Methods Data Analysis Using Dedoose: A Practical Approach for Research Across the Social Sciences*. London: Sage.

Schwarzer, G., Carpenter, J. and Rücker, G. (2015) *Meta-Analysis with R*. New York: Springer.

Seidman, I. (2019) *Interviewing as Qualitative Research: A Guide for Researchers in Education and the Social Sciences*, 5th edition. New York: Teachers College Press.

Shawn, W. (2008) *Research Is Ceremony: Indigenous Research Methods*. Black Point, Nova Scotia: Fernwood Publishing.

Shulman, J. and Asimov, I. (eds) (1988) *Isaac Asimov's Book of Science and Nature Quotations*. New York: Weidenfeld & Nicolson.

Sidnell, J. (2010) *Conversation Analysis: An Introduction*. Chichester: Wiley-Blackwell.

Sidnell, J. and Stivers, T. (eds) (2014) *The Handbook of Conversation Analysis*. Chichester: Wiley-Blackwell.

Silverman, D. (2024) *Interpreting Qualitative Data: Methods for Analysing Talk, Text and Interaction*, 7th edition. London: Sage.

Smith, D. (1999) *Writing the Social: Critique, Theory and Investigations*. Toronto: University of Toronto Press.

Smith, J., Flowers, P. and Larkin, M. (2009) *Interpretative Phenomenological Analysis: Theory, Method and Research*. London: Sage.

Smith, L. (2022) *Decolonizing Methodologies: Research and Indigenous Peoples*, 3rd edition. London: Zed Books.

Smith, W. W. (1949) 'Walter Winchell in New York', *Naugatuck Daily News*, 6 April: 4, Column 5.

Sofalvi, A. (2011) 'Health education films of the silent era: A historical analysis', *International Electronic Journal of Health Education, 14*: 135–41.

Sprague, J. (2016) *Feminist Methodologies for Critical Researchers: Bridging Differences*, 2nd edition. Lanham, MD: AltaMira Press.

Stake, R. E. (1995) *The Art of Case Study Research*. Thousand Oaks, CA: Sage.

Steinmetz, G. (ed.) (2005) *The Politics of Method in the Human Sciences: Positivism and its Epistemological Others*. Durham, NC: Duke University Press.

Stoudt, B. G., Fox, M. and Fine, M. (2012) 'Contesting privilege with critical participatory action research', *Journal of Social Issues, 68*(1): 178–93.

Stringer, E. (2013) *Action Research*. London: Sage.

Supple, L. (2013) *Music Journalism 101: The Definitive Resource for New and Established Writers*.

Swanborn, P. (2010) *Case Study Research: What, Why and How?* Thousand Oaks, CA: Sage.

Tashakkori, A. and Teddlie, C. (eds) (2010) *SAGE Handbook of Mixed Methods in Social and Behavioral Research*. Thousand Oaks, CA: Sage.

Ten Have, P. (2014) *Understanding Qualitative Research and Ethnomethodology*. London: Sage.

Terrell, S. (2015) *Writing a Proposal for your Dissertation: Guidelines and Examples*. New York: Guilford Press.

Thomas, J. (1993) *Doing Critical Ethnography*. Newbury Park, CA: Sage.

Thompson, S. K. (2012) *Sampling*. Hoboken, NJ: John Wiley & Sons.

Thomson, P. and Kamler, B. (2012) *Writing for Peer Reviewed Journals: Strategies for Getting Published*. Abingdon: Routledge.

Tokunaga, H. (2018) *Fundamental Statistics for the Social and Behavioral Sciences*. Thousand Oaks, CA: Sage.

Townsend, K. (2018) *How to Keep Your Research Project on Track: Insights from When Things Go Wrong*. Cheltenham: Edward Elgar.

Trahar, S., Juntrasook, A., Burford, J., von Kotze, A. and Wildemeersch, D. (2019) 'Hovering on the periphery? "Decolonising" writing for academic journals', *Compare: A Journal of Comparative and International Education, 49*(1): 149–67.

Underwood, M. (2017) 'Exploring the social lives of image and performance enhancing drugs: An online ethnography of the Zyzz fandom of recreational body builders', *International Journal of Drug Policy, 39*: 78–85.

van Manen, M. (2014) *Phenomenology of Practice: Meaning-Giving Methods in Phenomenological Research and Writing*. Abingdon: Routledge.

Vartanian, T. (2010) *Secondary Data Analysis*. Oxford: Oxford University Press.

Viloria, A., Naveda, A., Palma, H., Núñez W. and Núñez, L. (2020) 'Using Big Data to determine potential dropouts in higher education', *Journal of Physics: Conference Series, 1432*(1): 012077.

Wagner, W. E. (2019) *Using IBM® SPSS® Statistics for Research Methods and Social Science Statistics*. Thousand Oaks, CA: Sage.

Wales, E. and Brewer, B. (1976) 'Graffiti in the 1970s', *Journal of Social Psychology, 99*(1): 115–23.

Walker, C. A. (2015) 'Social constructionism and qualitative research', *Journal of Theory Construction & Testing, 19*(2): 37–8.

Weakliem, D. (2016) *Hypothesis Testing and Model Selection in the Social Sciences*. New York: Guilford Press.

Webb, E. J., Campbell, D. T., Schwartz, R. D. and Sechrest, L. ([1966] 2015) *Unobtrusive Measures: Nonreactive Research in the Social Sciences*. London: Sage.

Wertz, F., Charmaz, K., McMullen, L., Josselson, R., Anderson, R. and McSpadden, E. (2011) *Five Ways of Doing Qualitative Analysis: Phenomenological Psychology, Grounded Theory, Discourse Analysis, Narrative Research, and Intuitive Inquiry*. New York: Guilford Press.

White, G. (2017) *The Dissertation Warrior: The Ultimate Guide to Being the Kind of Person Who Finishes a Doctoral Dissertation or Thesis*. Happy Valley, OR: Triumphant Heart International.

White, P. (2017) *Developing Research Questions: A Guide for Social Scientists*. Basingstoke: Palgrave Macmillan.

Wickre, K. (2018) *Taking the Work Out of Networking: An Introvert's Guide to Making Connections That Count*. New York: Gallery Books.

Wilde, O. (1884) 'Oscar's morning work' (Acknowledgement to 'New York Graphic'), *The Syracuse Standard*, 21 May: 2, Column 5.

Wodak, R. and Meyer, M. (eds) (2015) *Methods of Critical Discourse Analysis*. London: Sage.

Wolcott, H. F. (2009) *Writing Up Qualitative Research*. London: Sage.

Wolf, C., Joye, D., Smith, T. and Fu, Y. (eds) (2016) *The SAGE Handbook of Survey Methodology*. London: Sage.

Wu, C. and Thompson, M. (2020) *Sampling Theory and Practice*. New York: Springer.

Yin, R. K. (2017) *Case Study Research: Design and Methods*. Thousand Oaks, CA: Sage.

Zack, D. (2019) *Networking for People Who Hate Networking: A Field Guide for Introverts, the Overwhelmed, and the Underconnected*. Oakland, CA: Berrett-Koehler Publishers.

INDEX

Page numbers in *italics* refer to figures and tables.

abstract *see* summary/abstract
academic career advancement 25
academic formats
  alternative 371
  and applied research formats 372–3
  traditional 370–1
academic knowledge advancement 52
academic publishing 389
academics: sourcing relevant literature 108
accommodation/office space 27
accurate and verifiable accounts 73–4
'action learning' 24
action research 4, 138–9, 198
  challenges 203–4
  exemplar 202
  improving practice 199
  key elements 200–2
  scope of 199
  shifting systems 199–200
age and trust building 68
AI and research 11–14
aims/objectives
  research proposal 92
  writing up 377
analytical data, online-generated 302
anonymity 77–8
applied research formats 372–3
archives 306–7
arguments, relevant and appropriate 71–3
arts, as secondary data 281
audience
  dissemination planning 388
  presentations 392, 394
  writing up 369
audio and video recording of interviews 260–1
audio-visual presentations 393–4
authenticity and multiple realities 67–8
automated text analysis 308–9
autonomy and independence 27, 28
axiology 5, *10*

bar graph 332
Beukes, L. 278
biases
  non-response 221
  qualitative data analysis (QDA) 349, 353
  questionnaires 246
  secondary data 278
  unwitting 223
bibliography *see* references
Big Data 300
  see also online-generated data
Blake, W. 144
books 107
Bradley, E. 252
breaching experiments 163
bricoleur: role of researcher 133
Butler, E.E. 379

Cameron, W.B. 341
Campbell Collaboration 291
Carlyle, T. 188
case studies 73, 153, 228–30
  ethical 79–80
  selection 230–1
central limit theorum 221
central tendency, measuring 324, *325*
change agent: role of researcher 133
change-driving research 188
choreographer: role of researcher 133
class *see* socioeconomic status/class
Cline, M. 298
cluster bar graph 332, *333*
cluster sampling *222*
Coates, T-N. 41
Cochrane Collaboration 290
coding themes 349–51, 353–4
communication skills 24
community engagement 43–4
competing positions 5, 6–7
computer technology 27
  ethnomethodology and conversation analysis (EMCA) 165
  see also software
concept map 42, 45–6
concept operationalization 243–5
concepts: qualitative data analysis (QDA) 350
conscientiousness 76
conclusions
  qualitative data analysis (QDA) 353, 355
  writing up 379
conferences 389, 390
confidence, lack of 34
confidentiality 76, 77–8
consent forms 83–4
consistency in methods 70–1
constructivism *see* qualitative tradition
contemporary/timely issues 43
control environment/group 146–7
'convenience' sampling *224–5*
conversation analysis 164, 165
copyrights laws 133
coverage error 221
creativity
  curiosity and 41–2
  and focus balance 347–8
credibility
  accurate and verifiable accounts 73–4
  appropriate indicators 60–1
  capturing 'truth' 66–70
  consistency in methods 70–1
  indicators and checklist 74–5

managing subjectivities 61–6
in mixed methodology 182–3
in online-generated data 304–5
in qualitative studies 153–4
relevant and appropriate arguments 71–3
in secondary data 279
critical ethnography 206–7
critical thinking 24
cultural anthropology/cultural groups *see* ethnography
cultural artefacts analysis 285–6
curiosity and creativity 41–2

data, literature as source of 107
data cleaning 322
data entry
qualitative 345
quantitative 322
data management
qualitative data/analysis 343–5
quantitative data/analysis 321–2
secondary data 279
data record 321–2
data scraping 308
data screening 322
data stored online vs online-generated data 297–8
databases 30, 109–10, *111*
'dead social scientist test' 278
deadlines 25
decision-making 3–4, 25, 40
deductive and inductive reasoning 347–8
descriptive statistics 324–7
direction, losing and finding 35
discipline-based reference materials 107
discipline-related databases 109–10, *111*
discussion, writing up 379
disorganization/organization 35
dispersion/distribution, measuring 324–7
dissemination 387–9
document analysis 157
vs literature review 117
see also textual/document analysis
documentary method 162
domain and methodological design 135, *137*
drafting and redrafting
research proposal 97–8
writing up 381–3

Economic and Social Research Council (ESRC), UK: standardized ethics applications 81
Einstein, A. 59, 60, 387
emancipatory research 204–5
critical ethnography 206–7
examples 207–8
issues in 208–9
participatory action research (PAR) 205–6
empiricism 5, 6, 7
see also quantitative tradition
epistemology 5, *6*, *10*
EPPI Centre 290–1
equity 76–7
erroneous assumptions 223
ethics
approval 26
processes 80–4
case studies 79–80
ethical obligations 77–9
key informants *228*
legal obligations 76
methodological design 133
moral obligations 76–7
research proposal 93
writing up 378
ethnicity/race
insensitivity to 63
trust-building 68
ethnography 154–5
conducting study 156
critical 206–7
exemplar 155–6
online 310–11
range of potential cultural groups 156–7
range of potential data collection/analysis methods 157
strengths and challenges 158
ethnomethodology 162
breaching experiments 163
exemplar 162–3
interpretative miscues 164
shared interpretations 163–4
strengths and challenges 164–5
evaluative research 4, 188–9
formative/process evaluation 191–2
politics of 192–4
real-world challenges 195–8
summative/outcome evaluation 189–91
evidence-based decision-making 25
examination process 26
Excel 321
existing data 149–50
see also secondary data
existing skills 24
experiments
conducting 145–7
design 144–5
strengths and challenges 148
experts
concept operationalization 244–5
key informants 225–8
sourcing relevant literature 108

fair use/fair dealing 113
feedback, first to final draft 380–1
feminist approaches 165–6
Feynmann, R. 3, 73
findings
generalizable 73
writing up 379
focus groups
ethical dilemmas 78–9
vs multiple interviews 263
see also interviews; surveys
formative/process evaluation 191–2
four-step question generation process 46–7
fraudulence 73
funds/budget 27, 93–4, 134

Gantt chart 32
Garfinkel, H. 162–3, 164
Geetz, C. 154–5
gender
insensitivity to 63
trust building 68
generalizable findings 73
Gibbon, E. 89
Goldman, E. 125
Google Scholar 30, 109

graphs 331–4
grey literature 107–8
grounded theory 138, 152
group research/teamworking 30–1
Guttman scale 244, 245

hand-picked sampling *224*
harm, protecting respondents from 77
Hawthorne studies 148, 179–80
Heisenberg, W. 126–7
histogram 334–5
historical analysis 285
honesty 77
Hurston, Z.N. 1, 2
hypothesis
  dilemma 49–50
  see also research question/hypothesis

IBM *see* SPSS Statistics
independence and autonomy 27, 28
'indexicality' 162
indicators
  appropriate 60–1
  and checklist 74–5
inductive and deductive reasoning 347–8
inferential statistics 221, 327–30
informants/insiders 225–8
informed consent 77
informed decision making 3–4
inspiration for research question 43–4
integrity 59–60
  see also credibility; ethics
interconnections and patterns: qualitative data
    analysis (QDA) 351, 354
interpretivism *see* qualitative tradition
interval response scale *see* Lickert scale
interviews 157, 252
  issues and complexities 254–5
  issues and types *252–3*
  online 262–3
  options and possibilities 252
  process 255–62
    conducting and analysing 258–9
    initial questions/answers 260–1
    managing 262
    piloting and modification 257–8
    planning 256
    preliminaries 260
    schedule and recording system 257
introduction/background/rationale
  research proposal 92
  writing up 377–8

Janesick, V. 8, 133
Jemison, M. 192
job market 397–8
Johansson, F. 180
journal articles 30, 107, 109–10, 389
judgement, listening without 69–70

King, S. 23
knowledge production 25
Konnikova, M. 264
Kuhn, T. 152
kurtosis 325

language
  characteristics of research question 52–3
  power of 65–6
  qualitative data analysis (QDA) 350–1
  questionnaires 246
learning and action cycles 201–2
legal obligations 76
Lévi-Strauss, C. 39
Lewin, K. 198
librarians 108
Library of Congress Web Archives 306
library resources 27
  see also databases
library search engines 109
Lickert scale 177, 244–5, 249
limitations/delimitations
  research proposal 93
  of study 72, 73
  writing up 378
line graph 332
literature
  managing 113–16
    annotating references 115–16
    assessing quality 114
    assessing relevance 113–14
    systematic 114–15
  research question 42–3, 105–6
  role of 105–7
  sourcing relevant 107–13
    copyrights laws 133
    databases 30, 109–10, *111*
    'experts' 108
    search skills 110–13
    types 107–8
  using 29–30
literature review
  importance of 103–7
  research proposal 92–3
  writing 106, 116–22
    coverage 118
    plagiarism 118–19
    process 119–21
    purpose 116–17
    styles 121
  writing up 377

machine data, online-generated 301
Marx, K. 204
measurement scales 247, 324
measuring dispersion/distribution 324–7
media/contemporary entertainment data 281
meta-analysis 291–2
'methodolatry' 8
methodological design 125–6
  fundamental questions 134–8
  paths 126–7
  pragmatics 133–4
  and research question 128
  researcher perspective 131–3
  working at level of method 129–31
  working at level of methodology 128–9
methodology 9–10
  research proposal 93
  working at level of 128–9
  writing up 378
  see also mixed methodology; qualitative tradition;
      quantitative tradition; *specific methodologies*
methods 9–10
  assistance 27
  literature, role of 106

research proposal 93
demonstrating merits of 91
working at level of 129–31
writing up 378
mind map 351–2
mixed methodology 7–8
arguments for 173–4
challenges and possibilities 174–6
credibility 182–3
data management and analysis 180–2
exemplar 179–80
perspectives and strategies 176–80
operational 176–8
phased 178
question-driven 179
theoretical 176
triangulation 178
moral obligations 76–7
motivation 34
multiple realities and authenticity 67–8
Myers, W.D. 103

National Ethics Approval Form (NEAF), Australia 82–3
netnography 310, 311
networking 396–7
non-random samples 152, 221–3, *224–5*
non-response bias 221
non-verbal clues: qualitative data analysis (QDA) 351
normal curve 325–7, 332–4
note taking in interviews 261
NVivo 344, *345*

objectives *see* aims/objectives
objectivity 7
observation 264–72
issues and complexities 265–7
issues and types *265*
options and possibilities 264
process 267–72
authenticating 272
planning 267–8
preliminary analysis 268–9
receiving 270–1
recording 268–9, 271–2
reflecting 271
reviewing, refining and continued analysis 269–70
research question 43
observation, participant 24, 157
office space 27
official data and records 280
official publications 108
online communities 309–11
online ethnography 310–11
online interviews 262–3
online-generated data
assessing 303–4
benefits and challenges of 298–9
credibility 304–5
data stored online vs 297–8
finding 302–3
types of 299–302
web mining 307–8
working with 305–9
archives 306–7
automated text analysis 308–9
data scraping 308
web mining 307–8
ontology and epistemology 5, *6*, *10*

organizational communication, documents and records 280
originality 26
outcome/summative evaluation 189–91

paradigm perspective 176
participant information statements and consent forms 83–4
participant observation 24, 157
participatory action research (PAR) 200–1, 205–6
patterns and interconnections: qualitative data analysis (QDA) 351, 354
Pearson's correlation 334
personal communication, documents and records 280
personal crises 35
personal interest/experiences and research question 43, 51–2
phenomenology 158–9
conducting study 160
exemplar 161
producing descriptions 160
second cycle 160
strengths and challenges 161–2
pie graph 331, *332*
pilot interviews 257–8
pilot surveys 241–2, 248
plagiarism 26, 118–19
population
defining 218
see also sample and population
population studies
data 148–51
strengths and challenges 151
positivism 6
see also quantitative tradition
post-interview data dump 261
postmodernists 5, 6–7
Potter, E. 278
power issues 62–6
and trust-building 69
presentations 390–6
elements of best practice 392–5
for impact and influence 390–1
importance of audience 392
shift in focus 392
primary data 108
gathering 150–1
opportunities and challenges of collecting 238
see also interviews; observation; surveys
problem solving and decision making 3–4
'problem-based learning' 24
process/formative evaluation 191–2
professional, transition from student to 396–8
professional knowledge advancement 52
progress reports/seminars 26
prompts and probes 238, 262
provider and recipient perspectives 190–1, 192
psychological harm, protecting respondence from 77

qualitative data analysis (QDA) 219–20, 341–3
data management 343–5
logic 346–8
creativity and focus balance 346–7
inductive and deductive reasoning 347–8
methods 348–56
drawing conclusions 353, 355
identifying biases and noting impressions 349, 353
looking for patterns and interconnections 351, 354
mapping and building themes 351–2, 354

reducing and coding themes 349–51, 353–4
theory development 352–3, 354
presenting 357–9
software 344–5
specific strategies 356–7
qualitative tradition 152–67
with acceptance of quantitative data 177–8
and quantitative tradition, compared 7, 142–3
quantitative data/analysis 219, 220, 318–20
data management 321–2
descriptive statistics 324–7
inferential statistics 327–30
presenting 331–7
statistical analysis/software 320–1
variables
cause and effect 322
measurement scales 324
quantitative tradition 143–8
with acceptance of qualitative data 177
and qualitative tradition, compared 7, 142–3
studies of populations 148–51
question-driven approach 179
questionnaires *see* surveys

race *see* ethnicity/race
random samples 221, *222*
randomized controlled trial 147
real-time data, online-generated 301
realism 5, 6
recommendations, writing up 379
recording interviews 257, 260–1
redefining research question 48–9
redrafting *see* drafting and redrafting
reference books 107
references
annotating 115–16
research proposal 94
writing up 379
reflective qualitative analysis 342–3
reflexive analysis 318–19
reflexivity 8–9, 62
relativism 7
reliability 70–1
representative samples 182
research
concept and definitions 2
'construct' of 4–8
research journal 32–3
research knowledge
need for 3
potential of 3–4
research process
and AI 11–14
navigating 25–36
research proposal
elements of 92–4
obstacles and challenges 98–100
change of direction/method 99–100
design and proposal requirements 98
emergent design 99
role of 89–92
writing 94–8
drafting and redrafting 97–8
example 94–6
guidelines 96
purposive writing 97
research question
answer to 215–16
characteristics of 51–5
academic/professional knowledge advancement 52
approval of authorities 54
doable 53
personal interest 51–2
well articulated 52–3
concept map 42, 45–6
defining topic 41–5
curiosity and creativity 41–2
inspiration 43–4
literature 42–3, 105–6
importance of 39–41
and methodological design 128
mixed methodology 176
research proposal demonstrating merits of 90–1
researchable questions 45–51
four-step generation process 46–7
hypothesis dilemma 49–50
narrowing in 45
redefining 48–9
research question/hypothesis
research proposal 92
writing up 377
research requirements 25–6
research skills 24
and job market 297–8
researcher
perspective in methodological design 131–3
research proposal demonstrating merits of 91–2
role as interviewer 262
resources 26–7, 134
Roy, A. 64

sample frame 218
sample and population 216–25
appropriate 73
methodological design 134–5, *136–7*
sample selection 217
sample size 218–20
sampling strategy 220–5
saturation 157
scatter graph 334
scientific methods 144
scientist: role of researcher 132–3
search skills 110–13
secondary data
analysis 287–8
benefits and challenges of 278–9
credibility in 279
definition of 278
meta-analysis 291–2
systematic reviews 289–91
types of 280–1
working with 281–8
see also existing data
seminars/progress reports 26
simple random sampling *222*
situation improvement, purpose of research 3
SMART objectives 92
snowball sampling *224*
social artefacts, as secondary data 281
social data, online-generated 300–1, 304, 305–6
social media *see* online communities; social data
socioeconomic status/class
insensitivity to 63
trust-building 69
software 27
bibliographic file management 115

qualitative data analysis (QDA) 344–5
statistical analysis 321–2, *323*
survey 250–1
SPSS Statistics 321
Data View *323*
Variable View 322, *323*
stakeholders
presentations to 390
research question 43
statistical analysis 219, 220, 320–2
statistical significance 328
statistical tests, selecting 328–30
'story' construction, writing up as 374–6
storytelling, presentations as 393
stratified sampling *222*
subjectivities 7
managing 61–6
summary/abstract
research proposal 92
writing up 377
summative/outcome evaluation 189–91
supervisory relationship and roles 27–9, 34, 35, 54, 108
support, sources of 34
surveys 157, 238–51
instrument 243–51
concept operationalization 243–5
information and instructions 249–50
layout and design 250
online software 250–1
organization and length 250
question formulation 245–7
response categories 247–9
issues and complexities 240
issues and types *239*
options and possibilities 238–40
process 240–3
administration and analysis 242–3
piloting and modification 241–2
planning 240–1
questionnaire development 241
systematic management of literature 114–15
systematic review 115–16, 289–91
systematic sampling *222*

tables, generating 335–7
teamworking 30–1
technical skills 27, 398
TED Talks 395
text analysis, automated 308–9
textual/document analysis 281–2
examples 286–7
gathering, reviewing and interrogating 283–4
historical analysis 285
planning 282–3
reflecting, refining and analysing 284–5
see also document analysis
themes
mapping and building 351–2, 354
reducing and coding 349–51, 353–4
theoretical perspectives
literature, role of 106
mixed methodology 176
research proposal 93
theorist: role of researcher 132
theory development: qualitative data analysis (QDA) 352–3, 354
'thick descriptions' 154–5
Thurstone scale 244, 245
time issues
methodological design 134, 135, *137*
research proposal 93
research question 43
title
research proposal 92
writing up 376
Toffler, A. 318
transactional data, online-generated 302
transferability 73
translation in interviews 261
triangulation 178
online archive tools 307
trust building 68–9
'truth', concept and capturing of 66–70
Tuhiwai Smith, L. 59, 60, 69

unwitting bias 223

validity 70–1
variables
cause and effect 322
dependent and independent 145
measurement scales 324
verifiable and accurate accounts 73–4
video recording interviews 260
voice
and power 64–5
presentations 394
writing up 375
volunteer sampling *224*

Wayback Machine 306–7
web mining 307–8
wider community perspective 191, 192
words
limits 25–6
qualitative data analysis (QDA) 350
work-home-university balance 33–4
workload management 31–3
workshops 27
writing aids 108
writing assistance 27
writing research proposal *see under* research proposal
writing up
challenge 367–8
as communication exercise 368–73
appropriate structure and style 369–73
knowing and engaging your audience 369
first to final draft 379–83
drafting and redrafting 381–3
seeking and using feedback 380–1
process 373–6
as analysis 374
as 'story' construction 374–6
as you go 374
section/chapter development 376–9
back end 378–9
front end 376–8
research design section 378
tips 383